38TH ANNUAL EDITION

2015

SONGWRITER'S MARKET

James Duncan, Editor

WD
WRITER'S DIGEST
BOOKS
WritersDigest.com
Cincinnati, Ohio

Writer's Market website: www.writersmarket.com
Writer's Digest website: www.writersdigest.com
Writer's Digest Bookstore: www.writersdigestshop.com

Publisher: Phil Sexton

Distributed in Canada by Fraser Direct
100 Armstrong Avenue
Georgetown, Ontario, Canada L7G 5S4
Tel: (905) 877-4411

Distributed in the UK and Europe by F&W Media International
Brunel House, Newton Abbot, Devon, TQ12 4PU, England
Tel: (+44) 1626-323200, Fax: (+44) 1626-323319
E-mail: postmaster@davidandcharles.co.uk

Distributed in Australia by Capricorn Link
P.O. Box 704, Windsor, NSW 2756 Australia
Tel: (02) 4577-3555

ISSN-10: 1-59963-842-8
ISBN-13: 978-1-59963-842-3

Attention Booksellers: This is an annual directory of F+W Media, Inc.
Return deadline for this edition is December 31, 2015.

Edited by James Duncan
Cover designed by Claudean Wheeler
Interior designed by Claudean Wheeler
Page layout by Geoff Raker
Production coordinated by Greg Nock and Debbie Thomas

(fw)
media

CONTENTS

FROM THE EDITOR

While researching the articles for this year's edition of *Songwriter's Market*, I spoke to a number of professional songwriters, music publishers, record producers, music educators, and musicians, and the phrase that kept coming up in regard to what songwriters must do to succeed was "educate themselves."

This applies to all aspects of the business, everything from avoiding scams to learning how to craft a meaningful song and exactly what a music publisher can and cannot do for you. Taking the time to educate yourself about the industry will help you in too may ways to express here, and we hope that this book will help point you in the right direction. This edition of *Songwriter's Market* is not the end-all be-all, but a starting point for your songwriting and music business education. There is so much to learn, so many conferences to attend, so many workshops to utilize, and so many songwriting books to read to help you along the way.

In fact, we asked Mark Simos, a professor at Berklee College of Music and the author of one such book, *Songwriting Strategies: A 360-Approach*, to help us fine-tune this edition of *Songwriter's Market*, as well as host a webinar on songwriting: Song Seeds: How to Jumpstart Your Songwriting Process. (You can find more about this exclusive webinar at www.writersmarket.com/sm15-webinar.) We found his advice invaluable, and we plan to continue making future upgrades in order to keep bringing you the insights of industry pros like Simos and others in this edition, including Jason Blume, Scott Mathews, Robert Clement, Deborah Evans, and more. It's our intent to provide you with the most relevant, accurate information about the music industry that we possibly can. So let this be the beginning of your education, not to mention a long and successful songwriting career.

James Duncan
Content Editor, Writer's Digest Community
http://writersdigest.com/editor-blogs/there-are-no-rules

FOREWORD

by Jason Blume

In the years that I've been writing songs, I've seen the music business evolve in ways I never would have imagined. I've witnessed the demise of 8-tracks, cassettes, record stores, and the Walkman—and the advent of MP3s, digital downloads, iTunes, streaming, "cloud" storage, and smart phones that provide instant access to more music than even the most avid fan could listen to in a lifetime.

During that same time, the music itself changed as dramatically as the modes of sales and delivery. The soulful stylings of classic R&B artists such as Aretha Franklin, James Brown, and Marvin Gaye gave way to the contemporary urban sounds of Beyoncé, Kanye West, and Pitbull. Loretta Lynn, Patsy Cline, and George Jones have been replaced on country radio by the pop-influenced sounds of Lady Antebellum, Florida Georgia Line, and Hunter Hayes. Music by artists such as Blake Shelton, Miranda Lambert, Jason Aldean, and Carrie Underwood bears little resemblance to the hits by their predecessors—Johnny Cash, Waylon Jennings, Tammy Wynette, and Merle Haggard. Similarly, the Motown Sound, the British Invasion, punk, grunge, and New Wave have been supplanted by hip-hop, EDM, and the slick, manufactured pop identified with Max Martin, Dr. Luke, and their peers.

There have also been surprising crossovers in styles and techniques. Most recently, hip-hop rhythms and even rap infiltrated mainstream country music in hits by artists such as Florida Georgia Line, Jason Aldean, and Colt Ford, while Mumford & Sons brought the sound of banjos to Top 40 radio. Several top country songwriters set down their guitars and wrote hit songs by starting with existing musical "backing tracks" and then adding the "top line" (melody and lyrics), incorporating the approach used with so much success by Max Martin, Dr. Luke, Ryan Tedder, and other pop superstar writer/producers.

Not only have styles progressed, but musical content as well. Some critics bemoaned that recent songs from Nashville's Music Row were one-dimensional, formulaic ditties that glorified trucks, girls in painted-on blue jeans, tailgating, and getting drunk—and at first glance, those topics certainly seem to define the genre today. But songs such as "I Drive Your Truck,"(recorded by Lee Brice) and "Merry Go 'Round" (recorded by Kacey Musgraves)—both nominated for Grammys—showed exceptional depth and originality, proving there is room on the charts—and on listeners' playlists—for songs that reach beyond the expected. And artists Macklemore & Ryan Lewis (featuring Mary Lambert) pushed beyond traditional boundaries and earned a Grammy nomination for "Same Love," a song that tackled the topic of gay and lesbian love and equality.

Clearly, music is always in flux, but one thing remains constant: Audiences still crave songs they love—melodies and lyrics that speak to them. There is still—and will always be—a demand for songs that move people, songs that insinuate themselves inside hearts and make a listener think, *How did that singer know what I was feeling?* There remains a hunger for songs that evoke tears, smiles, or hope, songs that propel listeners to the dance floor—or audiences to sing along.

As a songwriter and songwriting teacher, I look for common denominators—elements consistently found in songs that transform unknown artists into household names. I also identify the tools and techniques artists use in their songs that can make a profound impact on the charts—and on listeners. When I examine the breakthrough songs by artists such as Lorde, Adele, Avicii, Kacey Musgrave, Daft Punk, Florida Georgia Line, and so many others, I hear songs that differentiated themselves from everything else on the radio, songs that incorporated unique melodic and lyric elements, songs written by writers who, instead of copying what came before them, carved their own niche.

The songwriting business is fiercely competitive, and that elusive lucky break can seem impossible to attain. Yet somehow, every year brings a new crop of songwriters and singers who break through with their first hits. Luck is terrific—and I hope you get lots of it—but luck tends to find its way to those who write songs that are truly exceptional—while still having a place in the current market.

Writing perfectly crafted songs is not enough. We need to give our listeners—whether they are music publishers, recording artists, record label executives, or audiences—compelling reasons to choose our songs over countless others. These reasons typically include an original angle to the lyric, a new perspective, a unique way to express emotions that millions can relate to, and a catchy, hooky melody that breaks new ground and burns into listeners' brains.

Five students who have attended my songwriting workshops have gone on to write #1 singles; others have had their songs recorded by well-known artists, while others achieved their dream of signing a music-publishing deal. But having a dream is not enough. Those writers whom I've watched rise above the pack worked long and hard to hone their craft. They remained open to professional feedback and refused to settle for less than their very best. They put their work under the proverbial microscope and rewrote every line of their melodies and lyrics until they were as strong as they could possibly be.

But the successful writers I've worked with did something additional. After receiving professional feedback and ascertaining that their songs were indeed both outstanding and targeting the current market, they took care of business—networking, attending songwriter retreats, workshops, and camps, and joining songwriter organizations and availing themselves of every resource to get their music to the ears of decision-makers who could say "yes."

Few people write songs or become recording artists because they enjoy the process of pitching their music. But there's a reason why it's called "the music business"—and those who find commercial success embrace that they must market their music. Regardless of how incredible your songs might be, it's highly unlikely that Garth Brooks, Kelly Clarkson, Jay-Z, or a music publisher or record label executive is going to knock on your door. It is up to you to identify and pursue legitimate ways to promote your music.

It's not realistic to set a goal such as, "In six months I will have a number one single." That's a dream—not a goal. It can help to establish specific, measurable goals that are attainable.

For instance, "Tuesday evening I'll research the cost of having a professional demo recorded," or "Saturday afternoon, I'll attend the meeting of a local songwriters' organization." "Tonight, I'll research a trip to a music center to attend an event where I'll be able to pitch a song to a publisher," or "Today, I'll send an e-mail to five people I've met at songwriting workshops, and I'll ask if they'd be willing to refer me to publishers they work with."

With more recording artists writing or co-writing their songs, it's become more important than ever for nonperforming songwriters to create opportunities for their work. Educate yourself about potential outlets, and remember—music publishers need songs that are appropriate for artists who do not write their own material. You might have the perfect song for Coldplay, Taylor Swift, or Pharrell Williams—but these are artists who exclusively write their own songs.

If you are a nonperforming songwriter who writes in genres such as hip-hop, rock, or pop, or composes singer/songwriter-type songs that are typically written by the artists who record them, you might explore collaborating with up-and-coming artists. You can find additional outlets by using tip sheets that include leads to pitch songs internationally and by learning how songwriters' demos and independent artists' releases are placed in TV shows and films.

Songwriting success can't be guaranteed, but it is possible—for those who use their unique gifts and talents to create songs infused with originality and for those who harness their determination and persistence to continue working toward their goals—despite the inevitable disappointments and rejections that pave the way.

I don't have a crystal ball, but I can safely predict that someone somewhere will be the new "hot" writer—the one who finally broke through, the one whom everyone else wants to be. If you study your craft and the business of songwriting, write amazing songs, and do everything in your power to market them … it could be you.

Wishing you all the best on your songwriting journey.

Jason Blume

Jason Blume's songs are on three Grammy-nominated albums and have sold more than fifty million copies. He is one of only a few writers to ever have singles on the pop, country, and R&B charts all at the same time; his songs have been recorded by artists including Britney Spears, the Backstreet Boys, the Gipsy Kings, Jesse McCartney, and country stars including Collin Raye (six cuts), the Oak Ridge Boys, Steve Azar, and John Berry ("Change My Mind," a Top 5 single that earned a BMI "Million-Air" Award for garnering more than one million airplays). He's recently had three Top 10 singles and a "Gold" record in Europe by Dutch star, BYentl, including a #1 on the Dutch R&B iTunes chart.

His songs have been included in films and TV shows including *Scrubs, Friday Night Lights, Assassination Games,* Disney's *Kim Possible, Dangerous Minds, Kickin' it Old Skool, Guiding Light, The Miss America Pageant,* and many more.

Jason authored three best-selling songwriting books, *6 Steps to Songwriting Success*, *This Business of Songwriting*, and *Inside Songwriting*, as well as a series of instructional CDs, *Writing Hit Lyrics*, *Writing Hit Melodies*, *Taking Care of Business*, and *Placing Music in TV and Films*. He is in his nineteenth year of teaching the BMI Nashville Songwriters workshops. A regular contributor to BMI's *Music World* magazine, he presented a master class at the Liverpool Institute for Performing Arts (founded by Sir Paul McCartney) and teaches songwriting throughout the U.S., Australia, New Zealand, Norway, Ireland, the U.K., Canada, Bermuda, and Jamaica.

For songwriting tips and information about Jason's books, including the newly revised 2nd edition of *This Business of Songwriting*, instructional audio CDs, and upcoming workshops and events, visit www.jasonblume.com.

HOW TO USE *SONGWRITER'S MARKET*

Before you dive into the *Songwriter's Market* listings and start submitting songs, it's a good idea to take the time to assess if you are ready to submit songs and if you've completed all of the research necessary to position yourself for success. As you read through the articles and advice in this book's initial sections, continually ask yourself if you have all the materials you need to succeed—strong songs, a well-recorded demo, a professional presence both online and in person, the ability and desire to network, learn new technologies and skills, and perhaps most important, the dedication to commit to both your craft and to researching the business aspects of the music industry. By educating yourself and constantly assessing your needs and skills, you'll be better prepared when you actually do send off your songs.

Now let's take a look at what is inside *Songwriter's Market*, why these articles were put into the book in the first place, and how they can help your career.

THE LISTINGS

Beyond the articles, which we highly encourage you to read first, there are eight market sections in this book, from Music Publishers and Record Companies to Contests & Awards. Each section begins with an introduction detailing how the different types of companies function—what part of the music industry they work in, how they make money, and what you need to think about when approaching them with your music.

These listings are the heart of *Songwriter's Market*. They are the names, addresses, and contact information of music business companies looking for songs and artists, as well as descriptions of the types of music they are looking for.

So how do I use *Songwriter's Market?*

The quick answer is that you should use the indexes to find companies that are interested in your type of music; then read the listings for details about how they want the music submitted. For support and help, join a songwriting or other music industry association (see the Organizations section of this book). Also, read everything you can about songwriting (see the Publications of Interest section at the back of this book), and talk to other songwriters. Always conduct your own research (using this book is a great starting point), especially since businesses can change locations and contact info between a book's publication and when you pick it up. The industry moves fast!

How does *Songwriter's Market* work?

The listings in *Songwriter's Market* are packed with information. It can be intimidating at first, but they are structured to make them easy to work with. Take a few minutes to get used to how the listings are organized, and you'll save time in the long run. For more detailed information about how the listings are put together, skip ahead to the Where Should I Send My Songs? section.

The following are general guidelines about how to use the listings:

1. **READ THE ENTIRE LISTING** to decide whether to submit your music. Please do not use this book as a mass mailing list. If you blindly mail out demos by the hundreds, you'll waste a lot of money on postage and annoy a lot of people, and your demos will likely end up in the trash.

2. **PAY CLOSE ATTENTION TO THE "MUSIC" SECTION IN EACH LISTING.** This will tell you what kind of music the company is looking for. If they want rockabilly only and you write heavy metal, don't submit to that company. That's just common sense.

3. **PAY CLOSE ATTENTION TO SUBMISSION INSTRUCTIONS** shown under How to Contact. A lot of listings are particular about how they want submissions packaged. If you don't follow their instructions, your submission will probably be discarded. If you are confused about a listing's instructions, contact the company for clarification.

4. **IF IN DOUBT, CONTACT THE COMPANY FOR PERMISSION TO SUBMIT.** This is a good general rule. Many companies don't mind if you send an unsolicited submission, but some require you to get special permission prior to submitting. Contacting a company first is also a good way to determine their latest music needs, and it's an opportunity to briefly make contact on a personal level.

5. **BE COURTEOUS, BE EFFICIENT, AND ALWAYS HAVE A PURPOSE** to be in touch with your personal contact. Don't waste a contact's time. If you call, always have a legitimate reason: seeking permission to submit, checking on guidelines, following up on a

demo, etc. Once you have their attention, don't wear out your welcome. Always be polite.

6. **CHECK FOR A PREFERRED CONTACT.** Some listings have a designated contact person shown after a bolded Contact in the heading. This is the person you should contact with questions or to whom you should address your submission. Again, you may want to use the listing as a starting point and verify that the contact person is still with the company by checking the company's information online. Double-checking never hurts!

7. **READ THE "TIPS" SECTION.** This part of the listing provides extra information about how to submit or what it might be like to work with the company.

FREQUENTLY ASKED QUESTIONS

How do these companies get listed in the book anyway?

No company pays to be included—all listings are free. The listings come from a combination of research the editor does on the music industry and questionnaires requested by companies who want to be listed (many of them contact us to be included). All questionnaires are screened for known sharks and to make sure they meet our requirements.

Why aren't other companies I know about listed in the book?

There are many possible reasons. They may not have replied to the questionnaire we sent, they were removed due to reader complaints, went out of business, specifically asked not to be listed, could not be contacted for an update, were left out due to space restrictions, etc.

What's the deal with companies that don't take unsolicited submissions?

In the interest of completeness, the editor will sometimes include listings of crucial music companies and major labels he thinks you should be aware of. We want you to at least have some idea of what their policies are.

In one listing, a company claimed that they take unsolicited submissions, but my demo came back unopened. What happened?

Some companies' needs change rapidly and may have changed since we contacted them for this edition of the book. That's why it's often a good idea to contact a company before submitting.

So that's it. You now have the power at your fingertips to become the professional songwriter you've always wanted to be. Let us know how you're doing. Drop us a line at market-books@fwmedia.com and tell us about any successes you have had because you used the materials found in this book.

WHERE SHOULD I SEND MY SONGS?

//

It depends a lot on whether you write mainly for yourself as a performer or if you only want someone else to pick up your song for his or her recording (often the case in country music, for example). These two types of songwriters may have very different career trajectories, so it's important to assess who you'd like to write for and what you'd like to write. This is important for figuring out what kind of companies to contact, as well as how you contact them. (For more detail, skip to the Submission Strategies section.)

What if I'm strictly a songwriter/lyricist?

Many well-known songwriters are not performers. Some are not skilled instrumentalists or singers, but they understand melody, lyrics, and harmony and how those things go together. They can write great songs, but they need someone else to bring their music to life through skilled musicianship. This type of songwriter will usually approach music publishers first for access to artists looking for songs. Music publishers are to songwriters what literary agents are to authors. They take great songs and find homes for them while managing the rights and money flow for you. Some producers and record companies may also seek out songwriters directly, but music publishers might be your best bet. (For more details on the different types of companies and the roles they play for songwriters and performing artists, see the section introductions for Music Publishers, Record Companies, Record Producers, and Managers & Booking Agents.)

What if I am a performing artist/songwriter?

Many famous songwriters are also famous performers. They are skilled interpreters of their own material, and they also know how to write to suit their own particular talents as musicians. In this case, their intention is also usually to sell themselves as performers in hopes of recording and releasing an album, or they have an album and want to find gigs and people who can help guide their careers. They will want to approach record companies or record producers on the basis of recording an album. For gigs and career guidance, they will talk to booking agents and managers. A music publisher can still be helpful for this kind of artist, especially in managing a catalog of music. Some music publishers in recent years have also taken on the role of developing artists as both songwriters and performers or are connected to a major record label, so performing songwriters might go to them for these reasons, too.

How do I use *Songwriter's Market* to narrow my search?

Once you've identified whether you are primarily interested in getting others to perform your songs or you want to perform your own songs and want a record deal, etc., there are several steps you can take:

TYPES OF MUSIC COMPANIES

- **MUSIC PUBLISHERS** evaluate songs for commercial potential, find artists to record them, find other uses for the songs such as in film or TV, collect income from songs, protect copyrights from infringement

- **RECORD COMPANIES** sign artists to their labels, finance recordings, promotion, and touring, release songs/albums to radio and TV

- **RECORD PRODUCERS** work in the studio and record songs (independently or for a record company), may be affiliated with a particular artist, sometimes develop artists for record labels, locate or co-write songs if an artist does not write their own

- **MANAGERS & BOOKING AGENTS** work with artists to manage their careers, find gigs, locate songs to record if the artist does not write their own

1. **IDENTIFY WHAT KIND OF MUSIC COMPANY YOU WISH TO APPROACH.** As mentioned earlier, deciding whether you're a performing artist or strictly a songwriter will affect who you want to contact. Songwriters may wish to contact a music publisher for a publishing deal first. Performing artists may prefer to first contact record companies, managers, and record producers in order to find a record deal and/or record an album, and reaching out to music publishers might be a secondary, though still important, option.

ADDITIONAL RESOURCES

Songwriter's Market lists music publishers, record companies, producers, and managers (as well as advertising firms, play producers, and classical performing-arts organizations) along with specifications about how to submit your material to each.

The Recording Industry Sourcebook, an annual directory published by Norris-Whitney Communications, lists record companies, music publishers, producers, and managers, as well as attorneys, publicity firms, media, manufacturers, distributors, and recording studios around the U.S. Trade publications such as *Billboard* or *Variety,* available at most local libraries and bookstores, are great sources for up-to-date information. These periodicals list new companies as well as the artists, labels, producers and publishers for each song on the charts.

CD booklets and band websites can also be valuable sources of information, providing the name of the record company, publisher, producer, and usually the manager of an artist or group. Use your imagination in your research, and be creative—any contacts you make in the industry can only help your career as a songwriter. See the Publications of Interest section for more details.

2. CHECK FOR COMPANIES BASED ON LOCATION. Maybe you need a manager located close by. Maybe you need to find as many Nashville-based companies as you can because you write country music and most country publishers are in Nashville. In this case, start with the Geographic Index. You can also recognize Canadian and foreign listings by the icons in the listing (see "A Sample Listing Decoded" on the next page).

3. LOOK FOR COMPANIES BASED ON THE TYPE OF MUSIC THEY WANT. Some companies want country. Some record labels want only punk. Read the listings carefully to make sure you're maximizing your time and sending your work to the appropriate markets.

4. LOOK FOR COMPANIES BASED ON HOW OPEN THEY ARE TO BEGINNERS. Some companies are more open than others to beginning artists and songwriters. If you are a beginner, it would help to approach these companies first. Some music publishers are hoping to find that wild-card hit song and don't care if it comes from an unknown writer. A good song is a good song no matter who writes it. Maybe you are just starting out looking for gigs. In this case, try finidng a manager willing to help build your band's career from the ground up.

5. BUYER BEWARE. It is important to note that some companies out there are actually service companies for songwriters and not actual "markets." For example, many demo-recording companies that charge songwriters to professionally record their demos are legit, but there are others that may present themselves misleadingly as potential "markets" and over-promise exposure. Make sure you perform appropriate research before committing to any company for any reason.

A SAMPLE LISTING DECODED

What do the little symbols at the beginning of the listing mean?

Those are called "icons," and they give you quick information about a listing with one glance. Here is a list of the icons and what they mean:

Openness to Submissions

O means the company is open to beginners' submissions, regardless of past success

◑ means the company is mostly interested in previously published songwriters/ well-established acts but will consider beginners

● means the company does not want submissions from beginners, only from previously published songwriters/well-established acts

⊘ means the company only accepts material referred by a reputable industry source

Other Icons

☺ means the listing is Canadian

⊜ means the market is located outside of the U.S. and Canada

⊕ means the market is new to this edition

⊛ means the market places music in film/TV

EASY-TO-USE
REFERENCE ICONS

E-MAIL AND
WEBSITE
INFORMATION

TERMS OF
AGREEMENT

DETAILED
SUBMISSION
GUIDELINES

WHAT THEY'RE
LOOKING FOR

INSIDER ADVICE

O RUSTIC RECORDS

6337 Murray Lane, Brentwood, TN 37027. (615)371-8397. Fax: (615)370-0353. E-mail: rusticre-cordsam@aol.com. Website: www.rusticrecordsinc.com. President: Jack Schneider. Executive VP & Operations Manager: Nell Schneider. VP Publishing and Catalog Manager: Amanda Mark. VP Marketing and Promotions: Ross Schneider. Videography, Photography, and Graphic Design: Wayne Hall. Image consultant: Jo Ann Rossi. Independent traditional country music label and music publisher (Iron Skillet Music/ASCAP, Covered Bridge/BMI, Old Town Square/SESAC). Estab. 1979. Staff size: 6. Releases 2-3/year. Pays negotiable royalty to artists on contracts, statutory royalty to publisher per song on record.

DISTRIBUTED BY CD Baby.com and available on iTunes, MSN Music, Rhapsody, and more.

HOW TO CONTACT Submit professional demo package by mail. Unsolicited submissions are OK. CD only, no MP3s or e-mails. Include no more than 4 songs with corresponding lyric sheets and cover letter. Include appropriately sized SASE. Responds in 4 weeks.

MUSIC Good combination of traditional and modern country. 2008-09 releases: *Ready to Ride*—debut album from Nikki Britt, featuring "C-O-W-B-O-Y," "Do I Look Like Him," "Long Gone Mama," and "I'm So Lonesome I Could Cry."

TIPS "Professional demo preferred."

DEMO RECORDINGS

What is a "demo"?

The demo, shorthand for *demonstration recording*, is the most important part of your submission package. Demos are meant to give music-industry professionals a way to hear all the elements of your song as clearly as possible so they can decide if it has commercial potential.

What should I send?

Most music-industry people want CDs or DVDs, although many now request digital files or MP3 files via e-mail, a Dropbox account, etc. Either of these methods are cheap and easy to use. If a listing isn't specific, contact the company or check their website for details. For more details, see the next chapter, How Do I Submit My Demo?

How many songs should I send, and in what order and length?

Anywhere from three is enough, but the number varies. Most music professionals are short on time, and if you can't catch their attention in three songs, your songs probably don't have hit potential. Also, put at least three *complete songs* on your demo, not just snippets. Make sure to put your best, most commercial song first. An up-tempo number is usually best.

Should I sing my own songs on my demo?

If you can't sing well, you may want to hire someone who can. There are many resources for locating singers and musicians, including songwriter organizations, music stores, and songwriting magazines. Some aspiring professional singers will sing on demos in exchange for a copy they can use as a demo to showcase their talent.

Should I use a professional demo service?

Many songwriters find professional demo services convenient if they don't have the time or resources to hire musicians on their own. For a fee, a demo service will produce your songs in their studio using in-house singers and musicians (this is fairly common in Nashville). Many of these services advertise in music magazines, songwriting newsletters, and bulletin boards at music stores. Perform thorough research before selecting a service. Make sure to listen to samples of work they've done in the past, and look for reviews of the service online. Some are mail-order businesses—you send a rough recording of your song or the sheet music, and they produce and record a demo within a couple of months. Be sure to find a service that will allow some control over how the demo is produced, and tell them exactly how you want your song to sound. As with studios, look for a service that fits your needs and budget. Some will charge as low as $300 for three songs, while others may go as high as $3,000 and boast a high-quality sound. *Shop around and use your best judgment!*

Should I buy equipment and record demos myself?

If you have the drive and focus to learn good recording techniques, yes. Digital multitrack recorders are readily available and affordable, and many artists can set up a passable home studio using just some software, a laptop, and some basic recording equipment. If this is not something you feel comfortable doing yourself, it might be easier to have someone else do it, thus a demo-recording service becomes handy. For performing songwriters in search of record deals, the actual sound of their recordings can often be an important part of their artistic concept. Having the "means of production" within their grasp can be crucial to artists pursuing the independent route. But if you don't know how to use the equipment, it may be better to utilize a professional studio.

How elaborate and full should the demo production be if I'm not a performing artist?

Many companies listed in *Songwriter's Market* tell you what types of demos they're looking for. If in doubt, contact them and ask. In general, country songs and pop ballads can often be recorded with just a vocal plus a guitar or piano, although many songwriters in those genres still prefer a more complete recording with drums, guitars, and other backing instruments. Up-tempo pop, rock, and dance demos usually require a full production. If you write for a chorus, you will need a number of vocalists to help you create your demo.

What kind of production do I need if I'm a performing artist?

If you are a band or artist looking for a record deal, you will need a demo that is as fully produced as possible. Many singer/songwriters record their demos as if they are going to be released as an album. That way, if they don't get a deal, they can still release it on their own. Professionally pressed CDs are also now easily within reach of performing songwriters, and many companies offer graphic-design services for a professional-looking product.

What should I send if I'm seeking management?

Some companies want a video of an act performing their songs. Check with the companies for specific requirements.

HOW DO I SUBMIT MY DEMO?

You have three basic options for submitting your songs: submitting by mail, submitting in person, and submitting over the Internet.

SUBMITTING BY MAIL

Should I call, write, or e-mail first to ask for submission requirements?

This is always a good idea, and many companies require you to contact them first. If you call, be polite, brief, and specific. If you send a letter, make sure it is typed and to the point. Include a typed SASE (self-addressed stamped envelope) for reply. If you send an e-mail, again, be professional and to the point. Proofread your message before you send it, and then be patient. Give them some time to reply. Do not send out mass e-mails or otherwise overload their e-mail account with repeated requests.

What do I send with my demo?

Most companies have specific requirements, but here are some general pointers:

- Read the listing carefully and submit *exactly* what they ask for. It's also a good idea to check online in case they've changed their submission policies.
- Listen to each demo to make sure it sounds right and is in the right order (see the previous section, Demo Recordings).
- Enclose a *brief*, typed cover letter to introduce yourself. Indicate what songs you are sending and why you are sending them. If you are pitching your songs to a particular artist, say so in the letter. If you are an artist/songwriter looking for a record deal, you should say so. Be specific.

SUBMISSION MAILING POINTERS

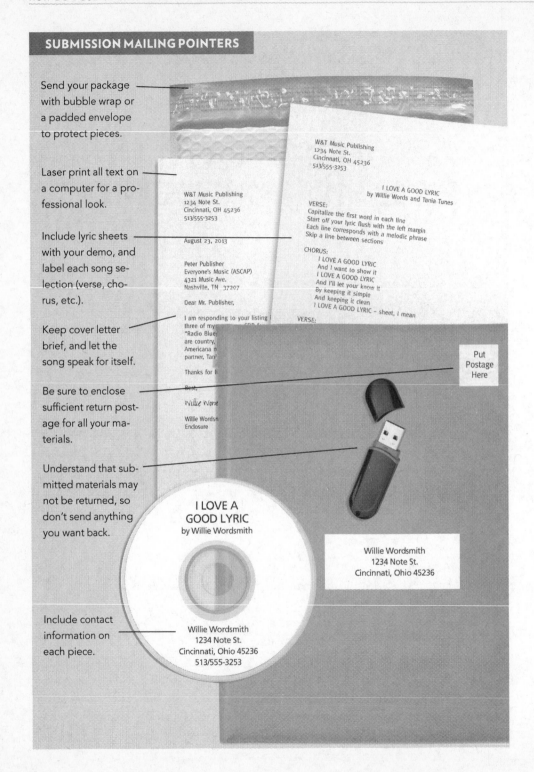

Send your package with bubble wrap or a padded envelope to protect pieces.

Laser print all text on a computer for a professional look.

Include lyric sheets with your demo, and label each song selection (verse, chorus, etc.).

Keep cover letter brief, and let the song speak for itself.

Be sure to enclose sufficient return postage for all your materials.

Understand that submitted materials may not be returned, so don't send anything you want back.

Include contact information on each piece.

W&T Music Publishing
1234 Note St.
Cincinnati, OH 45236
513/555-3253

W&T Music Publishing
1234 Note St.
Cincinnati, OH 45236
513/555-3253

August 23, 2013

Peter Publisher
Everyone's Music (ASCAP)
4321 Music Ave.
Nashville, TN 37207

Dear Mr. Publisher,

I am responding to your listing
three of my
"Radio Blue
are country,
Americana
partner, Tan

Thanks for li

Best,

Willie Words

Willie Wordsm
Enclosure

I LOVE A GOOD LYRIC
by Willie Words and Tania Tunes

VERSE:
Capitalize the first word in each line
Start off your lyric flush with the left margin
Each line corresponds with a melodic phrase
Skip a line between sections

CHORUS:
I LOVE A GOOD LYRIC
And I want to show it
I LOVE A GOOD LYRIC
And I'll let your know it
By keeping it simple
And keeping it clean
I LOVE A GOOD LYRIC – sheet, I mean

VERSE:

Put Postage Here

I LOVE A GOOD LYRIC
by Willie Wordsmith

Willie Wordsmith
1234 Note St.
Cincinnati, Ohio 45236
513/555-3253

Willie Wordsmith
1234 Note St.
Cincinnati, Ohio 45236

- Include *typed* lyric sheets or lead sheets, if requested. Make sure your name, address, and phone number are on each sheet.
- Neatly label each CD with your name, address, e-mail, and phone number, along with the song names in the order they appear on the recording.
- Include a SASE with sufficient postage, and make sure it's large enough to return all your materials. Warning: Many companies do not return materials, so read each listing carefully.
- If you submit to companies in other countries, include a self-addressed envelope (SAE) and International Reply Coupon (IRC), available at most post offices. Make sure the envelope is large enough to return all of your materials.
- Pack everything neatly. Neatly type or write the company's address and your return address so they are clearly visible. Your package is the first impression a company has of you and your songs, so neatness counts!
- Stamp or write "First Class Mail" on the package and the SASE you enclose.
- Do not use registered or certified mail unless requested. Most companies will not accept or open demos sent by registered or certified mail for fear of lawsuits.
- Keep records of the dates, songs, and companies you submit to.

Is it Okay to send demos to more than one person or company at a time?

It is usually acceptable to make simultaneous submissions. One exception is when a publisher, artist, or other industry professional asks you to put your song "on hold."

What does it mean when a song is "on hold"?

This means they intend to record the song and don't want you to give the song to anyone else. This is not a guarantee, though. Your song may eventually be returned to you, even if it's been on hold for months. Or it may be recorded and included on the album.

How can I protect my song from being put "on hold" indefinitely?

One approach is to establish a deadline for the person who asks for the hold, e.g., "You can put my song on hold for three months." Or you can modify the hold to specify that you will still pitch the song to others but won't sign another deal without allowing the person with the song on hold to make you an offer. Once you sign a contract with a publisher, they have exclusive rights to your song and you cannot pitch it to other would-be publishers.

SUBMITTING IN PERSON

Do I need to visit to New York, Nashville, or Los Angeles in order to submit in person?

A trip to one of the major music hubs can be valuable if you are organized and prepared to make the most of it. You should have specific goals and set up appointments before you go. Some industry professionals are difficult to see and may not consider meeting out-of-town writers a high priority. Others are more open and even encourage face-to-face meetings. By taking the time to travel, organize, and schedule meetings, you can appear more professional than songwriters who submit blindly through the mail.

What should I take?

Take several copies of your demo and typed lyric sheets of each of your songs. More than one company you visit may ask you to leave a copy for them to review. You can expect occasionally to find a person has canceled an appointment but wants you to leave a copy of your songs so they can listen and contact you later. (Never give someone the only (or last) copy of your demo if you absolutely want it returned, though.)

Where should I network while visiting?

Coordinate your trip with a music conference or make plans to visit ASCAP, BMI, or SESAC offices while you are there. For example, the South by Southwest Music Conference in Austin and NSAI Spring Symposium in Nashville often feature demo listening sessions, where industry professionals listen to demos submitted by songwriters attending the seminar. ASCAP, BMI, and SESAC also sometimes sponsor seminars or allow aspiring songwriters to make appointments with counselors who can give them solid advice.

How do I deal with rejection?

Many good songs have been rejected simply because they were not what the publisher or record company was looking for at that particular point. Do not take it personally. If few people like your songs, it does not mean they are not good. On the other hand, if you have a clear vision for what your particular songs are trying to convey, specific comments can also teach you a lot about whether your concept is coming across as you intended. If you hear the same criticisms of your songs over and over—for instance, the feel of the melody isn't right or the lyrics need work—give the advice serious thought. Listen carefully, and use what the reviewers say constructively to improve your songs.

SUBMITTING OVER THE INTERNET

Is it Okay to submit over the Internet?

More and more, this is becoming a standard practice, but many companies still require regular mail submissions, so make sure you verify which process the company prefers. Web-based companies like Songspace.com and TAXI, among many others, are making an effort to connect songwriters and industry professionals over the Internet. The Internet is proving important for networking. Garageband.com has extensive bulletin boards and allows members to post audio files of songs for critique.

If I want to try submitting over the Internet, what should I do?

First, send an e-mail to confirm whether a music company is equipped to stream or download audio files properly (whether MP3 or streaming at Bandcamp, Soundcloud, etc.). If they do accept demos online, it is possible to use sites such as Dropbox to set up an online folder for sharing. Many e-mail services also have larger maximum file sizes for attachments than they used to, making it easier to e-mail songs. Another strategy is to build a website with audio files that can be streamed or downloaded, or make YouTube videos using just a band photo or album cover image, or better yet, a memorable video. Then, when you have permission, send an e-mail with links to that website or to particular songs. All they have to do is click on the link, and it launches their web browser to the appropriate page. Do not try to send MP3s or other files as attachments if the company doesn't accept them or doesn't request them.

HOW DO I AVOID THE RIP-OFFS?

The music industry has its share of dishonest, greedy people who will try to rip you off by appealing to your ambition, by stroking your ego, or by claiming special powers to make you successful—for a price, of course. Most of them use similar methods, and you can prevent a lot of heartbreak by learning to spot them and stay away.

Service vs. Rip-off

First we should note that there are many legit services out there for songwriters that charge money in order to use them. For example, there are many high-quality demo-recording services that will record your demo with professional musicians for a reasonable cost, but there are also some who will overcharge and use low-quality talent and equipment. You must research their services, compare their fees with other companies thoroughly, and request samples that sound satisfactory for what you are paying. There are also helpful curatorial services like TAXI where you can pay a small per-opportunity fee or an annual fee to expose your work to industry professionals and gain feedback. Still, there are other services that will promise miracles and ask for a large sum of money in order to re-record your demo, include it in an anthology, or send it to producers. Never pay fees for these kinds of services, especially if you are not sure of the quality of the service or product, or if you find many complaints about them online. Make sure you take the following advice to heart before you agree to pay any company any fee for any service.

What is a "song shark"?

"Song sharks," as they're called, prey on beginners—songwriters unfamiliar with how the music industry works and what the ethical standards are. Two general signs of a song shark are:

- Song sharks will take *any* songs—quality doesn't count.
- They're not concerned with future royalties since they get their money up front from songwriters who think they're getting a great deal by having their song shopped around for them.

What are some of the most blatant rip-offs?

A request for money up front is the most common element. Song sharks may ask for money in the form of submission fees, an outright offer to publish your song for a fee, or an offer to re-record your demo for a sometimes hefty price (with the implication that they will make your song wildly successful if you only pay to have it re-demoed in *their* studio). While there are legitimate services such as professional demo-recording companies who will charge fees, some basic online research and company reviews will be able to help you decide whether or not they are the real deal or sharks. Always, always, always research companies first!

Here is a list of other tips and hints that can help you avoid a lot of scams:

- **DO NOT SELL YOUR SONGS OUTRIGHT!** It's unethical for anyone to offer such a proposition. If your song becomes successful after you've sold it outright, you will never get royalties for it.
- **NEVER PAY "SUBMISSION FEES," "REVIEW FEES," "SERVICE FEES," "FILING FEES," ETC.** Reputable companies review material free of charge. If you encounter a company in this book that charges to submit, report them to the editor. If a company charges "only" $15 to submit your song, consider this: *If "only" one hundred songwriters pay the $15, this company has made an extra $1,500 just for opening the mail!*
- **NEVER PAY TO HAVE YOUR SONGS PUBLISHED.** A reputable company interested in your songs assumes the responsibility and cost of promoting them, in hopes of realizing a profit once the songs are recorded and released. If they truly believe in your song, they will accept the costs involved. They will pay *you.*
- **DO NOT PAY A COMPANY TO PAIR YOU WITH A COLLABORATOR.** It's much better to contact a songwriting organization that offers collaboration services to their members.
- **NEVER PAY TO HAVE YOUR LYRICS OR POEMS SET TO MUSIC.** This is a classic rip-off. "Music mills"—for a price—may use the same melody for hundreds of lyrics and poems, whether it sounds good or not. Publishers recognize one of these melodies as soon as they hear it.
- **AVOID "PAY-TO-PLAY" CD COMPILATION DEALS.** It's totally unrealistic to expect this will open doors for you. These are mainly moneymakers for the music company. CDs are cheap to manufacture, so a company that charges $100 to include your recording on a CD is making a killing. They claim they send these CDs to radio stations, producers, etc., but they usually end up in the trash or as drink coasters. Music-industry professionals have no incentive to listen to them. Everybody on the

IF YOU WRITE LYRICS BUT NOT MUSIC

- Find a collaborator. The music business is looking for the complete package: music plus lyrics. If you don't write music, find a collaborator who does. The best way to find a collaborator is through songwriting organizations. Check the Organizations section for songwriting groups near you.
- Avoid rip-offs. "Music mills" advertise in the back of magazines or solicit you through the mail. For a fee they will set your lyrics or poems to music. The rip-off is that they may use the same melody for hundreds of lyrics and poems, whether it sounds good or not. Publishers recognize one of these melodies as soon as they hear it.

CD paid to be included, so it's not as if they were carefully screened for quality.

- **AVOID "SONGPLUGGERS" WHO OFFER TO "SHOP" YOUR SONG FOR AN UP FRONT FEE OR RETAINER.** This practice is not appropriate for *Songwriter's Market* readers, many of whom are beginners and live away from major music centers like Nashville. Professional, established songwriters in Nashville are sometimes known to work on a fee basis with songpluggers they have gotten to know over many years, *but the practice is controversial even for professionals.* Also, the songpluggers used by established professionals are very selective about their clients and have their own reputation to uphold. Companies who offer you these services but barely know you or your work are to be avoided. Also, contracting a songplugger long distance offers little or no accountability—you have no direct way of knowing what they're doing on your behalf.
- **AVOID PAYING A FEE UP-FRONT TO HAVE A PUBLISHER MAKE A DEMO OF YOUR SONG.** Some publishers may take your pro-rata share of demo expenses out of your future royalties (a negotiable contract point usually meant to avoid endless demo sessions). But you should avoid paying up-front for demo costs unless the company is solely a demo-publishing firm and not also a publisher. Avoid situations where it is implied or expressed that a company will publish your song when you pay up-front to use their demo services. The two services are separate.
- **NO RECORD COMPANY SHOULD ASK YOU TO PAY THEM OR AN ASSOCIATED COMPANY TO MAKE A DEMO.** The job of a record company is to make records and decide which artists to sign *after* listening to demo submissions.
- **READ ALL CONTRACTS CAREFULLY BEFORE SIGNING.** And don't sign any contract you're unsure about or that you don't fully understand. It is well worth paying an attorney for the time it takes her to review a contract if you can avoid a bad situation that may cost you thousands of dollars.
- **BEFORE ENTERING A SONGWRITING CONTEST, READ THE RULES CAREFULLY.** Be sure that what you're giving up in the way of entry fees, etc., is not more than what you stand to gain by winning the contest (see the Contests & Awards section).

- **VERIFY ANY SITUATION ABOUT AN INDIVIDUAL OR COMPANY IF YOU HAVE ANY DOUBTS.** Contact the company's Performing Rights Society—ASCAP, BMI, SESAC, or SOCAN (in Canada). Check with the Better Business Bureau in the company's town, or contact the state attorney general's office. Contact professional organizations of which you're a member and inquire about the company's reputation.
- **IF A RECORD COMPANY OR OTHER COMPANY ASKS YOU TO PAY EXPENSES UP-FRONT, BE CAREFUL.** Record producers commonly charge up-front to produce an artist's album. Small indie labels sometimes ask a band to help with recording costs (but seek less control than a major label might). It's up to you to decide whether or not it is a good idea. Talk to other artists who have signed similar contracts before you sign one yourself. Research companies to find out if they can deliver on their claims and what kind of distribution they have. Visit their website, if they have one. Beware of any company that won't let you know what it has done in the past. If a company has had successes and good working relationships with artists, it should be happy to brag about them.

HOW DO I FILE A COMPLAINT?

Write to the *Songwriter's Market* editor at: 10151 Carver Road, Suite 200, Blue Ash, OH 45262. Include:

- a complete description of the situation, as best you can describe it
- copies of any materials a company may have sent you that we may keep on file

If you encounter situations similar to any of the "song shark" scenarios described previously, let us know about it.

Should I hire a producer to produce me? Is that money well spent?

It depends. What are your goals? If you write songs, but do not sing or perform, you are looking for publishing opportunities with the producer instead of someone who can help you record an album or CD. If you are a performing artist or band, then you might be in the market to hire a producer, in which case you will most likely pay them up front (and possibly give them a share in royalties or publishing, depending on the specific deal you negotiate). For more information see the Record Producers section introduction and the Royalties section.

Will it help me avoid rip-offs if I join a songwriting organization?

Yes. You will have access to a lot of good advice from a lot of experienced people. You will be able to research and compare notes, which will help you avoid pitfalls.

What should I know about contracts?

Negotiating a fair contract is important. You must protect yourself, and there are specific things you should look for in a contract. See the Contracts section for more information.

Are companies that offer demo services automatically bad?

No, but you are not obligated to make use of their services. Many music companies have their own or related recording studios, and with good recording equipment becoming so cheap and easy to use in recent years, a lot of them are struggling to stay afloat. This doesn't mean a company is necessarily trying to rip you off, but use your best judgment. In some cases, a company will submit a listing to *Songwriter's Market* for the wrong reasons—to pitch their demo services instead of finding songs to sign—in which case you should report them to the *Songwriter's Market* editor.

SUBMISSION STRATEGIES

LYRICISTS & SONGWRITERS

Here's a short list of avenues nonperforming songwriters can pursue when submitting songs:

1. **SUBMIT TO A MUSIC PUBLISHER.** This is the obvious one, and songwriters with a growing portfolio of songs should start here. Look at the information under Music in the listing to see examples of a publisher's songs and the artists they work with. Do you recognize the songs? Have you heard of the artists? Who are the writers? Do they have cuts with artists you would like to get a song to? Research each thoroughly before you submit so you come across as knowledgeable as possible.

2. **SUBMIT TO A RECORD COMPANY.** See if artists listed with the record company perform and record many songs written by outside lyricists. If you are strictly a songwriter, ask if the record company has a group or artist in development who needs outside material.

3. **SUBMIT TO A RECORD PRODUCER.** Do the producer's credits in the listings show songs written by songwriters other than the artist? Does he produce name artists known for using outside material? Be aware that producers themselves often write with the artists, so your song might also be competing against the producer's songwriting.

4. **SUBMIT TO AN ARTIST'S MANAGER.** If an artist needs songs, his or her manager is a prime gateway for your song. Contact the manager and ask if he has an act in need of material.

5. **JOIN A SONGWRITING ORGANIZATION.** Songwriting organizations are a good way to make contacts. Through the contacts you make, you'll discover opportunities that others might not hear about. Some organizations can put you in direct con-

tact with publishers for song-critique sessions. You can increase your chances of a hit by co-writing with other songwriters. Your songs will get better because of the feedback from other members.

6. **APPROACH PERFORMING RIGHTS ORGANIZATIONS (PROS).** PROs like ASCAP and BMI have writer-relation representatives who can sometimes (if they think you're ready) give you a reference to a music company. This is one of the favored routes to success in the Nashville music scene.

PERFORMING ARTISTS & BANDS

This is a bit more complicated because there are a lot of different avenues available for artists who both write and perform their own songs.

Finding a Record Deal

This is often a performing songwriter's primary goal—to get a record deal and release an album. Here are some possible ways to approach it:

1. **APPROACH A RECORD COMPANY FOR A RECORD DEAL.** This is an obvious one. Independent labels will be a lot more approachable than major labels, which are usually deluged with demos. Independent labels give you more artistic freedom, while major labels will demand more compromise, especially if you do not have a previous track record. A compromise between the two is to approach one of the "fake indie" labels owned by a major. You'll get some of the benefits of an indie, but with more of the resources and connections of a major label.

2. **APPROACH A RECORD PRODUCER FOR A DEVELOPMENT DEAL.** Some producers sign artists, produce their albums, develop them like a record company, and then approach major labels for distribution deals. This has advantages and drawbacks. For example, the producer gives you guidance and connections, but it can also be harder to get paid because you are signed to the producer and not the label.

3. **GET A MANAGER WITH CONNECTIONS.** The right manager with the right connections can make all the difference in getting a record deal.

4. **ASK A MUSIC PUBLISHER.** Some publishers are helping to develop performing songwriters as artists. Many major publishers are sister companies to record labels and can shop you for a deal when they think you're ready. They do this in the hope of participating in the mechanical royalties from an album release, and these monies can be substantial when it's a major label release.

5. **APPROACH AN ENTERTAINMENT ATTORNEY.** Entertainment attorneys are a must when it comes to negotiating record contracts, and some moonlight by helping artists make connections for record deals (they will get their cut, of course).

Finding a Producer to Help with Your Album

Independently minded performing songwriters often find they need help navigating the studio when it comes time to produce their own album. In this case, the producer often works for an up-front fee from the artist, for a percentage of the royalty when the album is released and sold (referred to as "points," as in "percentage points"), or a combination of both.

Things to keep in mind when submitting a demo to a producer on this basis:

1. **IS THE PRODUCER KNOWN FOR A PARTICULAR GENRE OR "SOUND"?** Many producers have a signature sound to their studio productions and are often connected to specific genres. Phil Spector had the "Wall of Sound." Bob Rock pioneered a glossy metal sound for Metallica and the Cult. Daniel Lanois and Brian Eno are famous for the atmospheres they created on albums by U2. Look at your favorite CDs to see who produced them. Use these as touchstones when approaching producers to see if they are on your wavelength.

2. **WHAT ROLE DOES A PARTICULAR PRODUCER LIKE TO TAKE IN THE STUDIO?** The Tips information found at the end of many of the Record Producers listings often have notes from the producer about how they like to work with performing songwriters in the studio. Some work closely as a partner with the artist on developing arrangements and coaching performances. Some prefer final authority on creative decisions. Think carefully about what kind of working relationship you want.

Finding a Manager

Many performing songwriters eventually find it necessary to locate a manager who will help develop their careers and find gigs. Some things to keep in mind when looking:

1. **DOES THE MANAGER WORK WITH ARTISTS IN MY GENRE OF MUSIC?** A manager who typically works with punk rock bands may not have as many connections useful to an aspiring country singer-songwriter. A manager who mainly works with gospel artists might not know what to do with a hedonistic rock band.

2. **HOW BIG IS THE MANAGER'S AGENCY?** If a manager is working with multiple acts but has a small (or no) staff, you might not get the attention you want. Some of the listings include information about the agency's staff size.

3. **DOES THE MANAGER WORK WITH ACTS FROM MY REGION?** Many of the listings have information describing whether they work with regional acts only or artists from any region.

4. **DOES THE MANAGER WORK WITH NAME ACTS?** A manager with famous clients could work wonders for your career. Or you could get lost in the shuffle. Use your best judgment when sizing up a potential manager, and be clear with yourself about the

kind of relationship you would like to have and the level of attention you want for your career.

5. **IF I'M A BEGINNER, WILL THE MANAGER WORK FOR ME?** Check the listings for the Openness to Submissions icons ⊘ ◯ ◐ ● to find companies open to beginners. Some may suggest extensive changes to your music or image. On the other hand, you may have a strong vision of what you want to do and need a manager who will work with you to achieve that vision. Decide for yourself how much you are willing to compromise in good faith. Remember that a relationship between you and a manager is a two-way street. You will have to earn each other's trust and be clear about your goals for mutual success.

ROYALTIES

NONPERFORMING SONGWRITERS

How do songwriters make money?

The quick answer is that songwriters make money from rights available to them through copyright law. For more details, keep reading and see the upcoming Copyright section.

What specific rights make money for songwriters?

There are two primary ways songwriters earn money on their songs: performance royalties and mechanical royalties.

What is a performance royalty?

When you hear a song on the radio, on television, in the elevator, in a restaurant, etc., the songwriter receives royalties, called performance royalties. Performing Rights Organizations (ASCAP, BMI, and SESAC in the U.S.A.) collect payment from radio stations, television, etc., and distribute those payments to songwriters (see below).

What is a mechanical royalty?

When a record company puts a song onto a CD or online and distributes copies for sale, they owe a royalty payment to the songwriter for each copy they press of the album. It is called a mechanical royalty because of the mechanical process used to mass-produce a copy of a CD or sheet music. The payment is small per song (see the "Royalty Provisions" subhead of the sidebar in the Contracts section), but the earnings can add up and reach massive pro-

MUSIC PUBLISHING ROYALTIES

portions for songs appearing on successful label albums. Note: This royalty is totally different from the artist royalty on the retail price of the album.

Who collects the money for performance and mechanical royalties?

Performing Rights Organizations collect performance royalties, and there are three organizations that do this: ASCAP, BMI, and SESAC. These organizations arose many years ago when songwriters and music publishers gathered together to press for their rights and improve their ability to collect fees for the use of their songs. ASCAP, BMI, and SESAC collect fees for the use of songs and then pass along the money to their member songwriters and music publishers.

MECHANICAL RIGHTS ORGANIZATIONS COLLECT MECHANICAL ROYALTIES. There are three organizations that collect mechanical royalties: the Harry Fox Agency (HFA), the American Mechanical Rights Organization (AMRA), and the Songwriters Guild of America (SGA). These three organizations collect mechanical royalties from record companies of all sizes—major labels, midsize, and independents—and pass the royalties along to member music publishers and songwriters.

How do songwriters hook up with this system to earn royalties?

For performance royalties, individual songwriters need to create a publishing company and apply to a Performing Rights Organization of their choice as both a writer and a publisher and register their songs in the PRO database. Each PRO has a slightly different method of calculating payment, a different ownership, and a different membership structure, so choosing a PRO is an individual choice. Once a songwriter is affiliated and has registered his or her songs, the PROs then collect fees as described above and issue a check to the songwriter.

For mechanical royalties, different things can happen:

1. The songwriter is not signed to a publisher and owns exclusive rights to his songs and so works with AMRA or the Songwriters Guild of America, who cuts a check directly to the songwriter instead of passing him or her to the publisher first.
2. They are signed to a publisher, but the songs are being released on albums by independent labels. In this case, the songwriter often works with AMRA since they focus on the independent music publishing market.

PERFORMING ARTISTS

How do performing artists make money?

Performing artists (if they write their own songs) make money the same way songwriters do, by licensing their songs through a music publisher, but they also make money through royalties made on the retail price of an album when it is sold online, in a store, etc. Thus it is important for performing artists to contact both music publishers in order to license their songs *and* record companies and producers in order to record them. Be careful of "360-Degree" deals, in which labels seek to work with performing artists who write their own material and combine the licensing and retail royalty streams into one deal. It is in your interest to keep them separate.

What about all the stories of performing songwriters who get into bad deals?

The stories of artists and bands signing bad deals with record companies are generally true, but if they're smart, performing artists will try to hold on to performing and mechanical royalties. But when it comes to retail sale royalties, all they will usually see is an "advance"—essentially a loan—which must then be paid off from record sales. You will not see a royalty check on retail sales until your advance is paid off. If you are given a $600,000 advance, for example, you will have to pay back the record company $600,000 out of your sales royalties before you see any more money.

Do performing artists get to keep the advance?

Not really. If you have a manager who has gotten you a record deal, he or she will take a cut. You will probably be required in the contract to pay for the producer and studio time to make the album. Often the producer will take a percentage of subsequent royalties from album sales, which comes out of your pocket. There are also music video costs, promotion to radio stations, tour support, paying sidemen, etc. Just about anything you can think of is eventually paid for out of your advance or out of sales royalties. Deductions to royalties that make it harder to earn out an advance are usually built into record-company contracts.

What should a performing songwriter wanting to sign with a major label do?

Songwriters' best option is to negotiate a fair contract, get as large an advance as possible, and then manage that advance money the best they can. A good contract will keep the songwriting royalties described above separate from the flow of sales royalties and will also cut down on the number of royalty deductions the record company builds into the contract. And because of the difficulty in earning out any size advance or auditing the record company, it makes sense to get as much cash up front as you can. Basically, you will need a good lawyer.

RECORD COMPANIES, PRODUCERS, MANAGERS, & BOOKING AGENTS

How do music publishers make money?

A publisher works as a songwriter's agent, looks for profitable commercial uses for the songs he or she represents and then takes a percentage of the profits—often referred to as the *publisher's share*. The songwriter should receive no less than 50 percent of the income his or her song generates. That means the songwriter and publisher split the total royalties 50/50. A successful publisher stays in contact with several A&R reps at various labels, as well as producers and television/film professionals, in order to fine out what upcoming projects are in need of new material and whether any songs he or she represents will be appropriate.

How do record companies make money?

Record companies primarily make their money from profits made selling CDs, DVDs, downloads, etc. Record companies keep most of the profit after subtracting manufacturing costs, royalties to recording artists, distribution fees, and the costs of promoting songs to radio (for major labels this can reach up to $300,000 per song). Record companies sometimes have music-publishing divisions that make money performing all the functions of publishers.

How do record producers make money?

Producers make most of their money by charging a flat fee up front to helm a recording project, by sharing in the royalties from album sales, or both. A small independent producer might charge $10,000 (sometimes less) up front to produce a small indie band, while a "name" producer such as Bob Rock, who regularly works with major-label bands, might charge $300,000. Either of these might also take a share in sales royalties, referred to as "points"—as in "percentage points." A producer might say, "I'll produce you for $10,000 and two points." If an artist is getting a 15-percent royalty on album sales, then two of those percentage points will go to the producer instead. Producers also make money by co-writing with the artists to get publishing royalties. However, producers should not take any points or percentages on publishing royalties for songs they did not write or co-write, only retail/mechanical royalties.

How do managers make money?

Most managers make money by taking a percentage commission of their clients' income, usually 10–25 percent. If a touring band finishes a show and makes a $2,000 profit, a manager on 15-percent commission would get $300. If an artist gets a $40,000 advance from a midsize label, the manager would get $6,000. Whether an artist's songwriting income is included in the manager's commission comes down to negotiation. The commission should give the manager incentive to make things happen for your career, so avoid paying flat fees up front.

COPYRIGHT

How am I protected by copyright law?

Copyright protection applies to your songs the instant you put them down in fixed form—a recording, sheet music, lead sheet, etc. This protection lasts for your lifetime plus seventy years (or the lifetime of the last surviving writer, if you co-wrote the song with somebody else). When you prepare demos, place notification of copyright on all copies of your song—the lyric sheets, lead sheets, and labels for CDs, etc. The notice is simply the word "copyright" or the symbol © followed by the year the song was created (or published) and your name (Example: © 2013 by John Q. Songwriter).

What parts of a song are protected by copyright?

Traditionally, only the melody line and the lyrics are eligible for copyright. Period. Chords and rhythm are virtually never protected. An incredibly original arrangement can sometimes qualify. Sound recordings can also be copyrighted as Recording Copyrights, but this applies strictly to the actual sounds on the recording, not the song itself, which is considered the Composition Copyright. The Recording Copyright is usually owned by record companies, while the Composition is owned by the songwriter or music publisher.

What songs are not protected?

Song titles or mere ideas for music and lyrics cannot be copyrighted. Very old songs in the "public domain" are not protected. You could quote a melody from a Bach piece, but you could not then stop someone else from quoting the same melody in his song.

When would I lose or have to share the copyright?

If you collaborate with other writers, they are assumed to have equal interests unless you state some other arrangement (in writing). If you write under a work-for-hire arrangement, the company or person who hired you to write the song then owns the copyright. Sometimes your spouse may automatically be granted an interest in your copyright as part of his or her spousal rights, which might then become important if you get divorced.

Should I register my copyright?

Registering your copyright with the Library of Congress gives the best possible protection. Registration establishes a public record of your copyright—even though a song is legally protected, whether or not it is registered—and could prove useful in any future court cases involving the song. Registration also entitles you to a potentially greater settlement in a copyright infringement lawsuit.

How do I register my song?

To register your song, you can do so online or request government form PA from the Copyright Office. Visit them at www.copyright.gov, or call the 24-hour hotline at (202) 707-9100 and leave your name and address on the messaging system. To complete the form online or via postal mail, you must fill out the form, pay a registration fee, submit the song via upload or CD, and include a lead sheet of your song. Via postal mail, send them to the Register of Copyrights, Copyright Office, Library of Congress, Washington DC 20559. It may take several months to receive your certificate of registration from the Copyright Office, but your songs are protected from the date of creation (the date of registration will reflect the date you applied). For more information, call the Copyright Office's Public Information Office at (202) 707-3000 or visit their website at www.copyright.gov.

How likely is it that someone will try to steal my song?

Copyright infringement is very rare. But if you ever feel that one of your songs has been stolen—that someone has unlawfully infringed on your copyright—you must prove that you created the work and that the person you are suing had access to your song. Copyright registration is the best proof of a date of creation. You must have your copyright registered in order to file a lawsuit. Also, it's helpful if you keep your rough drafts and revisions of songs, either on page, CD, or digitally.

Why did song sharks begin soliciting me after I registered my song?

This is one potential, unintended consequence of registering your song with the Library of Congress. The copyright indexes are a public record of your songwriting, and song sharks often search the copyright indexes and mail solicitations for songwriters who live outside of the range of major music centers such as Nashville. They figure these songwriters don't know any better and are easy prey. *Do not allow this possibility to stop you from registering your songs!* Just be aware, educate yourself, and then throw the song sharks' mailings in the trash.

What if I mail a CD to myself to get a postmark date on a sealed envelope?

The "poor man's copyright" has not stood up in court and is not an acceptable substitute for registering your song. If you feel it's important to shore up your copyright, register it with the Library of Congress.

for the draw date printed on the reverse side OR the purchase date for EZPLAY® Games. Winning tickets and Pay-to-Bearer receipts must be presented for payment within 180 days of the draw date or purchase date of EZPLAY® Games. Ohio Lottery Games and players are subject to Ohio Laws and Lottery Commission rules and regulations. Your name and likeness may be utilized for administrative and/or promotional purposes. For automated current or past winning number information, call 1-800-589-6446. For cashing locations and further information, please visit www.ohiolottery.com or for customer service, call 1-800-686-4208.

Signature

Print (name)

OH!

LOTTERY®

615 W. Superior Ave · Cleveland, Ohio 44113-1879

PLEASE PLAY RESPONSIBLY

106885050571

Check your ticket carefully. An original winning Lottery ticket and is the only receipt you have to claim your prize.

PROPER CARE OF TICKET: ◆ Avoid heat ◆ Keep dry ◆ Avoid prolonged exposure to direct sunlight.

TO CLAIM YOUR PRIZE:

◆ To immediately collect your prize of up to $599 per wager, present your ticket to any Ohio Lottery Retailer

◆ For prizes between $600 and $5,000, winners may have their ticket validated by any Ohio Lottery Retailer and receive a Pay-to-Bearer receipt and a claim form. For payment options, please refer to back of claim form for detailed instructions.

◆ For prizes over $5,000, winners must submit their ticket to an Ohio Lottery office for validation and check processing.

OTHER IMPORTANT INFORMATION:

The Ohio Lottery is not responsible for lost or stolen tickets. Tickets are void if altered. This ticket is only valid for the draw date printed on the reverse side OR the purchase date for EZPLAY® Games. Winning tickets and Pay-to-Bearer receipts must be presented for payment within 180 days of the draw date or purchase date of EZPLAY® Games. Ohio Lottery Games and players are subject to Ohio Laws and Lottery Commission rules and regulations. Your name and likeness may be utilized for administrative and/or promotional purposes. For automated current or past winning number information, call 1-800-589-6446. For cashing locations and further information, please visit www.ohiolottery.com or for customer service, call 1-800-686-4208.

re

615 W. Superior Ave · Cleveland, Ohio 44113-1879

EASE PLAY RESPONSIBLY

106885050572

original winning Lottery ticket is a Bearer instrument to claim your prize.

Avoid heat ◆ Keep dry ◆ Avoid prolonged exposure to direct sunlight.

up to $599 per wager, present your ticket to any Ohio Lottery Retailer
winners may have their ticket validated by any Ohio Lottery Retailer
·1 a claim form. For payment options, please refer to back of claim

PRINTED ON 10/18/2018   14:56:09
40265 31874 06768 41472 22198 89626 61836

A. 21 27 34 45 58   AP MB: 25 AF

MEGAPLIER® - YES

FOR 1 DRAW (02236) Fri Oct 19 18

$3.00

THE MEGA MILLIONS JACKPOT IS AT AN A
TIME HIGH! THE FRIDAY OCTOBER
DRAWING JACKPOT IS OVER $8
PLAY MEGA MIL

Game Rul

DRAW RESULTS: 1-8

046630 -046630 C
1295A2BC7A7582B9C
40265 31874 06768 4

CAREER SONGWRITING

//

What career options are open to songwriters who do not perform?

The possibilities range from a beginning songwriter living away from a music center like Nashville who lands an occasional single-song publishing deal to a staff songwriter signed to a major publishing company, although these opportunities are much harder to come by and may require a substantial number of high-quality songs and a good deal of face-to-face networking to obtain such a position. There are many songwriters who operate independently, have developed a lot of connections, work with numerous artists, and have set up their own independent publishing operations. No matter the career path, it still starts with getting the one right song heard by the one right person.

What is "single-song" songwriting about?

In this case, a songwriter submits songs to many different companies. One or two songs gain interest from different publishers, and the songwriter signs separate contracts for each song with each publisher. The songwriter can then pitch other songs to other publishers. In Nashville, for instance, a single-song contract is usually the first taste of success for an aspiring songwriter on his or her way up the ladder. Success of this sort can induce a songwriter to move to a music center like Nashville or Los Angeles (if he or she hasn't already) and is a big boost for a struggling songwriter already living there. A series of single-song contracts often signals a songwriter's maturing skill and marketability.

What is a "staff songwriter"?

A staff songwriter usually works for a major publisher and receives a monthly stipend as an advance against the royalties he or she is likely to earn for the publisher. The music publisher has exclusive rights to everything the songwriter writes while signed to the company. The publisher also works actively on the writer's behalf to hook him or her up with co-writers and other opportunities. A staff songwriting position is highly treasured by many because it offers a steady income and these positions are very hard to come by as they require a solid track record and substantial networking. In Nashville, landing such a position is a sign the songwriter "has arrived." Songwriters who are lucky and talented enough to reach this level have a significant reputation for their ability to write hit songs. Famous artists seek them out, and they often write actively in several markets at once. They also write on assignment for film and television and commonly keep their own publishing companies to maximize their income.

As my career grows, what should I do about keeping track of expenses, etc.?

You should keep a ledger or notebook with records of all financial transactions related to your songwriting—royalty checks, demo costs, office supplies, postage, travel expenses, dues to organizations, class and workshop fees, plus any publications you purchase pertaining to songwriting. You may also want a separate checking account devoted to your songwriting activities. This will make record-keeping easier and help to establish your identity as a business for tax purposes. A music publisher will help you manage these aspects of the music business for you or will at least put you on the right track to an entertainment lawyer or accountant. But always keep your own records as well in order to protect yourself.

What should I know about taxes related to songwriting income?

Any royalties you receive will not reflect taxes or any other mandatory deductions. It is your responsibility to keep track of income and file the correct tax forms. For specific information, contact the IRS or talk to an accountant who serves music-industry clients.

CONTRACTS

CO-WRITING

What kind of agreements do I need with co-writers?

You may need to sign a legal agreement between you and a co-writer to establish percentages you will each receive of the writer's royalties. The co-writers will need to decide many other things moving forward: Who do we want to pitch to? Do we accept a hold? What is our demo budget? Will we change the song in response to plugger or publisher feedback? Tough, awkward situations may arise. For example, if a major artist or producer wants to cut your song for his or her album but also wants to rewrite some lyrics and take a share of the publishing (which many consider an unacceptable and predatory practice since no co-writer status should be given to anyone once the song is created)—you and your co-writer need to agree whether it is better to get a song on an album that might sell millions (and make a lot of money) or pass on it because you object on principle to being forced to give up credit. You and your co-writer should be on the same page on all of these minor and major issues, no matter how rare they may be.

When do I need a lawyer to look over agreements?

When it comes to doing business with a publisher, producer, or record company, you should always have the contract reviewed by a knowledgeable entertainment attorney. As long as the issues at stake are simple, the co-writers respect each other, and they discuss their business philosophies before writing a song together, they can probably write an agreement without the aid of a lawyer.

SINGLE-SONG CONTRACTS

What is a single-song contract?

A music publisher offers a single-song contract when he or she wants to sign one of your songs but doesn't want to hire you as a staff songwriter. You assign your rights to a particular song to the publisher for an agreed-upon number of years so that he or she may represent the song and find uses profitable for both of you. This is a common contract and quite possibly will be the first you encounter in your songwriting career.

What basic elements should every single-song contract contain?

Every contract should have the publisher's name, the writer's name, the song's title, the date, and the purpose of the agreement. The songwriter also declares that the song is an original work and that he or she is creator of the work. The contract *must* specify the royalties the songwriter will earn from various uses of the song, including performance, mechanical, print, and synchronization royalties.

How should the royalties usually be divided in the contract?

The songwriter should receive no less than 50 percent of the income his or her song generates. That means the songwriter and publisher split the total royalties 50/50. The songwriter's half is called the "writer's share," and the publisher's half is called the "publisher's share." If there is more than one songwriter, the songwriters split the writer's share. Sometimes successful songwriters will bargain for a percentage of the publisher's share, negotiating what is basically a co-publishing agreement. For a visual explanation of how royalties are collected and flow to the songwriter, see the chart called Music Publishing Royalties in the Royalties section.

What should the contract say about a "reversion clause"?

Songwriters should always negotiate for a "reversion clause," which returns all rights to the songwriter if some provision of the contract is not met. Most reversion clauses give a publisher a set amount of time (usually one or two years) to work the song and make money with it. If the publisher can't get the song recorded and released during the agreed-upon time period, the songwriter can then take his song to another publisher. The danger of not getting some sort of reversion clause is that you could wind up with a publisher sitting on your song for the entire life-plus-seventy-years term of the copyright—which may as well be forever.

Is a reversion clause difficult to get?

Some publishers agree to it and figure that if they can't get any action with the song in the first year or two, they're not likely to ever have much luck with it. Other publishers may be reluctant to agree to a reversion clause. They may invest a lot of time and money in producing the demo and pitching it to artists and may want to keep working at it for a longer period of time. Or, for example, a producer might put a song on hold for a while and then go into a lengthy recording project. A year can easily go by before the artist or producer decides which songs to release as singles. This means you may have to agree to a longer time period, be flexible, and trust that the publisher has your best mutual interests in mind. Use your judgment.

BASIC SONG CONTRACT POINTERS

The following list, taken from a Songwriters Guild of America publication, enumerates the basic features of an acceptable songwriting contract:

1) **WORK FOR HIRE.** When you receive a contract covering just one composition, you should make sure the phrases "employment for hire" and "exclusive writer agreement" are not included. Also, there should be no options for future songs.

2) **PERFORMING RIGHTS AFFILIATION.** If you previously signed publishing contracts, you should be affiliated with ASCAP, BMI, or SESAC. You must receive all performance royalties directly from your performing rights organization, and this should be written into your contract.

3) **REVERSION CLAUSE.** The contract should include a provision that if the publisher does not secure a release of a commercial sound recording within a specified time (one year, two years, etc.), you may terminated the contract.

4) **CHANGES IN THE COMPOSITION.** If the contract includes a provision that the publisher can change the title, lyrics, or music, this should be amended so that only with your consent can such changes be made.

5) **ROYALTY PROVISIONS.** You should receive 50 percent of all publisher's income on all licenses issued. If the publisher prints and sells his own sheet music, your royalty should be 10 percent of the wholesale selling price. The royalty should not be stated in the contract as a flat rate ($.05, $.07, etc.).

6) **NEGOTIABLE DEDUCTIONS.** Ideally, demos and all other expenses of publication should be paid 100 percent by the publisher. The only allowable fee is for the Harry Fox Agency collection fee, whereby the writer pays half of the amount charged to the publisher for mechanical rights. The current mechanical royalty collected by the Harry Fox Agency is $.091 cents per cut for songs under five minutes; and $.0175 cents per minute for songs over five minutes.

7) **ROYALTY STATEMENTS AND AUDIT PROVISION.** Once the song is recorded, you are entitled to receive royalty statements at least once every six months. In addition, an audit provision with no time restriction should be included in every contract.

8) **WRITER'S CREDIT.** The publisher should make sure that you receive proper credit on all uses of the composition.

9) **ARBITRATION.** In order to avoid large legal fees in case of a dispute with your publisher, the contract should include an arbitration clause.

10) **FUTURE USES.** Any use not specifically covered by the contract should be retained by the writer to be negotiated as it comes up.

What other basic issues should a single-song contract cover?

The contract should also address these issues:

- Will an advance be paid, and if so, how much will the advance be?
- When will royalties be paid (annually or semiannually)?
- Who will pay for demos—the publisher, songwriter, or both?
- How will lawsuits against copyright infringement be handled, including the cost of lawsuits?
- Will the publisher have the right to sell its interest in the song to another publisher without the songwriter's consent?
- Does the publisher have the right to make changes in a song or approve changes by someone else without the songwriter's consent?
- The songwriter should have the right to audit the publisher's books if he feels it is necessary and gives the publisher reasonable notice.

WHEN DOES 50 PERCENT EQUAL 100 PERCENT?

NOTE: The publisher's and songwriter's share of the income are sometimes referred to as each being 100 percent—for 200 percent total! You might hear someone say, "I'll take 100 percent of the publisher's share." Do not be needlessly confused! If the numbers confuse you, ask for the terms to be clarified.

Where else can I go for advice on contracts?

The Songwriters Guild of America has drawn up a Popular Songwriter's Contract, which it believes to be the best minimum songwriter contract available (see the Basic Song Contract Pointers sidebar). The Guild will send a copy of the contract at no charge to any interested songwriter upon request (see the Songwriters Guild of America listing in the Organizations section). SGA will also review—free of charge—any contract offered to its members and will check it for fairness and completeness. Also check out these two books published by Writer's Digest Books: *The Craft and Business of Songwriting*, 3rd edition, by John Braheny; and *The New Songwriter's Guide to Music Publishing*, 3rd edition, by Randy Poe.

MAKE THE MOST OF THE DIGITAL AGE

An Interview With Songspace.com Founder Robert Clement

by *Allison Malafronte*

Are you a songwriter who is looking to get your lyrics, music, and recordings organized in one place and heard by important people in the music industry? Are you someone in need of collaborators and co-writers during the creative process? Or maybe you're a label or producer looking to find the perfect lyrics or music for a specific project. Songspace is an online community built to bring everyone from the independent songwriter to the major corporate label together to make the music-publishing process easier and more effective.

The way our culture consumes content is changing constantly, and technology seems to present new ways of accessing, researching, and adopting information and inspiration almost daily. What's changing almost as quickly is the manner in which artists create and share content, as they can now avail themselves to numerous avenues of online connection and collaboration and then reach a far-broader audience with the finished results than ever before. For songwriters in particular, there is a whole new world of websites, social networks, apps, and programs designed to help connect them to other important players in the music-publishing industry—musicians, vocalists, producers, labels, publishers, and copyright and royalty lawyers—making the creative process more stream-lined and successful for all.

As a songwriter, it can be difficult to know where to begin when diving into the digital music space, or for that matter which tools are truly helpful. That's be-cause the songwriting and publishing process varies by individual. Some have advanced musical training and degrees and are extremely precise and particular about composing each note into structured sheet music. Others are more intuitive and could be anywhere when they hear or observe something that inspires them. There are several songwriters who prefer privacy and solitude when writing and aren't ready to share the story until it's fully finished. Others have a lyric or melody in mind and then search for collaborators, needing that missing voice, musician, or producer to bring the song to life.

The team at Songspace understands this process from all angles, and they have built a company and an online community based on first-hand understand-ing of what songwriters and musicians really want. Robert Clement, the CEO of Songspace, created the Nashville-based company after eight years as the co-own-er and publisher of *American Songwriter* magazine. He interacted with, listened to, and observed an international community of top singer-songwriters and in-dustry professionals before realizing that the culture was changing and that there was an opportunity to bring aspects of the new Digital Age into the music indus-try for everyone's benefit. He is a songwriter himself, a music connoisseur, and a genuine lover of great music. In this Q&A, Clement describes some of the ways Songspace can benefit you.

Please give us a little background on how, when, and why Songspace was created. What need did you notice in the songwriter industry that you felt Songspace could fulfill?

The idea for Songspace came from my background in media and technolo-gy around the songwriting community. I ran the Nashville-based *American Songwriter* magazine for about eight years, and during that time I realized (from people telling me repeatedly) that songwriters didn't have many tools to organize all their songs. When I say "all their songs," I'm referring to ev-erything an artist, musician, or writer uses in the creative process, such as demos, works in progress, ideas, lyrics, melodies, recordings, all the way to the finished songs and keeping track of who wrote what (in the case of songs with multiple contributors).

At the same time, I noticed that many songwriters use voice memos on their phones to capture ideas, lyrics, or melodies on the go. I started out building a simple Smartphone app for songwriters and as I got into it I realized there was an opportunity to simplify other parts of the creative process as well, like song splits and publishing rights. When I started meeting with music publishers about this product for songwriters the light bulb went off that Songspace could really help everyone from the independent writer to large music labels and enterprises.

I'm assuming part of the reason you were able to recognize and identify this need is because it resonated with you personally on some level. What is your background in the music industry, and why you are passionate about this topic in particular?

A friend and I purchased *American Songwriter* magazine in 2004. I'm a songwriter and a huge fan of great songs in general. Running the magazine put me in contact with thousands of phenomenal songwriters from all over the world, and I felt like I was the right guy to tackle this technology issue, to build something that would make the creative process better and more streamlined for songwriters and the people they work with. My passion for music bleeds over into a passion for the people who create it. My goal is to create a great product and company that makes a meaningful impact in as many people's lives as possible, first for our customers and partners and then for our employees and owners of the company.

What specific tools and resources do you offer your members to meet this goal? Who is your typical customer?

Our mission is to make music publishing more efficient. We offer songwriters a simple creative app that helps them collaborate with other writers and makes sure all of the files and data that go into creating a song—lyrics, recordings, copyright splits, etc.—are in one place and accessible to everyone involved. For publishers, we offer the same resource, just on an enterprise level. The key is linking everyone together—songwriters, artists, publishers, and labels—so everyone is on the same page when it comes to the process of creating and monetizing songs. Our typical customer is any songwriter who wants to better manage his or her professional career. We make that easy to do.

Tell us a little bit more about the Songspace GO app. How does it integrate with the other data and information members have saved in their Songspace account?

The Songspace GO app naturally supports the existing creative process of millions of songwriters worldwide. You can quickly record melodies or lyric ideas on the go, tie them to existing works or ideas, and share them with collaborators. And then everything is synced to the cloud in your account and accessible from any phone or computer. It's pretty cool because you never know when inspiration is going to strike. The Songspace GO app is designed to make sure you're ready wherever that happens.

In what ways does Songspace allow independent singer-songwriters to get their music, ideas, and lyrics in front of important and influential people in the industry? How does the online community and networking actually work?

We partner with music companies and brands to run contests (songspace.com/contests) that we believe are real, legitimate, and genuine opportunities to get your music heard. We also run a feature every day on AmericanSongwriter.com called the Daily Discovery, where we showcase great Songspace songwriters.

Can you give some examples of songwriters or publishers who are current customers of Songspace so readers can better understand the caliber and range of clients participating in your company?

A great example is the company Secret Road, a leading LA-based publisher that represents a lot of the music you hear on commercials, TV shows, and movies. They have about ninety writers who use Songspace every day to keep track of their work and co-writes. When they're ready to submit their music to the business folks at Secret Road, they turn their songs in via Songspace, which means the Secret Road team has everything they need to start pitching the music immediately.

I know that Songspace collaborates with important leaders in the songwriting industry on various projects and is a partner company with *American Songwriter* magazine. In what ways do you work together to offer opportunities for songwriters to get their music noticed and published?

Because of my history with *American Songwriter* magazine, we still have strong ties. We're a partner company of the magazine and work closely with them in a number of areas, including contests to help discover and give exposure to new talented songwriters, in addition to online collaborations.

How has the Nashville songwriting scene responded to this online community and resource? Do some of the more traditional labels and songwriters still pre-

fer in-person meetings and collaborations, or have you seen them embrace the concept that Songspace and similar companies are promoting?

So far the response has been great. A big part of what we're trying to do is naturally adapt to how songwriters and music business folks work. In-person meetings and co-writes are always going to be hugely important, but there's a lot of e-mailing and back-tracking that slows down the process. Songspace supports the way people already work, and the industry response has been really positive.

What are some of the projects Songspace is currently working on, and what tools and resources do you plan to offer customers in the future?

Right now we're really focused on making our existing platform as fast and easy as possible, but we're also planning on making it easier for independent songwriters to self-publish their songs. Technology gives us the opportunity to help people work better together, and that's what Songspace is all about. We're not trying to tell people how to create music, just trying to make it easier to connect and collaborate with songwriters and music businesses.

For more information on Songspace, visit www.songspace.com.

Allison Malafronte is a writer, editor, and singer-songwriter based in New York City.

GET THE MOST FROM MUSIC CONFERENCES

The Perfect Time to Showcase Your Work and Meet Industry Professionals

by Graydon James

Everyone knows about music festivals, but few artists and songwriters are as well informed about music conferences: what they are, where and when they take place, who goes, and most important, how you can benefit from attending one.

Like almost all types of conferences, music conferences have multiple purposes, but mainly they serve as a meeting ground for industry professionals and artists. Depending on the type of conference, you could rub shoulders with label representatives, publishers, festival programmers, house concert promoters, publicists, journalists, radio DJs, booking agents, entertainment lawyers, and a host of other professionals, each of whom could potentially help develop your career or act as a resource or mentor. Conferences are an excellent way to develop good relationships with all types of people in the music industry, so if you aren't attending them yet, strongly consider doing so!

TYPES OF CONFERENCES

In general, there are two types of conferences: (1) performance-based conferences, where you apply to showcase as an artist and presenters and other industry members are given a chance to see you perform, and (2) development conferences, where industry types and artists gather for professional development opportunities, usually in the form of seminars, classes, or workshops.

Depending on your career goals, you may favor one type of conference over the other, but development conferences are easier to get into—you simply register and go—and they are geared more toward songwriters interested in process, craft, and networking. Many of these types of conferences also have performance opportunities, either through official showcases, private showcases, or both. In fact, some conferences have a very active festival portion, but the festival is usually open to the public. The conference activities—and the opportunities they present to meet industry insiders—are only open to delegates who have registered for the conference.

The main conferences that you should know about are:

Folk Alliance (www.folkalliance.org)
APAP (www.apapnyc.org)
MIDEM (www.midem.com)
MusExpo (www.musexpo.net)
Americana Music Festival & Conference (www.americanamusic.org)
South by Southwest (www.sxsw.com)
North by Northeast (www.nxne.com)
Winter Music Conference (www.wintermusicconference.com)

There are multiple smaller conferences as well, and they are usually regional in scope. And aside from the previously mentioned North by Northeast, there are other important conferences in Canada such as Canadian Music Week, CAPA-COA, and Folk Music Ontario. In addition, there are a few specific to college and university presenters: the National Association for Campus Activities (NACA) and its Canadian counterpart, Canadian Organization of Campus Activies (COCA).

It would be very difficult and quite expensive to go to all of these conferences. Do your research, and determine which conferences serve the part of the industry you want to target. For example, the Americana Conference targets folk/roots music and singer-songwriters, whereas the Winter Music Conference is for electronic music. Most songwriters are not suited for both conferences!

BEFORE YOU GO TO A CONFERENCE

Keep in mind what you want to achieve by going to a conference in the first place. Conferences are a great place to learn more about your musical community and to become more involved in it. Don't be surprised if you don't suddenly get immediate songwriting or performance work from a conference—what you are trying to do is develop relationships with people that can help you in the long-term with your career. These people will hopefully become life-long friends as well as business partners! Remember this while you're at the conference, and act appropriately.

Your first step is to register for the conference and, if you are a performer, to apply for an opportunity to showcase. When researching a conference, make a note of all the deadlines and submission requirements. Most conferences do have an "early bird" date for registration; if you apply before that date you can save a significant amount of money on registration, membership, and even hotel rates.

If you're applying to showcase at a conference, then apply early. There are sometimes "early-bird" rates for those applications as well, and you will be heard by the selection committee before other artists. Most showcase submissions require recordings of your music, a bio, promotional photos, and a link to your website or electronic press kit (EPK). Some require videos of your performances, press clippings, a CV, stage plot, or other credentials. Be aware of what the selection committee wants, and stay within their restrictions. Don't give a full-page bio when they only want fifty words. Put your best foot forward and remember that the committee will have to listen to many submissions. Make it easy for them to choose you!

Keep copies of your submission documents (stage plot, bio, CV, etc.). You can use them for other submissions and easily update them year after year.

Materials

You will want multipurpose promotional materials that you can use as a calling card, a poster, and a promotional flyer. The most versatile item is a postcard-sized (4" x 6") flyer, professionally designed and printed on quality cardstock. These flyer cards are larger than business cards, so you can post them on bulletin boards and they can be seen from a distance, making them miniature posters to promote your name. They have plenty of room for a striking visual on the front and information on the back: name, website, a short bio, press quotes, tour dates, and showcase schedule.

One of the things you want from a conference is to increase your name recognition, but since you can't be everywhere and meet everyone, some promotional flyers can go a long way toward making you more visible.

In addition, a business card is exceptionally useful and portable, and is a well-known standard, so at the least you should have a nicely designed card that communicates all your information—you can even include showcase times/locations on the back of the card if you plan ahead.

Keep your own business cards, flyers, and CDs handy in a purse, a knapsack, or a small bag. It's helpful to hand someone a flyer in the middle of a conversation without having to dig around for it, but don't force your flyers on anyone. Ideally you should have a chat for a minute or two first and then, if they are interested, you can offer a flyer or business card.

Be aware that your materials (posters, postcards, flyers, business cards, and even your CDs) say as much about your professionalism as they do about your image. If you can't afford professionally printed flyers in full color, then focus on having a great business card.

You should bring CDs to the conference if you have them, but it's not necessary to hand out free CDs to everyone you meet. Your flyer/business card should have a link to a website with streaming tracks that will allow the person to listen to a sample of your music for free. If someone asks for a CD, that's a good sign! Give them one and make sure you get their business card to follow up. Always make a note on the back of the business card about who the person is, how you met, and what you should follow up about.

Some radio DJs will attend conferences, so have copies of your CD to give to them. Note that most radio DJs prefer CDs in full-sized jewel cases—many radio stations still use the spine of the CD to record pertinent information that can be seen even when filed into their music library. It can be helpful to indicate the genre, the instrumentation, where you're from, and even a short description of the music on a Post-It note inside the front of the jewel case.

Contacting Industry Members

If you are registered for a conference, then you will likely have access to a delegate list a month or more before the conference starts. It may not be complete—some people will register closer to the conference date—but it is a good place to start researching the industry members that you want to contact before and during the conference. Find the delegates you think will be most interested and most useful to you at the current stage of your career. There's no need to send a preconference e-mail to every single attendee! Not only is that a lot of work, but it can easily be seen as spam. Your goal, by the end of the conference, is to make seven to ten new connections. Be strategic and put your time into researching the most likely candidates, and it will pay off more than sending one blanket e-mail to hundreds of people.

Make sure you send personalized e-mails to each person you want to contact. Keep your e-mail brief, and include a link to your website so they can learn more about you if they want. Send ten to twenty e-mails out at a time, and wait a few days to see if you get any responses. Then send out an e-mail to the next ten to twenty names on your list. Keep track of the people you have sent e-mails because if you run into them at the conference it's nice to be able to say, "Oh, I recognize your name. I sent you an e-mail." This can easily begin a conversation and lead to a connection.

Showcases

If the conference has a performance aspect, official showcases will be determined well before the conference starts. If you don't have an official showcase, there may still be private showcase opportunities available. Conferences like Folk Alliance have numerous showcase opportunities: The official showcases happen during the day until about 11 P.M., and the private showcases happen in individual hotel rooms from 11 P.M. to as late as 4 A.M. and sometimes longer! Showcasing is the best way to connect with other artists.

Why connect with other artists? Your conference experience should hopefully be about getting more involved with your musical community, and your fellow artists are the bulk of that community. You can help each other with advice, show swaps, co-songwriting, opening slots, contact info for industry industry members and other artists, and much, much more.

Official showcases are a great way to perform in front of the industry, but private showcases don't generally have the same effect. While some industry folks will make it a priority to go to private showcases as well (so don't discount them), they are not as formalized and structured as the official showcases. You will have to do some research to find private showcases. The best way to start your search is to ask the conference organizers how to go about finding private showcases.

AT THE CONFERENCE

The first thing you will do when you arrive is register and receive a schedule and other information about the conference itself. The schedule is usually posted online before the conference begins, and you should have a rough knowledge of what workshops, showcases, or mentoring sessions you'd like to attend. Once you have the finalized schedule in hand, it's a good time to run through and find the specific events you don't want to miss. If there are mentoring sessions, you may be able to sign up for them at the registration desk—and you should! Mentoring sessions are an extremely effective way to meet someone in the industry who wants to give their time and experience, so take advantage of it.

Lanyards and Name Tags

If you get a lanyard or name tag, wear it on your chest or somewhere equally easy to see. There is no sense making someone work to find out what your name is. Conferences are all about making it easy for people to connect with you. In addition, name tags on lanyards are a great way to carry around business cards you receive—just tuck them in behind your name. Make sure you have a pen handy to make notes on the backs of the business cards you get so you can follow up effectively.

Meeting New People

It's not a bad idea to have a few stock questions you can ask if you meet someone new but aren't prepared and don't know anything about him or her. What brings you to the conference? What are you looking forward to seeing? What do you recommend I try to see? Any advice for a first-time conference attendee? What other conferences have you been to? Be honest, be yourself, be personable, and be open to wherever the conversation takes you. Even very experienced conference-goers are out of their home element at the conference, and it's always nice to meet a friendly and engaging person.

You should also prepare your "elevator pitch": a short description of who you are and what you do. For example: "I'm a songwriter, not a performer, and I'm here to meet artists and professionals who need country songs for their upcoming releases," or "I'm in a punk band that combines elements of hip-hop with a hard edge. We've been touring for two years ,and now we're looking for some representation. Feel free to come to our showcase!" Be descriptive, be honest, and don't be afraid to let them know that you are new to the experience. Most people enjoy being asked about their expertise or for advice.

Don't forget that amongst all the hobnobbing and meeting new, exciting people, you still need to factor in time for food and rest. If you are performing in official or private showcases you need to be able to put your best foot forward, so rest up and avoid over-indulging. Be aware of your limit and stay safely in it, otherwise you may embarrass yourself and reduce your chances of performing at your peak.

Showcases

Showcases can be anywhere from ten minutes to a full set, so be well aware of how much time you have and plan your set accordingly. Be aware of any technical restrictions or requirements as well. For example, many private showcases are unamplified, meaning you are performing with no amps, no microphones, and no loud instruments (like drum kits). If you know the equipment situation beforehand, then you can quickly set up and tear down, which makes you look more professional.

If you choose your best material and keep your between-song banter light and relevant, you have a good shot at charming the audience. If you have multiple showcases, it's a good idea to prepare one or two songs that are your very best "showcase" material and play them each time but vary the other songs and the setlist. If someone sees you twice they shouldn't think you have a scant amount of material and they shouldn't be bored.

Tear down quickly after your set, and then spend time in the audience so anyone who just saw you perform can approach you. Have your business cards, flyers, and CDs ready.

AFTER THE CONFERENCE

Rest! You will likely need it. Don't be too concerned with following up with everyone you met right away, unless they specifically asked you to do so. Take the information you received, either on business cards or in conversations, and put it into a spreadsheet so you can keep track of the people you met and the opportunities you developed.

Within two weeks start sending out e-mails to the people you met. Make sure you indicate in the subject line that you met them at the conference. Make it personal, keep it brief, and be yourself in your correspondence. If you don't have specific business to discuss, just let them know that it was nice to meet them and you hope to see them again at the next conference. Be especially thankful to anyone that gave you one-on-one mentoring sessions!

Following up is the second most important conference-related task you can do, coming only slightly behind meeting the people in the first place. Industry members are very busy, and you have to prove that you really are as professional and dedicated as you appeared at the conference. If you follow up and don't hear anything back, that's okay. Wait a few more weeks or even a month, and send a secondary follow-up e-mail.

Don't be upset if nothing comes from the follow-up. It may take a few meetings at conferences or events to make a firm connection. Remember that you are developing life-long relationships with people in the industry, and at some point it will hopefully make sense to work together. As one industry member put it to me: "We hire our friends because we have a relationship, we can trust each other, and we both want to see the other person succeed. It's just a natural fit."

Graydon James is a musician, author, recording engineer, and dad. He has toured Canada with his band (Graydon James & the Young Novelists), played dozens of festivals, showcased at folk conferences, released several albums, published a novel, and is currently tackling potty training. He has his own studio space (Typewriter Studio) where he records his own songs as well as other artists and bands. He's working on a new album, a play, a novel, and a few government grants. For more, visit www.theyoungnovelists.com.

DOING IT ALL: SCOTT MATHEWS

Adventures on Both Sides of the Studio Glass

·······

by James Duncan

Some musicians have a knack for lyrics, some can bang the drum all day but can't tell a mixing board from a surfboard, and some progress from one musical skill to the next and have the passion and desire to write, play, compose, produce, do it all. And why should you limit your aspirations when the entire industry is yours for the taking? That is, of course, if you have the talent and the guts to reach for it ...

Scott Mathews is a prime example of this kind of musical omnivore, and I asked for a few minutes of his time to share some of the lessons, adventures, and laughs he's had along the way. His insights will help you prepare for the leap from picking up your guitar to picking up a set of headphones on the other side of the studio glass. But who is Scott Mathews to offer such advice? The deluge of a response you'll get when you ask that question should convince even the greenest musical novice that the real fun in the music business might not be on stage but in a producer's booth. (Or better yet, both!)

Mathews is (drum roll please ...) a music producer, composer, arranger, multi–instrumentalist, publisher, media entrepreneur, recording studio owner/operator, and a music biz consultant/speaker/mentor. Over the course of his career, Mathews has earned more than 40 million units in sales and numerous Grammy and Oscar awards and nominations. Called a 'wunderkind' in *Rolling Stone* magazine in 1977, his work has consistently appeared in Billboard's Top 10 list, including several chart-topping number one hits, and he has worked with such artists as David Bowie, Billie Joe Armstrong (Green Day), The Beach Boys, Clint Black, Zac Brown, Jimmy Buffett, Johnny Cash, Rosanne Cash, Glen Campbell, Elvis Costello, Dick Dale, Snoop Dogg, Roky Erickson, Jerry Garcia, Billy Gibbons, Sammy Hagar, George Harrison, Etta James, Mick Jagger, Booker T. Jones, B.B. King, Patti LaBelle, Curtis Mayfield, Van Morrison, Graham Nash, Roy Orbison, Keith Richards, Kid Rock,

Todd Rundgren, Carlos Santana, Joe Satriani, Boz Scaggs, Barbra Streisand, Nancy Wilson (Heart), Brian Wilson, Dan Wilson, Bobby Womack, Stevie Ray Vaughn, Dwight Yoakam, Neil Young, and many other major artists, including more than seventy Rock & Roll Hall of Fame Inductees.

Music creativity is in his DNA, and with his custom-built TikiTown Studios in California, he is busier than ever discovering and developing new, emerging artists. But while working with state-of-the-art equipment, traveling the world, and recording with a galaxy of musical stars is his daily norm now, he grew up learning his craft by strumming on a ukulele and obsessively listening to his favorite records, like every other kid with a turntable. So who's to say you, your niece, or the kid playing drums next door too early on a Sunday morning might be the next Scott Mathews?

Tell us a little bit about how you got started with music. What was your first memory of playing an instrument?

My first memory of playing an instrument was in front of a large group of people at a campfire in Yellowstone Park. I was bangin' on a banjo uke with two strings busted and howlin' at the top of my lungs. Fearless! I might have been five years old.

At what point did you begin to write songs as well as play them?

I clearly remember the moment I wrote my first song, "Surf Hog." I was eight and wrote it on piano and had my dad hold down one vocal part while I sang the tenor bit. He was obviously a great guy and a very good sport, but I was serious. Telling others what to do from jump. Now, all these years later, it's clear I've made a career out of something I should have been treated for. Also, as I think about it, on my first song I became an arranger and producer too! Clearly, I peaked a bit early ...

Who were your initial inspirations?

Anything and everything I heard on the radio. I had a natural, open ear for all genres and back then it was all flowing out of the Top 40 pop stations. My now 'eclectic' taste was commonplace back in the sixties. It's a shame that diversity on one station went away ... I mean, music has no boundaries, so why try and impose them? Silly, huh? I subscribe to the Duke Ellington School: "There are only two kinds of music—good and bad." And I love a lot of bad music so ... [laughs]

Do you feel you're a better solo songwriter, or do you enjoy the collaborative process?

I honestly love the collaborative process so much that I will take my co-writer a finished song and see what they might want to do to change it. Perhaps it will work as 98 percent my original, but they earn 50 percent as my co-writer if they help in any way, as well it should be. Conversely, I love coming into a writing session and hearing a truly stunning piece. With my jaw on the floor, I drool and try my best to say it's perfect and I should go home.

But if you are fair, it all comes out in the wash. I may have a stellar session one day, then my partner the next ... all good.

What do you feel is the best way to approach a collaboration—in other words, how do people get past "This is my song" and get to to "This is our song"?

Well, if the arrangement is such that you have a co-writer for a project or for a stretch of time, I just like to ball it all up into whatever we work on, we split right down the middle. Otherwise you end up with, "Well I wrote the hook; you only changed an 'if' to a 'but' and I ..." and those messy situations inevitably lead to the girlfriend of the roadie getting a piece of the song. But seriously, it's very important to communicate well. After all, we are in the communications biz if you really think about it. I am clear and up front with any collaborator. The dealio is we write, and whatever comes out is 50/50 between us.

As a fellow writer, I find this question extremely difficult because all of my pieces feel special in their own way, but do you have a particular song or set of songs that you wrote that you are most proud of? Why or why not?

Hhmmm ... that's prone to change with the wind, but indeed there are very special nuggets of truth that I regard as the pure essence of my life in writing. Some songs have your heartstrings pulling for personal reasons and other songs may have your monkey nerve excited, but they are all your children and you want to see them get a job and do well for themselves out in the world!

I very rarely look through the rearview mirror at my work. Really, I hardly ever listen to my older work. And when I do, it guarantees me I *did* peak early and I turn it right off!

I sometimes hear how some songs just "happen" and come together in minutes. Should beginning songwriters roll with this, or is it best for songwriters to work a song for a while until they get it "just right"?

For songs that happen quickly, those songs appear because they are pulled out of thin air—we just get to "say" we wrote them. Ha! Call it what you want; the spirits of the song gods paid us a blessed visit and some songs can come in a snap. Many of the best do! Just ... *Pow ... what the hell was that*!? The writers that go with that and don't doubt it are my kind of people, as I also don't bother asking why or fussing about whether I meant this or that. They are gifts and I am always found pleasantly in receiving mode! Sometimes working a song can happen a lot, too, and I feel the need to conjure up the voice of Orson Welles and answer, "No song of mine shall be released before it's time." I'll spend the time on several rewrites if need be ... it's gotta resonate with me first, so until then, it remains in the lab. It's well worth the wait ... no animals were harmed.

As a songwriter, do you find it difficult to stay inspired, or do ideas come easily?

Given the gods aren't always available for comment, I'm sometimes left to my own devices and I'll work my craft until it's art. The only way to write great songs is to write a bunch of not-so-great songs first. Put the editor to sleep, and just roll. Come back later with fresh eyes and ears, and see what comes of it all. They say writers write, right? So ...

What situations/activities do you find most inspirational?

My old friend peripheral cognition rules! Doing e-mails, reading, watching wildlife out my window, and producing all at once makes my creative life just like a real life. I like to say it's not rocket surgery! But my creative thought patterns are best jumping all over the joint as opposed to overconcentrating. I don't want people overconcentrating on the music—I want it to seep into where they can't deny they feel it.

How did you transition from musician/songwriter to producer?

Well, now that I've already confessed I began directing as a child ... (laughs) ... no, it was crystal clear I wasn't born to be on the road for the smell of the crowd nor the roar of the grease paint. In my youth I began collecting and studying records like a fiend. As I said, I was serious—tunnel-vision serious. Oh, I had a ton of fun but it was a solitary thing when it came to my love affair with music. Once I got home from school it was just me and my records with a 'Do Not Disturb' sign on my door. I went away to another world and I frankly dug that world a whole lot more than the real one and I had a truly wonderful childhood in every respect.

As much as I loved it, I used to hear things that a producer hears ... like how McCartney sang flat here or how Charlie Watts rushed there, and I wondered why they kept the mistakes. Later those "mistakes" became charming to me, and of course now I miss the charming mistakes in music.

Was it a natural fit transitioning from performer to producer, or were there some hard lessons along the way?

I may have been a natural on the music front, but it was hard learning the process of politics and how to become successful in the sometimes foul face of this industry. It may have taken some hard lessons, not sure they are quite done ... I fear they are not. [laughs] No different than business anywhere, really. We aren't as terminally unique as we might wish to think ...

What sort of mind-set does one need to be able to work on either side of the soundboard?

Well, if your instincts don't stink, go with them. It saves you from needing your mind! Hey it's always worked for me!

What are some of the things a young artist should know to build a strong relationship with a producer?

Mutual trust is an absolute must. It is more than a rhyme—sure to reveal in time.

Is there a point when an artist (or producer) should put his foot down if he feels strongly about an idea, and how is that moment best navigated?

I'm going to put my foot right down on this point! If I feel strongly about something, I'll say something, and you better be ready to defend your position. And visa versa, of course. It's never a matter of right and wrong as all art is subjective (and why I had trouble perceiving accuracy), but it can be worth fighting for. My thing is *May the best idea win*. I don't care whose it is … as long as I get the credit! [laughs]

Have you had many negative, frustrating moments in a studio? If so, how did you work through them?

I work through them knowing everyone is doing their level best and it's my job to raise that bar wherever it may be set. One truism is *Never take it personally,* and I don't (anymore). And I try to help whoever may be struggling. It's tough. We've all been there, right? I don't have flowers in my hair, but I will say I do it with love. Love for the music—can't always love the people!

You've worked with a vast range of artists for a few decades now as a producer, musician, and a songwriter. Have there ever been moments where you have just been playing with someone or just helping with songwriting but had a strong opinion about production…but that wasn't your role on that particular project?

Yup … I've bitten my tongue more than a few times. But that's better than my early days when I hadn't a clue that I wasn't running the whole show at all times! Just ask Barbra Streisand. I was very young and full of all that cocky stuff (usually a cover up for insecurity), but she loved working with me because she said I made her look nice by comparison. I swear I was just trying to be professional, but I did boot some very high profile people out of sessions ... and because of that she was my biggest fan! [laughs] I made quite an impression alright, but I'm all groovy now, even if David Foster will never speak to me again. Where are those flowers? I need some for my hair.

Do you run a pretty tight ship in the studio, or are you more open to feedback and a slightly more 'anything-goes' process?

I'm an open book. I'm quite loose and will ask anyone their opinion. I'll have the mail carrier in from time to time to listen to a mix. No kidding—he's got a great ear. I love the wisdom of the crowds. I feel everyone's an expert but at the same time, I'm solely responsible for my projects. Unless the wheels are coming off the bus, we should enjoy the ride. My best work is done with no stress and I am acutely aware of not putting any undue strain on people or projects ... great music isn't born of that. And people are often taken aback by my peripheral cognition but I am inspired while doing several things at once and not stressing about one specific thing. It's like writing a song ... do you wanna stare at a page and force it or is the song going to come to you when you're driving around and the lightbulb jumps over your head and shines, ya know? It's quite often while we are busy doing drone activities that we somehow summon visitation rights of the song gods!

If you could play just one role—produce, play, or write—for your next dream project, what would you do?

Now that's just plain cruel! I love it all. Taking candy from a baby! [laughs] Why? There's so much to love. But no, I wanna answer because it's a fair question. Whatever is right for the project, I will gladly do. I'm a damn good soldier. No ego, no fuss ... serve the song.

Have any upcoming projects you're excited about?

My next. Isn't the next one always the most exciting? What a great gig!

Who do you feel are the best songwriters—in any genre—working right now?

Australians.

What makes them stand out?

So real, so fun, so spirited.

Is there anyone just coming into their own now who will be considered the next Dylan or Springsteen when we look back in thirty years?

I've got my ear on that Brian Wilson fella. There is something in him—far beyond that surf stuff ...

For more about Scott Mathews and TikiTown Studios, visit www.scottmathews.com.

James Duncan is a content editor with Writer's Digest Books and occasionally writes for *Writer's Digest* magazine and their editor's blog, "There Are No Rules." He is the author of the short story collection *The Cards We Keep* and numerous poetry collections from small presses around the country, including *Maybe a Bird Will Sing* (2009, Bird War Press), *Lantern Lit, Vol. 1* (2014, Dog On A Chain Press), and the forthcoming *Berlin* (Maverick Duck Press). For more of his work, visit www.jameshduncan.com.

CROSS-COUNTRY COLLABORATION

Using Technology to Create Long-Distance Musical Partnerships

by Jennifer Billock

The high-water mark for garage bands is behind us. Savvy musicians across the world are now looking to the Internet to craft their art. A drum track from California, vocals from Indiana, lead guitar from Alaska—with the power of the web, these can easily be combined without any travel (or dusty garages) at all. Here's how.

PRE-PRODUCTION

The first step in any online collaboration is picking the song and the players. You need to have a vision and a sound in mind from the beginning in order for the final product to be successful.

"I dream up an arrangement in my head and send a private [Facebook] message to my dream team," Nancy Gardos, a Los Angeles-based musician, says. "I usually ask for the instruments or parts I envision to give it some direction. And it just takes off from there."

Aside from talent, there needs to be a healthy dose of excitement about the project. Collaborations face the very real possibility of falling flat if not all the players are invested in the unconventional, innovative process. Atlanta-based keyboardist Bill Shaouy chooses to work with people who are clearly fired up about the possibilities. He says that inspiration and excitement translates into a better recording experience and final product.

Once the musicians and song are decided and the team is completely on board, the real work can begin.

THE PROCESS

To start a collaboration, a guide track is essential.

"What [the guide track] includes is dependent on the style of the song and what instruments are involved, but typically it's drums, rhythm guitar, and lead vocal," says Bob Fenster, a New Jersey-based musician. "From there, the other players/singers record their tracks, and the song is pieced together."

The band leader might also create a click track, a perfectly timed computer-generated metronome, that the musicians play along with to keep time.

Communication and clarity are crucial to ensuring that a song comes together as planned. Group messages on Facebook, Skype, and e-mail help bring a virtual band together. But these are not without their challenges.

"Because the communication medium is mostly long text message threads, if something is mentioned and then the conversation goes and goes, the bandmate may not scroll all the way up to see that little detail mentioned early on," Shaouy says. "You have to repeat yourself, even if it means being annoying, just so you're sure everybody is on the same page."

Once all the players have their tracks recorded, they can be placed in a Dropbox folder, an online tool for sharing files.

"It's like opening up a mystery box and unloading all the secret ingredients," Gardos says. "When I see that someone has uploaded their parts to Dropbox, I get this feeling like I'm about to open the best present ever."

After all the parts are in, it comes down to using the right software to make the real magic happen. Learning how to use the correct software is a vital step, so be sure to utilize any online tutorials or classes you find. Beginners in the collaboration process tend to use GarageBand and iMovie to put together audio tracks and video because they are simple and easy to use. Los Angeles-based musician Circe Link considers GarageBand and iMovie to be the "training wheels for music [and video] work stations."

She notes that if you apply yourself and learn, you can easily move up to more complex software. She and her collaboration partner, Christian Nesmith (the eldest son of ex-Monkee Michael Nesmith), used online tutorials to expand their knowledge base and have since moved up the video-software chain to Final Cut Pro X.

ENJOYING THE PERKS

If a fully finished and sparkling new cross-country production just isn't enough, the process itself carries a wealth of other benefits, including the sheer enjoyment of bringing people together with music no matter where they are, not to mention an increased audience. A band's ability to collaborate from anywhere and market themselves in their varied, distinct circles around the world will lead to a greater amount of material available for release and a greater reach among listeners. This increase in collaborative material has allowed an artist like Fenster to see a huge spike in his YouTube views, up to 120,000 in the last year, something that is beneficial for any musician.

As Nesmith says, "In this day and age of YouTube popularity ... the more you've got up there, the more you get seen."

THE BIRTH OF THE ONLINE BAND

With online collaborations comes a new avenue for people to join forces and create music as a unit. The Facebook group Theme Music, a place where musicians can come together and create music videos with players across the country, has spawned a number of new virtual bands. All the collaboration, from songwriting to playing to videos, is done online and shared via social media and YouTube.

"It's a sign of our new and growing culture," says Circe Link. "Communities can stretch across the country; we don't have to be in physical proximity to each other in order to be inspired by and create art with one another."

Virtual bands formed out of Theme Music include Sons of Lazaro, Sunshine on Mars, Unicorn Indifferent, Graveyard Shifters, and the Offenders, and have been producing collaborations, both covers and originals, with anywhere from two people up to forty different musicians. Here are some of Gardos', Shaouy's, Fenster's, Link's, and Nesmith's favorite collaborations to date:

"Write My Own Ticket," an original by Nancy Gardos: "This collaboration was successful because we spoke the same musical language and were inspired by similar grooves."

"Just One Person," (originally by The Muppets) covered by Bill Shaouy: "This collaboration had a cast of brilliance with more than thirty people. It was a combination of really great sounds and a really great, warm vibe and an insanely great video."

"Born to Run," (originally by Bruce Springsteen) by Bob Fenster: "This collaboration involved thirty-eight different people from all over the country. It was an enormous effort, but it sounds incredible."

"Suit Fugue," (originally by Kevin Gilbert) by Circe Link and Christian Nesmith: "We had six people involved and they all filmed in different locations, sang their parts in different locations, and all their parts were different."

Jennifer Billock is an award-winning writer, editor, author, and owner of Jennifer Billock Creative Services, a boutique content editing and consulting firm. Her work has appeared in publications including *World Travel Buzz, Tea Magazine, Taste of Home Magazine, Broughton Quarterly, Healthy Cooking Magazine,* and *The Ambler.* Her book, "Images of America: Keweenaw County," was released by Arcadia Publishing in May 2014. Follow her on Twitter @JenniferBillock.

MUSIC LICENSING FOR SONGWRITERS

by Michael St. James

The full scope of music licensing is very large and can be mind-numbingly confusing, but it doesn't have to be. As a songwriter, it is your responsibility to become acquainted with the rights associated with every song and recording you create, and how to use them correctly.

When you write and record a song, you are automatically granted exclusive rights guaranteed to you by U.S. Copyright Law. These rights give you, the creator, control over who can use parts of your music or recordings, and how they may use them. These rights are granted to you, the creator, at the time when you make a 'fixed copy' of your creation (such as writing lyrics and chords down on paper) all the way to the finalized master recording of that song. Generally, these rights include: public performance, reproduction or mechanicals, distribution, derivative works, grand rights, display, and digital transmission.

Here's the basic concept of music licensing: The party who owns the rights (music publisher, label, or songwriter) to a composition (song) and/or recording (track) enters into a formal agreement with another party (TV producer, gaming company, advertising agency, other music publisher or label) who wants to use that music.

A license typically outlines the terms of how the music may be used. This includes territory, length of use, exclusivity, right to publicize, and payment amount, among other usages. This is not a sale of a song, nor should it ever be. Think of it as a lease agreement that sets out rules for where and how your music creations can be used before those exclusive rights are returned to you.

Many situations exist where you may not even realize you "licensed" your music. If you upload your music to a digital download store, such as iTunes or Google Play, you have granted them many licenses, from distribution and reproduction to a nonroyalty sample. If your lyrics are displayed on a website or a t-shirt, you've granted a right of display. If you manufacture your own CDs or a country artist decides to record a cover of your song, you have granted a mechanical right of reproduction. If you upload a video on YouTube of your song, you've granted a master/synchronization license.

This is not an exhaustive list by any means, but here are two main types of licenses that the majority of songwriters should learn and understand. They are the master/synch agreement and the public performance royalty.

Most of the licensing that happens for use in film, advertising, television, gaming, etc., is normally a master/synch license. This licensing agreement concerns the recording itself (master) and the underlying composition of melody and lyrics (synch). Keep in mind that a song in full is rarely what's licensed. It is normally the recording of a composition. In order for this kind of deal to go through, two things must be in place: The song you've written must be good, and the recording and production must be excellent. If it doesn't sound clean and professional, even the best song ever written will not come across and will not likely attract this kind of licensing deal with an entertainment company. By joining a performing rights organization (ASCAP, BMI, or SESAC) and registering your songs, you grant the right to those organizations to collect and pay you public performance royalties for qualified plays in public (on the radio, in a bar, in the grocery store, on a broadcast, etc.). Understanding exactly how these organizations determine usages of your songs and royalty payments is far from an exact science. However, it is worth joining as a "writer member" and registering your songs. You should talk frequently with your representative about opportunities for your songs and make sure you've registered them correctly. If you do have a song that is played on a television show or even one that attains widespread radio play, you simply cannot adequately collect these public-performance fees on your own, so being part of these organizations is invaluable.

Just by writing and recording a song, you can add "record company" and "music publisher" alongside "songwriter" to your resume. To understand this, let's break down the master/synch agreement a little further. A master license is usually granted by the owner of the recording, and in many cases this is the record company. Assuming you are not signed to a record label and you paid for your own recording, you are the record company and the owner of the master license. A synchronization license is usually granted by one of the owners of the copyright to a song (the lyrics and underlying melody) in many cases this is performed by a music publisher. Assuming you are not signed to a publishing deal as a writer, you are the music publisher.

Now that you have a basic understanding of what rights you have when you write and record a song and how your music can be licensed for use, let's dive into how you can best write and prepare songs to make some income.

Songwriting at its best is a personal artistic pursuit, as it should be. Music licensing can often be a similar pursuit. I describe it as the art of finding the perfect song, at the perfect time, for the perfect scene. That's a heavy load to carry. For instance, a song about drunk driving will not be placed in an auto commercial, but it may be placed in a movie scene about that topic. Conversely, many love songs have been used to sell vacuums and mops. The uses for songs can vary widely, but those who write songs purely for licensing will ultimately find disappointment. In all forms of music licensing, emotion is the biggest factor. Can the song connect the scene with the listener? Does it add to the messaging of the commercial?

The most simple songwriting advice you need to hear is to always write authentic songs in your own voice. Edit your lyrics to best convey the message of your song. You already know you need a hook, a catchy chorus, and a story-reinforcing bridge. You already know that an intro should be as short as possible and to get to the chorus within the first minute or so. What makes a great song a hit is the same thing that makes it licensable.

Rather than tell you the exact topics or types of songs to write, here are some elements of songs that show up in licenses again and again. In no particular order, commercials tend to use these words and phrases most: *love, let's go, c'mon, want, need, time, shine, life, dreams, tonight, today*, and *new you*. While movies and television use songs that are normally about the situation: falling in love, rekindling love, friendship, attaining a big goal, getting out into the world, starting over, and heartbreak. Obviously these are generalizations, but keep them in mind when you are working on your choruses.

Preparation is important, especially when it concerns recording a song. Understand that master/synch licenses are used with video, dialogue and sound effects mixed alongside your music into the final product. This is a key point because now we're not just talking about a song anymore—we're talking about digital files and other people manipulating them for the best use.

Here's what you need to know about preparing your songs. Whenever you write and record a song you need to do these five steps:

1. **FILL OUT A SPLIT SHEET.** This is a document that specifies all of the parties who wrote the song, publishers involved in the rights management, and when it was written and recorded. Often, all of these parties will just be you. This lets a licensor know that you have the rights to the song.

2. **MAKE A LYRIC SHEET.** This is a separate document with the lyrics of the song.

3. **CREATE SEPARATE TRACKS.** Before recording, make sure the studio or producer has agreed to give you instrumental and vocal separate tracks, in addition to your finished mixes. These tracks will often be requested for mixing dialogue and narration in a film, and the lack thereof is the number one reason why many songs by independents are not licensed. And all of these tracks must be mastered.

4. **TAG YOUR TRACKS.** Tagging is the process of adding keywords to the digital file (MP3, m4a, FLAC, WAV), usually in the "grouping" section. You'll want to include keywords that describe the song like: up-tempo, uplifting, personal triumph, heartbreak, luxurious, sensual, etc. This helps music supervisors sort through thousands of songs to find what they are looking for.

5. **INCLUDE CONTACT INFORMATION.** In the notes section of your track, include your e-mail address and the name of your performing rights organization. This makes the process of researching and contacting the rightsholder of a song much easier.

Now you're armed with the information you need to protect yourself and to prepare your songs for licensing deals. Go write those incredible songs, and follow the five steps. I can't wait to hear your tune on that next big commercial or TV show!

Michael St. James is the Creative Director of St. James Media in Denver, CO—an award-winning music publishing, marketing, and licensing agency. He is a sought-after speaker and thought leader on the music business, having written for *Music Business Journal*, *Performer Magazine*, and founded NewMusicBusinessModel.com and SongwritersUniversity.com. St. James' songs and voice have been heard on radio and television worldwide. When not writing or recording, you can find him drinking coffee and playing guitar and Xbox. Follow him on Twitter @michael-stjames, if you dare.

BECOME A DIY PRODUCER
Preparing Yourself for the Perfect Home Demo

....

by Mark Bacino

With powerful recording tools just a laptop's click away and the line between home and studio recordings blurring daily, songwriters and performing artists are now finding themselves, more and more, in the role of de facto producer-engineer-mixer when looking to capture their latest creations. With that thought in mind, this article looks to dissect, simplify, and offer insight into the sometimes daunting process and art of DIY music production.

PRE-PRODUCTION

Okay, so you've just finished writing a great song and you're excited to begin getting it down. Before you hit that record button, here's a pre-production checklist worth a run-through to help ensure your new tune is ready to hit the hard drive:

- **EDIT FOR CONCISENESS.** Are there sections that could be discarded or shortened in efforts to tighten up the overall structure?

- **ORDER YOUR SONGS.** Are your song sections ordered in such a way that's consistent with the genre you're working in (e.g., in the pop genre, having a chorus that repeats at logical points throughout the song)?

- **EXAMINE YOUR STRUCTURE.** Write your song's structure down on paper (verse, chorus, etc.) and see if it makes sense from that perspective. If you're still not sure your structure's the best it can be, pick a similar tune from a favorite artist that falls within your genre and dissect that song's structure on paper as well. How does it differ from your song's makeup? What structural ideas can you borrow from that model song and apply to your tune?

- **ESTABLISH A TEMPO.** Using your recording software's click/metronome function, play around with how your tune feels when performed at different BPMs (beats per minute) until you find a tempo right for the song.

- **ESTABLISH A KEY.** Many times a song will be written in a key that may not suit the vocal range of whoever will be singing the tune on the recording. Play the song in various keys with a singer on hand to make sure you have the right fit.

- **TYPE UP A LYRIC SHEET.** Include chord changes. Having this information in print will be a big help to both singers and players alike during the recording sessions. Typing the lyrics will also afford you, the writer, the opportunity to re-analyze, edit, and improve your lyrics before recording commences.

- **RECORD A DEMO.** Before "official" recording begins, it's helpful to get a simple version of your song down with just an acoustic guitar or piano and a vocal. This exercise will help you road test all the choices and tweaks you've made in the points listed above and will also give you a better sense of the overall quality of the tune when listening back. If the song moves you with just one instrument and a voice, you'll know it's ready and worthy of a proper recording. If it doesn't excite you, better to learn that before you've recorded your fiftieth theremin overdub.

- **DETERMINE THE ARRANGEMENT.** Begin to plan the specific musical parts that will populate your song, and make decisions as to what instruments will play those parts on the recording (e.g., rhythm guitar parts will be played by acoustic guitars, bass lines will be played by synth bass, etc.). Try to create parts in addition to the basic drums, bass, rhythm guitar/keys and vocal. Think of possibly adding some melodic lines played by different instruments that will artfully weave in and out of your recording, lending it some excitement and color. The possibilities are endless, but don't go overboard.

- **GET YOUR IDEAS DOWN ON PAPER.** Create a road map of sorts for your tune. Once you begin recording, this document will point your song in the right direction (despite any detours, welcome or unwanted) and will help get your song where you want it to go.

- **REHEARSE.** If you're planning on recording the basics of your song (drums, bass, rhythm guitar/keys) with a band live in the studio as opposed to building the song from the ground up in the overdub process, rehearse the players. Then rehearse them some more. If you intend to record to a click/fixed time, have the drummer practice playing along with said click at the song's chosen tempo. When musicians are well prepared and know their parts, they tend to stop thinking their way through takes while recording and start to actually perform.

RECORDING

So you've done all your pre-production prep work, and you're ready to begin recording your song? Cool. Let's dive in.

- **DISCLAIMER.** Obviously, the art of capturing sound is a topic so vast it can never be thoroughly covered within the limited confines of this space. There are, however, many instructional recording resources available on the web and in print. Seek them out, and learn as much as you can. Since recording is so intertwined with what we do as songwriters/artists, it makes a lot of sense to educate oneself on the subject, especially if you ever intend to take on any DIY recording projects.

- **MONITORING.** It's very important that you become sonically familiar with the speakers you'll be listening through while recording. You don't necessarily need expensive studio monitors (although owning a pair couldn't hurt), just make sure to listen to a lot of music on whatever speakers you'll be working with before recording so you'll know what things are "supposed" to sound like in terms of lower, middle, and upper frequencies when evaluating your own work.

  Truth be told, there are many factors that come into play with monitoring: the amplifier you pair your speakers with, the placement of your speakers in the room, the use or lack of acoustic treatment in the space, etc. Educate yourself on the aforementioned when you can, but in the meantime intimately knowing how other music sounds on your speakers in your space will at least give you a solid chance at crafting recordings that will translate decently in the real world.

- **TAKING IT FROM THE TOP.** As the saying goes, "garbage in, garbage out." If you plan on recording a guitar that doesn't sound so hot before you put a mic in front of it, don't expect it to sound great when recorded. Make sure your instruments are up to snuff and sounding their best (fresh strings, tuned drums, etc.). These days there are a lot of affordable, quality instruments available. No reason not to use them. Same can be said of microphones. There are a slew of great mics on the market with very reasonable price points.

- **MIC PLACEMENT.** When preparing to record an instrument, mic it up (there are many good, instrument-specific web tutorials on this) and do a quick test record. Listen back. If the recording sounds close to what the instrument sounds like when played live in the room, great. If not, don't adopt a "fix it in the mix" mentality. Change the mic position, and repeat the test process until you achieve a recorded sound that's fairly true to the instrument and pleasing to your ears.

- **DRUMS, BASS, RHYTHM.** If you're recording a song with live drums as the foundation (as opposed to drum samples or no drums at all) there are two ways to approach this task. You can record the kit yourself in your own space, or you can book a commercial studio for a few hours to capture the drums and then bring those files back to your project studio and move forward with the rest of your production. I offer this second option, even within our DIY framework, because often folks find the concept of recording drums intimidating or beyond their skill set or they may have other concerns such as noise level or equipment limitation issues, etc. If you can't or would prefer not to record your own drums, find a reasonably priced, local studio and go there to lay down your kit. The studio will be glad to have your business and given its sonically optimized setting, you'll more than likely come home with some good drum tracks.

  When recording live drums, also record your bass and rhythm guitar (or keys) at the same time. This will hopefully make for a cohesive rhythm section. If capturing bass and your rhythm instrument while laying down drums is not possible for whatever reason (lack of physical space, technical limitations, etc.), track drums only with just your rhythm guitarist or bassist playing along, unrecorded, for your drummer's reference/benefit. Once you've got a good drum take, then overdub your bass and rhythm instrument(s).

- **SCRATCH VOCAL.** Now with a solid foundation in place (drums, either live or programmed, bass, and a chordal instrument), have your singer record a quick lead vocal. Since you'll be re-recording this vocal part for keeps later in the process, don't invest a lot of time perfecting the performance (although record it well, as you never know what kind of magic you might capture). This "scratch" vocal's sole purpose will be to act as guide while recording the remainder of your music tracks, helping you, the producer, gauge if the support parts you're laying down are either aiding or hindering the ever-important vocal line. If your tune is instrumental in nature, put down a scratch of your top-line melody for the same purposes listed above.

- **FOLLOWING THE MAP.** Now with drums, bass, a chordal instrument, and a scratch vocal in place, dig out the arrangement "road map" you created back in pre-production. Again, this document should contain a list of all the specific musical parts that will populate your song, the instruments that will play those parts, and any/all additional arrangement ideas. Begin to overdub your parts one by one. As you record, listen not only for accuracy of execution but for passion and feel as well. Remember that sometimes the best takes aren't always the "perfect" ones.

  After you finish recording each part, edit as needed in your DAW (digital audio workstation, aka your recording software) but don't overdo it; if something requires a lot of slicing/dicing, it probably needs to be re-recorded. Once edited, rough mix each new part into your track. Spot editing and rough mixing as you go will give you an immediate sense of whether or not your arrangement is actually working as a whole. It will also lessen your workload down the line when you enter the mix phase of the project.

- **CHECKING THE EGO AT THE DOOR.** While tracking, remember that everyone involved in the recording process, from producer to band member, is there to serve one master and one master only—the song. Acknowledge your limitations and always defer to the best player in the room for the sake of the tune. If the drummer can rock that odd little rhythmic guitar figure better than the guitar player, let him have a crack at it. If the arrangement calls for a part or instrument no one on hand can really play, don't try and fake it; hire someone who can. There are a ton of great, affordable musicians out there who can use the work, and your track will sound all the better as a result of their expertise.

  Also, be open to experimentation. If any of your collaborators offer up arrangement suggestions, don't dismiss their thoughts because they may deviate from your blueprint or vision of the song. Give things a try. Great producers will always harness the best ideas even if they're not their own.

- **VOCALS.** Once the instrumental components of your tune have been recorded, dismiss your scratch-vocal track and begin the task of capturing final vocal performances for the song. There are many ways to record vocals. As such, it's best to defer to the singer as to what approach they're personally most comfortable with. If your vocalist wants to sing the song in sections, let them do so. If they prefer to sing the whole song in one pass, record three or four takes and edit together a "best of" comp after the tracking session.

  As the singer lays down his or her tracks, once again, listen for accuracy (pitch and timing) in addition to passion and feel. As mentioned earlier, keep in mind that the best takes might not always be the ones that are technically perfect.

  Remember to try double tracking vocal parts if you're looking for a fatter sound. When applicable to the genre, add backing/harmony vocals. If there's more than one vocalist in the band, have someone other than the lead singer record the background parts so as to add a different color/texture.

- **THE EXTRAS.** Once lead and/or backing vocals are in the bag, think about any last minute arrangement or production ideas you may want to add to your song before moving on to the mix phase of the project. Often overlooked, simple percussion overdubs or subtle keyboard pads, etc. can serve as valued additions to an arrangement, lending some polish to your track.

- **WATCH YOUR BACK!** Always remember to save your work as often as you can both during and after every recording session. It is vital that you back-up your files to multiple external drives and/or DVDs and keep them in separate locations, just in case. A minute devoted to backing up all of your files may save you hours of rerecording in the event you're faced with power or equipment failure.

As mentioned in the disclaimer at the head of this section, the art of recording is a subject as vast as it is varied. The suggested approach above is just that, a suggestion culled from my own experiences as a producer. There are, of course, many approaches, both technical and procedural. Educate yourself, and experiment to find the ones that work best for you.

MIXING

With your song now fully recorded, we're ready to move into the next phase of the production process—mixing.

- **DISCLAIMER.** Not unlike recording, mixing is a subject/art so vast, with approaches so varied, one could never hope to cover the topic properly within the confines of a single article. There are many great mixing tutorials online, and one of my favorites can be found at http://therecordingrevolution.com/5minutes. Educate yourself and focus on learning the basics. In the meantime, here are some rudimentary thoughts to get you going.

- **MONITORING.** As was the case with recording, it's very important that you become sonically familiar with the speakers you'll be listening through while mixing. Again, you don't necessarily need expensive studio monitors (or headphones). Just make sure to listen to a lot of professionally recorded music on whatever speakers you'll be working with before starting to mix so you'll know what things are "supposed" to sound like in terms of bass, midrange, and high frequencies when evaluating your own work.

- **CLEAN HOUSE.** Before beginning your mix, take some time to go through each of your recorded tracks (use the "solo" function in your DAW software) and remove any stray pops, clicks, noises, etc. that may have accumulated during the recording process. The rustling of a lyric sheet, the clearing of a throat—it's best to address these problems now so they won't interrupt your creative flow once you get down to mixing.

- **ADJUSTING RECORDED VOLUME LEVELS.** While tending to your house-cleaning duties, also listen to your tracks for any glaringly obvious, internal-volume inconsistencies they may have acquired during the recording process. If your singer's vocal gets quiet on the bridge because the dynamics of the song call for that, great, but if one line of the chorus sounds a lot louder than its surrounding phrases, go in and tweak said line down in volume at the waveform level to make it consistent with its neighbors. There are tools/processors that can make these adjustments for you electronically, but you should always try and remedy the larger, more overt problems manually.

- **EQUALIZATION.** The process of adjusting the balance between frequency components within an audio signal is a deep and somewhat complex topic worthy (and the subject) of many books, blogs, videos, etc. Again, you must do your research and educate yourself about the basics, but first, here are a few EQ basics to prime the pump:

  Try cutting frequencies before boosting them; If, for example, an instrument in your mix sounds dark/muddy to your ears, don't immediately add top end; first try to remove some bottom or low-mid from the signal by either lowering the volume level of those frequencies or by utilizing a high-pass filter to gain the clarity you're looking for. Boost frequencies only when cutting fails to achieve your desired result. Cutting rather than boosting will keep your mixes phase coherent.

  Lastly, think of the sonic space in a mix as real estate. In order for instruments to be heard clearly, they must be assigned their own frequency-based parcel of land, so to speak. If too many instruments try to occupy the same space in the frequency spectrum, they'll sound muddled and lose their definition. Attempt to carve out unique frequency homes for as many elements of your mix as possible.

  Again, education is key, so try to learn as much as you can about EQ and the fascinating world of frequency that exists between 20Hz and 20KHz.

- **COMPRESSION.** A compressor (or limiter—a compressor on steroids) is a processor (hardware or plug-in) that electronically controls spikes in volume (transients) present in an audio signal. It can, for example, automatically tame peaks in level on a vocal track and reduce those peaks by an adjustable amount. Once those spikes in volume have been controlled by a compressor, you are now free to raise the new, more consistent overall level of said vocal in your mix without the danger of signal overload. In addition to its main leveling function, compression can also be used as an effect. Two million articles could probably be written on the subject of compression. Learn about the topic, and don't be afraid to experiment. That said, if you're confused about compression (and if you are, you're not alone), refrain from using it on that "mission critical" demo until you get a handle on the ins and outs.

- **DE-ESSING.** A de-esser (hardware or plug-in) is a processing tool used to remove excess sibilance from an audio signal. If, say, you find your recorded vocal track sounds a little harsh when your vocalist sings a word with an "s", "t," or "c" sound (or similar) in it, try using a de-esser on the track to electronically lessen those sibilant frequencies. Be sure to educate yourself and experiment before using this tool on an important vocal track. Misuse of a de-esser can give your singer a serious speech impediment.

- **EFFECTS.** Effects processors (hardware or plug-in)—reverbs, delays, chorus, distortion, wideners, etc.—are tools used to add sonic depth, color, and texture to a mix. There are a myriad of different effects and many applications for each. Jump on the web and look up each effect mentioned above as a start, and then find those effects in your DAW software and begin to investigate.

- **PANNING.** Panning refers to the practice of placing instruments/tracks left, center, or right (and all points in between) across the stereo field in efforts to create the perception of space within a mix. Note: While panning covers left-to-right placement, adding the aforementioned effects of reverb or delay to instruments can help place those elements back to front in the soundscape.

- **BALANCING ACT.** With some/all of the above processing and panning in effect, use your DAW's virtual console faders to balance the volume level of each instrument (relative to the others) in your song to taste. You should already be close to a semi-decent blend if you've been "rough mixing" each individual element in as recorded (suggested in our recording rundown) to assess if said parts were working from a production standpoint.

  While balancing, realize that one set volume-level placement of a track may not always sound right for the entire duration of a song. That track's instrument may have to move up or down in level several times over the course of a mix. Program you DAW software's automation function to perform these adjustments for you.

  Also, when balancing, monitor your mix at varied volume levels (loud, soft) to get different perspectives on instrument placement and remember to take frequent breaks from all the heavy listening. Ear fatigue can send you down some undesirable mix roads.

- **REFERENCE.** Use a professionally produced, stylistically similar, favorite song as a sonic reference. Compare your mix to the "pro" tune, and see how close or far off you are in terms of the overall picture; does your mix have too much or too little bottom-end compared to your reference track? Is the model track brighter than your mix, or are the top-ends similar? Adjust your work accordingly. Warning: At first it will be fairly discouraging (to say the least) when comparing your mixes to pro cuts, but the knowledge derived from these exercises will help you grow and shape your work for the better.

  Next, check out your mix on different playback systems to get a sense of how it's translating outside of your workspace. Listening on boom boxes, in cars, on computer speakers, and earbuds will lend you some valuable perspective. Obviously, your track will never sound the same on each of these systems, but if you've done a good job with your mix, your track should sound fairly balanced in terms of levels and frequencies wherever you play it. If an element of your mix is calling attention to itself when you're listening on speakers other than the ones you mixed on, you might need to revisit that instrument again and adjust.

- **MIX DOWN.** Lastly, once you've got your mix sounding the way you want it, bounce/render a stereo file of the tune (this will become your two-track "master") and save both your mix program file and your newly created stereo master file across numerous hard drives or DVDs for safe-keeping/future reference.

So that does it for "Written and Produced By ..." Hope you found this breakdown of the DIY production process helpful. Hey, you wrote it; why not produce, record, and mix it? Now go make some great music ... and don't forget to add more cowbell.

Mark Bacino is a singer-songwriter based in New York City with three album releases to his credit as an artist. When not crafting his own melodic brand of retro-pop, Mark can be found producing fellow artists or composing for television/advertising via his Queens English Recording Co. Mark is also a contributing writer for Guitar World as well as the founder-curator of intro.verse.chorus, a website dedicated to exploring the art of songwriting. For more, visit www.markbacino.com.

THE BUSINESS OF CREATIVITY

How a Music Publisher Can Help You Focus on Songwriting, Not Paperwork

An interview with music publisher Deborah Evans by James Duncan

While young bands and performers may hunger for a record deal, the working songwriter's relationship with a professional music publisher is just as vital (maybe more so) to a long and successful career. For those just starting out, a music publisher oversees the business and development aspect of songwriting, much like a literary agent would for an author. They handle copyright issues, seek out and manage licensing opportunities across all media, around the world, can help get new songs into the hands of recording artists, and ensure that the songwriters and composers receive payment when their compositions are used commercially.

Basically, a good publisher is there to protect and enhance the value of the artist's work and to free a songwriter from the burden of a paperwork avalanche.

Deborah Evans, President of Della Music Publishing (based in New Orleans), began working in the music publishing business in 1998 and worked for a variety of publishers while managing all areas of copyright, licensing, and royalties for such artists as Charles Strouse (the musicals *Annie* and *Bye Bye Birdie*), Paul Winter, the Scorpions, UFO, Lorin Maazel, and many indie-rock, alt-country, rock-a-billy, jazz, pop, and hip-hop artists. She is now an independent music publisher of her own, having started Della Music Publishing in August 2007, and she represents such artists as Reggie Noble (previously known as Redman), Grammy-Award-winner Faith Evans, producer/songwriter Keith Ross (who has worked with Pitbull, Nelli, Ashanti, and more), and award-winning composer Randy Klein.

We asked Deborah for a few minutes of her time to tell us a little about the life of a music publisher and how up-and-coming songwriters can best catch the ear (and eye) of a music publisher. And hey, you never know … maybe a few of you songwriters out there might realize that publishing is more exciting than scribbling and strumming. Stranger things have happened, and a career as diverse and fascinating as Deborah's is not a bad place to start if this is where your own interests lie.

For starters, when and how did you first become involved with music, both on a personal and professional level?

I've played piano since I was about six. After taking a break in junior high, probably due to boys, I got pretty serious in high school and wanted to go to Oberlin College to become an ethnomusicologist. I applied to both the conservatory and the liberal-arts college, but my SAT scores, grades, and my piano playing were not up to that caliber. I was disappointed but went on to Dickinson College in Carlisle, PA to major in English with a minor in music. My senior year I discovered the harpsichord and was instantly hooked, cutting classes in order to practice for five to six hours a day.

After Dickinson I went to Montclair State University in NJ to obtain an MA in Harpsichord Performance. After teaching, performing, and playing for dance classes up in Western Massachusetts for about five years, I decided that I wanted to head to NYC for the culture and also to have a steadier job. So when I was about twenty-seven, I chose the music business, and specifically, music publishing. I interviewed at a music publisher there, Bourne Co., learned copyright law (which strangely was not taught in music school) and loved that type of work. I've been on the publishing side of the business ever since.

Tell us a little about Della Music Publishing and how that began?

Della Music Publishing evolved out of putting together two or three music publishing administrative part-time jobs I had in addition to my full-time work at Stray Dog Music, a music company in Brooklyn. I was Director of Publishing at that company, but the company was changing focus and I was also commuting from NJ to Brooklyn every day, while pregnant with my daughter. Ultimately, I did not want to be two river crossings away from my infant daughter, so in 2007, I set up Della at my home office in Bloomfield, NJ. I pieced together the admin work I had for other music publishers and various copyright attorneys. I also started doing music clearance work for TV, film, video, live stage, audio CSS, and began to take on a few songwriters as their publisher. My experience lay in years of work with music publishers, a music licensing agency, and a label. So I had a pretty broad knowledge of the business and was confident in my abilities enough to branch off on my own.

On your website for Della Music Publishing, you say one of your goals as a music publisher is to "cultivate and free a songwriter to spend time creatively." How do you go about doing that? And what exactly does a music publisher provide a songwriter?

The songwriter, if trying to handle the publishing end, will become mired in paperwork. Much of it is legal and licensing related, and it takes time to understand the finer points of the deals. Someone who knows these types of deals and can not only explain them to the writer but can handle them for the writer, as well as oversee the accounting work involved, is invaluable for a songwriter who wants to focus on creation, not numbers. I also collect foreign revenue for my writers, which is something they would have difficulty doing on their own. An important part of the job is to help songwriters understand their rights and how to protect their copyrights so they are not taken advantage of. A good publisher will also know what types of fees are appropriate for what types of uses, whether they are for synchronization (music put to visual images), mechanical (music which is audio only), or performance (heard on radio and internet).

Do you work with established artists only, or do you also find and support talented if less successful artists who are on the rise?

At this point I mostly have publishing deals with established artists. For upcoming artists/songwriters, I offer guidance (I don't charge fees, up to a point) on registering songs, licensing, value of their copyrights, copyright law, and any other publishing or related concerns they have. It is important to me to educate where I can. I particularly like to help out New Orleans-based musicians. New Orleans is so much more of a live music town than a music business (i.e., recording) town that many of the musicians do not completely understand the rights that they have. The HBO show *Treme*, which constantly featured local musicians, was extremely important in helping locals understand the value of their music beyond the club and stage.

How can a songwriter best go about getting themselves heard, seen, and represented by a publisher?

Even more important to a songwriter than the actual licensing is getting the music out there and heard. I am a proponent of giving your music away for free but only when you are starting out. I think the most important thing to do is spend money to produce a great video for your song. If the video starts getting a large number of views on Vevo or YouTube, the inquiries to use the song and subsequent licensing will automatically follow. Publishers are very attuned to the visual as well as audio now, (e.g., see what Beyonce just did with her latest album. It's all videos.)

What will really turn heads is a very well mastered and produced recording, not just a demo.

What else can make an artist stand out and build a successful relationship with a publisher?

Aside from great songs, follow-through is actually the most important trait a song-writer can have but not aggressiveness. It is very frustrating for me to start working with a songwriter and then find him or her unavailable and hard to contact. I also do not work with dishonest people, and a savvy publisher can usually detect that right off the bat. I also have a hard time with a songwriter who thinks he's superior to the process or has a huge ego, and publishers can detect that too. I'd much rather work with someone who may not be as talented an artist but is respectful of and grateful of what I'm able to do for him or her.

Your catalog at Della Music Publishing is pretty diverse and includes hip-hop, blues, rock 'n' roll, R&B, world music, jazz, and more. Do you find your own musical tastes drive your career, or has your career broadened your musical tastes as you've worked with a wider variety of artists?

My musical tastes definitely drive my work. I like pretty much all genres of music with the exception of country music. (I love Johnny Cash, however!) As I've gotten older, my tastes have changed, and I prefer happy music and dance music. I now love the old-ies station—so weird, I never expected this. And I almost never like to listen to Pink Floyd anymore, which was all I listened to for years. I moved from classic rock to clas-sical music, then to jazz, Latin hip hop, world music, dance music, and rap music. Rap is difficult because of things like the language and general views of women, but the lyr-ics speak to me because they are stories about culture. I love Dr. John because he em-bodies New Orleans culture and it is expressed in his lyrics, rhythm, and harmonies. When I go to Jazzfest, I hang out at the gospel tent and the blues tent. I am friends with and admire Ani DiFranco—her social commentary in her lyrics is just amazing. She is a fascinating and very talented songwriter. What I love most of all is the groove, and this can be found in any type of music. I've always been drawn to the beat. I think my next instrument I learn will be drums.

Any final advice for songwriters out there who are seeking representation?

Make sure you are registered with BMI and ASCAP. BMI in particular holds regular songwriting workshops to pair songwriters together. AIMP (Association of Indepen-dent Music Publishers (www.aimp.org), which is based in LA and NYC, also has similar workshops, as well as monthly panel discussions featuring people from all sides of the music business. Finally, New York City, Los Angeles, and Nashville are the best places to be in order to find songwriter groups and co-writers to connect with, although Mi-ami is great for hip-hop and Latin music.

For more information about Deborah Evans, Della Music Publishing, and what kinds of services a music publisher can offer a songwriter, visit www.dellamusicpublishing.com.

James Duncan is a content editor with Writer's Digest Books and occasionally writes for *Writer's Digest* magazine and their editor's blog, "There Are No Rules." He is the author of the short-story collection *The Cards We Keep* and numerous poetry collections from small presses around the country, including *Maybe a Bird Will Sing* (2009, Bird War Press), *Lantern Lit, Vol. 1* (2014, Dog On A Chain Press), and the forthcoming *Berlin* (Maverick Duck Press). For more of his work, visit www.jameshduncan.com.

SO, YOU'RE MOVING TO NASHVILLE?

Advice From the Front Lines

....

by Scarlet Keys

Maybe you're moving to Nashville from New York or Chicago or California because you have been listening to Diana Krall, Patsy Cline, Tim McGraw, Jack White, Alison Krauss, Jeff Buckley, or Sara Barielles, and you decided you want to make your living on music row among the elite tunesmiths. All of our stories are a little different. I was born in Dallas but was raised in Southern California and had an uncle with car parts on his lawn and a cousin named Bubba, so I was sure I was qualified to write country songs—but I had a lot to learn about country music.

When I first moved to Nashville, I had been trying to make contact with a woman in the business but got no answer. When she called me back, she said, "I know, I was in and out like a little dog wettin' in the snow; I'm harder to find than hens teeth." I just stood there with my mouth open, thinking, *Does she know she just said that?*

These colorful metaphors that just seem to float out of locals' mouths come from being born in southern soil, and that vernacular translates into the vivid storytelling in country songwriting—something you may already know about if you're also dead set on moving to Nashville. And if you don't know, you will quickly find out after you arrive.

So let's say there is no talking you out of the crazy pursuit of a songwriter's life of subsiding on crackers and hearing "No" for several years until you hear "Maybe" and eventually "YES." If that sounds like you, then here is some professional advice I had to learn the hard way that you can pack along with your clothes, your notebooks, and your guitar picks.

COMMITMENT

Chris Dubois, hit writer and owner of Sea Gayle Music, says, "You have to move here and show Nashville that you are committed. So, settle in for your first job waiting tables at The

Cracker Barrel until you get a job performing at local hotels or singing song demos and eventually interning at a publishing company where you can start making contacts."

Anna Wilson, who has won a SESAC award and had songs recorded with Lady Antebellum, offered similar yet concise advice, saying, "Nashville is a five-year town." In other words, it's not going to happen overnight.

Then again, if you don't go, it never will happen.

TREAT WRITING LIKE A JOB

I packed my entire life in the trunk of my car and arrived in Music City on the same day that at least fifty other people arrived with the same big dream: to be a hit songwriter and hear your songs blasting out of the car stereo sung by Carrie Underwood, Luke Bryan, or Lady Antebellum. I thought, *How hard can it be?* Sure, every waiter, dental assistant, and water-delivery guy is also coincidentally a songwriter—just ask them; they will hand you a CD.

It sounds like basic advice, but it's an absolute must: "You need to have demos of your songs," insists Eddie Byers, a top studio drummer. "Whether a band or just guitar or piano, etc. That is one of the best calling cards to give to others to hear."

Genre and even location cna have an effect on your demo. Consider this: I find that writers from New York or L.A. whose focus has been primarily on groove, complicated chord progressions, and generally more emotional lyrics are soon humbled by the deceptive simplicity of country songs. Complexity is replaced by three or four chords, and some writers are daunted by how difficult it is to write a story song using that sparse format. Suddenly standing naked with just three chords, they quickly find out if they really have something to say, Nashville is just the place to learn how to say it.

But even after you create your demo, continue to treat writing like a job. Chris Dubois says, "Write as much as possible. I soon realized I wasn't going to wait around to be a signed staff writer ... so I turned my guest room into a writer's room. I wrote five days a week even if my appointments canceled. I met as many songwriters as possible and tried to meet writers with songs currently on the radio, and I filled my date book with co-writing sessions every day of the week."

Writing advice that Monty Powell, a Golden Globe nominee and hit writer for Keith Urban, is known to offer: "Write for the industry that exists eighteen months from now or you will be behind the curve. Work with people one level above your tier. When you collaborate, try and write a hit song every time, and if the songs you have started don't measure up, start over."

Greg Becker, who has worked with Rascal Flatts and Tim McGraw, advises you to avoid taking any publishing appointments until you've gone through a few months of writer's rounds and have determined where your songs stand by comparison to those who are getting deals and cuts.

"I always say join one of the performance rights organizations," Becker adds. "ASCAP, BMI or SESAC—and get a meeting with one of the writers representatives. The rep may set you up with a co-writer or arrange a meeting with a publisher, and since publishers don't take unsolicited material or cold calls, this is a great place to start.

"People ask me which one to join and I always tell them to get a meeting with each one and sign with whoever loves you the most; that's the one that will champion you."

Similarly, Jason Blume, author and hit writer for artists such as Britney Spears and Collin Raye, recommends joining PRI and NSAI and attending their events, as well as BMI songwriter Workshops. "Collaborate. Nashville is a co-writing town. You could probably count the solo written hits of the past few years on one hand."

But when you meet reps and co-writers, keep this advice in mind: "Don't be pushy. Be polite," says Darrell Brown, a producer and hit songwriter. "And don't go around saying you are the best thing next to sliced bread, even if you are. No one wants that around for long and if you are that special, people in time will discover it. Show up with an open heart and an open mind for every appointment, and never hold back your best."

CULTIVATING PATIENCE

Just remember, building a career in this city is a process. It takes time. And that doesn't apply just to the music business, but life itself in Nashville. Wherever you are coming from, the moment your tires cross the Tennessee state line, you will feel everything slow down and suddenly it will feel like you are driving in molasses. At the first diner I stopped at, the waitress said, "Whatcha gonna have, precious?" When I began to tell her she said, "Darlin', you're gonna have to slow down, 'cause we don't hear as fast as you talk."

And that was my first lesson on how you can't be in any hurry in the South, or to get the ASCAP award or the Grammy.

And that pace can be hard for many. As Mark D. Sanders, writer of the hit song "I Hope You Dance" says, "Professional songwriters have to deal with loads of disappointment, on a daily basis, so I would try to remind myself that how you feel about your career on any given day is not necessarily an accurate depiction of your career. And the same is true of your life, no matter how high or low you may be today, tomorrow may be better. Or worse. Only way to find out is to be there.

"Ironically, just after surrendering my songwriting dream for changing the world one vertebrae at a time [Sanders eventually became a chiropractor], I got a voice mail from a publisher who had gotten a copy of my song demo saying he really loved the simple piano and vocal songs on track 3 and 7. I had fully produced songs on that CD and had done co-writes with really successful writers, but he liked the two songs that had most of my heart in them. I thought, *Someone finally gets me.*

"After several meetings he called me at home and said: 'I want to hire you to write for my company.' For the first time in my six years in Nashville, I felt my arm punch straight up into the air like a champion when I heard those words and finally realized that I was officially a staff songwriter, and someone was going to pay me to write songs.

Victory and success may not always be as clear-cut, and will probably come in small increments. The important thing is to stay patient while still working, step-by-step, open mic by open mic, workshop after workshop. The good things in your career will happen because you make them happen, over time, and one day you may wake up and realize that you found your own brand of success without realizing it happened. It can be *that* subtle.

Or, as Mark D. Sanders says, "On your first day as a staff writer, you will be pouring your first cup of coffee in that music publishing company kitchen and some Grammy winning writer will be pouring his coffee right next to you he will smile and tell you, 'Good tlaking, now go write a hit.'

"And, eventually, you will."

Scarlet Keys has been a full-time professor in the Songwriting department at the Berklee College of Music in Boston, MA for the past ten years, teaching songwriting, lyric writing, performance, and upper-division songwriting courses. Scarlet is a former staff songwriter for Warner/Chappell music publishing in Nashville and performs as a solo singer-songwriter. Scarlet has had several songs recorded by other artists and has had a gold record, a number one song in Britain and many songs recorded by artists in Canada, Nashville, and elsewhere in the U.S.

SONGWRITING CALENDAR

The best way for songwriters to achieve success is by setting concrete goals and meeting them. Goals are usually met by songwriters who give themselves, or are given, deadlines. Something about having an actual date to hit helps create a sense of urgency for most writers. This songwriting calendar is a great place to keep your important deadlines.

Also, this calendar is a good tool for recording upcoming events you'd like to attend or contests you'd like to enter. Or use this calendar to block out time for yourself—to just create.

Of course, you can use this calendar to record other special events, especially if you have a habit of remembering to write but of forgetting birthdays or anniversaries. After all, this calendar is now yours. Do with it what you will.

OCTOBER 2014

SUN	MON	TUE	WED	THURS	FRI	SAT
			1	2	3	4
5	6	7	8	9	10	11
12	13	14	15	16	17	18
19	20	21	22	23	24	25
26	27	28	29	30	31	

Start a songwriting blog and make at least one post per week.

NOVEMBER 2014

SUN	MON	TUE	WED	THU	FRI	SAT
						1
2	3	4	5	6	7	8
9	10	11	12	13	14	15
16	17	18	19	20	21	22
23	24	25	26	27	28	29
30						

Try sending out one targeted demo per day.

DECEMBER 2014

SUN	MON	TUE	WED	THU	FRI	SAT
		1	2	3	4	5
6						
7	8	9	10	11	12	13
14	15	16	17	18	19	20
21	22	23	24	25	26	27
28	29	30	31			

Evaluate your 2014 accomplishments and make 2015 goals.

JANUARY 2015

SUN	MON	TUE	WED	THU	FRI	SAT
				1	2	3
4	5	6	7	8	9	10
11	12	13	14	15	16	17
18	19	20	21	22	23	24
25	26	27	28	29	30	31

Make 2015 your best songwriting year yet!

SUN	MON	TUE	WED	THU	FRI	SAT
1	2	3	4	5	6	7
8	9	10	11	12	13	14
15	16	17	18	19	20	21
22	23	24	25	26	27	28

Don't wait until April to file your 2014 taxes.

MARCH 2015

SUN	MON	TUE	WED	THU	FRI	SAT
1	2	3	4	5	6	7
8	9	10	11	12	13	14
15	16	17	18	19	20	21
22	23	24	25	26	27	28
29	30	31				

Are you on Twitter? Try leaving a meaningful tweet daily.

APRIL 2015

SUN	MON	TUE	WED	THU	FRI	SAT
			1	2	3	4
5	6	7	8	9	10	11
12	13	14	15	16	17	18
19	20	21	22	23	24	25
26	27	28	29	30		

Sign up for a songwriting workshop.

MAY 2015

SUN	MON	TUE	WED	THU	FRI	SAT
					1	2
3	4	5	6	7	8	9
10	11	12	13	14	15	16
17	18	19	20	21	22	23
24	25	26	27	28	29	30
31						

Develop one song idea each week.

JUNE 2015

SUN	MON	TUE	WED	THU	FRI	SAT
	1	2	3	4	5	6
7	8	9	10	11	12	13
14	15	16	17	18	19	20
21	22	23	24	25	26	27
28	29	30				

Create a social network platform for your songs.

JULY 2015

SUN	MON	TUE	WED	THU	FRI	SAT
			1	2	3	4
5	6	7	8	9	10	11
12	13	14	15	16	17	18
19	20	21	22	23	24	25
26	27	28	29	30	31	

Find a new co-writer to work with.

AUGUST 2015

SUN	MON	TUE	WED	THU	FRI	SAT
						1
2	3	4	5	6	7	8
9	10	11	12	13	14	15
16	17	18	19	20	21	22
23	24	25	26	27	28	29
30	31					

Find a songwriting conference to attend.

SEPTEMBER 2015

SUN	MON	TUE	WED	THU	FRI	SAT
		1	2	3	4	5
6	7	8	9	10	11	12
13	14	15	16	17	18	19
20	21	22	23	24	25	26
27	28	29	30			

Remember to hit the "save" button when you're writing.

OCTOBER 2015

SUN	MON	TUE	WED	THU	FRI	SAT
				1	2	3
4	5	6	7	8	9	10
11	12	13	14	15	16	17
18	19	20	21	22	23	24
25	26	27	28	29	30	31

If you don't have it yet, find a copy of *2016 Songwriter's Market.*

NOVEMBER 2015

SUN	MON	TUE	WED	THU	FRI	SAT
1	2	3	4	5	6	7
8	9	10	11	12	13	14
15	16	17	18	19	20	21
22	23	24	25	26	27	28
29	30					

Try an unfamiliar writing style to help you grow as a writer.

DECEMBER 2015

SUN	MON	TUE	WED	THU	FRI	SAT
		1	2	3	4	5
6	7	8	9	10	11	12
13	14	15	16	17	18	19
20	21	22	23	24	25	26
27	28	29	30	31		

Try listening to one new band a week in a genre you haven't explored.

JANUARY 2016

SUN	MON	TUE	WED	THU	FRI	SAT
					1	2
3	4	5	6	7	8	9
10	11	12	13	14	15	16
17	18	19	20	21	22	23
24	25	26	27	28	29	30
31						

Look for a songwriting organization to join, if you haven't already.

FEBRUARY 2016

SUN	MON	TUE	WED	THU	FRI	SAT
	1	2	3	4	5	6
7	8	9	10	1	12	13
14	15	16	17	18	19	20
21	22	23	24	25	26	27
28	29					

Attend a show or concert for inspiration.

MUSIC PUBLISHERS

Music publishers work with songwriters the same way literary agents work with authors: they find and review songs, represent artists, and find ways for artists to make money from their songs by plugging the songs to recording artists and entertainment firms. In return for a share of the money made from your songs, they take care of paperwork and accounting, help you vet new songs, seek out foreign licensing deals, set you up with co-writers (recording artists or other songwriters), fund demo productions, give advances against future royalties, and so on.

HOW DO MUSIC PUBLISHERS MAKE MONEY FROM SONGS?

Music publishers make money by getting songs recorded onto albums, film and TV soundtracks, commercials, and other areas. While this is their primary function, music publishers also handle administrative tasks such as copyrighting songs; collecting royalties for the songwriter; negotiating and issuing synchronization licenses for use of music in films, television programs and commercials; arranging and administering foreign rights; auditing record companies and other music users; suing infringers; and producing new demos of new songs. In a small, independent publishing company, one or two people may handle all these jobs. Larger publishing companies are more likely to be divided into the following departments: creative (or professional), copyright, licensing, legal affairs, business affairs, royalty, accounting, and foreign.

HOW DO MUSIC PUBLISHERS FIND SONGS?

The creative department is responsible for finding talented writers and signing them to the company. Once a writer is signed, it's up to the creative department to develop and nurture the writer so he will write songs that create income for the company. Staff members often put writers together to form collaborative teams. And, perhaps most important, the creative department is responsible for securing commercial recordings of songs and pitching them for use in film and other media. The head of the creative department—usually called the "professional manager"—is charged with locating talented writers for the company.

HOW DO MUSIC PUBLISHERS GET SONGS RECORDED?

Once a writer is signed, the professional manager arranges for a demo to be made of the writer's songs. Even though a writer may already have recorded his own demo, the publisher will often re-demo the songs using established studio musicians in an effort to produce the highest-quality demo possible.

Once a demo is produced, the professional manager begins shopping the song to various outlets. He may try to get the song recorded by a top artist on his or her next album or get the song used in an upcoming film. The professional manager uses all the contacts and leads he has to get the writer's songs recorded by as many artists as possible. Therefore, he must be able to deal efficiently and effectively with people in other segments of the music industry, including A&R personnel, recording artists, producers, distributors, managers and lawyers. Through these contacts, he can find out what artists are looking for new material, and who may be interested in recording one of the writer's songs.

HOW IS A PUBLISHING COMPANY ORGANIZED?

After a writer's songs are recorded, the other departments at the publishing company come into play.

- The licensing and copyright departments are responsible for issuing any licenses for use of the writer's songs in film or TV and for filing various forms with the copyright office.
- The legal affairs department and business affairs department works with the professional department in negotiating contracts with its writers.
- The royalty and accounting departments are responsible for making sure that users of music are paying correct royalties to the publisher and ensuring the writer is receiving the proper royalty rate as specified in the contract and that statements are mailed to the writer promptly.
- Finally, the foreign department's role is to oversee any publishing activities outside of the United States, to notify sub-publishers of the proper writer and ownership information of songs in the catalogue and update all activity and new releases, and to make sure a writer is being paid for any uses of his material in foreign countries.

FINDING THE RIGHT MUSIC PUBLISHER FOR YOU

How do you go about finding a music publisher that will work well for you? First, you must find a publisher suited to the type of music you write. If a particular publisher works mostly with alternative music and you're a country songwriter, the contacts he has within the industry will hardly be beneficial to you.

Each listing in this section details, in order of importance, the type of music that publisher is most interested in; the music types appear in **boldface** to make them easier to locate. It's also very important to submit only to companies interested in your level of experience (see A Sample Listing Decoded on page 13). You will also want to refer to the Category Indexes, which list companies by the type of music they work with. Publishers placing music in film or TV will be proceded by an ⊗ (see the Film & TV Index for a complete list of these companies).

Do your research!

It's important to study the market and do research to identify which companies to submit to.

- Many record producers have publishing companies or have joint ventures with major publishers who fund the signing of songwriters and who provide administration services. Because producers have an influence over what is recorded in a session, targeting the producer/publisher can be a useful avenue.

- Because most publishers don't open unsolicited material, try to meet the publishing representative in person (at conferences, speaking engagements, etc.) or try to have an intermediary intercede on your behalf (for example, an entertainment attorney; a manager, an agent, etc.).

- As to demos, submit no more than 3 songs unless that publisher makes it clear they want more songs.

- As to publishing deals, co-publishing deals (where a writer owns part of the publishing share through his or her own company) are relatively common if the writer has a well-established track recoRoad

- Are you targeting a specific artist to sing your songs? If so, find out if that artist even considers outside material. Get a copy of the artist's latest album, and see who wrote most of the songs. If they were all written by the artist, he's probably not interested in hearing material from outside writers. If the songs were written by a variety of different writers, however, he may be open to hearing new songs.

- Check the album liner notes, which will list the names of the publishers of each writer. These publishers obviously have had luck pitching songs to the artist, and they may be able to get your songs to that artist as well.

- If the artist you're interested in has a recent hit on the Billboard charts, the publisher of that song will be listed in the "Hot 100 A-Z" index. Carefully choosing which publishers will work best for the material you write may take time, but it will only increase your chances of getting your songs heaRoad "Shotgunning" your demo packages (sending out many packages without regard for music preference or submission policy) is a waste of time and money and will hurt, rather than help, your songwriting career.

Once you've found some companies that may be interested in your work, learn what songs have been successfully handled by those publishers. Most publishers are happy to provide you with this information in order to attract high-quality material. As you're researching music publishers, keep in mind how you get along with them personally. If you can't work with a publisher on a personal level, chances are your material won't be represented as you would like it to be. A publisher can become your most valuable connection to all other segments of the music industry, so it's important to find someone you can trust and feel comfortable with.

Independent or major company?

Also consider the size of the publishing company. The publishing affiliates of the major music conglomerates are huge, handling catalogs of thousands of songs by hundreds of songwriters. Unless you are an established songwriter, your songs probably won't receive enough attention from such large companies. Smaller, independent publishers offer several advantages. First, independent music publishers are located all over the country, making it easier for you to work face-to-face rather than by mail or phone. Smaller companies usually aren't affiliated with a particular record company and are therefore able to pitch your songs to many different labels and acts. Independent music publishers are usually interested in a smaller range of music, allowing you to target your submissions more accurately. The most obvious advantage to working with a smaller publisher is the personal attention they can bring to you and your songs. With a smaller roster of artists to work with, the independent music publisher is able to concentrate more time and effort on each particular project.

SUBMITTING MATERIAL TO PUBLISHERS

When submitting material to a publisher, always keep in mind that a professional, courteous manner goes a long way in making a good impression. When you submit a demo through the mail, make sure your package is neat and meets the particular needs of the publisher. Review each publisher's submission policy carefully, and follow it to the letter. Disregarding this information will only make you look like an amateur in the eyes of the company you're submitting to.

Listings of companies in Canada are preceded by a ICON, and international markets are designated with a ICON. You will find an alphabetical list of these companies at the back of the book, along with an index of publishers by state in the Geographic Index (see page XXXXX).

PUBLISHING CONTRACTS

Once you've located a publisher you like and he's interested in shopping your work, it's time to consider the publishing contract—an agreement in which a songwriter grants certain rights to a publisher for one or more songs. The contract specifies any advances offered to the writer, the rights that will be transferred to the publisher, the royalties a songwriter is to receive and the length of time the contract is valid.

- When a contract is signed, a publisher will ask for a 50-50 split with the writer. This is standard industry practice; the publisher is taking that 50% to cover the overhead costs of running his business and for the work he's doing to get your songs recorded.
- It is always a good idea to have a publishing contract (or any music business contract) reviewed by a competent entertainment lawyer.
- There is no "standard" publishing contract, and each company offers different provisions for their writers.

Make sure you ask questions about anything you don't understand, especially if you're new in the business. Songwriter organizations such as the Songwriters Guild of America (SGA) provide contract review services, and can help you learn about music business language and what constitutes a fair music publishing contract. Be sure to read the Contracts section on page 40 for more information on contracts. See the Organizations section, beginning on page 238 of this book, for more information on the SGA and other songwriting groups.

When signing a contract, it's important to be aware of the music industry's unethical practitioners. The "song shark," as he's called, makes his living by asking a songwriter to pay to have a song published. The shark will ask for money to demo a song and promote it to radio stations; he may also ask for more than the standard 50% publisher's share or ask you to give up all rights to a song in order to have it published. Although none of these practices is illegal, it's certainly not ethical, and no successful publisher uses these methods. Songwriter's Market works to list only honest companies interested in hearing new material. (For more on "song sharks," see How Do I Avoid the Rip-Offs? on page 22.)

ADDITIONAL PUBLISHERS

There are more publishers located in other sections of the book! Use the Index to find listings within other sections who are also music publishers.

Icons

For more instructional information on the listings in this book, including explanations of symbols beside many listings, read the article How To Use Songwriter's Market on page 7.

◐ ABEAR PUBLISHING (BMI)/SONG-TOWN PUBLISHING (ASCAP)

5631 Myrtlewood Dr., Nashville TN 37211 United States. **E-mail:** ronhebert@gmail.com.

HOW TO CONTACT Submit mp3 by e-mail. Unsolicited submissions are OK. Prefers 3 songs with lyric sheets. Responds in 1 week if interested.

MUSIC Mostly **country**, **country/pop**, **pop**, **dance**, and **Christian**.

◑◯ ALL ROCK MUSIC

United States. **E-mail:** info@collectorrecords.nl. **Website:** www.collectorrecords.nl. **Contact:** Cees Klop, president. music publisher, record company (Collector Records) and record producer. Estab. 1967. Publishes 40 songs/year; publishes several new songwriters/year. Staff size: 3. Pays standard royalty.

○ Also see the listings for Collector Records in the Record Companies and Record Producers sections of this book.

AFFILIATES All Rock Music (United Kingdom).

HOW TO CONTACT Submit demo package by mail. Unsolicited submissions are OK. Prefers CD. SAE and IRC. Responds in 2 months.

MUSIC Mostly **'50s rock**, **rockabilly** and **country rock**; also **piano boogie woogie**. Published Rock Crazy Baby (album), written and recorded by Art Adams (1950s rockabilly), released 2004; Marvin Jackson (album), by Marvin Jackson (1950s rockers), released 2005; Western Australian Snake Pit R&R (album), recorded by various (1950s rockers), released 2005, all on Collector Records.

TIPS "Send only the kind of material we issue/produce as listed."

◐✪ ALPHA MUSIC INC.

106 Apple Street, Suite 302, Tinton Falls NJ 07724 United States. **E-mail:** info@trfMusic.com. **Website:** www.trfMusic.com. **Contact:** Michael Nurko, music publisher. Pays standard royalty. Affiliate(s) Dorian Music Publishers, Inc. (ASCAP) and TRF Music Inc.

○ Also see listing for TRF Production Music Libraries in the Advertising, Audiovisual & Commercial Music Firms section of this book.

HOW TO CONTACT "We accept submissions of new compositions. Submissions are not returnable."

MUSIC All categories, mainly **instrumental** and **acoustic** suitable for use as **production music**, including **theme and background music for television**

and film. "Have published more than 50,000 titles since 1931."

◐ A NEW RAP JAM PUBLISHING

P.O. Box 683, Lima OH 45802. **E-mail:** newexperiencerecords@yahoo.com. **Contact:** A&R Department. Professional Managers: William Roach (rap, clean); James Milligan (country, 70s music, pop). Music publisher and record company (New Experience/Faze 4 Records, Pump It Up Records, and Rough Edge Records). Publishes 50-100 songs/year; Grind Blocc Records and Touch Tone Digital International Records publishes 5-10 new songwriters/year. Hires staff songwriters. Pays standard royalty.

AFFILIATES Songwriters Party House Publishing (BMI), Creative Star Management, and Rough Edge Records. Distribution through KVZ Distribution and States 51 Distribution.

HOW TO CONTACT Write first to arrange personal interview or submit demo CD by mail. Unsolicited submissions are OK. Prefers CD with 3-5 songs and lyric or lead sheet. Include SASE. Responds in 6-8 weeks. "Visit www.myspace.com/newexperiencerecords2 for more information."

MUSIC Mostly **R&B**, **pop**, **blues**, and **rock/rap** (clean); also **contemporary**, **gospel**, **country** and **soul**. Published "Lets Go Dancing" (single by Dion Mikel), recorded and released 2006 on Faze 4 Records/New Experience Records; "The Broken Hearted" (single) from The Final Chapter (album), recorded by T.M.C. the milligan connection (R&B/gospel); James Jr.; Girl Like You feat. Terry Zapp Troutman, additional appearances by Kurtis Blow, King MC, Sugarfoot Lead Singer (Ohio Players) Lavel Jackson 2009/10 on New Experience/Pump It Up Records. Other artists include singer-songwriter James, Jr. on Faze 4 Records/Rough Edge Records Grind Blocc Records.

TIPS "We are seeking hit artists from the 70s, 80s, and 90s who would like to be signed, as well as new talent and female solo artists. Send any available information supporting the group or act. We are a label that does not promote violence, drugs, or anything that we feel is a bad example for our youth. Establish music industry contacts, write and keep writing, and most of all believe in yourself. Use a good recording studio but be very professional. Just take your time and produce the best music possible. Sometimes you only get one chance. Make sure you place your best song on your demo first. This will increase your chances greatly. If you're the owner of your own small label and have a finished product, please send it. And if there is interest we will contact you. Also be on the lookout for new artists on Rough Edge Records and Touch Tone Records. Now reviewing blues and soul music. If you have a developing record label and would like distribution send us your artist listing record label information to be considered and thank you for considering us for your next project."

ANTELOPE PUBLISHING INC.

P.O. Box 55, Rowayton CT 06853 United States. Publishes 5-10 new songs/year; publishes 3-5 new songwriters/year. Pays standard royalty.

HOW TO CONTACT Submit demo by mail. Unsolicited submissions are OK. Prefers CD with lead sheet. Does not return material. Responds in 1 month "only if interested."

MUSIC Only **bebop** and **1940s swing**. Does not want anything electronic. Published "Somewhere Near" (single by Tony LaVorgna) from Just For My Friends (album), recorded by Jeri Brown (easy listening); "Cookie Monster" and "The Lady From Mars" (singles by Tony LaVorgna) from Just For My Friends (album), recorded by Tony LaVorgna (jazz/easy listening), released 2007 on Antelope.

TIPS "Put your best song first with a short intro."

ATTACK MEDIA GROUP

401 Richmond St. W, Suite 395, Toronto ON M5V 3A8 Canada. **E-mail:** info@attackmediagroup.com. **Website:** www.attackmediagroup.com. Already the owner of an extensive music publishing catalogue, Attack Media Groups mission is to target potential acquisitions in the music, film and television industries ranging from independent record labels, artists, DVD acquisitions, feature length films to purchases in the music publishing sector along with acquiring childrens and extreme sports content. We are a Toronto-based privately owned media and entertainment company.

BAITSTRING MUSIC

2622 Kirtland Road, Brewton AL 36426 United States. (251)867-2228. **Contact:** Roy Edwards, president.

Also the listings for Cheavroia Music in this section, Bolivia Records in the Record Companies section, and Known Artist Productions in the Record Producers section of this book.

AFFILIATES Cheavoria Music Co. (BMI).

HOW TO CONTACT Submit demo by mail. Unsolicited submissions are OK. Prefers CD with 3 songs and lyric sheet. Does not return material. Responds in 1 month.

MUSIC Mostly **R&B**, **pop** and **easy listening**; also **country** and **gospel**. Published "Forever and Always," written and recorded by Jim Portwood (pop); and "Make Me Forget" (by Horace Linsley) and "Never Let Me Go" (by Cheavoria Edwards), both recorded by Bobbie Roberson (country), all on Bolivia Records.

BEARSONGS

Box 944, Edgbaston, Birmingham B16 8UTT United Kingdom. +(44)0121-454-7020. **Website:** www.bigbearMusic.com. **Contact:** Jim Simpson, managing director; Russell Fletcher, professional manager. music publisher and record company (Big Bear Records). Member PRS, MCPS. Publishes 25 songs/year; publishes 15-20 new songwriters/year. Pays standard royalty.

Also see the listings for Big Bear Records in the Record Companies section and Big Bear in the Record Producers section of this book.

HOW TO CONTACT Submit demo by mail. Unsolicited submissions are OK. Prefers CD. Does not return material. Responds in 3 months.

MUSIC Mostly **blues**, **swing** and **jazz**. Published Blowing With Bruce and Cool Heights (by Alan Barnes), recorded by Bruce Adams/Alan Barnes Quintet; and Blues For My Baby (by Charles Brown), recorded by King Pleasure & The Biscuit Boys, all on Big Bear Records.

TIPS "Have a real interest in jazz, blues, swing."

BIG FISH MUSIC PUBLISHING GROUP

12720 Burbank Blvd., Suite 124, Valley Village CA 91607. (818) 508-9777. **E-mail:** clisag21@yahoo.com. **Website:** See their Facebook page for more information. **Contact:** Chuck Tennin. Producer: Gary Black (country, pop, adult contemporary, rock, crossover songs, other styles). Professional Music Manager: Lora Sprague (jazz, New Age, instrumental, pop rock, R&B). Professional Music Manager: B.J. (pop, TV, film, and special projects). Professional Music and Vocal Consultant: Zell Black (country, pop, gospel, rock, blues). Producer, Independent Artists: Darryl Harrelson—Major Label Entertainment (country, pop and other genres). Nashville Music Associate: Ron Hebert (Abear/Songtown Publishing). Songwriter/Consultant: Jerry Zanandrea (Z Best Muzic). Staff Songwriters: BillyO'Hara, Joe Rull, Lisa Faye, Claire Applewhite. Music Publisher, record company (California Sun Records) and production company. Publishes 20-30 songs/year; publishes 5-10 new songwriters/year. Staff size: 10. Pays standard royalty. "We also license songs and music copyrights to users of music, especially TV and film, commercials, and recording projects." Member: BMI, ASCAP, CMA and ACM.

AFFILIATES Big Fish Music (BMI) and California Sun Music (ASCAP).

HOW TO CONTACT Write first and obtain permission to submit. Include SASE for reply. "**Please do not call** or e-mail submissions. After permission to submit is confirmed, we will assign and forward to you a submission code numberallowing you to submit up to 4 songs maximum, preferably on CD. Include a properly addressed cover letter, signed and dated, with your source of referral with your assigned submission code number and an SASE for reply and/or return of material. Include lyrics. Unsolicited material will not be accepted. This is our submission policy to review outside and new material." Responds in 2 weeks.

FILM & TV Places 6 songs in TV/year. Recently published "Even the Angels Knew" (by Cathy Carlson/Craig Lackey/MartyAxelrod); "Stop Before We Start" (by J.D. Grieco); "Oh Santa" (by Christine Bridges/John Deaver), all recorded by The Black River Girls in Passions (NBC); licensed "A Christmas Wish" (by Ed Fry/Eddie Max), used in Passions (NBC); "Girls Will Be Girls" (by Cathy Carlson/John LeGrande), recorded by The Black River Girls, used in All My Children (ABC); "The WayYou're Drivin' Me" and "Ain't No Love 'Round Here" (by Jerry Zanandrea), bothrecorded by The Black River Girls, used in Passions (NBC); "Since You Stole My Heart"(by Rick Colmbra/Jamey Whiting), used in Passions (NBC); "Good Time To Fly", "All INeed Is A Highway," and "Eyes Of The Children" (by Wendy Martin), used in Passions (NBC); "It's An Almost Perfect Christmas" (by Michael Martin), used in Passions (NBC).

MUSIC Country, including **country pop, country A/C** and **country crossover** with "a cutting edge"; also **pop, rock, pop ballads, adult contemporary, uplifting, praise, worship, spiritual,** and **inspirational adult contemporary gospel** "with a powerful message," **instrumental background and theme Music** for TV, film, and commercials, **New Age/instrumental jazz** and **novelty, orchestral classical, R&B** and

children's music, for all kinds of commercial use. Published "If Wishes Were Horses" (single by Billy O'Hara); "Heroes to Us" (single by Joe Rull); "Leavin' You For Me" (single by J.D. Grieco).

TIPS "Demo should be professional, high quality, clean, simple, dynamic, and must get the song across on the first listen. Good clear vocals, a nice melody, a good musical feel, good musical arrangement, strong lyrics and chorus—a unique, catchy, clever song that sticks with you. Looking for unique country and pop songs with a different edge that can crossover to the mainstream market for ongoing Nashville Music projects and songs for hot female Country acts that can crossover to adult contemporary and pop with great lush harmonies. Also, catchy, up-tempo songs with an attitude and a groove, preferably rock, that can be marketed to today's youth."

⊘ 🄫 🄰 BIG YELLOW DOG

1313 16th Street South, Nashville TN 37212. **E-mail:** info@bigyellowdogMusic.com. **Website:** www.bigyellowdogMusic.com. Big Yellow Dog Music is an independent music publishing company based in Nashville, Tennessee, recognized with such accolades as four Grammys (including Song of the Year "Need You Now"), sixteen Number Ones, four Song of the Year awards (ACM, BMI and two ASCAPs), an ASCAP Global Award, an ASCAP Pop Award, and many more.

HOW TO CONTACT Does not accept outside submissions.

MUSIC Catalog includes songs performed by Lady Antebellum, Adele, Sheryl Crow, Carrie Underwood, Luke Bryan, Susan Boyle, Tim McGraw, The Mavericks, Eli Young Band, Toby Keith, George Strait, Darius Rucker, Willie Nelson, Alison Krauss, Guy Clark, Jimmy Buffett, Dierks Bentley, and many more.

⊘ 🄫 BIXIO MUSIC GROUP & ASSOCIATES/IDM MUSIC

111 E. 14th St., Suite 140, New York NY 10003 United States. (212)695-3911. **E-mail:** info@bixio.com. **Website:** www.bixio.com. (ASCAP) Music publisher, record company and rights clearances. Estab. 1985. Publishes a few hundred songs/year; publishes 2 new songwriters/year. Staff size: 6. Pays standard royalty.

HOW TO CONTACT Does not accept unsolicited material.

MUSIC Mostly **soundtracks.** Published "La Strada Nel Bosco," included in the TV show Ed (NBC); "La

Beguine Du Mac," included in the TV show The Chris Isaac Show (Showtime); and "Alfonsina Delle Camelie," included in the TV show UC: Undercover (NBC).

○ BLUEWATER MUSIC

PO Box 120904, Nashville TN 37212. (615)327-0808. **Fax:** (615)327-0809. **E-mail:** info@bluewaterMusic. com. **Website:** www.bluewaterMusic.com. **Contact:** Bennet Davidson, assistant, creative department. Now, approaching its 30th year, Bluewater is embarking on a new venture—Artist Management. With its extensive contacts in the music industry and creative promotional ideas, Bluewater is set to increase the fan base of bands and musical acts of all genres. Kink Ador is the company's first signing and the band's new album, "Free World," will be released in early 2014.

⊘ BMG CHRYSALIS US

BMG Chrysalis US, 1745 Broadway, 19th Floor, New York NY 10019 United States. **Website:** www. bmgchrysalis.com. (ASCAP, BMI) 8447 Wilshire Boulevard, Suite 400, Beverly Hills CA 90211. (323)658-9125. **Fax:** (323)658-8019. **Website:** http:// chrysalisMusicusa.com. **Contact:** David Stamm, Vice President of A&R. Music publisher. Estab. 1968.

HOW TO CONTACT Chrysalis Music does not accept any unsolicited submissions.

MUSIC Published "Sum 41" (single), written and recorded by OutKast; "Light Ladder" (single), written and recorded by David Gray. Administer, David Lee Roth, Andrea Boccelli, Velvet Revolver, and Johnta Austin.

◖ BOUQUET-ORCHID PUBLISHING

P.O. Box 1335, Norcross GA 30091 United States. (770)814-2420. Music publisher, record company, record producer (Bouquet-Orchid Enterprises) and artist management. Member: CMA, AFM. Publishes 10-12 songs/year; publishes 3 new songwriters/year. Pays standard royalty.

HOW TO CONTACT Submit demo by mail. Unsolicited submissions are OK. Prefers CD with 3-5 songs and lyric sheet. "Send biographical information if possible—even a photo helps." Include SASE. Responds in 1 month.

MUSIC Mostly **religious** ("Amy Grant, etc., contemporary gospel"); **country** ("Garth Brooks, Trisha Yearwood-type material"); and **top 100/pop** ("Bryan Adams, Whitney Houston-type material"). Published "Blue As Your Eyes" (single), written and recorded by

Adam Day; "Spare My Feelings" (single by Clayton Russ), recorded by Terri Palmer; and "Trying to Get By" (single by Tom Sparks), recorded by Bandoleers, all on Bouquet Records.

⊘ BOURNE CO. MUSIC PUBLISHERS

5 W. 37th St., New York NY 10018 United States. (212)391-4300. **Fax:** (212)391-4306. **E-mail:** bourne@ bourneMusic.com. **Website:** www.bourneMusic.com. Publishes educational material and popular Music.

AFFILIATES ABC Music, Ben Bloom, Better Half, Bogat, Burke & Van Heusen, Goldmine, Harborn, Lady Mac and Murbo Music.

HOW TO CONTACT Does not accept unsolicited submissions.

MUSIC Piano/vocal, **band pieces** and **choral pieces.** Published "Amen" and "Mary's Little Boy Child" (singles by Hairston); "When You Wish Upon a Star" (single by Washington/Harline); and "San Antonio Rose" (single by Bob Willis, arranged John Cacavas).

○ BRANDON HILLS MUSIC, LLC (BMI)

N 3425 Searle County Line Road, Brandon WI 53919 United States. **E-mail:** martab@centurytel.net. **Website:** www.brandonhillsMusic.com. **Contact:** Marsha L. Brown. Publishes 4 new songwriters/year. Staff size: 2. Pays standard royalty of 50%.

HOW TO CONTACT Submit demo package by mail. Unsolicited submissions are OK. Prefers CD with 1-4 songs and cover letter. Does not return submissions. Responds only if interested.

MUSIC Mostly **country (traditional, modern, country rock), contemporary Christian, blues**; also **children's** and **bluegrass** and **rap.** Published "Let It Rain," recorded by Steff Nevers, written by Larry Migliore and Kevin Gallarello (Universal Records, Norway); "Do You Like My Body," recorded by Ginger-Ly, written by Nisa McCall (SEI Corp and Big Daddy G Music, CA); "Did I Ever Thank You Lord," recorded by Jacob Garcia, written by Eletta Sias (TRW Records); "Honky Tonk In Heaven," recorded by Buddy Lewis, written by Mike Heath and Bob Alexander (Ozark Records).

TIPS "We prefer studio-produced CDs. The lyrics and the CD must match. Cover letter, lyrics, and CD should have a professional look. Demos should have vocals up front and every word should be distinguishable. Please make sure your lyrics match your song. Submit only your best. The better the demo, the better of chance of getting your music published and recorded."

⊘ BUG MUSIC INC.

7750 Sunset Blvd., Los Angeles CA 90046 United States. (323)969-0988. **Fax:** (323)969-0968. **E-mail:** buginfo@bugMusic.com. **Website:** www.bugMusic.com. **Contact:** Senior Vice President of Creative: Eddie Gomez. Creative Manager: Mara Schwartz. Creative Coordinator: Laura Scott. **Nashville:** 33 Music Square W Suite 104B, Nashville TN 37203. (615)313-7676. **Fax:** (615)313-7670. Director of Creative Services: Ed Williams; Creative Manager: Tyler Pickens. **New York:** 347 W. 36th St., Suite 1203, New York NY 10018. (212)643-0925. **Fax:** (212)643-0897. Senior Vice President: Garry Valletri. Music publisher. "We handle administration."

AFFILIATES Bughouse (ASCAP).

HOW TO CONTACT Does not accept unsolicited submissions.

MUSIC All genres. Published "You Were Mine" (by E. Erwin/M. Seidel), recorded by Dixie Chicks on Monument.

○ CALIFORNIA COUNTRY MUSIC

112 Widmar Pl., Clayton CA 94517 United States. **Contact:** Edward J. Brincat, owner. (BMI) Publisher and record company (Roll On Records). Pays standard royalty. Affiliate(s) Sweet Inspirations Music (ASCAP).

○ Also see the listing for Roll On Records in the Record Companies section of this book.

HOW TO CONTACT Submit demo by mail. Unsolicited submissions are OK. "Do not call or write. Any calls will be returned collect to caller." Send CD with 3 songs and lyric sheet. Include SASE. Responds in 6 weeks.

MUSIC Mostly **MOR**, **contemporary country** and **pop.** Does not want rap, metal or rock. Published For Realities Sake (album by F.L. Pittman/R. Barretta) and Maddy (album by F.L. Pittman/M. Weeks), both recorded by Ron Banks & L.J. Reynolds on Life & Bellmark Records; and Quarter Past Love (album by Irwin Rubinsky/Janet Fisher), recorded by Darcy Dawson on NNP Records.

○ CARNIVAL MUSIC

Carnival Music, 24 Music Square West, Nashville TN 37203. (615)259-0841. **Fax:** (615)259-0843. **Website:** www. .com. Carnival music isn't a publishing company, or a record label, though it does the work of both. It's a music company, front to back, founded by industry veterans Frank Liddell and Travis Hill in 1997, not with the intent of using music to prop up a business, but to build a business that could find and nurture compelling, lasting music, and set the stage for compelling, lasting careers.

MUSIC Carnival's current roster includes country voices David Nail, Brent Cobb and Hailey Whitters, roots-rooted talents Stoney LaRue, Rob Baird, and Mando Saenz and the style-blending Logan Brill and Derik Hultquist. Each Carnival writer puts forth his or her own stylistic stamp; all possess that undeniable talent.

◐ ⊛ CHRISTMAS & HOLIDAY MUSIC

26642 Via Noveno, Mission Viejo CA 92691 United States. (949)859-1615. **E-mail:** justinwilde@christmassongs.com. **Website:** www.christmassongs.com. **Contact:** Justin Wilde. Publishes 8-12 songs/year; publishes 8-12 new songwriters/year. Staff size: 1. "All submissions must be complete songs (i.e., music and lyrics)." Pays standard royalty.

AFFILIATES Songcastle Music (ASCAP).

HOW TO CONTACT Submit demo CD by mail. Unsolicited submissions are OK. Do not call. Do not send unsolicited mp3s or links to Websites. See website for submission guidelines. "First Class Mail only. Registered or certified mail not accepted." Prefers CD with no more than 3 songs with lyric sheets. Do not send lead sheets or promotional material, bios, etc." Include SASE but does not return material out of the US. Responds only if interested.

FILM & TV Places 10-15 songs in TV/year. Published Barbara Streisand's "It Must Have Been the Mistletoe."

MUSIC Strictly **Christmas**, **Halloween**, **Hanukkah**, **Mother's Day**, **Thanksgiving**, **Father's Day** and **New Year's Eve Music** in every style imaginable: easy listening, rock, pop, blues, jazz, country, reggae, rap, children's secular or religious. Please do not send anything that isn't a holiday song. Published "It Must Have Been the Mistletoe" (single by Justin Wilde/Doug Konecky) from Christmas Memories (album), recorded by Barbra Streisand (pop Christmas), by Columbia; "What Made the Baby Cry?" (single by Toby Keith) and "Mr. Santa Claus" (single by James Golseth) from Casper's Haunted Christmas soundtrack (album), recorded by Scotty Blevins (Christmas) on Koch International.

TIPS "We only sign one out of every 200 submissions. Please be selective. If a stranger can hum your melody back to you after hearing it twice, it has 'standard' potential. Couple that with a lyric filled with unique, inventive imagery, that stands on its own, even without music. Combine the two elements, and workshop the finished result thoroughly to identify weak points. Submit to us only when the song is polished to perfection. Submit positive lyrics only. Avoid negative themes like 'Blue Christmas'."

◑ COME ALIVE COMMUNICATIONS, INC. (ASCAP)

348 Valley Road, Suite A, P.O. Box 436, West Grove PA 19390-0436 United States. (610)724-1581. E-mail: info@comealiveMusic.com. **Website:** www. comealiveusa.com. Professional Managers: Joseph L. Hooker (pop, rock, jazz); Bridget G. Hylak (spiritual, country, classical). Music publisher, record producer and record company. Estab. 1985. Publishes 4 singles/year. Staff: 7. Pays standard royalty of 50%.

◐ Come Alive Communications received a IHS Ministries Award in 1996, John Lennon Songwriting Contest winnter, 2003.

HOW TO CONTACT Call first to obtain permission to submit a demo. For song publishing submissions, prefers CD with 3 songs, lyric sheet, and cover letter. Does not return submissions. Responds only if interested.

MUSIC Mostly **pop**, **easy listening**, **contemporary Christian**, and **patriotic**; also **country** and **spiritual**. Does not want obscene, suggestive, violent, or morally offensive lyrics. Produced "In Search of America" (single) from Long Road to Freedom (album), written and recorded by J. Hooker (patriotic), released 2003 on ComeAliveMusic.com; "Our Priests/Nuestros Sacerdotes," named CMN's official theme song for the Vatican Designated Year of the Priest (2009-10). See www.ourpriests.com.

⊘ COPPERFIELD MUSIC GROUP/PENNY ANNIE MUSIC (BMI)/TOP BRASS MUSIC (ASCAP)/BIDDY BABY MUSIC (SESAC)

1400 South St., Nashville TN 37212 United States. E-mail: hkenbiddy@comcast.net. **Website:** www.copperfieldMusic.com. **Contact:** Ken Biddy.

HOW TO CONTACT Contact ken@copperfieldMusic.com first and obtain permission to submit a demo by e-mail. Company does not return submissions or accept phone calls. Responds only if interested.

MUSIC Mostly **country**; also **modern bluegrass**. Does not want rap or heavy/metal/rock. Recently published "Daddy Won't Sell the Farm" from Tat-

toos and Scars (album), recorded by Montgomery Gentry (country).

◒ CORELLI MUSIC GROUP

P.O. Box 2314, Tacoma WA 98401-2314 United States. (253)735-3228. **E-mail:** JerryCorelli@yahoo.com; corellisMusicgroup@yahoo.com. **Website:** www.corelliMusicgroup.blogspot.com. **Contact:** Jerry Corelli. (BMI/ASCAP) Music publisher, record company (Omega III Records), record producer (Jerry Corelli/Angels Dance Recording Studio) and booking agency (Tone Deaf Booking). Estab. 1996. Publishes 12 songs/year; publishes 6 new songwriters/year. Staff size: 3. Pays standard royalty.

AFFILIATES My Angel's Songs (ASCAP); Corelli's Music Box (BMI).

HOW TO CONTACT Submit demo by mail. Unsolicited submissions are OK. "No phone calls, e-mails, or letters asking to submit." CD only with no more than 3 songs, lyric sheet and cover letter. "We DO NOT accept mp3s vie e-mail. We want love songs with a message and overtly Christian songs. Make sure all material is copyrighted. You MUST include SASE or we DO NOT respond!" Responds in 2 months

MUSIC Mostly **contemporary Christian**, **Christian soft rock** and **Christmas**; also **love songs**, **ballads** and **new country**. Does not want songs without lyrics or lyrics without music. Published "I'm Not Dead Yet" (by Jerry Corelli), "Fried Bologna" (by Jerry Corelli), and "His Name is Jesus" (by Jerry Corelli), all from I'm Not Dead Yet (album), released 2010 on Omega III Records.

TIPS "Success is obtained when opportunity meets preparation! If a SASE is not sent with demo, we don't even listen to the demo. Be willing to do a rewrite. Don't send material expecting us to place it with a Top Ten artist. Be practical. Do your songs say what's always been said, except differently? Don't take rejection personally. Always send a #10 self-adhesive envelope for your SASE."

◑ THE CORNELIUS COMPANIES/ GATEWAY ENTERTAINMENT, INC.

Dept. SM, 9 Music Square S, Suite 92, Nashville TN 37203 United States. (615)321-5333. **E-mail:** corneliuscompanies@bellsouth.net. **Website:** www.corneliuscompanies.com. (BMI, ASCAP, SESAC) Music publisher and record producer (Ron Cornelius). Publishes 60-80 songs/year; publishes 2-3 new songwriters/year. Occasionally hires staff writers. Pays standard royalty.

AFFILIATES RobinSparrow Music (BMI), Strummin' Bird Music (ASCAP) and Bridgeway Music (SESAC).

HOW TO CONTACT Contact by e-mail or call for permission to submit material. Submit demo package by mail. Unsolicited submissions are OK. "Send demo on CD format only with 2-3 songs." Include SASE. Responds in 2 months.

MUSIC Mostly **country** and **pop**; also **positive country**, **gospel** and **alternative**. Published songs by Confederate Railroad, Faith Hill, David Allen Coe, Alabama and over 50 radio singles in the positive Christian/country format.

TIPS "Looking for material suitable for film."

CRINGE MUSIC (PRS, MCPS)

The Cedars, Elvington Lane, Hawkinge, Kent CT18 7AD United Kingdom. (01)(303)893-472. **E-mail:** info@cringeMusic.co.uk. **Website:** www.cringeMusic.co.uk. **Contact:** Christopher Ashman. Music publisher and record company (Red Admiral Records). Estab. 1979. Staff size: 2.

HOW TO CONTACT Submit demo package by e-mail. Unsolicited submissions are OK. Submission materials are not returned. Responds if interested.

MUSIC All styles.

CURB MUSIC

48 Music Square East, Nashville TN 37203 United States. (615)321-5080. **Website:** www.curb.com. (ASCAP, BMI, SESAC)

Curb Music only accepts submissions through reputable industry sources and does not accept unsolicited demos.

AFFILIATES Mike Curb Music (BMI); Curb Songs (ASCAP); and Curb Congregation Songs (SESAC).

JOF DAVE MUSIC

1055 Kimball Ave., Kansas City KS 66104 United States. (913)593-3180. **Contact:** David Johnson, CEO. Music publisher, record company (Cymbal Records). Estab. 1984. Publishes 30 songs/year; publishes 12 new songwriters/year. Pays standard royalty.

HOW TO CONTACT Contact first and obtain permission to submit. Prefers CD. Include SASE. Responds in 1 month.

MUSIC Mostly **gospel** and **R&B**. Published "The Woman I Love" (single) from Sugar Bowl (album), written and recorded by King Alex, released 2001 on Cymbal Records; and "Booty Clap" (single by Johnny Jones) from Gotta Move On (album), recorded by Jacuzé, released 2005 on Cymbal Records.

DAYWIND MUSIC PUBLISHING

114A Commerce Ave., Hendersonville TN 37075. (615)826-8101. **E-mail:** info@daywindpublishing.com. **Website:** www.daywindpublishing.com. **Contact:** Rick Shelton, vice president. Since its inception in 1995, Daywind Music Publishing has emerged as the premier source of new songs for the Southern Gospel and Church Print/Choral markets. In early 2012, Daywind expanded publishing to include Christian Contemporary staff and writers and has already made an impressive start to their year including cuts by Hawk Nelson, Hyland, Jamie Slocum, and Nate Sallie. DMP boasts of an exclusive staff of 13 prestigious songwriters. Daywind Music Publishing has been blessed with more than 75 Singing News Song of the Year and Gospel Music Association (Dove) nominations as well as 37 radio singles hitting the top position on the charts—#1. BMI awarded DMP's Christian Taylor Music, Christian Music Publisher of the Year in both 2002 and 2004.

MUSIC Daywind Music Publishing remains committed to the exhortation and encouragement of the church through the advancement of quality Christian Music.

DEFINE SOMETHING IN NOTHING MUSIC

11213 W. Baden Street, Avondale AZ 85323 United States. (360)421-9225. **E-mail:** definesinm@gmail.com. **Website:** http://dsinm.weebly.com. **Contact:** Jaime Reynolds. Music agency. Staff Size: 5. Pays 75% of gross revenue.

HOW TO CONTACT Prefers MP3s sent to e-mail only. "Please do not contact for permission, just send your music." Does not return submissions. Responds in 2 weeks if interested.

MUSIC Interested in all styles. "We welcome everything all over the world."

TIPS "Please e-mail a zip file via yousendit.com. No phone calls or mail, no CDs."

DELEV MUSIC COMPANY

7231 Mansfield Ave., Philadelphia PA 19138-1620 United States. (215)780-0183. **E-mail:** delevMusic@msn.com. **Contact:** William Lucas, president/CEO; Darryl Lucas, A&R. (ASCAP, BMI) Music publisher.

Publishes 6-10 songs/year; publishes 6-10 new song-writers/year. Pays standard royalty.

AFFILIATES Sign of the Ram Music (ASCAP) and Delev Music (BMI).

HOW TO CONTACT Does not accept unsolicited material. Write or call first to obtain permission to submit. Prefers CDs with 1-4 songs and lyric sheet. "We will not accept certified mail or SASE." Does not return material. Responds in 1-2 months.

MUSIC Mostly **R&B ballads** and **dance-oriented**; also **pop ballads**, **christian/gospel**, **crossover** and **country/western**. We do not accept rap song material. Published "Angel Love" (single by Barbara Heston/Geraldine Fernandez) from The Silky Sounds of Debbie G (album), recorded by Debbie G (light R&B/easy listening), released 2000 on Blizzard Records; Variety (album), produced by Barbara Heston, released on Luvya Records; and "Ever Again" by Bernie Williams, released 2003 on SunDazed Records. (Original version of "Ever Again" by Gene Woodbury has been re-released by several record companies, with last cover in Latter 2013).

TIPS "Persevere regardless if it is sent to our company or any other company. Most of all, no matter what happens, believe in yourself."

⊘⊗ DELLA MUSIC PUBLISHING

Della Music Publishing LLC, 509 Mandeville St, New Orleans LA 70117. **E-mail:** deborahevansMusic@gmail.com. **Website:** https://sites.google.com/site/dellaMusicpublishingllc/. **Contact:** Deborah Evans. Deborah Evans started Della Music Publishing in August 2007, and represents both domestic and foreign catalogues. Maintains and promotes the catalogues of many rap and hip hop artists such as Reggie Noble (pka Redman) and Erick Sermon, the Keep On Kicking Music classic reggae catalogue, Sweet River Music, and professional artists and songwriters such as Randy Klein and Anya Singleton. She represents several overseas publishers such as Cee Dee Music from the UK and Editions Ozella from Germany. She is a member of the Association of Independent Music Publishers (AIMP), the Copyright Society of the USA (CSUSA), and the National Music Publishers' Association (NMPA).

⊘ DISNEY MUSIC PUBLISHING

500 S. Buena Vista St., Burbank CA 91521 United States. (818)569-3241. **Fax:** (818)845-9705. **Website:** http://home.disney.go.com/Music. (ASCAP, BMI).

Affiliate(s) Seven Peaks Music and Seven Summits Music.

◖ Part of the Buena Vista Music Group.

HOW TO CONTACT "We cannot accept any unsolicited material."

⊘ DOWNTOWN MUSIC PUBLISHING

485 Broadway, 3rd Fl, New York NY 10013. Established in 2007, Downtown Music Publishing is a leading independent music publisher. Over the past six years, Downtown's catalog has grown to include more than 60,000 copyrights, including the works of John Lennon & Yoko Ono, hard rock legends Mötley Crüe, renowned film composer Hans Zimmer, influential punk rockers Social Distortion, pop songstress Ellie Goulding and the critically acclaimed artist and actor Mos Def. Downtown writers have penned hit singles for artists such as Beyonce, Bruno Mars, Carrie Underwood, Katy Perry, Keith Urban, and Rihanna. Managed by a team of executives with backgrounds in music supervision, advertising, and licensing, Downtown works to match its clients' interests with a broad range of media. In addition to traditional placement in film, TV, advertising, and video games, Downtown excels in digital and mobile licensing, product placement, merchandising, and integrated brand partnerships. Affiliates include Songtrust and MAS: Music and Strategy.

● DUANE MUSIC, INC.

382 Clarence Ave., Sunnyvale CA 94086 United States. (408)739-6133. Music publisher and record producer. Publishes 10-20 songs/year; publishes 1 new songwriter/year. Pays standard royalty.

AFFILIATES Morhits Publishing (BMI).

HOW TO CONTACT Submit demo by mail. Unsolicited submissions are OK. Prefers CD with 1-2 songs. Include SASE. Responds in 2 months.

MUSIC Mostly **blues**, **country**, **disco** and easy listening; also **rock**, **soul** and **top 40/pop**. Published "Little Girl" (single), recorded by The Syndicate of Sound & Ban (rock); "Warm Tender Love" (single), recorded by Percy Sledge (soul); and "My Adorable One" (single), recorded by Joe Simon (blues).

◑ EARTHSCREAM MUSIC PUBLISHING CO.

8375 Westview Dr., Houston TX 77055 United States. **Website:** www.soundartsrecording.com. (BMI) 8375 Westview Dr., Houston TX 77055. (713)464-GOLD. **E-mail:** jeffwells@soundartsrecording.com. **Website:**

www.soundartsrecording.com. **Contact:** Jeff Wells; Brian Baker, Nick Cooper. Music publisher, record company and record producer. Estab. 1975. Publishes 12 songs/year; publishes 4 new songwriters/year. Pays standard royalty.

○ Also see the listing for Sound Arts Recording Studio in the Record Producers section of this book.

AFFILIATES Reach For The Sky Music Publishing (ASCAP).

HOW TO CONTACT Submit demo by mail. Unsolicited submissions are OK. Prefers CD or videocassette with 2-5 songs and lyric sheet. Does not return material. Responds in 6 weeks.

MUSIC Mostly **new rock**, **country**, **blues**. Published "Baby Never Cries" (single by Carlos DeLeon), recorded by Jinkies on Surface Records (pop); "Telephone Road" (single), written and recorded by Mark May(blues) on Icehouse Records; "Do You Remember" (single by Barbara Pennington), recorded by Perfect Strangers on Earth Records (rock), and "Sheryl Crow" (single), recorded by Dr. Jeff and the Painkillers (pop); "Going Backwards" (single), written and recorded by Tony Vega (Gulf swamp blues), released on Red Onion Records.

◑ ELECTRIC MULE PUBLISHING COMPANY (BMI)/NEON MULE MUSIC (ASCAP)

1019 17th Ave. S, Nashville TN 37212 United States. (615)321-4455. **E-mail:** emuleme@aol.com.
MUSIC Country, pop.

◑ EMF PRODUCTIONS

1000 E. Prien Lake Road, Suite D, Lake Charles LA 70601 United States. (337)474-0435. **Website:** www.emfproductions.com. **Contact:** Ed Fruge, president. (ASCAP) Music publisher and record producer. Estab. 1984. Pays standard royalty.

HOW TO CONTACT Submit demo package by mail. Unsolicited submissions are OK. Prefers CD or DVDs with 3 of your best songs and lyric sheets. Does not return material. Responds in 6 weeks.

MUSIC Mostly **R&B**, **pop** and **rock**; also **country** and **gospel**.

⊘ EMI CHRISTIAN MUSIC PUBLISHING

P.O. Box 5084, Brentwood TN 37024 United States. (615)371-4300. **Website:** www.emicmg.com. (ASCAP, BMI, SESAC) Music publisher. Publishes more than 100 songs/year. Represents more than 35,000 songs

and more than 300 writers. Hires staff songwriters. Pays standard royalty.

AFFILIATES Birdwing Music (ASCAP), Sparrow Song (BMI), His Eye Music (SESAC), Ariose Music (ASCAP), Straightway Music (ASCAP), Shepherd's Fold Music (BMI), Songs of Promise (SESAC), Dawn Treader Music (SESAC), Meadowgreen Music Company (ASCAP), River Oaks Music Company (BMI), Stonebrook Music Company (SESAC), Bud John Songs, Inc. (ASCAP), Bud John Music, Inc. (BMI), Bud John Tunes, Inc. (SESAC), WorshipTogether Songs, ThankYou Music, Thirst Moon River.

HOW TO CONTACT "We do not accept unsolicited submissions."

MUSIC Published Chris Tomlin, Toby Mac, David Crowder, Jeremy Camp, Stephen Curtis Chapman, Delirious, Tim Hughes, Matt Redman, Demon Hunter, Underoath, Switchfoot, Third Day, Casting Crowns, and many others.

TIPS "Do what you do with passion and excellence and success will follow; just be open to new and potentially more satisfying definitions of what 'success' means."

⊘ EMI MUSIC PUBLISHING

75 Ninth Ave., 4th Floor, New York NY 10011 United States. (212)492-1200. **Fax:** (212)492-1865. **Website:** www.emiMusicpub.com. See website for global offices.

HOW TO CONTACT EMI does not accept unsolicited material. Only accepts songs submitted via an attorney, manager, and/or at the recommendation of an existing artist.

MUSIC Published "All Night Long" (by F. Evans/R. Lawrence/S. Combs), recorded by Faith Evans featuring Puff Daddy on Bad Boy; "You" (by C. Roland/J. Powell), recorded by Jesse Powell on Silas; and "I Was" (by C. Black/P. Vassar), recorded by Neal McCoy on Atlantic.

TIPS "Don't bury your songs. Less is more—we will ask for more if we need it. Put your strongest song first."

◑ EMSTONE MUSIC PUBLISHING

Box 398, Hallandale FL 33008 United States. **E-mail:** webmaster@emstoneMusicpublishing.com. **Website:** www.emstoneMusicpublishing.com. **Contact:** Mitchell Stone; Madeline Stone. (BMI)

HOW TO CONTACT Submit demo CD by mail with any number of songs. Unsolicited submissions are OK. Does not return material. Responds only if interested.

"Also check our sister company at SongwritersBest-Song.com."

MUSIC All types. Published Greetings from Texas (2009) (album), by Greetings From Texas; "Gonna Recall My Heart" (written by Dan Jury) from No Tears (album), recorded by Cole Seaver and Tammie Darlene, released on CountryStock Records; and "I Love What I've Got" (single by Heather and Paul Turner) from The Best of Talented Kids (compilation album) recorded by Gypsy; "My Christmas Card to You" (words and music by Madeline and Mitchell Stone); and "Your Turn to Shine" (words and music by Mitchell Stone).

TIPS "Keep the materials inside your demo package as simple as possible. Just include a brief cover letter (with your contact information) and lyric sheets. Avoid written explanations of the songs; if your music is great, it'll speak for itself. We only offer publishing contracts to writers whose songs exhibit a spark of genius. Anything less can't compete in the music industry."

FATT CHANTZ MUSIC

2535 Winthrope Way, Lawrenceville GA 30044 United States. (770)982-7055. **Website:** www.jeromepromotions.com. **Contact:** Bill Jerome, president. (BMI) Staff size: 3. Pays standard royalty of 50%.

HOW TO CONTACT Contact first and obtain permission to submit a demo. Include CD or mp3 and cover letter. Does not return submissions. Responds in 1 week.

MUSIC Top 40, alt country. Also alternative, crossover **R&B** and **hip-hop**. Does not want rap, gospel, country. Published "She's My Girl," written by Lefkowith/Rogers, recorded by Hifi on Red/Generic (2009).

●●❀ FIRST TIME MUSIC (PUBLISHING) U.K.

Ebrel House, 2a Penlee Close, Praa Sands, Penzance, Cornwall TR20 9SR England, United Kingdom. +44(01736)762826. **Fax:** +44(01736)763328. **E-mail:** panamus@aol.com. **Website:** www.panamaMusic.co.uk. Music publisher, record company (Digimix Records Ltd www.digimaxrecords.com, Rainy Day Records, Mohock Records, Pure Gold Records). Estab. 1986. Publishes 500-750 songs/year; 20-50 new songwriters/year. Staff size: 6. Hires staff writers. Pays standard royalty; "50-60% to established and up-and-coming writers with the right attitude."

AFFILIATES Scamp Music Publishing, Panama Music Library, Musik Image Library, Caribbean Music Library, PSI Music Library, ADN Creation Music Library, Promo Sonor International, Eventide Music, Melody First Music Library, Piano Bar Music Library, Corelia Music Library, Panama Music Ltd, Panama Music Productions, Digimix Worldwide DigitalPublishing.

HOW TO CONTACT Submit demo package by mail. Unsolicited submissions are OK. Submit on CD only, "of professional quality" with unlimited number of songs/instrumentals and lyric or lead sheets. Responds in 1 month. SAE and IRC required for reply.

FILM & TV Places 200 songs in film and TV/year. "Copyrights and phonographic rights of Panama Music Limited and its associated catalogue idents have been used and subsist in many productions broadcasts and adverts produced by major and independent production companies, television, film/video companies, radio broadcasters (not just in the UK, but in various countries world-wide) and by commercial record companies for general release and sale. In the UK & Republic of Ireland they include the BBC networks of national/regional television and radio, ITV network programs and promotions (Channel 4, Border TV, Granada TV, Tyne Tees TV, Scottish TV, Yorkshire TV, HTV, Central TV, Channel TV, LWT, Meridian TV, Grampian TV, GMTV, Ulster TV, Westcountry TV, Channel TV, Carlton TV, Anglia TV, TV3, RTE (Ireland), Planet TV, Rapido TV, VT4 TV, BBC Worldwide, etc.), independent radio stations, satellite Sky Television (BskyB), Discovery Channel, Learning Channel, National Geographic, Living Channel, Sony, Trouble TV, UK Style Channel, Hon Cyf, CSI, etc., and cable companies, GWR Creative, Premier, Spectrum FM, Local Radio Partnership, Fox, Manx, Swansea Sound, Mercury, 2CRFM, Broadland, BBC Radio Collection, etc. Some credits include copyrights in programs, films/videos, broadcasts, trailers and promotions such as Desmond's, One Foot in the Grave, EastEnders, Hale and Pace, Holidays from Hell, A Touch of Frost, 999 International, and Get Away."

MUSIC All styles. Published "I Get Stoned" (hardcore dance), recorded by AudioJunkie & Stylus, released by EMI records (2009) on Hardcore Nation 2009; "Long Way to Go" (country/MOR) on Under Blue Skies, recorded by Charlie Landsborough, released on Rosette Records (2008); "Mr Wilson" (folk) from Only the Willows are Weeping, released on

Digimix Records (2009); "Blitz" (progressive rock/goth rock), recorded by Bram Stoker on Rock Paranoia, released by Digimix Records and many more.

TIPS "Have a professional approach—present well produced demos. First impressions are important and may be the only chance you get. Writers are advised to join the Guild of International Songwriters and Composers in the United Kingdom (www.songwriters-guild.co.uk and www.myspace.com/guildofsongwriters)."

◑ FRICON MUSIC COMPANY

11 Music Square E, Nashville TN 37203 United States. (615)826-2288. **Fax:** (615)826-0500. **E-mail:** fricon@comcast.net. **Website:** http://friconent.com. **Contact:** Terri Fricon, president; Madge Benson, professional manager. Publishes 25 songs/year; publishes 1-2 new songwriters/year. Staff size: 6. Pays standard royalty.

AFFILIATES Fricout Music Company (ASCAP) and Now and Forever Songs (SESAC).

HOW TO CONTACT Contact first and obtain permission to submit. Prefers CD with 3-4 songs and lyric or lead sheet. "Prior permission must be obtained or packages will be returned." Include SASE. Responds in 2 months.

MUSIC Mostly **country**.

○ GLAD MUSIC CO.

14340 Torrey Chase, Suite 380, Houston TX 77014 United States. (281)397-7300. **Fax:** (281)397-6206. **E-mail:** hwesdaily@gladMusicco.com. **Website:** www.gladMusicco.com. **Contact:** Wes Daily; Don Daily. Music publisher, record company and record producer. Publishes 3 songs/year; publishes 2 new songwriters/year. Staff size: 2. Pays standard royalty.

AFFILIATES Bud-Don (ASCAP), Rayde (SESAC), and Glad Music (BMI).

HOW TO CONTACT Submit via CD or mp3 with 3 songs maximum, lyric sheet and cover letter. Lyric sheet should be folded around CD and submitted in a rigid case and secured with rubber band. Does not return material. Responds in 6 weeks. SASE or e-mail address for reply.

MUSIC Mostly **country**. Does not want weak songs. Published **Love Bug** (album by C. Wayne/W. Kemp), recorded by George Strait, released 1995 on MCA; Walk Through This World With Me (album), recorded by George Jones; and Race Is On (album by D. Rollins), recorded by George Jones, both released 1999 on Asylum.

◑ G MAJOR PUBLISHING

P.O. Box 3331, Fort Smith AR 72913 United States. **E-mail:** Alex@Gmajor.org. **Website:** https://sites.google.com/a/gmajor.org/www/. **Contact:** Alex Hoover.

HOW TO CONTACT No unsolicited submissions. Submit inquiry by mail with SASE. Prefers CD or mp3. Submit up to 3 songs with lyrics. Include SASE. Responds in 4-6 weeks.

MUSIC Mostly **country** and **contemporary Christian**. Published Set The Captives Free (album by Chad Little/Jeff Pitzer/Ben Storie), recorded by Sweeter Rain (contemporary Christian), for Cornerstone Television; "Hopes and Dreams" (single by Jerry Glidewell), recorded by Carrie Underwood (country), released on Star Rise; and "Be Still" (single by Chad Little/Dave Romero/Bryan Morse/Jerry Glidewell), recorded CO3 (contemporary Christian), released on Flagship Records.

TIPS "We are looking for 'smash hits' to pitch to the Country and Christian markets."

◐⊛ GOODNIGHT KISS MUSIC

10153 1/2 Riverside Dr. #239, Toluca Lake CA 91602 United States. (831)479-9993; (808)331-0707. **Website:** www.goodnightkiss.com; www.smalluses.com. (BMI, ASCAP) Publishes 6-8 songs/year; publishes 4-5 new songwriters/year. Pays standard royalty.

Goodnight Kiss Music specializes in placing Music in movies and TV.

AFFILIATES Scene Stealer Music (ASCAP).

HOW TO CONTACT "Check our website or subscribe to newsletter (www.goodnightkiss.com) to see what we are looking for and to obtain codes. Packages must have proper submission codes, or they are discarded." Only accepts material that is requested on the website. Does not return material. Responds in 6 months.

FILM & TV Places 3-5 songs in film/year. Published "I Do, I Do, Love You" (by Joe David Curtis), recorded by Ricky Kershaw in Road Ends; "Bee Charmer's Charmer" (by Marc Tilson) for the MTV movie Love Song; "Right When I Left" (by B. Turner/J. Fisher) in the movie Knight Club.

MUSIC All modern styles. Published and produced Addiction: Highs & Lows (CD), written and recorded by various artists (all styles), released 2004; Tall Tales of Osama Bin Laden (CD), written and recorded by various artists (all styles parody), released 2004; and Rythm of Honor (CD), written and recorded by various artists (all styles), slated release 2005, all on Goodnight Kiss Records.

TIPS "The absolute best way to keep apprised of the company's needs is to subscribe to the online newsletter. Only specifically requested material is accepted, as listed in the newsletter (what the industry calls us for is what we request from writers). We basically use an SGA contract, and there are never fees to be considered for specific projects or albums. However, we are a real music company, and the competition is just as fierce as with the majors."

L.J. GOOD PUBLISHING

33 Appleway Road, Okanogan WA 98840 United States. (509)422-1400. **E-mail:** ljgood@wingsforchrist.com. **Website:** www.wingsforchrist.com. **Contact:** Lonnie Good. (ASCAP) Publishes 5 songs/year. Publishes 1 new songwriters/year. Staff size: 1. Pays standard royalty of 50%.

AFFILIATES L.J. Good Publishing (ASCAP).

HOW TO CONTACT Prefers CD or mp3 with 3 songs and lyric sheet, cover letter. Does not e-mailed mp3s. Does not return submissions.

MUSIC Mostly **country**, **blues**, **soft rock**, **contemporary Christian/Praise and Worship**.

R L HAMMEL ASSOCIATES, INC.

P.O. Box 531, Alexandria IN 46001 United States. **Website:** www.rlhammel.com. "Consultants to the Music, Recording & Entertainment Industries," P.O. Box 531, Alexandria IN 46001. **E-mail:** rlh@rlhammel.com. **Website:** www.rlhammel.com. **Contact:** A&R Department. President: Randal L. Hammel. Music publisher, record producer and consultant. Estab. 1974. Staff size: 3-5. Pays standard royalty.

AFFILIATES LADNAR Music (ASCAP) and LEMMAH Music (BMI).

HOW TO CONTACT Submit demo package and brief bio by mail. Unsolicited submissions are OK. Prefers a maximum of 3 songs and typed lyric sheets. "Please notate three (3) best songs—no time to listen to a full project." Does not return material. Responds ASAP. "No fixed timeline."

MUSIC Mostly **pop**, **R&B** and **Christian**; also **MOR**, **light rock**, **pop country** and **feature film title cuts**. Produced/arranged The Wedding Collection Series for WORD Records. Published Lessons For Life (album by Kelly Hubbell/Jim Boedicker) and I Just Want Jesus (album by Mark Condon), both recorded by Kelly Connor, released on iMPACT Records. Pro-

duced major oratorio "Testament" written by David Featherstone.

HEUPFERD MUSIKVERLAG GMBH

Ringwaldstr. 18, Dreieich 63303 Germany. Ringwaldstr. 18, Dreieich 63303. Germany. **E-mail:** heupferd@t-online.de. **Website:** www.heupferd-musik.de. **Contact:** Christian Winkelmann, general manager. Music publisher and record company (Viva La Difference). GEMA. Publishes 30 songs/year. Staff size: 3. Pays "royalties after GEMA distribution plan."

AFFILIATES Song Buücherei (book series). "Vive La Difference!" (label).

HOW TO CONTACT Does not accept unsolicited submissions.

FILM & TV Places 1 song in film/year. Published "El Grito Y El Silencio" (by Thomas Hickstein), recorded by Tierra in Frauen sind was Wunderbares .

MUSIC Mostly **folk**, **jazz** and **fusion**; also **New Age**, **rock** and **ethnic Music**. Published "Mi Mundo" (single by Denise M'Baye/Matthias Furstenberg) from Havana—Vamos A Ver (album), recorded by Havana (Latin), released 2003 on Vive La Difference. Printed Andy Irvine: Aiming For the Heart—Irish Song Affairs, released in 2007.

HICKORY LANE PUBLISHING AND RECORDING

19854 Butternut Lane, Pitt Meadows BC V3Y 2S7 Canada. (604)465-1258. **E-mail:** kobzar@telus.net. **Website:** http://chrisurbanski.weebly.com. **Contact:** Chris Urbanski. (ASCAP, SOCAN) Music publisher, record company and record producer. Estab. 1988. Hires staff writers. Publishes 30 songs/year; publishes 5 new songwriters/year. Pays standard royalty.

HOW TO CONTACT Does not accept unsolicited submissions.

MUSIC Mostly **country** and **country rock**. Published "Just Living For Today" (single by Chris Urbanski), recorded by Chris Michaels (country), released 2005 on Hickory Lane Records; "This is My Sons" (single by Tyson Avery/Chris Urbanski/Alex Bradshaw), recorded by Chris Michaels (country), released 2005 on Hickory Lane Records; "Stubborn Love" (single by Owen Davies/Chris Urbanski/John Middleton), recorded by Chris Michaels (country), released 2005 on Hickory Lane Records.

TIPS "Send us a professional quality demo with the vocals upfront. We are looking for hits, and so are the major record labels we deal with. Be original in your approach, don't send us a cover tune."

○❀ HIP SONG MUSIC

Boston MA **E-mail:** info@hipsonMusic.com. **Website:** www.hipsonMusic.com. Hip Son Music is a music publishing, music production and record company based in Boston USA. Both Hip Son Music and Hip Son Publishing (BMI) work with talented music artists, producers, songwriters and performers involved in electronic, world, alternative and pop music. Our vocal and instrumental music catalog has been licensed for various movies, documentaries and TV shows on the networks including MTV, VH1, Fox TV, BBC, and ITV UK.

MUSIC Hip Son Music offers instrumental and vocal electronic and pop music for use in TV, film, TV commercials, Flash presentations, ring tones and other digital mediums. Our vocal and instrumental music catalog has been licensed for various movies and TV shows including: independent movies "Exploring Love," "Road To Victory," "Ghost In Cabin," MTV shows (The Real World, Road Rules, MADE, RR/RW Challenge, Pimp My Ride, Making the Band, Undressed), VH1 (Band Reunited, Born To Diva), Fox TV (Girl Next Door—Playboy special), BBC (The World), featured in the documentary "Picture Me Enemy" (the winner of Philadelphia's Film Festival), on Flash movies. DVD products and promo campaigns produced by BerkleeMusic.

○ HITSBURGH MUSIC CO.

P.O. Box 1431, 233 N. Electra, Gallatin TN 37066 United States. (615)452-0324. **Contact:** Harold Gilbert. Publishes 12 songs/year. Staff size: 4. Pays standard royalty.

AFFILIATES 7th Day Music (BMI).

HOW TO CONTACT Submit demo by mail. Unsolicited submissions are OK. Prefers CD with 2-4 songs and lead sheet. Prefers studio produced demos. Include SASE. Responds in 6 weeks.

MUSIC Mostly **country gospel** and **MOR**. Published "That Kind'a Love" (single by Kimolin Crutchet and Dan Serafini), from Here's Cissy (album), recorded by Cissy Crutcher (MOR), released 2005 on Vivaton; "Disorder at the Border" (single), written and recorded by Donald Layne, released 2001 on Southern City; and "Blue Tears" (single by Harold Gilbert/Elaine Harmon), recorded by Hal, released 2006 (reissue) on Southern City.

IAMA (INTERNATIONAL ACOUSTIC MUSIC AWARDS)

2881 E. Oakland Park Blvd., Suite 414, Ft. Lauderdale FL 33306 United States. **Website:** www.inacoustic.com. 2881 E. Oakland Park Blvd., Ft. Lauderdale FL 33306.(954)537-3127. **E-mail:** info@inacoustic.com. **Website:** www.inacoustic.com.

IDOL PUBLISHING

P.O. Box 140344, Dallas TX 75214 United States. (214)321-8890. **E-mail:** info@idolrecords.com. **Website:** www.IdolRecords.com. **Contact:** Erv Karwelis, president. Record publisher. Releases 30 singles, 80 LPs, 20 EPs and 10-15 CDs/year. Pays negotiable royalty to artists on contract; negotiable rate to publisher per song on recoRoad

HOW TO CONTACT See website for submission policy. No phone calls or e-mail follow-ups.

MUSIC Mostly **rock, pop**, and **alternative**. Released The Boys Names Sue-The Hits Vol. Sue! (album), The O's—We are the Os (album), Little Black Dress—Snow in June (album), The Manrecorded by Sponge (alternative); Movements (album), recorded by Black Tie Dynasty (alternative); In Between Days (album), recorded by Glen Reynolds (rock), all released 2006/2006 on Idol Records. Other artists include Flickerstick, DARYL, Centro-matic, The Deathray Davies, GBH, PPT, The Crash that Took Me, Shibboleth, Trey Johnson.

⊘ INGROOVES

55 Francisco St, #710, San Francisco CA 94113. (415)489-7000. **E-mail:** info@ingrooves.com. **Website:** www.ingrooves.com. INgrooves Music Group is comprised of INgrooves Distribution Services, INresidence Artist Services, and INgrooves Rights Services. All divisions of the company work together to provide clients with global distribution, customized marketing, promotion, sync licensing, music publishing, rights management and administrative support to help maximize the earnings potential of specific music and video releases in today's dynamic Music marketplace. Our end-to-end digital asset management platform automates many distribution and administration functions. Utilizing the Client Console, INgrooves clients have total visibility on the status of their releases—how, when and where they are distributed, the ability to opt in and out of retail deals and review and export monthly sales reports for retailers. Our platform is a content hub that connects directly

to all leading online and mobile stores worldwide, optimizing the consumer reach for our partners.

HOW TO CONTACT If you are interested in partnering with INgrooves, fill out the online form at www.ingrooves.com. A representative will get back to you ASAP.

INSIDE RECORDS/OK SONGS

St.-Jacobsmarkt 76 (B1), 2000, Antwerp Belgium. 32+(0)3-226-77-19. **Fax:** 32+(0)3-226-78-05. **E-mail:** info@inside-records.be. **Website:** www.inside-records.be. Music publisher and record company. Publishes 50 songs/year; publishes 30-40 new songwriters/year. Hires staff writers. Royalty varies "depending on teamwork."

HOW TO CONTACT Submit demo by mail. Unsolicited submissions are OK. Prefers CD with complete name, address, telephone and fax number. SAE and IRC. Responds in 2 months.

MUSIC Mostly **dance**, **pop** and **MOR contemporary**; also **country**, **reggae** and **Latin**. Published Fiesta De Bautiza (album by Andres Manzana); I'm Freaky (album by Maes-Predu'homme-Robinson); and Heaven (album by KC One-King Naomi), all on Inside Records.

INTOXYGENE SARL

27 rue Eugène carrière, Paris 75018 France. **E-mail:** infos@intoxygene.com. **Website:** www.intoxygene.com or www.theyounggods.com. **Contact:** Patrick Jammes. Music publisher and record company. Estab. 1990. Staff size: 1. Publishes 30 songs/year. Pays 50% royalty.

HOW TO CONTACT Does not accept unsolicited submissions.

FILM & TV Places 3/5 songs in film and in TV/year.

MUSIC Mostly **new industrial** and **metal**, **lounge**, **electronic**, and **ambient**. Publisher for Peepingtom (trip-hop), Djaimin (house), Missa Furiosa by Thierry Zaboitzeff (progressive), The Young Gods (alternative), Alex Carter, Love Motel, Steve Tallis, and lo'n, amongst others.

ISLAND CULTURE MUSIC PUBLISHERS

E-mail: islandking@islandkingrecords.com. **Website:** www.islandkingrecords.com. (BMI) Music publisher and record company (Island King Records). Estab. 1996. Publishes 10 songs/year; publishes 3 new songwriters/year. Hires staff songwriters. Staff size: 3. Pays standard royalty.

HOW TO CONTACT Submit demo package by mail. Unsolicited submissions are OK. Prefers CD with 8 songs and lyric sheet. Send bio and 8×10 glossy. Does not return material. Responds in 1 month.

MUSIC Mostly **reggae**, **calypso**, and **zouk**; also **house**. Published De Paris a Bohicon (album), recorded by Rasbawa (reggae), released 2006 on Island King Records; "Jah Give Me Life" (single by Chubby) from Best of Island King (album), recorded by Chubby (reggae), released 2003 on Island King Records; "When People Mix Up" (single by Lady Lex/L. Monsanto/Chubby) and "I Am Real" (single by L. Monsanto) from Best of Island King (album), recorded by Lady Lex (reggae), released 2003 on Island King Records.

IVORY PEN ENTERTAINMENT

P.O. Box 1097, Laurel MD 20725 United States. **E-mail:** ivorypen@comcast.net. (ASCAP) Professional Managers: Steven Lewis (R&B, pop/rock, inspirational); Sonya Lewis (AC, dance) Wandaliz Colon (Latin, Ethnic); Cornelius Roundtree (gospel/inspirational). music publisher. Publishes 10 songs/year. Staff size: 4. Pays standard royalty.

HOW TO CONTACT E-mail electronic press kit or mp3 no less than 128k. Unsolicited submissions are OK. Prefers CD with 3-5 songs and cover letter. Does not return material. Responds in 4 months. "Don't forget contact info with e-mail address for faster response! Always be professional when you submit your work to any company. Quality counts."

MUSIC Mostly **R&B**, **dance**, **pop/rock**, **Latin**, **adult contemporary**, and **inspirational**. Published Ryan Vetter (single), writer recorded by Alan Johnson (/pop/rock), released on Ivory Pen Entertainment; and "Mirror" (single), by Angel Demone, on Vox Angel Inc./Ivory Pen Entertainment.

TIPS "Learn your craft. Always deliver high quality demos. 'Remember, if you don't invest in yourself, don't expect others to invest in you. Ivory Pen Entertainment is a music publishing company that caters to the new songwriter, producer, and aspiring artist. We also place music tracks (no vocals) with artists for release."

JANA JAE MUSIC

P.O. Box 35726, Tulsa OK 74153 United States. (918)786-8896. **E-mail:** janajae@janajae.com. **Website:** www.janajae.com. **Contact:** Kathleen Pixley, secretary. music publisher, record company (Lark Record Productions, Inc.) and record producer (Lark Talent and Advertising). Publishes 5-10 songs/year; publishes 1-2 new songwriters/year. Staff size: 8. Pays standard royalty.

HOW TO CONTACT Submit demo by mail. Unsolicited submissions are OK. Prefers CD or DVD with 3-4 songs and typed lyric and lead sheet if possible. Does not return material. Responds only if accepted for use.

MUSIC Mostly **country, bluegrass, jazz** and **instrumentals** (**classical** or **country**). Published Mayonnaise (album by Steve Upfold), recorded by Jana Jae; and Let the Bible Be Your Roadmap (album by Irene Elliot), recorded by Jana Jae, both on Lark Records.

☺○ JA/NEIN MUSIK VERLAG GMBH

Oberstr. 14 A, D - 20144, Hamburg Germany. (GEMA) Oberstr. 14 A, D - 20144, Hamburg Germany. **Fax:** (49)(40)448 850. **E-mail:** janeinmv@aol.com. General Manager: Mary Dostal. Music publisher, record company and record producer. Member of GEMA. Publishes 50 songs/year; publishes 5 new songwriters/year. Staff size: 3. Pays 50-66% royalty.

AFFILIATES Pinorrekk Mv., Star-Club Mv. (GEMA).

HOW TO CONTACT Submit audio (visual) carrier by mail. Unsolicited submissions are OK. "We do not download unsolicited material, but visit known websites." Prefers CD or DVD. Enclose e-mail address. Responds in maximum 2 months.

MUSIC Mostly **jazz, world** (**klezmer**), **pop, rap** and **rock**.

TIPS "We do not return submitted material. Send your best A-Side works only, please. Indicate all rights owners, like possible co-composer/lyricist, publisher, sample owner. Write what you expect from collaboration. If artist, enclose photo. Enclose lyrics. Be extraordinary! Be fantastic!"

⊘ QUINCY JONES MUSIC

6671 Sunset Blvd., #1574A, Los Angeles CA 90028 United States. (323)957-6601. **Fax:** (323)962-5231. **E-mail:** info@quincyjonesMusic.com. **Website:** www.quincyjonesMusic.com. (ASCAP)

HOW TO CONTACT Quincy Jones Music does not accept unsolicited submissions.

MUSIC The Quincy Jones Music Publishing catalogue is home to over 1,600 titles spanning five decades of music covering numerous musical genres including Jazz, R&B, Pop, Rock-n-Roll, Brazilian, Alternative and Hip-Hop. Over the years, such legendary performers as Frank Sinatra, Count Basie, Sarah Vaughan, Louis Jordan, Lesley Gore, Barbra Streisand, Billy Eckstine and Tony Bennett have recorded our songs. We remain a presence in today's market by way of such artists as Michael Jackson, 98°, Tevin Campbell, K-Ci & Jo Jo, George Benson, Ivan Lins, S.W.V., Vanessa Williams, Patti Austin, The Manhattan Transfer, James Ingram, Barry White and Ray Charles. Our current roster of talent includes lyricists, composers, musicians, performers, and producers.

○ KAUPPS & ROBERT PUBLISHING CO.

P.O. Box 5474, Stockton CA 95205 United States. (209)948-8186. **E-mail:** kauppsrobertbmi@yahoo.com. (BMI) Melissa Glenn, A&R coordinator (all styles). Production Manager (country, pop, rock): Rick Webb. Professional Manager (country, pop, rock): Bruce Bolin. President: Nancy L. Merrihew. music publisher, record company (Kaupp Records), manager and booking agent (Merri-Webb Productions and Most Wanted Bookings). Estab. 1990. Publishes 15-20 songs/year; publishes 5 new songwriters/year. Pays standard royalty.

HOW TO CONTACT Write first and obtain permission to submit. Prefers CD with 3 songs maximum and lyric sheet. "If artist, send PR package." Include SASE. Responds in 6 months.

MUSIC Mostly **country, R&B** and **A/C rock**; also **pop, rock** and **gospel**. Published "Rushin' In" (singles by N. Merrihew/B. Bolin), recorded by Valerie; "Goin Postal" (singles by N. Merrihew/B. Bolin), recorded by Bruce Bolin (country/rock/pop); and "I Gotta Know" (single by N. Merrihew/B. Bolin), recorded by Cheryl (country/rock/pop), all released on Kaupp Records.

TIPS "Know what you want, set a goal, focus in on your goals, be open to constructive criticism, polish tunes and keep polishing."

◐ KINGSPIRIT MUSIC

(615)712-7870. **E-mail:** kingspiritMusic@gmail.com. **Website:** www.kingspiritMusic.com. **Contact:** Todd Wilkes, president. Nearly 30 years after achieving more than 400 cuts leading to more than 100 Million album sales to date, Owner and Founder Todd Wilkes, combined his vast knowledge of publishing and strong industry relationships in 2012 to create KingSpirit Music. KingSpirit Music is a dynamic independent Music publishing company, consulting company, artist development and Independent song pitching company that focuses on the representation of songwriters, artists and other publishing affiliations to secure the correct placement of their Music. King-

Spirit Music is known for delivering only the highest quality of songs to artists, labels, managers and producers. Upon the companies commencement, King-Spirit partnered with Nashville's Universal Music Publishing Group, and jointly signed Kalisa Ewing to an exclusive worldwide publishing deal.

TIPS "Be a sponge. Listen. I have learned more by listening than talking. The music business is fundamentally no different really from any other business…you have to show up and be ready to answer the door when opportunity knocks. Know your weaknesses and strengthen them."

LAKE TRANSFER PRODUCTIONS & MUSIC

11300 Hartland St., North Hollywood CA 91605 United States. (818)508-7158. **E-mail:** info@laketransfer.com. **Website:** www.laketransfer.com. **Contact:** Jim Holvay, professional manager (pop, R&B, soul); Tina Antoine (hip-hop, rap); Steve Barri Cohen (alternative rock, R&B). Music publisher and record producer (Steve Barri Cohen). Estab. 1989. Publishes 11 songs/year; publishes 3 new songwriters/year. Staff size: 6. Pay "depends on agreement, usually 50% split."

AFFILIATES Lake Transfer Music (ASCAP) and Transfer Lake Music (BMI).

HOW TO CONTACT Accepting unsolicited submissions through mid-2008.

MUSIC Mostly **alternative pop, R&B/hip-hop** and **dance**. Does not want country & western, classical, New Age, jazz or swing. Published "Tu Sabes Que Te Amo (Will You Still Be There)" (single by Steve Barri Cohen/Rico) from Rico: The Movement II (album), recorded by Rico (rap/hip-hop), released 2004 on Lost Empire/Epic-Sony; "When Water Flows" (single by Steve Barri Cohen/Sheree Brown/Terry Dennis) from Sheree Brown "83" (album), recorded by Sheree Brown (urban pop), released 2004 on BBEG Records (a division of Saravels, LLC); and "Fair Game" (single by LaTocha Scott/Steve Barri Cohen) Soundtrack from the movie Fair Game (album), recorded by LaTocha Scott (R&B/hip-hop), released 2004 on Raw Deal Records, College Park, Georgia. "All our staff are songwriters/producers. Jim Holvay has written hits like 'Kind of a Drag' and 'Hey Baby They're Playin our Song' for the Buckinghams. Steve Barri Cohen has worked with every one from Evelyn 'Champagne' King (RCA), Phantom Planets (Epic),

Meredith Brooks (Capitol) and Dre (Aftermath/Interscope)."

TIPS "Trends change, but it's still about the song. Make sure your music and lyrics have a strong (POV) point of view."

LAUREN KEISER MUSIC PUBLISHING

St. Louis MO (203)560-9436. **E-mail:** info@laurenkeiserMusic.com. **Website:** www.laurenkeiserMusic.com. **Contact:** Lauren Keiser. Veteran Music publisher, Lauren Keiser, started Lauren Keiser Music Publishing (ASCAP) and Keiser Classical (BMI) from the purchase of MMB Musicâ€™s assets of St. Louis and is joining it with new deals and editions he is creating and developing. His almost forty years of being involved with Alfred, Cherry Lane and Carl Fischer Music publishing companies has provided a basis and foundation for a new music publishing company based on his experience. The firm publishes performance and music copyrights of gifted concert and symphonic composers in addition to producing publications of talented writers and artists.

MUSIC Classical composers represented include Claude Baker, David Baker, Daniel Dorff, Peng-Peng Gong, Sheila Silver, David Schiff, David Stock, George Walker, and many more.

LEVY MUSIC PUBLISHING

22509 Carbon Mesa Road, Malibu CA 90265. (310)571-5389. **E-mail:** info@levyMusic.tv. Levy Music Publishing, LLC. is a companion entity to the Levy Entertainment Group. With more than 400 artists and composers our clients are given the option to easily license all types of music from our exclusive publishing catalog. Longstanding relationships with major and indie record labels & music publishers, ensuring the most excellent & affordable results.

LITA MUSIC

P.O. Box 40251, Nashville TN 37204 United States. (615)269-8682. **Fax:** (615)269-8929. **E-mail:** justinpeters@songsfortheplanet.com; songsfortheplanet@songsfortheplanet.com. **Website:** http://songsfortheplanet.com. **Contact:** Justin Peters. (ASCAP)

AFFILIATES Justin Peters Music, Platinum Planet Music and Tourmaline (BMI).

HOW TO CONTACT Submit demo package by mail. Unsolicited submissions are OK. Prefers CD with 5 songs and lyric sheet. Does not return material.

MUSIC Mostly **country, classic rock, Southern rock, inspirational AC Pop, Southern gospel/Christian** and **worship songs**. Published "The Bottom Line" recorded by Charley Pride on Music City Records (written by Art Craig, Drew Bourke, and Justin Peters); "No Less Than Faithful" (single by Don Pardoe/Joel Lyndsey), recorded by Ann Downing on Daywind Records, Jim Bullard on Genesis Records and Melody Beizer (#1 song) on Covenant Records; "No Other Like You" (single by Mark Comden/Paula Carpenter), recorded by Twila Paris and Tony Melendez (#5 song) on Starsong Records; "Making A New Start" and "Invincible Faith" (singles by Gayle Cox), recorded by Kingdom Heirs on Sonlite Records; "I Don't Want To Go Back" (single by Gayle Cox), recorded by Greater Vision on Benson Records; and "HE HAD MERCY ON ME" (by Constance and Justin Peters) recorded by Shining Grace.

○ M & T WALDOCH PUBLISHING, INC.

4803 S. Seventh St., Milwaukee WI 53221 United States. (BMI)4803 S. Seventh St., Milwaukee WI 53221. (414)482-2194. VP, Creative Management (rockabilly, pop, country): Timothy J. Waldoch. Professional Manager (country, top 40): Mark T. Waldoch. Music publisher. Estab. 1990. Publishes 2-3 songs/year; publishes 2-3 new songwriters/year. Staff size: 2. Pays standard royalty.

HOW TO CONTACT Submit demo package by mail. Unsolicited submissions are OK. Prefers CD with 3-6 songs and lyric or lead sheet. Include SASE. Responds in 3 months.

MUSIC Mostly **country/pop, rock, top 40 pop**; also **melodic metal, dance, R&B**. Does not want rap. Published "It's Only Me" and "Let Peace Rule the World" (by Kenny LePrix), recorded by Brigade on SBD Records (rock).

TIPS "Study the classic pop songs from the 1950s through the present time. There is a reason why good songs stand the test of time. Today's hits will be tomorrow's classics. Send your best well-crafted, polished song material."

○○ MAJOR BOB MUSIC

(615)329-4150. **Fax:** (615)329-1021. **Website:** www.majorbob.com. **Contact:** Tina Crawford, director of A&R.

○ MANY LIVES MUSIC PUBLISHERS (SOCAN)

RR #1, Kensington PE COB 1MO Canada. (902)836-4571. **E-mail:** Musicpublisher@amajorsound.com.

Website: www.amajorsound.com/manylivespublishers.html. **Contact:** Paul C. Milner, publisher. "Owners of Shell Lane Studio www.shelllanestudio.com complete in-house production facility. Many Lives Music Publishers was also involved in the production and recording of all projects listed below." Pays standard royalty.

HOW TO CONTACT Submit demo by mail, myspace, or SonicBids. Unsolicited submissions are OK. Prefers CD and lyric sheet (lead sheet if available). Does not return material. Responds in 3 months if interested.

MUSIC All styles. Six Pack EP and Colour(album), written and recorded by Chucky Danger (Pop/Rock), released 2005 on Landwash Entertainment. Chucky Danger's Colour album was named Winner Best Pop Recording at the East Coast Music Awards 2006, "Sweet Symphony" was nominated for Single of the Year, and Chucky Danger was nominated for Best New Group. Released Temptation (album by various writers), arrangement by Paul Milner, Patrizia, Dan Cutrona (rock/opera), released 2003 on United One Records; The Edge Of Emotion (album by various writers), arrangement by Paul Milner, Patrizia, Dan Cutrona (rock/opera), released 2006 on Nuff entertainment /United One Records. The Single "Temptation" won a SOCAN #1 awaRoad Saddle River Stringband (album) written and recorded by The Saddle River Stringband (Bluegrass) released on Panda Digital/Save As Music 2007. Winners of best Bluegrass recording East Coast Music Awards 2007. Pat Deighan and the Orb Weavers (album) "In A Fever In A Dream" (Alternative Rock) written by Pat Deighan, released on Sandbar Music April 2008.

MATERIAL WORTH PUBLISHING

46 First St., Walden NY 12586. (845)778-7768. **E-mail:** materialworthpub@aol.com. **Website:** www.materialworth.com. **Contact:** Frank Sardella, owner. (ASCAP) Music publisher. Staff size: 3. Pays standard royalty of 50%.

HOW TO CONTACT E-mail or visit website for how to obtain permission to submit. Must have permission before sending. Do not call first. Prefers mp3 or online player. CD, lyric sheet, and cover letter are also accepted; "no cassette tapes please." Does not return submissions. Responds in 6-8 weeks.

MUSIC Mostly **female pop** or **pop/country crossover, singer-songwriter, male pop alternative rock**.

MAUI ARTS & MUSIC ASSOCIATION/ SURVIVOR RECORDS/TEN OF DIAMONDS MUSIC

PMB 208, P.O. Box 79-1540, Paia, Maui HI 96779 United States. **Website:** www.dreammaui.org. Music publisher and record producer. Estab. 1974. Publishes 1-2 artists/year. Staff size: 2. Pays standard royalty.

HOW TO CONTACT Send e-mail with a little about yourself or your group (pictures or a video of you performing, your Music genre, a brief bio) and your best contact information. Subject line: Musician.

MUSIC Mostly **pop**, **country**, **R&B**, and **New Age**. Does not want rock. Published "In the Morning Light" (by Jack Warren), recorded by Jason (pop ballad); "Before the Rain" (by Giles Feldscher), recorded by Jason (pop ballad), both on Survivor; and "Then I Do" (single), written and recorded by Lono, released on Ono Music.

TIPS "Looking for a great single only!"

MCCLURE & TROWBRIDGE PUBLISHING, LTD (ASCAP, BMI)

P.O. Box 148548, Nashville TN 37214 United States. (615)902-0509. **E-mail:** manager@trowbridgeplanetearth.com. **Website:** http://trowbridgeplanetearth.com. Music publisher, and record label (JIP Records) and production company (George McClure, producer). Publishes 35 songs/year. Publishes 5 new songwriters/year. Staff size: 8. Pays standard royalty of 50%.

HOW TO CONTACT Follow directions ONLINE ONLY—obtain Control Number to submit a demo via US Mail. Requires CD with 1-5 songs, lyric sheet, and cover letter. Does not return submissions. Responds in 3 weeks if interested.

MUSIC Country, gospel, roots and swing. Publisher of Women in Country and Band of Writers (BOW) series. Published "Experience (Should Have Taught Me)"album 2010 on JIP Records; "The Lights Of Christmas" album; "PlayboySwing," released 2008 on JIP Records; "Miles Away" (single) on Discovery-Channel's "The Deadliest Catch"; and "PlayboySwing," released 2008 on JIP Records.

JIM MCCOY MUSIC

25 Troubadour Lane, Berkeley Springs WV 25411 United States. **Website:** www.troubadourlounge.com. (BMI)25 Troubadour Lane, Berkeley Springs WV 25411. (304)258-9381 or (304)258-8314. **E-mail:** mccoytroubadour@aol.com. **Website:** www.troubadour-lounge.com. **Contact:** Bertha and Jim McCoy, owners. Music publisher, record company (Winchester Records) and record producer (Jim McCoy Productions). Estab. 1973. Publishes 20 songs/year; publishes 3-5 new songwriters/year. Pays standard royalty.

AFFILIATES New Edition Music (BMI).

HOW TO CONTACT Submit demo by mail with lyric sheet. Unsolicited submissions are OK. Prefers CD with 6 songs. Include SASE. Responds in 1 month.

MUSIC Mostly **country**, **country/rock** and **rock**; also **bluegrass** and **gospel**. Published Jim McCoy and Friends Remember Ernest Tubb; "She's the Best" recorded by Matt Hahn on Troubadour Records (written by Jim McCoy); "Shadows on My Mind" recorded by Sandy Utley (written by Jim McCoy), "Rock and Roll Hillbilly Redneck Girl" recorded by Elaine Arthur (written by Jim McCoy), released in 2007.

MCJAMES MUSIC INC.

1724 Stanford St., Suite B, Santa Monica CA 90404 United States. (310)712-1916. **Fax:** (419)781-6644. **E-mail:** tim@mcjamesMusic.com; steven@mcjamesMusic.com. **Website:** www.mcjamesMusic.com. **Contact:** Tim Jame; Steven McClintock. (ASCAP) Writers include: Pamela Phillips Oland, Stephen Petree, Jeremy Dawson, Chad Petree, Brian Stoner, Tom Templeman, Cathy-Anne McClintock, Tim James, Steven McClintock, Ryan Lawhon. Publishes 50 songs/year. Staff size: 4. Pays standard royalty. Does administration and collection for all foreign markets for publishers and writers.

AFFILIATES 37 Songs (ASCAP) and McJames Music, Inc. (BMI).

HOW TO CONTACT Only accepts material referred by a reputable industry source. Prefers CD with 2 songs and cover letter. Does not return material. Responds in 6 months.

FILM & TV Places 2 songs in film and 3 songs in TV/year. Music Supervisor: Tim James/Steven McClintock. Blood and Chocolate, 3 Day Weekend, Dirty Sexy Money, Brothe3rs and Sisters, Dancing with the Stars, Dexter, Always Sunny in Philadelphia, America's Top Model. Commercials include Honda Australia, Scion California, Motorola Razr 2 worldwide.

MUSIC Mostly **modern rock, country, pop, jazz** and **euro dance**; also **bluegrass** and **alternative**. Will accept some mainstream rap but no classical. Published "Le Disko"; "You are the One"; "Rainy Monday" (singles from Shiny Toy Guns on Universal), "Be Sure";

"What It Is" (singles from Cris Barber), "Keeps Bringing Me Back" (from Victoria Shaw on Taffita), "Christmas Needs Love to be Christmas" (single by Andy Williams on Delta), recent cover by ATC on BMG/Universal with "If Love is Blind"; single by new Warner Bros. act Sixwire called "Look at me Now."

TIPS "Write a song we don't have in our catalog or write an undeniable hit. We will know it when we hear it."

⊘✿ MIDI TRACK PUBLISHING (BMI)

P.O. Box 1545, Smithtown NY 11787 United States. (718)767-8995. **E-mail:** info@allrsMusic.com. **Website:** www.allrsMusic.com. **Contact:** Renee Silvestri-Bushey, president; F. John Silvestri, founder; Leslie Migliorelli, director of operations. Music publisher, record company (MIDI Track Records), Music consultant, artist management, record producer. Voting member of NARAS/National Academy of Recording Arts and Sciences (The Grammy Awards), voting member of the Country Music Association (CMA Awards); SGMA/Southern Gospel Music Association, SGA/Songwriters Guild of America (Diamond Member). Estab. 1994. Staff size: 6. Publishes 3 songs/year; publishes 2 new songwriters/year. Pays standard royalty. Affiliate(s) ALLRS Music Publishing Co. (ASCAP).

HOW TO CONTACT "Write or e-mail first to obtain permission to submit. We do not accept unsolicited submissions." Prefers CD with 3 songs, lyric sheet and cover letter. Does not return material. Responds in 6 months only if interested.

FILM & TV Places 1 song in film/year. Published "Why Can't You Hear My Prayer" (single by F. John Silvestri/Leslie Silvestri), recorded by Iliana Medina in a documentary by Silvermine Films.

MUSIC Mostly **country, gospel, top 40, R&B, MOR** and **pop**. Does not want showtunes, jazz, classical or rap. Published "Why Can't You Hear My Prayer" (single by F. John Silvestri/Leslie Silvestri), recorded by eight-time Grammy nominee Huey Dunbar of the group DLG (Dark Latin Groove), released on MIDI Track Records (including other multiple releases); "Chasing Rainbows" (single by F. John Silvestri/Leslie Silvestri/Darin Kelly), recorded by Tommy Cash (country), released on MMT Records (including other multiple releases); "Because of You" (single by F. John Silvestri/Leslie Silvestri), recorded by Iliana Medina, released 2002 on MIDI Track Records (including oth-

er multiple releases also recorded by Grammy nominee Terri Williams, of Always, Patsy Cline, Grand Ole Opry member Ernie Ashworth), released on KMA Records and including other multiple releases; "My Coney Island" (single by F. John Silvestri/Leslie Silvestri), recorded by eight-time Grammy nominee Huey Dunbar, released 2005-2009 on MIDI Track Records.

TIPS "Attend workshops, seminars, and visit our blog on our website for advise, tips, and info on the Music industry."

◑● MONTINA MUSIC

P.O. Box 32, Montreal QC H3X 3T3 Canada. (SOCAN) Music publisher and record company (Monticana Records). Estab. 1963. Pays negotiable royalty.

AFFILIATES Saber-T Music (SOCAN).

HOW TO CONTACT Unsolicited submissions are OK. Prefers CD. SAE and IRC. Responds in 3 months.

MUSIC Mostly **top 40**; also **bluegrass, blues, country, dance-oriented, easy listening, folk, gospel, jazz, MOR, progressive, R&B, rock** and **soul**. Does not want heavy metal, hard rock, jazz, classical or New Age.

TIPS "Maintain awareness of styles and trends of your peers who have succeeded professionally. Understand the markets to which you are pitching your material. Persevere at marketing your talents. Develop a network of industry contacts, first locally, then regionally, nationally, and internationally."

◯ MOONJUNE

The ongoing goal of MoonJune is to support music that transcends stylistic pigeon-holing, but operates within an evolutionary progressive musical continuum that places jazz at one end and rock at the other. The ever-expanding boundaries of these two musical categories have since come to include everything from progressive rock to ethno-jazz, from experimental avante-garde to jazz-rock, and anything in between.

⊘ THE MUSIC ROOM PUBLISHING GROUP

525 S. Francisca Ave., Redondo Beach CA 90277 United States. (310)316-4551. **E-mail:** mrp@aol.com. **Website:** http://Musicroomonline.com; www.Musicroom.us. **Contact:** John Reed. (ASCAP)/MRP Music (BMI) Music publisher and record producer. Estab. 1982. Pays standard royalty.

AFFILIATES MRP Music (BMI).

HOW TO CONTACT Not accepting unsolicited material.

MUSIC Mostly **pop/rock/R&B** and **crossover**. Published "That Little Tattoo," "Mona Lisa" and "Sleepin' with an Angel" (singles by John E. Reed) from Rock With An Attitude (album), recorded by Rawk Dawg (rock), released 2002; "Over the Rainbow" and "Are You Still My Lover" (singles) from We Only Came to Rock (album), recorded by Rawk Dawg, released 2004 on Music Room Productions [PIRg].

◑○ NERVOUS PUBLISHING

5 Sussex Crescent, Northolt, Middlesex UB5 4DL United Kingdom. +44(020) 8423 7373. **Fax:** +44(020) 8423 7773. **E-mail:** info@nervous.co.uk. **Website:** www.nervous.co.uk. **Contact:** Roy Williams, owner. Music publisher, record company (Nervous Records) and record producer. MCPS, PRS and Phonographic Performance Ltd. Publishes 100 songs/year; publishes 25 new songwriters/year. Pays standard royalty; royalties paid directly to US songwriters.

◔   Nervous Publishing's record label, Nervous Records, is listed in the Record Companies section.

HOW TO CONTACT Submit demo by mail. Unsolicited submissions are OK. Prefers CD with 3-10 songs and lyric sheet. "Include letter giving your age and mentioning any previously published material." SAE and IRC. Responds in 3 weeks.

MUSIC Mostly **psychobilly, rockabilly** and **rock** (impossibly fast music—e.g.: Stray Cats but twice as fast); also **blues, country**, **R&B** and **rock** ('50s style). Published Trouble (album), recorded by Dido Bonneville (rockabilly); Rockabilly Comp (album), recorded by various artists; and Nervous Singles Collection (album), recorded by various artists, all on Nervous Records.

TIPS "Submit no rap, soul, funk—we want rockabilly."

◐ NEWBRAUGH BROTHERS MUSIC

228 Morgan Lane, Berkeley Springs WV 25411 United States. (304)261-0228. **E-mail:** Nbtoys@verizon.net. **Contact:** John S. Newbraugh. (ASCAP, BMI) Music publisher, record company (NBT Records, BMI/ASCAP). Publishes 124 songs/year. Publishes 14 new songwriters/year. Staff size: 1. Pays standard royalty.

AFFILIATES NBT Music (ASCAP) and Newbraugh Brothers Music (BMI).

HOW TO CONTACT Submit demo by mail. Unsolicited submissions are OK. Prefers CD with any amount of songs, a lyric sheet and a cover letter. Include SASE. Responds in 6 weeks. "Please don't call for permission to submit. Your materials are welcomed."

MUSIC Mostly **rockabilly, hillbilly, folk** and **bluegrass**; also **rock**, **country**, and **gospel**. "We will accept all genres of music except songs with vulgar language." Published Released "Ride the Train Series Vol. 25; Layin' It On the Line by Night Drive (2009); "Love Notes" The Sisters Two; "The Country Cowboy" by Jack Long; "Original Praise Songs" by Russ and Donna Miller.

TIPS "Find out if a publisher/record company has any special interest. NBT, for instance, is always hunting 'original' train songs. Our 'registered' trademark is a train and from time to time we release a compilation album of all train songs. We welcome all genres of music for this project."

○ NEWCREATURE MUSIC

P.O. Box 1444, Hendersonville TN 37077 United States. (615)585-9301. **E-mail:** ba@landmarkcommunicationsgroup.com. **Website:** www.landmarkcommunicationsgroup.com. **Contact:** Bill Anderson, Jr., president; G.L. Score, professional manager. Music publisher, record company, record producer (Landmark Communications Group) and radio and TV syndicator. Publishes 25 songs/year; publishes 2 new songwriters/year. Pays standard royalty.

AFFILIATES Mary Megan Music (ASCAP).

HOW TO CONTACT Contact first and obtain permission to submit. Prefers CD or videocassette with 4-10 songs and lyric sheet. Include SASE. Responds in 6 weeks.

MUSIC Mostly **country, gospel, jazz, R&B, rock** and **top 40/pop**. Published Let This Be the Day by C.J. Hall; When a Good Love Comes Along by Gail Score; The Wonder of Christmas by Jack Mosley.

◐ NEXT DECADE ENTERTAINMENT

65 West 55th Street, Suite 4F, New York NY 10019. (212)583-1887 x10. **Fax:** (212)813-9788. **E-mail:** info@nextdecade-ent.com. **Website:** www.nextdecade-ent.com. **Contact:** Stu Cantor, president. Next Decade is more than just a music publisher. We're experts with years of experience and knowledge about music and licensing. Our approach is hands-on and service oriented. We work with clients closely to make sure their copyrights are not only protected and properly exploited, but that opportunities for

growth and development are identified and that we are involved with the newest companies and people for licensing opportunities.

MUSIC Represents such artists as Boston, Harry Belafonte, Millie Jackson, Ray Griff, Eric Lindell, Vic Mizzy, and more.

⊘⊛ OLD SLOWPOKE MUSIC

P.O. Box 52626, Utica Square Station, Tulsa OK 74152 United States. (918)742-8087. **Fax:** (888)878-0817. **E-mail:** ryoung@oldslowpokeMusic.com. **Website:** www.oldslowpokeMusic.com. **Contact:** Rodney Young, president. (BMI) Music publisher and record producer. Estab. 1977. Publishes 10- 20 songs/year; publishes 2 new songwriters/year. Staff size: 2. Pays standard royalty.

HOW TO CONTACT CDs only, no cassettes.

FILM & TV 1 song in film/year. Recently published "Samantha," written and recorded by George W. Carroll in Samantha. Placed two songs for Tim Drummond in movies "Hound Dog Man" in Loving Lu Lu and "Fur Slippers" in a CBS movie Shake, Rattle & Roll.

MUSIC Mostly **rock**, **country** and **R&B**; also **jazz**. Published Promise Land (album), written and recorded by Richard Neville on Cherry Street Records (rock).

TIPS "Write great songs. We sign only artists who play an instrument, sing, and write songs."

⊘⊛ OLE

E-mail: majorlyindie@olemm.com. **Website:** www.majorlyindie.com. Ole is the world's fastest growing rights management company. Founded in 2004, and with offices in Toronto, Nashville, New York and Los Angeles, Ole boasts a team of 45 experienced industry professionals focused on acquisitions, creative development and worldwide copyright administration. Ole has recently entered the Production Music space with the acquisition of MusicBox and Auracle which have operations in NY, Toronto and LA. Ole is committed to the creative development of its 60+ staff songwriters, legacy writers and composers and the cultivation of our catalogs and client catalogs. Ole has ongoing co-ventures with Last Gang Publishing (Alt Rock), Roots Three Music (Country) and tanjola (Pop/Rock/Urban).

HOW TO CONTACT Does not accept unsolicited submissions.

MUSIC Notable copyrights with Ole include those by Taylor Swift, Rascal Flatts, Justin Timberlake, Jay-Z, Eric, Church, Kelly Clarkson, Pink, Aerosmith, Tim McGraw, and many more.

○ PATRICK JOSEPH MUSIC

1200 Villa Pl., Ste. 204, Nashville TN **E-mail:** pat@pjmsongs.com. **Website:** www.songspub.com/PJM. **Contact:** Pat Higdon. In August of 2013, music publishing veteran, Pat Higdon re-launched his Patrick Joseph Music brand in the Nashville marketplace. The renewal of this successful publishing company marks a new partnership with New York and Los Angeles-based SONGS Music Publishing. Patrick Joseph Music will be dedicated to writer service, actively signing new writers as well as developing the reach for existing catalogs and songs.

⊘ PEERMUSIC

2397 Shattuck Ave., Suite 202, Berkeley CA 94704 United States. (510)848-7337. **Fax:** (510)848-7355. **E-mail:** sfcorp@peerMusic.com. **Website:** www.peerMusic.com. Music publisher and artist development promotional label. Estab. 1928. Hires staff songwriters. "All deals negotiable." Affiliate(s) Songs of Peer Ltd. (ASCAP) and PeerMusic III Ltd. (BMI).

HOW TO CONTACT "We do NOT accept unsolicited submissions. We only accept material through agents, attorneys and managers." Prefers CD and lyric sheet. Does not return material.

MUSIC Mostly **pop**, **rock** and **R&B**. Published Music by David Foster (writer/producer, pop); Andrew Williams (writer/producer, pop); Christopher "Tricky" Stewart (R&B, writer/producer).

⊘ PERLA MUSIC

134 Parker Ave., Easton PA 18042 United States. (212)957-9509. **Fax:** (917)338-7596. **E-mail:** PM@PMRecords.org. **Website:** www.pmrecords.org. **Contact:** Gene Perla. (ASCAP) Music publisher, record company (PMRecords.org), record producer (Perla.org), studio production (TheSystemMSP.com) and Internet Design (CCINYC.com). Estab. 1971. Publishes 5 songs/year. Staff size: 5.

HOW TO CONTACT E-mail first and obtain permission to submit.

MUSIC Mostly **jazz** and **rock**.

○ JUSTIN PETERS MUSIC

P.O. Box 40251, Nashville TN 37227 United States. (615)269-8682. **Fax:** (615)269-8929. **E-mail:** justin-

peters@songsfortheplanet.com; songsfortheplanet@
songsfortheplanet.com. **Website:** http://songsforth-
eplanet.com. **Contact:** Justin Peters. (BMI) Music
publisher. Estab. 1981.

AFFILIATES Platinum Planet Music (BMI), Tourmaline (BMI) and LITA Music (ASCAP).

HOW TO CONTACT Submit demo package by mail.
Unsolicited submissions are OK. Prefers CD with 5
songs and lyric sheet. Does not return material.

MUSIC Mostly **pop**, **reggae**, **country** and **comedy**.
Published "Saved By Love" (single), recorded by Amy
Grant on A&M Records; "From the Center of my
Heart," by Shey Baby on JAM Records; "A Gift That
She Don't Want" (single), recorded by Bill Engvall on
Warner Brother Records; "The Bottom Line," record-
ed by Charley Pride on Music City Records, cowrit-
ten by Justin Peters; "Heaven's Got to Help Me Shake
These Blues" (single), written by Vickie Shaub and
Justin Peters, recorded by B.J. Thomas; "Virginia
Dreams" and "Closer to You" (Jimmy Fortune/Jus-
tin Peters), recorded by Jimmy Fortune.

○ PLATINUM PLANET MUSIC, INC.

P.O. Box 40251, Nashville TN 37204 United States.
(615)269-8682. **Fax:** (615)269-8929. **E-mail:** justin-
peters@songsfortheplanet.com. **Website:** http://
songsfortheplanet.com. **Contact:** Justin Peters.
(BMI) Music publisher. Estab. 1997.

AFFILIATES Justin Peters Music (BMI), Tourmaline
(BMI) and LITA Music (ASCAP). SONGWRITERS
Lee Anna Culp, Rich Fehle, Bill McCorvey, Tommy
Stillwell, Dez Dickerson.

HOW TO CONTACT Submit demo package by mail.
Unsolicited submissions are OK. Prefers CD with 5
songs and lyricsheet. Does not return material.

MUSIC Mostly film/TV Americana/Alternative,
R&B, reggae, sports themes, educational themes,
dance and country; also represents many Chris-
tian artists/writers. Published "Happy Face" (single
by Dez Dickerson/Jordan Dickerson), recorded by
Squirt on Absolute Records; "Carry Me Away" & "I
DO' (Lee Anna Culp), recorded by Lee Anna Culp
on Platinum Planet Records; "Love's Not A Game"
(single), written by Art Craig and J. Peters and re-
corded by Kashief Lindo on Heavybeat Records;
"Merry Christmas, Merry Christmas" (single) "What
Makes You Good Enough" (single) written by Lee
Anna Culp & Justin Peters recorded by Lee Anna
Culp on Platinum Planet Records. and "Loud" (sin-

gle), written and recorded by These Five Down on
Absolute Records.

○✪ QUARK, INC.

P.O. Box 452, Newtown CT 06470 United States.
(917)687-9988. **E-mail:** quarkent@aol.com. Music
publisher, record company (Quark Records) and record producer (Curtis Urbina). Estab. 1984. Publishes
12 songs/year; 2 new songwriters/year. Staff size: 4.
Pays standard royalty.

AFFILIATES Quarkette Music (BMI), Freedurb Music (ASCAP), and Quark Records.

HOW TO CONTACT Prefers CD only with 2 songs.
No cassettes. Include SASE. Responds in 2 months.

FILM & TV Places 10 songs in film/year. Music Supervisor: Curtis Urbina.

MUSIC Pop. Does not want anything short of a hit.

✪✪ RAINBOW MUSIC CORP.

45 E. 66 St., New York NY 10021 United States.
(212)988-4619. **E-mail:** fscam45@aol.com. **Contact:**
Fred Stuart. Music publisher. Publishes 25 songs/year.
Staff size: 2. Pays standard royalty.

AFFILIATES Tri-Circle (ASCAP).

HOW TO CONTACT Only accepts material referred
by a reputable industry source. Prefers CD with 2
songs and lyric sheet. Include SASE. Responds in 1
week.

FILM & TV Published "You Wouldn't Lie To An Angel, Would Ya?" (single by Diane Lampert/Paul Overstreet) from Lady of the Evening (album), recorded by
Ben te Boe (country), released 2003 on Mega International Records; "Gonna Give Lovin' A Try" (single
by Cannonball Adderley/Diane Lampert/Nat Adderley) from The Axelrod Chronicles (album), recorded
by Randy Crawford (jazz), released 2003 on Fantasy
Records; "Breaking Bread" (single by Diane Lam-
pert/Paul Overstreet) from Unearthed (album), recorded by Johnny Cash (country), released 2003 on
Lost Highway Records; "Gonna Give Lovin' A Try"
(single by Cannonball Adderley/Diane Lampert/Nat
Adderley) from Day Dreamin' (album), recorded by
Laverne Butler (jazz), released 2002 on Chesky Records; "Nothin' Shakin' (But the Leaves on the Trees)"
(single by Diane Lampert;John Gluck, Jr./Eddie Fon-
taine/Cirino Colcrai) recorded by the Beatles, from
Live at the BBC (album).

MUSIC Mostly **pop**, **R&B** and **country**; also **jazz**.
Published "Break It To Me Gently" (single by Diane
Lampert/Joe Seneca) from TIME/LIFE compilations

Queens of Country (2004), Classic Country (2003), and Glory Days of Rock 'N Roll (2002), recorded by Brenda Lee.

☺○✦ RANCO MUSIC PUBLISHING

(formerly Lilly Music Publishing), 61 Euphrasia Dr., Toronto ON M6B 3V8 Canada. **E-mail:** panfilo@sympatico.ca; obbieMusic@sympatico.ca. **Website:** www.myspace.com/rancorecords; www.obbieMusic.com. **Contact:** Panfilo Di Matteo, president. Music publisher and record company (P. & N. Records). Publishes 20 songs/year; publishes 8 new songwriters/year. Staff size: 3. Pays standard royalty.

AFFILIATES San Martino Music Publishing and Paglieta Music Publishing (CMRRA).

HOW TO CONTACT Submit demo by mail. Unsolicited submissions are OK. Prefers CD (or videocassette if available) with 3 songs and lyric and lead sheets. "We will contact you only if we are interested in the material." Responds in 1 month.

FILM & TV Places 12 songs in film/year.

MUSIC Mostly **dance**, **ballads**, and **rock**; also **country**. Published "I'd Give It All" (single by Glenna J. Sparkes), recorded by Suzanne Michelle (country crossover), released on Lilly Records.

RAZOR & TIE ENTERTAINMENT

214 Sullivan St., Suite 4A, New York NY 10012 United States. (212)598-2259. **Fax:** (212)473-9173. **E-mail:** bprimont@razorandtie.com. **Website:** www.razorandtieMusicpublishing.com.

HOW TO CONTACT Does not accept unsolicited material.

MUSIC Songwriters and groups represented include Dar Williams, Bad Books, David Ford, Finch, Brand New, Emerson Lake & Palmer, BeBe Winans, Joe Jackson, Joan Baez, Nonpoint, Yellowcard, Foreigner, HIM, Saves the Day, Suzanne Vega, and many more.

○ RED SUNDOWN RECORDS

1920 Errel Dowlen Rd, Pleasant View TN 37146 United States. (615)746-0844. **E-mail:** rsdr@bellsouth.net. (BMI)

HOW TO CONTACT Does not accept unsolicited submissions. Submit CD and cover letter. Does not return submissions.

MUSIC Country, **rock**, and **pop**. Does not want rap or hip-hop. Published "Take A Heart" (single by Kyle Pierce) from Take Me With You (album), recorded by

Tammy Lee (country) released in 1998 on Red Sundown Records.

○✦ ROCHAMBEAU MUSIC

228 Dexter Ave N, Seattle WA 98119. **E-mail:** info@rochambeauMusic.com. **Contact:** Glenn Lorbecki, CEO. Rochambeau Music represents songwriters, composers, and artists in the areas of music publishing, licensing, placement and production. In conjunction with our full-service recording studio, Glenn Sound/Seattle, we offer services from artist development to full-scale album production and strive to work with the best new and established talent in taking their creativity to the next level. Capitalizing on our industry-wide contacts, we are opening new opportunities for master placement in film/TV/game soundtracks, forging new relationships for song placement with global artists, and seeking to introduce the music of our partners to the international marketplace.

MUSIC Represents such artists as Emi Meyer (jazz), Tim Huling (composer), Mycle Wastman (R&B), Jeffrey Alan (pop/rock), and more.

⊘ RONDOR MUSIC INTERNATIONAL/ ALMO/IRVING MUSIC, A UNIVERSAL MUSIC GROUP COMPANY

Part of Universal Music Publishing Group, 2440 Sepulveda Blvd., Suite 119, Los Angeles CA 90064 United States. (310)235-4800. **Fax:** (310)235-4801. **E-mail:** rondorla@uMusic.com. **Website:** www.universalMusicpublishing.com. (ASCAP,BMI)

AFFILIATES Almo Music Corp. (ASCAP) and Irving Music, Inc. (BMI).

HOW TO CONTACT Does not accept unsolicited submissions.

⊘ ROUND HILL MUSIC

400 Madison Avenue, 18th Floor, New York NY 10017. (212)380-0080. **E-mail:** info@roundhillMusic.com. **Website:** www.roundhillMusic.com. Round Hill Music is a full-service, creative music company with a core focus on music publishing. We take a thoughtful, long-term approach to building both a stellar song catalogue and a roster of talented active writers that our team is proud to work so closely with on a daily basis. Our ultimate goal is to deliver value from every single song in our catalogue, while simultaneously providing all of our writers with the individualized attention they need to succeed. The Round Hill team achieves this goal through everything from synch li-

censing and song placements, to setting up co-writes and performing international song registration, all while maintaining one of the most transparent and accurate royalty accounting systems in the music publishing marketplace. We're on a mission to bring back the kind of personalized creative attention that was so inherent to the initial heyday of music publishing, and our boutique size gives us the agility we need to realize that mission. From the iconic hits of yesterday, to the future chart toppers of tomorrow, our love for our music is at the center of everything we do.

○ RUSTIC RECORDS, INC. PUBLISHING

6337 Murray Lane, Brentwood TN 37027 United States. (615)371-0646. **E-mail:** rusticrecordsam@aol.com. **Website:** www.rusticrecordsinc.com. (ASCAP,BMI,SESAC) **Contact:** Jack Schneider, president. Vice President: Claude Southall. Office Manager: Nell Tolson. Music publisher, record company (Rustic Records Inc.) and record producer. Estab. 1984. Publishes 20 songs/year. Pays standard royalty. **AFFILIATES** Covered Bridge Music (BMI), Town Square Music (SESAC), Iron Skillet Music (ASCAP). How to Contact Submit demo by mail. Unsolicited submissions are OK. Prefers CD with 3-4 songs and lyric sheet. Include SASE. Responds in 3 months. **MUSIC** Mostly **country**. Published "In Their Eyes" (single by Jamie Champa); "Take Me As I Am" (single by Bambi Barrett/Paul Huffman); and "Yesterday's Memories" (single by Jack Schneider), recorded by Colte Bradley (country), released 2003. **TIPS** "Send three or four traditional country songs, novelty songs 'foot-tapping, hand-clapping' gospel songs with strong hook for male or female artist of duet. Enclose SASE (manilla envelope)."

○ SABTECA MUSIC CO. (ASCAP)

P.O. Box 10286, Oakland CA 94610 United States. **E-mail:** sabtecarecords@aol.com. **Website:** http://sabtecaMusiccompany.com. **Contact:** Duane Herring, owner; Romare Herring, representative. Music publisher and record company (Sabteca Record Co., Andre Romare). Estab. 1980. Publishes 8-10 songs/year; 1-2 new songwriters/year. Pays standard royalty. **AFFILIATES** Toyiabe Publishing (BMI). **HOW TO CONTACT** Write first and obtain permission to submit. Prefers CD with 2 songs and lyric sheet. Include SASE. Responds in 1 month. **MUSIC** Mostly **R&B, pop** and **country**. Published "Walking My Baby Home" (single by Reggie Walker)

from Reggie Walker (album), recorded by Reggie Walker (pop), 2002 on Andre Romare Records/Sabteca; "Treat Me Like a Dog" (single by Duane Herring/Thomas Roller), recorded by John Butterworth (pop), released 2004 Sabteca Music Co; "Sleeping Beauty", recorded by C Haynace, released 2008, Sabteca Music Co. **TIPS** "Listen to music daily, if possible. Keep improving writing skills."

○ SALT WORKS MUSIC

80 Highland Dr., Jackson OH 45640-2074 United States. 80 Highland Dr., Jackson OH 45640-2074. (740)286-1514 or (740)286-6561. Professional Managers: Jeff Elliott (country/gospel); Mike Morgan (country). Music publisher and record producer (Mike Morgan). Staff size: 2. Pays standard royalty. **AFFILIATES** Salt Creek Music (ASCAP) and Sojourner Music (BMI). **HOW TO CONTACT** Submit demo package by mail. Unsolicited submissions are OK. Prefers CD. Include SASE. Responds in 2 weeks. **MUSIC** Mostly **country, gospel** and **pop**. Does not want rock, jazz, or classical. Published "The Tracks You Left On Me" (single by Ed Bruce/Jeff Elliott/MikeMorgan) and "Truth Is I'm A Liar" (single by Jeff Elliott/Mike Morgan) from This Old Hat (album), recorded by Ed Bruce (country), released 2002 on Sony/Music Row Talent.

○ SANDALPHON MUSIC PUBLISHING

P.O. Box 18197, Panama City Beach FL 32417. **E-mail:** sandalphonMusic@yahoo.com. **Contact:** Ruth Otey. Music publisher, record company (Sandalphon Records), and management agency (Sandalphon Management). Staff size: 2. Pays standard royalty of 50%. **HOW TO CONTACT** Submit demo by mail. Unsolicited submissions are fine. Prefers CD with 1-5 songs, lyric sheet, and cover letter. Include SASE or SAE and IRC for outside United States. Responds in 6-8 weeks. **MUSIC** Mostly **rock, country**, and **alternative**; also **pop, blues**, and **gospel**.

○⊛ SAVANNAH MUSIC GROUP

(615)504-7732. **E-mail:** info@savannahMusicgroup.com. **Website:** www.savannahMusicgroup.com. **Contact:** Daisy Dern, creative director. Savannah Music Group is a grass roots music publishing company located in the heart of Nashville's Music Row.

MUSIC The current songwriting roster includes Kevin "Swine" Grantt, Jack Williams, and Dave Gibson. The company has had releases by Montgomery Gentry, The Blind Boys of Alabama, Brad Paisley, The Randy Rogers Band, Tommy Steele, The Mulch Brothers, Kristina Cornell, and The Dirt Drifters, and has songs in the motion picture releases "Country Strong," "Sucker," and TV series "Good Christian Belles." Savannah Music Group is positioned to be competitive at the highest level in the publishing community with its current roster of writers and executive team.

◖⊛ SB21 MUSIC PUBLISHING

1610 16th Ave. South (2nd Floor), Nasjville TN 37212. **E-mail:** info@sb21Music.com. **Website:** www.sb-21Music.com. SB21 Music is an independent music publishing company started by Steve Pasch in 2010. Writers with SB21 have had country cuts with major artists Tim McGraw, Wynonna, John Michael Montgomery, and Clay Walker, including 2006 Billboard Country's "Most Played Song of the Year" Rodney Adkins' "Watching You."

◖ SHAWNEE PRESS, INC.

1221 17th Ave. S, Nashville TN 37212 United States. **E-mail:** info@shawneepress.com. **Website:** www.ShawneePress.com. 1221 17th Ave. S, Nashville TN 37212. (615)320-5300. **Fax:** (615)320-7306. **E-mail:** info@shawneepress.com. **Website:** www.ShawneePress.com. **Contact:** Director of Church Music Publications (sacred choral music): Joseph M. Martin. Director of School Music Publications (secular choral music): Greg Gilpin. Music publisher. Estab. 1939. Publishes 150 songs/year. Staff size: 12. Pays negotiable royalty. **AFFILIATES** GlorySound, Harold Flammer Music, Mark Foster Music, Wide World Music, Concert Works.
HOW TO CONTACT Submit manuscript. Unsolicited submissions are OK. See website for guidelines. Prefers manuscript; recording required for instrumental submissions. Include SASE. Responds in 4 months. "No unsolicited musicals or cantatas."
MUSIC Mostly **church/liturgical**, **educational choral** and **instrumental**.
TIPS "Submission guidelines appear on our website."

◖ SILICON MUSIC PUBLISHING CO.

222 Tulane St., Garland TX 75043 United States. **E-mail:** support@siliconMusic.us. **Website:** http://siliconMusic.us. Public Relations: Steve Summers. Music publisher and record company (Front Row Records). Estab. 1965. Publishes 10-20 songs/year; publishes 2-3 new songwriters/year. Pays standard royalty.

◖ Also see the listing for Front Row Records in the Record Companies section of this book.

HOW TO CONTACT Submit demo package by mail. Unsolicited submissions are OK. Prefers CD with 1-2 songs. Does not return material. Responds ASAP.
MUSIC Mostly **rockabilly** and **'50s material**; also **old-time blues/country** and MOR. Published "Rockaboogie Shake" (single by James McClung) from Rebels and More (album), recorded by Lennerockers (rockabilly), released 2002 on Lenne (Germany); "Be-Bop City" (single by Dan Edwards), "So" (single by Dea Summers/Gene Summers), and "Little Lu Ann" (single by James McClung) from Do Right Daddy (album), recorded by Gene Summers (rockabilly/'50s rock and roll), released 2004 on Enviken (Sweden).
TIPS "We are very interested in '50s rock and rockabilly original masters for release through overseas affiliates. If you are the owner of any '50s masters, contact us first! We have releases in Holland, Switzerland, United Kingdom, Belgium, France, Sweden, Norway and Australia. We have the market if you have the tapes! Our staff writers include James McClung, Gary Mears (original Casuals), Robert Clark, Dea Summers, Shawn Summers, Joe Hardin Brown, Bill Becker and Dan Edwards."

⊘⊛ SILVER BLUE MUSIC/OCEANS BLUE MUSIC

3940 Laurel Canyon Blvd., Suite 441, Studio City CA 91604. (818)980-9588. **E-mail:** jdiamond20@aol.com. **Website:** http://www.joeldiamond.com. **Contact:** Joel Diamond. (ASCAP, BMI) Music publisher and record producer (Joel Diamond Entertainment). Estab. 1971. Publishes 50 songs/year. Pays standard royalty.
HOW TO CONTACT Does not accept unsolicited material. "No CDs returned."
FILM & TV Places 4 songs in film and 6 songs in TV/year.
MUSIC Mostly **pop** and **R&B**; also **rap** and **classical**. Produced and managed The 5 Browns-3 #1 CDs on Sony. Published "After the Lovin" (by Bernstein/Adams), recorded by Engelbert Humperdinck; "This Moment in Time" (by Alan Bernstein/Ritchie Adams), recorded by Engelbert Humperdinck. Other artists include David Hasselhoff, Kaci (Curb Records), Ike

Turner, Andrew Dice Clay, Gloria Gaynor, Tony Orlando, Katie Cassidy, and Vaneza.

🌑🌑 SINUS MUSIK PRODUKTION, ULLI WEIGEL

Geitnerweg 30a, D-12209, Berlin Germany. **Website:** www.ulli-weigel.de. Geitnerweg 30a, D-12209, Berlin Germany. +49-30-7159050. **Fax:** +49-30-71590522. **E-mail:** ulli.weigel@arcor.de. **Website:** www.ulli-weigel.de. **Contact:** Ulli Weigel, owner. Music publisher, record producer and screenwriter. Wrote German lyrics for more than 500 records. Member: GEMA, GVL. Estab. 1976. Publishes 20 songs/year; publishes 6 new songwriters/year. Staff size: 3. Pays standard royalty.
AFFILIATES Sinus Musikverlag H.U. Weigel GmbH.
HOW TO CONTACT Submit demo package by mail. Prefers CD with up to 10 songs and lyric sheets. If you want to send mp3 attachments, you should contact me before. Attachments from unknown senders will not be opened. Responds in 2 months by e-mail. "If material should be returned, please send 2 International Reply Coupons (IRC) fs and 3 for a CD. No stamps."
MUSIC Mostly **rock**, **pop** and **New Age**; also **background Music for movies and audio books**. Published "Simple Story" (single), recorded by MAANAM on RCA (Polish rock); Die Musik Maschine (album by Klaus Lage), recorded by CWN Productions on Hansa Records (pop/German), "Villa Woodstock" (film music/comedy) Gebrueder Blattschuss, Juergen Von Der Lippe, Hans Werner Olm (2005).
TIPS "Take more time working on the melody than on the instrumentation. I am also looking for master-quality recordings for non-exclusive release on my label (and to use them as soundtracks for multimedia projects, TV and movie scripts I am working on)."

⊙⊘⊛ S.M.C.L. PRODUCTIONS, INC.

P.O. Box 84, Boucherville QC J4B 5E6 Canada. P.O. Box 84, Boucherville QC J4B 5E6 Canada. (450)641-2266. **Contact:** Christian Lefort, president. Music publisher and record company. SOCAN. Estab. 1968. Publishes 25 songs/year. Pays standard royalty.
AFFILIATES A.Q.E.M. Ltee, Bag Music, C.F. Music, Big Bazaar Music, Sunrise Music, Stage One Music, L.M.S. Music, ITT Music, Machine Music, Dynamite Music, Cimafilm, Coincidence Music, Music and Music, CineMusic Inc., Cinafilm, Editions La Fete Inc., Groupe Concept Musique, Editions Dorimen, C.C.H. Music (PRO/SDE) and Lavagot Music.

HOW TO CONTACT Write first and obtain permission to submit. Prefers CD with 4-12 songs and lead sheet. SAE and IRC. Responds in 3 months.
FILM & TV Places songs in film and TV. Recently published songs in French-Canadian TV series and films, including Young Ivanhoe, Twist of Terror, More Tales of the City, Art of War, Lance & Comte (Nouvelle Generation), Turtle Island (TV series), Being Dorothy, The Hidden Fortress, Lance et Compte:La Revanche (TV series), and A Vos Marques, Party (film).
MUSIC Mostly **dance**, **easy listening** and MOR; also **top 40/pop** and **TV and movie soundtracks**. Published Always and Forever (album by Maurice Jarre/Nathalie Carien), recorded by N. Carsen on BMG Records (ballad); Au Nom De La Passion (album), written and recorded by Alex Stanke on Select Records.

⊘ SONY/ATV MUSIC PUBLISHING

8 Music Square W, Nashville TN 37203 United States. **Website:** www.sonyatv.com. (ASCAP, BMI, SESAC)8 Music Square W, Nashville TN 37203. (615)726-8300. **Fax:** (615)726-8329. **E-mail:** info@sonyatv.com. **Website:** www.sonyatv.com. **Santa Monica:** 10635 Santa Monica Blvd., Suite 300, Los Angeles CA 90025. (310)441-1300. **New York:** 550 Madison Ave., 5th Floor, New York NY 10022. (212)833-7730.
HOW TO CONTACT Sony/ATV Music does not accept unsolicited submissions.

⊘⊛ STILL WORKING MUSIC GROUP

1625 Broadway, Suite 200, Nashville TN 37203 United States. (615)242-0567. **Website:** http://stillworkingMusicgroup.com. (ASCAP, BMI, SESAC) Music publisher and record company (Orby Records, Inc.). Estab. 1994.
AFFILIATES Still Working for the Woman Music (ASCAP), Still Working for the Man Music (BMI) and Still Working for All Music (SESAC).
HOW TO CONTACT Does not accept unsolicited submissions.
FILM & TV Published "First Noel," recorded by The Kelions in Felicity.
MUSIC Mostly **rock**, **country** and **pop**; also **dance** and **R&B**. Published "If You See Him/If You See Her" (by Tommy Lee James), recorded by Reba McIntire/Brooks & Dunn; "Round About Way" (by Wil Nance), recorded by George Strait on MCA; and "Wrong Again" (by Tommy Lee James), recorded by Martina McBride on RCA (country).

TIPS "If you want to be a country songwriter you need to be in Nashville where the business is. Write what is in your heart."

⬤ SUPREME ENTERPRISES INT'L CORP.

P.O. Box 1373, Agoura Hills CA 91376 United States. (818)707-3481. **E-mail:** seicorp@earthlink.net. **Website:** www.seicorp.ne. (ASCAP, BMI) Music publisher, record company and record producer. Publishes 20-30 songs/year; publishes 2-6 new songwriters/year. Pays standard royalty.

AFFILIATES Fuerte Suerte Music (BMI), Big Daddy G. Music (ASCAP).

HOW TO CONTACT No phone calls. Submit demo by mail. Unsolicited submissions are OK. Prefers CD. Does not return material and you must include an e-mail address for a response. **Mail Demos To:** P.O. Box 1373, Agoura Hills CA 91376. "Please copyright material before submitting and include e-mail." Responds in 12-16 weeks if interested.

MUSIC Mostly **reggae**, **rap**, and **dance**. Published "Paso La Vida Pensando," recorded by Jose Feliciano on Universal Records; "Cucu Bam Bam" (single by David Choy), recorded by Kathy on Polydor Records (reggae/pop); "Volvere Alguna Vez" recorded by Matt Monro on EMI Records and "Meneaito" (single), recorded by Gaby on SEI Records.

TIPS "A good melody is a hit in any language."

⬤ T.C. PRODUCTIONS/ETUDE PUBLISHING CO.

121 Meadowbrook Dr., Hillsborough NJ 08844 United States. (908)359-5110. **Fax:** (908)359-1962. **E-mail:** tony@tcproductions2005.com. **Website:** www.tony-camillo.com. (BMI) Music publisher and record producer. Estab. 1992. Publishes 25-50 songs/year; publishes 3-6 new songwriters/year. Pays negotiable royalty.

AFFILIATES We Iz It Music Publishing (ASCAP), Etude Publishing (BMI), and We B Records (BMI).

HOW TO CONTACT Write or call first and obtain permission to submit. Prefers CD with 3-4 songs and lyric sheet. Include SASE. Responds in 1 month.

MUSIC Mostly **R&B** and **dance**; also **country** and **outstanding pop ballads**. Published "I Just Want To Be Your Everything" (single) from A Breath of Fresh Air (album), recorded by Michelle Parto (spiritual), released 2006 on Chancellor Records; and New Jersey Jazz (album).

TIPS "Michelle Parto will soon be appearing in the film Musical Sing Out, directed by Nick Castle and written by Kent BerhaRoad"

⊘ TEN TEN MUSIC GROUP

33 Music Square West, Suite 110, Nashville TN **E-mail:** info@tentenMusic.com. **Website:** www.tenten-Musicgroup.com. **Contact:** Dave Pacula, creative director. Since 1984, Ten Ten Music Group, Inc. has established itself as one of the most successful independent music publishing companies in Nashville. Appearing on Billboard's list of Top Song Publishers from 2004 to 2006, Ten Ten Music continues to expand its footprint across multiple genres. With cuts by major rock groups like Papa Roach, Shinedown, Halestorm, and Cavo as well as other superstars, including One Direction, Bonnie Raitt and Selena Gomez, the diverse talent of Ten Ten Music's writing staff has ventured far beyond Nashville.

MUSIC The writing staff at Ten Ten has also enjoyed recent success with cuts by country artists such as Tim McGraw, Miranda Lambert, Pistol Annie's, Reba McEntire, David Nail and many others. Continuing a tradition of developing and nurturing the careers of such superstars as Alan Jackson and Keith Urban, Ten Ten has also been working to shape the careers of up-and-coming artists Clare Dunn and Femke Weidema.

⬤✤ THISTLE HILL (BMI)

P.O. Box 120931, Arlington TN 76012 United States. (615)889-7105. **E-mail:** billyherzig@hotmail.com.

HOW TO CONTACT Submit demo by mail. Unsolicited submissions OK. Prefers CD with 3-10 songs. No lyric sheets. Responds only if interested.

MUSIC Country, **pop**, and **rock**; also **songs for film/TV**. We pitch a select group of songs in Nashville and Texas. Published "Angry Heart " (single) from See What You Wanna See (album), recorded by Radney Foster (Americana); and I Wanna be Free (album), recorded by Jordon MyCoskie (Country); "Restless .Soul" (single) recorded by Tori Martin (Red Dirt Country); others

⬤ TINDERBOX MUSIC

3148 Bryant Ave. S, Minneapolis MN 55408. (612)375-1113. **E-mail:** brady@tinderboxMusic.com; patrick@tinderboxMusic.com. **Website:** www.tinderboxMusic.com. Tinderbox is a music promotions and distribution company. We work with unsigned, indie label, and major label artists across the country by obtaining press and radio airplay in appropriate markets and formats. We specialize in college radio and the artists that fit the CMJ (College Music Journal) and secondary FM and community formats. We also provide local and national distribution for artists as well as publishing and music licensing opportunities.

HOW TO CONTACT There are two ways to submit; physically or digitally. As we live in a digital age, it is probably easier for you to submit your music to us via Bandcamp, Facebook, Reverbnation, Soundcloud, or Sonicbids. Got links? We'll take them! Just e-mail them to us. If you are a Hip Hop or Electronic artist, please submit your music to jordan@tinderboxMusic.com. (We don't like Myspace links though, sorry Myspace). DO NOT ATTACH YOUR SONGS TO YOUR SUBMISSION E-MAIL. Links only please. Please include a little bit about yourself as well. If you have a one sheet that is less than 7MB in size, you may attach that. If you like to do things old school, you can also send us physical submissions. Your CD must be radio ready. By this we mean that it should have been professionally recorded, mixed, and mastered. Watch out for profanity. When sending a physical submission, please send us two or three copies of your CD (depending on which departments you're interested in). More than one person will probably want to review your CD. We do promise that we will get back to everyone who submits material via phone, e-mail, or snail mail regarding your submission and you can typically expect to hear from us within 48 hours. More details available at the website.

MUSIC We specialize in indie, pop/alternative, modern rock, triple-A, rock, and acoustic-based rock, hip hop and electronic music. All though we love Jazz, we don't regularly promote jazz, sorry. Featured artists include Imagine Dragons, Gentleman Hall, Twenty One Pilots, Stars Go Dim, others.

◉ TOURMALINE MUSIC, INC.

2831 Dogwood Place, Nashville TN 37204 United States. (615)269-8682. **Fax:** (615)269-8929. **E-mail:** justinpeters@songsfortheplanet.com. **Website:** http://songsfortheplanet.com. **Contact:** Justin Peters. (BMI) Music publisher. Estab. 1980.

AFFILIATES Justin Peters Music (BMI), LITA Music (ASCAP) and Platinum Planet Music (BMI). SONGWRITERS Ben Peters, George Searcy, Mike Hunter, Art Craig, J. Craig Dunnagan, and many others.

HOW TO CONTACT Submit demo package by mail. Unsolicited submissions are OK. Prefers CD with 5 songs and lyric sheet. Does not return material.

MUSIC Mostly rock and roll, classy alternative, adult contemporary, classic rock, country, Spanish gospel, and some Christmas music. Published "Making War In The Heavenlies," written by George Searcy, recorded by Ron Kenoly (Integrity); "The Hurt is Worth The Chance," by Justin Peters/Billy Simon, recorded by Gary Chapman on RCA/BMG Records, and "The Bottom Line," by Art Craig, Drew Bourke, and Justin Peters, recorded by Charley Pride (Music City Records).

◐❀ TOWER MUSIC GROUP

PO Box 2435, Hendersonville TN 37077 United States. (615)401-7111. **Fax:** (615)401-7111. **E-mail:** castlerecords@castleRecords.com. **Website:** www.castlerecords.com. **Contact:** Dave Sullivan. (ASCAP, BMI) Professional Managers: Ed Russell; Eddie Bishop. Music publisher, record company (Castle Records) and record producer. Estab. 1969. Publishes 50 songs/year; publishes 10 new songwriters/year. Staff size: 15. Pays standard royalty.

AFFILIATES Cat's Alley Music (ASCAP) and Alley Roads Music (BMI).

HOW TO CONTACT See submission policy on website. Prefers CD with 3 songs and lyric sheet. Does not return material. "You may follow up via e-mail." Responds in 3 months only if interested.

FILM & TV Places 2 songs in film and 26 songs in TV/year. Published "Run Little Girl" (by J.R. Jones/Eddie Ray), recorded by J.R. Jones in Roadside Prey.

MUSIC Mostly **country** and **R&B**; also **blues**, **pop** and **gospel**. Published "If You Broke My Heart" (single by Condrone) from If You Broke My Heart (album), recorded by Kimberly Simon (country); "I Wonder Who's Holding My Angel Tonight" (single) from Up Above (album), recorded by Carl Butler (country); and "Psychedelic Fantasy" (single by Paul Sullivan/Priege) from The Hip Hoods (album), recorded by The Hip Hoods (power/metal/y2k), all released 2001 on Castle Records. "Visit our website for an up-to-date listing of published songs."

TIPS "Please follow our Submission Policy at our website www.CastleRecords.com."

◯ TRANSITION MUSIC CORPORATION

P.O. Box 2586, Toluca Lake CA 91610 United States. (323)860-7074. **E-mail:** submissions@transitionMusic.com. **Website:** www.transitionMusic.com. Publishes 250 songs/year; publishes 50 new songwriters/ year. Variable royalty based on song placement and writer.

AFFILIATES Pushy Publishing (ASCAP), Creative Entertainment Music (BMI) and One Stop Shop Music (SESAC).

HOW TO CONTACT Submit one song (make it your best) online only to submissions@transitionMusic. com. We accept all genres and unsolicited music. Responses will not be given due to the high volume of submissions daily. Please do not call/e-mail to inquire about us receiving your submission. TMC will only contact who they intend on signing.

FILM & TV "TMC provides music for all forms of visual media. Mainly Television."Music—all styles.

MUSIC TMC is a music library and publishing company generating more than 95,000 performances in film, TV, commercials, games, internet, and webisodes over the past year. In the last few months, TMC launched it's newest division, Ultimate Exposure, exposing new independent artists to the world of visual media.

TIPS "Supply master quality material with great songs."

⊘ TRIO PRODUCTIONS, INC/SONGSCAPE MUSIC, LLC

1026 15th Ave. S., Nashville TN 37212 United States. **E-mail:** info@trioproductions.com; robyn@trioproductions.com. **Website:** www.trioproductions.com. **Contact:** Robyn Taylor-Drake.

AFFILIATES ASCAP, BMI, SESAC, Harry Fox Agency, CMA, WMBA, IPA

HOW TO CONTACT Contact first by e-mail to obtain permission to submit demo. Unsolicited material will not be listened to or returned. Submit CD with 3-4 songs and lyric sheet. Submit via mp3 once permission to send has been received. Include a lyric sheet.

MUSIC Country, **pop**, and **Americana**.

⊘ UNIVERSAL MUSIC PUBLISHING

2100 Colorado Ave., Santa Monica CA 90404 United States. (310)235-4700. **Fax:** (310)235-4900. **Website:** www.uMusicpub.com. (ASCAP, BMI,SESAC)

HOW TO CONTACT Does not accept unsolicited submissions.

◐ UNKNOWN SOURCE MUSIC (ASCAP)

120-4d Carver Loop, Bronx NY 10475 United States. **E-mail:** unknownsourceMusic@hotmail.com. **Website:** www.unknownsourceMusic.com. Music publisher, record company (Smokin Ya Productions) and record producer. Estab. 1993. Publishes 5-10 songs/year; publishes 5-10 new songwriters/year. Pays standard royalty.

AFFILIATES SONGWRITERS Unks (ASCAP), Critique Records, WMI Records.

HOW TO CONTACT Send e-mail first then mail. Unsolicited submissions are OK. Prefers mp3s. Responds within 6 weeks.

MUSIC Mostly **rap/hip-hop**, **R&B**, and **alternative**. Published "LAH" recorded by Daforce; "Nothing Better" recorded by Curtis Dayne.

TIPS "Keep working with us, be patient, be willing to work haRoad Send your very best work."

◐ VAAM MUSIC GROUP

P.O. Box 29550, Hollywood CA 90029 United States. **E-mail:** request@vaamMusic.com. **Website:** www. vaamMusic.com. **Contact:** Pete Martin, president. (BMI) Music publisher and record producer (Pete Martin/Vaam Productions). Estab. 1967. Publishes 9-24 new songs/year. Pays standard royalty.

AFFILIATES Pete Martin Music (ASCAP). <tab>

HOW TO CONTACT Send CD with 2 songs and lyric sheet. Include SASE. Responds in 1 month. "Small packages only."

MUSIC Mostly **top 40/pop**, **country**. "Submitted material must have potential of reaching top 5 on charts."

TIPS "Study the top 10 charts in the style you write. Stay current and up-to-date with today's market."

◐ VINE CREEK MUSIC

P.O. Box 171143, Nashville TN 37217 United States. **E-mail:** vinecreek1@aol.com. **Website:** www. myspace.com/vinecreekMusic; www.darleneaustin. com. **Contact:** Louise Cook. (ASCAP) Administration: Jayne Negri. Creative Director: Brenda Madden.

HOW TO CONTACT Vine Creek Music does not accept unsolicited submissions. "Only send material of good competitive quality. We do not return CDs unless SASE is enclosed."

○ WALKERBOUT MUSIC GROUP

P.O. Box 24454, Nashville TN 37202 United States. (615)269-7074. **Fax:** (888)894-4934. **E-mail:** matt@

walkerboutMusic.com. **Website:** www.walker-boutMusic.com. **Contact:** Matt Watkins, director of operations. (ASCAP, BMI, SESAC) Publishes 50 songs/year; 5-10 new songwriters/year. Pays standard royalty.

AFFILIATES Goodland Publishing Company (ASCAP), Marc Isle Music (BMI), Gulf Bay Publishing (SESAC), Con Brio Music (BMI), Wiljex Publishing (ASCAP), Concorde Publishing (SESAC).

HOW TO CONTACT "Please see website for submission information."

MUSIC Mostly **country/Christian** and **adult contemporary**.

⊕⊘ WARNER/CHAPPELL MUSIC, INC.

10585 Santa Monica Blvd., Los Angeles CA 90025 United States. (310)441-8600. **Fax:** (310)470-8780. **Website:** www.warnerchappell.com.

HOW TO CONTACT Warner/Chappell does not accept unsolicited material.

⊕ WEAVER OF WORDS MUSIC

2239 Bank St., Baltimore MD 21231 United States. (276)970-1583. **E-mail:** weaverofwordsMusic@gmail.com. **Website:** www.weaverofwordsMusic.com. **Contact:** H.R. Cook, president. (BMI) Music publisher and record company (Fireball Records). Publishes 12 songs/year. Pays standard royalty.

AFFILIATES Weaver of Melodies Music (ASCAP).

HOW TO CONTACT Submit demo by mail. Unsolicited submissions are OK. Prefers CD with 3 songs and lyric or lead sheets. "We prefer CD submissions but will accept mp3s—limit 2." Include SASE. Responds in 3 weeks.

MUSIC Mostly **country**, **pop**, **bluegrass**, **R&B**, **film and television** and **rock**. Published "Zero To Love" (single by H. Cook/Brian James Deskins/Rick Tiger) from It's Just The Night (album), recorded by Del McCoury Band (bluegrass), released 2003 on Mc-Coury Music; "Muddy Water" (Alan Johnston) from The Midnight Call (album), recorded by Don Rigsby (bluegrass), released 2003 on Sugar Hill; "Ol Brown Suitcase" (H.R. Cook) from Lonesome Highway (album), recorded by Josh Williams (bluegrass), released 2004 on Pinecastle; and "Mansions of Kings" from Cherry Holmes II (album), recorded by IBMA 2005 Entertainer of the Year Cherry Holmes (bluegrass), released 2007 on Skaggs Family Records.

⊜◯ BERTHOLD WENGERT (MUSIKVERLAG)

Hauptstrasse 36, Pfinztal-Sollingen D-76327 Germany. Hauptstrasse 36, Pfinztal-Söllingen, D-76327 Germany. **Contact:** Berthold Wengert. Music publisher. Pays standard GEMA royalty.

HOW TO CONTACT Prefers CD and complete score for piano. SAE and IRC. Responds in 1 month. "No cassette returns!"

MUSIC Mostly **light Music** and **pop**.

⊘ WRENSONG/REYNSONG

1229 17th Avenue South, Nashville TN 37212. **E-mail:** christina.wrensong@gmail.com. **Contact:** Christina Mitchell. WRENSONG/REYNSONG is an independent music publishing company with offices in Nashville & Minneapolis. Conceived in 1983 by Father/Daughter team, Reyn Guyer and Ree Guyer Buchanan, the company began with only 20 songs and is now home to over 3,000. Our current writer roster consists of Jon Randall, Ashely Monroe, John Wiggins, Clint & Bob Moffatt (Like Strangers), Trevor Rosen, Jacob Davis amd Shelley Skidmore. Wrensong/Reynsong offers full in-house administration services for our writers and the catalogs we represent as well as outside writers and catalogs.

HOW TO CONTACT Does not accept unsolicited material.

⊕ YOUR BEST SONGS PUBLISHING

1402 Auburn Way N., Suite 396, Auburn WA 98002 United States. (ASCAP) 1402 Auburn Way N, Suite 396, Auburn WA 98002. **Contact:** John Markovich, general manager. Music publisher. Estab. 1988. Publishes 1-5 songs/year; publishes 1-3 new songwriters/year. Query for royalty terms.

HOW TO CONTACT Write first and obtain permission to submit. Prefers CD with 1-3 songs and lyric sheet. "Submit your 1-3 best songs per type of music. Use separate CDs per music type and indicate music type on each CD." Include SASE. Responds in 3 months.

MUSIC Mostly **country**, **rock/blues**, and **pop/rock**; also **progressive**, **A/C**, some **heavy metal** and **New Age**.

TIPS "We just require good lyrics, good melodies and good rhythm in a song. We absolutely do not want music without a decent melodic structure. We do not want lyrics with foul language or lyrics that do not inspire some form of imaginative thought."

RECORD COMPANIES

//

Record companies release and distribute records and CDs—the tangible products of the music industry. They sign artists to recording contracts, decide what songs those artists will record, and determine which songs to release. They are also responsible for providing recording facilities, securing producers and musicians, and overseeing the manufacture, distribution and promotion of new releases.

MAJOR LABELS & INDEPENDENT LABELS

Major labels and independent labels—what's the difference between the two?

The majors

As of this writing, there are three major record labels, commonly referred to as the "Big 3":
- Sony Music (Columbia Records, Epic Records, RCA Records, Arista Records, J Records, Provident Label Group, etc.)
- Universal Music Group (Universal Records, Interscope/Geffen/A&M, Island/Def Jam, Dreamworks Records, MCA Nashville Records, Verve Music Group, etc.)
- Warner Music Group (Atlantic Records, Bad Boy, Asylum Records, Warner Bros. Records, Maverick Records, Sub Pop, etc.)

Each of the "Big 3" is a large, publicly-traded corporation beholden to shareholders and quarterly profit expectations. This means the major labels have greater financial resources and promotional muscle than a smaller "indie" label, but it's also harder to get signed to a major. A big major label may also expect more contractual control over an artist or band's sound and image.

As shown in the above list, they also each act as umbrella organizations for numerous other well-known labels—former major labels in their own right, well-respected former independent/boutique labels, as well as subsidiary "vanity" labels fronted by successful major label recording artists. Each major label also has its own related worldwide product distribution system, and many independent labels will contract with the majors for distribution into stores.

If a label is distributed by one of these major companies, you can be assured any release coming out on that label has a large distribution network behind it. It will most likely be sent to most major retail stores in the United States.

The independents

Independent labels go through smaller distribution companies to distribute their product. They usually don't have the ability to deliver records in massive quantities as the major distributors do. However, that doesn't mean independent labels aren't able to have hit records just like their major counterparts. A record label's distributors are found in the listings after the "Distributed by" heading.

Which do I submit to?

Many of the companies listed in this section are independent labels. They are usually the most receptive to receiving material from new artists. Major labels spend more money than most other segments of the music industry; the music publisher, for instance, pays only for items such as salaries and the costs of making demos. Record companies, at great financial risk, pay for many more services, including production, manufacturing and promotion. Therefore, they must be very selective when signing new talent. Also, the continuing fear of copyright infringement suits has closed avenues to getting new material heard by the majors. Most don't listen to unsolicited submissions, period. Only songs recommended by attorneys, managers and producers who record company employees trust and respect are being heard by A&R people at major labels (companies with a referral policy have a ⊘ preceding their listing). But that doesn't mean all major labels are closed to new artists. With a combination of a strong local following, success on an independent label (or strong sales of an independently produced and released album) and the right connections, you could conceivably get an attentive audience at a major label.

But the competition is fierce at the majors, so you shouldn't overlook independent labels. Since they're located all over the country, indie labels are easier to contact and can be important in building a local base of support for your music (consult the Geographic Index at the back of the book to find out which companies are located near you). Independent labels usually concentrate on a specific type of music, which will help you target those companies your submissions should be sent to. And since the staff at an indie label is smaller, there are fewer channels to go through to get your music heard by the decision makers in the company.

HOW RECORD COMPANIES WORK

Independent record labels can run on a small staff, with only a handful of people running the day-to-day business. Major record labels are more likely to be divided into the following departments: A&R, sales, marketing, promotion, product management, artist development, production, finance, business/legal and international.

- The *A&R department* is staffed with A&R representatives who search out new talent. They go out and see new bands, listen to demo, and decide which artists to sign. They also look for new material for already signed acts, match producers with artists and oversee recording projects. Once an artist is signed by an A&R rep and a record is recorded, the rest of the departments at the company come into play.
- The *sales department* is responsible for getting a record into stores. They make sure record stores and other outlets receive enough copies of a record to meet consumer demand.
- The *marketing department* is in charge of publicity, advertising in magazines and other media, promotional videos, album cover artwork, in-store displays, and any other means of getting the name and image of an artist to the public.
- The *promotion department*'s main objective is to get songs from a new album played on the radio. They work with radio programmers to make sure a product gets airplay.
- The *product management department* is the ringmaster of the sales, marketing and promotion departments, assuring that they're all going in the same direction when promoting a new release.
- The *artist development department* is responsible for taking care of things while an artist is on tour, such as setting up promotional opportunities in cities where an act is performing.
- The *production department* handles the actual manufacturing and pressing of the record and makes sure it gets shipped to distributors in a timely manner.
- People in the *finance department* compute and distribute royalties, as well as keep track of expenses and income at the company.
- The *business/legal department* takes care of contracts, not only between the record company and artists but with foreign distributors, record clubs, etc.
- And finally, the *international department* is responsible for working with international companies for the release of records in other countries.

LOCATING A RECORD LABEL

With the abundance of record labels out there, how do you go about finding one that's right for the music you create? First, it helps to know exactly what kind of music a record label releases. Become familiar with the records a company has released, and see if they fit in with what you're doing. Each listing in this section details the type of music a particular record company is interested in releasing. You will want to refer to the Category Index to help you find those companies most receptive to the type of music you write. You should only approach companies open to your level of experience (see A Sample Listing Decoded on page 13). Visiting a company's website can also provide valuable information about a company's philosophy, the artists on the label and the music they work with.

Networking

Recommendations by key music industry people are an important part of making contacts with record companies. Songwriters must remember that talent alone does not guarantee success in the music business. You must be recognized through contacts, and the only way to make contacts is through networking. Networking is the process of building an interconnecting web of acquaintances within the music business. The more industry people you meet, the larger your contact base becomes, and the better are your chances of meeting someone with the clout to get your demo into the hands of the right people. If you want to get your music heard by key A&R representatives, networking is imperative.

Networking opportunities can be found anywhere industry people gather. A good place to meet key industry people is at regional and national music conferences and workshops. There are many held all over the country for all types of music (see the Workshops and Conferences section for more information). You should try to attend at least one or two of these events each year; it's a great way to increase the number and quality of your music industry contacts.

Creating a buzz

Another good way to attract A&R people is to make a name for yourself as an artist. By starting your career on a local level and building it from there, you can start to cultivate a following and prove to labels that you can be a success. A&R people figure if an act can be successful locally, there's a good chance they could be successful nationally. Start getting booked at local clubs, and start a mailing list of fans and local media. Once you gain some success on a local level, branch out. All this attention you're slowly gathering, this "buzz" you're generating, will not only get to your fans but to influential people in the music industry as well.

SUBMITTING TO RECORD COMPANIES

When submitting to a record company, major or independent, a professional attitude is imperative. Be specific about what you are submitting and what your goals are. If you are strictly a songwriter and the label carries a band you believe would properly present your song, state that in your cover letter. If you are an artist looking for a contract, showcase your strong points as a performer. Whatever your goals are, follow submission guidelines closely, be as neat as possible and include a top-notch demo. If you need more information concerning a company's requirements, write or call for more details. (For more information on submitting your material, see the article Where Should I Send My Songs? on page 10 and Demo Recordings on page 14.)

RECORD COMPANY CONTRACTS

Once you've found a record company that is interested in your work, the next step is signing a contract. Independent label contracts are usually not as long and complicated as major label ones, but they are still binding, legal contracts. Make sure the terms are in the best interest of both you and the label. Avoid anything in your contract that you feel is too restrictive. It's important to have your contract reviewed by a competent entertainment lawyer. A basic recording contract can run from 40-100 pages, and you need a lawyer to help you understand it. A lawyer will also be essential in helping you negotiate a deal that is in your best interest.

Recording contracts cover many areas, and just a few of the things you will be asked to consider will be: What royalty rate is the record label willing to pay you? What kind of advance are they offering? How many records will the company commit to? Will they offer tour support? Will they provide a budget for video? What sort of a recording budget are they offering? Are they asking you to give up any publishing rights? Are they offering you a publishing advance? These are only a few of the complex issues raised by a recording contract, so it's vital to have an entertainment lawyer at your side as you negotiate.

ADDITIONAL RECORD COMPANIES

There are more record companies located in other sections of the book! Use the Index to find additional Record Companies within other sections who are also record companies.

The Case for Independents

If you're interested in getting a major label deal, it makes sense to look to independent record labels to get your start. Independent labels are seen by many as a stepping stone to a major recording contract. Very few artists are signed to a major label at the start of their careers; usually, they've had a few independent releases that helped build their reputation in the industry. Major labels watch independent labels closely to locate up-and-coming bands and new trends. In the current economic atmosphere at major labels—with extremely high overhead costs for developing new bands and the fact that only 10 percent of acts on major labels actually make any profit—they're not willing to risk everything on an unknown act. Most major labels won't even consider signing a new act that hasn't had some indie success.

But independents aren't just farming grounds for future major label acts; many bands have long term relationships with indies, and prefer it that way. While they may not be able to provide the extensive distribution and promotion that a major label can (though there are exceptions), indie labels can help an artist become a regional success, and may even help the performer to see a profit as well. With the lower overhead and smaller production costs an independent label operates on, it's much easier to "succeed" on an indie label than on a major.

Icons

For more instructional information on the listings in this book, including explanations of symbols, read the article How To Use Songwriter's Market on page 10.

4AD

17-19 Alma Road, London SW18 1AA United Kingdom. **E-mail:** 4AD@4AD.com. **Website:** www.4ad.com.

HOW TO CONTACT Submit demo (CD or vinyl only) by mail, attention A&R, 4AD. "Sadly, there just aren't enough hours in the day to respond to everything that comes in. We'll only get in touch if we really like something."

MUSIC Mostly rock, indie/alternative. Current artists include Blonde Redhead, Bon Iver, Camera Obscura, The Breeders, The National, TV On The Radio, and more.

ALBANY RECORDS

915 Broadway, Albany NY 12207. **E-mail:** infoalbany@aol.com. Do you enjoy classical music that is off the beaten path? Are you frustrated by the lack of imaginative releases by the major classical labels? Albany Records is where you should look. Interesting, imaginative releases—many, many world premieres. The music on Albany Records is uncommonly classical. Albany Records is devoted to music by American composers (with a few notable exceptions) performed by the best of America's artists. From premiere recordings of orchestral music by Roy Harris, Morton Gould and Don Gillis to music by George Lloyd and Andrei Eshpai, there is something for everyone on Albany Records—provided your interests are just a bit out of the ordinary.

MUSIC Choral, chamber, opera, instrumental, organ, wind & brass, percussion, classical, world, etc.

AMERICAN RECORDINGS

3300 Warner Blvd., Burbank CA 91505-4832 United States. **Website:** www.americanrecordings.com. A&R: Dino Paredes, George Drakoulias, Antony Bland. Labels include Too Pure, Infinite Zero, UBL, Venture and Onion. American Recordings is a subsidiary of Republic Records/Sony BMG.

DISTRIBUTED BY Sony.

HOW TO CONTACT Submit demo by mail. Unsolicited submissions are OK. Prefers CD with lyric and lead sheet.

MUSIC Released *Unchained*, recorded by Johnny Cash, released on American Recordings. Other artists include ZZ Top, Howlin Rain, The Avett Brothers, Dan Wilson, and The (International) Noise Conspiracy.

ARIANA RECORDS

1312 S. Avenida Polar, #A-8, Tucson AZ 85710. (520)790-7324. **E-mail:** jtiom@aol.com. **Website:** www.arianarecords.net. **Contact:** James M. Gasper, president; Tom Dukes, vice president (pop, rock); Tom Privett (funk, experimental, rock) and Scott Smith (pop, rock, AOR), partners. Record company, Music publisher (Myko Music/BMI) and record producer. Estab. 1980. Releases 5 CDs a year and 1 compilation/year. Pays negotiable rates.

DISTRIBUTED BY LoneBoy Records London, The Yellow Record Company in Germany, and Groovetune music distributors in Alberta, Canada. Started talks with RCD Records for German distribution in early 2012.

HOW TO CONTACT "Send finished masters only. No demos! Unsolicited material okay."

MUSIC Mostly rock, funk, jazz, anything weird, strange, or lo-fi (must be mastered to CD). Released *Rustling Silk* (electronic) by BuddyLoveBand; *PornMuzik 2* (ambient); *T.G.I.F4* (electronica); *UnderCover Band*; *2010* (pop rock and funk); *Catch the Ghost* (hard rock). New releases *Musika* 2011 CD compilation, *Fun and Games* EP by Alien Workshop, and the single, "Hey Mr. President" by the Bailout Boys. Recently signed Perfect Paris (an electronic duo) and A Thousand Poets (an industrial/electronic duo).

TIPS "Keep on trying."

ARKADIA ENTERTAINMENT CORP.

11 Reservoir Road, Saugerties NY 12477. (845)246-9955. **Fax:** (845)246-9966. **E-mail:** info@view.com. **E-mail:** acquisitions@view.com. **Website:** www.arkadiarecords.com. A&R Song Submissions, acquisitions@view.com. Labels include Arkadia Jazz and Arkadia Chansons. Record company, music publisher (Arkadia Music), record producer (Arkadia Productions), and Arkadia Video. Estab. 1995.

HOW TO CONTACT Write or call first and obtain permission to submit.

MUSIC Mostly jazz, classical, and pop/R&B; also world.

ASTRALWERKS

101 Avenue of the Americas, 10th Floor, New York NY 10013 United States. **E-mail:** astralwerks@astralwerks.net; A&R@astralwerks.net. **Website:** www.astralwerks.com.

Astralwerks is a subsidiary of the EMI Group, one of the "Big 3" major labels. EMI is a British-based company.

HOW TO CONTACT Does not accept unsolicited submisisons.

MUSIC Mostly alternative/indie/electronic. Artists include VHS or BETA, Badly Drawn Boy, The Beta Band, Chemical Brothers, Turin Breaks, and Fatboy Slim.

○ ATLAN-DEC/GROOVELINE RECORDS

2529 Green Forest Court, Snellville GA 30078-4183. (877)751-5169. **E-mail:** atlandec@prodigy.net. **Website:** www.atlan-dec.com. **Contact:** Wileta J. Hatcher, art director. This company has grown to boast a roster of artists representing different genres of music. "Our artists' diversity brings a unique quality of musicianship to our CDs. This uniqueness excites our listeners and has gained us the reputation of releasing only the very best in recorded music." Atlan-Dec/Grooveline Records CDs are distributed worldwide through traditional and virtual online retail stores. Record company, music publisher and record producer. Staff size: 2. Releases 3-4 singles, 3-4 LPs and 3-4 CDs/year. Pays 10-25% royalty to artists on contract; statutory rate to publisher per song on recoRoad

DISTRIBUTED BY C.E.D. Entertainment Dist.

HOW TO CONTACT Submit demo package by mail. Unsolicited submissions are OK. Prefers CD with lyric sheet. Does not return material. Responds in 3 months.

MUSIC Mostly R&B/urban, hip-hop/rap, and contemporary jazz; also soft rock, gospel, dance, and new country. Released "Temptation" by Shawree, released 2004 on Atlan-Dec/Grooveline Records; *Enemy of the State* (album), recorded by Lowlife (rap/hip-hop); *I'm The Definition* (album), recorded by L.S. (rap/hip-hop), released 2007; "AHHW" (single), recorded by LeTebony Simmons (R&B), released 2007. Other artists include Furious D (rap/hip-hop), Mark Cocker (new country), and Looka, "From the Top" (rap/hip-hop) recorded in 2008.

○○ ATLANTIC RECORDS

1290 Avenue of the Americas, New York NY 10104 United States. (212)707-2000. **Fax:** (212)581-6414. **E-mail:** contact@atlanticrecords.com. **Website:** www. atlanticrecords.com. Labels include Big Beat Records, LAVA, Nonesuch Records, Atlantic Classics, and Rhino Records. Record company. Pays negotiable royalty to artists on contract; negotiable rate to publisher per song on recoRoad

Atlantic Records is a subsidiary of Warner Music Group, one of the "Big 3" major labels.

DISTRIBUTED BY WEA.

HOW TO CONTACT *Does not accept unsolicited material.* "No phone calls please."

MUSIC Artists include Missy Elliott, Simple Plan, Lupe Fiasco, Phil Collins, B.O.B., Jason Mraz, and Death Cab For Cutie.

○ AVITA RECORDS

P.O. Box 764, Hendersonville TN 37077-0764. (615)824-1435. **Website:** www.avitajazz.com.

Also see the listing for Riohcat Music in the Managers & Booking Agents section of this book.

HOW TO CONTACT *Contact first and obtain permission to submit.* "We only accept material referred to us by a reputable industry source." Prefers CD. Does not return materials. Responds only if interested.

MUSIC Mostly jazz. Recently released Stories by the Jerry Tachoir Group. Other artists include Van Manakas and Marlene Tachoir.

●○ AWAL UK LIMITED

Sheffield Technology Park, Arundel St., Sheffield S1 2NS United Kingdom. **E-mail:** info@awal.com. **Website:** www.awal.com.

DISTRIBUTED BY Primarily distributes via digital downloads but physical distribution available.

HOW TO CONTACT Submit demo by mail. Unsolicited submissions are OK. Prefers CD with 5 songs, lyric sheet, cover letter and press clippings. Does not return materials.

MUSIC Mostly pop, world, and jazz; also techno, teen, and children's. Released *Go Cat Go* (album by various), recorded by Carl Perkins on ArtistOne.com; *Bliss* (album), written and recorded by Donna Delory (pop); and *Shake A Little* (album), written and recorded by Michael Ruff, both on Awal Records.

○ AWARE RECORDS

1316 Sherman Ave., #215, Evanston IL 60201. (847)424-2000. **E-mail:** awareinfo@awareMusic.com. **Website:** www.awareMusic.com.

HOW TO CONTACT *Does not accept unsolicited submissions.*

MUSIC Mostly rock/pop. Artists include Mat Kearney and Guster.

BAD TASTE RECORDS

Box 1243, S - 221 05 Lund, Sweden. **E-mail:** info@bad-tasterecords.se. **Website:** www.badtasterecords.se. **HOW TO CONTACT** We listen to everything we receive. It usually takes a while because we receive a lot of demos, but eventually we always listen to it. Send CDs to the address above. Do not e-mail MP3s. With the amount of demos we receive there is rarely time to write back, unless of course we're interested in releasing your band or including a song on one of our compilations. Please don't be too disappointed by this. We would love to be able to write back to everyone, but we are already working days, nights and weekends to try and get things done. Just in case though, please include your e-mail address. More details are posted at the website. **MUSIC** Works with bands such as Danko Jones, Logh, Quit Your Dayjob, Embee, Lemonheads, Langhorns, and more.

BIG COFFEE RECORDS

4867 Ashford Dunwoody Road #6202, Atlanta GA 30338. **E-mail:** info@bigcoffeerecords.com. **Website:** www.bigcoffeerecords.com. Big Coffee Records is an Independent Record Label located in Atlanta, Georgia, dedicated to releasing like-minded quality local music in many genres, including: Rock, Southern Rock, Blues, Rhythm & Blues, Americana, Contemporary Jazz, Smooth Jazz, Groove, Club, as well as New Age, Stress Relief, Meditation, Healing, with music for Film, TV, and Advertising placement. **MUSIC** Artists include Mose Jones, Steve McRay, Java Monkey, Cole/Taylor, Francine Reed, etc.

BIG FACE ENTERTAINMENT

100 State St Suite 360, Albany NY 12207. **E-mail:** info@bigfaceonline.com. **Website:** www.bigfaceonline.com. Big Face Entertainment, your hybrid record label that offers multi dimensional services that caters to the artists. "In other words, we are the house that creates the product and put's it out there! We focus on what is truly important at our company opposed to others; investing in the music and talented artists that create the content. We believe in creating a collaborative and innovative environment where our artist can thrive and reach their full capacity in a stress free atmosphere." **MUSIC** Artists include Legend, Island Boy, Daytona, and more. Rap, hip-hop, pop, etc.

BIG HEAVY WORLD

P.O. Box 428, Burlington VT 05402-0428. **E-mail:** info@bigheavyworld.com. **Website:** www.bigheavyworld.com. Big Heavy World has been pulling together compilations of Vermont artists since 1996 with the release of Sonic Tonic, the indie-alt-core battle cry of our veteran scene-pimping phalanx. We've plowed lovingly through more than fifteen titles and continue to unite regional musicians within projects that ultimately, we hope, bring recognition to Vermont's deserving music community and maybe make the world a better place in the process. Most Big Heavy World compilations and their release parties have created exposure and fiscal support for worthy humanitarian organizations like Spectrum Youth and Family Services, the Make A Wish Foundation, the Women's Rape Crisis Center, 242 Main, and Viet Nam Assistance for the Handicapped.

BLACKHEART RECORDS

636 Broadway, New York NY 10012 United States. (212)353-9600. **Fax:** (212)353-8300. **E-mail:** blackheart@blackheart.com. **Website:** www.blackheart.com. **HOW TO CONTACT** Unsolicited submissions are OK. Prefers CD with 1-3 songs and lyric sheets. Include SASE. Responds only if interested. **MUSIC** Mostly rock. Artists include Joan Jett & the Blackhearts, The Dollyrots, The Vacancies, Girl In A Coma, and The Eyeliners.

BLANK TAPE RECORDS

E-mail: blanktaperecords@gmail.com. **Website:** www.blanktaperecords.org. Blank Tape Records a collectively owned and operated independent record label based in Southern Colorado, dedicated to creating and sharing music. Our artists make up songs, wander and sing cross-country, conjure spirits and invent albums. So that we might do the impossible and make a living out of our curiosities. Since 2008 Blank Tape has released over 20 albums, the majority featuring the diverse and talented music scene of the front range. **MUSIC** Roster includes The Changing Colors, The Haunted Windchimes, Mike Clark & The Sugar Sounds, Grant Sabin, Desirae Garcia, and more. **TIPS** "We are friends helping friends put out records, working through an organic process. We don't make our artists sign contracts, so our relationships are based on friendship, good work ethic and trust. We all contribute to the Blank Tape Family in some way shape or form; we are artists, designers, social media managers, photographers, envelope stuffers, web designers, audio engineers and videographers dedicated to each other's vision and dream. New bands and artists come into the fold when they have made a mark within our community and there is a mutual agreement that we can benefit from one other."

CAMBRIA RECORDS & PUBLISHING

P.O. Box 374, Lomita CA 90717. (310)831-1322. **Fax:** (310)833-7442. **E-mail:** cambriamus@aol.com. **Website:** www.cambriamus.com.

DISTRIBUTED BY Albany Distribution.

HOW TO CONTACT *Write first and obtain permission to submit.* Accepts CD. Include SASE. Responds in 1 month.

MUSIC Mostly *classical*. Released *Songs of Elinor Remick Warren* (album) on Cambria Records. Other artists include Marie Gibson (soprano), Leonard Pennario (piano), Thomas Hampson (voice), Mischa Leftkowitz (violin), Leigh Kaplan (piano), North Wind Quintet, and Sierra Wind Quintet.

CANTILENA RECORDS

740 Fox Dale Ln., Knoxville TN 37934 United States. **Website:** www.cantilenarecords.com. Record company. Estab. 1993. Releases 3 CDs/year. Pays Harry Fox standard royalty to artists on contract; statutory rate to publishers per song on recoRoad

HOW TO CONTACT *Write first and obtain permission to submit or to arrange personal interview.* Prefers CD. Does not return material.

MUSIC Classical, jazz. Released "Caliente!" (single by Christopher Caliendo) from *Caliente! World Music for Flute & Guitar* (album), recorded by Laurel Zucker and Christopher Caliendo! (world crossover); *Suites No. 1 & 2 For Flute & Jazz Piano Trio*(album by Claude Bolling), recorded by Laurel Zucker, Joe Gilman, David Rokeach, Jeff Neighbor (jazz); and *HOPE! Music for Flute, Soprano, Guitar* (album by Daniel Akiva, Astor Piazzolla, Haim Permont, Villa-Lobos) (classical/world), recorded by Laurel Zucker, Ronit Widmann-Levy, Daniel Akiva, all released in 2004 by Cantilena Records. Other artists include Tim Gorman, Prairie Prince, Dave Margen, Israel Philharmonic, Erkel Chamber Orchestra, Samuel Magill, Renee Siebert, Robin Sutherland, and Gerald Ranch.d

CAPITOL RECORDS

1750 N. Vine St., Hollywood CA 90028. (323)462-6252. **Fax:** (323)469-4542. **Website:** www.hollywoodandvine.com. Labels include Blue Note Records, Grand Royal Records, Pangaea Records, The Right Stuff Records and Capitol Nashville Records.

Capitol Records is a subsidiary of the EMI Group, one of the "Big 3" major labels.

DISTRIBUTED BY EMD.

HOW TO CONTACT *Capitol Records does not accept unsolicited submissions.*

MUSIC Artists include Coldplay, The Decemberists, Beastie Boys, Katy Perry, Interpol, Lily Allen, and Depeche Mode.

CAPP RECORDS

P.O. Box 150871, San Rafael CA 94915-0871. (415)457-8617. **Website:** www.capprecords.com.

HOW TO CONTACT Submit demo package by mail. Unsolicited submissions are OK. Prefers CD or NTSC videocassette with 3 songs and cover letter. "E-mail (on website) us in advance for submissions, if possible." Include SASE. Only responds if interested.

FILM & TV Places 20 songs in film and 7 songs in TV/year. Music Supervisors: Dominique Toulon (pop, dance, New Age). "Currently doing music placement for television—*MTV, VH1, Oprah, A&E Network, and Discovery Channel.*"

MUSIC Mostly pop, dance, and techno; also New Age. Does not want country. Released "It's Not a Dream" (single by Cary August/Andre Pessis), recorded by Cary August on CAPP Records (dance). "Visit our website for new releases."

COLLECTOR RECORDS

P.O. Box 1200, 3260 AE Oud Beijerland The Netherlands. (31)186 604266. **E-mail:** info@collectorrecords.nl. **Website:** www.collectorrecords.nl.

HOW TO CONTACT Submit demo package by mail. Unsolicited submissions are OK. Prefers CD. SAE and IRC. Responds in 2 months.

MUSIC Mostly '50s rock, rockabilly, hillbilly boogie and country/rock; also piano boogie woogie. Released *Rock Crazy Baby* (album), by Art Adams (1950s rockabilly), released 2005; *Marvin Jackson* (album), by Marvin Jackson (1950s rockers), released 2005; *Western Australian Snake Pit R&R* (album), recorded by various (1950s rockers), released 2005, all on Collector Records. Other artists include Henk Pepping, Rob Hoeke, Eric-Jan Overbeek, and more. "See our website."

⊘ COLUMBIA RECORDS

550 Madison Ave., 10th Floor, New York NY 10022 United States. (212)833-4000. **Fax:** (212)833-4389. **E-mail:** sonyMusiconline@sonyMusic.com. **Website:** www.columbiarecords.com. Santa Monica: 2100 Colorado Ave., Santa Monica CA 90404. (310)449-2100. **Fax:** (310)449-2743. Nashville: 34 Music Square E., Nashville TN 37203. (615)742-4321. **Fax:** (615)244-2549. Record company.

◖ Columbia Records is a subsidiary of Sony BMG, one of the "Big 3" major labels.

DISTRIBUTED BY Sony.

HOW TO CONTACT *Columbia Records does not accept unsolicited submissions.*

MUSIC Artists include Aerosmith, Marc Anthony, Beyonce, Bob Dylan, and Patti Smith.

⊘ COSMOTONE RECORDS

2951 Marina Bay Dr., Suite 130, PMB 501, League City TX 77573-2733. **E-mail:** marianland@earthlink.net. **Website:** www.marianland.com/Music.html; www.cosmotonerecords.com. Record company, Music publisher (Cosmotone Music, ASCAP), and record producer (Rafael Brom).

DISTRIBUTED BY marianland.com

HOW TO CONTACT "Sorry, we do not accept material at this time." Does not return materials.

MUSIC Mostly Christian pop/rock. Released *Rafael Brom I*, *Padre Pio* Lord Hamilton, *Dance for Padre Pio*, *Peace of Heart*, *Music for Peace of Mind*, *The Sounds of Heaven*, *The Christmas Songs*, *Angelophany*, *The True Measure of Love*, *All My Love to You Jesus* (albums), and *Rafael Brom Unplugged* (live concert DVD), *Life is Good, Enjoy it While You Can, Change*, by Rafael Brom, *Refugee from Socialism* by Rafael Brom, and *Move Your Ass*, by Rafael Brom, *Peanut Regatta* by Rafael Brom, and *Best of Rafael Brom*, Volume I, II, III and IV.

◖ CREATIVE IMPROVISED MUSIC PROJECTS (CIMP) RECORDS

Cadence Building, Redwood NY 13679. (315)287-2852. **Fax:** (315)287-2860. **E-mail:** cimp@cadencebuilding.com. **Website:** www.cimprecords.com. Labels include Cadence Jazz Records. Record company and record producer (Robert D. Rusch). Releases 25-30 CDs/year. Pays negotiable royalty to artists on contract; pays statutory rate to publisher per song on recoRoadDistributed by North Country Distributors.

◖ CIMP specializes in jazz and creative improvised music.

HOW TO CONTACT Submit demo by mail. Unsolicited submissions are OK. Prefers CD. "We are not looking for songwriters but recording artists." Include SASE. Responds in 1 week.

MUSIC Mostly jazz and creative improvised music. Released *The Redwood Session* (album), recorded by Evan Parker, Barry Guy, Paul Lytton, and Joe McPhee; *Sarah's Theme* (album), recorded by the Ernie Krivda Trio, Bob Fraser, and Jeff Halsey; and *Human Flowers* (album), recorded by the Bobby Zankel Trio, Marily Crispell, and Newman Baker, all released on CIMP (improvised jazz). Other artists include Arthur Blythe, Joe McPhee, David Prentice, Anthony Braxton, Roswell Rudd, Paul Smoker, Khan Jamal, Odean Pope, etc.

TIPS "CIMP Records are produced to provide music to reward repeated and in-depth listenings. They are recorded live to two-track which captures the full dynamic range one would experience in a live concert. There is no compression, homogenization, eq-ing, post-recording splicing, mixing, or electronic fiddling with the performance. Digital recording allows for a vanishingly low noise floor and tremendous dynamic range. This compression of the dynamic range is what limits the 'air' and life of many recordings. Our recordings capture the dynamic intended by the musicians. In this regard these recordings are demanding. Treat the recording as your private concert. Give it your undivided attention and it will reward you. CIMP Records are not intended to be background music. This method is demanding not only on the listener but on the performer as well. Musicians must be able to play together in real time. They must understand the dynamics of their instrument and how it relates to the others around them. There is no fix-it-in-the-mix safety; either it works or it doesn't. What you hear is exactly what was played. Our main concern is music not marketing."

⊘ CURB RECORDS

49 Music Square E., Nashville TN 37203. (615)321-5080. **Fax:** (615)327-1964. **Website:** www.curb.com.

HOW TO CONTACT *Curb Records does not accept unsolicited submissions; accepts previously* *published material only. Do not submit without permission.*

MUSIC Released *Everywhere* (album), recorded by Tim McGraw; *Sittin' On Top of the World* (album), recorded by LeAnn Rimes; and *I'm Alright* (album), recorded by Jo Dee Messina, all on Curb Records. Other artists include Mary Black, Merle Haggard, David Kersh, Lyle Lovett, Tim McGraw, Wynonna, and Sawyer Brown.

DENTAL RECORDS

P.O. Box 20058, New York NY 10017. (212) 486-4513. **E-mail:** rsanford@dentalrecords.com. **Website:** www.dentalrecords.com.

HOW TO CONTACT "Check website to see if your material is appropriate." *Not currently accepting unsolicited submissions.*

MUSIC Pop-derived structures, jazz-derived harmonies, and neo-classic-wannabee-pretenses. Claims no expertise, nor interest, in urban, heavy metal, or hard core. Released *Perspectivism* (album), written and recorded by Rick Sanford (instrumental), released 2003 on Dental Records. Other artists include Les Izmor.

DRUMBEAT INDIAN ARTS, INC.

4143 N. 16th St., Suite 1, Phoenix AZ 85016. (602)266-4823. **E-mail:** info@drumbeatindianarts.com.

   Note that Drumbeat Indian Arts is a very specialized label, and only wants to receive submissions by Native American artists.

HOW TO CONTACT *Call first and obtain permission to submit.* Include SASE. Responds in 2 months.

MUSIC Music by American Indians—any style (must be enrolled tribal members). Does not want New Age "Indian style" material. Released Pearl Moon (album), written and recorded by Xavier (native Amerindian). Other artists include Black Lodge Singers, R. Carlos Nakai, Lite Foot, and Joanne Shenandoah.

TIPS "We deal only with American Indian performers. We do not accept material from others. Please include tribal affiliation."

EARACHE RECORDS

4402 11th St., #507A, Long Island City NY 11101. (718)786-1707. **Fax:** (718)786-1756. **E-mail:** usaproduction@earache.com. **Website:** www.earache.com.

MUSIC Rock, industrial, heavy metal techno, death metal, grindcore. Artists include Municipal Waste, Dillinger Escape Plan, Bring Me the Horizon, Deicide, Oceano, and more.

ELEKTRA RECORDS

75 Rockefeller Plaza, 17th Floor, New York NY 10019. **Website:** www.elektra.com.

   Elektra Records is a subsidiary of Warner Music Group, one of the "Big 3" major labels.

DISTRIBUTED BY WEA.

HOW TO CONTACT *Elektra does not accept unsolicited submissions.*

MUSIC Mostly alternative/modern rock. Artists include Bruno Mars, Cee Lo, Justice, Little Boots, and *True Blood.*

EPIC RECORDS

550 Madison Ave., 22nd Floor, New York NY 10022. (212)833-8000. **Fax:** (212)833-4054. **Website:** www.epicrecords.com. Labels include Beluga Heights, Daylight Records and E1 Music. Record company.

   Epic Records is a subsidiary of Sony BMG, one of the "Big 3" major labels.

DISTRIBUTED BY Sony Music Distribution.

HOW TO CONTACT *Write or call first and obtain permission to submit* (New York office only). Does not return material. Responds only if interested. *Santa Monica and Nashville offices do not accept unsolicited submissions.*

MUSIC Artists include Sade, Shakira, Modest Mouse, The Fray, Natasha Bedingfield, Sean Kingston, Incubus, The Script.

TIPS "Do an internship if you don't have experience or work as someone's assistant. Learn the business and work hard while you figure out what your talents are and where you fit in. Once you figure out which area of the record company you're suited for, focus on that, work hard at it and it shall be yours."

EPITAPH RECORDS

2798 Sunset Blvd., Los Angeles CA 90026. (213)355-5000. **E-mail:** publicity@epitaph.com. **Website:** www.epitaph.com. Record company. Contains imprints Hellcat Records and Anti. "Epitaph Records was founded by Bad Religion guitarist Brett Gurewitz with the aim of starting an artist-friendly label from a musicians point of view. Perhaps most well known for being the little indie from L.A. that spawned the 90s punk explosion."

HOW TO CONTACT "Post your demos on-line at one of the many free music portals, then simply fill out the Demo Submission-form" on website.

MUSIC Artists include Social Distortion, Alkaline Trio, Rancid, The Weakerthans, Weezer, Bad Religion, Every Time I Die.

○ EQUAL VISION RECORDS

P.O. Box 38202, Albany NY 12203-8202. (518)458-8250. **E-mail:** info@equalvision.com. **E-mail:** Music@equalvision.com. "We're an independent record label entirely owned and operated with no outside financial support. We are however distributed by the Alternative Distribution Alliance (ADA Music), which is a subsidiary of Warner Music Group. ADA also distributes some of our favorite independent labels like Sub Pop, Epitaph, Saddle Creek, Atlantic, Doghouse, Fearless, Hopeless, Matador, Merge, Polyvinyl, and more."

HOW TO CONTACT In an effort to become more environmentally friendly, Equal Vision Records no longer accepts unsolicited physical demos. Instead, please e-mail Music@equalvision.com with a link to where we can check out songs on the web. It's much faster, cheaper, and easier for us to listen to music online. If we like your tunes, we'll request a CD or demo package.

TIPS "We love talking about music, but unfortunately we can't respond or give tips to every band that sends in a submission ... there just aren't enough hours in the day, and we need to devote our time to our current artists. Instead, spend your time writing the best music you can. Travel, tour, flyer, and build your band on your own. The harder you work, the more likely we are to notice."

◉ ETERNAL OTTER RECORDS

8 Mayo Street #2, Portland ME 04101. **Website:** www.eternalotterrecords.com. Eternal Otter Records is an online music label devoted to limited edition recordings of exceptional musical talents, drawn primarily from the Portland, Maine area. The criterion for all Eternal Otter releases is not simply the talent of the individual artist. It is, to a larger extent, defined by the enduring, timeless nature of the music itself.

HOW TO CONTACT Contact via online form.

MUSIC Artists include Cerebus Soul, Lady Lamb and Beekeeper, The Milkman's Union, Jesse Pilgrim & the Bonfire, Panda Bandits, and more.

◉ EUCLID RECORDS

Website: www.label/euclidrecords.com. After 30 years of serving the St. Louis area and the world with great music, Euclid Records is now a label. Still based in St. Louis with a nod towards New Orleans (Euclid NOLA opened in September of 2010), the store has formed its own label.

HOW TO CONTACT Contact using online form.

MUSIC Artists include Sleepy Kitty, Cotton Mather, NRBQ, Troubador Dali, and more.

⊘ FAT WRECK CHORDS

P.O. Box 193690, San Francisco CA 94119. **E-mail:** mailbag@fatwreck.com. **Website:** www.fatwreck.com.

MUSIC Punk, rock, alternative. Artists include NOFX, Rise Against, The Lawrence Arms, Anti-Flag, Me First and the Gimme Gimmes, Propagandhi, Dillinger Four, Against Me!, and more.

FEARLESS RECORDS

13772 Goldenwest St. #545, Westminster CA 92683. **Website:** www.fearlessrecords.com.

HOW TO CONTACT Send all demos to mailing address. "Do not e-mail us about demos or with links to mp3s."

MUSIC Alternative, pop, indie, rock, metal. Artists include Plain White T's, Mayday Parade, Blessthefall, Breathe Carolina, The Summer Set, Forever The Sickest Kids, The Downtown Fiction, Real Friends, Jason Lancaster (Go Radio), Motionless In White, and more.

○ FIREANT

2009 Ashland Ave., Charlotte NC 28205. (704)335-1400. **E-mail:** lewh@fireantMusic.com. **Website:** www.fireantMusic.com.

DISTRIBUTED BY The Orchard, City Hall Records, and eMusic.com.

HOW TO CONTACT Submit demo by mail. Unsolicited submissions are OK. Does not return material.

MUSIC Mostly progressive, traditional, and Musical hybrids. "Anything except New Age and MOR." Released *Loving the Alien: Athens Georgia Salutes David Bowie* (album), recorded by various artists (rock/alternative/electronic), released 2000 on Fireant; and *Good Enough* (album), recorded by Zen Frisbee. Other artists include Mr. Peters' Belizean Boom and Chime Band.

◯ FLYING HEART RECORDS

4015 NE 12th Ave., Portland OR 97212. **E-mail:** fly-heart@teleport.com. **Website:** www.home.teleport.com/~flyheart.

DISTRIBUTED BY Burnside Distribution Co.

HOW TO CONTACT Submit demo by mail. Unsolicited submissions are OK. Prefers CD with 1-10 songs and lyric sheets. Does not return material. "SASE required for *any* response." Responds in 3 months.

MUSIC Mostly R&B, blues, and jazz; also rock. Released *Vexatious Progr.* (album), written and recorded by Eddie Harris (jazz); *Juke Music* (album), written and recorded by Thara Memory (jazz); and *Lookie Tookie* (album), written and recorded by Jan Celt (blues), all on Flying Heart Records. Other artists include Janice Scroggins, Tom McFarland, Thara Memory, and Snow Bud & The Flower People.

◯ FORGED ARTIFACTS

5000 Lyndale Ave S Unit 1, Minneapolis MN 55419. **E-mail:** forgedartifacts@gmail.com. **Website:** www.forgedartifacts.com. **Contact:** Matt Linden. An indie record company based in Minneapolis, MN.

HOW TO CONTACT Feel free to send demos/sounds to forgedartifacts@gmail.com. Streamable links please. If you have physical demos, send 'em to the address above.

MUSIC Artists include Some Pulp, Baked, Gloss, France Camp, Nice Purse, and more.

◯ FRESH ENTERTAINMENT

1315 Joseph E. Boone Blvd., NW, Suite 5, Atlanta GA 30314. **E-mail:** whunter1122@yahoo.com. **Contact:** Willie W. Hunter, managing director. Record company and music publisher (Hserf Music/ASCAP, Blair Vizzion Music/BMI). Releases 5 singles and 2 LPs/year. Pays 7-10% royalty to artists on contract; statutory rate to publisher per song on recoRoad

DISTRIBUTED BY Ichiban International and Intersound Records.

HOW TO CONTACT Submit demo package by mail. Unsolicited submissions are OK. Prefers CDs or DVDs with at least 3 songs and lyric sheet. Include SASE. Responds in 2 months.

MUSIC Mostly R&B, rock and pop; also jazz, gospel and rap. Recent releases include "Wreckless" by Cap1; "Cut Her Off" by Cinco; *Nubian Woman* by Bob Miles; *You Know I'm From the A* by Joe "Da Bingo" Bing; Future's *Pluto*, 3 tracks: "Tony Montana," "Astronaut Chick," "Fishscale."

◉ FUELED BY RAMEN

1290 Avenue of the Americas, New York NY 10104. **Website:** www.fueledbyramen.com.

HOW TO CONTACT Send demos by mail to address above. Do not e-mail about demos. Make sure there's a bio, contact information, touring information, and more. "Your music will speak for itself, but the packaging is our first impression of your band. There is no bigger frustration than opening a package and seeing a demo that looks like it was sent without even trying."

MUSIC Alternative, Rock, Indie. Artists include The Academy Is..., Cobra Starship, Gym Class Heroes, Panic! at the Disco, Paramore, Sublime with Rome, This Providence, and more.

TIPS "To be honest, each one of our bands have been signed for different reasons, and there are numerous things that we always look for—from your music, to your work ethic, to your personalities, to everything in between. The most important thing you can do is to work hard and accomplish as much as you can for your band before trying to get signed to a label. Develop a local following, tour the country, record an EP, start a street team, get interviewed by your local publications, etc.—we look for bands that are creating their own buzz and aren't depending on somebody else to do it for them. Putting all you can into your band will attract labels wishing to do the same."

◉ MARTY GARRETT ENTERTAINMENT

320 W. Utica Place, Broken Arrow OK 74011. (918)451-6780. **E-mail:** martygarrett@earthlink.net. **Website:** www.martygarrettentertainment.com; www.Musicbusinessmoney.com. **Contact:** Marty R. Garrett, president. Labelsinclude MGE Records and Lonesome Wind Records. Record company, record producer, music publisher, and entertainment consultant. Authorized Agent for Christian music Artist David Ingles. Releases 1 CD/year. Pays negotiable royalty toartists on contract; statutory rate to publisher per song on recoRoad

HOW TO CONTACT Call orcheck website first to review submission instructions and if submissions arecurrently being accepted. Prefers CD only with maximum 10 songs and lyric orlead sheets with chord progressions listed. Does not return material. Do notsend press packs or bios unless specifically instructed to do so. Responds in 4-6 weeks.

MUSIC MostlyScripture based Christian and Gospel, honky tonk, and traditional country. Co-produced and released The Very Best Of David Ingles on DIP Records.

TIPS "We help artists record and release major label quality CD products to the public for sale through any number of methods, including Radio and 1-800 Television. Although we do submit finished products to major record companies for review, our main focus is to establish and surround each artist with their own long-term production, promotion and distribution organization. Professional studio demos are not required, but make sure vocals are distinct, up-front, and up-to-date. I personally listen to each submission received, so call or check website FIRST to see if I am conducting reviews."

○ GOTHAM RECORDS

P.O. Box 7185, Santa Monica CA 90406. **E-mail:** ar@gothamrecords.com; info@gothamrecords.com. **Website:** www.gothamrecords.com. Releases 8 LPs and 8 CDs/year. Pays negotiable royalty to artists on contract; statutory rate to publisher per song on recoRoad "Gotham Music Placement is Gotham Records' main focus. Gotham Music Placement places recorded material with motion picture, TV, advertising, and video game companies. GMP supervises full feature films and releases full soundtracks, and represents artists from all over the world and all types of genres."

DISTRIBUTED BY Sony RED.

HOW TO CONTACT Submit demo by mail "in a padded mailer or similar package." Unsolicited submissions are OK. Prefers CD and bios, pictures, and touring information. Does not return material.

MUSIC All genres. Artists include SLANT, Red Horizon, The Day After..., and The Vicious Martinis.

TIPS "Send all submissions in regular packaging. Spend your money on production and basics, not on fancy packaging and gift wrap."

○ GRAVEFACE

5 West 40th St, Savannah GA 31401. **E-mail:** mail@graveface.com. **Website:** www.graveface.com. Graveface is an extremely small recording label. We are constantly searching for brilliant music to release to the world. If you are a fan of the music we already release, feel free to send us samples of your brilliance. We might reply back to you and we might not. We are happy with our little roster but if you really impress us, you will certainly be getting an e-mail.

MUSIC Artists include The Appleseed Cast, Creepoid, Dosh, The Loose Salute, The Casket Girls, The Stargazer Lilies, Hospital Ships, Gramma's Boyfriend, Dreamend, and many more.

○ HACIENDA RECORDS & RECORDING STUDIO

1236 S. Staples St., Corpus Christi TX 78404. (361)882-7066. **Fax:** (361)882-3943. **E-mail:** info@haciendarecords.com. **Website:** www.hacienda-records.myshopify.com.

HOW TO CONTACT Submit demo package by mail. Unsolicited submissions are OK. Prefers CD with cover letter. Does not return material. Responds in 6 weeks.

MUSIC Mostly tejano, regional Mexican, country (Spanish or English), and pop. Released "Chica Bonita" (single), recorded by Albert Zamora and D.J. Cubanito, released 2001 on Hacienda Records; "Si Quieres Verme Llorar" (single) from *Lisa Lopez con Mariachi* (album), recorded by Lisa Lopez (mariachi), released 2002 on Hacienda; "Tartamudo" (single) from *Una Vez Mas* (album), recorded by Peligro (norteno); and "Miento" (single) from *Si Tu Te Vas* (album), recorded by Traizion (tejano), both released 2001 on Hacienda. Other artists include, Gary Hobbs, Steve Jordan, Grammy Award nominees Mingo Saldivar and David Lee Garza, Michelle, Victoria Y Sus Chikos, La Traizion.

◑ HARDROC RECORDS

Website: www.hardrocrecords.com. HardRoc Records is an Independent Record Label based out of Newark, New Jersey. Its deep connection to street music and support of mainstream flair, Hardroc has made itself the base for the most relevant and promising artists from NJ and the Tri-State area.

HOW TO CONTACT Use online form to contact.

MUSIC Artists include Nice and Ill, Roky Reign, Chad B., 22 McGraw, Aitch, and more. Hip-hop, rap, pop, trance, etc.

⊘ HEADS UP INT., LTD.

Concord Music Group, 100 North Crescent Drive, Garden Level, Beverly Hills CA 90210. **Website:** www.concordMusicgroup.com/labels/Heads-Up/.

MUSIC Mostly jazz, R&B, pop and world. Does not want anything else. Released *Long Walk to Freedom* (album), recorded by Ladysmith Black Mambazo (world); *Pilgrimage* (album), recorded by Michael Brecker (contemporary jazz); *Rizing Sun* (album), recorded by Najee (contemporary jazz). Other artists include Diane Schuur, Mateo Parker, Victor Wooten, Esperanza Spalding, Incognito, George Doke, Take 6, Fourplay.

⊘ HEART MUSIC, INC.

P.O. Box 160326, Austin TX 78716-0326. (512)795-2375. **E-mail:** info@heartMusic.com. **Website:** www.heartMusic.com. **Contact:** Tab Bartling, president. Record company and music publisher (Coolhot Music). "Studio available for artists." Staff size: 2. Releases 1-2 CDs/year. Pays statutory rate to publisher per song on recoRoad

HOW TO CONTACT *Not interested in new material at this time.* Does not return material. Responds only if interested.

MUSIC Mostly Folk-rock, pop, and jazz; also blues and contemporary folk. Libby Kirkpatrick's Heroine in early 2011; released *The Fisherman* (album), recorded by Darin Layne/Jason McKensie; released The Fisherman by Darin Layne;Joe LoCascio Woody Witt Seasons Ago In the City of Lost Things (jazz), recorded by Joe LoCascio, both released in 2007; Collaborations (album), recorded by Will Taylor and Strings Attached , featuring Eliza Gilkyson, Shawn Colvin, Patrice Pike, Ian Moore, Guy Forsyth, Ruthie Foster, Libby Kirkpatrick, Jimmy LaFave, Slaid Cleaves, and Barbara K., released 2006; *Goodnight Venus* (album), recorded by Libby Kirkpatrick, released in 2003, and *Be Cool Be Kind* (album), recorded by Carla Helmbrecht (jazz), released January 2001.

◐ HOLOGRAPHIC RECORDS

Longworth Hall, 700 West Pete Rose Way, Suite 390, P.O. Box 18, Cincinnati OH 45203. (513)442-3886. **Fax:** (513)834-9390. **E-mail:** info@holographicrecords.com. **Website:** www.holographicrecords.com.

HOW TO CONTACT Call or e-mail first and obtain permission to submit.

MUSIC Jazz, progressive. Current acts include Acumen (progressive jam rock), John Novello (fusion), Alex Skolnick Trio (progressive jazz), Jeff Berlin (jazz), Poogie Bell Band (urban jazz), Dave LaRue (fusion), Mads Eriksen (fusion).

◐ HOPELESS RECORDS

PO Box 7495, Van Nuys CA 91409. **E-mail:** information@hopelessrecords.com. **E-mail:** ar@hopelessrecords.com. **Website:** www.hopelessrecords.com. Founded in 1993, Hopeless Records is a Southern Cal-

ifornia independent record label home to Yellowcard, All Time Low, Silverstein, Bayside, Enter Shikari, The Wonder Years, Taking Back Sunday, The Used, and many more. Throughout the 20 year history of Hopeless Records the label has released more than 100 albums and launched the careers of Avenged Sevenfold, Thrice, and Melee. In 1999, Hopeless Records formally started supporting non-profit organizations under the Sub City name with charitable albums, tours, and events. Now itself a registered 501c3 non profit organization, Sub City continues this mission of raising funds and awareness for worthy causes and to date has raised more than $2 million dollars for over 50 non-profit organizations.

HOW TO CONTACT E-mail ar@hopelessrecords.com with your band name in the subject. Send us your bio, Myspace, Youtube videos, EPKs, etc. If you attach mp3's, do not attach more than 1-2 of your best songs to the e-mail. We are no longer accepting physical submissions.

MUSIC Works with such artists as Divided by Friday, Bayside, Driver Friendly, New Found Glory, The Used, Taking Back Sunday, Neck Deep, and more.

○ HOTTRAX RECORDS

1957 Kilburn Dr. NE, Atlanta GA 30324. **E-mail:** hotwax@hottrax.com. **Website:** www.hottrax.com.

◖　　Also see the listing for Alexander Janoulis Productions/Big Al Jano Productions in the Record Producers section of this book.

DISTRIBUTED BY Get Hip Inc., DWM Music and Super D.

HOW TO CONTACT *E-mail first to obtain permission to submit.* Prefers an e-link to songs and lyrics in the e-mail. Does not return CDs or printed material. Responds in 6 months. "When submissions get extremely heavy, we do not have the time to respond/return material we pass on. We do notify those sending the most promising work we review, however. Current economic conditions may also affect song acceptance and response."

MUSIC Mostly blues/blues rock, some top 40/pop, rock, and country; also hardcore punk and jazz-fusion. Released *Power Pop Deluxe* (album), by Secret Lover featuring Delanna Protas, *Some of My Best Friends Have the Blues* (album), by Big Al Jano, *Hot to Trot* (album), written and recorded by Starfoxx (rock); *Lady That Digs The Blues* (album), recorded by Big Al Jano's Blues Mafia Show (blues rock); and

Vol. III, Psychedelic Era. 1967-1969 (album), released 2002 on Hottrax. Other artists include Big Al Jano, Sammy Blue, and Sheffield & Webb. Released in 2010: *So Much Love* (album), by Michael Rozakis & Yorgos; Beyond the Shadows—Then and Now, by Little Phil. Scheduled: *Rare Pidgeon* (CD) by Rick Ware.

◐ IDOL RECORDS

P.O. Box 140344, Dallas TX 75214. (214)370-5417. **E-mail:** info@idolrecords.com. **Website:** www.idolrecords.com. **Contact:** Erv Karwelis, president. Releases 30 singles, 80 LPs, 20 EPs and 10-15 CDs/year. Pays negotiable royalty to artists on contract; negotiable rate to publisher per song on recoRoad

DISTRIBUTED BY Super D (SDID).

HOW TO CONTACT See website at www.IdolRecords.com for submission policy. No phone calls or e-mail follow-ups.

MUSIC Mostly rock, pop, and alternative; also some hip-hop. The O's *Between The Two* (album), Here Holy Spain *Division* (album), Calhoun *Heavy Sugar* (album), Little Black Dress *Snow in June* (album), all released 2009-12 on Idol Records. Other artists include Flickerstick, DARYL, Centro-matic, The Deathray Davies, GBH, PPT, The Crash that Took Me, Shibboleth, Trey Johnson, Black Tie Dynasty, Old 97's.

◐ IMAGEN RECORDS

3905 National Dr. Ste. 440, Burtonsville MD 20866. **E-mail:** info@imagenrecords.com. **Website:** www.imagenrecords.com. Imagen Records is a full service Indie label based in the Washington, D.C. area. Imagen artists represent the best in rock, pop, hip-hop and R&B. With a growing roster of innovative artists, Imagen Records has significant resources and experience that supports our artists to maximize success. Founded by a musician and business person, Imagen artists enjoy a fully collaborative artist development process with a 360 degree perspective. In the current market environment, Imagen has the ability to make significant investments in new talent which gives a strong competitive edge in the marketplace. As a label that was founded in 2007, Imagen employs the newest most innovative methods to maximize use of new media and technologies including new fanbase management and content delivery methods.

HOW TO CONTACT Contact via online form.

MUSIC Rock, pop, hip-hop, and R&B. Artists include Framing & Hanley, New Medicine, 3 Years Hollow, Separation, and Candlelight Red.

◷⊘ INTERSCOPE/GEFFEN/A&M RECORDS

2220 Colorado Ave., Santa Monica CA 90404. (310)865-1000. **Fax:** (310)865-7908. **Website:** www.interscoperecords.com. Labels include Blackground Records, Cherrytree Records, will.i.am's music group and Aftermath Records. Record company.

◖ Interscope/Geffen/A&M is a subsidiary of Universal Music Group, one of the "Big 3" major labels.

HOW TO CONTACT *Does not accept unsolicited submissions.*

MUSIC Artists include Beck, U2, M.I.A, Keane, Lady Gaga, and ...And You Will Know Us By The Trail Of Dead.

⊘ ISLAND/DEF JAM MUSIC GROUP

825 Eighth Ave., New York NY 10019. (212)333-8000. **Fax:** (212)603-7654. **Website:** www.islanddefjam.com.

◖ Island/Def Jam is a subsidiary of Universal Music Group, one of the "Big 3" major labels.

HOW TO CONTACT *Island/Def Jam Music Group does not accept unsolicited submissions. Do not send material unless requested.*

MUSIC Artists include Bon Jovi, Rick Ross, Fall Out Boy, The Gaslight Anthem, Kanye West, Rihanna, The Killers, Jay-Z, Babyface, Snow Patrol, and Ludacris.

JEROME PROMOTIONS & MARKETING INC.

2535 Winthrope Way, Lawrenceville GA 30044. (770)982-7055. **Fax:** (770)982-1882. **Website:** www.jeromepromotions.com.

HOW TO CONTACT Use mailing address or online form (allows attachment of MP3s.) Contact first and obtain permission to submit a demo. Include CD with 5 songs and cover letter. Does not return submissions. Responds in 1 week.

MUSIC Mostly interested in top 40, adult contemporary, hot AC; also R&B, alternativeand hip-hop crossover. Does not want rap, country, gospel, hard rock.

◐ KILL ROCK STARS

107 SE Washington St. Suite 155, Portland OR 97214. **Website:** www.killrockstars.com.

DISTRIBUTED BY Redeye Distribution.

HOW TO CONTACT *Does not accept or listen to demos sent by mail.* Will listen to links online only if in a touring band coming through Portland. "If you are not touring through Portland, don't send us anything." Prefers link to Web page or EPK. Does not return material.

MUSIC Mostly punk rock, neo-folk or anti-folk and spoken woRoad Artists include Deerhoof, The Decemberists, Boats, Xiu Xiu, The Gossip, Horse Feathers, Erase Errata, The Thermals, Kinski, Marnie Stern, and Two Ton Boa.

TIPS "We will only work with touring acts, so let us know if you are playing Portland. Particularly interested in young artists with indie-rock background."

KORDA RECORDS

po box 2346, Minneapolis MN 55402. **E-mail:** info@kordarecords.com; allison@kordarecords.com. **Website:** www.kordarecords.com. **Contact:** Allison LaBonne. Korda Records is a Minneapolis based record label cooperative launched in 2012 by Allison LaBonne (Typsy Panthre, The Starfolk, The Owls), David Schelzel (The Ocean Blue), Brian Tighe (The Starfolk, The Hang Ups, The Owls) and the Legendary Jim Ruiz (Jim Ruiz Set).

○ LANDMARK COMMUNICATIONS GROUP

P.O. Box 1444, Hendersonville TN 37077. **E-mail:** lmarkcom@bellsouth.net. **Website:** www.landmarkcommunicationsgroup.com. Labels include Jana and Landmark Records. Record company, record producer, music publisher (Newcreature Music/BMI and Mary Megan Music/ASCAP) and management firm (Landmark Entertainment). Releases 6 singles, 8 CDs/year. Pays 5-7% royalty to artists on contract; statutory rate to publisher for each record sold.

HOW TO CONTACT Submit demo by mail. Unsolicited submissions are OK. Prefers mp3 or CD with 2-4 songs and lyric sheet. Responds in 1 month.

MUSIC Mostly country/crossover, Christian. Recent projects: *Smoky Mountain Campmeeting* by Various Artists; *The Pilgrim & the Road* by Tiffany Turner; *Fallow Ground* by C.J. Hall; *Prince Charming is Dead* by Kecia Burcham.

TIPS "Be professional in presenting yourself."

○ LARK RECORD PRODUCTIONS, INC.

P.O. Box 35726, Tulsa OK 74153. (918)786-8896. **Fax:** (918)786-8897. **E-mail:** janajae@janajae.com. **Website:** www.janajae.com.

HOW TO CONTACT Submit demo by mail. Unsolicited submissions are OK. Prefers CD or DVD with 3 songs and lead sheets. Does not return material. Responds only if interested.

MUSIC Mostly country, bluegrass, and classical; also instrumentals. Released "Ashokan Farewell," "Fiddlestix" (single by Jana Jae); "Mayonnaise" (single by Steve Upfold); and "Flyin' South" (single by Cindy Walker), all recorded by Jana Jae on Lark Records (country). Other artists include Sydni, Hotwire, and Matt Greif.

◑ MAGNA CARTA RECORDS

A-1 Country Club Road, East Rochester NY 14445. (585)381-5224. **E-mail:** info@magnacarta.net. **Website:** www.magnacarta.net.

HOW TO CONTACT Submit physical demo CD to the address above. Requirements: Artist must be touring. Artist must be established in their local scene. Artist must have a web presence: Myspace, Facebook, Twitter, YouTube, etc. When sending a physical demo please the take time and effort to package it properly. Include all relevant materials.

MUSIC Mostly progressive metal, progressive rock, and progressive jazz.

⊘ MATADOR RECORDS

304 Hudson St., 7th Floor, New York NY 10013. (212)995-5882. **Fax:** (212)995-5883. **E-mail:** info@matadorrecords.com. **Website:** www.matadorrecords.com.

HOW TO CONTACT "We are sorry to say that we *no longer accept unsolicited demo submissions.*"

MUSIC Alternative rock. Artists include Lou Reed, Pavement, Belle and Sebastian, Cat Power, Jay Reatard, Sonic Youth, Yo La Tengo, Mogwai, The New Pornographers, and more.

◒⊘ MCA NASHVILLE

1904 Adelicia St., Nashville TN 37212. (615)340-5400. **Fax:** (615)340-5491. **Website:** www.umgnashville.com.

○   MCA Nashville is a subsidiary of Universal Music Group, one of the "Big 3" major labels.

HOW TO CONTACT *MCA Nashville cannot accept unsolicited submissions.*

MUSIC Artists include Tracy Byrd, George Strait, Vince Gill, Sugarland, The Mavericks, and Shania Twain.

○ MEGAFORCE RECORDS

P.O. Box 63584, Philadelphia PA 19147. (215)922-4612. **Fax:** (509)757-8602. **Website:** www.megaforcerecords.com.

DISTRIBUTED BY Red/Sony Distribution.

HOW TO CONTACT *Contact first and obtain permission to submit.* Submissions go to the Philadelphia office.

MUSIC Mostly rock. Artists include Truth and Salvage, The Meat Puppets, and The Disco Biscuits.

◐ METAL BLADE RECORDS

5737 Kanan Road #143, Agoura Hills CA 91301. (805)522-9111. **Fax:** (805)522-9380. **E-mail:** metalblade@metalblade.com. **Website:** www.metalblade.com.

HOW TO CONTACT Submit demo through website form. Does not accept physical copies of demos. Unsolicited submissions are OK. Response time varies, but "be patient."

MUSIC Mostly heavy metal and industrial; also hardcore, gothic and noise. Released "Gallery of Suicide," recorded by Cannibal Corpse; "Voo Doo," recorded by King Diamond; and "A Pleasant Shade of Gray," recorded by Fates Warning, all on Metal Blade Records. Other artists include As I Lay Dying, The Red Chord, The Black Dahlia Murder, and Unearth.

TIPS "Metal Blade is known throughout the underground for quality metal-oriented acts."

◑ MINT 400 RECORDS

E-mail: mint400recs@yahoo.com. **Website:** www.fairmontMusic.com/1/m4r.html. **Contact:** Neil Sabatino, owner. A northern New Jersey indie rock record label focusing on the digital marketplace.

HOW TO CONTACT Send links to streaming music.

MUSIC Acts include Fairmont, Any Day Parade, The Trashpickers, Dave Charles, Jack Skuller, Ladybirds, Depression State Troopers, Sink Tapes, and many more.

TIPS "I like a lot of different kinds of music and on the label we have everything from old timey country to surf to indie rock to 60's motown. What I am most interested in is great songwriting and an original singing voice. We do digital distro, recording, producing, engineering, mastering, video editing, web design, art and graphic design, music licensing, radio promotion and a little PR. Some bands need all of our services and some do not, but we are more then willing to help with every aspect of your music career. We do not give cash advances or tour support. We as well deal only in digital records and do not press anything. However for bands who foot the bill for pressings of vinyl we do have distro."

◯ MODAL MUSIC, INC.

P.O. Box 6473, Evanston IL 60204-6473. (847)864-1022. **E-mail:** info@modalMusic.com. **Website:** www.modalMusic.com.

HOW TO CONTACT Submit demo package by mail. Unsolicited submissions are OK. Prefers CD with bio, PR, brochures, any info about artist and music. Does not return material. Responds in 4 months.

MUSIC Mostly ethnic and world. Released "St. James Vet Clinic" (single by T. Doehrer/Z. Doehrer) from *Wolfpak Den Recordings* (album), recorded by Wolfpak, released 2005; "Dance The Night Away (single by T. Doehrer) from *Dance The Night Away* (album), recorded by Balkan Rhythm Band™; "Sid Beckerman's Rumanian" (single by D. Jacobs) from *Meet Your Neighbor's Folk Music* (album), recorded by Jutta & The Hi-Dukes; and *Hold Whatcha Got* (album), recorded by Razzemetazz, all on Modal Music Records. Other artists include Ensemble M'chaiya, Nordland Band™ and Terran's Greek Band.

TIPS "Please note our focus is primarily traditional and traditionally-based ethnic which is a very limited, non-mainstream market niche. You waste your time and money by sending us any other type of music. If you are unsure of your music fitting our focus, please call us before sending anything. Put your name and contact info on every item you send!"

◕◯ NERVOUS RECORDS

5 Sussex Crescent, Northolt, Middx UB5 4DL United Kingdom. 44(020)8423 7373. **Fax:** 44(020)8423 7713. **E-mail:** info@nervous.co.uk. **Website:** www.nervous.co.uk. **Contact:** R. Williams. Record company (Nervous Records), record producer and music publisher (Nervous Publishing and Zorch Music). Member: MCPS, PRS, PPL, ASCAP, NCB. Releases 2 albums/year. Pays 8-12% royalty to artists on contract; statutory rate to publisher per song on records. Royalties paid directly to US songwriters and artists or through US publishing or recording affiliate.

◌ Nervous Records' publishing company, Nervous Publishing, is listed in the Music Publishers section.

HOW TO CONTACT Unsolicited submissions are OK. Prefers CD with 4-15 songs and lyric sheet. SAE and IRC. Responds in 3 weeks.

MUSIC Mostly psychobilly and rockabilly. "No heavy rock, AOR, stadium rock, disco, soul, pop—only wild rockabilly and psychobilly." Released *Extra Chrome*, written and recorded by Johnny Black; *It's Still Rock 'N' Roll to Me*, written and recorded by The Jime. Other artists include Restless Wild and Taggy Tones.

OGLIO RECORDS

23759 Madison St., Torrance CA 90505. (310)791-8600. **Fax:** (310)791-8670. **Website:** www.oglio.com.

HOW TO CONTACT *No unsolicited demos. Use online form to contact.*

MUSIC Mostly alternative rock and comedy. Released *Shine* (album), recorded by Cyndi Lauper (pop); *Live At The Roxy* (album), recorded by Brian Wilson (rock); *Team Leader* (album), recorded by George Lopez (comedy).

OUTSTANDING RECORDS

P.O. Box 2111, Huntington Beach CA 92647. **Website:** www.outstandingrecords.com.

DISTRIBUTED BY All full CDs listed on the website can be ordered directly through the website. Most of them are now available via download through iTunes, Napster, Rhapsody, Amazon/mp3, EMusic, or Yahoo. Whenever wholesale distributors contact me for specific orders, I am happy to work with them, especially distributors overseas.

HOW TO CONTACT Submit demo by mail. Unsolicited submissions are OK. Prefers CD (full albums), lyric sheet, photo and cover letter. Include SASE. Responds in 3 weeks.

MUSIC Mostly jazz, rock and country; also everything else especially Latin. Does not want music with negative, anti-social or immoral messages. "View our website for a listing of all current releases."

TIPS "We prefer to receive full CDs, rather than just three numbers. A lot of submitters suggest we release their song in the form of singles, but we just can't bother with singles at the present time. Especially looking for performers who want to release their material on my labels. Some songwriters are pairing up with performers and putting out CDs with a 'Writer Presents the Performer' concept. No dirty language. Do not encourage listeners to use drugs, alcohol or engage in immoral behavior. I'm especially looking for upbeat, happy, danceable music."

THE PANAMA MUSIC GROUP OF COMPANIES

Ebrel House, 2a Penlee Close, Praa Sands, Penzance, Cornwall TR20 9ST England. +44 (0)1736 762826. **Fax:** +44 (0)1736 763328. **E-mail:** panamus@aol.com.

Website: www.songwriters-guild.co.uk; www.panamaMusic.co.uk. **Contact:** Roderick G. Jones, CEO, A&R. Labels include Pure Gold Records, Panama Music Library, Rainy Day Records, Panama Records, Mohock Records, Digimix Records Ltd. (www.digimixrecords.com and www.myspace.com/digimixrecords). Registered members of Phonographic Performance Ltd. (PPL). Record company, Music publisher, production and development company (Panama Music Library, Melody First Music Library, Eventide Music Library, Musik Image Music Library, Promo Sonor International Music Library, Caribbean Music Library, ADN Creation Music Library, Piano Bar Music Library, Corelia Music Library, PSI Music Library, Scamp Music, First Time Music Publishing U.K.), Digimix Music Publishing, registered members of the Mechanical Copyright Protection Society (MCPS) and the Performing Right Society (PRS) (London, England UK), management firm and record producer (First Time Management & Production Co.). Staff size: 6. Pays variable royalty to artists on contract; statutory rate to publisher per song on record subject to deal.

DISTRIBUTED BY Media U.K. Distributors and Digimix Worldwide Digital Distribution.

HOW TO CONTACT Submit demo package by mail. Unsolicited submissions are OK. CD only with unlimited number of songs/instrumentals and lyric or lead sheets where necessary. "We do not return material so there is no need to send return postage. We will, due to volume of material received only respond to you if we have any interest. Please note: no MP3 submissions, attachments, downloads, or referrals to Websites in the first instance via e-mail. Do not send anything by recorded delivery or courier as it will not be signed for. If we are interested, we will follow up for further requests and offers as necessary."

MUSIC All styles. Published by Scamp Music: "F*ck Me I'm Famous" written by Paul Clarke & Matthew Dick (film/DVD [Universal Films, Hollywood] & single & album track [Universal Records]), released worldwide in *Get Him to the Greek*, Universal films Hollywood, starring Russell Brand, recorded by Dougal & Gammer, "We Killed The Rave" (voted best hardcore track of 2013), recorded by Dougal & Gammer, released as an album track on Clubland Xtreme Hardcore 9 by Universal Records in 2013, Published by Scamp Music. Also published "Get Your Lovekicks" (soul/R&B), recorded by Leonie Parker, released by

Digimix Records Ltd; "Country Blues" (country), recorded by The Glen Kirton Country Band on Digimix Records Ltd, published by Scamp Music; "Guitar Hero" (hardcore), recorded by Dougal & Gammer, released by Universal Records/All Around the World; published by Scamp Music: "I Get Stoned" (hardcore dance) recorded by AudioJunkie & Stylus, released by EMI records on *Hardcore Nation 2009*, published by Panama Music Library; "Everytime I Hear Your Name" (pop dance), recorded by Cascada, released by All Around The World/Universal Records, published by Scamp Music; "The Leaves of Paradise" 9 track album (mind, body, & soul) by Kevin Kendle release 2013 by Eventide Music and Digimix Records Ltsd, published by Panama Music Library, and many more.

PAPER + PLASTICK

E-mail: paperandplastick@gmail.com. **Website:** www.paperandplastick.com.

MUSIC Rock, punk, and more. Artists include: Dopamines, Andrew Dost, Coffee Project, Foundation, Gatorface, Blacklist Royals, Landmines, We are the Union, and more.

◐ PARLIAMENT RECORDS

357 S. Fairfax Ave. #430, Los Angeles CA 90036. (323)653-0693. **Fax:** (323)653-7670. **Website:** www.parliamentrecords.com.

HOW TO CONTACT Submit demo package by mail. Unsolicited submissions are OK. Prefers CD with 3-10 songs and lyric sheet. Include SASE. "Mention Songwriter's Market. Please make return envelope the same size as the envelopes you send material in, otherwise we cannot send everything back." Responds in 6 weeks.

MUSIC Mostly R&B, soul, dance, and top 40/pop; also gospel and blues. Arists include Rapture 7 (male gospel group), Wisdom Gospel Singers (male gospel group), Chosen Gospel Recovery (female gospel group), Jewel With Love (female gospel group), Apostle J. Dancy (gospel), TooMiraqulas (rap), The Mighty Voices of Joy (male gospel group) L'Nee (hip hop/soul).

TIPS "Parliament Records will also listen to 'tracks' only. If you send tracks, please include a letter stating what equipment you record on—ADAT, Protools or Roland VS recorders."

◐ PARTISAN RECORDS

Website: www.partisanrecords.com. **Contact:** Tim Putnam and Ian Wheeler. Partisan Records is a Brooklyn-based artist-run independent label dedicated to the unique visions of those we are soprivileged to represent. We believe that artistry in its many forms essentially has a singular purpose: to create and share the next new story. At Partisan, our artists create the stories that others will tell.

MUSIC Current artists include Callers, Ages of Ages, Deer Tick, Amy Wells, Dolorean, Middle Brother, Heartless Bastards, Lumerians, Phox, Mountain Man, more.

PEAPOD RECORDINGS

PO BOX 2631, South Portland MA 04116-2631. **E-mail:** info@peapodrecordings.com. **Website:** www.peapodrecordings.com. **Contact:** Ron Harrity. Peapod Recordings is a small label based out of Portland, Maine.

HOW TO CONTACT "At this time we're not looking for new artists. However we do love to hear new music, so if you just feel like sharing what you've been up to, please e-mail us with MP3 or .zip file links only. Please no attached MP3s. Also keep in mind that we can't always return e-mails regarding your music. Thanks!"

MUSIC Artists include Dead End Armory, Foam Castles, Brown Bird, If and It, Olas, Dan Blakeslee, Hearts by Darts, Honey Clouds, and many more.

◐ QUARK RECORDS

P.O. Box 452, Newtown CT 06470. (917)687-9988. **E-mail:** quarkent@aol.com. **Website:** www.quarkrecordsusa.com. **Contact:** Curtis Urbina, CEO. Record company and music publisher (Quarkette Music/BMI and Freedurb Music/ASCAP). Releases 3 singles and 3 LPs/year. Pays negotiable royalty to artists on contract; 3/4 statutory rate to publisher per song on recoRoad

HOW TO CONTACT Prefers CD with 2 songs (max). Include SASE. "Must be an absolute 'hit' song!" Responds in 6 weeks.

MUSIC Pop and electronica music only.

◯ RADICAL RECORDS

77 Bleecker St., New York NY 10012. (212)475-1111. **Fax:** (212)475-3676. **E-mail:** info@radicalrecords.com; keith@radicalrecords.com. **Website:** www.radicalrecords.com. **Contact:** Keith Masco, president; Bryan Mechutan, general manager/sales and marketing. "We do accept unsolicited demos, however please allow ample time for a response, also please note that we deal almost exclusively with punk rock. Feel free to send us your Hip-Hop, Folk, Jazz Fusion, demo but don't be surprised when we don't show up at your

door with a contract. Please make sure you have an e-mail address clearly printed on the disc or case. Most importantly, don't call us, we'll call you."

DISTRIBUTED BY City Hall, Revelation, Select-O-Hits, Choke, Southern, Carrot Top, and other indie distributors.

HOW TO CONTACT *E-mail first for permission to submit demo.* Prefers CD. Does not return material. Responds in 1 month.

MUSIC Mostly punk, hardcore, glam and rock.

TIPS "Create the best possible demos you can and show a past of excellent self-promotion."

RANCO RECORDS

61 Euphrasia Dr., Toronto ON M6B 3V8 Canada. (416)782-5768. **Fax:** (416)782-7170. **E-mail:** panfilo@sympatico.ca. **Contact:** Panfilo Di Matteo, president, A&R. Record company, record producer, and music publisher (Lilly Music Publishing). Staff size: 2. Releases 10 singles, 20 12" singles, 15 LPs, 20 EPs, and 15 CDs/year. Pays 25-35% royalty to artists on contract; statutory rate to publisher per song on recoRoad

HOW TO CONTACT Submit demo by mail. Unsolicited submissions are OK. Prefers CD with 3 songs and lyric or lead sheet. Does not return material. Responds in 1 month only if interested.

MUSIC Mostly dance, ballads, and rock. Released *Only This Way* (album), written and recorded by Angelica Castro; *The End of Us* (album), written and recorded by Putz, both on P. & N. Records (dance); and "Lovers" (single by Marc Singer), recorded by Silvana (dance), released on P. and N. Records.

RAVE RECORDS, INC.

Attn: Production Dept., 13400 W. Seven Mile Road, Detroit MI 48235. **E-mail:** info@raverecords.com. **Website:** www.raverecords.com. **Contact:** Carolyn and Derrick, production managers. Record company and music publisher (Magic Brain Music/ASCAP).

DISTRIBUTED BY Action Music Sales.

HOW TO CONTACT *"We do not accept unsolicited submissions."*

MUSIC Mostly alternative rock and dance. Artists include Cyber Cryst, Dorothy, Nicole, and Bukimi 3.

RCA RECORDS

550 Madison Ave., New York NY 10022. **Website:** www.rcarecords.com. Labels include RCA Records Nashville and RCA Victor. Record company.

RCA Records is a subsidiary of Sony BMG, one of the "Big 3" major labels.

DISTRIBUTED BY BMG.

HOW TO CONTACT *RCA Records does not accept unsolicited submissions.*

MUSIC Artists include The Strokes, Dave Matthews Band, Christina Aguilera, and Foo Fighters.

RED ADMIRAL RECORDS LLP

The Cedars, Elvington Lane, Hawkinge, Folkestone, Kent CT18 7AD United Kingdom. (01) (303) 893-472. **E-mail:** info@redadmiralrecords.com. **Website:** www.redadmiralrecords.com. **Contact:** Chris Ashman. Registered members of MCPS, PRS, and PPL. Record company and music publisher [Cringe Music (MCPS/PRS)].

HOW TO CONTACT Submit demo package by e-mail. Unsolicited submissions are OK. Responds if interested.

MUSIC All styles.

RED ONION RECORDS

8377 Westview, Houston TX 77055. (713)464-4653. **E-mail:** jeffwells@soundartsrecording.com. **Website:** www.soundartsrecording.com. **Contact:** Jeff Wells.

DISTRIBUTED BY Earth Records.

HOW TO CONTACT Submit demo by mail. Unsolicited submissions are OK. Prefers CD with 4 songs and lyric sheet. Does not return material. Responds in 6 weeks.

MUSIC Mostly country, blues and pop/rock. Released *Glory Baby* (album), recorded by Tony Vega Band (blues); *Two For Tuesday* (album), recorded by Dr. Jeff and the Painkilllers (blues), all released 2007 on Red Onion Records.

REPRISE RECORDS

3300 Warner Blvd., 4th Floor, Burbank CA 91505. (818)846-9090. **Website:** www.warnerbrosrecords.com. Reprise Records is a subsidiary of Warner Music Group, one of the "Big 3" major labels.

DISTRIBUTED BY WEA.

HOW TO CONTACT *Reprise Records does not accept unsolicited submissions.*

MUSIC Artists include Eric Clapton, My Chemical Romance, Michael Bublé, The Used, Green Day, Alanis Morissette, Fleetwood Mac, and Neil Young.

RISE RECORDS

15455 NW Greenbrier Pkwy., Suite 115, Beaverton OR 97006. **E-mail:** Matthew@RiseRecords.com. **Website:** www.riserecords.com. **Contact:** Matthew Gordner.

HOW TO CONTACT E-mail a link to your music (Facebook, Bandcamp, Youtube, Myspace or Purevolume) using the e-mail form on the website. "Please save your money and don't mail a press kit. Also less is more, Just send the link to your music, If we need more information we'll let you know."

MUSIC Rock, metal, alternative. Artists include Bouncing Souls, Memphis May Fire, Of Mice & Men, Secrets, Poison The Well, Transit, Hot Water Music, and more.

◐ ROADRUNNER RECORDS

902 Broadway, 8th Floor, New York NY 10010. **Website:** www.roadrunnerrecords.com.

HOW TO CONTACT Submit demo by e-mail at signmeto@roadrunnerrecords.com. Submissions are currently open.

MUSIC Rock, metal, alternative. Artists include Korn, Killswitch Engage, Opeth, Nickelback, Lenny Kravitz, Lynyrd Skynyrd, Megadeth, Slipknot, and more.

● ROBBINS ENTERTAINMENT LLC

35 Worth St., 4th Floor, Attn: A&R Dept., New York NY 10013. (212)675-4321. **Fax:** (212)675-4441. **E-mail:** info@robbinsent.com. **Website:** www.robbinsent.com.

DISTRIBUTED BY Sony/BMG.

HOW TO CONTACT If you're interested in submitting a demo to Robbins Entertainment, please follow these instructions. 1. Make sure that everything is labeled properly from artist and title, to your contact information. 2. Please send us no more than 3 tracks, and make sure they are representative of your very best. 3. Radio edits preferred. If you'd like to send a digital demo, please use download links ONLY (YouSendit, SoundCloud, or FTP etc.) and write to info@robbinsent.com. DO NOT send mp3's attached to an e-mail. These will automatically be discarded. We do listen to everything that comes through, but please keep in mind that we get a lot of submissions every week. If we like what we hear, we will contact you.

MUSIC Commercial dance only. Released top 10 pop smashes, "Heaven" (single), recorded by DJ Sammy; "Everytime We Touch" (single), recorded by Cascada; "Listen To Your Heart" (single), recored by DHT; as well as Hot 100 records from Rockell, Lasgo, Reina and K5. Other artists includel, September, Andain, Judy Torres, Jenna Drey, Marly, Dee Dee, Milky, Kreo and many others.

TIPS "Do not send your package 'Supreme-Overnight-Before-You-Wake-Up' delivery. Save yourself some money. Do not send material if you are going to state in your letter that, 'If I had more (fill in the blank) it would sound better.' We are interested in hearing your best and only your best. Do not call us and ask if you can send your package. The answer is yes. We are looking for dance music with crossover potential."

◐ ROLL CALL RECORDS

Los Angeles CA **E-mail:** info@rollcallrecords.com. **Website:** www.rollcallrecords.com. Come download some music for free at our website: www.rollcallrecords.com.

MUSIC Released albums by such artists as Army Navy, Isbells, Royal Canoe, Typhoon, Wintersleep, and more.

ROTTEN RECORDS

P.O. Box 56, Upland CA 91786. (909)920-4567. **Fax:** (909)920-4577. **E-mail:** rotten@rottenrecords.com. **Website:** www.rottenrecords.com. **Contact:** Ron Peterson, president.

DISTRIBUTED BY RIOT (Australia), Sonic Rendezvous (NL), RED (US) and PHD (Canada).

HOW TO CONTACT Submit demo package by mail. Unsolicited submissions are OK. Prefers CD or MySpace link. Does not return material.

MUSIC Mostly rock, alternative and commercial; also punk and heavy metal. Released *Paegan Terrorism* (album), written and recorded by Acid Bath; *Kiss the Clown* (album by K. Donivon), recorded by Kiss the Clown; and *Full Speed Ahead* (album by Cassidy/Brecht), recorded by D.R.T., all on Rotten Records.

TIPS "Be patient."

◑ ROUGH TRADE RECORDS

66 Golborne Road, London W10 5PS United Kingdom. **Website:** www.roughtraderecords.com.

HOW TO CONTACT Demo submissions are welcome, however we are not entitled to return any materials submitted to us. Please make sure you keep copies for yourself. Demos should be marked for attention of Paul Jones. "Due to the postal delays, you're advised to send MP3 demos online using our Soundcloud page (info at website)." To e-mail, use online form at the website.

MUSIC Alternative. Artists include Super Furry Animals, Jarvis Cocker, The Hold Steady, Emiliana Torrini, British Sea Power, The Libertines, My Morning

Jacket, Jenny Lewis, The Strokes, The Mystery Jets, The Decemberists, and more.

RUSTIC RECORDS

6337 Murray Lane, Brentwood TN 37027. (615)371-0646. **E-mail:** zach@rusticrecordsinc.com. **Contact:** Jack Schneider, president and founder; Nell Schneider; Brien Fisher.

DISTRIBUTED BY CDBaby.com and available on iTunes, MSN Music, Rhapsody, and more.

HOW TO CONTACT Submit professional demo package by mail. Unsolicited submissions are OK. CD only; no mp3s or e-mails. Include no more than 4 songs with corresponding lyric sheets and cover letter. Include appropriately-sized SASE. Responds in 4 weeks.

MUSIC Good combination of traditional and modern country. 2008-09 releases: *Ready to Ride*—debut album from Nikki Britt, featuring "C-O-W-B-O-Y," "Do I Look Like Him," "Star in My Car," and "You Happened"; *Hank Stuff* from DeAnna Cox—featuring "I'm a Long Gone Mama," and "I'm so Lonesome I Could Cry."

TIPS "Professional demo preferred."

SANDALPHON RECORDS

P.O. Box 18197, Panama City Beach FL 32417. (850)307-3030. **Contact:** A&R Department.

DISTRIBUTED BY "We are currently negotiating for distribution."

HOW TO CONTACT Submit demo package by mail. Unsolicited submissions are fine. Prefers CD with 1-5 songs with lyric sheet and cover letter. Returns submissions if accompanied by a SASE or SAE and IRC for outside the United States. Responds in 6-8 weeks.

MUSIC Mostly rock, country, and alternative; also pop, gospel, and blues.

SECRET STASH RECORDS

711 W Lake Street, Suite B, Minneapolis MN 55408. **Website:** www.secretstashrecords.com. Secret Stash Records is an independent record label owned and operated in Minneapolis, MN. We are dedicated to one thing, releasing great music in great collectible LP packages. Whether you are a DJ looking for rare grooves to sample, or just an average Joe looking for great music, we've got you covered.

HOW TO CONTACT Use online form to contact.

MUSIC Funk, soul, blues.

SILVER WAVE RECORDS

P.O. Box 7943, Boulder CO 80306. (303)443-5617. **Fax:** (303)443-0877. **E-mail:** valerie@silverwave.com. **Website:** www.silverwave.com. **Contact:** Valerie Sanford, art director.

MUSIC Mostly Native American and world.

SIMPLY GRAND MUSIC INC

P.O. Box 770208, Memphis TN 38177-0208. (901)763-4787. **E-mail:** info@simplygrandMusic.com. **Website:** www.simplygrandMusic.com. **Contact:** Linda Lucchesi, president. Record company (Simply Grand Music) and music publisher (Beckie Publishing Company). Staff size: 2. Released 9 CDs last year. Royalties are negotiable. Distributed by Ace Records and various others.

HOW TO CONTACT Contact first and obtain permission to submit a demo. Include CD and limit 3 songs per submission. Please give 2-4 weeks for a response. please include Lyrics and a sase if you want any materials returned.

MUSIC Mostly interested in country, soul/R&B, pop; also interested in top 40, soft rock. Recently published "Get Your Praise On," written by Corey Lee Barker and Jody Harris, recorded by Suzette Michaels (Christian) for *Stronger Every Day* (album) on High Mountain Records; "Pity A Fool," written by Dan Greer, recorded by Barbara & The Browns (soul), featured in "Against The Wall" on USA Network; "I Love You", written by Charles Chalmers and Domingo Samudio, performed by Richard & Walter (soul), featured in *Happy and Bleeding* movie; "Can't Find Happiness," written by Charlie Chalmers and Paul Selph, Jr., recorded by Barbara & The Browns (soul) for Can't Find Happiness (album) on Ace Records.

SMALL STONE RECORDS

P.O. Box 02007, Detroit MI 48202. (248)219-2613. **Fax:** (248)541-6536. **E-mail:** sstone@smallstone.com. **Website:** www.smallstone.com.

DISTRIBUTED BY ADA, Bertus, Cargo Records GmbH.

HOW TO CONTACT Submit CD/CD Rom by mail. Unsolicited submissions are OK. Does not return material. Responds in 2 months.

MUSIC Mostly alternative, rock and blues; also funk (not R&B). Released *Fat Black Pussy Cat*, written and recorded by Five Horse Johnson (rock/blues); *Wrecked & Remixed*, written and recorded by Morsel (indie rock, electronica); and *Only One Division*, written and recorded by Soul Clique (electronica), all on Small Stone Records. Other artists include Acid King, Perplexa, and Novadriver.

TIPS "Looking for esoteric music along the lines of Bill Laswell to Touch & Go/Thrill Jockey records material. Only send along material if it makes sense with what we do. Perhaps owning some of our records would help."

◐ SMOG VEIL RECORDS

1093 A1A Beach Blvd #343, St. Augustine Beach FL 32080. (904)547-1393. **E-mail:** franklisa@aol.com. **Website:** www.svrshop.myshopify.com. Smog Veil Records has been releasing records since 1991, most geared to the post-young, most of which are ridiculous, bombastic, and otherwise under appreciated rock and roll from Northeastern Ohio. You may have bought one.

HOW TO CONTACT Submit CD or CD-R to Frank Mauceri by mail. Does not accept submissions by e-mail or links to website. Submissions must inlcud a contact, press kit, and plans for touring. Response time is slow. Demo submissions cannot be returned to the submitter.

MUSIC Artists include Batusis, David Thomas, Thor, This Moment in Black History, Butcher Boys, and Prisoners.

◐◯ SONIC UNYON RECORDS CANADA

P.O. Box 57347, Jackson Station, Hamilton ON L8P 4X2 Canada. (905)777-1223. **Fax:** (905)777-1161. **E-mail:** jerks@sonicunyon.com. **Website:** www.sonicunyon.com. **Contact:** Tim Potocic and Mark Milne, co-owners.

DISTRIBUTED BY Caroline Distribution.

HOW TO CONTACT *Call first and obtain permission to submit.* Prefers CD. "Research our company before you send your demo. We are small; don't waste my time and your money." Does not return material. Responds in 4 months.

MUSIC Mostly rock, heavy rock and pop rock. Released *Doberman* (album), written and recorded by Kittens (heavy rock); *What A Life* (album), written and recorded by Smoother; and *New Grand* (album), written and recorded by New Grand on sonic unyon records (pop/rock). Other artists include Ad Astra Per Aspera, Wooden Stars, The Ghost is Dancing, The Nein, Simply Saucer, Raising the Fawn, and Aereogramme.

TIPS "Know what we are about. Research us. Know we are a small company. Know signing to us doesn't mean that everything will fall into your lap. We are only the beginning of an artist's career."

⊘ SONY BMG

550 Madison Ave., New York NY 10022. **Website:** www.sonyMusic.com.

◖ Sony BMG is one of the primary "Big 3" major labels.

HOW TO CONTACT For specific contact information see the listings in this section for Sony subsidiaries Columbia Records, Epic Records, Sony Nashville, RCA Records, J Records, Arista, and American Recordings.

⊘ SONY MUSIC NASHVILLE

1400 18th Ave. S, Nashville TN 37212-2809. Labels include Columbia Nashville, Arista Nashville, RCA, BNA, and Provident Music Group.

◖ Sony Music Nashville is a subsidiary of Sony BMG, one of the "Big 3" major labels.

HOW TO CONTACT *Sony Music Nashville does not accept unsolicited submissions.*

⊘◑ STAX RECORDS

Stax Records / Concord Music Group, 100 N. Crescent Drive, Beverly Hills CA 90210. **E-mail:** publicity@concordMusicgroup.com. **Website:** www.staxrecords.com. Stax Records is critical in American Music history as it's one of the most popular soul music record labels of all time—second only to Motown in sales and influence, but first in gritty, raw, stripped-down soul music. In 15 years, Stax placed more than 167 hit songs in the Top 100 on the pop charts, and a staggering 243 hits in the Top 100 R&B charts. It launched the careers of such legendary artists as Otis Redding, Sam & Dave, Rufus & Carla Thomas, Booker T, & the MGs, and numerous others. Among the many artists who recorded on the various Stax Records labels were the Staple Singers, Luther Ingram, Wilson Pickett, Albert King, Big Star, Jesse Jackson, Bill Cosby, Richard Pryor, the Rance Allen Group, and Moms Mabley.

MUSIC Current Stax recording artists include Ben Harper, Booker T. Jones, and others.

◐ STONES THROW RECORDS

2658 Griffith Park Blvd #504, Los Angeles CA 90039. **E-mail:** losangeles@stonesthrow.com. **Website:** www.stonesthrow.com.

HOW TO CONTACT Stones Throw recieves a lot of unsolicited demos that we don't always have time to listen to, but don't let that discourage you from sending us your music. Please take the time to check the following points before sending anything. Acceptable formats are vinyl, CD, even cassette. NO MP3 files via e-mail. They will be blocked & unheaRoad We get a lot of Bandcamp, Soundcloud, Myspace and other links with music—too many to listen to, but we hear them too. We receive hundreds of demos every year, so put your best track first. We cannot acknowledge receipt of your submission. Calling or e-mailing to make sure the package has been received will not improve your chances of it being heaRoad

MUSIC One of the leading names in underground hip-hop. Artists include 7 Days of Funk, Anika, J Rocc, The Stepkids, James Pants, Madvillain, Arabian Prince, Jonwayne, more.

⊘ SUGAR HILL RECORDS

NC **E-mail:** info@sugarhillrecords.com. **Website:** www.sugarhillrecords.com.

🔾 Welk Music Group acquired Sugar Hill Records in 1998.

HOW TO CONTACT *No unsolicited submissions.* "If you are interested in having your music heard by Sugar Hill Records or the Welk Music Group, we suggest you establish a relationship with a manager, publisher, or attorney that has an ongoing relationship with our company. We do not have a list of such entities."

MUSIC Mostly Americana, bluegrass, and country. Artists include Nitty Gritty Dirt Band, Sarah Jarosz, Donna the Buffalo, The Infamous Stringdusters, Joey + Rory, and Sam Bush.

◐ TEXAS ROSE RECORDS

2002 Platinum St., Garland TX 75042. (972)898-2032. **E-mail:** txrrl@aol.com. **Website:** www.texasroserecords.com. **Contact:** Nancy Baxendale, president. Record company, music publisher (Yellow Rose of Texas Publishing) and record producer (Nancy Baxendale). Staff size: 1. Releases 3 CDs/year. Pays negotiable royalty to artists on contract; statutory rate to publisher per song on recoRoad

DISTRIBUTED BY Self distribution.

HOW TO CONTACT *E-mail first for permission to submit.* Submit maximum of 2 songs via mp3 file with copy of lyrics in Word format. Does not return material. Responds only if interested.

MUSIC Mostly country, soft rock, pop, and R&B. Does not want hip-hop, rap, heavy metal. Released *Flyin' High Over Texas* (album), recorded by Dusty Martin (country); *High On The Hog* (album), recorded by Steve Harr (country); *Time For Time to Pay* (album), recorded by Jeff Elliot (country); *Double XXposure* (album), recorded by Jeff Elliott and Kim Neeley (country), Pendulum Dream (album) recorded by Maureen Kelly (Americana) and "Cowboy Super Hero" (single) written and recorded by Robert Mauldin.

TIPS "We are interested in songs written for today's market with a strong musical hook and a great chorus. No home recordings, please."

⊘ TOMMY BOY ENTERTAINMENT LLC

120 Fifth Ave., 7th Floor, New York NY 10011. **E-mail:** info@tommyboy.com. **Website:** www.tommyboy.com.

DISTRIBUTED BY WEA, Subway Records.

HOW TO CONTACT E-mail to obtain current demo submission policy.

MUSIC Artists include Chavela Vargas, Afrika Bambaataa, Biz Markie, Kool Keith, and INXS.

◑ TOPCAT RECORDS

P.O. Box 670234, Dallas TX 75367. (972)484-4141. **Website:** www.topcatrecords.com.

DISTRIBUTED BY City Hall.

HOW TO CONTACT *Call first and obtain permission to submit.* Prefers CD. Does not return material. Responds in 1 month.

MUSIC Mostly blues, swing, rockabilly, Americana, Texana and R&B. Released *If You Need Me* (album), written and recorded by Robert Ealey (blues); *Texas Blueswomen* (album by 3 Female Singers), recorded by various (blues/R&B); and *Jungle Jane* (album), written and recorded by Holland K. Smith (blues/swing), all on Topcat. Released CDs: *Jim Suhler & Alan Haynes—Live*; Bob Kirkpatrick *Drive Across Texas*; *Rock My Blues to Sleep* by Johnny Nicholas; *Walking Heart Attack*, by Holland K. Smith; *Dirt Road* (album), recorded by Jim Suhler; *Josh Alan Band* (album), recorded by Josh Alan; *Bust Out* (album), recorded by Robin Sylar. Other artists include Grant Cook, Muddy Waters, Big Mama Thornton, Big Joe Turner, Geo. "Harmonica" Smith, J.B. Hutto and Bee Houston. "View our website for an up-to-date listing of releases."

TIPS "Send me blues (fast, slow, happy, sad, etc.) or good blues oriented R&B. No pop, hip-hop, or rap."

TRANSDREAMER RECORDS

P.O. Box 1955, New York NY 10113. **Website:** www.transdreamer.com. Transdreamer Records started in October, 2002, as a small alternative label with a vision to develop extremely high quality artists. The name, Transdreamer, symbolizes artists and projects that attempt to transcend normal genre conventions. The Transdreamer logo does not subscribe to the typical "steady product flow, cram-as-many-releases-into the market as possible, hopefully one will hit" mentality. Fewer releases hopefully means focus, and a high level of excellence and great music.

DISTRIBUTED BY Red/Sony.

HOW TO CONTACT Feel free to send in your demo to the above address, but please don't call us asking if it's any good. If we are interested, we will harass you. Thanks.

MUSIC Mostly alternative/rock. Artists include The Delgados, Arab Strap, Dressy Bessy, The Dig, and Holly Golightly.

UAR RECORDS

Box 1264, 6020 W. Pottstown Road, Peoria IL 61654-1264. (309)673-5755. **Fax:** (309)673-7636. **Website:** www.unitedcyber.com/uarltd.

⚬ Also see the listings for Kaysarah Music (ASCAP) and Jerjoy Music (BMI) in the Music Publishers section of this book.

HOW TO CONTACT "If you are an artist seeking a record deal, please send a sample of your vocal and/or songwriting work-guitar and vocal is fine, no more than 4 songs. Fully produced demos are NOT necessary. Also send brief information on your background in the business, your goals, etc. If you are NOT a songwriter, please send 4 songs maximum of cover tunes that we can use to evaluate your vocal ability. If you wish a reply, please send a SASE, otherwise, you will not receive an answer. If you want a critique of your vocal abilities, please so state as we do not routinely offer critiques. Unsolicited submissions are OK. If you wish all of your material returned to you, be sure to include mailing materials and postage. WE DO NOT RETURN PHONE CALLS."

MUSIC Mostly American and Irish country. Released "When Jackie Sang The Walking Talking Dolly," "Far Side Banks of Jordan," "There's You," all recorded by Jerry Hanlon. "Lisa Dance With Me," "Philomena From Ireland," "Rainbow," "I'd Better Stand Up," all recorded by the Heggarty Twins from Northern Ireland and Jerry Hanlon. "An Ordinary Woman," "All Your Little Secrets," recorded by Anne More.

TIPS "We are a small independent company, but our belief is that every good voice deserves a chance to be heard and our door is always open to new and aspiring artists."

UNIVERSAL MOTWON RECORDS

1755 Broadway, #6, New York NY 10019. (212)373-0600. **Fax:** (212)373-0726. **Website:** www.universalmotown.com.

⚬ Universal Motown Records is a subsidiary of Universal Music Group, one of the "Big 3" major labels.

HOW TO CONTACT *Does not accept unsolicited submissions.*

MUSIC Artists include Lil' Wayne, Erykah Badu, Days Difference, Kem, Paper Route, and Kelly Rowland.

VAGRANT RECORDS

6351 Wilshire Blvd., Los Angeles CA 90048. **E-mail:** publicity@vagrant.com; info@vagrant.com. **Website:** www.vagrant.com.

HOW TO CONTACT Send demos to demosubmissions@vagrant.com.

MUSIC Rock, alternative. Artists include PJ Harvey, The 1975, Active Child, Bad Suns, Blitzen Trapper, California Wives, Eels, James Vincent McMorrow, Wake Owl, Bombay Bicycle Club, Benjamin Francis Leftwich, AlunaGeorge, Edward Sharpe and the Magnetic Zeros, Black Joe Lewis, Reptar, and more.

THE VERVE MUSIC GROUP

1755 Broadway, 3rd Floor, New York NY 10019. (212)331-2000. **E-mail:** contact@verveMusicgroup.com. **Website:** www.verveMusicgroup.com. Record company. Labels include Verve, GRP, and Impulse! Records.

⚬ Verve Music Group is a subsidiary of Universal Music Group, one of the "Big 3" major labels.

HOW TO CONTACT *The Verve Music Group does not accept unsolicited submissions.*

MUSIC Artists include Boney James, Diana Krall, Ledisi, Herbie Hancock, Queen Latifah, and Bruce Hornsby & The Noisemakers.

VICTORY RECORDS

346 N. Justine St., Suite #504, Chicago IL 60607. **Website:** www.victoryrecords.com.

HOW TO CONTACT Submit demo using online submission manager.

MUSIC Alternative, metal, rock. Artists include The Audition, Bayside, Catch 22, Funeral For A Friend, Otep, Hawthorne Heights, Ringworm, Secret Lives of the Freemasons, Silverstein, The Tossers, Voodoo Glow Skulls, William Control, Streetlight Manifesto, and more.

⊘ VIRGIN MUSIC GROUP

5750 Wilshire Blvd., Los Angeles CA 90036. (323)462-6252. **Fax:** (310)278-6231. **Website:** www.virginrecords.com.

○   Virgin Records is a subsidiary of the EMI Group, one of the "Big 3" major labels.

DISTRIBUTED BY EMD.

HOW TO CONTACT *Virgin Music Group does not accept recorded material or lyrics unless submitted by a reputable industry source.* "If your act has received positive press or airplay on prior independent releases, we welcome your written query. Send a letter of introduction accompanied by all pertinent artist information. Do not send a demo until requested. All unsolicited materials will be returned unopened."

MUSIC Mostly rock and pop. Artists include Lenny Kravitz, Placebo, Joss Stone, Ben Harper, Iggy Pop, and Gorillaz.

WARNER BROS. RECORDS

3300 Warner Blvd., Burbank CA 91505. (818)953-3361; (818)846-9090. **Fax:** (818)953-3232. **Website:** www.wbr.com.

DISTRIBUTED BY WEA.

HOW TO CONTACT *Warner Bros. Records does not accept unsolicited material.* "All unsolicited material will be returned unopened. Those interested in having their demos heard should establish a relationship with a manager, publisher or attorney that has an ongoing relationship with Warner Bros. Records."

MUSIC Released *Van Halen 3* (album), recorded by Van Halen; *Evita* (soundtrack); and *Dizzy Up the Girl* (album), recorded by Goo Goo Dolls, both on Warner Bros. Records. Other artists include Faith Hill, Tom Petty & the Heartbreakers, Jeff Foxworthy, Porno For Pyros, Travis Tritt, Yellowjackets, Bela Fleck and the Flecktones, Al Jarreau, Joshua Redmond, Little Texas, and Curtis Mayfield.

⊘ WATERDOG RECORDS

329 W. 18th St., #313, Chicago IL 60616. (312)421-7499. **E-mail:** waterdog@waterdogMusic.com. **Website:** www.waterdogMusic.com. **Contact:** Rob Gillis.

○   "At present Waterdog Music is solely concentrating on the career of Ralph Covert and his Bad Examples, Ralph's World and theatrical music projects."

HOW TO CONTACT "Not accepting unsolicited materials, demos at this time. If submission policy changes, it will be posted on our website."

MUSIC Mostly rock and pop. *Smash Record*, by The Bad Examples, released 2011. Other artists have included Middle 8, Al Rose & The Transcendos, Kat Parsons, Torben Floor (Carey Ott), MysteryDriver, Joel Frankel, Dean III, Suzy Brack & the New Jack Lords and Matt Pingel

TIPS "Ralph Covert's children's music (Ralph's World) (past releases onwill be reissued on Waterdog in 2013). We are not looking for any other children's music performers or composers."

◑ WINCHESTER RECORDS

25 Troubadour Lane, Berkeley Springs WV 25411. **E-mail:** info@winchesterrecords.com. **Website:** www.winchesterrecords.com.

HOW TO CONTACT *Write first and obtain permission to submit.* Prefers CD with 5-10 songs and lead sheet. Include SASE. Responds in 1 month.

MUSIC Mostly bluegrass, church/religious, country, folk, gospel, progressive and rock.

⊘ WIND-UP ENTERTAINMENT

72 Madison Ave., 7th Floor, New York NY 10016. **Website:** www.winduprecords.com. Wind-up Records is a privately-owned, full-service music entertainment firm founded in 1997. The Company has successfully launched numerous multi-platinum artists, including Evanescence, Creed, Seether, and Finger Eleven and has further built on the successes of Five for Fighting and O.A.R. In addition to these marquee acts, Wind-up has scouted and developed several award-winning, newer artists, such as Civil Twilight, Company of Thieves, and Thriving Ivory. Since its inception nearly 15 years ago, the Company has shipped over 60 million units worldwide generating over $700 million in gross revenue. Wind-up

has garnered seven multi-platinum albums (including one diamond—sales over 10 million) and seven gold albums. The Company has licensed music to high-profile television shows and motion pictures and has released several motion picture soundtracks, most notably, the platinum selling, "Walk the Line" and "Daredevil," which went on to sell over 700,000 copies. Combining a team of creative A&R scouts, in-house writers, and engineers with its own recording studio and housing in New York City, Wind-up cultivates a fluid and collaborative recording process with its artists, independent of points in their career.

DISTRIBUTED BY BMG.

HOW TO CONTACT *Write first and obtain permission to submit.* Use online form. Prefers CD or DVD. Does not return material or respond to submissions.

MUSIC Mostly rock, folk and hard rock. Artists include Seether, Evanescence, Finger Eleven, Creed, and People In Planes.

TIPS "We rarely look for songwriters as opposed to bands, so writing a big hit single would be the rule of the day."

WORLD BEATNIK RECORDS

121 Walnut Lane, Rockwall TX 75032. Phone/fax: (972)771-3797. **E-mail:** tropikalproductions@gmail.com. **Website:** www.tropikalproductions.com. Record company and record producer (Jimi Towry). Staff size: 4. Releases 6 singles, 6 LPs, 6 EPs and 6 CDs/year. Pays negotiable royalty to artists on contract; statutory rate to publisher per song on recoRoad

DISTRIBUTED BY Midwest Records, Southwest Wholesale, Reggae OneLove, Ejaness Records, Ernie B's, and CD Waterhouse.

HOW TO CONTACT Submit demo by mail. Unsolicited submissions are OK. Prefers CD with lyric sheet. Include SASE. Responds in 2 weeks.

MUSIC Mostly world beat, reggae and ethnic; also jazz, hip-hop/dance, and pop. Released *Alive Montage* by Watusi; *Pura Vida* by Wave; *Jamma* by Panorama; *I and I* (album by Abby I/Jimbe), recorded by Abby I (African pop); *Rastafrika* (album by Jimbe/Richard Ono), recorded by Rastafrika (African roots reggae); and *Vibes* (album by Jimbe/Bongo Cartheni), recorded by Wave (worldbeat/jazz), all released 2001/2002 on World Beatnik. Other artists include

Ras Richi (Cameroon), Wisdom Ogbor (Nigeria), Joe Lateh (Ghana), Dee Dee Cooper, Ras Lyrix (St. Croix), Ras Kumba (St. Kitts), Gary Mon, Darbo (Gambia), Ricki Malik (Jamaica), Arik Miles, Narte's (Hawaii), Gavin Audagnotti (South Africa), and Bongo (Trinidad).

XEMU RECORDS

2 E. Broadway, Suite 901, New York NY 10038. (212)807-0290. **E-mail:** XemuRecord@aol.com. **Website:** www.xemu.com. **Contact:** Cevin Solling. Xemu Records is an independent record label, founded in 1990 in New York City by writer, filmmaker, philosopher, musician, music producer and artist Cevin Soling as a vehicle for his music and music production endeavors. Originally conceived as a "record label" nod to underground cult movements of the 60's and 70's the label has since grown to be a home to burgeoning young bands in the psychedelic music and independent music scenes.

DISTRIBUTED BY Redeye Distribution.

HOW TO CONTACT *Write first and obtain permission to submit.* Prefers CD with 3 songs. Does not return material. Responds in 2 months.

MUSIC Mostly alternative. Released *Happy Suicide, Jim!* (album) by The Love Kills Theory (alternative rock); *Howls From The Hills* (album) by Dead Meadow; *The Fall* (album), recorded by Mikki James (alternative rock); *A is for Alpha* (album), recorded by Alpha Bitch (alternative rock); *Hold the Mayo* (album), recorded by Death Sandwich (alternative rock); *Stockholm Syndrome* (album), recorded by Trigger Happy (alternative rock) all released on Xemu Records. Other artists include Morning After Girls, Spindrift, and Rumpleville.

XL RECORDINGS

One Codrington Mews, London W11 2EH United Kingdom. **Website:** www.xlrecordings.com.

HOW TO CONTACT Contact via online form.

MUSIC Alternative rock. Artists include Adele, Basement Jaxx, Radiohead, Beck, M.I.A, Peaches, Radiohead, Sigur Ros, The Horrors, The Raconteurs, The White Stripes, Thom Yorke, Vampire Weekend, and more.

RECORD PRODUCERS

///

The independent producer can best be described as a creative coordinator. He's often the one with the most creative control over a recording project and is ultimately responsible for the finished product. Some record companies have in-house producers who work with the acts on that label (although, in more recent years, such producer-label relationships are often non-exclusive). Today, most record companies contract out-of-house, independent record producers on a project-by-project basis.

WHAT RECORD PRODUCERS DO

Producers play a large role in deciding what songs will be recorded for a particular project and are always on the lookout for new songs for their clients. They can be valuable contacts for songwriters because they work so closely with the artists whose records they produce. They usually have a lot more freedom than others in executive positions and are known for having a good ear for potential hit songs. Many producers are songwriters and musicians themselves. Since they wield a great deal of influence, a good song in the hands of the right producer at the right time stands a good chance of being cut. And even if a producer is not working on a specific project, he is well-acquainted with record company executives and artists and can often get material through doors not open to you.

SUBMITTING MATERIAL TO PRODUCERS

It can be difficult to get your demo to the right producer at the right time. Many producers write their own songs and even if they don't write, they may be involved in their own publishing companies so they have instant access to all the songs in their catalogs. Also, some genres are more dependent on finding outside songs than others. A producer working with a rock group or a singer-songwriter will rarely take outside songs.

It's important to understand the intricacies of the producer/publisher situation. If you pitch your song directly to a producer first, before another publishing company publishes the song, the producer may ask you for the publishing rights (or a percentage thereof) to your song. You must decide whether the producer is really an active publisher who will try to get the song recorded again and again or whether he merely wants the publishing because it means extra income for him from the current recording project. You may be able to work out a co-publishing deal, where you and the producer split the publishing of the song. That means he will still receive his percentage of the publishing income, even if you secure a cover recording of the song by other artists in the future. Even though you would be giving up a little bit initially, you may benefit in the future.

Some producers will offer to sign artists and songwriters to "development deals." These can range from a situation where a producer auditions singers and musicians with the intention of building a group from the ground up, to development deals where a producer signs a band or singer-songwriter to his production company with the intention of developing the act and producing an album to shop to labels (sometimes referred to as a "baby record deal").

You must carefully consider whether such a deal is right for you. In some cases, such a deal can open doors and propel an act to the next level. In other worst-case scenarios, such a deal can result in loss of artistic and career control, with some acts held in contractual bondage for years at a time. Before you consider any such deal, be clear about your goals, the producer's reputation, and the sort of compromises you are willing to make to reach those goals. If you have any reservations whatsoever, don't do it.

The listings that follow outline which aspects of the music industry each producer is involved in, what type of music he is looking for, and what records and artists he's recently produced. Study the listings carefully, noting the artists each producer works with, and consider if any of your songs might fit a particular artist's or producer's style. Then determine whether they are open to your level of experience (see the A Sample Listing Decoded on page 13).

Consult the Category Index to find producers who work with the type of music you write, and the Geographic Index at the back of the book to locate producers in your area.

ADDITIONAL RECORD PRODUCERS

There are more record producers located in other sections of the book! Use the Index to find additional Record Producers within other sections who are also record producers.

Icons

For more instructional information on the listings in this book, including explanations of symbols, read the article How To Use Songwriter's Market on page 10.

WILLIAM ACKERMAN

P.O. Box 419, Bar Mills ME 04004. **E-mail:** will@williamackerman.com. **Website:** www.williamackerman.com.

MUSIC Has worked with George Winston, Michael Hedges, Heidi Anne Breyer, Fiona Joy Hawkins, Devon Rice, Erin Aas. **Music:** acoustic, alternative, instrumental.

⊘ ADR STUDIOS

250 Taxter Road, Irvington NY 10533. (914)591-5616. **Fax:** (914)591-5617. **E-mail:** adrstudios@adrinc.org. **Website:** www.adrinc.org. **Contact:** Stuart J. Allyn. Produces 6 singles and 3-6 CDs/year. Fee derived from sales royalty and outright fee from recording artist and record company.

○   *Does not accept unsolicited submissions.*

MUSIC Mostly **pop**, **rock**, **jazz**, and **theatrical**; also **R&B** and **country**. Produced *Thad Jones Legacy* (album), recorded by Vanquard Jazz Orchestra (jazz), released on New World Records. Other artists include Billy Joel, Aerosmith, Carole Demas, Michael Garin, The Magic Garden, Bob Stewart, The Dixie Peppers, Nora York, Buddy Barnes and various video and film scores.

ALLRS MUSIC PUBLISHING CO. (ASCAP)

P.O. Box 1545, Smithtown NY 11787. (718)767-8995. **E-mail:** info@allrsMusic.com. **Website:** www.allrsMusic.com. **Contact:** Renee Silvestri-Bushey, president. Music publisher, record company (MIDI Track Records), music consultant, artist management, record producer. Voting member of: NARAS (The Grammy Awards); the Country Music Association (The CMA Awards); SGMA; and Songwriters Guild of America (Diamond member). Staff size: 5. Publishes 3 songs/year; publishes 2 new songwriters/year. Pays standard royalty. Affiliate(s) Midi-Track Publishing Co. (BMI).

HOW TO CONTACT "Write/e-mail to obtain permission to submit. *We do not accept unsolicited submissions.*" Prefers CD with 3 songs, lyric sheet and cover letter. Responds via e-mail in 6 months only if interested.

MUSIC Mostly **country**, **gospel**, **top 40**, **R&B**, **MOR**, and **pop**. Does not want showtunes, jazz, classical or rap. Published "Why Can't You Hear My Prayer" (single by F. John Silvestri/Leslie Silvestri), recorded by 10-time Grammy nominee Huey Dunbar of the group DLG (Dark Latin Groove) released on Midi Track

Records including other multiple releases); "Chasing Rainbows" (single by F. John Silvestri/Leslie Silvestri), recorded by Tommy Cash (country), released on MMT Records (including other multiple releases); "Because of You" (single by F. John Silvestri/Leslie Silvestri), recorded by Iliana Medina, released on MIDI Track Records, also recorded by Grammy nominee Terri Williams of Always...Patsy Cline, released on MIDI Track Records; also recorded by Grand Ole Opry member Ernie Ashworth, and other multiple releases.

TIPS "Attend workshops, seminars, and visit our blog on our website for advise and info on the music industry."

☉● A MAJOR SOUND CORPORATION

RR # 1, Kensington PE COB 1MO Canada. **E-mail:** info@amajorsound.com; Musicpublisher@amajorsound.com. **Website:** www.amajorsound.com. **Contact:** Paul Milner, producer/engineer/mixer. Record producer and music publisher. Produces 8 CDs/year. Fee derived in part from sales royalty when song or artist is recorded, and/or outright fee from recording artist or record company, or investors. Submit demo package by mail. Unsolicited submissions are OK. Prefers CD with 5 songs and lyric sheet (lead sheet if available). Does not return material. Responds only if interested in 3 months.

MUSIC Mostly **rock**, **A/C**, **alternative** and **pop**; also **Christian** and **R&B**. Produced *COLOUR* (album written by J. MacPhee/R. MacPhee/C. Buchanan/D. MacDonald), recorded by The Chucky Danger Band (pop/rock); winner of ECMA award; *Something In Between* (album, written by Matt Andersen), recorded by Matt Andersen and Friends (Blues), released on Weatherbox/Andersen; *In A Fever In A Dream* (album,written by Pat Deighan), recorded by Pat Deighan and The Orb Weavers (Rock), released on Sandbar Music; *Saddle River String Band* (album, written by Saddle River Stringband), recorded by Saddle River Stringband (Blue Grass) released on Save As Music; winner of ECMA awaRoad

TIM ANDERSEN

(651)271-0515. **E-mail:** tandersen2005@yahoo.com. **Website:** www.timandersenrecordingengineer.com. "Can offer all those techniques to make your project rise above "the usual" to something extraordinary, the way real records are made."

MUSIC Has worked with House of Pain, Shaq, Judgement Night, SDTRK, De Jef, Patti LaBelle, Temptations, Hiroshima, Krazy Bone, Snoop Dogg. **Music:** rock, r&b, hip-hop, rap, acoustic.

ANDREW LANE

Atlanta GA (213)400-4007. **E-mail:** andrewlanester@gmail.com. **Contact:** Andrew Lane, Queen Throngkompol (Exec. Assistant).

HOW TO CONTACT E-mail Andrew Lane at andrewlanester@gmail.com or his executive assistant, Queen Throngkompol at (213)400-4007.

MUSIC Has produced such artists as The Backstreet Boys, Irene Cara, Keith Sweat, Kelly Rowland, Keana, The Clique Girls, and more. Tv and Film clients include Disney, Nikelodeon, MTV, BET, Country Music Network, HBO, ESPN, ABC Family, etc.

AUDIO 911

P.O. Box 212, Haddam CT 06438. (860)916-9947. **E-mail:** request@audio911.com. **Website:** www.audio911.com. Produces 4-8 singles, 3 LPs, 3 EPs and 4 CDs/year. Fee derived from outright fee from recording artist or record company. Submit demo by mail. Unsolicited submissions are OK. Prefers CD or DVDs with several songs and lyric or lead sheet. "Include live material if possible." Does not return material. Responds in 3 months.

MUSIC Mostly **rock**, **pop**, **top 40** and **country/acoustic**. Produced *Already Home* (album), recorded by Hannah Cranna on Big Deal Records (rock); *Under the Rose* (album), recorded by Under the Rose on Utter Records (rock); and *Sickness & Health* (album), recorded by Legs Akimbo on Joyful Noise Records (rock). Other artists include King Hop!, The Shells, The Gravel Pit, G'nu Fuz, Tuesday Welders and Toxic Field Mice.

WILLIE BASSE

Los Angeles CA (818)731-9116. **E-mail:** williebasse@gmail.com. **Website:** www.williebasse.com. **Contact:** James Wright.

MUSIC Has worked with: Canned Heat, Finis Tasby, Frank Goldwasser, Paul Shortino, Jeff Nothrup, Black Sheep. Prefers: rock, blues, heavy metal.

EVAN BEIGEL

P.O. BOX 801556, Santa Clarita CA 91380. (818)321-5472. **E-mail:** mail@evanjbeigel.com. **Website:** www.evanjbeigel.com.

MUSIC Has worked with Troup, Badi Assad, Ray Kurzweil, Gilli Moon, Michelle Featherstone, Killer Tracks. **Music:** rock, indie, alternative, folk, dance/electronica.

BEN LINDELL

EMW Music Group, 42 Broadway 22nd Floor, New York NY 10004. **E-mail:** ben@benlindell.com. **Website:** www.benlindell.com. **Contact:** Ben Lindell. Ben Lindell is a NYC based producer/mixer/engineer who has worked with hundreds of artists including MGMT, 50 Cent, Wale, Bebel Giberto and many more. In addition to being a fantastic musician he is also a tremendous geek. It's his marriage of musical creativity and technical know-how that makes him an in-demand producer/mixer/engineer.

HOW TO CONTACT Use online form to contact.

MUSIC Select clients include: 50 Cent, Soulja Boy, Wale, Ryan Leslie, Genasis, Lloyd Banks, Tony Yayo, Roshon, Illmind, Red Cafe, J.Period, Olivia, Kelly Rowland, Locnville, Chromeo, MGMT, Bebel Giberto, Rufus Wainright, Edie Brickell, and more.

BIG BEAR

P.O. Box 944, Edgbaston, Birmingham, B16 8UT United Kingdom. (0)(121)454-7020. **Fax:** (0)(121)454-9996. **E-mail:** jim@bigbearMusic.com. **Website:** www.bigbearMusic.com. **Contact:** Jim Simpson, managing director. Record producer, music publisher (Bearsongs) and record company (Big Bear Records). Produces 10 LPs/year. Fee derived from sales royalty. *Write first about your interest, then submit demo and lyric sheet.* Does not return material. Responds in 2 weeks.

Also see the listings for Bearsongs in the Music Publishers section of this book and Big Bear Records in the Record Companies section of this book.

MUSIC **Blues**, **swing**, and **jazz**.

BLUES ALLEY RECORDS

Rt. 1, Box 288, Clarksburg WV 26301. (304)598-2583. **E-mail:** hswiger@bluesalleyMusic.com. **Website:** www.bluesalleyMusic.com. Record producer, record company and music publisher (Blues Alley Publishing/BMI). Produces 4-6 LPs and 2 EPs/year. Fee derived from sales royalty when song or artist is recorded. Submit demo package by mail. Unsolicited submissions are OK. Will only accept CDs with lead sheets and typed lyrics. Does not return material. Responds in 6 weeks.

MUSIC Mostly **country, pop, Christian**, and **rock**. Produced *Monongalia*, recorded by The New Relics (country), 2009; *Chasing Venus*, recorded by The New Relics (acoustic rock), 2006; *Sons of Sirens*, recorded by Amity (rock), 2004; and *It's No Secret*, recorded by Samantha Caley (pop country), 2004.

CLIFF BRODSKY

Beverly Hills CA **E-mail:** cliff@brodskyentertainment.com. **Website:** www.cliffbrodsky.com.

MUSIC Has worked with Rose Rossi, Daize Shayne, Jason Kirk, Burning Retna, Future Kings of Spain, Jordy Towers, Brentley Gore, Cat Switzer, Justin Lanning, Warner Brothers, Universal, Sony, MCA, Virgin, Interscope. **Music:** indie, pop, rock.

◑ CHRIS GAGE

Austin TX **Website:** www.chrisgage.biz.

MUSIC Artists produced include 8 1/2 Souvenirs (co-produced with Jack Hazzard for RCA Records) Bill Small, Jody Mills, Steve Brooks, Michael Austin, Cowboy Johnson, Albert and Gage, Christine Albert, Abi Tapia, Rio King, Sharon Bousquet, Lawrence J. Clark, Boyd Bristow, Jimmie Dale Gilmore (2 songs) and Willie Nelson (one duet with Jimmie Dale Gilmore).

◑ ERIC CORNE

Los Angeles CA (310)500-8831. **E-mail:** eric@ericcorneMusic.com. **Website:** www.ericcorneMusic.com. **Contact:** Eric Corne, producer.

MUSIC Has worked with Glen Campbell, Lucinda Willaims, Joanna Wang, Michelle Shocked, DeVotchKa, Instant Karma. **Music:** rock, indie, Americana, country, blues, jazz, folk.

◑ CREATIVE SOUL

Nashville TN 37179. (615)400-3910. **E-mail:** firstcontact@creativesoulrecords.com. **Website:** www.creativesoulonline.com. Record producer. Produces 10-25 singles and 10-15 albums/year. Fee derived from outright fee from recording artist or company. Other services include consulting/critique/review services. *Contact first by e-mail to obtain permission to submit demo.* Prefers 2-3 MP3s via e-mail. Responds only if interested.

MUSIC Mostly contemporary Christian, including pop, rock, jazz, world, and ballads in the Christian and gospel genre. No southern gospel, rap, or hip hop please. Produced Arise & Shine, recorded by Adrielle K (contemporary Christian/World); Portraits of White, recorded by Frances Drost (contemporary Christian/Seasonal); Unshakable, recorded by Jeannette Petkau (contemporary Christian/Pop); all released on Creative Soul Records. Other artists include Leslie McKee, Stephen Bautista, Stephanie Newton, Mike Westendorf, Jessie Laine Powell, and Kristyn Leigh.

TIPS "Contact us first by e-mail; we are here in Nashville for you. We offer weekly free online information and monthly consults in Nashville for Christian artists and writers. We want to meet you and talk with you about your dreams. E-mail us and let's start talking about your music and ministry!"

MARC DESISTO

Sherman Oaks CA (818)522-0214. **E-mail:** marcdmix@gmail.com. **Website:** www.marcdesisto.com.

MUSIC Has worked with Stevie Nicks, Michelle Branch, Unwritten Law, Melissa Ethridge, Rick Knowles, Don Henley, Patti Smith, Mark Opitz, Tom Petty, U2. **Music:** rock, alternative, pop, indie.

JEANNIE DEVA

P.O. Box 4636, Sunland CA 91041. (818)446-0932. **E-mail:** sing@jeanniedeva.com. **Website:** www.jeanniedeva.com. **Contact:** Jeannie Deva.

MUSIC Has worked with Rounder Records, Charisse Arrington, MCA, Dar Williams, Razor and Tie Records, Alldaron West. **Music:** all contemporary styles.

⊘ JOEL DIAMOND ENTERTAINMENT

3940 Laurel Canyon Blvd., Suite 441, Studio City CA 91604. (818)980-9588. **E-mail:** jdiamond20@aol.com. **Website:** www.joeldiamond.com. **Contact:** Joel Diamond, president and CEO. Record producer, music publisher and manager. Fee derived from sales royalty when song is recorded or outright fee from recording artist or record company.

◑　　Also see the listing for Silver Blue Music/Oceans Blue Music in the Music Publishers section of this book.

MUSIC Mostly **dance, R&B, soul** and **top 40/pop**. The 5 Browns—3 number 1 CDs for Sony/BMG, David Hasselhoff; produced "One Night In Bangkok" (single by Robey); "I Think I Love You," recorded by Katie Cassidy (daughter of David Cassidy) on Artemis Records; "After the Loving" (single), recorded by E. Humperdinck; "Forever Friends," recorded by Vaneza (featured on Nickelodeon's *The Brothers Garcia*); and "Paradise" (single), recorded by Kaci.

LES DUDEK

EFLAT Productions, P.O. Box 726, Auburndale FL 33823-0726. **Website:** www.lesdudek.com.
MUSIC Has worked with Stevie Nicks, Steve Miller Band, Cher, Dave Mason, The Allman Brothers, Mike Finnigan, Bobby Whitlock. **Music:** southern rock.

● FINAL MIX INC.

2219 W. Olive Ave., Suite 102, Burbank CA 91506. **E-mail:** rob@finalmix.com. **Website:** www.finalmix.com. Releases 70 singles and 5-7 LPs and CDs/year. Fee derived from sales royalty when song or artist is recorded.

○ *Does not accept unsolicited submissions.*

MUSIC Primarily **pop**, **rock**, **dance**, **R&B**, and **rap**. Produced and/or mixer/remixer for Mary Mary, New Boyz, Kirk Franklin, Charlie Wilson, LeAnn Rimes, Charice, Train, Aaliyah, Hilary Duff, Jesse McCartney, Christina Aguilera, American Idol, Ray Charles, Quincy Jones, Michael Bolton, K-Ci and Jo Jo, Will Smith, and/or mixer/remixer for Janet Jackson, Ice Cube, Queen Latifah, Jennifer Paige, and The Corrs.

MAURICE GAINEN

4470 Sunset Blvd., Suite 177, Hollywood CA 90027. (323)662-3642. **E-mail:** mauricegainen@gmail.com. **Website:** www.mauricegainen.com. "We provide complete start to finish CD Production, including help in choosing songs and musicians through CD mastering. We also pride ourselves on setting a budget and keeping to it."

MUSIC Has worked with Stacy Golden, Yuka Takara, Donna Loren, James Webber, Andy McKee, Rafael Moreira, Alex Skolnick Trio, Metro, Mel Elias, Shelly Rudolph, Kenny Tex, Rachael Owens. **Music:** r&b, jazz, alternative, rock, pop.

BRIAN GARCIA

Los Angeles CA (626)487-0410. **E-mail:** brian@briangarcia.net. **Website:** www.briangarcia.net.
MUSIC "Producer-Mixer-Engineer Brian Garcia specializes in the genres of rock and pop. He has been part of 22 million records sold, debuts at No. 1 in 30 countries, a Grammy winning album, and a No. 1 single on iTunes as a co-writer/producer/mixer. Brian has taken artists from development to securing record deals and producing albums for EMI and Sony/BMG." Has worked with Our Lady Peace, Earshot, Until June, Galactic Cowboys, Avril Lavigne, Kelly Clarkson, Michelle Branch, Dizmas, Chantal Kreviazuk, King's X, Diana Degarmo, The Library, Pushmonkey, The Day-lights, Precious Death, Joy Drop. **Music:** rock, pop, indie.

MCKAY GARNER

1873 Eighth Ave. Suite A, San Francisco CA 94122. (323)912-9119. **E-mail:** info@mckaygarner.com. **Website:** www.mckaygarner.com.
MUSIC Producer, engineer that has worked with Red Hot Chili Peppers, Styles of Beyond, Flogging Molly, doppio, Valencia, Mike Shinoda, MichaelBublé, Sara Melson.

CARMEN GRILLO

Big Surprise Music, 1616 Ventura Blvd. Suite 522, Encino CA 91436. (818)905-7676. **E-mail:** info@carmengrillo.com. **Website:** www.carmengrillo.com.
MUSIC Has worked with Manhattan, Transfer, Chicago, Bill Champlin, Mike Finnigan, Tower of Power. **Music:** R&B, pop, rock, jazz, blues.

● HEART CONSORT MUSIC

410 First St. SW, Mt. Vernon IA 52314. **E-mail:** mail@heartconsortMusic.com. **Website:** www.heartconsortMusic.com. **Contact:** James Kennedy. Produces 2-3 CDs/year. Fee derived from sales royalty when song or artist is recorded. Submit demo package by mail. Unsolicited submissions are OK. Prefers CD with 3 songs and 3 lyric sheets. Include SASE. Responds in 3 months.

MUSIC Mostly **jazz**, **New Age** and **contemporary**. Produced *New Faces* (album), written and recorded by James Kennedy on Heart Consort Music (world/jazz).

TIPS "We are interested in jazz/New Age artists with quality demos and original ideas. We aim for an international audience."

HEATHER HOLLEY

New York NY **E-mail:** info@heatherholley.com. **Website:** www.heatherholley.com. Heather Holley is a multi-platinum selling pop Music producer and songwriter based in LA and NYC. She specializes in artist development and is known for her role in launching Christina Aguilera's career. Her songs have been featured in global ad campaigns for Pepsi, Mercedes; feature films and trailers "Pursuit of Happyness," "Honey," "Kiss of the Dragon;" TV series "Grey's Anatomy," "The Office," "90210," "Private Practice," and many more. Her article about the craft of songwriting, "Soaring With Christina Aguilera," was published in The Wall Street Journal.

MUSIC Has worked with CChristina Aguilera, Skylar Grey, Itaal Shur, Katie Costello, Nikki Williams. **Music:** pop, dance, indie, R&B.

JIMMY HUNTER

Hollywood CA (323)655-0615. **E-mail:** jimmy@jimmyhunter.com. **Website:** www.jimmyhunter.com. "When you work with Jimmy Hunter, you find a fellow artist who will help you to achieve and refine your vision. He has the experience and tools to get the ultimate sound for your music and bring out the very best in you."

MUSIC Has worked with Cher, Savannah Phillips, Smoove, Jared Justice, Lisa Rine, Lynn Tracy, Mark R. Kent, Della Reese, Lisa Gold, Jamie Palumbo, The Ramblers. **Music:** rock, pop, R&B.

ⓞ SIMON ILLA

Atlanta GA **E-mail:** info@simonilla.com. **Website:** www.simonilla.com.

MUSIC Has worked with Onyx, Vivian Green, Floetry, Roscoe P. Coldchain, The Answer. **Music:** hiphop, R&B, pop, folk, rock, gospel, emo.

ⓞ INTEGRATED ENTERTAINMENT

1815 JFK Blvd., #1612, Philadelphia PA 19103. (267)408-0659. **E-mail:** lawrence@gelboni.com. **Website:** www.gelboni.com. Estab. 1991. Produces up to 6 projects/year. Compensation is derived from outright fee from recording artist or record company and sales royalties.

HOW TO CONTACT Submit demo package by mail. Solicited submissions only. CD only with 3 songs. "Draw a guitar on the outside of envelope so we'll know it's from a songwriter." Will respond if interested.

MUSIC Mostly **rock** and **pop**. Produced *Gold Record* (album), written and recorded by Dash Rip Rock (rock) on Ichiban Records and many others.

CHRIS JULIAN

4872 Topanga Canyon Blvd., Suite 406, Woodland Hills CA 91364. (310)924-7849. **E-mail:** chris@ChrisJulian.com. **Website:** www.chrisjulianproductions.com. "Owned and operated solely by engineer/producer Chris Julian, the studio is oriented toward personal service."

MUSIC Has worked with David Bowie, Vanessa Williams, Jimmy Webb, De La Soul, Queen Latifah, Biz Markie, A Tribe Called Quest, Fat Joe, Peter Moffitt, Art Garfunkle, David Crosby, Danielle Livingston, Ray Davies, Don Was, Bobbi Humphrey, Mint, Just James, Brenda K. Star, Jimmy Webb, Naughty By Nature. **Music:** R&B, pop, rock, soul, hip-hop, jazz.

ⓞ KAREN KANE PRODUCER/ENGINEER

(910)681-0220. **E-mail:** karenkane@mixmama.com. **Website:** www.mixmama.com. **Contact:** Karen Kane. Record producer and recording engineer. Produces 3-5 CDs/year. Fee derived from sales royalty when song or artist is recorded or outright fee from recording artist or record company. *E-mail first and obtain permission to submit. Unsolicited submissions are not OK.* "Please note: I am not a song publisher. My expertise is in album production." Does not return material. Responds in 1 week.

MUSIC Mostly **acoustic Music of any kind**, **rock**, **blues**, **pop**, **alternative**, **R&B/reggae**, **country**, and **bluegrass**. Produced *Good to Me* (album), recorded by Nina Repeta; *Topless* (Juno-nominated album), recorded by Big Daddy G, released on Reggie's Records; *Mixed Wise and Otherwise* (Juno-nominated album), recorded by Harry Manx (blues). Other artists include Tracy Chapman (her first demo), Katarina Bourdeaux, Crys Matthews, Laura Bird, L Shape Lot, The Hip Hop Co-op, Barenaked Ladies (live recording for a TV special), and The Coolidge Band.

TIPS "Get proper funding to be able to make a competitive, marketable product."

TIM DAVID KELLY

Los Angeles CA (818)601-7047. **E-mail:** info@timdavidkelly.com. **Website:** www.timdavidkelly.com.

MUSIC Has worked with Kicking Harold, Shiny Toy Guns, Dokken. **Music:** alternative, metal, Americana, rock, acoustic pop.

ⓞ L.A. ENTERTAINMENT, INC.

7095 Hollywood Blvd., #826, Hollywood CA 90028. **E-mail:** info@warriorrecords.com. **Website:** www.warriorrecords.com. Record producer, record company (Warrior Records [distributed via Universal Music Distribution]) and music publisher (New Entity Music/ASCAP, New Copyright Music/BMI, New Euphonic Music/SESAC). Fee derived from sales royalty when song or artist is recorded. Submit demo package by mail. Unsolicited submissions are OK. Prefers CD and/or DVD with original songs, lyric and lead sheet if available. "We do not review Internet sites. Do not send MP3s, unless requested. All written submitted materials (e.g., lyric sheets, letter, etc.) should be typed." Does not return material unless SASE is included. Responds in 2 months only via e-mail or SASE.

MUSIC All styles. "All genres are utilized with our music supervision company for Film & TV, but our original focus is on **alternative rock** and **urban genres** (e.g., **R&B**, **rap**, **gospel**).

○ LANDMARK COMMUNICATIONS GROUP

P.O. Box 1444, Hendersonville TN 37077. (615)585-9301. **E-mail:** ba@landmarkcommunicationsgroup.com. **Website:** www.landmarkcommunications-group.com. **Contact:** Bill Anderson Jr., producer. Record producer, record company, music publisher (Newcreature Music/BMI) and TV/radio syndication. Produces 6 singles and 6 LPs/year. Fee derived from sales royalty. *Write first and obtain permission to submit.* Prefers CD, mp3 with 4-10 songs and lyric sheet. Include SASE.

○ Also see the listings for Landmark Communications Group in the Record Companies section of this book.

MUSIC Country crossover. Recent projects: *Smoky Mountain Campmeeting* by Various Artists; *The Pilgrim & the Road* by Tiffany Turner; *Fallow Ground* by C.J. Hall; *Prince Charming is Dead* by Kecia Burcham.

○ LINEAR CYCLE PRODUCTIONS

P.O. Box 2608, North Hills CA 91393. **E-mail:** accessiblyliveoffline@gmail.com. **Website:** www.linearcycle-productions.com.

MUSIC Mostly **rock/pop**, **R&B/blues** and **country**; also **gospel** and **comedy**. Produced "Giving it All to Me" (single by Pandanceski/Katz/Purewhite), recorded by Monea Later (pop/dance), released on Tozic Googh Sounds. "P for the Bits" (G Glix) (single by Hyram Yip Pea) from his Last Sound Collection, recorded and released on "Swip" brand mp3s; and "Back into the Box Sho Nuff" (single by Blyma/Warmwater/Posh) recorded by Mister Quit.

TIPS "We only listen to songs and other material recorded on quality CDs. We will not accept any submissions via e-mail. If your demo is recorded on an mp3 or AIFF sound file, you must either burn the file onto a CD, or download the sound file into an mp3 player and send the player with the songs to our attention. Otherwise, anything sent via e-mail will be disposed of and will not be considered."

BOB LUNA

Los Angeles CA (310)202-8043 or (310)508-1356. **E-mail:** bobluna@earthlink.net. **Website:** www.boblunaMusic.net.

MUSIC Music: live and midi orchestration. Live performance/arranging/recording credits include Paul McCartney, Dionne Warwick, Reba McEntire, Denice Willaims, Randy Crawford, Alanis Morissette, Sister Sledge, others.

PETER MALICK

Los Angeles CA (866)884-9919, ext. 2. **E-mail:** petermalick@gmail.com. **Website:** www.petermalick.com. **MUSIC** Has worked with Fast Heart Mart, Henry Gummer, Chelsea Williams, Hope Waits, Norah Jones, Kirsten Proffit, Whitey Conwell, Free Dominguez, Suzanne Santos. **Music:** indie, rock, roots, Americana.

⊘ COOKIE MARENCO

P.O. Box 874, Belmont CA 94002. (650)595-8475. **E-mail:** info@bluecoastrecords.com. **Website:** www.cookiemarenco.com.

HOW TO CONTACT *"No speculative projects." Does not accept unsolicited material.* Must have budget.

MUSIC Mostly acoustic, high resolution, live-performance oriented **alternative modern rock**, **country**, **folk**, **rap**, **ethnic** and **avante-garde**; also **classical**, **pop** and **jazz**. Produced *Winter Solstice II* (album), written and recorded by various artists for Windham Hill Records (instrumental). Artists include Tony Furtado, Brain, Buckethead, Alex Degrassi, Turtle Island String Quartet, Praxis, Oregon, Mary Chapin Carpenter, Max Roach and Charle Haden & Quartet West.

TIPS "Specialist in high quality ANALOG recording. Mixing to 1/2" or DSD digital. Full service mastering and dynamic website development."

⊘○ SCOTT MATHEWS, D/B/A HIT OR MYTH PRODUCTIONS INC.

246 Almonte Blvd., Mill Valley CA 94941. **E-mail:** scott@scottmathews.com. **Website:** www.scottmathews.com. Record producer, "song doctor", multi-instrumentalist, studio owner, music industry executive, and professional consultant. Produces 6-9 CDs/year. Fee derived from recording artist or record company (with royalty points).

○ Scott Mathews has more than 20 gold and multi-platinum rawards for sales of more than 30 million records. He has worked with more than 70 Rock & Roll Hall of Fame inductees and on several Grammy and Oscar-winning releases. He is currently working primarily with emerging artists while still making Music with his legendary established artists such as James Hatfield (Metallica), Pat Monohan (Train), Sammy Hagar, Ann Wilson, Joe Satriani, and Van Dyke Parks. The pan-Asian pop group, Blush, was his latest a #1 Billboard hit in 2012.

HOW TO CONTACT "No publishing submissions, please. We do not place songs with artists because we work with artists that write their own material." Submit artist demo for production consideration with a CD by mail or an mp3 by e-mail. "Unsolicited submissions are often the best ones and readily accepted. Include SASE if e-mail is not an option. Also include your e-mail address on your demo CD as all early stage business is handled by e-mail." Responds in 2 months.

MUSIC Mostly **rock/pop**, **alternative**, **country** and **singer/songwriters of all styles**. In 2014, he was awarded seven more gold and multi-platinum records by Eric Clapton, Van Morrison, David Bowie, B.B. King, The Beach Boys, Bonnie Raitt, and Sammy Hagar. In 2004 Mathews earned a gold album for "Smile" by Brian Wilson. Has produced Elvis Costello, Roy Orbison, Rosanne Cash, Jerry Garcia, Huey Lewis, Sammy Hagar, Bob Weir, and many more. Has worked with Barbra Streisand, John Lee Hooker, Keith Richards, George Harrison, Mick Jagger, Van Morrison, Bonnie Raitt, Ringo Starr, Brian Wilson, Zac Brown, Chris Isaak, and Eric Clapton.

TIPS "These days if you are not independent, you are dependent. The new artists that are coming up and achieving success in the music industry are the ones that prove they have a vision and can make incredible records without the huge financial commitment of a major label. When an emerging artist makes great product for the genre they are in, they are in the driver's seat to be able to make a fair and equitable deal for distribution, be it with a major or independent label. My philosophy is to go where you are loved. The truth is, a smaller label that is completely dedicated to you and shares your vision may help your career far more than a huge label that will not keep you around if you don't sell millions of units. Perhaps no label is needed at all, if you are up for the challenge of wearing a lot of hats. I feel too much pressure is put on the emerging artist when they have to pay huge sums back to the label in order to see their first royalty check. We all know those records can be made for a fraction of that cost without compromising quality or commercial

appeal and I am proving that every day. I still believe in potential and our company is in business to back up that belief. It is up to us as record makers/visionaries to take that potential into the studio and come out with music that can compete with anything else on the market. Discovering, developing and producing artists that can sustain long careers is our main focus at Hit or Myth Productions. We are proud to be associated with so many legendary and timeless artists and our track record speaks for itself. If you love making music, don't let anyone dim that light. We look forward to hearing from you if you are an emerging artist looking for production to kick your career into high gear. (Please check out www.scottmathews.com for more info, and also www.allMusic.com-keyword; Scott Mathews.) Accept no substitutes!"

⦿ MEGA TRUTH RECORDS

P.O. Box 4988, Culver City CA 90231. **E-mail:** jonbare@aol.com. **Website:** www.jonbare.net. **Contact:** Jon Bare, CEO. Submit demo package by mail. Unsolicited submissions are OK. Prefers CD. "We specialize in recording world-class virtuoso musicians and bands with top players." Does not return material. Responds in 2 weeks only if interested.

MUSIC Mostly **rock**, **blues** and **country rock**; also **swing**, **dance** and **instrumental**. Produced Party Platter recorded by Hula Monsters (swing); and Killer Whales, Shredzilla and Orcastra (by Jon Bare and the Killer Whales) (rock), all on Mega Truth Records. Other artists include The Rich Harper Blues Band, Aeon Dream & the Dream Machine and Techno Dudes.

TIPS "Create a unique sound that blends great vocals and virtuoso musicianship with a beat that makes us want to get up and dance."

BILL METOYER

16209 Victory Blvd. #132, Lake Balboa CA 91406. (818)780-5394. **E-mail:** bill@skullseven.com. **Website:** www.billmetoyer.com.

MUSIC Has worked with Slayer, W.A.S.P., Fates Warning, Six Feet Under, Armored Saint, DRI, COC, Tourniquet, Skrew, Rigor Mortis, Sacred Steel, Cement. **Music:** hard rock, metal.

BILLY MITCHELL

P.O. Box 284, S. Pasadena CA 91031. (626)574-5040. **Fax:** (626)446-2584. **E-mail:** billymitchell2k@aol.com. **Website:** www.billy-mitchell.com.

MUSIC Has worked with Chartmaker Records, Vista Records, PRC Records, USA Music Group. **Music:** contemporary jazz, pop.

ADAM MOSELEY

Los Angeles CA (323)316-4932. **E-mail:** adammoseley@mac.com. **Website:** www.adammoseley.com.
MUSIC Has worked with Claudio Valenzuela, Lisbeth Scott, Wolfmother, Nikka Costa, Abandoned Pools, John Cale, AJ Croce, Lucybell, The Cure, KISS, Rush, Roxette, Maxi Priest. **Music:** rock, alternative, electronica, acoustic.

○ MUSICJONES RECORDS

P.O. Box 5163, Chatsworth CA 91313. (818)920-8058. **E-mail:** mike@Musicjones.com. **Website:** www.Musicjones.com.
MUSIC Mostly **country**, **folk** and **pop**; also **rock**. Recent album releases: *The Highway* featuring Mike Jones and "Oops My Bad" Featuring Ginger Granger. Also produced "Lonelyville," and "Alabama Slammer" (singles), both written and recorded by Wake Eastman; and "Good Looking Loser" (single), written and recorded by Renee Rubach, all on Sound Works Records (country). Other artists include Matt Dorman, Steve Gilmore, The Tackroom Boys, The Las Vegas Philharmonic, and J.C. Clark.
TIPS "Put your ego on hold. Don't take criticism personally. Advice is meant to help you grow and improve your skills as an artist/songwriter. Be professional and business-like in all your dealings."

ZAVE NATHAN

2 Village Lane, Bear Valley Springs CA 93561. (661)839-6370. **E-mail:** zave2004@yahoo.com. **Website:** www.zaveMusic.net.
MUSIC Songwriter/Arranger/Producer. Has worked with Headsandwich, Sahaloop, The Joy House, Dan Bern, Indya, Edouardo Torres. **Music:** rock, blues, R&B, funk, acoustic, hard rock.

○ NEU ELECTRO PRODUCTIONS

P.O. Box 1582, Bridgeview IL 60455. (630)257-6289. **E-mail:** neuelectro@email.com. **Website:** www.neuelectro.com. **Contact:** Bob Neumann.
MUSIC Mostly **dance**, **house**, **techno**, **rap** and **rock**; also **experimental**, **New Age** and **top 40**. Produced "Juicy" (single), written and recorded by Juicy Black on Dark Planet International Records (house); "Make Me Smile" (single), written and recorded by Roz Baker (house); *Reactovate-6* (album by Bob Neumann), re-

corded by Beatbox-D on N.E.P. Records (dance); and *Sands of Time* (album), recorded by Bob Neumann (New Age). Other artists include Skid Marx and The Deviants.

◐ NEW EXPERIENCE RECORDS/FAZE 4 RECORDS/PUMP IT UP RECORDS/TOUCH TONE RECORDS

1017 Myrtle Street, Marks MS 38646. **E-mail:** newexperiencerecords@yahoo.com. **Contact:** James L. Milligan Jr., president, CEO, and Music publisher. Record producer, music publisher (A New Rap Jam Publishing/ASCAP), management firm (Creative Star Management) and record company (New Experience Records, Rough Edge Records, Grand-Slam Records, and Pump It Up Records). Produces 15-30 12" singles, 3 EPs and 2-5 CDs/year. Fee derived from sales royalty when song or artist is recorded or outright fee from record company, "depending on services required." Distributed by KVZ Distribution and States 51 Distribution.
○ Also see the listings for A New Rap Jam Publishing (ASCAP) in the Music Publishers section of this book.
HOW TO CONTACT Contact A&R Department or write first to arrange personal interview. Address material to A&R Department or Talent Coordinator. Prefers CD with a minimum of 3 songs and lyric or lead sheet (if available). "If CDs are to be returned, proper postage should be enclosed and all CDs and letters should have SASE for faster reply." Responds in 6-8 weeks.
MUSIC Mostly **pop**, **R&B**, and **rap**; also **gospel**, **soul**, **contemporary gospel** and **rock**. Produced "The Son of God" (single by James Milligan/Anthony Milligan/Melvin Milligan) from *The Final Chapter* (album), recorded by T.M.C. Milligan Conection (R&B, Gospel), released 2002 on New Experience/Pump It Up Records. Other artists include Dion Mikel, Paulette Mikel, Melvin Milligan and Venesta Compton.
TIPS "Do your homework on the music business. Be aware of all the new sampling laws. There are too many sound alikes. Be yourself. I look for what is different, vocal ability, voice range and sound stage presence, etc. Be on the look out for our new blues label Rough Edge Records/Rough Edge Entertainment. Blues material is now being reviewed. Send your best studio recorded material. Also be aware of the new digital downloading laws. People are being jailed and fined for recording music that has not been

paid for. Do your homework. Labels: New Experience Records, Touch Tone Records, Grind Blocc Records, Pump It Up Records; now we can better serve our customers with great distribution. You can also e-mail us at newexperiencerecords@yahoo.com for further information on our services. We are reviewing hip-hop and rap material that is positive, clean, and commercial; please no Gangsta rap if you want a deal with us as well as airplay. Also reviewing gospel Music, gospel rap and anything with commercial appeal."

NICK EIPERS

Website: www.nickeipers.com. "I am a freelance recording engineer and producer, specializing in music. Currently based in the Chicago area, I am on staff at Tranquility One Studios, and am available to work freelance almost anywhere. I have worked at Chicago Recording Company, Studiomedia Recording Company, Hinge Studios, Rax Trax Recording, IV Lab Studios, Gallery of Carpet Recording, Shantyville Recording Studio, Gravity Studios, Studiochicago, Star Trax Recording and Chicago Trax, as well as various remote locations and private studios. We choose the recording space based on the aesthetic and practical needs of your music."

MUSIC Specializing in Jazz, Fusion, World, Indie, Alternative, Singer/Songwriter, Folk, Classical

NIGHTWORKS RECORDS

355 W. Potter Dr., Anchorage AK 99518. (907)562-3754. **E-mail:** surrealstudiosak@gmail.com. **Website:** www.surrealstudios.com. **Contact:** Kurt Riemann, owner/engineer.

HOW TO CONTACT Submit demo package by mail. Unsolicited submissions are OK. Prefers CD with 2-3 songs "produced as fully as possible. Send jingles and songs on separate CDs." Does not return material. Responds in 1 month.

MUSIC Produces a variety of music from **native Alaskan** to **techno** to **Christmas**.

CARLA OLSON

11684 Ventura Blvd. Suite 583, Studio City CA 91604. **E-mail:** carlawebsite@aol.com. **Website:** www.carlaolson.com.

MUSIC Has worked with Paul Jones, Jake Andrews, Davis Gaines, Joe Louis Walker, Astrella Celeste, Youngblood Hart, Billy Joe Royal, Kim Wilson.

PHILEK

E-mail: info@philek.com. **Website:** www.philek.com. **Contact:** Steve Moir, Moir Entertainment, Inc..

HOW TO CONTACT E-mail Steve Moir at info@philek.com.

MUSIC Worked with such acts as Fleet Foxes, Band of Horses, Boy & Bear, The Walkmen, The Cave Singers, Run River South, Father John Misty, Shout Out Louds, Modest Mouse, The Dodos, Sea Wolf, Animal Kingdom, Mudhoney, The Shins, Spanish for 100, David Cross, Jana McCall, Dinosaur Jr., Feed, Built to Spill, Sick Bees, Fumes, and others.

PLATINUM STUDIOS

Los Angeles CA (818)994-5368. **E-mail:** paulhilton123@sbcglobal.net. **Website:** www.paulhiltonMusic.com. "Platinum sound at affordable rates."

MUSIC Has worked with Janet Klein, Matt Zane & Society 1, Bon Jovi, Spencer Davis, Big Joe Turner, Billy Vera, Metallica, Ratt, Motley Crue, Morgana King, Jack Mack & the Heart Attack, Rodney O & Joe Cooley, WASP, Carlos Rico, Mera, Sam Glaser. **Music:** Latin, rock, blues.

WILL RAY

106 Sunset Hills CT., Asheville NC 28803. (828)299-1422. **E-mail:** will@willray.biz. **Website:** www.willray.biz.

MUSIC Has worked with The Hellecasters, Solomon Burke, Wylie & the Wild West Show, Candye Kane, Jeffrey Steele, Clay DuBose, The Buzzards, Carrie James. **Music:** country, folk, blues.

TODD ROSENBERG

Los Angeles CA (310)926-5059. **E-mail:** todd@toddrosenberg.net. **Website:** www.toddrosenberg.net.

MUSIC Has worked with Pressure 45, Devil Driver, Mad Caddies, Motograter, Honda, Mitsubishi, Panasonic, Grooveworks. **Music:** indie, rock, Americana, country, ska, punk.

STEVE SATKOWSKI RECORDINGS

P.O. Box 3403, Stuart FL 34995. (772)225-3128. **Website:** www.clearsoulproductions.com/SteveSatkowski.html.

HOW TO CONTACT Submit demo by mail. Unsolicited submissions are OK. Prefers CD. Does not return material. Responds in 2 weeks.

MUSIC Mostly **classical**, **jazz** and **big band**. Produced recordings for National Public Radio and affiliates. Engineered recordings for Steve Howe, Patrick Moraz, Kenny G, and Michael Bolton.

MARK SAUNDERS

Beat 360 Studios, 630 Ninth Ave., Suite 710, New York NY 10036. **E-mail:** ollie@spark-mgmt.com. **Website:** www.marksaunders.com. **Contact:** Ollie Hammett.

MUSIC Has worked with The Cure, Tricky, Depeche Mode, Marilyn Manson, David Byrne, Cyndi Lauper, Shiny Toy Guns, Yaz, The Mission, John Lydon, The Farm, The Sugarcubes, Gravity Kills, Neneh Cherry. **Music:** electronic, rock.

SKYELAB MUSIC GROUP

Skyelab Music Group, 247 W. 38th St. Suite 601, New York NY 10018. (212)789-8942. **E-mail:** info@skyelab.com. **Contact:** Arty Skye. Arty Skye has worked with major stars such as Will Smith, Madonna, Alicia Keys, Santana, 98 Degrees, Queen Latifah, Missy Elliot, Public Enemy, Wu-Tang Clan and many more. Arty opened Skyelab Sound Studios in 1994, and has hosted such stars as James Taylor, Tito Puente, Mya, Pink, Hayle Duff, 98 Degrees , Lil 'Mo and many more.

SLANG MEDIA GROUP

1915 West Superior St., Chicago IL 60622. (312)482-9001. **Website:** www.slangMusicGroup.com. **Contact:** Vince Lawrence. Chicago based Music producers that specialize in creating remix and original music for television commercials, artists, film, and gaming.Noted for achievements in house music, owner/producer Vince Lawrence has created a destination for electronic music makers of every genre. The Slang Musicgroup has multiple producer/artists and we have recieved many RIAA Gold & Platinum awards. Along with music for commercials, members of The Slang MusicGroup have also been working with burgeoning new talent from all over the world.

HOW TO CONTACT Contact via online form.

TIPS "House Music is the heartbeat of every dancer... no fluff or glitter, just the beat of the drum and the true passionate voice of a life worth living.House Music is a tale of distant lovers trying to get back together, broken hearts mending, people finding true joy while they are just getting by. House knows no race, religion or sexual preference. House Music isn't just for the rich or the poor, dumb or intellectual ... house Music is the backing track to life. It moves in all directions."

SOUND ARTS RECORDING STUDIO

8377 Westview Dr., Houston TX 77055. (713)464-4653. **E-mail:** brianbaker@soundartsrecording.com. **Website:** www.soundartsrecording.com. **Contact:** Brian Baker.

MUSIC Mostly **pop/rock**, **country** and **blues**. Produced Texas Johnny Brown (album), written and recorded by Texas Johnny Brown on Quality (blues); and "Sheryl Crow" (single), recorded by Dr. Jeff and the Painkillers. Other artists include Tim Nichols, Perfect Strangers, B.B. Watson, Jinkies, Joe "King" Carasco (on Surface Records), Mark May (on Icehouse Records), The Barbara Pennington Band (on Earth Records), Tempest, Atticus Finch, Tony Vega Band (on Red Onion Records), Saliva (Island Records), Earl Gillian, Blue October (Universal Records), and The Wiggles.

CHRIS STAMEY

Modern Recording, Chapel Hill NC (919)929-5008. **E-mail:** mrstamey@gmail.com. **Website:** www.chrisstamey.com. "The central philosophy behind my production and mixing these days is that the best records combine the recording of transcendent musical moments with the structuring of the carefully considered arrangement details that frame those moments. And the point of recording is to add new entries to that select list of best records." See website for rates.

MUSIC Has worked with Alejandro Excovedo, Ryan Adams/Whiskeytown, Amy Ray, Yo La Tengo, Squirrel Nut Zippers, Patrick Park, Le Tigre, Jeremy Larson, Chatham Country Line. **Music:** rock, indie, alternative.

STUART AUDIO SERVICES

Houndog Recording, 134 Mosher Road, Gorham ME 04038. (207)892-0960. **E-mail:** js@stuartaudio.com. **Website:** www.stuartaudio.com.

HOW TO CONTACT *Write or call first and obtain permission to submit or to arrange a personal interview.* Prefers CD with 4 songs and lyric sheet. Include SASE. Responds in 2 months.

MUSIC Mostly **alternative folk-rock**, **rock** and **country**; also **contemporary Christian**, **children's** and **unusual**. Produced *One of a Kind* (by various artists), recorded by Elizabeth Boss on Bosco Records (folk); *Toad Motel*, written and recorded by Rick Charrette on Fine Point Records (children's); and *Holiday Por-*

trait, recorded by USM Chamber Singers on U.S.M. (chorale). Other artists include Noel Paul Stookey, Beavis and Butthead (Mike Judge), Don Campbell, Jim Newton, and John Angus.

○ STUDIO SEVEN

417 N. Virginia, Oklahoma City OK 73106. (405)236-0643. **Website:** www.lunacyrecords.com.

HOW TO CONTACT *Contact first and obtain permission to submit.* Prefers CD with lyric sheet. Include SASE. Responds in 6 weeks.

MUSIC Mostly **rock, jazz-blues, country,** and **Native American**.

RANDALL MICHAEL TOBIN

2219 W. Olive Ave. Suite 226, Burbank CA 91506. (818)955-5888. **E-mail:** rmt@rmtobin.com. **Website:** www.thetadata.com.

MUSIC Has worked with Mel Carter, Bettie Ross, Isla St. Clair, Margaret MacDonald, Katheryne Levin. **Music:** pop, rock, R&B, jazz, alternative, country.

DAVE TOUGH

5801 Tee Pee Dr., Nashville TN 37013. (615)554-6693. **E-mail:** dave@davetough.com. **Website:** www.davetough.com.

HOW TO CONTACT See website for rates.

MUSIC Has worked with Come & Go, Cindy Alter, Matt Heinecke, Craig Winquist, Jeff Dane, Lost Trailers, Analise Malik, Billdiluigi, and Rhyme Partners. **Music:** country, pop, rock, hip-hop.

BIL VORNDICK

6090 Fire Tower Road, Nashville TN 37221. (615)352-1227. **E-mail:** bilinstudio@comcast.net. **Website:** www.bilvorndick.com. "Helping artists realize their dreams."

MUSIC Has worked with Alison Krauss, Rhonda Vincent, Jerry Douglas, Bela Fleck, Jim Lauderdale, Ralph Stanley, Claire Lynch, Lynn Anderson, Bob Dylan, John Oates.

DICK WAGNER

Desert Dreams Books & Music, 10645 N. Tatum Blvd., Suite 200, Phoenix AZ 85028. (888)458-7900. **E-mail:** wagnerrocks@gmail.com. **Website:** www.wagnerMusic.com.

MUSIC Has worked with Wensday, Robert Wagner, Chris de Marco, Bleedstreet, Janis Leigh, DWB, Matt Besey, Darin Scott, Skinner Rat, Gwen Goodman, Adam Smith. **Music:** rock, pop, modern country, spiritual.

DAVE WATERBURY

Laurel Canyon and Magnolia, Valley Village CA 91607. **E-mail:** davewaterbury91607@yahoo.com. **Website:** www.davewaterbury.net.

MUSIC Has worked with The XOTX, Robbie Krieger, Pink, Mark Krendal, David Eagle, Irv Kramer. **Music:** rock, dance, electronica, pop.

◖ WESTWIRES RECORDING USA

1042 Club Ave., Allentown PA 18109. (610)435-1924. **E-mail:** westwires@aol.com. **Website:** www.westwires.com.

MUSIC Mostly **rock, R&B, dance, alternative, folk** and **eclectic**. Produced Ye Ren (Dimala Records), Weston (Universal/Mojo), Zakk Wylde (Spitfire Records). Other artists include Ryan Asher, Paul Rogers, Anne Le Baron, and Gary Hassay

TIPS "We are interested in singer/songwriters and alternative artists living in the mid-Atlantic area. Must have steady gig schedule and established fan base."

◖ WLM MUSIC/RECORDING

2808 Cammie St., Durham NC 27705-2020. (919)471-3086. **Fax:** (919)471-4326. **E-mail:** wlm-Musicrecording@nc.rr.com; wlm-band@nc.rr.com. **Contact:** Watts Lee Mangum, owner. Record producer. Fee derived from outright fee from recording artist. "In some cases, an advance payment requested for demo production."

HOW TO CONTACT Submit demo by mail. Unsolicited submissions are OK. Prefers CD with 2-4 songs and lyric or lead sheet (if possible). Include SASE. Responds in 6 months.

MUSIC Mostly **country, country/rock,** and **blues/rock**; also **pop, rock, blues, gospel** and **bluegrass**. Produced "911," and "Petals of an Orchid" (singles), both written and recorded by Johnny Scoggins (country); and "Renew the Love" (single by Judy Evans), recorded by Bernie Evans (country), all on Independent. Other artists include Southern Breeze Band and Heart Breakers Band.

MICHAEL WOODRUM

(818)848-3393. **Website:** www.soundmovesaudio.com. "Michael Woodrum is a producer who's also an accomplished engineer. He gets sounds faster than you can think them up. You won't sit around waiting for something to sound right."

MUSIC Has worked with 3LW, Juvenile, 2Pac, Linkin Park, MC Lyte, Mary J. Blige, Eric Clapton, Joss Stone,

Snoop Dogg, Bobby Rydell, B2K, Rocio Banquells, Queen Latifah, JoJo, Dr. Dre, John Guess, Tiffany Evans, Samantha Jade. **Music**: rock, pop, R&B, rap, hiphop, alternative, acoustic, indie, Americana, country, soul.

● WORLD RECORDS

5450 Harris Road, Traverse City MI 49684. **E-mail:** jack@worldrec.org. **Website:** www.worldrec.org. "We produce and distribute CD recordings from a limited number of outstanding Musicians."

MUSIC Mostly **classical**, **folk**, and **jazz**. Produced *2 to Celebrate* (album), recorded by Traverse Symphony Orchestra (classical); *Reflections on Schubert* (album) recorded by Michael Coonrod (classical). Other artists include Joe Welsh and Mark Ducommun.

● ZIG PRODUCTIONS

P.O. Box 120931, Arlington TX 76012. **E-mail:** billyherzig@hotmail.com. **Website:** www.zigproductions.com. "Occasionally I produce a single that is recorded separate from a full CD project." Produces 6-10 albums. Fee derived from sales royalty when song or artist is recorded and/or outright fee from recording artist. "Sometimes there are investors."

MUSIC Mostly **country**, **Americana**, and **rock**; also **pop**, **r&b**, and **alternative**. Produced "Ask Me to Stay" (single by King Cone/Josh McDaniel) from *Gallery*, recorded by King Cone (Texas country/Americana). released on King Cone; "A Cure for Awkward Silence" (single), recorded by Tyler Stock (acoustic rock), released on Payday Records; "Take Me Back" (single) from *Peace, Love & Crabs*, written and recorded by Deanna Dove (folk-rock), released on Island Girl. Also produced Robbins & Jones (country), Jordan Mycoskie (country), Carla Rhodes (comedy), Four Higher (alternative), Charis Thorsell (country), Shane Mallory (country), Rachel Rodriguez (blues-rock), Jessy Daumen (country), Frankie Moreno (rock/r&b), Shawna Russell (country), and many others.

SAUL ZONANA

606 Stone Mill Circle, Murfreesboro TN 37130. (800)965-5114. **E-mail:** zonana@comcast.net. **Website:** www.saulzonana.com.

MUSIC Has worked with Crash Test Dummies, Adrian Belew, Blue Oyster Cult, Nicole McKenna, Ace Frehley, Haeley Vaughn, Taylor Dayne, and more. **Music**: rock, pop, progressive rock.

MANAGERS &
BOOKING AGENTS

Before submitting to a manager or booking agent, be sure you know exactly what you need. If you're looking for someone to help you with performance opportunities, the booking agency is the one to contact. They can help you book shows either in your local area or throughout the country. If you're looking for someone to help guide your career, you need to contact a management firm. Some management firms may also handle booking; however, it may be in your best interest to look for a separate booking agency. A manager should be your manager—not your agent, publisher, lawyer or accountant.

MANAGERS

Of all the music industry players surrounding successful artists, managers are usually the people closest to the artists themselves. The artist manager can be a valuable contact, both for the songwriter trying to get songs to a particular artist and for the songwriter/performer. A manager and his connections can be invaluable in securing the right publishing deal or recording contract if the writer is also an artist. Getting songs to an artist's manager is yet another way to get your songs recorded, since the manager may play a large part in deciding what material his client uses. For the performer seeking management, a successful manager should be thought of as the foundation for a successful career.

The relationship between a manager and his client relies on mutual trust. A manager works as the liaison between you and the rest of the music industry, and he must know exactly what you want out of your career in order to help you achieve your goals. His handling of publicity, promotion, and finances, as well as the contacts he has within the industry, can make or break your career. You should never be afraid to ask questions about any aspect of the relationship between you and a prospective manager.

Always remember that a manager works *for the artist.* A good manager is able to communicate his opinions to you without reservation, and should be willing to explain any confusing terminology or discuss plans with you before taking action. A manager needs to be able to communicate successfully with all segments of the music industry in order to get his client the best deals possible. He needs to be able to work with booking agents, publishers, lawyers and record companies.

Keep in mind that you are both working together toward a common goal: success for you and your songs. Talent, originality, professionalism and a drive to succeed are qualities that will attract a manager to an artist—and a songwriter.

BOOKING AGENTS

The function of the booking agent is to find performance venues for their clients. They usually represent many more acts than a manager does, and have less contact with their acts. A booking agent charges a commission for his services, as does a manager. Managers usually ask for a 15-20 percent commission on an act's earnings; booking agents usually charge around 10 percent. In the area of managers and booking agents, more successful acts can negotiate lower percentage deals than the ones set forth above.

SUBMITTING MATERIAL TO MANAGERS & BOOKING AGENTS

The firms listed in this section have provided information about the types of music they work with and the types of acts they represent. You'll want to refer to the Category Index to find out which companies deal with the type of music you write, and the Geographic Index to help you locate companies near where you live. Then determine whether they are open to your level of experience (see A Sample Listing Decoded on page 13). Each listing also contains submission requirements and information about what items to include in a press kit and will also specify whether the company is a management firm or a booking agency. Remember that your submission represents you as an artist, and should be as organized and professional as possible.

ADDITIONAL MANAGERS & BOOKING AGENTS

There are more managers & booking agents located in other sections of the book. Consult the Index to find additional Managers & Booking Agents listings within other sections.

Icons

For more instructional information on the listings in this book, including explanations of symbols, read the article *How To Use Songwriter's Market* on page 10.

◑ AIR TIGHT MANAGEMENT

115 West Road, P.O. Box 113, Winchester Center CT 06094. (860)738-9139. **Fax:** (860)738-9135. **E-mail:** mainoffice@airtightmanagement.com. **Website:** www.airtightmanagement.com. **Contact:** Jack Forchette, president. Represents individual artists, groups or songwriters from anywhere; currently represents 7 acts. Receives 15-20% commission. Reviews material for acts.

HOW TO CONTACT *Write e-mail first and obtain permission to submit.* Prefers CD or DVD. If seeking management, press kit should include photos, bio, and recorded material. "Follow up with a fax or e-mail, not a phone call." Does not return material. Responds in 1 month.

MUSIC Mostly **rock**, **country**, and **jazz**. Current acts include P.J. Loughran (singer/songwriter), Kal David (blues singer/songwriter/guitarist), Kaitlyn Lusk (singer/songwriter and featured vocalist for Howard Shore's orchestral presentation of *Lord of the Rings*), Warren Hill (jazz singer/songwriter/saxophonist), Harvey Mason (percussionist/composer), George Marinelli (Americana/rock singer/songwriter/guitarist), and Rocco Prestia (songwriter/bassist).

◐◑ ALERT MUSIC INC.

305-41 Britain St., Suite 305, Toronto ON M5A 1R7 Canada. **E-mail:** contact@alertMusic.com. **Website:** www.alertMusic.com. **Contact:** W. Tom Berry, president. Management firm, record company and recording artist. Represents local and regional individual artists and groups; currently handles 3 acts. Reviews material for acts.

HOW TO CONTACT *Write first and obtain permission to submit.* Prefers CD. If seeking management, press kit should include finished CD, photo, press clippings, and bio. Include SASE.

MUSIC All types. Works primarily with bands and singer/songwriters. Current acts include Holly Cole (jazz vocalist) and Kim Mitchell (rock singer/songwriter). Also worked with Michael Kaeshammer (pianist/singer) and Rozanne Potvin.

◑ MICHAEL ALLEN ENTERTAINMENT DEVELOPMENT

P.O. Box 111510, Nashville TN 37222. (615)754-0059. **E-mail:** gmichaelallen@comcast.net. **Website:** www.gmichaelallen.com. **Contact:** Michael Allen. Management firm and public relations. Represents individual artists, groups and songwriters. Receives 15-25% commission. Reviews material for acts.

HOW TO CONTACT Submit demo package by mail. Unsolicited submissions are OK. Prefers CD/DVD with 3 songs and lyric or lead sheets. If seeking management, press kit should include photo, bio, press clippings, letter and CD/DVD. Include SASE. Responds in 3 months.

MUSIC Mostly **country** and **pop**; also **rock** and **gospel**. Works primarily with vocalists and bands. Currently doing public relations for Brenda Lee, The Imperials, Ricky Lynn Gregg, Kyle Rainer, and Lee Greenwood.

○ AMERICAN BANDS MANAGEMENT

3300 S. Gessner, Suite 207, Houston TX 77063. (713)785-3700. **Fax:** (713)785-4641. **E-mail:** americanbandmgmt@aol.com. **Website:** www.americanbandsmanagement.com. **Contact:** John Blomstrom Sr., CEO; Cheryl Blomstrom, vice president and CFO. Represents groups from anywhere. Receives 15-25% commission. Reviews material for acts.

HOW TO CONTACT Submit demo package by mail prior to making phone contact. Unsolicited submissions are OK. Prefers live videos. If seeking management, press kit should include cover letter, bio, photo, demo CD, press clippings, video, résumé, and professional references with names and numbers. Does not return material. Responds in 1 month.

MUSIC Mostly **rock (all forms)** and **modern country**. Works primarily with bands. Current acts include The Scars Heal In Time, Trey Gadler & Dead Man's Hand, Kenny Cordrey & Love Street, The Standells, Paul Cotton (from Poco), and Pearl (Janis Joplin tribute).

◑ BILL ANGELINI ENTERPRISES/ BOOKYOUREVENT.COM

P.O. Box 132, Seguin TX 78155. (210)363-4978. **Fax:** (830)401-0069. **E-mail:** bill@bookyourevent.com. **Website:** www.bookyourevent.com. **Contact:** Bill Angelini, owner. Management firm and booking agency. Represents individual artists and groups from anywhere. Receives 10-15% commission. Reviews material for acts.

HOW TO CONTACT Submit demo package by mail or EPK. Unsolicited submissions are OK. Press kit should include pictures, bio, and discography. Does not return material. Responds in 1 month.

MUSIC Mostly **Latin American**, **Tejano**, and **international**; also **Norteno** and **country**. Current acts include Jay Perez (Tejano), Ram Herrera (Tejano), Michael Salgado (Tejano), Electric Cowboys (tex-mex), Los Caporales (Tejano), Grupo Solido (Tejano), and Texmaniacs (Tex-Mex).

◑ APODACA PROMOTIONS INC.

717 E. Tidwell Road, Houston TX 77022. (713)691-6677. **Fax:** (713)692-9298. **E-mail:** houston@apodacapromotions.com. **Website:** www.apodacapromotions.com. **Contact:** Domingo A. Barrera, manager. Management firm, booking agency, music publisher (Huina Publishing, Co. Inc.). Represents songwriters and groups from anywhere; currently handles 40 acts. Reviews material for acts.

HOW TO CONTACT Submit demo package by mail. Unsolicited submissions are OK. Prefers CD and lyric and lead sheet. Include SASE. Responds in 2 months.

MUSIC Mostly **international** and **Hispanic**; also **rock**. Works primarily with bands and songwriters. Current acts include Alicia Villarreal, Boby Pulldo, Fanny Lu, Elephant, Angel Y Khriz, Golden Horse, and Ninel Conde.

◑ ARTIST REPRESENTATION AND MANAGEMENT

1257 Arcade St., St. Paul MN 55106. (651)483-8754. **Fax:** (651)776-6338. **E-mail:** Molly@armentertainment.com; jdr@armentertainment.com. **Website:** www.armentertainment.com. **Contact:** Roger Anderson, agent/manager. Management firm and booking agency. Estab. 1983. Represents artists from USA/Canada. Receives 15% commission. Reviews material for acts.

HOW TO CONTACT Submit CD and DVD by mail. Unsolicited submissions are OK. Please include minimum 3 songs. If seeking management, current schedule, bio, photo, press clippings should also be included. "Priority is placed on original artists with product who are currently touring." Does not return material. Responds only if interested within 30 days.

MUSIC Mostly **melodic rock**. Current acts include Alannah Myles, Warrant, Firehouse, Winger, Skid Row, Head East, Frank Hannon of Tesla, LA Guns featuring Phil Lewis, Dokken, Adler's Appetite, and Vince Neil.

◑ BACKSTREET BOOKING

Longworth Hall Office Complex, 700 W. Pete Rose Way, Cincinnati OH 45203. (513)442-4405. **Fax:** (513)834-9390. **E-mail:** info@backstreetbooking.com. **Website:** www.backstreetbooking.com. **Contact:** Jim

Sfarnas, president. Represents individual artists and groups from anywhere; currently handles 30 acts. Receives 10-15% commission. Reviews material for acts.

HOW TO CONTACT *Call first and obtain permission to submit.* Accepts only signed acts with product available nationally and/or internationally.

MUSIC Mostly **niche-oriented music**. Current acts include Bobby Womack (soul), 500 Miles To Memphis (country punk), Niacin (fusion), John Novello (fusion), Novello B3 Soul (Urban Jazz), Jeff Berlin (jazz), Greg Howe (fusion), Cares Of Steel (tribute to Rush).

TIPS "Build a base on your own."

⊘ BILL SILVA

Website: www.billsilvaentertainment.com. Bill Silva Management (BSM) was formed in 1993 and offers a full house of specialized services helping to guide the careers of an eclectic roster of music artists and producers. Our roster includes GRAMMY Award-winning artist Jason Mraz; RCA Records rapper Brooke Candy; Greyson Chance; Olivia Holt; and Atlantic Records band Night Terrors of 1927. For all of our musical clients we also offer music licensing services by placing their music in television programs, movies, video games and commercials.

HOW TO CONTACT Use online form to contact.

MUSIC Artists include Jason Mraz, Midlake, Annie Stela, Ryan Hewitt, Brooke Candy, Olivia Holt, M. Ward, and many more.

◑ BLOWIN' SMOKE PRODUCTIONS/RECORDS

7438 Shoshone Ave., Van Nuys CA 91406-2340. (818)881-9888. **Fax:** (818)881-0555. **E-mail:** blowinsmokeband@ktb.net. **Website:** www.blowinsmokeband.com. **Contact:** Larry Knight, presiden. Management firm and record producer. Estab. 1990. Represents local and West Coast individual artists and groups; currently handles 6 acts. Receives 15-20% commission. Reviews material for acts.

○ Also see the listing for Hailing Frequency Music Productions in the Record Producers section of this book.

HOW TO CONTACT *Write or call first and obtain permission to submit.* Prefers CD. If seeking management, press kit should include cover letter, demo tape/CD, lyric sheets, press clippings, video if available, photo, bios, contact telephone numbers and any info on legal commitments already in place. Include SASE. Responds in 1 month.

MUSIC Mostly **R&B**, **blues**, and **blues-rock**. Works primarily with single and group vocalists and a few R&B/blues bands. Current acts include Larry "Fuzzy" Knight (blues singer/songwriter), Spirits Rebellious, La Quita Davis, Dwanna Parker, The Blowin' Smoke Rhythm & Blues Band, The Fabulous Smokettes, Joyce Lawson, Sky King (rock/blues), and Guardians of the Clouds (alternative rock).

◯ BREAD & BUTTER PRODUCTIONS

P.O. Box 1539, Wimberley TX 78676. (512)787-0761. **E-mail:** sgladson@gmail.com. **Contact:** Steve Gladson, managing partner. Management firm and booking agency. Represents individual artists, songwriters and groups from anywhere; currently handles 6 acts. Receives 10-20% commission. Reviews material for acts.

HOW TO CONTACT Submit demo package by e-mail or mail. Unsolicited submissions OK. Prefers e-mail. If seeking management, press kit should include cover letter, demo tape/CD, lyric sheets, press clippings, video, résumé, picture, and bio or a list of your social networking sites. Does not return material. Responds in 1 month.

MUSIC Mostly **alternative rock**, **country**, and **R&B**; also **classic rock**, **folk** and **Americana**. Works primarily with singer/songwriters and original bands. Current acts include Lou Cabaza (songwriter/producer/manager), Duck Soup (band) and Gaylan Ladd (songwriter/singer/producer).

TIPS "Remember why you are in this biz. The art comes first."

◑ BROTHERS MANAGEMENT ASSOCIATES

141 Dunbar Ave., Fords NJ 08863. (732)738-0880. **Fax:** (732)738-0970. **E-mail:** bmaent@yahoo.com. **Website:** www.bmaent.com. **Contact:** Allen A. Faucera, president. Management firm and booking agency. Represents artists, groups and songwriters; currently handles 25 acts. Receives 15-20% commission. Reviews material for acts.

HOW TO CONTACT *Write first and obtain permission to submit.* Prefers CD or DVD with 3-6 songs and lyric sheets. Include photographs and résumé. If seeking management, include photo, bio, tape, and return envelope in press kit. Include SASE. Responds in 2 months.

MUSIC Mostly **pop**, **rock**, **MOR**, and **R&B**. Works primarily with vocalists and established groups. Cur-

rent acts include Nils Lofgren of the E Street Band, Cover Girls, Harold Melvin's Blue Notes, and Gloria Gaynor.

TIPS "Submit very commercial material—make demo of high quality."

◑◐ CIRCUIT RIDER TALENT & MANAGEMENT CO.

123 Walton Ferry Road, Hendersonville TN 37075. (615)824-1947. **Fax:** (615)264-0462. **E-mail:** dotwool@bellsouth.net. **Contact:** Linda S. Dotson, president. Consultation and deal negotiation firm, booking agency and music publisher (Channel Music, Cordial Music, Dotson & Dotson Music Publishers, Shalin Music Co.). Represents individual artists, songwriters and actors; currently handles 10 acts. Works with a large number of recording artists, songwriters, actors, and producers. (Includes the late multi-Grammy-winning producer/writer Skip Scarborough.) Receives 10-15% commissionas booking agent (union rates). Reviews material for acts (free of charge) as publisher.

HOW TO CONTACT *E-mail or call first and obtain permission to submit.* Prefers DVD or CD with 3 songs and lyric sheet. If seeking consultation, press kit should include bio, cover letter, résumé, lyric sheets if original songs, photo and CD or DVD with 3 songs. "Full press kit or EPK to my e-mail address required of artist's submissions." Include SASE. Responds "ASAP, sometimes 8 weeks, but if by EPK or internet, will be more timely."

MUSIC Mostly **Latin blues**, **pop**, **country** and **gospel**; also **R&B** and **comedy**. Works primarily with vocalists, special concerts, movies and TV. Current acts include Razzy Bailey (award winning blues artist/writer), Clint Walker (actor/recording artist), Ben Colder (comedy/novelty), and Freddy Weller (formerly Paul Revere & The Raiders/hit songwriter), and Dickie Lee.

TIPS "Artists, have your act together. Have a full press kit, videos and be professional. Attitudes are a big factor in my agreeing to work with you (no egotists). This is a business, and we will be building your career."

◯ CLASS ACT PRODUCTIONS/ MANAGEMENT/PETER KIMMEL'S MUSIC CATALOG

P.O. Box 55252, Sherman Oaks CA 91413. (818)980-1039. **E-mail:** peter.kimmel@sbcglobal.net. **Contact:** Peter Kimmel, president. Management firm; Independent Music Licensing Professional and composer rep.

Currently represents music material of artists for licensing to media; must have broadcast-quality, mastered recordings. Receives 50/50 split of licensing fees income from placements onto soundtracks of motion pictures, TV shows, commercials, etc.

HOW TO CONTACT "Music artists: Submit broadcast-quality, mastered recordings via mail or links to high quality MP3s derived from your mastered recordings, via e-mail. Unsolicited submissions are OK. For mail, include CD, cover letter (mention *Songwriter's Market*), lyric sheets (mandatory) or submit electronic press kit by e-mail. Responds in 1 month.

MUSIC **All styles**. Represents select first rate music material to music supervisors of films, television, commercials, etc.

TIPS "We cannot use song lyrics only or demos. Songwriting must be professional quality, recorded music must be highly accomplished, andrecordings must be professional, broadcast-quality and mastered."

◑ CLOUSHER PRODUCTIONS

P.O. Box 1191, Mechanicsburg PA 17055. (717)766-7644. **Fax:** (717)766-1490. **E-mail:** cpinfo@msn.com. **Website:** www.clousherentertainment.com. **Contact:** Fred Clousher, owner. Booking agency and production company. Represents groups from anywhere; currently handles more than 100 acts.

HOW TO CONTACT Submit demo package by mail. Please, no electronic press kits. Unsolicited submissions are OK. Prefers CDs or DVD. Press kit should also include bio, credits, pictures, song list, references, and your contact information. Does not return material. "Performer should check back with us!"

MUSIC Mostly **country**, **oldies rock & roll** and **ethnic** (German, Hawaiian, etc.); also **dance bands** (regional), **Dixieland**, and **classical musicians**. "We work mostly with country, old time R&R, regional variety dance bands, tribute acts, and all types of variety acts." Current acts include Stanky & the Coal Miners (polka), Lee Alverson (tribute artist), and Orville Davis & The Wild Bunch (country/rockabilly).

TIPS "The songwriters we work with are entertainers themselves, which is the aspect we deal with. They usually have bands or do some sort of show, either with tracks or live music. We engage them for stage shows, concerts, etc. We do not review songs you've written. We do not publish music, or submit performers to recording companies for contracts. We strictly set up live performances for them."

◐ CONCEPT 2000 INC.

P.O. Box 2950, Columbus OH 43216-2950. (614)276-2000. **Fax:** (614)275-0163. **E-mail:** info2k@concept2k. com. **Website:** www.concept2k.com. **Contact:** Brian Wallace, president. Management firm and booking agency. Represents international individual artists, groups and songwriters. Receives 20% commission. Reviews material for acts.

HOW TO CONTACT Submit demo by mail. Unsolicited submissions are OK. Prefers CD with 4 songs. If seeking management, include demo, press clips, photo and bio. Does not return material. Responds in 2 weeks.

MUSIC Mostly **rock, country, pop**, and **contemporary gospel**. Current acts include Satellites Down (rock); Gene Walker (jazz); Endless Summer (show group); Thomas Wynn and the Believers (country).

TIPS "Send quality songs with lyric sheets. Production quality is not necessary."

◯ COUNTDOWN ENTERTAINMENT

110 West 26th Street, New York NY 10001-6805. **E-mail:** lovie@countdownentertainment.com. **Website:** www.countdownentertainment.com. Founded by James Citkovic in 1983, Countdown Entertainment is a full service artist management firm representing established musicians, bands, producers and songwriters. Countdown Entertainment also brokers intellectual properties such as publishing catalogues and music masters. Countdown Entertainment accepts all styles of music from singers, songwriters, musicians, unsigned bands, signed bands, independent record labels, producers, film composers and others.

HOW TO CONTACT All unsolicited materials are accepted as long as they arrive to us with fully completed submissions forms (available at website).

MUSIC Deals secured include those for The Ramones, Joe Strummer, Steve Ronsen, The Fixx, Wood Ready, etc.

⊘ DAS COMMUNICATIONS, LTD.

83 Riverside Dr., New York NY 10024. 83 Riverside Dr., New York, NY 10024. (212)877-0400. **Fax:** (212)595-0176. Management firm. Estab. 1975. Represents individual artists, groups and producers from anywhere; currently handles 25 acts. Receives 20% commission.

HOW TO CONTACT *Does not accept unsolicited submissions.*

MUSIC Mostly **rock, pop, R&B, alternative** and **hip-hop**. Current acts include Joan Osborne (rock), Wyclef

Jean (hip-hop), Black Eyed Peas (hip-hop), John Legend (R&B), Spin Doctors (rock), The Bacon Brothers (rock).

◐ DCA PRODUCTIONS

676A 9th Ave., #252, New York NY 10036. (800)659-2063. **Fax:** (609)259-8260. **E-mail:** info@dcaproductions.com. **Website:** www.dcaproductions.com. **Contact:** Suzanne Perrotta, office manager. Management firm. Represents individual artists, groups, and songwriters from anywhere.

HOW TO CONTACT If seeking management, press kit should include cover letter, bio, photo, demo CD, and video. Prefers CD or DVD with 2 songs. "All materials are reviewed and kept on file for future consideration. Does not return material. We respond only if interested."

MUSIC Mostly **acoustic**, **rock**, and **mainstream**; also **cabaret** and **theme**. Works primarily with acoustic singer/songwriters, top 40 or rock bands. Current acts include And Jam Band (soulful R&B), Lorna Bracewell (singer/songwriter), and Jimmy and The Parrots (Jimmy Buffett cover band). "Visit our website for a current roster of acts."

TIPS "Please do not call for a review of material."

◐◐ DIVINE INDUSTRIES

(formerly Gangland Artists), Unit 191, #101-1001 W. Broadway, Vancouver BC V6H 4E4 Canada. (604)737-0091. **Fax:** (604)737-3602. **E-mail:** allenm@divineindustries.com. **Website:** www.divineindustries.com. **Contact:** Allen Moy. Management firm, production house and music publisher. Represents artists and songwriters; currently handles 5 acts. Reviews material for acts.

HOW TO CONTACT *Write first and obtain permission to submit.* Prefers audio links. "Videos are not entirely necessary for our company. It is certainly a nice touch. If you feel your CD is strong—send the video upon later request." Does not return material. Responds in 2 months.

MUSIC Rock, **pop**, and **roots**. Works primarily with rock/left-of-center folk show bands. Current acts include 54-40 (rock/pop), Blackie & The Rodeo Kings (folk rock), Ridley Bent, John Mann (of Spirit of the West).

◐ JOHN ECKERT ENTERTAINMENT CONSULTANTS

(formerly Pro Talent Consultants), 7723 Cora Dr., Lucerne CA 95458. (323)325-6662. **E-mail:** talentconsultants@gmail.com. **Contact:** John Eckert, coordinator.

Management firm and talent coordination. Represents individual artists and groups; currently handles 12 acts. Receives 15% commission. Reviews material for acts.

HOW TO CONTACT Submit demo package by mail. Unsolicited submissions are OK. "We prefer CD (4 songs). Submit DVD with live performance only." If seeking management, press kit should include an 8x10 photo, a CD of at least 4-6 songs, a bio on group/artist, references, cover letter, press clippings, video, and business card, or a phone number with address. Does not return material. Responds in 5 weeks.

MUSIC Mostly **country**, **country/pop**, and **rock**. Works primarily with vocalists, show bands, dance bands, and bar bands. Current acts include The Rose Garden (pop/rock/country band); The Royal Guardsmen (pop/rock/top 40); Sam the Sham (vocalist); Russ Varnell (country); and Buddy Allan Owens (country).

◐ SCOTT EVANS PRODUCTIONS

P.O. Box 814028, Hollywood FL 33081-4028. (954)963-4449. **E-mail:** evansprod@hotmail.com; evansprod@aol.com. **Website:** www.theentertainmentmall.com. **Contact:** Jeffrey Birnbaum, new artists; Jeanne K., Internet marketing and sales. Management firm and booking agency. Represents local, regional or international individual artists, groups, songwriters, comedians, novelty acts and dancers; currently handles more than 200 acts. Receives 10-50% commission. Reviews material for acts.

HOW TO CONTACT New artists can make submissions through the "Auditions" link located on the website. Unsolicited submissions are OK. "Please be sure that all submissions are copyrighted and not your original copy as we do not return material."

MUSIC Mostly **pop**, **R&B**, and **Broadway**. Deals with "all types of entertainers; no limitations." Current acts include Scott Evans and Company (variety song and dance), Dorit Zinger (female vocalist), Jeff Geist, Actors Repertory Theatre, Entertainment Express, Joy Deco (dance act), Flashback (musical song and dance revue), and Around the World (international song and dance revue).

TIPS "Submit a neat, well put together, organized press kit."

◐◐ THE FELDMAN AGENCY & MACKLAM FELDMAN MANAGEMENT

200-1505 W. 2nd Ave., Vancouver BC V6H 3Y4 Canada. (604)734-5945. **Fax:** (604)732-0922. **E-mail:** info@mfmgt.com; feldman@slfa.com. **Website:** www.

mfmgt.com; www.slfa.com. Booking agency and artist management firm. Agency represents mostly established Canadian recording artists and groups.

HOW TO CONTACT *Write or call first to obtain permission to submit a demo.* Prefers CD, photo and bio. If seeking management, contact Watchdog for consideration and include video in press kit. SAE and IRC. Responds in 2 months.

MUSIC Current Macklam Feldman Management acts include The Chieftains, Diana Krall, Elvis Costello, Better Midler, Sarah McLachlan, Ylvis, James Taylor, Colin James, Ry Cooder, Tommy LiPuma, and Melody Gardot.

◐ ◐ B.C. FIEDLER MANAGEMENT

53 Seton Park Road, Toronto ON M3C 3Z8 Canada. (416)421-4421. **Fax:** (416)421-0442. **E-mail:** info@bc-fiedler.com. **Website:** www.bcfiedler.com. **Contact:** B.C. Fiedler. Management firm, music publisher (B.C. Fiedler Publishing) and record company (Sleeping Giant Music Inc.). Represents individual artists, groups and songwriters from anywhere. Receives 20-25% or consultant fees. Reviews material for acts.

HOW TO CONTACT *Call first and obtain permission to submit.* Prefers CD or DVD with 3 songs and lyric sheet. If seeking management, press kit should include bio, list of concerts performed in past 2 years including name of venue, repertoire, reviews and photos. Does not return material. Responds in 2 months.

MUSIC Mostly **classical/crossover**, **voice** and **pop**. Works primarily with classical/crossover ensembles, instrumental soloists, operatic voice and pop singer/songwriters. Current acts include Gordon Lightfoot, Dan Hill, Quartetto Gelato, and Patricia O'Callaghan.

TIPS "Invest in demo production using best quality voice and instrumentalists. If you write songs, hire the vocal talent to best represent your work. Submit CD and lyrics. Artists should follow up 6-8 weeks after submission."

◑ ◐ FIRST TIME MANAGEMENT

Ebrel House, 2a Penlee Close, Praa Sands, Penzance, Cornwall TR20 9SR England, United Kingdom. (01736)762826. **Fax:** (01736)763328. **E-mail:** panamus@aol.com. **Website:** www.songwriters-guild.co.uk. **Contact:** Roderick G. Jones, managing director. Management firm, record company (Digimix Records Ltd www.digimixrecords.com, Rainy Day Records, Mohock Records, Pure Gold Records), and music publisher (Panama Music Library, Melody First Music Library, Eventide Music Library, Musik' Image Music Library, Promo Sonor International Music Library, Caribbean Music Library, ADN Creation Music Library, Piano Bar Music Library, Corelia Music Library, PSI Music Library, Scamp Music Publishing, First Time Music [Publishing] U.K. [www.panamaMusic.co.uk and www.myspace.com/scampMusicpublishing]—registered members of the Mechanical Copyright Protection Society [MCPS] and the Performing Right Society [PRS]). Represents local, regional, and international individual artists, groups, composers, DJs, and songwriters. Receives 15-25% commission. Reviews material for acts.

⬤   Also see the listings for First Time Music (Publishing) in the Music Publishers section of this book.

HOW TO CONTACT Submit demo package by mail. Unsolicited submissions are OK. Prefers CD with 3 songs, lyric sheets and also complete album projects where writer/performer has finished masters. If seeking management, press kit should include cover letter, bio, photo, demo tape/CD, press clippings and anything relevant to make an impression. Does not return material. Responds in 1 month only if interested.

MUSIC All styles. Works primarily with songwriters, composers, DJs, rappers, vocalists, bands, groups and choirs. Current acts include Leonie Parker (soul), The Glen Kirton Country Band (country), Bram Stoker (prog rock/gothic rock group), Kevin Kendle (New Age, holistic) Peter Arnold (folk/roots), David Jones (urban/R&B), Shanelle (R&B/dance), AudioJunkie & Stylus (dance/hardcore/funky house/electro house) Ray Guntrip (jazz); DJ Gammer (hardcore/hardhouse/dance); Toots Earl & Clown.

TIPS "Become a member of the Guild of International Songwriters and Composers (www.songwriters-guild.co.uk). Keep everything as professional as possible. Be patient and dedicated to your aims and objectives."

⊘ FOUNDATIONS ARTIST MANAGEMENT

307 7th Avenue Suite 403, New York NY 10001. **E-mail:** info@foundationsMusic.com. **Website:** www.foundationsMusic.com. Foundations Artist Management was launched in 2000 by Steve Bursky, and has since grown into a full-service artist representation company focusing on building artists' careers from the ground-up. The New York based company prides itself on its work with its acts from the very early stages of their careers, helping them lay the neces-

sary groundwork for a successful future in the music industry. With the addition of Brian Winton in 2004 as partner, and Drew Simmons in 2011 as General Manager, Foundations has continued to build on its original vision: providing uncompromising support to great artists, assisting them in growing their careers as we grow our own. Our goal is to work with our acts to develop a strategy for success, one that takes into account where they have been, but even more importantly, where they want to go next. It goes without saying that the primary ingredient for success is talent. But even the most gifted performers can face seemingly insurmountable obstacles without an experienced, creative management team in their corner, helping to guide their artistic endeavors through a constantly changing music industry.

HOW TO CONTACT We do not accept unsolicited submissions! If you would like to submit music for review and consideration, please e-mail us.

MUSIC Represents such acts as Pacific Air, White Rabbits, Foy Vance, Dr. Dog, Dispatch, Owl City, Young The Giant, The Colourist, others.

◑ BILL HALL ENTERTAINMENT & EVENTS

138 Frog Hollow Road, Churchville PA 18966-1031. (215)357-5189. **Fax:** (215)357-0320. **E-mail:** billhallevents@verizon.net. **Contact:** William B. Hall III, owner/president. Booking agency and production company. Represents individuals and groups. Receives 15% commission. Reviews material for acts.

HOW TO CONTACT Submit demo package by mail. Unsolicited submissions are OK. Prefers CD with 2-3 songs and photos and promo material. We need quality material, preferably before a 'live' audience." Does not return material. Responds only if interested.

MUSIC Marching band, circus, and novelty. Works primarily with "unusual or novelty attractions in Musical line, preferably those that appeal to family groups." Current acts include Fralinger and Polish-American Philadelphia Championship Mummers String Bands (marching and concert group), "Mr. Polynesian" Show Band and Hawaiian Revue (ethnic group), the "Phillies Whiz Kids Band" of Philadelphia Phillies Baseball team, Mummermania Musical Quartet, Philadelphia German Brass Band (concert band), Vogelgesang Circus Calliope, Kromer's Carousel Band Organ, Reilly Raiders Drum & Bugle Corps, Hoebel Steam Calliope, Caesar Rodney Brass Band,

Philadelphia Police & Fire Pipes Band, Tim Laushey Pep & Dance Band, Larry Stout (show organist/keyboard player), Jersey Surf Drum & Bugle Corp, Caesar Rodney Brass Marching Band, Corporales San Simon Bolivian Dancers, Robinson's Grandmaster Concert Band Organ, and Bobby Burnett, vocalist/comedian.

TIPS "Please send whatever helps us to most effectively market the attraction and/or artist. Provide something that gives you a clear edge over others in your field!"

◑ HARDISON INTERNATIONAL ENTERTAINMENT CORPORATION

P.O. Box 1732, Knoxville TN 37901-1732. (865)293-7062 (prefers e-mail contact). **E-mail:** dennishardison@bellsouth.net. **Website:** www.dynamoreckless.com. **Contact:** Dennis K. Hardison, CEO/founder; Dennis K. Hardison II, president; Travis J. Hardison, president, Denlatrin Record (a division of Hardison International Entertainment Corp.). Management firm, booking agency, Music publisher (Denlatrin Music) BMI, record label (Denlatrin Records), and record producer. Represents individual artists from anywhere; currently handles 3 acts. Receives 20% commission. Reviews material for acts. "We are seeking level-minded and patient individuals. Our primary interests are established recording acts with prior major deals."

◒   This company has promoted many major acts and unsigned acts for more than 38 years.

HOW TO CONTACT Submit demo package by mail. Unsolicited submissions are OK. Prefers CD with 3 songs only. If seeking management, press kit should include bio, promo picture, and CD. Does not return materials. Responds in 6 weeks to the "best material". Critiques available via dennishardison@bellsouth.net.

MUSIC Mostly **R&B**, **hip-hop**, and **rap**. Current acts include Dynamo (hip-hop), Triniti (record producer, Universal Music, Public Enemy, Dynamo, among others; current engineer for Chuck D), and RapStation artists.

TIPS "We respond to the hottest material, so make it hot!"

HUNT TALENT MANAGEMENT

Website: www.hunttalentmanagement.com. **Contact:** Tammy Hunt. Hunt Talent Management brings more than 25 years of professional experience in the film and music industry. As a management firm dedicated to the business side of the entertainment industry, we are determined to assist our clients achieve their career goals. Hunt Talent Management understands how to create a profitable business while strategically marketing your individual talents. We represent talent from all areas of the entertainment industry. In addition, Hunt Talent Management is partners with Gandolfo-Helin Literary Management to help promote our talented authors.

HOW TO CONTACT Contact via online form.

MUSIC Clients include Ray Brown, Jr. (jazz), Sonya Kahn (singer/songwriter), Aziza (singer) and more.

⊘ INTERNATIONAL ENTERTAINMENT BUREAU

3612 N. Washington Blvd., Indianapolis IN 46205-3592. (317)926-7566. **E-mail:** ieb@prodigy.net. **Contact:** David Leonards. Booking agency. Represents individual artists and groups from anywhere; currently handles 145 acts. Receives 20% commission.

HOW TO CONTACT *No unsolicited submissions.*

MUSIC Mostly **rock**, **country**, and **A/C**; also **jazz**, **nostalgia**, and **ethnic**. Works primarily with bands, comedians and speakers. Current acts include Five Easy Pieces (A/C), Scott Greeson (country), and Cool City Swing Band (variety).

◐ JANA JAE ENTERPRISES

P.O. Box 35726, Tulsa OK 74153. (918)786-8896. **Fax:** (918)786-8897. **E-mail:** janajae@janajae.com. **Website:** www.janajae.com. **Contact:** Kathleen Pixley, agent. Booking agency, music publisher (Jana Jae Publishing/BMI) and record company (Lark Record Productions, Inc.). Represents individual artists and songwriters; currently handles 12 acts. Receives 15% commission. Reviews material for acts.

◯ Also see the listings for Jana Jae Music in the Music Publishers section, Lark Record Productions in the Record Companies section and Lark Talent & Advertising in the Record Producers section of this book.

HOW TO CONTACT Submit demo by mail. Unsolicited submissions are OK. Prefers CD or DVD of performance. If seeking management, press kit should include cover letter, bio, photo, demo tape/CD, lyric sheets and press clippings. Does not return material.

MUSIC Mostly **country**, **classical**, and **jazz instrumentals**; also **pop**. Works with vocalists, show and concert bands, solo instrumentalists. Represents Jana Jae (country singer/fiddle player), Matt Greif (classical guitarist), Sydni (solo singer) and Hotwire (country show band).

◐ KENDALL WEST AGENCY

P.O. Box 1673, Colleyville TX 76034. **E-mail:** Michelle@KendallWestAgency.com. **Contact:** Michelle Vellucci. Booking agency and television producer. Represents individual artists and groups from anywhere. Receives 20% commission. Reviews material for acts.

HOW TO CONTACT *Write first and obtain permission to submit or write to arrange personal interview.* Prefers CD with 5 songs and lead sheet. If seeking management, press kit should include bio, photo, cover letter, CD and resume. Include SASE. Responds in 1 month.

MUSIC Mostly **country**, **blues/jazz**, and **rock**; also **trios**, **dance** and **individuals**. Works primarily with bands. Current acts include Chris & the Roughnecks (Texas Music), Shawna Russell (southern rock), Ty England (country), and Jaz-Vil (jazz/blues).

◯ KUPER PERSONAL MANAGEMENT/ RECOVERY RECORDINGS

515 Bomar St., Houston TX 77006. (713)520-5791. **E-mail:** info@recoveryrecordings.com. **Website:** www.recoveryrecordings.com. **Contact:** Koop Kuper, owner. Management firm, music publisher (Kuper-Lam Music/BMI, Uvula Music/BMI, and Meauxtown Music/ASCAP), and record label (Recovery Recordings). Represents individual artists, groups, and songwriters from Texas. Receives 20% commission. Reviews material for acts.

HOW TO CONTACT Submit demo package by mail. Unsolicited submissions are OK. Prefers CD. If seeking management, press kit should include cover letter, press clippings, photo, bio (1 page) tearsheets (reviews, etc.) and demo CD. Does not return material. Responds in 2 months.

MUSIC Mostly **singer/songwriters**, **AAA**, **roots rock**, and **Americana**. Works primarily with self-contained and self-produced artists. Current acts include Philip Rodriguez (singer/songwriter), David Rodriguez (singer/songwriter), Def Squad Texas (hip-hop). US representative for the group The Very Girls (Dutch vocal duo).

TIPS "Create a market value for yourself, produce your own master tapes, and create a cost-effective situation."

ⓘ LEVINSON ENTERTAINMENT VENTURES INTERNATIONAL, INC.

1440 Veteran Ave., Los Angeles CA 90024. (323)663-6940. **E-mail:** leviinc@aol.com. **Contact:** Jed Leland, Jr. Management firm. Represents national individual artists, groups and songwriters. Receives 15-25% commission. Reviews material for acts.

HOW TO CONTACT *Write first and obtain permission to submit.* Prefers CD or DVD with 6 songs and lead sheet. If seeking management, press kit should include bio, pictures and press clips. Include SASE. Responds in 1 month.

MUSIC Mostly **rock**, **MOR**, **R&B**, and **country**. Works primarily with rock bands, and vocalists.

TIPS "Should be a working band, self-contained and, preferably, performing original material."

ⓘ RICK LEVY MANAGEMENT

4250 A1AS, D-11, St. Augustine FL 32080. (904)806-0817. **Fax:** (904)460-1226. **E-mail:** rick@ricklevy.com. **Website:** www.ricklevy.com. **Contact:** Rick Levy, president. Management firm, music publisher (Flying Governor Music/BMI), and record company (Luxury Records). Voting member of the Grammys. Represents local, regional, or international individual artists and groups; currently handles 5 acts. Also provides worldwide music promotion services. Receives 15-20% commission. Reviews material for acts.

HOW TO CONTACT *Write or call first and obtain permission to submit.* Prefers CD or DVD with 3 songs and lyric sheet. If seeking management, press kit should include cover letter, bio, demo CD, DVD demo, photo and press clippings. Include SASE. Responds in 2 weeks.

MUSIC Mostly **R&B** (no rap), **pop**, **country**, and **oldies**. Current acts include Jay & the Techniques ('60s hit group), The Limits (pop), Freddy Cannon ('60s), The Fallin Bones (Blues/rock), Tommy Roe ('60s), Wax (rock).

TIPS "If you don't have 200% passion and commitment, don't bother. Be sure to contact only companies that deal with your type of music."

ⓘ LOGGINS PROMOTION

5018 Franklin Pike, Nashville TN 37220. (310)325-2800. **E-mail:** staff@LogginsPromotion.com. **Website:** www.logginspromotion.com. **Contact:** Paul Loggins, CEO. Management firm and radio promotion. Represents individual artists, groups and songwriters from anywhere; currently handles 6 acts. Receives 20% commission. Reviews material for acts.

HOW TO CONTACT If seeking management, press kit should include picture, short bio, cover letter, press clippings and CD (preferred). "Mark on CD which cut you, as the artist, feel is the strongest." Does not return material. Responds in 2 weeks.

MUSIC Mostly **adult**, **top 40** and **AAA**; also **urban**, **rap**, **alternative**, **college**, **smooth jazz** and **Americana**. Works primarily with bands and solo artists.

ⓘ MANAGEMENT BY JAFFE

68 Ridgewood Ave., Glen Ridge NJ 07028. (973)743-1075. **Fax:** (973)743-1075. **E-mail:** jerjaf@aol.com. **Contact:** Jerry Jaffe, president. Management firm. Represents individual artists and groups from anywhere. Receives 20% commission. Reviews material for acts "rarely." Reviews for representation "sometimes."

HOW TO CONTACT *Write or call first to arrange personal interview.* Prefers CD or DVD with 3-4 songs and lyric sheet. Does not return material. Responds in 2 months.

MUSIC Mostly **rock/alternative**, **pop**, and **Hot AC**. Works primarily with groups and singers/songwriters.

TIPS "If you are influenced by Jesus & Mary Chain, please e-mail. Create some kind of 'buzz' first."

ⓘⓘ THE MANAGEMENT TRUST, LTD.

471 Queen St. E., Unit 01, Toronto ON M5A 1T9 Canada. (416)979-7070. **Fax:** (416)979-0505. **Website:** www.mgmtrust.ca. **Contact:** Lisa Ioannou, Admin. Management firm. Represents individual artists and/or groups.

HOW TO CONTACT Submit demo package by mail (Attn: A&R Dept.). Unsolicited submissions are OK. If seeking management, press kit should include CD, bio, cover letter, photo and press clippings. Does not return material. Responds in 2 months.

MUSIC All types.

MARMOSET

2105 SE 7th Ave, Portland OR 97214. (971)260-0201. **E-mail:** compass@marmosetMusic.com. **Website:** www.marmosetMusic.com. Marmoset is an off-the-beaten-path boutique music agency born among the green, mountainous landscapes of the rain soaked Pacific Northwest. While we enjoy working on all kinds of inspired and creative endeavors, we spend most of our time crafting original music for story-driven mediums in the public eye. We also curate a hand picked roster of some of the most fascinating independent artists on the planet, whose recordings are made available for licensing. Marmoset is made of real people, living real lives, making a real living crafting music and sound. We're talking about hard working, blue collar artists, crafting music with their hands and hearts. While some of these are full-time musicians, many are baristas and bartenders too. Programmers and farmers. Fathers and mothers. Sisters and brothers.

○ RICK MARTIN PRODUCTIONS

125 Fieldpoint Road, Greenwich CT 06830. **Website:** www.rickmartinproductions.com; www.myspace. com/rickmartinproductions. **Contact:** Rick Martin, president. Personal manager and independent producer. Held the Office of Secretary of the National Conference of Personal Managers for 22 years. Represents vocalists; currently produces pop and country crossover music artists in private project studio and looking for a female vocalist in the general area of Greenwich, CT, for production project. Receives 15% commission as a personal manager and/or customary production and publishing distributions.

HOW TO CONTACT "Please e-mail for initial contact with your web link. Do not submit unless permission received to do so."

MUSIC Any genre but hip-hop or rap.

TIPS "Your demo does not have to be professionally produced to submit to producers, publishers, or managers. In other words, save your money. It's really not important what you've done. It's what you can do now that counts."

◑ PHIL MAYO & COMPANY

P.O. Box 304, Bomoseen VT 05732 United States. P.O. Box 304, Bomoseen VT 05732. (802)468-2554. **Fax:** (802)468-2554. **E-mail:** pmcamgphil@aol.com. **Contact:** Phil Mayo, President. Management firm and record company (AMG Records). Estab. 1981. Represents individual artists, groups and songwriters from anywhere; currently handles 4 acts. Receives 15-20% commission. Reviews material for acts.

HOW TO CONTACT *Contact first and obtain permission to submit.* Prefers CD with 3 songs (professionally recorded) and lyric or lead sheet. If seeking management, include bio, photo and lyric sheet in press kit. Does not return material. Responds in 2 months.

MUSIC Mostly **contemporary Christian pop**. Current and past acts have included John Hall, Guy Burlage, Jonell Mosser, Pam Buckland, Orleans, Gary Nicholson, and Jon Pousette-Dart.

○ MID-COAST, INC.

1002 Jones Road, Hendersonville TN 37075. (615)400-4664. **E-mail:** mid-co@ix.netcom.com. **Contact:** Bruce Andrew Bossert, managing director. Management firm and music publisher (MidCoast, Inc./BMI). Represents individual artists, groups, and songwriters. Reviews material for acts.

HOW TO CONTACT Submit demo package by mail. Unsolicited submissions are OK. Prefers CD or DVD with 2-4 songs and lyric sheet. If seeking management, press kit should include cover letter, "short" bio, tape, video, photo, press clippings, and announcements of any performances in Nashville area. Does not return material. Responds in 6 weeks if interested.

MUSIC Mostly **rock**, **pop**, and **country**. Works primarily with original rock and country bands and artists.

● NOTEWORTHY PRODUCTIONS

124 1/2 Archwood Ave., Annapolis MD 21401. (410)268-8232. **Fax:** (410)268-2167. **E-mail:** mcshane@mcnote.com. **Website:** www.mcnote.com. **Contact:** McShane Glover, president. Management firm and booking agency. Represents individual artists, group,s and songwriters from everywhere. Receives 15-20% commission. Reviews material for acts.

HOW TO CONTACT *Write first and obtain permission to submit.* Prefers CD/CDR with lyric sheet. If seeking management, press kit should include CD, photo, bio, venues played and press clippings (preferably reviews). "Follow up with a phone call 3-5 weeks after submission." Does not return material. Responds in 2 months.

MUSIC Mostly **Americana**, **folk**, and **Celtic**. Works primarily with performing singer/songwriters. Current acts include Toby Walker (blues) and Vicki Genfan (folk/jazz/soul).

◑ PARADIGM TALENT AGENCY

360 N. Crescent Dr., North Bldg., Beverly Hills CA 90210. (310)288-8000. **Fax:** (310)288-2000. **Website:** www.paradigmagency.com. **Nashville:** 124 12th Ave. S., Suite 410, Nashville TN 37203. (615)251-4400. **Fax:** (615)251-4401. **New York:** 260 Park Ave. S., 16th Floor, New York, NY 10010. (212)897-6400. **Fax:** (212)764-

8941. **Monterey:** 404 W. Franklin St., Monterey, CA 93940. (831)375-4889. **Fax:** (831)375-2623. Booking agency. Represents individual artists, groups from anywhere. Receives 10% commission. Reviews material for acts.

HOW TO CONTACT *Write or call first to arrange personal interview.*

MUSIC Current acts include Ricky Skaggs, Junior Brown, Toby Keith, Kasey Chambers, Umphrey's McGee, Black Eyed Peas, Kirk Franklin, Lily Allen, My Chemical Romance, and Lauryn Hill.

⊘⊛ PRIMARY WAVE

116 East 16th Street, 9th Floor, New York NY 10003. (212)661-6990. **E-mail:** management@primarywave-Music.com. **Website:** www.primarywaveMusic.com. Primary Wave Talent Management passionately and meticulously guides the careers of our clients to enhance, shape, and extend their brand—providing a solid foundation for longevity in an ever-changing industry. From multi-platinum selling recording artists to hit-making songwriters and producers, we represent some of the biggest and brightest brands in entertainment. We leverage the full strength of Primary Wave's internal resources to ensure our clients' creative and commercial success. Our talent management division is powered by all divisions of Primary Wave including our in-house press division, A&R/writer-producer relations team, our branding company Brand Synergy Group, digital marketing arm BrightShop, as well as our in-house film, television, video game, commercial advertising and TV development team.

MUSIC Primary Wave's unique music repertoire includes an interest in the Beatles songs written by John Lennon, the catalogs of Kurt Cobain/Nirvana, Steven Tyler/Aerosmith, Daryl Hall & John Oates, Chicago, Maurice White (Earth, Wind & Fire), Def Leppard, Steve Earle, Daniel Johnston, Marvin Hamlisch, The Matrix, Lamont Dozier and Steven Curtis Chapman, as well as artists such as Airborne Toxic Event, Albert Hammond Jr., John Forte, The Boxer Rebellion, New Boyz, Taddy Porter, Anberlin, writers such as Gregg Alexander, Ryan & Smitty, LP, RoccStar, among others; as well as marketing and administration agreements with Jimmy Webb, Katrina and The Waves, Graham Parker, Evolution Entertainment/Twisted Pictures, Hammer Films, Matt Serletic and Emblem Music Group, and many others

◑ PRIME TIME ENTERTAINMENT

2430 Research Dr., Livermore CA 94550. (925)449-1724. **Fax:** (925)605-0379. **E-mail:** info@prime-timeentertainment.com. **Website:** www.primetimeentertainment.com. Management firm and booking agency. Represents individual artists, groups and songwriters from anywhere. Receives 10-20% commission. Reviews material for acts.

HOW TO CONTACT Submit demo package by mail. Unsolicited submissions are OK. Prefers CD with 3-5 songs. If seeking management, press kit should include 8x10 photo, reviews, and CDs/tapes. Include SASE. Responds in 1 month.

MUSIC Mostly **jazz**, **country**, and **alternative**; also **ethnic**.

TIPS "It's all about the song."

◑ RAINBOW TALENT AGENCY LLC

146 Round Pond Lane, Rochester NY 14626. (585)723-3334. **E-mail:** carl@rainbowtalentagency.com; info@rainbowtalentagency.com. **Website:** www.rainbowtalentagency.com. **Contact:** Carl Labate, president. Management firm and booking agency. Represents artists and groups. Receives 15-25% commission.

HOW TO CONTACT Submit demo package by mail. Unsolicited submissions are OK. Prefers CD with minimum 3 songs. May send DVD if available; "a still photo and bio of the act; if you are a performer, it would be advantageous to show yourself or the group performing live. Theme videos are not helpful." If seeking management, include photos, bio, markets established, CD/DVD. Does not return material. Responds in 1 month.

MUSIC Mostly **blues**, **rock**, and **R&B**. Works primarily with touring bands and recording artists. Current acts include Russell Thompkins Jr. & The New Stylistics (R&B), Josie Waverly (country), and Spanky Haschmann Swing Orchestra (high energy swing).

TIPS "My main interest is with groups or performers that are currently touring and have some product. And are at least 50% original. Strictly songwriters should apply elsewhere."

◯ REIGN MUSIC AND MEDIA, LLC

P.O. Box 2394, New York NY 10185. **E-mail:** online@reignmm.com. **Website:** www.reignmm.com. **Contact:** Talent Relations Department. Multi-media/artist development firm. Promotes/develops primarily local and regional vocalists, producers, and songwriters. Receives 20-25% commission. Reviews material for artists.

HOW TO CONTACT Submit demo package by mail or e-mail. Unsolicited submissions are OK. Prefers CD, mp3, or video. Standard hard copy press kit or EPK should include cover letter, press clippings and/or reviews, bio, demo (in appropriate format), picture, and accurate contact telephone number. Include SASE. Usually responds in 3 weeks.

MUSIC Mostly **pop**, **R&B**, **club/dance**, and **hip-hop/rap**; some **Latin**. Works primarily with singer/songwriters, producers, rappers, and bands.

◑ RIOHCAT MUSIC

P.O. Box 764, Hendersonville TN 37077-0764. (615)824-1435. **E-mail:** tachoir@bellsouth.net. **Website:** www.tachoir.com. **Contact:** Robert Kayne, manager. Management firm, booking agency, record company (Avita Records) and music publisher. Represents individual artists and groups. Receives 15-20% commission.

○ Also see the listing for Avita Records in the Record Companies section of this book.

HOW TO CONTACT *Contact first and obtain permission to submit.* Prefers CD and lead sheet. If seeking management, press kit should include cover letter, bio, photo, demo CD, and press clippings. Does not return material. Responds in 6 weeks.

MUSIC Mostly **contemporary jazz** and **fusion**. Works primarily with jazz ensembles. Current acts include Group Tachoir (jazz), Tachoir/Manakas Duo (jazz) and Jerry Tachoir (jazz vibraphone artist).

◐○ ROBERTSON ENTERTAINMENT

106 Harding Road Kendenup 6323, Western Australia Australia. (618)9851-4311. **Fax:** (618)9851-4225. **E-mail:** info@robertsonentertainment.com. **Website:** www.robertsonentertainment.com. **Contact:** Eddie Robertson. Booking agency. Represents individual artists and/or groups; currently handles 50 acts. Receives 20% commission. Reviews material for acts.

HOW TO CONTACT *Write first and obtain permission to submit.* Unsolicited submissions are OK. If seeking management, press kit should include photos, bio, cover letter, press clippings, video, demo, lyric sheets and any other useful information. Does not return material. Responds in 1 month.

MUSIC Mostly **top 40/pop**, **jazz**, and **60s-90s**; also **reggae** and **blues**. Works primarily with show bands and solo performers. Current acts include Faces

(dance band), Heart & Soul (easy listening), and Ruby Tuesday (contemporary pop/rock/classics).

TIPS "Send as much information as possible. If you do not receive a call after 4-5 weeks, follow up with letter or phone call."

◑ SA'MALL MANAGEMENT

468 N. Camden Dr., Suite 200, Beverly Hills CA 90210. (818)506-8533. **Fax:** (310)860-7400. **E-mail:** pplzmi@aol.com. **Website:** www.pplentertainmentgroup.com. **Contact:** Ted Steele, vice president of talent. Management firm, music publisher (Pollybyrd Publications) and record company (PPL Entertainment Group). Represents individual artists, groups and songwriters worldwide; currently handles 10 acts. Receives 10-25% commission. Reviews material for acts.

○ Also see the listing for Pollybyrd Publications Limited in the Music Publishers section of this book.

HOW TO CONTACT *E-mail first and obtain permission to submit.* "Only professional full-time artists who tour and have a fan base need apply. No weekend warriors, please." Prefers CD . If seeking management, press kit should include picture, bio and tape. Include SASE. Responds in 2 months.

MUSIC All types. Current acts include Riki Hendrix (rock), Buddy Wright (blues), Fhyne, Suzette Cuseo, The Band AKA, LeJenz, B.D. Fuoco, MoBeatz, and Kenyatta Jarrett (Prince Ken).

○ SANDALPHON MANAGEMENT

P.O. Box 18197, Panama City Beach FL 32417. **E-mail:** sandalphonMusic@yahoo.com. **Contact:** Ruth Otey. Management firm, Music publisher (Sandalphon Music Publishing/BMI), and record company (Sandalphon Records). Represents individual artists, groups, songwriters; works with individual artists and groups from anywhere. Receives negotiable commission. Reviews material for acts.

HOW TO CONTACT Submit demo by mail. Unsolicited submissions are fine. Prefers CD with 1-5 songs and lyric sheet, cover letter. "Include name, address, and contact information." Include SASE or SAE and IRC for outside the United States. Responds in 6-8 weeks.

MUSIC Mostly **rock**, **country**, and **alternative**; also **pop**, **gospel**, and **blues**. "We are looking for singers, bands, and singer/songwriters who are original but would be current in today's music markets. We help singers, bands, and singer-songwriters achieve their personal career goals."

TIPS "Submit material you feel best represents you, your voice, your songs, or your band. Fresh and original songs and style are a plus. We are a West Coast management company looking for singers, bands, and singer-songwriters who are ready for the next level. We are looking for those with talent who are capable of being national and international contenders."

●●⊛ SERGE ENTERTAINMENT GROUP

P.O. Box 5147, Canton GA 30114. (678)880-8207. **Fax:** (678)494-9289. **E-mail:** sergeent@aol.com. **Website:** www.sergeentertainmentgroup.com. **Contact:** Sandy Serge, president. Management and PR firm and song publishers. Represents individual artists, groups, songwriters from anywhere; currently handles 20 acts. Receives 20% commission for management. Monthly fee required for PR acts.

HOW TO CONTACT *E-mail first for permission to submit.* Submit demo package by mail. Unsolicited submissions are OK. Prefers CD with 4 songs and lyric sheet. If seeking management, press kit should include 8x10 photo, bio, cover letter, lyric sheets, max of 4 press clips, DVD, performance schedule and CD. "All information submitted must include name, address and phone number on each item." Does not return material. Responds in 6 weeks if interested.

MUSIC Mostly **rock**, **pop**, and **country**; also **New Age**. Works primarily with singer/songwriters and bands. Current acts include Julius Curcio (alt), Erik Norlander (prog rock), and Lana Lane (prog rock).

☯● SIEGEL ENTERTAINMENT LTD.

1736 W. 2nd Ave, Vancouver BC V6J 1H6 Canada. (604)736-3896. **Fax:** (604)736-3464. **E-mail:** siegelent@telus.net. **Website:** www.siegelent.com. **Contact:** Robert Siegel, president. Management firm and booking agency. Represents individual artists, groups and songwriters from anywhere; currently handles more than 100 acts (for bookings). Receives 15-20% commission. Reviews material for acts.

HOW TO CONTACT *Does not accept unsolicited submissions. E-mail or write for permission to submit.* Does not return material. Responds in 1 month.

MUSIC Mostly **rock**, **pop**, and **country**; also **specialty** and **children's**. Current acts include Johnny Ferreira & The Swing Machine, Lee Aaron, Kenny Blues Boss Wayne (boogie) and Tim Brecht (pop/children's).

○ GARY SMELTZER PRODUCTIONS

P.O. Box 201112, Austin TX 78720-11112. (512)478-6020. **Fax:** (512)478-8979. **E-mail:** info@garysmeltzerproductions.com. **Website:** www.garysmeltzerproductions.com. **Contact:** Gary Smeltzer, president. Management firm and booking agency. Represents individual artists and groups from anywhere. Currently handles 20 acts. "We book about 100 different bands each year—none are exclusive." Receives 20% commission. Reviews material for acts.

HOW TO CONTACT Submit demo package by mail. Unsolicited submissions are OK. Prefers CD or DVD. If seeking management, press kit should include cover letter, résumé, CD/DVD, bio, picture, lyric sheets, press clippings, and video. Does not return material. Responds in 1 month.

MUSIC Mostly **alternative**, **R&B** and **country**. Current acts include Rotel & the Hot Tomatoes (nostalgic '60s showband).

TIPS "We prefer performing songwriters who can gig their Music as a solo or group."

○ SOUND ADVICE MANAGEMENT

538 Frenchman St, New Orleans LA 70116. (504)298-6652. **E-mail:** kp@soundadvicemanagement.com. **Website:** www.soundadvicemanagement.com. **Contact:** Kimball PackaRoad For artists just starting out or looking to take it to the next level, we have a variety of a la carte options available on a contract basis, including creating your website, press kit, bio, identity and more. We are available for consultation on an hourly basis as well, to guide you through any number of projects; your first CD release (recording, packaging, duplication, promotion) online presence, publishing questions, touring, etc. Call or e-mail for more information.

◑ SOUTHEASTERN ATTRACTIONS

1025 23rd St. S., Suite 302, Birmingham AL 35205. (205)307-6790. **Fax:** (205)307-6798. **E-mail:** info@seattractions.com. **Website:** www.seattractions.com. **Contact:** Agent. Booking agency. Represents groups from anywhere. Receives 20% commission.

HOW TO CONTACT Submit demo package by mail. Unsolicited submissions are OK. Prefers CD or DVD. Does not return material. Responds in 2 months.

MUSIC Mostly **rock**, **alternative**, **oldies**, **country**, and **dance**. Works primarily with bands. Current acts include The Undergrounders (variety to contempo-

rary), The Connection (Motown/dance), andRollin'
in the Hay (bluegrass).

ⓘ STARKRAVIN' MANAGEMENT

11135 Weddington St., Suite 424, North Hollywood
CA 91601. 11135 Weddington St., Suite 424, North
Hollywood, CA 91601. (818)587-6801. **Fax:** (818)587-
6802. **E-mail:** bcmclane@aol.com. **Website:** www.
benmclane.com. **Contact:** B.C. McLane, Esq. Management and law firm. Estab. 1994. Represents individual artists, groups and songwriters. Receives 20%
commission (management); $300/hour as attorney.
HOW TO CONTACT Submit demo package by mail.
Unsolicited submissions are OK. Prefers CDs. Does
not return material. Responds in 1 month if interested.
MUSIC Mostly **rock**, **pop** and **R&B**. Works primarily with bands.

ⓞ ST. JOHN ARTISTS

P.O. Box 619, Neenah WI 54957-0619. (920)722-2222.
Fax: (920)725-2405. **E-mail:** jon@stjohn-artists.com.
Website: www.stjohn-artists.com. **Contact:** Jon
St. John and Gary Coquoz, agents. Booking agency.
Represents local and regional individual artists and
groups; currently handles 20 acts. Receives 15-20%
commission. Reviews material for acts.
HOW TO CONTACT *Call first and obtain permission to submit.* Prefers CD or DVD. If seeking
management, press kit should include cover letter, bio,
photo, demo CD, video and résumé. Include SASE.
MUSIC Mostly **rock** and **MOR**. Current acts include
Boogie & the Yo-Yo's (60s to 2000s), Vic Ferrari (Top
40 '80s-2000s), Little Vito & the Torpedoes (variety
'50s-2000s), and Da Yoopers (Musical comedy/nov-
elty).

ⓘ TAS MUSIC CO./DAVID TASSÉ
ENTERTAINMENT

N2467 Knollwood Dr., Lake Geneva WI 53147.
(888)554-9898; (262)245-1335. **E-mail:** info@bay-
breezerecords.com. **Website:** www.baybreezerecords.
com. **Contact:** David Tassé. Booking agency, record
company and music publisher. Represents artists,
groups, and songwriters; currently handles 21 acts.
Receives 10-20% commission. Reviews material for
acts.
HOW TO CONTACT Submit demo by mail. Unsolicited submissions are OK. Prefers CD with 2-4 songs
and lyric sheet. Include performance videocassette
if available. If seeking management, press kit should

include tape, bio, and photo. Does not return material.
Responds in 3 weeks.
MUSIC Mostly **pop** and **jazz**; also **dance, MOR, rock,
soul**, and **top 40**. Works primarily with show and
dance bands. Current acts include Maxx Kelly (po-
prock) and Glenn Davis (blues band).

ⓞ UNIVERSAL MUSIC MARKETING

P.O. Box 2297, Universal City TX 78148. Phone/fax:
(210)653-3989. **Website:** www.universalMusicmar-
keting.net. **Contact:** Frank Wilson, president. Management firm, record company (BSW Records), booking agency, music publisher and record producer
(Frank Wilson). Represents individual artists and
groups from anywhere. Receives 15% commission.
Reviews material for acts.
HOW TO CONTACT Submit demo package by mail.
Unsolicited submissions are OK. Prefers CD or DVD
with 3 songs and lyric sheet. If seeking management,
include tape/CD, bio, photo and current activities. Include SASE. Responds in 6 weeks.
MUSIC Mostly **country** and **light rock**; also **blues**
and **jazz**. Works primarily with vocalists, singer/
songwriters and bands.
TIPS "Visit our website for an up-to-date listing of
current acts."

WHITESMITH ENTERTAINMENT

E-mail: Info@WhitesmithEnt.com. **Website:** www.
whitesmithentertainment.com. **Contact:** LA: Keri
Smith Esguia (keri@whitesmithent.com); NY: Em-
ily White (emily@whitesmithent.com). Whitesmith
Entertainment is a full-service talent management
firm based in Los Angeles and New York, spanning
the music, comedy, film, TV, literary, & sports industries. We take pride in working with artists who have a
unique voice, style and meaning to their fans. Whitesmith balances a youthful edge while maintaining a
deep knowledge within the fields of touring, merchandising, online marketing, social networking, branding, sponsorship, as well as physical and modern content releases. Whitesmith Entertainment is available
for outside consulting services in all areas of artist
development, content releases, touring services, online marketing, and beyond.
MUSIC Artists represented include Brandan Benson,
The Big Sleep, Hockey, The Autumn Defense, GOLD
MOTEL, Urge Overkill, Future Monarchs, and many
more.

◐ WORLDSOUND, LLC

17837 1st Ave. South, Suite 3, Seattle WA 98148. (206)444-0300. **Fax:** (206)244-0066. **E-mail:** a-r@ worldsound.com. **Website:** www.worldsound.com. **Contact:** Warren Wyatt, A&R manager. Management firm. Represents individual artists, groups and songwriters from anywhere. Receives 20% commission. Reviews material for acts.

HOW TO CONTACT "Online, send us an e-mail containing a link to your website where your songs can be heard and the lyrics are available; please do not e-mail song files! By regular mail, unsolicited submissions are OK." Prefers CD with 2-10 songs and lyric sheet. "If seeking management, please send an e-mail with a link to your website—your site should contain song samples, band biography, photos, video (if available), press and demo reviews. By mail, please send the materials listed above and include SASE." Responds in 1 month.

MUSIC Mostly **rock**, **pop**, and **world**; also **heavy metal**, **hard rock**, and **top 40**. Works primarily with pop/rock/world artists.

TIPS "Always submit new songs/material, even if you have sent material that was previously rejected; the music biz is always changing."

◐ ZANE MANAGEMENT, INC.

One Liberty Place, 1650 Market St., 56th Floor, Philadelphia PA 19103. (215)575-3803. **Fax:** (215)575-3801. **Website:** www.zanemanagement.com. **Contact:** Lloyd Z. Remick, Esq., president. Entertainment/sports consultants and managers. Represents artists, songwriters, producers and athletes; currently handles 7 acts. Receives 10-15% commission.

HOW TO CONTACT Submit demo tape by mail. Unsolicited submissions are OK. Prefers CD and lyric sheet. If seeking management, press kit should include cover letter, bio, photo, demo tape and video. Does not return material. Responds in 3 weeks.

MUSIC Mostly **dance**, **easy listening**, **folk**, **jazz (fusion)**, **MOR**, **rock (hard and country)**, **soul** and **top 40/pop**. Current acts include Bunny Sigler (disco/funk), Peter Nero and Philly Pops (conductor), Pieces of a Dream (jazz/crossover), Don't Look Down (rock/pop), Christian Josi (pop-swing), Bishop David Evans (gospel), Kevin Roth (children's music), and Rosie Carlino (standards/pop).

MUSIC FIRMS

///

It's happens a million times—you hear a jingle on the radio or television and can't get it out of your head. That's the work of a successful jingle writer, writing songs to catch your attention and make you aware of the product being advertised. But the field of commercial Music consists of more than just memorable jingles. It also includes background Music that many companies use in videos for corporate and educational presentations, as well as films and TV shows.

SUBMITTING MATERIAL

More than any other market listed in this book, the commercial Music market expects composers to have made an investment in the recording of their material before submitting. A sparse piano/vocal demo won't work here; when dealing with commercial Music firms, especially audiovisual firms and Music libraries, high quality production is important. Your demo may be kept on file at one of these companies until a need for it arises, and it may be used or sold as you sent it. Therefore, your demo tape or reel must be as fully produced as possible.

The presentation package that goes along with your demo must be just as professional. A list of your credits should be a part of your submission, to give the company an idea of your experience in this field. If you have no experience, look to local television and radio stations to get your start. Don't expect to be paid for many of your first jobs in the commercial Music field; it's more important to get the credits and exposure that can lead to higher-paying jobs.

Commercial Music and jingle writing can be a lucrative field for the composer/songwriter with a gift for writing catchy melodies and the ability to write in many different Music styles. It's a very competitive field, so it pays to have a professional presentation package that makes your work stand out.

Three different segments of the commercial Music world are listed here: advertising agencies, audiovisual firms and commercial Music houses/Music libraries. Each looks for a different type of Music, so read these descriptions carefully to see where the Music you write fits in.

ADVERTISING AGENCIES

Ad agencies work on assignment as their clients' needs arise. Through consultation and input from the creative staff, ad agencies seek jingles and Music to stimulate the consumer to identify with a product or service.

When contacting ad agencies, keep in mind they are searching for Music that can capture and then hold an audience's attention. Most jingles are short, with a strong, memorable hook. When an ad agency listens to a demo, it is not necessarily looking for a finished product so much as for an indication of creativity and diversity. Many composers put together a reel of excerpts of work from previous projects, or short pieces of Music that show they can write in a variety of styles.

AUDIOVISUAL FIRMS

Audiovisual firms create a variety of products, from film and video shows for sales meetings, corporate gatherings and educational markets, to motion pictures and TV shows. With the increase of home video use, how-to videos are a big market for audiovisual firms, as are spoken word educational videos. All of these products need Music to accompany them. For your quick reference, companies working to place Music in movies and TV shows (excluding commercials) have a preceding their listing (also see the Film & TV Index in the back of the book for a complete list of these companies).

Like ad agencies, audiovisual firms look for versatile, well-rounded songwriters. When submitting demos to these firms, you need to demonstrate your versatility in writing specialized background Music and themes. Listings for companies will tell what facet(s) of the audiovisual field they are involved in and what types of clients they serve. Your demo tape should also be as professional and fully produced as possible; audiovisual firms often seek demo tapes that can be put on file for future use when the need arises.

COMMERCIAL MUSIC HOUSES & MUSIC LIBRARIES

Commercial Music houses are companies contracted (either by an ad agency or the advertiser) to compose custom jingles. Because they are neither an ad agency nor an audiovisual firm, their main concern is Music. They use a lot of it, too—some composed by inhouse songwriters and some contributed by outside, freelance writers.

Music libraries are different in that their Music is not custom composed for a specific client. Their job is to provide a collection of instrumental Music in many different styles that, for an annual fee or on a per-use basis, the customer can use however he chooses.

In the following listings, commercial Music houses and Music libraries, which are usually the most open to works by new composers, are identified as such by **bold** type.

The commercial Music market is similar to most other businesses in one aspect: experience is important. Until you develop a list of credits, pay for your work may not be high. Don't pass up opportunities if a job is non- or low-paying. These assignments will add to your list of credits, make you contacts in the field, and improve your marketability.

Money & rights

Many of the companies listed in this section pay by the job, but there may be some situations where the company asks you to sign a contract that will specify royalty payments. If this happens, research the contract thoroughly, and know exactly what is expected of you and how much you'll be paid.

Depending on the particular job and the company, you may be asked to sell one-time rights or all rights. One-time rights involve using your material for one presentation only. All rights means the buyer can use your work any way he chooses, as many times as he likes. Be sure you know exactly what you're giving up, and how the company may use your Music in the future.

In the commercial world, many of the big advertising agencies have their own publishing companies where writers assign their compositions. In these situations, writers sign contracts whereby they do receive performance and mechanical royalties when applicable.

ADDITIONAL LISTINGS

For additional names and addresses of ad agencies that may use jingles and/or commercial Music, refer to the *Standard Directory of Advertising Agencies* (National Register Publishing). For a list of audiovisual firms, check out the latest edition of *AV Marketplace* (R.R. Bowker). Both these books may be found at your local library. To contact companies in your area, see the Geographic Index at the back of this book.

THE AD AGENCY

P.O. Box 470572, San Francisco CA 94147. **E-mail:** michaelcarden@msn.com. **Contact:** Michael Carden, creative director. Advertising agency and jingle/commercial Music production house. Clients include business, industry and retail. Uses the services of Music houses, independent songwriter/composers and lyricists for scoring of commercials, background Music for video production, and jingles for commercials. Commissions 20 composers and 15 lyricists/year. Pays by the job or by the hour. Buys all or one-time rights.

HOW TO CONTACT Submit demo tape of previous work. Prefers CD with 5-8 songs and lyric sheet. Include SASE. Responds in 3 weeks. Uses variety of Musical styles for commercials, promotion, TV, video presentations.

TIPS "Our clients and our needs change frequently."

CEDAR CREST STUDIO

#17 CR 830, Henderson AR 72544. (870)488-5777. **E-mail:** cedarcrest@springfield.net. **Website:** www.cedarcreststudio.com. **Contact:** Bob Ketchum, owner. **Audiovisual firm and jingle/commercial Music production house.** Clients include corporate, industrial, sales, Music publishing, training, educational, legal, medical, Music and Internet. Sometimes uses the services of independent songwriters/composers for background Music for video productions, jingles for TV spots and commercials for radio and TV. Pays by the job or by royalties. Buys all rights or one-time rights. Query with résumé of credits or submit demo tape of previous work. Prefers CD or DVD. Does not return material. "We keep it on file for future reference." Responds in 2 months. Uses up-tempo pop (not too "rocky"), unobtrusive—no solos for commercials and background Music for video presentations.

TIPS "Hang, hang, hang. Be open to suggestions. Improvise, adapt, overcome."

COMMUNICATIONS FOR LEARNING

395 Massachusetts Ave., Arlington MA 02474. (781)641-2350. **E-mail:** comlearn@thecia.net. **Website:** www.communicationsforlearning.com. **Contact:** Jonathan L. Barkan, executive producer/director. Video, multimedia, exhibit and graphic design firm. Clients include multi-nationals, industry, government, institutions, local, national and international nonprofits. Uses services of Music houses and independent songwriters/composers as theme and background Music for videos and multimedia. Commissions 1-2 composers/year. Pays $2,000-5,000/job and one-time use fees. Rights purchased vary. Submit demo and work available for library use. Prefers CD to Web links. Does not return material; prefers to keep on file. "For each job we consider our entire collection." Responds in 3 months.

TIPS "Please don't call. Just send your best material available for library use on CD. We'll be in touch if a piece works and negotiate a price. Make certain your name and contact information are on the CD itself, not only on the cover letter."

DBF A MEDIA COMPANY

9683 Charles St., LaPlata MD 20646. (301)645-6110. **E-mail:** service@dbfmedia.com. **Website:** www.db-fmedia.com. Video production. Uses the services of Music houses for background Music for industrial, training, educational, and promo videos, jingles and commercials for radio and TV. Buys all rights. "All genre for MOH, industrial, training, video/photo montages and commercials."

HOW TO CONTACT Submit demo CD of previous work. Prefers CD or DVD with 5-8 songs and lead sheet. Include SASE, but prefers to keep material on file. Responds in 6 months.

⊙⊛ DISK PRODUCTIONS

1100 Perkins Road, Baton Rouge LA 70802. **E-mail:** disk_productions@yahoo.com. **Contact:** Joey Decker, director. **Jingle/production house.** Clients include advertising agencies and film companies. Uses the services of Music houses, independent songwriters/composers and lyricists for scoring and background Music for TV spots, films and jingles for radio and TV. Commissions 7 songwriters/composers and 7 lyricists/year. Pays by the job. Buys all rights.

HOW TO CONTACT Submit demo of previous work. Prefers DVD or CD. Does not return material. Responds in 2 weeks.

MUSIC Needs all types of Music for jingles, Music beds or background Music for TV and radio, etc.

TIPS "Advertising techniques change with time. Don't be locked in a certain style of writing. Give me Music that I can't get from pay needle-drop."

HOME, INC.

566 Columbus Ave., Boston MA 02118. (617)427-4663. **Fax:** (617)427-4664. **E-mail:** alanmichel@homeinc.org. **Website:** www.homeinc.org. **Contact:** Alan Michel, director and co-founder. Audiovisu-

al firm and video production company. Clients include cable television, nonprofit organizations, pilot programs, entertainment companies and industrial. Uses the services of Music houses and independent songwriters/composers for scoring of Music videos, background Music and commercials for TV. Commissions 2-5 songwriters/year. Pays up to $200-600/job. Buys all rights and one-time rights. Submit demo tape of previous work. Prefers CD or website URL with 6 pieces. Does not return material; prefers to keep on file. Responds as projects require.

MUSIC Mostly synthesizer. Uses all styles of Music for educational videos.

TIPS "Have a variety of products available and be willing to match your skills to the project and the budget."

K&R ALL MEDIA PRODUCTIONS LLC

28533 Greenfield Road, Southfield MI 48076. (248)557-8276. **E-mail:** recordav@knr.net. **Website:** www.knr.net. Scoring service and **jingle/commercial Music production house**. Clients include commercial and industrial firms. Services include sound for pictures (Foley, Music, dialogue). Uses the services of independent songwriters/composers and lyricists for scoring of film and video, commercials and industrials and jingles and commercials for radio and TV. Commissions 1 composer/month. Pays by the job. Buys all rights.

HOW TO CONTACT Submit demo tape of previous work. Prefers CD or VHS videocassette with 5-7 short pieces. "We rack your tape for client to judge." Does not return material.

TIPS "Keep samples short. Show me what you can do in 5 minutes. Go to knr.net 'free samples' and listen to the sensitivity expressed in emotional Music."

KEN-DEL PRODUCTIONS INC.

1500 First State Blvd., First State Industrial Park, Wilmington DE 19804-3596. (302)999-1111. **E-mail:** info@ken-del.com. **Website:** www.ken-del.com. Clients include publishers, industrial firms and advertising agencies, how-to's and radio/TV. Uses services of songwriters for radio/TV commercials, jingles and multimedia. Pays by the job. Buys all rights.

HOW TO CONTACT Submit all inquiries and demos in any format to general manager." Does not return material. Will keep on file for 3 years. Generally responds in 1 month or less.

LAPRIORE VIDEOGRAPHY

67 Millbrook St. Ste. 114, Worcester MA 01606. (508)755-9010. **E-mail:** peter@lapriorevideo.com. **Website:** www.lapriorevideo.com. **Contact:** Peter Lapriore, owner/producer. Video production company. Clients include corporations, retail stores, educational and sports. Uses the services of Music houses, independent songwriters/composers for background Music for marketing, training, educational videos and TV commercials and for scoring video. "We also own several Music libraries." Commissions 2 composers/year. Pays $150-1,000/job. Buys all or one-time rights.

HOW TO CONTACT Submit demo of previous work. Prefers CD, or DVD with 5 songs and lyric sheet. Does not return material; prefers to keep on file. Responds in 3 weeks.

MUSIC Uses slow, medium, up-tempo, jazz and classical for marketing, educational films and commercials.

TIPS "Be very creative and willing to work on all size budgets."

⊙ NOVUS VISUAL COMMUNICATIONS

59 Page Ave., Suite 300, Tower One, Yonkers NY 10704. (212)473-1377. **E-mail:** novuscom@aol.com. **E-mail:** robert@nakinc.com. **Website:** www.novuscommunications.com. **Contact:** Robert Antonik, managing director. Integrated marketing, communications and consultation company. Clients include Fortune 500 companies and nonprofits. Uses the services of Music houses, independent songwriters/composers and lyricists for scoring, background Music for documentaries, commercials, multimedia applications, website, film shorts, and commercials for radio and TV. Commissions 2 composers and 4 lyricists/year. Pay varies per job. Buys one-time rights.

HOW TO CONTACT *Request a submission of demo.* Query with a brief of sample and songs. Prefers CD with 2-3 songs or link to website. "We prefer to keep submitted material on file, but will return material if SASE is enclosed. Responds in 6 weeks.

MUSIC Uses all styles for a variety of different assignments.

TIPS "Always present your best and don't add quantity to your demo. Novus is a creative marketing and integrated communications company. We work with special events companies, PR firms, artists' management and media companies."

OMNI COMMUNICATIONS

P.O. Box 302, Carmel IN 46082-0302. (317)846-2345. **Fax:** (317)846-6664. **E-mail:** omni@omniproductions.com. **Website:** www.omniproductions.com. OMNI Productions is an experienced interactive, digital media solutions provider offering the complete infrastructure for production and delivery of digital media services including interactive multipoint Internet training; live event and archived web casting; video, DVD & CD-ROM production; and encoding, hosting and distribution of streaming video content. OMNI is recognized by Microsoft as a Windows Media Service Provider. This partnership with Microsoft was obtained through vigorous training, testing and experience to ensure that those we serve receive the highest quality service from OMNI's experienced professionals. OMNI's staff includes technology experts certified by Microsoft and other industry vendors.

TIPS "Submit good demo tape with examples of your range to command the attention of our producers."

UTOPIAN EMPIRE CREATIVEWORKS

P.O. Box 9, Traverse City MI 49865. (231)715-1614. **E-mail:** creativeservices@utopianempire.com; clientworks@utopianempire.com. **Website:** www.utopianempire.com. **Contact:** Ms. M'Lynn Hartwell, president. Web design, multimedia firm, and motion picture/video production company. Primarily serves commercial, industrial and nonprofit clients. "We provide the following services: advertising, marketing, design/packaging, distribution and booking. Uses services of Music houses, independent songwriters/composers for jingles and scoring of and background Music for multi-image/multimedia, film and video." Negotiates pay. Buys all or one-time rights.

HOW TO CONTACT Submit CD of previous work, demonstrating composition skills or query with resume of credits. Prefers CD. Does not return material; prefers to keep on file. Responds only if interested.

MUSIC Uses mostly industrial/commercial themes.

✇ VIDEO I-D, TELEPRODUCTIONS

105 Muller Road, Washington IL 61571. (309)444-4323. **E-mail:** videoid@videoid.com. **Website:** www.videoid.com. **Contact:** Sam B. Wagner, president. Post production/teleproductions. Clients include law enforcement, industrial and business. Uses the services of Music houses and independent songwriters/composers for background Music for video productions. Pays per job. Buys one-time rights.

HOW TO CONTACT Submit demo of previous work. Prefers CD with 5 songs and lyric sheet. Does not return material. Responds in 1 month.

PLAY PRODUCERS
& PUBLISHERS

//

Finding a theater company willing to invest in a new production can be frustrating for an unknown playwright. But whether you write the plays, compose the music or pen the lyrics, it is important to remember not only where to start but how to start. Theater in the US is a hierarchy, with Broadway, Off Broadway, and Off Off Broadway being pretty much off limits to all but the Stephen Sondheims of the world.

Aspiring theater writers would do best to train their sights on nonprofit regional and community theaters to get started. The encouraging news is there are a great number of local theater companies throughout the US with experimental artistic directors who are looking for new works to produce, and many are included in this section. This section covers two segments of the industry: theater companies and dinner theaters are listed under Play Producers, and publishers of musical theater works are listed under the Play Publishers heading. All these markets are actively seeking new works of all types for their stages or publications.

BREAKING IN

Starting locally will allow you to research each company carefully and learn about their past performances, the type of musicals they present, and the kinds of material they're looking for. When you find theaters you think may be interested in your work, attend as many performances as possible, so you know exactly what type of material each theater presents. Or volunteer to work at a theater, whether it be moving sets or selling tickets. This will give you valuable insight into the day-to-day workings of a theater and the creation of a new show. On a national level, you will find prestigious organizations offering workshops and apprenticeships covering every subject from arts administration to directing to costuming. But it could be more helpful to look into professional internships at theaters and attend theater workshops in your area. The more knowledgeable you are about the workings of a particular company or theater, the easier it will be to tailor your work to fit its style and the more responsive they will be to you and your work. (See the Workshops & Conferences section on page 260 for more information.) As a composer for the stage, you need to know as much as possible about a theater and how it works, its history and the different roles played by the people involved in it. Flexibility is the key to successful productions, and knowing how a theater works will only help you in cooperating and collaborating with the director, producer, technical people and actors.

If you're a playwright looking to have his play published in book form or in theater publications, see the listings under the Play Publishers section. To find play producers and publishers in your area, consult the Geographic Index at the back of this book.

ARKANSAS REPERTORY THEATRE

601 Main St., P.O. Box 110, Little Rock AR 72201. (501)378-0445. **E-mail:** bhupp@therep.org. **Website:** www.therep.org. Produces 6-10 plays and musicals/year. "We perform in a 354-seat house and also have a 99-seat second stage." Pays 5-10% royalty or $75-150 per performance.

HOW TO CONTACT Query with synopsis, character breakdown and set description. Include SASE. Responds in 6 months.

MUSICAL THEATER "Small casts are preferred, comedy or drama and prefer shows to run 1:45 to 2 hours maximum. Simple is better; small is better, but we do produce complex shows. We aren't interested in children's pieces, puppet shows or mime. We always like to receive a tape of the music with the book."

PRODUCTIONS *Disney's Beauty & the Beast*, by Woolverton/Ashman/Rice/Menken (musical retelling of the myth); *Crowns*, by Taylor/Cunningham/Marberry (on the significance of African-American women's hats); and *A Chorus Line*, by Kirkwood/Hamlisch/Kleban (auditions).

TIPS "Include a good CD of your music, sung well, with the script."

WILLIAM CAREY UNIVERSITY DINNER THEATRE

William Carey College, Hattiesburg MS 39401 United States. (601)318-6051. **E-mail:** cdt@wmcarey.edu. **Website:** www.wmcarey.edu. "Our dinner theater operates only in summer and plays to family audiences." Payment negotiable.

HOW TO CONTACT Query with synopsis, character breakdown and set description. Does not return material. Responds in 1 month.

MUSICAL THEATER "Plays should be simply-staged, have small casts (8-10 maximum), and be suitable for family viewing; two hours maximum length. Score should require piano only, or piano, synthesizer."

PRODUCTIONS *Ring of Fire: The Johnny Cash Musical*; *Smoke on the Mountain*; *Spitfire Grill*; and *Pump Boys and Dinettes*.

CIRCA '21 DINNER PLAYHOUSE

1828 Third Ave., Rock Island IL 61201 United States. (309)786-7733. **Website:** www.circa21.com. Plays produced for a general audience. Three children's works/year, concurrent with major productions. Payment is negotiable.

HOW TO CONTACT Query with synopsis, character breakdown and set description or submit complete manuscript, score and tape of songs. Include SASE. Responds in 3 months.

MUSICAL THEATER "We produce both full length and one act children's musicals. Folk or fairy tale themes. Works that do not condescend to a young audience yet are appropriate for entire family. We're also seeking full-length, small cast musicals suitable for a broad audience." Would also consider original music for use in a play being developed.

PRODUCTIONS *A Closer Walk with Patsy Cline*, *Swingtime Canteen*, *Forever Plaid* and *Lost Highway*.

TIPS "Small, upbeat, tourable musicals (like *Pump Boys*) and bright musically-sharp children's productions (like those produced by Prince Street Players) work best. Keep an open mind. Stretch to encompass a musical variety—different keys, rhythms, musical ideas and textures."

LA JOLLA PLAYHOUSE

P.O. Box 12039, La Jolla CA 92039 United States. (858)550-1070. **Fax:** (858)550-1075. **E-mail:** information@ljp.org. **Website:** www.lajollaplayhouse.org. Produces 6-show season including 1-2 new musicals/year. Audience is University of California students to senior citizens. Performance spaces include a large proscenium theatre with 492 seats, a 3/4 thrust (384 seats), and a black box with up to 400 seats.

HOW TO CONTACT Query with synopsis, character breakdown, 10-page dialogue sample, demo CD. Include SASE. Responds in 1-2 months.

MUSICAL THEATER "We prefer contemporary music but not necessarily a story set in contemporary times. Retellings of classic stories can enlighten us about the times we live in. For budgetary reasons, we'd prefer a smaller cast size."

PRODUCTIONS *Cry-Baby*, book and lyrics by Thomas Meehan and Mark O'Donnell, music by David Javerbaum and Adam Schlesinger; *Dracula, The Musical*, book and lyrics by Don Black and Christopher Hampton, music by Frank Wildhorn (adaptation of Bram Stoker's novel); *Thoroughly Modern Millie*, book by Richard Morris and Dick Scanlan, new music by Jeanine Tesori, new lyrics by Dick Scanlan (based on the 1967 movie); and *Jane Eyre*, book and additional lyrics by John Cairo, music and lyrics by Paul Gordon (adaptation of Charlotte Bronte's novel).

NORTH SHORE MUSIC THEATRE

62 Dunham Rd., Beverly MA 01915 United States. (978)232-7200. **Fax:** (978)921-9999. **E-mail:** NorthShoreMusicTheatre@nsmt.org. **Website:** www.nsmt. org.

HOW TO CONTACT Submit synopsis and CD of songs. Include SASE. Responds within 6 months.

MUSICAL THEATER Prefers full-length adult pieces not necessarily arena-theatre oriented. Cast sizes from 1-30; orchestra's from 1-16.

PRODUCTIONS *Tom Jones*, by Paul Leigh, George Stiles; *I Sent A Letter to My Love*, by Melissa Manchester and Jeffrey Sweet; *Just So*, by Anthony Drewe & George Stiles (musical based on Rudyard Kipling's fables); *Letters from 'Nam*, by Paris Barclay (Vietnam War experience as told through letters from GI's); and *Friendship of the Sea*, by Michael Wartofsky & Kathleen Cahill (New England maritime adventure musical).

TIPS "Keep at it!"

THE OPEN EYE THEATER

P.O. Box 959, 960 Main St., Margaretville NY 12455 United States. **E-mail:** openeye@catskill.net. **Website:** www.theopeneye.org. P.O. Box 959, 960 Main St., Margaretville NY 12455. **Phone/Fax:** (845)586-1660. **E-mail:** openeye@catskill.net. **Website:** www. theopeneye.org. **Contact:** Amie Brockway, producing artistic director. Play producer. Estab. 1972. Produces approximately 3 full length or 3 new plays for multigenerational audiences. Pays on a fee basis.

HOW TO CONTACT Query first. "A manuscript will be accepted and read only if it is a play for all ages and is: 1) Submitted by a recognized literary agent; 2) Requested or recommended by a staff or company member; or 3) Recommended by a professional colleague with whose work we are familiar. Playwrights may submit a one-page letter of inquiry including a very brief plot synopsis. Please enclose a self-addressed (but not stamped) envelope. We will reply only if we want you to submit the script (within several months)."

MUSICAL THEATER "The Open Eye Theater is a not-for-profit professional company working in a community context. Through the development, production and performance of plays for all ages, artists and audiences are challenged and given the opportunity to grow in the arts. In residence, on tour, and in the classroom, The Open Eye Theater strives to stimulate, educate, entertain, inspire and serve as a creative resource."

PRODUCTIONS *The Tempest* and *As You Like It* by Shakespeare; John Dilworth Newman's *A Year Down Yonder* based on the novel for young readers by Richard Peck; Willy Russell's *Shirley Valentine*; Sandra Fenichel Asher's *The Princess and the Goblin* and *Keeping Mr. Lincoln*; Robert Harling's *Steel Magnolias*; Amie Brockway's *The Cricket on the Hearth*, based on the book by Charles Dickens.

PRIMARY STAGES

307 W. 38th St., Suite 1510, New York NY 10018 United States. (212)840-9705. **Fax:** (212)840-9725. **E-mail:** info@primarystages.org. **Website:** www.primarystages.org. New York theater-going audience representing a broad cross-section, in terms of age, ethnicity, and economic backgrounds. 199-seat, Off-Broadway theater.

HOW TO CONTACT *No unsolicited scripts accepted. Submissions by agents only.* Include SASE. Responds in up to 8 months.

MUSICAL THEATER "We are looking for work of heightened theatricality, that challenges realism— musical plays that go beyond film and televisions standard fare. We are looking for small cast shows under 6 characters total, with limited sets. We are interested in original works, that have not been produced in New York."

PRODUCTIONS *Harbor*, by Chad Beguelin; *Bronx Bombers*, by Fran Kirmser and Eric Simmonson; *The Model Apartment*, by Donald Margulies; *The Tribute Artist*, by Charles Busch.

PRINCE MUSIC THEATER

1412 Chestnut St., Philadelphia PA 19102. (215)569-9700. **E-mail:** info@princemusictheater.org. **Website:** www.princemusictheater.org. **Contact:** Nancy Lee Kathan, artistic administrator. "Professional musical productions. Drawing upon operatic and popular traditions as well as European, African, Asian, and South American forms, new work, and new voices take center stage." Play producer. Produces 4-5 musicals/year. "Our average audience member is in their mid-40s. We perform to ethnically diverse houses."

HOW TO CONTACT Submit 2-page synopsis with tape or CD of 4 songs. Include SASE. "May include complete script, but be aware that response is at least 10 months."

TIPS "Innovative topics and use of media, music, technology a plus. Sees trends of arts in technology (interactive theater, virtual reality, sound design); works are shorter in length (60 to 90 minutes with no intermissions or 2 hours with intermission)."

THUNDER BAY THEATRE

400 N. Second Ave., Alpena MI 49707 United States. (989)354-2267. **E-mail:** TBT@ThunderBayTheatre. com; ArtisticDirector@ThunderBayTheatre.com. **Website:** www.thunderbaytheatre.com.

HOW TO CONTACT Submit complete ms, score and tape of songs. Include SASE.

MUSICAL THEATER Small cast. Not equipped for large sets. Considers original background music for use in a play being developed or for use in a pre-existing play.

CLASSICAL PERFORMING ARTS

//

Finding an audience is critical to the composer of orchestral Music. Fortunately, baby boomers are swelling the ranks of classical Music audiences and bringing with them a taste for fresh, innovative music. So the climate is fair for composers seeking their first performance.

Finding a performance venue is particularly important because once a composer has his work performed for an audience and establishes himself as a talented newcomer, it can lead to more performances and commissions for new works.

BEFORE YOU SUBMIT

Be aware that most classical music organizations are nonprofit groups, and don't have a large budget for acquiring new works. It takes a lot of time and money to put together an orchestral performance of a new composition, therefore these groups are quite selective when choosing new works to perform. Don't be disappointed if the payment offered by these groups is small or even non-existent. What you gain is the chance to have your music performed for an appreciative audience. Also realize that many classical groups are understaffed, so it may take longer than expected to hear back on your submission. It pays to be patient, and employ diplomacy, tact and timing in your follow-up.

In this section you will find listings for classical performing arts organizations throughout the US. But if you have no prior performances to your credit, it's a good idea to begin with a small chamber orchestra, for example. Smaller symphony and chamber orchestras are usually more inclined to experiment with new works. A local university or conservatory of music, where you may already have contacts, is a great place to start.

All of the groups listed in this section are interested in hearing new works from contemporary classical composers. Pay close attention to the music needs of each group, and when you find one you feel might be interested in your music, follow submission guidelines carefully. To locate classical performing arts groups in your area, consult the Geographic Index at the back of this book.

ACADIANA SYMPHONY ORCHESTRA

P.O. Box 53632, Lafayette LA 70505. (337)232-4277. **Website:** www.acadianasymphony.org. 412 Travis St., Lafayette LA 70503. (337)232-4277. **Fax:** (337)237-4712. **Website:** www.acadianasymphony. org. **Contact:** Jenny Krueger, executive director. Estab. 1984. Members are amateurs and professionals. Performs 20 concerts/year, including 1 new work. Commissions 1 new work/year. Performs in 2,230-seat hall with "wonderful acoustics." Pays "according to the type of composition."

HOW TO CONTACT Call first. Does not return material. Responds in 2 months.

MUSIC Full orchestra: 10 minutes at most. Reduced orchestra, educational pieces: short, up to 5 minutes.

PERFORMANCES Quincy Hilliard's *Universal Covenant* (orchestral suite); James Hanna's *In Memoriam* (strings/elegy); and Gregory Danner's *A New Beginning* (full orchestra fanfare).

THE AMERICAN BOYCHOIR

75 Mapleton Road, Princeton NJ 08540. (609)924-5858. **E-mail:** admissions@americanboychoir.org. **Website:** www.americanboychoir.org. 75 Mapleton Road, Princeton NJ 08540. (609)924-5858. **Fax:** (609)924-5812. **E-mail:** admissions@americanboychoir.org. **Website:** www.americanboychoir.org. General Manager: Christie Starrett. Music director: Fernando Malvar-Ruiz. Professional boychoir. Estab. 1937. Members are musically talented boys in grades 4-8. Performs 150 concerts/year. Commissions 1 new work approximately every 3 years. Actively seeks high quality arrangements. Performs national and international tours, orchestral engagements, church services, workshops, school programs, local concerts, and at corporate and social functions.

HOW TO CONTACT Submit complete score. Include SASE. Responds in 1 year.

MUSIC Choral works in unison, SA, SSA, SSAA or SATB division; unaccompanied and with piano or organ; occasional chamber orchestra or brass ensemble. Works are usually sung by 28-60 boys. Composers must know boychoir sonority.

PERFORMANCES *Four Seasons*, by Michael Torke (orchestral-choral); *Garden of Light*, by Aaron Kernis (orchestral-choral); *Reasons for Loving the Harmonica*, by Libby Larsen (piano); and *Songs Eternity*, by Steven Paulus (piano).

ANDERSON SYMPHONY ORCHESTRA

1124 Meridian Plaza, Anderson IN 46016 United States. **Website:** www.andersonsymphony.org. 1124 Meridian Plaza, Anderson IN 46016. (765)644-2111. **E-mail:** aso@andersonsymphony.org. **Website:** www. andersonsymphony.org. **Contact:** Dr. Richard Sowers, Music director. Symphony orchestra. Estab. 1967. Members are professionals. Performs 7 concerts/year. Performs for typical mid-western audience in a 1,500-seat restored Paramount Theatre. Pay negotiable.

HOW TO CONTACT Query first. Include SASE. Responds in several months.

MUSIC "Shorter lengths better; concerti OK; difficulty level: mod high; limited by typically 3 full service rehearsals."

THE ATLANTA YOUNG SINGERS OF CALLANWOLDE

1085 Ponce de Leon Ave NE, Atlanta GA 30306 United States. **Website:** www.aysc.org. 1085 Ponce de Leon Ave NE, Atlanta GA 30306. (404)873-3365. **Fax:** (404)873-0756. **E-mail:** info@aysc.org. **Website:** www.aysc.org. **Contact:** Paige F. Mathis, Music director. Children's chorus. Estab. 1975. Performs 3 major concerts/year as well as invitational performances and co-productions with other Atlanta arts organizations. Audience consists of community members, families, alumni, and supporters. Performs most often at churches. Pay is negotiable.

HOW TO CONTACT Submit complete score and tape of piece(s). Include SASE. Responds in accordance with request.

MUSIC Subjects and styles appealing to 3rd- to 12th-grade boys and girls. Contemporary concerns of the world of interest. Unusual sacred, folk, classic style. Internationally and ethnically bonding. Medium difficulty preferred, with or without keyboard accompaniment.

TIPS "Our mission is to promote service and growth through singing."

AUGSBURG CHOIR

Augsburg Colleg, 2211 Riverside Ave. S, Minneapolis MN 55454 United States. **Website:** www.augsburg. edu. Augsburg College, 2211 Riverside Ave. S, Minneapolis MN 55454. (612)330-1265. **E-mail:** Musicdept@ augsburg.edu. **Website:** www.augsburg.edu. **Director of Choral Activities:** Peter A. Hendrickson. Vocal ensemble (SATB choir). Members are amateurs. Performs 25 concerts/year, including 1-6 new works.

Commissions 0-2 composers or new works/year. Audience is all ages, "sophisticated and unsophisticated." Concerts are performed in churches, concert halls and schools. Pays for outright purchase.

HOW TO CONTACT Query first. Include SASE. Responds in 1 month.

MUSIC Seeking "sacred choral pieces, no more than 5-7 minutes long, to be sung a cappella or with obbligato instrument. Can contain vocal solos. We have 50-60 members in our choir."

PERFORMANCES Carol Barnett's *Spiritual Journey*; Steven Heitzeg's *Litanies for the Living* (choral/orchestral); and Morton Lanriclsen's *O Magnum Mysteries* (a cappella choral).

BILLINGS SYMPHONY

2721 Second Ave. N, Suite 350, Billings MT 59101 United States. **Website:** www.billingssymphony.org. 2721 Second Ave N., Suite 350, Billings MT 59101. (406)252-3610. **Fax:** (406)252-3353. **E-mail:** symphony@billingssymphony.org. **Website:** www.billingssymphony.org. **Contact:** Darren Rich, executive director. Symphony orchestra, orchestra and chorale. Estab. 1950. Members are professionals and amateurs. Performs 12-15 concerts/year, including 6-7 new works. Traditional audience. Performs at Alberta Bair Theater (capacity 1,416). Pays by outright purchase (or rental).

HOW TO CONTACT Query first. Include SASE. Responds in 2 weeks.

MUSIC Any style. Traditional notation preferred.

PERFORMANCES 2013 Symphony in the Park includes Billings Community Band and Young Conductors' Contest (led by Maestra Anne Harrigan).

TIPS "Write what you feel (be honest) and sharpen your compositional and craftsmanship skills."

BIRMINGHAM-BLOOMFIELD SYMPHONY ORCHESTRA

P.O. Box 1925, Birmingham MI 48012 United States. **Website:** www.bbso.org. P.O. Box 1925, Birmingham MI 48012. (248)352-2276. **E-mail:** bbso@bbso.org. **Website:** www.bbso.org. **Contact:** John Thomas Dodson, Music director and conductor. Conductor Laureate: Felix Resnick. Executive director: Dana Gill. Symphony orchestra. Estab. 1975. Members are professionals. Performs 5 concerts including 1 new work/year. Commissions 1 composer or new work/year "with grants." Performs for middle- to upper-

class audience at Temple Beth El's Sanctuary. Pays per performance "depending upon grant received."

HOW TO CONTACT *Query first.* Does not return material. Responds in 6 months.

MUSIC "We are a symphony orchestra but also play pops. Usually 3 works on program (2 hours) Orchestra size 65-75. If pianist is involved, they must rent piano."

PERFORMANCES Brian Belanger's *Tuskegee Airmen Suite* (symphonic full orchestra); Larry Nazer & Friend's *Music from "Warm" CD* (jazz with full orchestra); and Mark Gottlieb's *Violin Concerto for Orchestra*.

THE BOSTON PHILHARMONIC

295 Huntington Ave., Suite 210, Boston MA 02115 United States. **Website:** www.bostonphil.org. 295 Huntington Ave., Suite 210, Boston MA 02115. (617)236-0999. **E-mail:** info@bostonphil.org. **Website:** www.bostonphil.org. **Music Director:** Benjamin Zander. Symphony orchestra. Estab. 1979. Members are professionals, amateurs and students. Performs 2 concerts/year. Audience is ages 30-70. Performs at New England Conservatory's Jordan Hall, Boston's Symphony Hall and Sanders Theatre in Cambridge. Both Jordan Hall and Sanders Theatre are small (approximately 1,100 seats) and very intimate.

HOW TO CONTACT *Does not accept new Music at this time.*

MUSIC Full orchestra only.

PERFORMANCES Dutilleuxs' *Tout un monde lointain* for cello and orchestra (symphonic); Bernstein's *Fancy Free* (symphonic/jazzy); Copland's *El Salon Mexico* (symphonic); Gershwin's *Rhapsody in Blue*; Shostakovitch's *Symphony No. 10*; Harbison's *Concerto for Oboe*; Holst's *The Planet Suite*; Schwantner's *New Morning for the World*; Berg's *Seven Early Songs*; and Ive's *The Unanswered Question*.

BRAVO! L.A.

CA United States. **Website:** www.bravo-la.com. (818)892-8737. **Fax:** (818)892-1227. **E-mail:** info@bravo-la.com. **Website:** www.bravo-la.com. **Contact:** Cellist Dr. Janice Foy, director. An umbrella organization of recording/touring musicians, formed in 1994. Includes the following musical ensembles: the New American Quartet (string quartet); The Ascending Wave (harp/cello duo); Celllissimo! L.A. (cello ensemble); and Jazz Kats (trio band).

HOW TO CONTACT Submit scores/tape of pieces. Include SASE. Responds in a few months. "We also record DEMOS for those needing entry into various situations and we use a DEMO rate through the musicians Union Local 47 as our contract for that. If you want to do a Limited Pressing recording, that also goes through the Union with an appropriate contract."

MUSIC "We do all styles from classical to jazz. You can hear examples of most of the above ensembles on the site. You may also read about the latest musical antics of these musicians at the site."

TIPS "Let Bravo! L.A. know about your latest or upcoming performances and if you have a tape/CD of it, please forward or send an audio clip! If you have trouble getting through the spam blocker, let me know! We do not provide funding but there are many different grants out there for different situations. Good luck!"

☺ CALGARY BOYS CHOIR

4825 Mt. Royal Gate SW, Calgary AB T3E 6K6 Canada. **Website:** www.wix.com/levendis99/calgary-boyschoir#!. 4825 Mt. Royal Gate SW, Calgary, AB, T3E 6K6 Canada. (403)440-6821. **Fax:** (403)440-6594. **E-mail:** gm.calgaryboyschoir@gmail.com. **Website:** www.levendis99.wix.com/calgary-boyschoir. **Contact:** Paul Grindlay, artistic director. Boys choir. Estab. 1973. Members are amateurs age 5 and up. Performs 5-10 concerts/year including 1-2 new works. Pay negotiable.

HOW TO CONTACT Query first. Submit complete score and tape of piece(s). Include SASE. Responds in 6 weeks. Does not return material.

MUSIC "Style fitting for boys choir. Lengths depending on project. Orchestration preferable a cappella/for piano/sometimes orchestra."

☺ CANADIAN OPERA COMPANY

227 Front St. E., Toronto ON M5A 1E8 Canada. **Website:** www.coc.ca. 227 Front St. E, Toronto ON M5A 1E8 Canada. (800)250-4653. **E-mail:** info@coc.ca; Music@coc.ca. **Website:** www.coc.ca. **Contact:** Alexander Neef, general director. Opera company. Estab. 1950. Members are professionals. 68-72 performances, including a minimum of 1 new work/year. Pays by contract.

HOW TO CONTACT Submit complete CDs or DVDs of vocal and/or operatic works. "Vocal works please." Include SASE. Responds in 5 weeks.

MUSIC Vocal works, operatic in nature. "Do not submit works which are not for voice. Ask for requirements for the Composers-In-Residence program."

PERFORMANCES Dean Burry's *Brothers Grimm* (children's opera, 50 minutes long); Dean Burry's Isis and the Seven Scorpions (45-minute opera for children); James Rolfe's *Swoon:* James Rolfe's *Donna* (work title for forthcoming work); Nixon in China by John Adams; L'Amour Do Loin by Saariaho.

TIPS "We have a Composers-In-Residence program which is open to Canadian composers or landed immigrants."

CANTATA ACADEMY

P.O. Box 1958, Royal Oak MI 48084 United States. **Website:** www.cantataacademy.org. CHORALE P.O. Box 1958, Royal Oak MI 48084. (313)248-7282. **E-mail:** director@cantataacademy.org or cantata@cantataacademy.org. **Website:** www.cantataacademy.org. **Contact:** Ashley M. Prescott, business manager; Susan Catanese, director. Vocal ensemble. Estab. 1961. Members are professionals. Performs 10-12 concerts/year including 1-3 new works. "We perform in churches and small auditoriums throughout the Metro Detroit area for audiences of about 500 people." Pays variable rate for outright purchase.

HOW TO CONTACT Submit complete score. Include SASE. Responds in 3 months.

MUSIC Four-part a cappella and keyboard accompanied works, two- and three-part works for men's or women's voices. Some small instrumental ensemble accompaniments acceptable. Work must be suitable for 40 voice choir. No works requiring orchestra or large ensemble accompaniment. No pop.

PERFORMANCES Libby Larsen's *Missa Gaia: Mass for the Earth* (SATB, string quartet, oboe, percussion, 4-hand piano); Dede Duson's *To Those Who See* (SATB, SSA); and Sarah Hopkins' *Past Life Melodies* (SATB with Harmonic Overtone Singing); Eric Whiteacre *Five Hebrew Love Songs*; Robert Convery's *Songs of the Children.*

TIPS "Be patient. Would prefer to look at several different samples of work at one time."

CARMEL SYMPHONY ORCHESTRA

760 3rd Avenue SW, Suite 102, Carmel IN 46032 United States. **Website:** www.carmelsymphony.org. 760 3rd Avenue SW, Suite 102, Carmel IN 46032. (317)844-9717. **Fax:** (317)844-9916. **E-mail:** info@

carmelsymphony.org. **Website:** www.carmelsymphony.org. **Contact:** Alan Davis, president/CEO. Symphony orchestra. Estab. 1976. Members are paid and non-paid professionals. Performs 15 concerts/year, including 1-2 new works. Performs in a 1,600-seat Palladium at the Center for the Performing Arts.

HOW TO CONTACT *Query first.* Include SASE. Responds in 3 months.

MUSIC "Full orchestra works, 5-60 minutes in length. Parents are encouraged to bring a child. 85-piece orchestra, medium difficult to difficult.

PERFORMANCES Brahms' *Concerto in D Major for Violin and Orchestra*, Op. 77; Debussy's "La Mer"; Ravel's Second Suite from "Daphnis and Chloe"; Dvorak's *Carnival Overture*, Op. 92; and Sibelius' *Symphony No. 5* in E-flat Major, Op. 82. Outstanding guest artists include Michael Feinstein, Sylvia McNair, Cameron Carpenter, Dale Clevenger, and Angela Brown.

CHATTANOOGA GIRLS CHOIR

1831 Hickory Valley Road, Suite 400, Chattanooga TN 37421 United States. **Website:** www.chattanoogagirlschoir.com. 1831 Hickory Valley Road, Suite 400, Chattanooga TN 37421. (423)296-1006. **E-mail:** ChattanoogaGirlsChoir@gmail.com. **Website:** chattanoogagirlschoir.com. **Contact:** Laura Stephenson, executive director. Vocal ensemble. Estab. 1986. Members are amateurs. Performs 2 concerts/year including at least 1 new work. Audience consists of cultural and civic organizations and national and international tours. Performance space includes concert halls and churches. Pays for outright purchase or per performance.

HOW TO CONTACT Query first. Include SASE. Responds in 6 weeks.

MUSIC Seeks renaissance, baroque, classical, romantic, twentieth century, folk and musical theatre for young voices of up to 8 minutes. Performers include 5 treble choices: 4th grade (2 pts.); 5th grade (2 pts.) (SA); grades 6-9 (3 pts.) (SSA); grades 10-12 (3-4 pts.) (SSAA); and a combined choir: grades 6-12 (3-4 pts.) (SSAA). Medium level of difficulty. "Avoid extremely high Tessitura Sop I and extremely low Tessitura Alto II."

PERFORMANCES Jan Swafford's *Iphigenia Book: Meagher* (choral drama); Penny Tullock's *How Can I Keep from Singing* (Shaker hymn).

CHEYENNE SYMPHONY ORCHESTRA

1904 Thomes Ave., Cheyenne WY 82001 United States. **Website:** www.cheyennesymphony.org. 1904 Thomes Ave., Cheyenne WY 82001. (307)778-8561. **E-mail:** executivedirector@cheyennesymphony.org. **Website:** www.cheyennesymphony.org. **Contact:** Elizabeth McGuire, executive director. Symphony orchestra. Estab. 1955. Members are professionals. Performs 5-6 concerts/year. "Orchestra performs for a conservative, mid-to-upper income audience of 1,200 season members."

HOW TO CONTACT Query first to music director William Intriligator. Does not return material.

CIMARRON CIRCUIT OPERA COMPANY

P.O. Box 1085, Norman OK 73070 United States. **Website:** www.ccocopera.org. P.O. Box 1085, Norman OK 73070. (405)364-8962. **Fax:** (405)321-5842. **E-mail:** info@cimarronopera.org. **Website:** www.ccocopera.org. **Contact:** Kevin W. Smith, Music director. Opera company. Estab. 1975. Members are semi professional. Performs 75 concerts/year including 1-2 new works. Commissions 1 or less new work/year. "CCOC performs for children across the state of Oklahoma and for a dedicated audience in central Oklahoma. As a touring company, we adapt to the performance space provided, ranging from a classroom to a full raised stage." Pay is negotiable.

HOW TO CONTACT Query first. Does not return material. Responds in 6 months.

MUSIC "We are seeking operas or operettas in English only. We would like to begin including new, American works in our repertoire. Children's operas should be no longer than 45 minutes and require no more than a synthesizer for accompaniment. Adult operas should be appropriate for families, and may require either full orchestration or synthesizer. CCOC is a professional company whose members have varying degrees of experience, so any difficulty level is appropriate. There should be a small to moderate number of principals. Children's work should have no more than four principals. Our slogan is 'Opera is a family thing to do.' If we cannot market a work to families, we do not want to see it."

PERFORMANCES Menotti's *Amahl & the Night Visitors*; and Barab's *La Pizza Con Funghi*.

TIPS "45-minute fairy tale-type children's operas with possibly a 'moral' work well for our market.

Looking for works appealing to K-8 grade students. No more than four principles."

CONNECTICUT CHORAL ARTISTS/ CONCORA

233 Pearl St., Hartford CT 06103. **Website:** www.concora.org. **Contact:** Ann Drinan, executive director. City Arts on Pearl, 233 Pearl St., Hartford CT 06103. (860)293-0567. **Fax:** (860)244-0073. **E-mail:** contact@concora.org. **Website:** www.concora.org. Estab. 1974. Professional concert choir. Members are professionals. Performs 5 concerts per year, including 3-5 new works.

HOW TO CONTACT Query first. "No unsolicited submissions accepted." Include SASE. Responds in 1 year.

MUSIC Seeking "works for mixed chorus of 36 singers; unaccompanied or with keyboard and/or small instrumental ensemble; text sacred or secular/any language; prefers suites or cyclical works, total time not exceeding 15 minutes. Performance spaces and budgets prohibit large instrumental ensembles. Works suited for 750-seat halls are preferable. Substantial organ or piano parts acceptable. Scores should be very legible in every way."

PERFORMANCES Don McCullough's *Holocaust Contata* (choral with narration); Robert Cohen's *Sprig of Lilac: Peter Quince at the Clavier* (choral); Greg Bartholomew's *The 21st Century: A Girl Born in Afghanistan* (choral).

TIPS "Use conventional notation and be sure ms is legible in every way. Recognize and respect the vocal range of each vocal part. Work should have an identifiable rhythmic structure."

♥ EUROPEAN UNION CHAMBER ORCHESTRA

Hollick, Yarnscombe EX31 3LQ United Kingdom. **Website:** www.etd.gb.com. Hollick, Yarnscombe, Devon EX31 3LQ, United Kingdom. (44)1271 858249. **Fax:** (44)1271 858375. **E-mail:** eucorch1@aol.com. **Website:** www.euco.org.uk. Chamber orchestra. Members are professionals. Performs 70 concerts/year, including 6 new works. Commissions 2 composers or new works/year. Performs regular tours of Europe, Americas and Asia, including major venues. Pays per performance or for outright purchase, depending on work.

HOW TO CONTACT Query first. Does not return material. Responds in 6 weeks.

MUSIC Seeking compositions for strings, 2 oboes and 2 horns with a duration of about 8 minutes.

PERFORMANCES Peeter Vahi "Prayer Wheel"; James MacMillan "Kiss on Wood."

TIPS "Keep the work to less than 15 minutes in duration, it should be sufficiently 'modern' to be interesting but not too difficult as this could take up rehearsal time. It should be possible to perform without a conductor."

FONTANA CONCERT SOCIETY

359 S. Kalamazoo Mall, Suite 200, Kalamazoo MI 49007 United States. **Website:** www.fontanachamberarts.org. 359 S. Kalamazoo Mall, Suite 200, Kalamazoo MI 49007. (269)382-7774. **Fax:** (269)382-0812. **Website:** www.fontanachamberarts.org. Chamber Music ensemble presenter. Estab. 1980. Members are professionals. Fontana Chamber Arts presents over 45 events, including the 6-week Summer Festival of Music and Art, which runs from mid-July to the end of August. Regional and guest artists perform classical, contemporary, jazz and nontraditional music. Commissions and performs new works each year. Fontana Chamber Arts presents 7 classical and 2 jazz concerts during the Fall/Winter season. Audience consists of well-educated individuals who accept challenging new works, but like the traditional as well. Summer—180 seat hall; fall/winter—various venues, 400-1,500 seats.

HOW TO CONTACT Submit complete score, résumé and tapes of piece(s). Include SASE. Responds in approximately 1 month. Music Chamber Music—any combination of strings, winds, piano. No "pop" music, new age type. Special interest in composers attending premiere and speaking to the audience.

TIPS "Provide a résumé and clearly marked tape of a piece played by live performers."

FORT WORTH CHILDREN'S OPERA

1300 Gendy St., Ft. Worth TX 76107 United States. **Website:** www.fwopera.org. 1300 Gendy St., Fort Worth TX 76107. (817)731-0833, ext. 19. **Fax:** (817)731-0833. **E-mail:** info@fwopera.org. **Website:** www.fwopera.org. **Contact:** Darren K. Woods, general director. Opera company. Estab. 1946. Members are professionals. Performs over 180 in-school performances/year." Audience consists of elementary school children; performs in major venues for district-wide groups and individual school auditoriums, cafetoriums and gymnasiums. Pays $40/performance.

HOW TO CONTACT Submit complete score and tape of piece(s). Include SASE. Responds in 6 months.

MUSIC "Familiar fairy tales or stories adapted to music of opera composers, or newly-composed music of suitable quality. Ideal length: 40-45 minutes. Piano or keyboard accompaniment. Should include moral, safety, or school issues. Can be ethnic in subject matter and must speak to pre-K and grade 1-6 children. Prefer pieces with good, memorable melodies. Performed by young, trained professionals on 9-month contract. Requires work for 4 performers, doubled roles OK, SATB plus accompanist/narrator. Special interest in biligual (Spanish/English) works."

GREATER GRAND FORKS SYMPHONY ORCHESTRA

3350 Campus Road, Mail Stop 7084, Grand Forks ND 58202 United States. **Website:** www.ggfso.org. PO Box 5302, Grand Forks ND 58206-5302. (701)732-0579 or (701)777-3359. **E-mail:** symphony@ggfso.org. **Website:** www.ggfso.org. **Contact:** Alexander Platt, Music director. Symphony orchestra. Estab. 1908. Members are professionals and/or amateurs. Performs 6 concerts/year. "New works are presented in 2-4 of our programs." Audience is "a mix of ages and musical experience. In 1997-98 we moved into a renovated, 420-seat theater." Pay is negotiable, depending on licensing agreements.

HOW TO CONTACT Submit complete score or complete score and tape of pieces. Include SASE. Responds in 6 months.

MUSIC "Style is open, instrumentation the limiting factor. Music can be scored for an ensemble up to but not exceeding: 3,2,3,2/4,3,3,1/3 perc./strings. Rehearsal time limited to 3 hours for new works."

PERFORMANCES Michael Harwood's *Amusement Park Suite* (orchestra); Randall Davidson's *Mexico Bolivar Tango* (chamber orchestra); and John Corigliano's *Voyage* (flute and orchestra); Linda Tutas Haugen's *Fable of Old Turtle* (saxophone concerto); Michael Wittgraf's *Landmarks*; Joan Tower's *Made in America*.

HEARTLAND MEN'S CHORUS

P.O. Box 32374, Kansas City MO 64171 United States. **Website:** www.hmckc.org. P.O. Box 32374, Kansas City MO 64171-5374. (816)931-3338. **Fax:** (816)531-1367. **E-mail:** hmc@hmckc.org. **Website:** www.hmckc.org. **Contact:** Joseph Nadeau, artistic director. Men's chorus. Estab. 1986. Members are professionals

and amateurs. Performs 3 concerts/year; 9-10 are new works. Commissions 1 composer or new works/year. Performs for a diverse audience at the Folly Theater (1,100 seats). Pay is negotiable.

HOW TO CONTACT Query first. Include SASE. Responds in 2 months.

MUSIC "Interested in works for male chorus (ttbb). Must be suitable for performance by a gay male chorus. We will consider any orchestration, or a cappella."

PERFORMANCES Mark Hayes' *Two Flutes Playing* (commissioned song cycle); Alan Shorter's *Country Angel Christmas* (commissioned chidren's musical); Kevin Robinson's *Life is a Cabaret: The Music of Kander and Ebb* (commissioned Musical).

TIPS "Find a text that relates to the contemporary gay experience, something that will touch peoples' lives."

HELENA SYMPHONY

2 N Last Chance Gulch Suite 1, Helena MT 59601 United States. **Website:** www.helenasymphony.org. P.O. Box 1073, Helena MT 59624. (406)442-1860. **E-mail:** llily@helenasymphony.org. **Website:** www.helenasymphony.org. **Contact:** Allan R. Scott, Music director and conductor; Ginny Abbot, executive director. Symphony orchestra. Estab. 1955. Members are professionals and amateurs. Performs 7-10 concerts/year including new works. Performance space is an 1,800 seat concert hall. Payment varies.

HOW TO CONTACT Query first. Include SASE. Responds in 3 months.

MUSIC "Imaginative, collaborative, not too atonal. We want to appeal to an audience of all ages. We don't have a huge string complement. Medium to difficult OK—at frontiers of professional ability we cannot do."

PERFORMANCES Eric Funk's *A Christmas Overture* (orchestra); Donald O. Johnston's *A Christmas Processional* (orchestra/chorale); and Elizabeth Sellers' *Prairie* (orchestra/short ballet piece).

TIPS "Try to balance tension and repose in your works. New instrument combinations are appealing."

HENDERSONVILLE SYMPHONY ORCHESTRA

P.O. Box 1811, Hendersonville NC 28793 United States. **Website:** www.hendersonvillesymphony.org. P.O. Box 1811, Hendersonville NC 28739. (828)697-5884. **Fax:** (828)697-5765. **E-mail:** info@hendersonvillesymphony.org. **Website:** www.hendersonvillesymphony.org. Symphony orchestra. Estab. 1971. Members are professionals and amateurs. Performs

6 concerts/year. "We would welcome a new work per year." Audience is a cross-section of retirees, professionals, and some children. Performance space is a 857-seat high school audiorium.

HOW TO CONTACT Query first. Include SASE. Responds in 1 month.

MUSIC "We use a broad spectrum of Music (classical concerts and pops)."

PERFORMANCES Nelson's *Jubilee* (personal expression in a traditional method); Britten's "The Courtly Dances" from Glorina (time-tested); and Chip Davis' arrangement for Mannheim Steamroller's *Deck the Halls* (modern adaptation of traditional melody).

TIPS "Submit your work even though we are a community orchestra. We like to be challenged. We have the most heavily patronized fine arts group in the county. Our emphasis is on education."

HERSHEY SYMPHONY ORCHESTRA

P.O. Box 93, Hershey PA 17033 United States. **Website:** www.hersheysymphony.org. P.O. Box 93, Hershey PA 17033. (717)533-8449. **Website:** www.hersheysymphony.org. **E-mail:** hsogm@itech.net. **Contact:** Dr. Sandra Dackow, Music director. Symphony orchestra. Estab. 1969. Members are professionals and amateurs. Performs 8 concerts/year, including 1-3 new works. Commissions "possibly 1-2" composers or new works/year. Audience is family and friends of community theater. Performance space is a 1,900 seat grand old movie theater. Pays commission fee.

HOW TO CONTACT Submit complete score and tape of piece(s). Include SASE. Responds in 3 months.

MUSIC "Symphonic works of various lengths and types which can be performed by a non-professional orchestra. We are flexible but like to involve all our players."

PERFORMANCES Paul W. Whear's *Celtic Christmas Carol* (orchestra/bell choir) and Linda Robbins Coleman's *In Good King Charlie's Golden Days* (overture).

TIPS "Please lay out rehearsal numbers/letter and rests according to phrases and other logical Musical divisions rather than in groups of ten measures, etc., which is very unMusical and wastes time and causes a surprising number of problems. Also, please do not send a score written in concert pitch; use the usual transpositions so that the conductor sees what the players see; rehearsal is much more effective this way. Cross cue all important solos; this helps in rehearsal where instruments may be missing."

HUDSON VALLEY PHILHARMONIC

35 Market St., Poughkeepise NY 12601 United States. **Website:** www.bardavon.org. 35 Market St., Poughkeepise NY 12601. (845)473-5288. **Fax:** (845)473-4259. **Website:** www.bardavon.org. **Contact:** AStephen LaMarca, managing director of theater production. Symphony orchestra. Estab. 1969. Members are professionals. Performs 20 concerts/year including 1 new work. "Classical subscription concerts for all ages; Pops concerts for all ages; New Wave concerts—crossover projects with a rock 'n' roll artist performing with an orchestra. HVP performs in 3 main theatres which are concert auditoriums with stages and professional lighting and sound." Pay is negotiable.

HOW TO CONTACT Query first. Include SASE. Responds only if interested.

MUSIC "HVP is open to serious classical Music, pop Music, and rock 'n' roll crossover projects. Desired length of work: 10-20 minutes. Orchestrations can be varied by should always include strings. There is no limit to difficulty since our Musicians are professional. The ideal number of Musicians to write for would include up to a Brahms-size orchestra 2222, 4231, T, 2P, piano, harp, strings."

PERFORMANCES Joan Tower's *Island Rhythms* (serious classical work); Bill Vanaver's *P'nai El* (symphony work with dance); and Joseph Bertolozzi's *Serenade* (light classical, pop work).

TIPS "Don't get locked into doing very traditional orchestrations or styles. Our Music director is interested in fresh, creative formats. He is an orchestrator as well and can offer good advice on what works well. Songwriters who are into crossover projects should definitely submit works. Over the past four years, HVP has done concerts featuring the works of Natalie Merchant, John Cale, Sterling Morrison, Richie Havens, and R. Carlos Naka (Native American flute player), all reorchestrated by our Music director for small orchestra with the artist."

INDIANA UNIVERSITY NEW MUSIC ENSEMBLE

Indiana University Bloomington, School of Music, Bloomington IN 47405 United States. **Website:** www.indiana.edu/~nme. Indiana University Bloomington, School of Music, Bloomington IN 47405. **E-mail:** ddzubay@indiana.edu. **Website:** www.indiana.edu/~nme. **Contact:** David Dzubay, director. Performs solo, chamber and large ensemble works.

Estab.1974. Members are students. Presents 4 concerts/year.

PERFORMANCES Peter Lieberson's *Free and Easy Wanderer*; Sven-David Sandstrom's *Wind Pieces*; Atar Arad's *Sonata*; and David Dzubay's *Dancesing in a Green Bay*.

KENTUCKY OPERA

323 W. Broadway, Suite 601, Louisville KY 40202 United States. **Website:** www.kyopera.org. 323 West Broadway, Suite 601, Louisville KY 40202. (502)584-4500. **Fax:** (502)584-7484. **E-mail:** alise_oliver@kyopera.org. **Website:** www.kyopera.org. **Contact:** Alise Oliver, artistic administrator. Opera. Estab. 1952. Members are professionals. Performs 3 main stage/year. Performs at Brown Theatre, 1,400. Pays by royalty, outright purchase or per performance.

HOW TO CONTACT *Write or call first before submitting. No unsolicited submissions.* Submit complete score. Include SASE. Responds in 6 months.

MUSIC Seeks opera—1 to 3 acts with orchestrations. No limitations.

PERFORMANCES *Cavalleria Rusticana, The Elixir of Love, Madame Butterfly.*

LEXINGTON PHILHARMONIC SOCIETY

161 N. Mill St., Lexington KY 40507 United States. **Website:** www.lexphil.org. 161 N. Mill St., Arts Place, Lexington KY 40507. (859)233-4226. **E-mail:** sterrell@lexphil.org. **Website:** www.lexphil.org. **Contact:** Scott Terrell, Music director. Symphony orchestra. Estab. 1961. Members are professionals. Series includes "8 serious, classical subscription concerts (hall seats 1,500); 3 concerts called Pops the Series; 3 Family Concerts; 10 outdoor pops concerts (from 1,500 to 5,000 tickets sold); 5-10 run-out concerts (1/2 serious/1/2 pops); and 10 children's concerts." Pays via ASCAP and BMI, rental purchase and private arrangements.

HOW TO CONTACT Submit complete score and tape of piece(s). Include SASE.

MUSIC Seeking "good current pops material and good serious classical works. No specific restrictions, but overly large orchestra requirements, unusual instruments and extra rentals help limit our interest."

PERFORMANCES "Visit our website for complete concert season listing."

TIPS "When working on large-format arrangement, use cross-cues so orchestra can be cut back if required. Submit good quality copy, scores and parts. Tape is helpful."

LIMA SYMPHONY ORCHESTRA

133 N. Elizabeth St., Lima OH 45801 United States. **Website:** www.limasymphony.com. 133 N. Elizabeth St., Lima OH 45801. (419)222-5701. **Fax:** (419)222-6587. **Website:** www.limasymphony.com. **Contact:** Crafton Beck, Music conductor. Symphony orchestra. Estab. 1953. Members are professionals. Performs 17-18 concerts including at least 1 new work/year. Commissions at least 1 composer or new work/year. Middle to older audience; also Young People's Series. Mixture for stage and summer productions. Performs in Veterans' Memorial Civic & Convention Center, a beautiful hall seating 1,670; various temporary shells for summer outdoors events; churches; museums and libraries. Pays $2,500 for outright purchase (Anniversary commission) or grants $1,500-5,000.

HOW TO CONTACT Submit complete score if not performed; otherwise submit complete score and tape of piece(s). Include SASE. Responds in 3 months.

MUSIC "Good balance of incisive rhythm, lyricism, dynamic contrast and pacing. Chamber orchestra to full (85-member) symphony orchestra." Does not wish to see "excessive odd meter changes."

PERFORMANCES Frank Proto's *American Overture* (some original Music and fantasy); Werner Tharichen's *Concerto for Timpani and Orchestra*; and James Oliverio's *Pilgrimage—Concerto for Brass* (interesting, dynamic writing for brass and the orchestra).

TIPS "Know your instruments, be willing to experiment with unconventional textures, be available for in depth analysis with conductor, be at more than 1 rehearsal. Be sure that individual parts are correctly matching the score and done in good, neat calligraphy."

LYRIC OPERA OF CHICAGO

20 N. Wacker Dr., Chicago IL 60606 United States. **Website:** www.lyricopera.org. 20 N. Wacker Dr., Chicago IL 60606. (312)332-2244. **Fax:** (312)419-8345. **Website:** www.lyricopera.org. **E-mail:** orchaud@lyricopera.org. Opera company. Estab. 1953. Members are professionals. Performs 80 operas/year including 1 new work in some years. Commissions 1 new work every 4 or 5 years. "Performances are held in a 3,563 seat house for a sophisticated opera audience, predominantly 30+ years old." Payment varies.

HOW TO CONTACT Query first. Does not return material. Responds in 6 months.

MUSIC "Full-length opera suitable for a large house with full orchestra. No Musical comedy or Broadway Musical style. We rarely perform one-act operas. We are only interested in works by composers and librettists with extensive theatrical experience. We have few openings for new works, so candidates must be of the highest quality. Do not send score or other materials without a prior contact."

PERFORMANCES William Bolcom's *View from the Bridge*; John Corigliano's *Ghosts of Versailles*; and Leonard Bernstein's *Candide*.

TIPS "Have extensive credentials and an international reputation."

MILWAUKEE YOUTH SYMPHONY ORCHESTRA

325 W. Walnut St., Milwaukee WI 53212 United States. **Website:** www.myso.org. 325 W. Walnut St., Milwaukee WI 53212. (414)267-2950. **Fax:** (414)267-2960. **E-mail:** general@myso.org. **Website:** www.myso.org. **Contact:** Linda Edelstein, executive director. Multiple youth orchestras and other instrumental ensembles. Estab. 1956. Members are students. Performs 12-15 concerts/year including 1-2 new works. "Our groups perform in Uihlein Hall at the Marcus Center for the Performing Arts in Milwaukee plus area sites. The audiences usually consist of parents, Music teachers and other interested community members, with periodic reviews in the Milwaukee Journal Sentinel." Payment varies.

HOW TO CONTACT Query first. Include SASE. Does not return material. Responds in 1 month.

PERFORMANCES James Woodward's *Tuba Concerto*.

TIPS "Be sure you realize you are working with *students* (albeit many of the best in southeastern Wisconsin) and not professional Musicians. The Music needs to be on a technical level students can handle. Our students are 8-18 years of age, in 2 full symphony orchestras, a wind ensemble and 2 string orchestras, plus two flute choirs, advanced chamber orchestra and 15-20 small chamber ensembles."

MOORES OPERA CENTER

Moores School of Music, University of Houston, 120 School of Music Building, Houston TX 77204 United States. **Website:** www.uh.edu/Music/Mooresopera. University of Houston, 120 Moores School of Music Bldg., Houston TX 77204. (713)743-3009. **Fax:** (713)743-3166. **E-mail:** bross@uh.edu. **Website:** www.uh.edu/Music/Mooresopera. **Director of Opera:** Buck Ross. Opera/Music theater program. Members are professionals, amateurs, and students. Performs 12-14 concerts/year including 1 new work. Performs in a proscenium theater which seats 800. Pit seats approximately up to 75 players. Audience covers wide spectrum, from first time opera-goers to very sophisticated. Pays per performance.

HOW TO CONTACT Submit complete score and tapes of piece(s). Include SASE. Responds in 6 months.

MUSIC "We seek Music that is feasible for high graduate level student singers. Chamber orchestras are very useful. No more than 2 1/2 hours. No children's operas."

PERFORMANCES *The Grapes of Wrath*, *Florencia en el Amazonas*, *Elmer Gantry*, *A Wedding*.

OPERA MEMPHIS

6745 Wolf River Pkwy., Memphis TN 38120 United States. **Website:** www.operamemphis.org. 6745 Wolf River Pkwy., Memphis TN 38120. (901)257-3100. **Fax:** (901)257-3109. **E-mail:** info@operamemphis.org. **Website:** www.operamemphis.org. **Contact:** Ned Canty, director of artistic administration. Opera company. Estab. 1955. Members are professionals. Performs 8-12 concerts/year including new works. Occasionally commissions composers. Audience consists of older, wealthier patrons, along with many students and young professionals. Pay is negotiable.

HOW TO CONTACT Query first. Include SASE. Responds in 1 year or less.

MUSIC "Accessible practical pieces for educational or second stage programs. Educational pieces should not exceed 90 minutes or 4-6 performers. We encourage songwriters to contact us with proposals or work samples for theatrical works. We are very interested in crossover work."

PERFORMANCES Mike Reid's *Different Fields* (one act opera); David Olney's *Light in August* (folk opera); and Sid Selvidge's *Riversongs* (one act blues opera).

TIPS "Spend many hours thinking about the synopsis (plot outline)."

ORCHESTRA SEATTLE/SEATTLE CHAMBER SINGERS

P.O. Box 15825, Seattle WA 98115 United States. **Website:** www.osscs.org. P.O. Box 15825, Seattle WA 98115. (206)682-5208. **E-mail:** osscs@osscs.org. **Website:**

www.osscs.org. **Contact:** Jeremy Johnsen, managing director. Symphony orchestra, chamber Music ensemble, and community chorus. Estab. 1969. Members are amateurs and professionals. Performs 8 concerts/year including 2-3 new works. Commissions 1-2 composers or new works/year. "Our audience is made up of both experienced and novice classical Music patrons. The median age is 45 with an equal number of males and females in the upper income range. Most concerts now held in Benaroya Hall."

HOW TO CONTACT Query first. Include SASE. Responds in 1 year.

PERFORMANCES Beyer's *The Turns of a Girl*; Bernstein's Choruses from *The Lark*; Edstrom's Concerto for Jazz Piano and Orchestra.

PALMETTO MASTERSINGERS

P.O. Box 7441, Columbia SC 29202 United States. **Website:** www.palmettomastersingers.org. P.O. Box 7441, Columbia, SC 29202. (803)765-0777. **E-mail:** info@palmettomastersingers.org. **Website:** www.palmettomastersingers.org. **Contact:** Walter Cuttino, Music director. 80 voice male chorus. Estab. 1981 by the late Dr. Arpad Darasz. Members are professionals and amateurs. Performs 8-10 concerts/year. Commissions 1 composer of new works every other year (on average). Audience is generally older adults, "but it's a wide mix." Performance space for the season series is the Koger Center (approximately 2,000 seats) in Columbia, SC. More intimate venues also available. Fee is negotiable for outright purchase.

HOW TO CONTACT Query first. Include SASE. Or e-mail to info@palmettomastersingers.org.

MUSIC Seeking Music of 10-15 minutes in length, "not too far out tonally. Orchestration is negotiable, but chamber size (10-15 players) is normal. We rehearse once a week and probably will not have more than 8-10 rehearsals. These rehearsals (2 hours each) are spent learning a 11/2-hour program. Only 1-2 rehearsals (max) are with the orchestra. Piano accompaniments need not be simplified, as our accompanist is exceptional."

PERFORMANCES Randal Alan Bass' *Te Deum* (12-minute, brass and percussion); Dick Goodwin's *Mark Twain Remarks* (40 minute, full symphony); and Randol Alan Bass' *A Simple Prayer* (a capella 6 minute).

TIPS "Contact us as early as possible, given that programs are planned by July. Although this is an am-

ateur chorus, we have performed concert tours of Europe, performed at Carnegie Hall, The National Cathedral and the White House in Washington, DC. We are skilled amateurs."

PICCOLO OPERA COMPANY INC.

24 Del Rio Blvd., Boca Raton FL 33432-4734 United States. 24 Del Rio Blvd., Boca Raton FL 33432-4734. (800)282-3161. **Fax:** (561)394-0520. **E-mail:** leejon51@msn.com. **Contact:** Marjorie Gordon, executive director. Traveling opera company. Estab. 1962. Members are professionals. Performs 1-50 concerts/year including 1-2 new works. Commissions 0-1 composer or new work/year. Operas are performed for a mixed audience of children and adults. Pays by performance or outright purchase. Operas in English.

HOW TO CONTACT *Query first.* Include SASE.

MUSIC "Productions for either children or adults. Musical theater pieces, lasting about one hour, for adults to perform for adults and/or youngsters. Performers are mature singers with experience. The cast should have few performers (up to 10), no chorus or ballet, accompanied by piano or local orchestra. Skeletal scenery. All in English."

PERFORMANCES Menotti's *The Telephone*; Mozart's *Cosi Fan Tutte*; and Puccini's *La Boheme* (repertoire of more than 22 productions).

PRINCETON SYMPHONY ORCHESTRA

P.O. Box 250, Princeton NJ 08542 United States. **Website:** www.princetonsymphony.org. P.O. Box 250, Princeton NJ 08542. (609)497-0020. **Fax:** (609)497-0904. **E-mail:** info@princetonsymphony.org. **Website:** www.princetonsymphony.org. **Contact:** Rossen Milanov, Music director. Symphony orchestra. Estab. 1980. Members are professionals. Performs 6-10 concerts/year including some new works. Commissions 1 composer or new work/year. Performs in a "beautiful, intimate 800-seat hall with amazing sound." Pays by arrangement.

MUSIC "Orchestra usually numbers 40-60 individuals."

PRISM SAXOPHONE QUARTET

257 Harvey St., Philadelphia PA 19144 United States. **Website:** www.prismquartet.com. 2 Ellwood Street, 5D, New York NY 10040; or, 257 Harvey St., Philadelphia PA 19144. (215)438-5282. **E-mail:** info@prismquartet.com. **Website:** www.prismquartet.com. **Contact:** Matthew Levy. Chamber Music en-

semble. Estab. 1984. Members are professionals. Performs 80 concerts/year including 10-15 new works. Commissions 4 composers or new works/year. "Ours are primarily traditional chamber Music audiences." Pays royalty per performance from BMI or ASCAP or commission range from $100 to $15,000.

HOW TO CONTACT Submit complete score (with parts) and tape of piece(s). Does not return material. Responds in 3 months.

MUSIC "Orchestration—sax quartet, SATB. Lengths—5-25 minutes. Styles—contemporary, classical, jazz, crossover, ethnic, gospel, avant-garde. No limitations on level of difficulty. No more than 4 performers (SATB sax quartet). No transcriptions. The Prism Quartet places special emphasis on crossover works which integrate a variety of Musical styles."

PERFORMANCES David Liebman's *The Gray Convoy* (jazz); Bradford Ellis's *Tooka-Ood Zasch* (ethnic-world Music); and William Albright's *Fantasy Etudes* (contemporary classical).

SACRAMENTO MASTER SINGERS

P.O. Box 417997, Sacramento CA 95841 United States. **Website:** www.mastersingers.org. P.O. Box 417997, Sacramento CA 95841. (916)788-7464. **E-mail:** smsbusiness@surewest.net. **Website:** www.mastersingers.org. **Contact:** Dr. Ralph Edward Hughes, conductor/artistic director. Vocal ensemble. Estab. 1984. Members are professionals and amateurs. Performs 9 concerts/year including 5-6 new works. Commissions 2 new works/year. Audience is made up of mainly college age and older patrons. Performs mostly in churches with 500-900 seating capacity. Pays $200 for outright purchase.

HOW TO CONTACT Submit complete score and tape of piece(s). Include SASE. Responds in 5 weeks.

MUSIC "A cappella works; works with small orchestras or few instruments; works based on classical styles with a 'modern' twist; multi-cultural Music; shorter works probably preferable, but this is not a requirement. We usually have 38-45 singers capable of a high level of difficulty, but find that often simple works are very pleasing."

PERFORMANCES Joe Jennings' *An Old Black Woman, Homeless and Indistinct* (SATB, oboe, strings, dramatic).

TIPS "Keep in mind we are a chamber ensemble, not a 100-voice choir."

SAN FRANCISCO GIRLS CHORUS

44 Page St., Suite 200, San Francisco CA 94102 United States. **Website:** www.sfgirlschorus.org. 44 Page St., Suite 200, San Francisco CA 94102. (415)863-1752. **E-mail:** info@sfgirlschorus.org. **Website:** www.sfgirlschorus.org. **Contact:** Lisa Bielawa, artistic director. Choral ensemble. Estab. 1978. Advanced choral ensemble of young women's voices. Performs 8-10 concerts/year including 3-4 new works. Commissions 2 composers or new works/year. Concerts are performed for "choral/classical Music lovers, plus family audiences and audiences interested in international repertoire. Season concerts are performed in a 800-seat church with excellent acoustics and in San Francisco's Davies Symphony Hall, a 2,800-seat state-of-the-art auditorium." Pay negotiable for outright purchase. **Editorial Comment:** The San Francisco Girls Chorus has won 5 Grammy Awards as guest performers on the San Francisco Symphony's recordings

HOW TO CONTACT Submit complete score and CD recording, if possible. Does not return material. Responds in 6 months.

MUSIC "Music for treble voices (SSAA); a cappella, piano accompaniment, or small orchestration; 3-10 minutes in length. Wide variety of styles; 45 singers; challenging Music is encouraged."

PERFORMANCES See website under "Music/Commissions" for a listing of SFGC commissions. Examples: Jake Heggie's *Patterns* (piano, mezzo-soprano soloist, chorus); and Chen Yi's *Chinese Poems* (a cappella).

TIPS "Choose excellent texts and write challenging Music. The San Francisco Girls Chorus has pioneered in establishing girls choral Music as an art form in the U.S. The Girls Chorus is praised for its 'stunning Musical standard' (San Francisco Chronicle) in performances in the San Francisco Bay Area and on tour. SFGC's annual concert season showcases the organization's concert/touring ensemble, Chorissima, in performances of choral masterworks from around the world, commissioned works by contemporary composers, and 18th-century Music from the Venetian Ospedali and Mexican Baroque which SFGC has brought out of the archives and onto the concert stage. Chorissima tours through California with partial support provided by the California Arts Council Touring Program and have represented the U.S. and the City of San Francisco nationally and abroad. The chorus provides ensemble and solo singers for performances and recordings with the San Francisco Symphony and San Francisco Opera, Women's Philharmonic, and many other Music ensembles. The Chorus has produced many solo CD recordings including: Voices of Hope and Peace, a recording that includes 'Anne Frank: A Living Voice' by an American composer Linda Tutas Haugen; Christmas, featuring diverse holiday selections; Crossroads, a collection of world folk Music; and Music from the Venetian Ospedali, a disc of Italian Baroque Music of which the New Yorker described the Chorus as 'tremendously accomplished.'"

SOLI DEO GLORIA CANTORUM

3402 Woolworth Ave., Omaha NE 68105 United States. **Website:** www.berkey.com. 3402 Woolworth Ave., Omaha NE 68105. (402)341-4111. **Fax:** (402)341-9381. **E-mail:** cantorum@berkey.com. **Website:** www.berkey.com. **Contact:** Linda Gardels, Music director. Professional choir. Estab. 1988. Members are professionals. Performs 5-7 concerts/year; several are new works. Commissions 1-2 new works/year. Performance space: "cathedral, symphony hall, smaller intimate recital halls as well." Payment is "dependent upon composition and composer."

HOW TO CONTACT Submit complete score and tape of piece(s). Include SASE. Responds in 2 months. **MUSIC** "Chamber Music mixed with topical programming (e.g., all Celtic or all Hispanic programs, etc.). Generally a cappella compositions from very short to extended range (6-18 minutes) or multi-movements. Concerts are of a formal length (approximately 75 minutes) with 5 rehearsals. Difficulty must be balanced within program in order to adequately prepare in a limited rehearsal time. 28 singers. Not seeking orchestral pieces, due to limited budget."

PERFORMANCES Jackson Berkey's *Native Am Ambience* (eclectic/classical); John Rutter's *Hymn to the Creator of Light* (classical); and Arvo Part's *Te Deum* (multi-choir/chant-based classical).

ST. LOUIS CHAMBER CHORUS

P.O. Box 11558, Clayton MO 63105 United States. **Website:** www.chamberchorus.org. P.O. Box 11558, Clayton MO 63105. (636)458-4343. **E-mail:** stlchamberchorus@gmail.com. **Website:** www.chamberchorus.org. **Contact:** Philip Barnes, artistic director. Vocal ensemble, chamber Music ensemble. Estab. 1956.

Members are professionals and amateurs. Performs 6 concerts/year including 5-10 new works. Commissions 3-4 new works/year. Audience is "diverse and interested in unaccompanied choral work and outstanding architectural/acoustic venues." Performances take place at various auditoria noted for their excellent acoustics—churches, synagogues, schools, and university halls. Pays by arrangement.

HOW TO CONTACT Query first. Does not return material. "Panel of 'readers' submit report to artistic director. Responds in 3 months. 'General Advice' leaflet available on request."Music "*Only a cappella writing! No contemporary 'popular' works; historical editions welcomed. No improvisatory works. Our programs are tailored for specific acoustics—composers should indicate their preference.*"

PERFORMANCES Sir Richard Rodney Bennett's *A Contemplation Upon Flowers* (a cappella madrigal); Ned Rorem's *Ode to Man* (a cappella chorus for mixed voices); and Sasha Johnson Manning's *Requiem* (a cappella oratorio).

TIPS "We only consider a cappella works which can be produced in five rehearsals. Therefore pieces of great complexity or duration are discouraged. Our seasons are planned 2-3 years ahead, so much lead time is required for programming a new work. We will accept hand-written manuscript, but we prefer typeset Music."

SUSQUEHANNA SYMPHONY ORCHESTRA

P.O. Box 963, Abingdon MD 21009 United States. **Website:** www.ssorchestra.org. P.O. Box 963, Abingdon MD 21009. **Fax:** (410)306-6069. **E-mail:** sheldon.bair@ssorchestra.org. **Website:** www.ssorchestra.org. **Contact:** Sheldon Bair, founder/Music director. Symphony orchestra. Estab. 1978. Members are amateurs. Performs 6 concerts/year including 1-2 new works. Composers paid depending on the circumstances. "We perform in 1 hall, 600 seats with fine acoustics. Our audience encompasses all ages." **HOW TO CONTACT** Query first. Include SASE. Responds in 3 or more months. **MUSIC** "We desire works for large orchestra, any length, in a 'conservative 20th and 21st century' style. Seek fine Music for large orchestra. We are a community orchestra, so the Music must be within our grasp. Violin I to 7th position by step only; Violin II—stay within 5th position; English horn and harp are OK. Full orchestra pieces preferred."

PERFORMANCES *Stabat Mater*, by Stanislaw Moryto; *Elegy*, Amanda Harberg; *I Choose the Mountain*, by Stacey Zyriek; *Little Gift*, by Benny Russell.

☉ TORONTO MENDELSSOHN CHOIR

Toronto ON Canada. **Website:** www.tmchoir.org. 720 Bathurst St., Suite 404, Toronto ON M5S 2R4, Canada. (416)598-0422. **Fax:** (416)598-2992. **E-mail:** manager@tmchoir.org. **Website:** www.tmchoir.org. **Contact:** Cynthia Hawkins, executive director. Vocal ensemble. Members are professionals and amateurs. Performs 25 concerts/year including 1-3 new works. "Most performances take place in Roy Thomson Hall. The audience is reasonably sophisticated, Musically knowledgeable but with moderately conservative tastes." Pays by commission and ASCAP/SOCAN.

HOW TO CONTACT Query first or submit complete score and tapes of pieces. Include SASE. Responds in 6 months.

MUSIC All works must suit a large choir (180 voices) and standard orchestral forces or with some other not-too-exotic accompaniment. Length should be restricted to no longer than 1/2 of a nocturnal concert. The choir sings at a very professional level and can sight-read almost anything. "Works should fit naturally with the repertoire of a large choir which performs the standard choral orchestral repertoire."

PERFORMANCES Holman's *Jezebel*; Orff's *Catulli Carmina*; and Lambert's *Rio Grande*.

☉ VANCOUVER CHAMBER CHOIR

1254 W. 7th Ave., Vancouver BC V6H 1B6 Canada. **Website:** www.vancouverchamberchoir.com. 1254 W. Seventh Ave., Vancouver BC V6H 1B6 Canada. **E-mail:** info@vancouverchamberchoir.com. **Website:** www.vancouverchamberchoir.com. **Contact:** Jon Washburn, artistic director. Vocal ensemble. Members are professionals. Performs 40 concerts/year including 5-8 new works. Commissions 2-4 composers or new works/year. Pays SOCAN royalty or negotiated fee for commissions.

HOW TO CONTACT Submit complete score and tape of piece(s). Does not return material. Responds in 6 months if possible.

MUSIC Seeks "choral works of all types for small chorus, with or without accompaniment and/or soloists. Concert Music only. Choir made up of 20 singers. Large or unusual instrumental accompaniments are less likely to be appropriate. No pop Music."

PERFORMANCES The VCC has commissioned and premiered over 200 new works by Canadian and international composers, including Alice Parker's *That Sturdy Vine* (cantata for chorus, soloists and orchestra); R. Murray Schafer's *Magic Songs* (SATB a cappella); and Jon Washburn's *A Stephen Foster Medley* (SSAATTBB/piano).

TIPS "We are looking for choral Music that is performable yet innovative, and which has the potential to become 'standard repertoire.' Although we perform much new Music, only a small portion of the many scores which are submitted can be utilized."

☉ VANCOUVER YOUTH SYMPHONY ORCHESTRA SOCIETY

3214 W. 10th Ave., Vancouver BC V6K 2L2 Canada. **Website:** www.vyso.com. 3214 W. 10th Ave., Vancouver BC V6K 2L2 Canada. (604)737-0714. **Fax:** (604)737-0739. **E-mail:** vyso@telus.net. **Website:** www.vyso.com. **Music directors:** Roger Cole, artistic director and senior orchestra conductor; Jin Zhang, intermediate orchestra conductor; Margitta Krebs, debut and junior orchestra conductor. Youth orchestra. Four divisions consisting of Musicians ranging in ages 8-22. Estab. 1930. Members are amateurs. Performs 10-15 concerts/year in various lower mainland venues. Concert admission by donation.

MUSIC "Extensive and varied orchestral repertoire is performed by all divisions. Please contact the VYSO for more information."

VIRGINIA OPERA

P.O. Box 2580, Norfolk VA 23501 United States. **Website:** www.vaopera.org. P.O. Box 2580, Norfolk VA 23501. (757)627-9545. **E-mail:** info@vaopera.com. **Website:** www.vaopera.org. **Contact:** Andrew Chugg, artistic administration director. Opera company. Estab. 1974. Members are professionals. Performs more than 560 concerts/year. Commissions vary on number of composers or new works/year. Concerts are performed for school children throughout Virginia, grades K-5, 6-8, and 9-12 at the Harrison Opera House in Norfolk and at the Carpenter Theatre in Richmond. Pays on commission.

HOW TO CONTACT Query first. Include SASE. Response time varies.

MUSIC "Audience accessible style approximately 45 minutes in length. Limit cast list to 3 vocal artists of any combination. Accompanied by piano and/or keyboaRoad Works are performed before school children of all ages. Pieces must be age appropriate both aurally and dramatically. Musical styles are encouraged to be diverse, contemporary as well as traditional. Works are produced and presented with sets, costumes, etc." Limitations: "Three vocal performers (any combination). One keyboardist. Medium to difficult acceptable, but prefer easy to medium. Seeking only pieces which are suitable for presentation as part of an opera education program for Virginia Opera's education and outreach department. Subject matter must meet strict guidelines relative to Learning Objectives, etc. Musical idiom must be representative of current trends in opera, Musical theater. Extreme dissonance, row systems not applicable to this environment."

PERFORMANCES Seymour Barab's *Cinderella*; John David Earnest's *The Legend of Sleepy Hollow*; and Seymour Barab's *The Pied Piper of Hamelin*.

TIPS "Theatricality is very important. New works should stimulate interest in Musical theater as a legitimate art form for school children with no prior exposure to live theatrical entertainment. Composer should be willing to create a product which will find success within the educational system."

WHEATON SYMPHONY ORCHESTRA

344 Spring Ave., Glen Ellyn IL 60137 United States. **Website:** www.wheatonsymphony.org. 344 Spring Ave., Glen Ellyn IL 60137. (630)790-1430. **Fax:** (630)790-9703. **E-mail:** info@wheatonsymphony.org. **Website:** www.wheatonsymphony.org. **Contact:** Don Mattison, manager. Symphony orchestra. Estab. 1959. Members are professionals and amateurs. Performs 6 concerts/year including a varying number of new works. "No pay for performance but can probably record your piece."

HOW TO CONTACT Query first. Include SASE. Responds in 1 month.

MUSIC "This is a good amateur orchestra that wants pieces to be performed in the mode of John Williams or Samuel Barber, Corliango, etc. Large scale works for orchestra only. No avant garde, 12-tone or atonal material. Pieces should be 20 minutes or less and must be prepared in 3 rehearsals. Instrumentation needed for woodwinds in 3s, full brass 4-3-3-1, 4 percussion and strings—full-instrumentation only. Selections for full orchestra only. No pay for reading your piece, but we will record it at our expense. We will rehearse and give a world premiere of your piece if it is in the stated orchestration, probably with keyboard added."

PERFORMANCES Richard Williams's *Symphony in G Minor* (4 movement symphony); Dennis Johnson's *Must Jesus Bear the Cross Alone, Azon* (traditional); and Michael Diemer's *Skating* (traditional style).

CONTESTS & AWARDS

///

Participating in contests is a great way to gain exposure for your Music. Prizes vary from contest to contest, from cash to Musical merchandise to studio time, and even publishing and recording deals. For Musical theater and classical composers, the prize may be a performance of your work. Even if you don't win, valuable contacts can be made through contests. Many times, contests are judged by Music publishers and other industry professionals, so your Music may find its way into the hands of key industry people who can help further your career.

HOW TO SELECT A CONTEST

It's important to remember when entering any contest to do proper research before signing anything or sending any money. We have confidence in the contests listed in *Songwriter's Market*, but it pays to read the fine print. First, be sure you understand the contest rules and stipulations once you receive the entry forms and guidelines. Then you need to weigh what you will gain against what they're asking you to give up. If a publishing or recording contract is the only prize a contest is offering, you may want to think twice before entering. Basically, the company sponsoring the contest is asking you to pay a fee for them to listen to your song under the guise of a contest, something a legitimate publisher or record company would not do. For those contests offering studio time, Musical equipment or cash prizes, you need to decide if the entry fee you're paying is worth the chance to win such prizes.

Be wary of exorbitant entry fees, and if you have any doubts whatsoever as to the legitimacy of a contest, it's best to stay away. Songwriters need to approach a contest, award or grant in the same manner as they would a record or publishing company. Make your submission as professional as possible; follow directions and submit material exactly as stated on the entry form.

Contests in this section encompass all types of Music and levels of competition. Read each listing carefully and contact them if the contest interests you. Many contests now have Websites that offer additional information and even entry forms you can print. Be sure to read the rules carefully and be sure you understand exactly what a contest is offering before entering.

AGO/ECS PUBLISHING AWARD IN CHORAL COMPOSITION

American Guild of Organists, 475 Riverside Dr., Suite 1260, New York NY 10115. (212)870-2310. **Fax:** (212)870-2163. **E-mail:** info@agohq.org; christian. lane@mac.com. **Website:** www.agohq.org. **Contact:** Christian Lane, councillor for competitions. Biannual awaRoad

REQUIREMENTS Composers are invited to submit a work for SATB choir and organ in which the organ plays a significant and independent role. Work submitted must be unpublished and are usually no longer than 8 minutes in length. There is no age restriction. Deadline: July 1. Application information on the website.

AWARDS Prize: $2,000 cash, publication by ECS Publishing, and premier performance at the AGO National Convention. Further details are published in *The American Organist.*

AGO/MARILYN MASON AWARD IN ORGAN COMPOSITION

American Guild of Organists, 475 Riverside Dr., Suite 1260, New York NY 10115. (212)870-2310. **Fax:** (212)870-2163. **E-mail:** info@agohq.org; christian. lane@mac.com. **Website:** www.agohq.org. **Contact:** Christian Lane, councillor for competitions. For composers and performing artists. Biennial awaRoad

REQUIREMENTS Organ solo, not less than 4 minutes and not more than 6 minutes in duration. Specifics vary from year to year. Deadline: July 1. Visit website for application.

AWARDS Prize: $2,000; publication by Hinshaw Music Inc.; performance at the biennial National Convention of the American Guild of Organists.

AMERICAN SONGWRITER LYRIC CONTEST

113 19th Ave. S., Nashville TN 37203. (615)321-6096. **Fax:** (615)321-6097. **E-mail:** info@americansongwriter.com. **Website:** www.americansongwriter.com. For songwriters and composers. Award for each bimonthly issue of *American Songwriter* magazine, plus grand prize winner at year-end.

PURPOSE To promote and encourage the craft of lyric writing.

REQUIREMENTS Contest is open to any amateur songwriter. *AS* defines an amateur as one who has not earned more than $5,000 from songwriting related to royalties, advances, or works for hire. Lyrics must be typed and a check for $15 (per entry) must be enclosed. Deadlines: January, March, May, July, September, November. See website for exact dates. Submit online through AmericanSongspace.com. Lyrics only. "If you enter 2 or more lyrics, you automatically receive a 1-year subscription to *American Songwriter* magazine (Canada: 3 or more; other countries: 4 or more)."

AWARDS The annual winner will be chosen from the 6 bimonthly contest winners. First place winners also receive 1 legendary Shure SM58 microphone and a Gibson J-45 standard acoustic electrica cobraburst guitar. Grand Prize: The annual winner, chosen from the 6 contest winners, will receive round trip airfare to Nashville and a dream co-writing session.

TIPS "You do not have to be a subscriber to enter or win. You may submit as many entries as you like. All genres of Music accepted."

ANNUAL NSAI SONG CONTEST

1710 Roy Acuff Place, Nashville TN 37203. (615)256-3354. **Fax:** (615)256-0034. **E-mail:** songcontest@nashvillesongwriters.com. **Website:** www.nashvillesongwriters.com; www.nsai.cmt.com. **Contact:** David Petrelli, NSAI event director.

PURPOSE "A chance for aspiring songwriters to be heard by Music industry decision makers."

REQUIREMENTS Entry fee: $35 per song (NSAI member); $45 per song (nonmember). Submissions accepted from August 1-October 31. In order to be eligible contestants must not be receiving income from any work submitted—original material only. Mail-in submissions must be in CD form and include entry form, lyrics and melody. Online submissions available through nsai.cmt.com. Visit website for complete list of rules and regulations. Deadline is different each year; check website or send for application. Samples are required with application in the format of cassette or CD.

AWARDS Grand Prize winner receives a one-on-one mentoring session with Music superstar, Darius Rucker. CMT Listener's Choice award gives fans a chance to vote for their favorite song entry. Visit website for complete list of rules and prizes.

ARTISTS' FELLOWSHIPS

New York Foundation for the Arts, 20 Jay St., 7th Floor, Brooklyn NY 11201. (212)366-6900. **Fax:** (212)366-1778. **E-mail:** fellowships@nyfa.org. **Website:** www.nyfa.org. For songwriters, composers, and

Musical playwrights. Annual award, but each category funded biennially.

PURPOSE Artists' Fellowships are $7,000 grants awarded by the New York Foundation for the Arts to individual originating artists living in New York State. The Foundation is committed to supporting artists from all over New York State at all stages of their professional careers. Fellows may use the grant according to their own needs; it should not be confused with project support.

REQUIREMENTS Must be 18 years of age or older; resident of New York State for 2 years prior to application; and cannot be enrolled in any graduate or undergraduate degree program. Applications will be available in July. Deadline: October. Samples of work are required with application. One or 2 original compositions on separate audiotapes or audio CDs and at least 2 copies of corresponding scores or fully harmonized lead sheets.

AWARDS All Artists' Fellowships awards are for $7,000. Fellowships are awarded on the basis of the quality of work submitted. Applications are reviewed by a panel of 5 composers representing the aesthetic, ethnic, sexual and geographic diversity within New York State. The panelists change each year and review all allowable material submitted.

TIPS "Please note that Musical playwrights may submit only if they write the Music for their plays; librettists must submit in our playwriting category."

ARTIST TRUST FELLOWSHIP AWARD

1835 12th Ave., Seattle WA 98122. (209)467-8734 ext. 11. **Fax:** (866)218-7878. **E-mail:** info@artisttrust.org. **Website:** www.www.artisttrust.org. **Contact:** Miguel Guillen, Program Manager. Fellowships award $7,500 to practicing professional artists of exceptional talent and demonstrated ability. The Fellowship is a merit-based, not a project-based awaRoad Recipients present a Meet the Artist Event to a community in Washington State that has little or no access to the artist and their work. Awards 14 fellowships of $7,500 and 2 residencies with $1,000 stipends at the Millay Colony.

THE ASCAP DEEMS TAYLOR AWARDS

American Society of Composers, Authors & Publishers, One Lincoln Plaza, New York NY 10023. (212)621-6318. **E-mail:** jsteinblatt@ascap.com. **Website:** www. ascap.com. **Contact:** Jim Steinblatt. The ASCAP Deems Taylor Awards program recognizes books, articles, broadcasts, and websites on the subject of Music selected for their excellence.

PURPOSE Honors the memory of composer/critic/commentator Deems Taylor.

THE BLANK THEATRE COMPANY YOUNG PLAYWRIGHTS FESTIVAL

P.O. Box 38756, Hollywood CA 90038. (323)662-7734. **Fax:** (323)661-3903. **E-mail:** info@theblank.com. **E-mail:** submissions@youngplaywrights.com. **Website:** www.youngplaywrights.com. For both Musical and non-Musical playwrights. Annual awaRoad

PURPOSE Purpose is to give young playwrights an opportunity to learn more about playwriting and to give them a chance to have their work mentored, developed, and presented by professional artists.

REQUIREMENTS Playwrights must be 19 years old or younger at time of submission. Send legible, original plays of any length and on any subject (co-written plays are acceptable provided all co-writers meet eligibility requirements). Submissions must be postmarked by March 15 and must include a cover sheet with the playwright's name, date of birth, school (if any), home address, home phone number, e-mail address and production history. Pages must be numbered and submitted unbound (unstapled). For Musicals, a tape or CD of a selection from the score should be submitted with the script. Mss will not be returned; do not send originals. Semi-finalists and winners will be contacted in May.

AWARDS Winning playwrights receive a workshop presentation of their work.

CRS COMPETITION FOR COMPOSERS' RECORDINGS

724 Winchester Road, Broomall PA 19008. (610)205-9897. **Fax:** (707)549-5920. **E-mail:** crsnews@verizon. net. **Website:** www.crsnews.org. **Contact:** Caroline Hunt, administrative assistant; Jack Shusterman, senior representative. For songwriters, composers, and performing artists. College faculty and gifted artists. Each annual competition is limited to the first 300 applicants—all fees beyond this limit will be returned.

REQUIREMENTS "Each category requires a separate application fee. The work submitted must be non-published (prior to acceptance) and not commercially recorded on any label. The work submitted must not exceed 9 performers. Each composer/performer may submit 1 work for each application submitted. (Taped performances by composers are additionally encouraged.) Composition must not exceed 16 minutes in length. CRS reserves the right not to accept a First Prize Winner. Write with SASE for application or visit website. Add $5 for postage and handling. Must send a detailed résumé with application form available on our Web page under 'Events' category. Samples of work required with application. Send score and parts with optional CD or DAT. Application fee: $50."

AWARDS First prize will consist of a commercially distributed new compact disc recording grant featuring one composition along with other distinguished composers and performing artists. Second and Third Prizes will be awarded Honorable Mention toward future recordings with CRS and Honorary Life Membership to the Society. Applications are judged by panel of judges determined each year.

DELTA OMICRON INTERNATIONAL COMPOSITION COMPETITION

910 Church St., P.O. Box 752, Jefferson City TN 37760. (865)471-6155. **Fax:** (865)475-9716. **E-mail:** doexecsec@att.net. **Website:** www.delta-omicron.org. **Contact:** Debbie Beckner, executive secretary. For composers. Triennial awaRoad Next contest: 2015.

PURPOSE "To encourage composers worldwide to continually add to our wonderful heritage of Musical creativity instrumentally and/or vocally."

REQUIREMENTS People from college age on (or someone younger who is enrolled in college). Work must be unpublished and unperformed in public. "View our website for specific submission guidelines such as instrument selection and deadline Click on 'Composition Competition' on homepage." Mss should be legibly written in ink or processed, signed with *nom de plume*, and free from any marks that would identify the composer to the judges. Entry fee: $25 per composition. Send for application. Composition is required with application. A total of 3 copies of composition are required, one for each judge. Music copies should *not* be spiral bound. Deadline: March 31.

AWARDS Prize: 1st Place: $1,000 and world premiere at Delta Omicron Triennial Conference. Judged by 2-3 judges (performers, conductors, and/or composers).

EUROPEAN INTERNATIONAL COMPETITION FOR COMPOSERS/IBLA FOUNDATION

568 Grand St., Suite 2001, New York NY 10002. (212)387-0111. **E-mail:** iblanewyork@gmail.com.

Website: www.ibla.org. **Contact:** Dr. Salvatore Moltisanti, president. For songwriters and composers. Annual awaRoad

PURPOSE "To promote the winners' career through exposure, publicity, recordings with Athena Records, and nationwide distribution with the Empire Group."

REQUIREMENTS Deadline: April 30. Send for application. Entry fee: $120. Music score and/or recording of one work are required with application. Application fee is refunded if not admitted into the program.

AWARDS Winners are presented in concerts in Europe-Japan, USA.

FULBRIGHT SCHOLAR PROGRAM, COUNCIL FOR INTERNATIONAL EXCHANGE OF SCHOLARS

1400 K St. NW, Suite 5L, Washington DC 20005. (202)686-4000. **Fax:** (202)686-4029. **E-mail:** scholars@iie.org. **Website:** www.cies.org.

PURPOSE "Annual awards for university lecturing and advanced research abroad are offered annually in virtually all academic disciplines including Musical composition."

REQUIREMENTS "U.S. citizenship at time of application; M.F.A., Ph.D. or equivalent professional qualifications; for lecturing awards, university teaching experience (some awards are for professionals non-academic)." Applications become available in March each year, for grants to be taken up 11/2 years later. See website for application deadlines. Write or call for application. Samples of work are required with application.

AWARDS "Benefits vary by country, but generally include round-trip travel for the grantee and for most full academic-year awards, one dependent; stipend in U.S. dollars and/or local currency; in many countries, tuition allowance for school age children; and book and baggage allowance. Grant duration ranges from 3 months-1 academic year."

GRASSY HILL KERRVILLE NEW FOLK COMPETITION

P.O. Box 291466, Kerrville TX 78029. (830)257-3600. **Fax:** (830)257-8680. **E-mail:** info@kerrville-Music.com. **Website:** www.kerrville-Music.com/newfolk.htm. **Contact:** Dalis Allen, producer. For songwriters. Annual awaRoad

◯ Also see the listing for Kerrville Folk Festival in the Workshops section of this book.

PURPOSE "To provide an opportunity for emerging songwriters to be heard and rewarded for excellence."

REQUIREMENTS Songwriter enters 2 original songs burned to CD (cassettes no longer accepted), or uploaded to Sonicbids, with entry fee; no more than one submission may be entered; 6-8 minutes total for 2 songs. Application online, no lyric sheets or press material needed. Submissions accepted between December 1 and March 8 or first 800 entries received prior to that date. Call or e-mail to request rules. Entry fee: $25.

AWARDS Thirty-two finalists invited to sing the 2 songs entered during The Kerrville Folk Festival in May. Six writers are chosen as award winners. Each of the 6 receives a cash award of $450 or more and performs at a winner's concert during the Kerrville Folk Festival in June. Initial round of entries judged by the Festival Producer and a panel of online listeners from the Music industry. Thirty-two finalists judged by panel of 3 performer/songwriters.

TIPS "Do not allow instrumental accompaniment to drown out lyric content. Don't enter without complete copy of the rules. Former winners and finalists include Lyle Lovett, Nanci Griffith, Hal Ketchum, John Gorka, David Wilcox, Lucinda Williams and Robert Earl Keen, Tish Hinojosa, Carrie Newcomer, and Jimmy Lafave."

GREAT AMERICAN SONG CONTEST

PMB 135, 6327-C SW Capitol Hill Hwy., Portland OR 97239-1937. **E-mail:** info@greatamerican-song.com. **Website:** www.greatamericansong.com. For songwriters, composers and lyricists. Annual awaRoad

- Also see the listing for Songwriters Resource Network in the Organizations section of this book.

PURPOSE To help songwriters get their songs heard by Music-industry professionals; to generate educational and networking opportunities for participating songwriters; to help songwriters open doors in the Music business.

REQUIREMENTS Entry fee: $30 each for first 2 entries; $25 after first 2. "Annual deadline. Check our website for details or send SASE along with your mailed request for information."

AWARDS Winners receive a mix of cash awards and prizes. The focus of the contest is on networking and educational opportunities. (All participants receive detailed evaluations of their songs by industry professionals.) Songs are judged by knowledgeable Music-industry professionals, including prominent hit songwriters, producers and publishers.

TIPS "Focus should be on the song. The quality of the demo isn't important. Judges will be looking for good songwriting talent. They will base their evaluations on the song—not the quality of the recording or the voice performance."

HARVEY GAUL COMPOSITION CONTEST

The Pittsburgh New Music Ensemble, Inc., 527 Coyne Terrace, Pittsburgh PA 15207. (412)889-7231. **E-mail:** contactpnme@gmail.com. **Website:** www.pnme.org. **Contact:** Kevin Noe, artistic director. For composers. Biennial.

PURPOSE Objective is to encourage composition of new Music.

REQUIREMENTS "Must be citizen of the U.S. Please submit score and recording, if available (CDs only) of a representative instrumental score." Send SASE for application or download from website. Samples of work are required with application. Entry fee: $20. Deadline: January 1.

AWARDS Prize: $6,000. Winner also receives commission for new work to be premiered by the PNME.

IAMA (INTERNATIONAL ACOUSTIC MUSIC AWARDS)

2881 E. Oakland Park Blvd., Suite 414, Fort Lauderdale FL 33306. **E-mail:** info@inacoustic.com. **Website:** www.inacoustic.com. For singer-songwriters, Musicians, performing Musicians in the acoustic genre.

PURPOSE "The purpose is to promote the excellence in acoustic Music performance and songwriting." Genres include: Folk, Alternative, Bluegrass, etc.

REQUIREMENTS Visit website for entry form and details. "All songs submitted must be original. There must be at least an acoustic instrument (voice) in any song. Electric and electronic instruments, along with loops, is allowed, but acoustic instruments (or voice) must be clearly heard in all songs submitted. Contestants may enter as many songs in as many categories as desired but each entry requires a separate CD, entry form, lyric sheet, and entry fee. CDs and lyrics will not be returned. Winners will be chosen by a Blue Ribbon Judging Committee comprised of Music industry professionals including A&R managers from record labels, publishers and producers. Entries are judged equally on Music performance, production, originality, lyrics, melody and composition. Songs may be in any language. Winners will be notified by e-mail and must sign and return an affidavit confirming that winner's song is original and he/she holds rights to the song. Entry fee: $35/entry.

AWARDS Overall Grand Prize receives $11,000 worth of merchandise. First prizes in all categories win $900 worth of merchandise and services. Runner-up prizes in all categories receive $600 worth of merchandise and services. All first prizes and runner-up winners will receive a track on IAMA compilation CD which goes out to radio stations.

TIPS "Judging is based on Music performance, Music production, songwriting, and originality/artistry."

KATE NEAL KINLEY MEMORIAL FELLOWSHIP

University of Illinois, College of Fine and Applied Arts, 100 Architecture Bldg., 608 E. Lorado Taft Dr., Champaign IL 61820. (217)333-1661. **E-mail:** faa@illinois.edu. **Website:** www.faa.illinois.edu/kate_neal_kinley_memorial_fellowship. For students of architecture, art or Music. Annual awaRoad

PURPOSE Purpose is for the advancement of study in the fine arts.

REQUIREMENTS "The Fellowship will be awarded upon the basis of unusual promise in the fine arts. Open to college graduates whose principal or major studies have been in the fields of architecture, art or Music." Deadline: December 6. Call or visit website for application. Samples of work are required with application.

AWARDS "One major fellowship which yield the sum of $20,000 each which is to be used by the recipients toward defraying the expenses of advanced study of the fine arts in America or abroad." Two or 3 smaller fellowships may also be awarded upon committee recommendations. Good for 1 year. Grant is nonrenewable.

THE JOHN LENNON SONGWRITING CONTEST

180 Brighton Road, Suite 801, Clifton NJ 07012. (888)884-5572. **E-mail:** info@jlsc.com; tiana@jlsc.com. **Website:** www.jlsc.com. **Contact:** Tiana Lewis, assistant director. Open year-round with two sessions. The first begins February 14 with a June 15

deadline. The second begins June 16 with a December 15 deadline.

PURPOSE "The purpose of the John Lennon Songwriting Contest is to promote the art of songwriting by assisting in the discovery of new talent as well as providing more established songwriters with an opportunity to advance their careers."

REQUIREMENTS "Each entry must consist of the following: completed and signed application; audio cassette, CD or mp3 containing 1 song only, 5 minutes or less in length; lyric sheet typed or printed legibly (English translation is required when applicable); $30 entry fee per song. Applications can be found in various Music-oriented magazines and on our website. Prospective entrants can also send for an application by e-mailing Tiana Lewis at tiana@jlsc.com."

AWARDS Entries are accepted in the following 12 categories: rock, country, jazz, pop, world, gospel/inspirational, R&B, hip-hop, Latin, electronic, folk and children's Music. Winners will receive EMI Publishing Contracts, Studio Equipment from Brian Moore Guitars, Roland, Edirol and Audio Technica, 1,000 CDs in full color with premium 6-panel Digipaks courtesy of Discmakers, and gift certificates from Musiciansfriend.com. One entrant will be chosen to TOUR and PERFORM for 1 week on Warped Tour. One Lennon Award winning song will be named "Song of the Year" and take home an additional $20,000 in cash.

MID-ATLANTIC SONG CONTEST

4200 Wisconsin Ave., NW, PMB 106-137, Washington DC 20016. **E-mail:** contact@saw.org. **Website:** www.saw.org. For songwriters and composers. Annual awaRoad

Also see the listing for Songwriters Association of Washington in the Organizations section.

PURPOSE "This is one of the longest-running contests in the nation; SAW has organized 27 contests since 1982. The competition is designed to afford rising songwriters in a wide variety of genres the opportunity to receive awards and exposure in an environment of peer competition."

REQUIREMENTS Amateur status is important. Applicants should request a brochure/application using the contact information above. Rules and procedures are clearly explained in the brochure and also online. CD and 3 copies of the lyrics are to be submitted with an application form and fee for each entry, or submit mp3 entries by applying online or through Sonicbids. Reduced entry fees are offered to members of Songwriters' Association of Washington; membership can be arranged simultaneously with entering. Multiple song discounts are also offered. Applications are mailed out and posted on their website around June 1; the submission deadline is September 15; awards are typically announced late in the fall.

AWARDS The 2 best songs in each of 10 categories win prize packages donated by the contest's corporate sponsors: BMI, Oasis CD Manufacturing, Omega Recording Studios, Mary Cliff, and Sonic Bids. Winning songwriters are invited to perform in Washington, DC at the Awards Ceremony Gala, and the winning songs are included on a compilation CD. The best song in each category is eligible for three grand cash prizes. Certificates are awarded to other entries meriting finalis and honorable mention.

TIPS "Enter the song in the most appropriate category. Make the sound recording the best it can be (even though judges are asked to focus on melody and lyric and not on production.) Avoid clichés, extended introductions, and long instrumental solos."

THELONIOUS MONK INTERNATIONAL JAZZ COMPETITION

5225 Wisconsin Ave. NW, Suite 605, Washington DC 20015. (202)364-7272. **Fax:** (202)364-0176. **E-mail:** lebrown@monkinstitute.org; info@monkinstitute.org. **Website:** www.monkinstitute.org. **Contact:** Leonard Brown, program director. For songwriters and composers. Annual award sponsored by BMI.

PURPOSE "This is the world's most prestigious jazz competition, recognized for discovering the next generation of jazz masters." The competition focuses on a different instrument each year and features an all-star judging panel.

REQUIREMENTS Deadline: See website. Send for application. Submission must include application form, résumé of Musical experience, CD or mp3, entry, 4 copies of the full score, and a photo. The composition features a different instrument each year. Entry fee: $50.

AWARDS Prize: $10,000.

NACUSA YOUNG COMPOSERS' COMPETITION

Box 49256 Barrington Station, Los Angeles CA 90049. (541)765-2406. **E-mail:** nacusa@Music-usa.

org. **Website:** www.Music-usa.org/nacusa. **Contact:** Greg Steinke.

○ Also see the National Association of Composers/USA (NACUSA) listing in the Organization section.

PURPOSE Encourages the composition of new American concert hall Music.

PULITZER PRIZE IN MUSIC

Columbia University, 709 Pulitzer Hall, 2950 Broaday, New York NY 10027. (212)854-3841. **Fax:** (212)854-3342. **E-mail:** pulitzer@pulitzer.org. **Website:** www.pulitzer.org. For composers and Musical playwrights. Annual awaRoad

REQUIREMENTS "For distinguished Musical composition by an American that has had its first perfomance or recording in the United States during the year." Entries should reflect current creative activity. Works that receive their American premiere between January 1 and December 31 of the contest year are eligible. A public performance or the public release of a recording shall constitute a premiere. Deadline: December 31. Samples of work are required with application, biography and photograph of composer, date and place of performance, score or manuscript and recording of the work, entry form, and $50 entry fee.

AWARDS Prize: $10,000. Applications are judged first by a nominating jury, then by the Pulitzer Prize BoaRoad

RICHARD RODGERS AWARDS FOR MUSICAL THEATER

American Academy of Arts and Letters, 633 W. 155 St., New York NY 10032. (212)368-5900. **Fax:** (212)491-4615. **E-mail:** academy@artsandletters.org. **Website:** www.artsandletters.org. **Contact:** Jane Bolster, coordinator. "The Richard Rodgers Awards subsidize staged reading, studio productions, and full productions by nonprofit theaters in New York City of works by composers and writers who are not already established in the field of Musical theater. The awards are only for Musicals—songs by themselves are not eligible. The authors must be citizens or permanent residents of the United States." Guidelines for this award may be obtained by sending a SASE to above address or downloaded from the website. Deadline: November 1.

ROCKY MOUNTAIN FOLKS FESTIVAL SONGWRITER SHOWCASE

Folks Showcase Contest, P.O. Box 769, Lyons CO 80540. (800)624-2422; (303)823-0848. **Fax:** (303)823-0849. **E-mail:** planet@bluegrass.com. **Website:** www.bluegrass.com. **Contact:** Steve Szymanski, director. For songwriters, composers, and performers. Annual awaRoad

PURPOSE Award based on having the best song and performance.

REQUIREMENTS Deadline: June. Finalists notified by July. Rules available on website. Samples of work are required with application. Send CD with $10/song entry fee. Can now submit online at www.sonicbids.com. "Contestants cannot be signed to a major label or publishing deal. No backup Musicians allowed. Awards: 1st Place is a Festival Main Stage set, Taylor Guitar, and $300; 2nd Place is $500; 3rd Place is $400; 4th Place is $300; 5th Place is $200; 6th to 10th Place is $100 each. Each finalist will also receive a complimentary 3-day Folks Festival pass that includes onsite camping, and a Songwriter In The Round slot during the Festival on our workshop stage."

ROME PRIZE COMPETITION FELLOWSHIP

American Academy in Rome, 7 E. 60th St., New York NY 10022-1001. (212)751-7200. **Fax:** (212)751-7220. **E-mail:** info@aarome.org. **Website:** www.aarome.org. For composers. Annual awaRoad

PURPOSE "Through its annual Rome Prize Competition, the academy awards up to 30 fellowships in 11 disciplines, including Musical composition. Winners of the Rome Prize pursue independent projects while residing at the Academy's 11 acre center in Rome."

REQUIREMENTS "Applicants for 11-month fellowships must be U.S. citizens and hold a bachelor's degree in Music, Musical composition, or its equivalent." Deadline: November 1. Entry fee: $60. Application guidelines are available through the Academy's website.

AWARDS "Up to 2 fellowships are awarded annually in Musical composition. Fellowship consists of room, board, and a studio at the Academy facilities in Rome as well as a stipend of $16,000 for a 6 month fellowship or $28,000 for an 11 month fellowship. In all cases, excellence is the primary criterion for selection, based on the quality of the materials submitted. Winners are announced in mid-April and fellowships generally begin in early September."

TELLURIDE TROUBADOUR CONTEST

ATTN: Troubadour Competition, P.O. Box 769, Lyons CO 80540. (303)823-0848; (800)624-2422. **Fax:** (303)823-0849. **E-mail:** planet@bluegrass.com. **Website:** www.bluegrass.com. **Contact:** Steve Szymanski, director. The Telluride Troubadour Competition is a nationally recognized songwriter competition open to anyone who writes and performs original Music and who is not currently signed to a major recording or publishing deal. Contestants are judged on the quality of the song's composition, vocal delivery, and the overall performance. Finalists are awarded cash and prizes, as well as critical acclaim, well-deserved recognition, and a chance to perform on the festival main stage.

REQUIREMENTS Deadline: must be postmarked by April 11; notified May 3, if selected. Rules available on website. Send CD and $10/song entry fee (limit of 2 songs). Can now submit Music online at www.sonicbids.com. No backup Musicians allowed.

AWARDS 1st Prize: custom Shanti Guitar, $300, and Festival Main Stage Set; 2nd Prize: $500 and Martin Travel Guitar; 3rd Prize: $400 and Martin Travel Guitar; 4th Prize: $300 and Martin Travel Guitar; 5th Prize: $200 and Martin Travel Guitar. Applications judged by panel of judges.

USA SONGWRITING COMPETITION

2881 E. Oakland Park Blvd., Suite 414, Ft. Lauderdale FL 33306. (954)537-3127. **Fax:** (954)537-9690. **E-mail:** info@songwriting.net. **Website:** www.songwriting.net. **Contact:** Contest Manager. For songwriters, composers, performing artists, and lyricists. Annual awaRoad

PURPOSE "To honor good songwriters/composers all over the world, especially the unknown ones."

REQUIREMENTS Open to professional and beginner songwriters. No limit on entries. Each entry must include an entry fee, a CD, mp3, or audio cassette tape of song(s) and lyric sheet(s). Judged by Music industry representatives. Past judges have included record label representatives and publishers from Arista Records, EMI and Warner/Chappell. Deadline: See website. Entry fee: $35 per song. See website or e-mail for entry forms at any time. Samples of work are not required.

AWARDS Prizes include cash and merchandise in 15 different categories: pop, rock, country, Latin, R&B, gospel, folk, jazz, "lyrics only" category, instrumental, and many others.

TIPS "Judging is based on lyrics, originality, melody, and overall composition. CD-quality production is great but not a consideration in judging."

U.S.-JAPAN CREATIVE ARTISTS EXCHANGE FELLOWSHIP PROGRAM

Japan-U.S. Friendship Commission, 1201 15th St. NW, Suite 330, Washington DC 20005. (202)418-9800. **Fax:** (202)418-9802. **E-mail:** mmihori@jusfc. gov; jusfc@jusfc.gov. **Website:** www.jusfc.gov. **Contact:** Margaret Mihori, associate executive director. For all creative artists. Annual awaRoad

PURPOSE "For artists to go as seekers, as cultural visionaries, and as living liaisons to the traditional and contemporary life of Japan."

REQUIREMENTS "Artists' works must exemplify the best in U.S. arts." Deadline: See website. Send for application and guidelines. Applications available on website. Samples of work are required with application. Requires 2 pieces on CD or DVD.

AWARDS Five artists are awarded a 3-month residency anywhere in Japan. Awards monthly stipend for living expenses, housing, and professional support services; up to $2,000 for round-trip transportation will be provided for the artist.

TIPS "Applicants should anticipate a highly rigorous review of their artistry and should have compelling reasons for wanting to work in Japan."

WESTERN WRITERS OF AMERICA

271CR 219, Encampment WY 82325. (307)329-8942. **Fax:** (307)327-5465 (call first). **E-mail:** wwa. moulton@gmail.com. **Website:** www.westernwriters.org. **Contact:** Candy Moulton, executive director.

17 Spur Award categories in various aspects of the American West.

PURPOSE The nonprofit Western Writers of America has promoted and honored the best in Western literature with the annual Spur Awards, selected by panels of judges. Awards, for material published last year, are given for works whose inspirations, image and literary excellence best represent the reality and spirit of the American West.

Y.E.S. FESTIVAL OF NEW PLAYS

Northern Kentucky University, Department of Theatre and Dance, Nunn Dr., Highland Heights KY 41099-1007. (859)572-6303. **Fax:** (859)572-6057. **E-mail:** forman@nku.edu. **Contact:** Sandra Forman, project director. For Musical playwrights. Biennial award (odd numbered years).

PURPOSE "The festival seeks to encourage new playwrights and develop new plays and Musicals. Three plays or Musicals are given full productions."

REQUIREMENTS "No entry fee. Submit a script with a completed entry form. Musicals should be submitted with a piano/conductor's score and/or a vocal parts score. Scripts may be submitted May 1 through Sept. 30, for the New Play Festival occuring in April of the following year. Send SASE for application."

AWARDS Three awards of $500. "The winners are brought to NKU at our expense to view late rehearsals and opening night." Submissions are judged by a panel of readers.

TIPS "Plays/Musicals which have heavy demands for mature actors are not as likely to be selected as an equally good script with roles for 18-30 year olds."

ORGANIZATIONS

One of the first places a beginning songwriter should look for guidance and support is a songwriting organization. Offering encouragement, instruction, contacts and feedback, these groups of professional and amateur songwriters can help an aspiring songwriter hone the skills needed to compete in the ever-changing music industry.

The type of organization you choose to join depends on what you want to get out of it. Local groups can offer a friendly, supportive environment where you can work on your songs and have them critiqued in a constructive way by other songwriters. They're also great places to meet collaborators. Larger, national organizations can give you access to Music business professionals and other songwriters across the country.

Most of the organizations listed in this book are non-profit groups with membership open to specific groups of people—songwriters, Musicians, classical composers, etc. They can be local groups with a membership of less than 100 people, or large national organizations with thousands of members from all over the country. In addition to regular meetings, most organizations occasionally sponsor events such as seminars and workshops to which Music industry personnel are invited to talk about the business, and perhaps listen to and critique demo tapes.

Check the following listings, bulletin boards at local music stores and your local newspapers for area organizations. If you are unable to locate an organization within an easy distance of your home, you may want to consider joining one of the national groups. These groups, based in New York, Los Angeles and Nashville, keep their members involved and informed through newsletters, regional workshops and large yearly conferences. They can help a writer who feels isolated in his hometown get his Music heard by professionals in the major Music centers.

In the following listings, organizations describe their purpose and activities, as well as how much it costs to join. Before joining any organization, consider what they have to offer and how becoming a member will benefit you. To locate organizations close to home, see the Geographic Index at the back of this book.

ACADEMY OF COUNTRY MUSIC

5500 Balboa Blvd., Encino CA 91316. (818)788-8000. **Fax:** (818)788-0999. **E-mail:** info@acmcountry.com. **Website:** www.acmcountry.com. Serves country Music industry professionals. Eligibility for professional members is limited to those individuals who derive some portion of their income directly from country Music. Each member is classified by one of the following categories: artist/entertainer, club/venue operator, Musician, on-air personality, manager, talent agent, composer, Music publisher, public relations, publications, radio, TV/motion picture, record company, talent buyer or affiliated (general). The purpose of ACM is to promote and enhance the image of country Music. The Academy is involved year-round in activities important to the country Music community. Some of these activities include charity fund-raisers, participation in country Music seminars, talent contests, artist showcases, assistance to producers in placing country Music on television and in motion pictures and backing legislation that benefits the interests of the country Music community. The ACM is governed by directors and run by officers elected annually. Applications are accepted throughout the year. Membership: $75/year.

NEW MUSIC USA (FORMERLY AMERICAN MUSIC CENTER, INC.)

90 John St., Suite 312, New York NY 10038. (212)645-6949. **Fax:** (212)490-0998. **E-mail:** info@newMusicusa.org. **Website:** www.newMusicusa.org. The American Music Center, founded by a consortium led by Aaron Copland in 1939, is the first-ever national service and information center for new classical Music and jazz by American composers. The Center has a variety of innovative new programs and services, including a montly Internet magazine (www.newMusicbox.org) for new American Music, online databases of contemporary ensembles and ongoing opportunities for composers, an online catalog of new Music for educators specifically targeted to young audiences, a series of professional development workshops, and an online listening library. Each month, AMC provides its over 2,500 members with a listing of opportunities including calls for scores, competitions, and other new Music performance information. Each year, AMC's Information Services Department fields thousands of requests concerning composers, performers, data, funding, and support programs. The

AMC Collection at the New York Public Library for the Performing Arts presently includes over 60,000 scores and recordings, many unavailable elsewhere. "AMC also continues to administer several grant programs: the Aaron Copland Fund for Music; the Henry Cowell Performance Incentive Fund; and its own programs Live Music for Dance and the Composer Assistance Program." Members also receive a link their Websites on www.amc.net. The American Music Center is not-for-profit and has an annual membership fee.

AMERICAN SOCIETY OF COMPOSERS, AUTHORS AND PUBLISHERS (ASCAP)

One Lincoln Plaza, New York NY 10023. (212)621-6000 (administration). **Fax:** (212)621-8453. **Website:** www.ascap.com. **Regional offices—West Coast:** 7920 W. Sunset Blvd., 3rd Floor, Los Angeles CA 90046, (323)883-1000; **Nashville:** Two Music Square W., Nashville TN 37203, (615)742-5000; **Atlanta:** 950 Joseph E. Lowery Blvd. NW, Suite 23, Atlanta GA 30318, (404)685-8699; **Miami:** 420 Lincoln Road, Suite 385, Miami Beach FL 33139, (305)673-3446; **London:** 8 Cork St., London W1S 3LJ England, 011-44-207-439-0909; **Puerto Rico:** Ave. Martinez Nadal, c/ Hill Side 623, San Juan, Puerto Rico 00920, (787)707-0782. ASCAP is a membership association of over 240,000 composers, lyricists, songwriters, and Music publishers, whose function is to protect the rights of its members by licensing and collecting royalties for the nondramatic public performance of their copyrighted works. ASCAP licensees include radio, television, cable, live concert promoters, bars, restaurants, symphony orchestras, new media, and other users of Music. ASCAP is the leading performing rights society in the world. All revenues, less operating expenses, are distributed to members (about 86 cents of each dollar). ASCAP was the first U.S. performing rights organization to distribute royalties from the Internet. Founded in 1914, ASCAP is the only society created and owned by writers and publishers. The ASCAP Board of Directors consists of 12 writers and 12 publishers, elected by the membership. ASCAP's Member Card provides exclusive benefits geared towards working Music professionals. Among the benefits are health, Musical instrument and equipment, tour and studio liability, term life and long term care insurance, discounts on Musical instruments, equipment and supplies, access to a credit union, and much more. ASCAP hosts a wide array of showcases and workshops throughout the year, and offers grants, special awards, and networking opportunities in a variety of genres. Visit their website listed above for more information.

ARIZONA SONGWRITERS ASSOCIATION

428 E. Thunderbird Road #737, Phoenix AZ 85022. **E-mail:** azsongwriters@cox.net. **Website:** www.azsongwriters.com. **Contact:** John Iger, president. Members are all ages; all styles of Music, novice to pro; many make money placing their songs in film and TV. Most members are residents of Arizona. Purpose is to educate about the craft and business of songwriting and to facilitate networking with business professionals and other songwriters, Musicians, singers and studios. Offers instruction, e-newsletter, workshops, performance, and song pitching opportunities. Applications accepted year-round. Membership fee: $25/year.

⟳ ASSOCIATION DES PROFESSIONEL. LE.S DE LA CHANSON ET DE LA MUSIQUE

450 Rideau St., Suite 401, Ottawa ON K1N 5Z4 Canada. (613)745-5642. **Fax:** (613)745-9715. **E-mail:** communications@apcm.ca. **Website:** www.apcm.ca. **Contact:** Mathilde Hountchegnon, head of communications and promotion. Members are French Canadian singers and Musicians. Members must be French singing and may have a CD to be distributed. Purpose is to gather French speaking artists (outside of Quebec, mainly in Ontario) to distribute their material, other workshops, instructions, lectures, etc. Offers instruction, newsletter, lectures, workshops, and distribution. Applications accepted year-round. Membership fee: $60 (Canadian).

ASSOCIATION OF INDEPENDENT MUSIC PUBLISHERS

P.O. Box 69473, Los Angeles CA 90069. (818)771-7301. **E-mail:** LAinfo@aimp.org; NYinfo@aimp.org; NAinfo@aimp.org. **Website:** www.aimp.org. The organization's primary focus is to educate and inform Music publishers about the most current industry trends and practices by providing a forum for the discussion of the issues and problems confronting the Music publishing industry. Offers monthly panels and networking events. Applications accepted year-round. Professional Membership fee: $75/year. Online only: $60/year.

AUSTIN SONGWRITERS GROUP

P.O. Box 2578, Austin TX 78768. (512)698-4237. **E-mail:** info@austinsongwritersgroup.com. **Website:** www.austinsongwritersgroup.com. **Contact:** Lee Duffy, executive director. The Austin Songwriters Group is in its 26th year of serving songwriters. ASG is a non-profit organization created by songwriters for songwriters. Serves all ages and all levels, from just beginning to advanced. "Prospective members should have an interest in the field of songwriting, whether it be for profit or hobby. The main purpose of this organization is to educate members in the craft and business of songwriting; to provide resources for growth and advancement in the area of songwriting; and to provide opportunities for performance and contact with the Music industry." The primary benefit of membership to a songwriter is exposed to Music industry professionals, which increases contacts and furthers the songwriter's education in both craft and business aspects. Offers competitions, instruction, lectures, library, newsletter, performance opportunities, evaluation services, workshops and contact with musi c industry professionals through special guest speakers at meetings, plus our yearly Austin Songwriters Symposium, which includes instruction, song evaluations, and song pitching direct to those pros currently seeking material for their artists, publishing companies, etc." Applications accepted year-round. Membership fee: $50/year.

TIPS "Our newsletter is top-quality-packed with helpful information on all aspects of songwriting-craft, business, recording and producing tips, and industry networking opportunities. Go to our website and sign up for emails to keep you informed about on going and up coming events!"

BALTIMORE SONGWRITERS ASSOCIATION

P.O. Box 22496, Baltimore MD 21203. **E-mail:** info@baltimoresongwriters.org. **Website:** www.baltimoresongwriters.org. "The BSA is an inclusive organization with all ages, skill levels and genres of Music welcome. We are trying to build a Musical community that is more supportive and less competitive. We are dedicated to helping songwriters grow and become better in their craft." Offers instruction, newsletter, lectures, workshops, performance opportunities. Applications accepted year-round; membership not limited to location or Musical status. Membership fee: $25.

THE BLACK ROCK COALITION

P.O. Box 1054, Cooper Station, New York NY 10276. **E-mail:** brcmembersinfo@gmail.com. **Website:** www. blackrockcoalition.org. **Contact:** Darrell M. McNeil, director of operations. Serves Musicians, songwriters-male and female ages 18-40 (average). Also engineers, entertainment attorneys and producers. Looking for members who are "mature and serious about Music as an artist or activist willing to help fellow Musicians. The BRC independently produces, promotes and distributes Black alternative Music acts as a collective and supportive voice for such Musicians within the Music and record business. The main purpose of this organization is to produce, promote, and distribute the full spectrum of black Music along with educating the public on what black Music is. The BRC is now soliciting recorded Music by bands and individuals for Black Rock Coalition Records. Please send copyrighted and original material only." Offers instruction, newsletter, lectures, free seminars and workshops, monthly membership meeting, quarterly magazine, performing opportunities, evaluation services, business advice, full roster of all members. Applications accepted year-round. Bands must submit a tape, bio with picture and a self-addressed, stamped envelope before sending their membership fee. Membership fee: $25.

BROADCAST MUSIC, INC. (BMI)

7 World Trade Center, 250 Greenwich St., New York NY 10007. (212)220-3000. **E-mail:** newyork@bmi. com. **Website:** www.bmi.com. **Los Angeles:** 8730 Sunset Blvd., 3rd Floor West, Los Angeles CA 90069. (310)659-9109. **E-mail:** losangeles@bmi.com. **Nashville:** 10 Music Square East, Nashville TN 37203. (615)401-2000. **E-mail:** nashville@bmi.com. **Miami:** 1691 Michigan Av., Miami FL 33139. (305)673-5148. **E-mail:** miami@bmi.com. **Atlanta:** 3340 Peachtree Road, NE, Suite 570, Atlanta GA 30326. (404)261-5151. **E-mail:** atlanta@bmi.com. **Puerto Rico:** 1250 Ave. Ponce de Leon, San Jose Building Santurce PR 00907. (787)754-6490. **United Kingdom:** 84 Harley House, Marylebone Road, London NW1 5HN United Kingdom. 011-44-207-486-2036. **E-mail:** london@ bmi.com. President and CEO: Del R. Bryant. Senior vice presidents: Phillip Graham, New York, writer/publisher relations; Alison Smith, rerforming rights.

Vice presidents: Charlie Feldman, New York; Barbara Cane and Doreen Ringer Ross, Los Angeles; Paul Corbin, Nashville; Diane J. Almodovar, Miami; Catherine Brewton, Atlanta. Senior executive, London: Brandon Bakshi. BMI is a performing rights organization representing approximately 300,000 songwriters, composers and Music publishers in all genres of Music, including pop, rock, country, R&B, rap, jazz, Latin, gospel and contemporary classical. "Applicants must have written a Musical composition, alone or in collaboration with other writers, which is commercially published, recorded or otherwise likely to be performed." Purpose: BMI acts on behalf of its songwriters, composers and Music publishers by insuring payment for performance of their works through the collection of licensing fees from radio stations, Internet outlets, broadcast and cable TV stations, hotels, nightclubs, aerobics centers and other users of Music. This income is distributed to the writers and publishers in the form of royalty payments, based on how the Music is used. BMI also undertakes intensive lobbying efforts in Washington D.C. on behalf of its affiliates, seeking to protect their performing rights through the enactment of new legislation and enforcement of current copyright law. In addition, BMI helps aspiring songwriters develop their skills through various workshops, seminars and competitions it sponsors throughout the country. Applications accepted year-round. There is no membership fee for songwriters; a one-time fee of $150 is required to affiliate an individually-owned publishing company; $250 for partnerships, corporations and limited-liability companies. "Visit our website for specific contacts, e-mail addresses and additional membership information."

CALIFORNIA LAWYERS FOR THE ARTS

Fort Mason Center, C-265, San Francisco CA 94123. (415)775-7200. **Fax:** (415)775-1143. **E-mail:** support@ calawyersforthearts.org; sanfrancisco@calawyersforthearts.org. **Website:** www.calawyersforthearts. org. CLA's mission is to empower the creative community by providing education, representation and dispute resolution. CLA's vision is that creative artists and arts organizations serve as agents of democratic involvement, innovation, and positive social change, and the growth of an empowered arts sector is essential to healthy communities. CLA's leadership and services strengthen the arts for the benefit of communities throughout California. CLA serves creative artists of all disciplines, skill levels, and ages, supporting individuals, businesses, inventors, and creative arts organizations. CLA also serves groups and individuals who support the arts. CLA works most closely with the California arts and innovation community. Offers online education, newsletters, in person workshops and seminars, library, mediation and arbitration service, attorney referral service, publications and arts advocacy. Membership fees: $20 for senior citizens and full-time students, $30 for working artists, $45 for general individual, $70 for non-panel attorney, $75 for panel attorney, $100 for patrons; organizations: $50 for small organizations (budget under $100,000), $90 for large organizations (budget of $100,000 or more), $100 for corporate sponsors

☺ CANADA COUNCIL FOR THE ARTS/ CONSEIL DES ARTS DU CANADA

150 Elgin St., P.O. Box 1047, Ottawa ON K1P 5V8 Canada. (800)263-5588 or (613)566-4414, ext. 5060. **Fax:** (613)566-4390. **Website:** www.canadacouncil. ca. An independent agency that fosters and promotes the arts in Canada by providing grants and services to professional artists including songwriters and Musicians. "Individual artists must be Canadian citizens or permanent residents of Canada, and must have completed basic training and/or have the recognition as professionals within their fields. The Canada Council offers grants to professional Musicians to pursue their individual artistic development and creation. There are specific deadline dates for the various programs of assistance. Visit our website for more details."

☺ CANADIAN ACADEMY OF RECORDING ARTS AND SCIENCES (CARAS)

345 Adelaide St. W, 2nd Floor, Toronto ON M5V 1R5 Canada. (416)485-3135. **Fax:** (416)485-4978. **E-mail:** info@carasonline.ca; meghan@junoawards.ca. **Website:** www.carasonline.ca. **Contact:** Meghan McCabe, manager, communications. Membership is open to all employees (including support staff) in broadcasting and record companies, as well as producers, personal managers, recording artists, recording engineers, arrangers, composers, Music publishers, album designers, promoters, talent and booking agents, record retailers, rack jobbers, distributors, recording studios and other Music industry related professions (on approval). Applicants must be affiliated with the Canadian recording industry. Offers newsletter, nomination and voting privileges for Juno Awards and dis-

count tickets to Juno Awards show. "CARAS strives to foster the development of the Canadian Music and recording industries and to contribute toward higher artistic standards." Applications accepted year-round. Membership fee: $50/year (Canadian) + HST ($56.50 total). Applications accepted from individuals only, not from companies or organizations.

☺ CANADIAN COUNTRY MUSIC ASSOCIATION

120 Adelaide St. E., Suite 200, Toronto ON M5C 1K9 Canada. (416)947-1331. **Fax:** (416)947-5924. **E-mail:** country@ccma.org. **Website:** www.ccma.org. Members are artists, songwriters, Musicians, producers, radio station personnel, managers, booking agents and others. Offers newsletter, workshops, performance opportunities and the CCMA awards every September. "Through our newsletters and conventions we offer a means of meeting and associating with artists and others in the industry. The CCMA is a federally chartered, nonprofit organization, dedicated to the promotion and development of Canadian country Music throughout Canada and the world and to providing a unity of purpose for the Canadian country Music industry." See website for membership information and benefits.

☺ CANADIAN MUSICAL REPRODUCTION RIGHTS AGENCY LTD.

56 Wellesley St. W, #320, Toronto ON M5S 2S3 Canada. (416)926-1966. **Fax:** (416)926-7521. **E-mail:** inquiries@cmrra.ca. **Website:** www.cmrra.ca. **Contact:** Michael Mackie, membership services and copyright. Members are Music copyright owners, Music publishers, sub-publishers and administrators. Representation by CMRRA is open to any person, firm or corporation anywhere in the world, which owns and/or administers one or more copyrighted Musical works. CMRRA is a Music licensing agency—Canada's largest—which represents Music copyright owners, publishers and administrators for the purpose of mechanical and synchronization licensing in Canada. Offers mechanical and synchronization licensing. Applications accepted year-round.

CENTRAL CAROLINA SONGWRITERS ASSOCIATION (CCSA)

131 Henry Baker Road, Zebulon NC 27597. (919)727-6647. **Website:** www.ccsa-raleigh.com. "CCSA welcomes songwriters of all experience levels from beginner to professional within the local RDU/Triad/

Eastern area of North Carolina to join our group. Our members' Musical background varies, covering a wide array of Musical genres. CCSA meets monthly in Raleigh, NC. We are unable to accept applications from incarcerated persons or those who do not reside in the local area as our group's primary focus is on songwriters who are able to attend the monthly meetings-to ensure members get the best value for their yearly dues." CCSA strives to provide each songwriter and Musician a resourceful organization where members grow Musically by networking and sharing with one another. Offers annual songwriters forum, periodic workshops, critiques at the monthly meetings, opportunities to perform and network with fellow members. Applications are accepted year round. Dues are $24/year (pro-rated for new members at $2/month by date of application) with annual renewal each January.

CENTRAL OREGON SONGWRITERS ASSOCIATION

1900 NE Third St., Suite 106-132, Bend OR 97701. **E-mail:** bookjanellybean@gmail.com. **Website:** http://oregonsongwriters.org. **Contact:** Janelle Musson, president. "Our members range in age from their 20s into their 80s. Membership includes aspiring beginners, accomplished singer/songwriter performing artists and all in between. Anyone with an interest in songwriting (any style) is invited to and welcome at COSA. COSA is a nonprofit organization to promote, educate and motivate members in the skills of writing, marketing and improving their craft." Offers competitions, instruction, newsletter, lectures, library, workshops, performance opportunities, songwriters round, awards, evaluation services, and collaboration. Applications accepted year-round. Membership fee: $25.

THE COLLEGE MUSIC SOCIETY

312 E. Pine St., Missoula MT 59802. (406)721-9616. **Fax:** (406)721-9419. **E-mail:** cms@Music.org. **Website:** www.Music.org. **Contact:** Shannon Devlin, member services. The College Music Society promotes Music teaching and learning, Musical creativity and expression, research and dialogue, and diversity and interdisciplinary interaction. A consortium of college, conservatory, university, and independent Musicians and scholars interested in all disciplines of Music, the Society provides leadership and serves as an agent of change by addressing concerns facing Music in higher education." Offers an online journal,

newsletter, lectures, workshops, performance opportunities, job listing service, databases of organizations and institutions, Music faculty, and mailing lists. Applications accepted year-round. Membership fees: $70 (regular dues), $35 (student dues), $35 (retiree dues).

CONNECTICUT SONGWRITERS ASSOCIATION

P.O. Box 511, Mystic CT 06355. **E-mail:** info@ctsongs.com. **Website:** www.ctsongs.com. **Contact:** Bill Pere, president and executive director. "We are an educational, nonprofit organization dedicated to improving the art and craft of original Music. Founded in 1979, CSA has had almost 2,000 active members and has become one of the best known and respected songwriters' associations in the country. Membership in the CSA admits you to 12-18 seminars/workshops/song critique sessions per year throughout Connecticut and surrounding region. Out-of-state members may mail in songs for free critiques at our meetings. Noted professionals deal with all aspects of the craft and business of Music including lyric writing, Music theory, Music technology, arrangement and production, legal and business aspects, performance techniques, song analysis and recording techniques." CSA offers song screening sessions for members and songs that pass become eligible for inclusion on the CSA sampler anthology through various retail and online outlets and are brought to national Music conferences. CSA is well connected in both the independent Music scene and the traditional Music industry. CSA also offers showcases and concerts which are open to the public and designed to give artists a venue for performing their original material for an attentive, listening audience. CSA benefits help local soup kitchens, group homes, hospice, world hunger, libraries, nature centers, community centers and more. CSA encompasses ballads to bluegrass and Bach to rock. Membership fee: $45/year.

DALLAS SONGWRITERS ASSOCIATION

Sammons Center for the Arts, 3630 Harry Hines Blvd. #20, Dallas TX 75219. (214)750-0916. **E-mail:** info@dallassongwriters.org. **Website:** www.dallassongwriters.org. Serves songwriters and lyricists of Dallas/Ft. Worth metroplex. Members are adults ages 18-75, Dallas/Ft. Worth area songwriters/lyricists who are or aspire to be professionals. Purpose is to provide songwriters an opportunity to meet other songwriters, share information, find co-writers and support each other through group discussions at monthly meetings; to provide songwriters an opportunity to have their songs heard and critiqued by peers and professionals by playing cassettes and providing an open mike at monthly meetings and open mics, showcases, and festival stages, and by offering contests judged by publishers; to provide songwriters opportunities to meet other Music business professionals by inviting guest speakers to monthly meetings and workshops; and to provide songwriters opportunities to learn more about the craft of songwriting and the business of Music by presenting mini-workshops at each monthly meeting. "We offer a chance for the songwriter to learn from peers and industry professionals and an opportunity to belong to a supportive group environment to encourage the individual to continue his/her songwriting endeavors." Offers competitions (including the Annual Song Contest with over $5,000 in prizes, and the Quarterly Lyric Contest), field trips, instruction, lectures, newsletter, performance opportunities, social outings, workshops and seminars. "Our members are eligible for discounts at several local Music stores and seminars." Applications accepted year-round. Membership fee: $50. "When inquiring by phone, please leave complete mailing address and phone number or e-mail address where you can be reached day and night."

THE DRAMATISTS GUILD OF AMERICA, INC.

1501 Broadway, Suite 701, New York NY 10036. (212)398-9366. **Fax:** (212)944-0420. **E-mail:** rtec@ dramatistsguild.com. **Website:** www.dramatistsguild.com. **Contact:** Roland Tec, director of membership. For over three-quarters of a century, The Dramatists Guild has been the professional association of playwrights, composers and lyricists, with more than 6,000 members across the country. All theater writers, whether produced or not, are eligible for Associate membership ($90/year); students enrolled in writing degree programs at colleges or universities are eligible for Student membership ($45/year); writers who have been produced on Broadway, Off-Broadway or on the main stage of a LORT theater are eligible for Active membership ($130/year). The Guild offers its members the following activities and services: use of the Guild's contracts (including the Approved Production Contract for Broadway, the Off-Broadway contract, the LORT contract, the collaboration agreements for both Musicals and drama, the 99 Seat Theatre Plan contract, the Small Theatre contract, commissioning agreements, and the Underlying Rights Agreements contract; advice on all theatrical contracts including Broadway, Off-Broadway, regional, showcase, Equity-waiver, dinner theater and collaboration contracts); a nationwide toll-free number for all members with business or contract questions or problems; advice and information on a wide spectrum of issues affecting writers; free and/or discounted ticket service; symposia led by experienced professionals in major cities nationwide; access to health insurance programs; and a spacious meeting room which can accommodate up to 50 people for readings and auditions on a rental basis. The Guild's publications are: *The Dramatist*, a bimonthly journal containing articles on all aspects of the theater (which includes The Dramatists Guild Newsletter, with announcements of all Guild activities and current information of interest to dramatists); and an annual resource directory with up-to-date information on agents, publishers, grants, producers, playwriting contests, conferences and workshops, and an interactive website that brings our community of writers together to exchange ideas and share information.

THE FIELD

75 Maiden Lane, Suite 906, New York NY 10038. (212)691-6969. **E-mail:** kelley@thefield.org. **Website:** www.thefield.org. **Contact:** Kelley Girod, Artist Services Associate. "Founded by artists for artists, The Field has been dedicated to providing impactful services to thousands of performing artists in New York City and beyond since 1986. From fostering creative exploration to stewarding innovative fundraising strategies, we are delighted to help artists reach their fullest potential. More than 1,900 performing artists come to The Field annually to build their businesses, 2,000+ new art works are developed under our stewardship each year, and our services are replicated in 11 cities across the US and in Europe. At the same time, we remain true to our grassroots origin and artist-centered mission: to strategically and comprehensively serve the myriad artistic and administrative needs of independent performing artists and companies who work in the fields of dance, theater, Music, text, and performance art. Our core values of affordability, accessibility and rigorous delivery infuse all of our interactions. Field services include career-building workshops (grant writing, touring, internet strate-

gies, etc.), fiscal sponsorship, creative residences in New York City and out of town, an 'Artists' Kinkos' Resource Center, and Membership benefits." Offers fiscal sponsorship, arts management and creative workshops, residencies, and performance opportunities. Applications accepted year-round. Membership fee: $100/year.

TIPS "The Field offers the most affordable and accessible fiscal sponsorship program in New York City. The Sponsored Artist Program offered by The Field enables performing artists and groups to accumulate the funds they need to make their artistic and career goals a reality. Fiscal sponsorship provides independent performing artists and groups with: eligibility to apply for most government, foundation, and corporate grants which require a 501(c)(3), not-for-profit status; eligibility to receive tax-deductible donations of both money and goods from individuals; and other services where 501(c)(3) status is necessary."

⊛ FILM MUSIC NETWORK

13101 Washington Blvd. Suite 466, Los Angeles CA 90066. **Website:** www.filmMusic.net. "The Film Music Network, established in 1997, is a leading worldwide professional association of composers, songwriters, bands, recording artists, and more who are seeking to place their Music or compose custom Music for film or television projects. One of the Film Music Network's most popular member benefits is providing leads for projects seeking Music or composers, including film projects, television projects, corporate videos, Music libraries and more. Additional member benefits include a free introductory legal consultation, discounted move theater and event tickets, resources including a directory of film Music agents and managers, our Film Music Salary and Rate survey, and more." Full membership fee: $11.95/month. Audio-only fee: $4.95/month.

FLORIDA SONGWRITERS ASSOCIATION

200 South Harbor City Blvd Suite 403, Melbourne FL 32901. **E-mail:** info@flsw.org. **Website:** www.flsw.org. Florida Songwriters Association is a collaboration of several companies in the industry. We all share the common goal of helping to further educate, motivate, and elevate songwriters. Annual memberships start at $100 per year.

TIPS "Learn what it takes to be a songwriter. Not just how to write songs, but how to protect your works as well. Learn the business…what it means to be repre-

sented by a publisher and what are your rights. Register with a Performing Rights Organization (PRO) and do your research on how the business works. This will go a long way when dealing with industry professionals."

FORT WORTH SONGWRITERS' ASSOCIATION

P.O. Box 330233, Fort Worth TX 76163. (817)654-5400. **E-mail:** fwsanewsletter@gmail.com. **Website:** www.fwsa.com. Members are ages 18-83, beginners up to and including published writers. Interests cover gospel, country, western swing, rock, pop, bluegrass, and blues. Purpose is to allow songwriters to become more proficient at songwriting; to provide an opportunity for their efforts to be performed before a live audience; to provide songwriters an opportunity to meet co-writers. "We provide our members free critiques of their efforts. We provide a monthly newsletter outlining current happenings in the business of songwriting. We offer competitions and mini workshops with guest speakers from the Music industry. We promote a weekly open mic for singers of original material, and hold invitational songwriter showcase events a various times throughout the year. Each year, we hold a Christmas Song Contest, judged by independent Music industry professionals. We also offer free web pages for members or links to member websites." Applications accepted year-round. Membership fee: $35.

GOSPEL MUSIC ASSOCIATION

4012 Granny White Pike, Nashville TN 37204-3924. (615)242-0303. **Fax:** (615)254-9755. **E-mail:** info@gospelMusic.org. **Website:** www.gospelMusic.org. Serves songwriters, Musicians and anyone directly involved in or who supports gospel Music. Professional members include advertising agencies, Musicians, songwriters, agents/managers, composers, retailers, Music publishers, print and broadcast media, and other members of the recording industry. Associate members include supporters of gospel Music and those whose involvement in the industry does not provide them with income. The primary purpose of the GMA is to expose, promote, and celebrate the Gospel through Music. A GMA membership offers newsletters, performance experiences and workshops, as well as networking opportunities. Applications accepted year-round. Membership fees: $95/year for professionals; $25/year for iMembers (supporters of gospel

Music and those whose involvement in the industry does not provide them a source of income).

❂ THE GUILD OF INTERNATIONAL SONGWRITERS & COMPOSERS

Ebrel House, 2a Penlee Close, Praa Sands, Penzance, Cornwall TR20 9SR United Kingdom. (01)(736)762826. **Fax:** (01)(736)763328. **E-mail:** songmag@aol.com. **Website:** www.songwriters-guild.co.uk. The Guild of International Songwriters & Composers is an international Music industry organisation based in England in the United Kingdom. Guild members are songwriters, composers, lyricists, poets, performing songwriters, Musicians, Music publishers, studio owners, managers, independent record companies, Music industry personnel, etc., from many countries throughout the world. The Guild of International Songwriters & Composers has been publishing Songwriting and Composing Magazine since 1986, which is issued free to all Guild members throughout their membership. The Guild of International Songwriters and Composers offers advice, guidance, assistance, copyright protection service, information, encouragement, contact information, Intellectual property/copyright protection of members works through the Guild's Copyright Registration Centre along with other free services and more to Guild members with regard to helping members achieve their aims, ambitions, progression and advancement in respect to the many different aspects of the Music industry. Information, advice and services available to Guild members throughout their membership includes assistance, advice and help on many matters and issues relating to the Music industry in general. Annual membership fees: are £55.

INTERNATIONAL BLUEGRASS MUSIC ASSOCIATION (IBMA)

608 W. Iris Dr., Nashville TN 37204. (615)256-3222 or (888)438-4262. **Fax:** (615)256-0450. **E-mail:** info@ibma.org. **Website:** www.ibma.org. Serves songwriters, Musicians and professionals in bluegrass Music. "IBMA is a trade association composed of people and organizations involved professionally and semi-professionally in the bluegrass Music industry, including performers, agents, songwriters, Music publishers, promoters, print and broadcast media, local associations, recording manufacturers and distributors. Voting members must be currently or formerly involved in the bluegrass industry as full or part-time profes-

sionals. A songwriter attempting to become professionally involved in our field would be eligible. Our mission statement reads: *IBMA: Working together for high standards of professionalism, a greater appreciation for our Music, and the success of the worldwide bluegrass Music community.* IBMA publishes a bimonthly International Bluegrass, holds an annual trade show/convention with a songwriters showcase in the fall, represents our field outside the bluegrass Music community, and compiles and disseminates databases of bluegrass related resources and organizations. Market research on the bluegrass consumer is available and we offer Bluegrass in the Schools information and matching grants. The primary value in this organization for a songwriter is having current information about the bluegrass Music field and contacts with other songwriters, publishers, Musicians and record companies." Offers workshops, liability insurance, rental car discounts, consultation and databases of record companies, radio stations, press, organizations and gigs. Applications accepted year-round. Membership fee: for a non-voting patron, $40/year; for an individual voting professional, $75/year; for an organizational voting professional, $205/year.

❂ INTERNATIONAL SONGWRITERS ASSOCIATION LTD.

P.O. Box 46, Limerick City, Ireland 00-353-61-228837 United Kingdom. (01)(71)486-5353. **E-mail:** jliddane@songwriter.iol.ie. **Website:** www.songwriter.co.uk. **Contact:** Bill Miller, Ray Coleman—membership department. Serves songwriters and Music publishers. "The ISA headquarters is in Limerick City, Ireland, and from there it provides its members with assessment services, copyright services, legal and other advisory services and an investigations service, plus a magazine for one yearly fee. Our members are songwriters in more than 60 countries worldwide, of all ages. There are no qualifications, but applicants under 18 are not accepted. We provide information and assistance to professional or semi-professional songwriters. Our publication, Songwriter, which was founded in 1967, features detailed exclusive interviews with songwriters and Music publishers, as well as directory information of value to writers." Applications accepted year-round. Membership fee for European writers is £19.95; for non-European writers, U.S. $30.

JUST PLAIN FOLKS MUSIC ORGANIZATION

5327 Kit Dr., Indianapolis IN 46237. **E-mail:** JPFolksPro@aol.com. **Website:** www.jpfolks.com. "Just Plain Folks is among the world's largest Music Organizations. Our members cover nearly every Musical style and professional field, from songwriters, artists, publishers, producers, record labels, entertainment attorneys, publicists and PR experts, performing rights organization staffers, live and recording engineers, educators, Music students, Musical instrument manufacturers, TV, Radio and Print Media, and almost every major Internet Music entity. Representing all 50 U.S. states and over 160 countries worldwide, we have members of all ages, Musical styles and levels of success, including winners and nominees of every major Music industry award, as well as those just starting out. A complete demographics listing of our group is available on our website. Whether you are a #1 hit songwriter or artist, or the newest kid on the block, you are welcome to join. Membership does require an active e-mail account." The purpose of this organization is "to share wisdom, ideas and experiences with others who have been there, and to help educate those who have yet to make the journey. Just Plain Folks provides its members with a friendly networking and support community that uses the power of the Internet and combines it with good old-fashioned human interaction. We help promote our members ready for success and educate those still learning." **TIPS** *Just Plain Notes Newsletter:* "Members receive our frequent e-mail newsletters full of expert info on how to succeed in the Music business, profiles of members successes and advice, opportunities to develop your career and tons of first-person networking contacts to help you along the way. (Note: we send this out 2-3 times/month via e-mail only.) "Our motto is 'We're All In This Together!'"

KNOXVILLE SONGWRITERS ASSOCIATION

P.O. Box 603, Knoxville TN 37901. **E-mail:** edna1riddick@yahoo.com. **Website:** www.knoxvillesongwritersassociation.com. **Contact:** Edna Riddick, president. Serves songwriters of all ages. "Some have been members since 1982, others are beginners. Members must be interested in learning the craft of songwriting. Not only a learning organization but a support group of songwriters who wants to learn what to do with their song after it has been written. We open doors for as-

piring writers. The primary benefit of membership is to supply information to the writer on how to write a song. Many members have received major cuts." Offers showcases, instruction, lectures, library, newsletter, performance opportunities, evaluation services and workshops. Applications accepted year-round. Membership fee: $30/year.

THE LAS VEGAS SONGWRITERS ASSOCIATION

P.O. Box 42683, Las Vegas NV 89116-0683. (702)223-7255. **E-mail:** lasvegassongwriters@yahoo.com. "We are an educational, nonprofit organization dedicated to improving the art and craft of the songwriter. We want members who are serious about their craft. We want our members to respect their craft and to treat it as a business. Members must be at least 18 years of age. We offer quarterly newsletters, monthly information meetings, workshops three times a month and quarterly seminars with professionals in the Music business. We provide support and encouragement to both new and more experienced songwriters. We critique each song or lyric that's presented during workshops, we make suggestions on changes—if needed. We help turn amateur writers into professionals. Several of our songwriters have had their songs recorded on both independent and major labels." Membership fee: $30/year.

LOS ANGELES MUSIC NETWORK

P.O. Box 2446, Toluca Lake CA 91610. (818)769-6095. **E-mail:** info@lamn.com. **Website:** www.lamn.com. "Connections. Performance opportunities. Facts. Career advancement. All that is available with your membership in the Los Angeles Music Network (LAMN). Our emphasis is on sharing knowledge and information, giving you access to top professionals and promoting career development. LAMN is an association of Music industry professionals, i.e., artists, singers, songwriters, and people who work in various aspects of the Music industry with an emphasis on the creative. Members are ambitious and interested in advancing their careers. LAMN promotes career advancement, communication and education among artists and creatives. LAMN sponsors industry events and educational panels held at venues in the Los Angeles area and now in other major Music hubs around the country (New York, Las Vegas, Phoenix, and San Francisco). LAMN Jams are popular among our members. Experience LAMN Jams in L.A. or N.Y. by performing your original Music in front of industry experts who can advance your career by getting your Music in the hands of hard-to-reach Music supervisors. The singer-songwriter contest gives artists an opportunity to perform in front of industry experts and receive instant feedback to their Music, lyrics and performance. As a result of the exposure, Tim Fagan won the John Mayer Songwriting Contest and was invited to tour with the Goo Goo Dolls, Lifehouse, and platinum recording artist Colbie Caillat. This paired him with multi-platinum songwriter and recording artist John Mayer, with whom Fagan co-wrote 'Deeper.' Publisher Robert Walls has pitched Music from LAMN Jam performers to hit TV shows like 'The O.C.' and 'Grey's Anatomy,' and the flick *The Devil Wears Prada*. Other performers have received offers including publishing and production deals and studio gigs. Offers performance opportunities, instruction, newsletter, lectures, seminars, Music industry job listings, career counseling, resume publishing, mentor network, and many professional networking opportunities. See our website for current job listings and a calendar of upcoming events." Applications accepted year-round. Annual membership fee: $25.

LOUISIANA SONGWRITERS ASSOCIATION

P.O. Box 82009, Baton Rouge LA 70884. **E-mail:** info@louisianaMusichalloffame.org. **Website:** http://louisianaMusichalloffame.org. Serves songwriters. Membership fee: $25/year.

☾ MANITOBA MUSIC

1-376 Donald St., Winnipeg MB R3B 2J2 Canada. (204)942-8650. **Fax:** (204)942-6083. **E-mail:** info@manitobaMusic.com. **Website:** www.manitobaMusic.com. **Contact:** Donna Evans, membership & operations coordinator. Organization consists of "songwriters, producers, agents, Musicians, managers, retailers, publicists, radio, talent buyers, media, record labels, etc. (no age limit, no skill level minimum). Must have interest in the future of Manitoba's Music industry." The main purpose of Manitoba Music is to foster growth in all areas of the Manitoba Music industry primarily through education, promotion and lobbying. Offers newsletter, extensive website, directory of Manitoba's Music industry, workshops and performance opportunities. Manitoba Music is also involved with the Western Canadian Music Awards fes-

tival, conference and awards show. Applications accepted year-round. Membership fee: $50 (Canadian).

MINNESOTA ASSOCIATION OF SONGWRITERS

P.O. Box 4262, St. Paul MN 55104. **E-mail:** info@mnsongwriters.org. **Website:** www.mnsongwriters.org. "Includes a wide variety of members, ranging in age from 18 to 80; type of Music is very diverse, ranging from alternative rock to folk, blues, theatrical and contemporary Christian; skill levels range from beginning songwriters to writers with recorded and published material. Main requirement is an interest in songwriting. Although most members come from the Minneapolis-St. Paul area, others come from nearby Wisconsin and other parts of the country. Some members are full-time Musicians, but most represent a wide variety of occupations. MAS is a nonprofit community of songwriters which informs, educates, inspires, and assists its members in the art and business of songwriting." Offers instruction, workshops with pro songwriters, public performance opportunities, online and in-meeting evaluation services, Internet radio and a public-access television show being aired around the nation. Applications accepted year-round. Membership fee: $35.

TIPS "Members are kept current on resources and opportunities. Original works are played at meetings or submitted via email, then reviewed by involved members. Through this process, writers hone their skills and gain experience and confidence in refining their works and putting them into the Music market."

☾ MUSIC BC INDUSTRY ASSOCIATION

#100-938 Howe St., Vancouver BC V6Z 1N9 Canada. (604)873-1914. **Fax:** (604)873-9686. **E-mail:** info@Musicbc.org. **Website:** www.Musicbc.org. Music BC(formerly PMIA) is a nonprofit society that supports and promotes the spirit, development, and growth of the BC Music community provincially, nationally, and internationally. Music BC provides education, resources, advocacy, opportunities for funding, and a forum for communication. Visit website for membership benefits.

MUSICIANS CONTACT

P.O. Box 788, Woodland Hills CA 91365. (818)888-7879. **E-mail:** information@Musicianscontact.com. **Website:** www.Musicianscontact.com. "The primary source of paying jobs for Musicians and vocalists nationwide. Job opportunities are posted daily on the Internet. Also offers exposure to the Music industry for solo artists and complete acts seeking representation."

NASHVILLE SONGWRITERS ASSOCIATION INTERNATIONAL (NSAI)

1710 Roy Acuff Place, Nashville TN 37203. (615)256-3354. **E-mail:** nsai@nashvillesongwriters.com. **Website:** www.nashvillesongwriters.com. Purpose: a not-for-profit service organization for both aspiring and professional songwriters in all fields of Music. Membership: Spans the U.S. and several foreign countries. Songwriters may apply in 1 of 4 annual categories: Active ($200 U.S currency for songwriters are actively working to improve in the craft of writing and/or actively pursing a career within the songwriting industry); Professional ($100 U.S. currency for songwriters who are staff writers for a publishing company or earn 51% of their annual income from songwriting, whether from advances, royalties, or performances, or are generally regarded as a professional songwriter within the Music industry); Lifetime (please contact NSAI for details). Membership benefits: Music industry information and advice, song evaluations, eNews, access to industry professionals through weekly Nashville workshops and several annual events, regional workshops, use of office facilities, and discounts on books and NSAI's 3 annual events. There are also "branch" workshops of NSAI. Workshops must meet certain standards and are accountable to NSAI.

TIPS Also see the listing for NSAI Songwriters Song-Posium (formerly NSAI Spring Symposium) in the Workshops section of this book.

THE NATIONAL ASSOCIATION OF COMPOSERS/USA (NACUSA)

P.O. Box 49256, Barrington Station, Los Angeles CA 90049. **E-mail:** nacusa@Music-usa.org; gregsteinke@mail.Music-usa.org. **Website:** www.Music-usa.org/nacusa. **Contact:** Greg A. Steinke, Ph.D, membership coordinator. "We are of most value to the concert hall composer. Members are serious Music composers of all ages and from all parts of the country, who have a real interest in composing, performing, and listening to modern concert hall Music. The main purpose of our organization is to perform, publish, broadcast and write news about composers of serious concert hall music—mostly chamber and solo pieces. Composers may achieve national notice of their work through our newsletter and concerts, and the fairly rare feeling of supporting a non-commercial Music enterprise dedicated to raising the Musical and social position of the serious composer. 99% of the money earned in Music is earned, or so it seems, by popular songwriters who might feel they owe the art of Music something, and this is one way they might help support that art. It's a chance to foster fraternal solidarity with their less prosperous, but wonderfully interesting classical colleagues at a time when the very existence of serious art seems to be questioned by the general populace." Offers competitions, lectures, performance opportunities, library and newsletter. Applications accepted year-round. Membership fee: National (regular): $30; National (students/seniors): $15.

TIPS Also see the listing for NACUSA Young Composers' Competition in the Contests section of this book.

NEW MUSIC USA

90 John St., Suite 312, New York NY 10038. (212)645-6949. **Fax:** (646)490-0998. **E-mail:** info@newMusicusa.org. **Website:** www.newMusicusa.org. **Contact:** Lorna Krier, program manager. "New Music USA was formed by the merger of the American Music Center and Meet the Composer. We provide over $1 million each year in grant support for the creation and performance of new work and community building throughout the country. We amplify the voice of the new Music community through NewMusicBox, profiling the people and ideas that energize and challenge Music makers today. We stream a wide-ranging catalog of new Music around the clock on Counterstream Radio and provide an online home for composers to feature their own Music. This is not a membership organization; all Musicians are eligible for support." Offers grant programs and information services. Deadlines vary for each grant program.

OPERA AMERICA

330 Seventh Ave., New York NY 10001. (212)796-8620. **Fax:** (212)796-8631. **E-mail:** info@operaamerica.org; SSnook@operaamerica.org. **Website:** www.operaamerica.org. **Contact:** Sam Snook, membership manager. Members are composers, librettists, Musicians, singers, and opera/Music theater producers. Offers conferences, workshops, and seminars for artists. Publishes online database of opera/Music theater companies in the U.S. and Canada, database of opportunities for performing and creative artists, online directory of opera and Musical performances worldwide and U.S., and an online directory of new works

created and being developed by current-day composers and librettists, to encourage the performance of new works. Applications accepted year-round. Publishes quarterly magazine and a variety of electronic newsletters. Membership fees are on a sliding scale by membership level.

OUTMUSIC

1206 Pacific St., Suite 3D, New York NY 11216. **E-mail:** info@outMusicfoundation.org. **Website:** www.out-Musicfoundation.org. "OUTMusic--The LGBT Academy of Recording Artists (LARA) is a 501c3 nonprofit, charitable foundation that serves as an advocacy and awareness platform, and offers programming to support its mission to promote the advancement and appreciation of LGBT Music culture and heritage,create opportunities to support the development of young aspiring artists, increase the viability and visibility of the LGBT Music and entertainment platform and honor, document and archive the contributions and achievements of out and proud LGBT Music artists." Offers newsletter, lectures, workshops, performance opportunities, networking, industry leads. Sponsors OUTMusic Awards. Applications accepted year-round. Membership: $100 for individual artist; $150 for duo or group; $100 for individual patrons; $150 for business patrons.

PORTLAND SONGWRITERS ASSOCIATION

P.O. Box 28355, Portland OR 97228. **E-mail:** info@portlandsongwriters.org. **Website:** http://portland-songwriters.org. "The PSA is a nonprofit organization providing education and opportunities that will assist writers in creating and marketing their songs. The PSA offers an annual National Songwriting Contest, monthly workshops, songwriter showcases, special performance venues, quarterly newsletter, mail-in critique service, discounted seminars by Music industry pros." Membership fee: $25 (no eligibility requirements).

TIPS "Although most of our members are from the Pacific Northwest, we offer services that can assist songwriters anywhere. Our goal is to provide information and contacts to help songwriters grow artistically and gain access to publishing, recording and related Music markets. For more information, please call, write, or e-mail."

RHODE ISLAND SONGWRITERS' ASSOCIATION

P.O. Box 9246, Warwick RI 02889. **E-mail:** generalinfo@risongwriters.com; memberships@risongwriters.com. **Website:** www.risongwriters.com. "Membership consists of novice and professional songwriters. RISA provides opportunities to the aspiring writer or performer as well as the established regional artists who have recordings, are published and perform regularly. The only eligibility requirement is an interest in the group and the group's goals. Non-writers are welcome as well." The main purpose is to "encourage, foster and conduct the art and craft of original Musical and/or lyrical composition through education, information, collaboration and performance." Offers instruction, newsletter, lectures, workshops, performance opportunities and evaluation services. Applications accepted year-round. Membership fees: $25/year (individual); $35/year (family/band). "The group holds twice monthly critique sessions; twice monthly performer showcases (one performer featured) at a local coffeehouse; songwriter showcases (usually 6-8 performers); weekly open mikes; and a yearly songwriter festival called 'Hear In Rhode Island,' featuring approximately 50 Rhode Island acts, over two days."

SAN DIEGO SONGWRITERS GUILD

3952 Clairemont Mesa Blvd, D413, San Diego CA 92117. (858)376-7374. **Website:** http://sdsongwriters.org. "Members range from their early 20s to senior citizens with a variety of skill levels. Several members perform and work full time in Music. Many are published and have songs recorded. Some are getting major artist record cuts. Most members are from San Diego county. New writers are encouraged to participate and meet others. All Musical styles are represented." The purpose of this organization is to "serve the needs of songwriters and artists, especially helping them in the business and craft of songwriting through industry guest appearances." Offers competitions, newsletter, workshops, performance opportunities, discounts on services offered by fellow members, in-person song pitches and evaluations by publishers, producers and A&R executives. Applications accepted year-round. Membership dues: $50/year.

SESAC INC.

55 Music Square East, Nashville TN 37203. (615)320-0055. **Fax:** (615)963-3527. **Website:** www.sesac.com. "SESAC is a selective organization taking pride in hav-

ing a repertory based on quality rather than quantity. Serves writers and publishers in all types of Music who have their works performed by radio, television, nightclubs, cable TV, etc. Purpose of organization is to collect and distribute performance royalties to all active affiliates. As a SESAC affiliate, the individual may obtain equipment insurance at competitive rates. Music is reviewed upon invitation by the Writer/Publisher Relations department."

SOCAN

41 Valleybrook Dr., Toronto ON M3B 2S6 Canada. (866)307-6226. **E-mail:** info@socan.ca; members@socan.ca. **Website:** www.socan.ca. "SOCAN is the Canadian copyright collective for the communication and performance of Musical works. We administer these rights on behalf of our members (composers, lyricists, songwriters, and their publishers) and those of affiliated international organizations by licensing this use of their Music in Canada. The fees collected are distributed as royalties to our members and to affiliated organizations throughout the world. We also distribute royalties received from those organizations to our members for the use of their Music worldwide. SOCAN has offices in Toronto, Montreal, Vancouver, and Dartmouth."

SOCIETY OF COMPOSERS & LYRICISTS

8447 Wilshire Blvd., Suite 401, Beverly Hills CA 90211. (310)281-2812. **Fax:** (310)284-4861. **E-mail:** execdir@thescl.com. **Website:** www.thescl.com. The professional nonprofit trade organization for members actively engaged in writing Music/lyrics for films, TV, and/or video games, or are students of film composition or songwriting for film. Primary mission is to advance the interests of the film and TV Music community. Offers an award-winning quarterly publication, educational seminars, screenings, special member-only events, and other member benefits. Applications accepted year-round. Membership fees: $150 Full Membership (composers, lyricists, songwriters-film/TV Music credits must be submitted); $90 Associate/Student Membership for composers, lyricists, songwriters without credits only; $150 Sponsor/Special Friend Membership (Music editors, Music supervisors, Music attorneys, agents, etc.).

SODRAC INC.

Tower B, Suite 1010, 1470 Peel, Montreal QC H3A 1T1 Canada. (514)845-3268. **Fax:** (514)845-3401. **E-mail:** sodrac@sodrac.ca; members@sodrac.ca. **Website:**

www.sodrac.ca. **Contact:** Alain Lauzon, general manager. "SODRAC is a reproduction rights collective society facilitating the clearing of rights on Musical and artistic works based on the Copyright Board of Canada tariffs or through collective agreements concluded with any users and is responsible for the distribution of royalties to its national and international members. The Society counts over 6,000 Canadian members and represents Musical repertoire originating from nearly 100 foreign countries and manages the right of over 25,000 Canadian and foreign visual artists. SODRAC is the only reproduction rights society in Canada where both songwriters and Music publishers are represented, equally and directly." Serves those with an interest in songwriting and Music publishing no matter what their age or skill level is. "Members must have written or published at least one Musical work that has been reproduced on an audio (CD, cassette, or LP) or audio-visual support (TV, DVD, video), or published 5 Musical works that have been recorded and used for commercial purposes. The new member will benefit from a society working to secure his reproduction rights (mechanicals) and broadcast mechanicals." Applications accepted year-round.

SONGWRITERS ASSOCIATION OF WASHINGTON

4200 Wisconsin Ave. NW, PMB 106-137, Washington DC 20016. **E-mail:** contact@SAW.org. **Website:** www.saw.org. The Songwriters' Association of Washington (SAW) is a nonprofit organization established in 1979 to benefit aspiring and professional songwriters. "Our mission: Strengthen the craft of songwriting; foster the talents of our members; provide an active forum for songwriters and their work; celebrate the power of Music." Membership: $35/year, $20/year for students.

THE SONGWRITERS GUILD OF AMERICA

5120 Virginia Way, Suite C22, Brentwood TN 37027. (615)742-9945. **Fax:** (615)630-7501. **E-mail:** membership@songwritersguild.com. **Website:** www.songwritersguild.com. "The Songwriters Guild of America Foundation offers a series of workshops with discounts for some to SGA members, including online classes and song critique opportunities. There is a charge for some songwriting classes and seminars; however, online classes and some monthly events may be included with an SGA membership. Charges vary depending on the class or event. Current class offerings and workshops vary. Visit website to sign up for the newsletter and e-events, and for more information on current events and workshops. Some current events in Nashville are the Ask-a-Pro and ProCritique sessions that give SGA members the opportunity to present their songs and receive constructive feedback from industry professionals. Various performance opportunities are also available to members, including an SGA Showcase at the BluebiRoad The New York office hosts a weekly Pro-Shop, which is coordinated by producer/Musician/award winning singer Ann Johns Ruckert. For each of 6 sessions an active publisher, producer or A&R person is invited to personally screen material from SGA writers. Participation is limited to 10 writers and an audit of 1 session. Audition of material is required. Various performance opportunities and critique sessions are also available from time to time. SGAF Week is held periodically and is a week of scheduled events and seminars of interest to songwriters that includes workshops, seminars and showcases."

SONGWRITERS HALL OF FAME (SONGHALL)

330 W. 58th St., Suite 411, New York NY 10019. (212)957-9230. **Fax:** (212)957-9227. **E-mail:** info@songhall.org. **Website:** www.songhall.org. **Contact:** Jimmy Webb, chairman. "SongHall membership consists of songwriters of all levels, Music publishers, producers, record company executives, Music attorneys, and lovers of popular Music of all ages. There are different levels of membership, all able to vote in the election for inductees, except supporters and Associates, who pay only $15 and $25 in dues (respectively), but are unable to vote. SongHall's mission is to honor the popular songwriters who write the soundtrack for the world, as well as providing educational and networking opportunities to our members through our workshop and showcase programs." Offers: newsletter, workshops, performance opportunities, networking meetings with industry pros and scholarships for excellence in songwriting. Applications accepted year-round. Membership fees: $15 and up.

SONGWRITERS OF WISCONSIN INTERNATIONAL

P.O. Box 1027, Neenah WI 54957. **E-mail:** sowi2012@gmail.com. **Website:** www.SongwritersOfWisconsin.org. Serves songwriters. "Membership is open to songwriters writing all styles of Music. Residency in Wisconsin is recommended but not required. Mem-

bers are encouraged to bring tapes and lyric sheets of their songs to the meetings, but it is not required. We are striving to improve the craft of songwriting in Wisconsin. Living in Wisconsin, a songwriter would be close to any of the workshops and showcases offered each month at different towns. The primary value of membership for a songwriter is in sharing ideas with other songwriters, being critiqued and helping other songwriters." Offers competitions (contest entry deadline: June 15), field trips, instruction, lectures, newsletter, performance opportunities, social outings, workshops and critique sessions. Applications accepted year-round. Membership dues: $30/year.

SONGWRITERS RESOURCE NETWORK

Portland OR **E-mail:** info@songwritersresourcenetwork.com. **Website:** www.SongwritersResourceNetwork.com. "For songwriters and lyricists of every kind, from beginners to advanced." No eligibility requirements. "Purpose is to provide free information to help songwriters develop their craft, market their songs, and learn about songwriting opportunities." Sponsors the annual Great American Song Contest, offers marketing tips and website access to Music industry contacts. "We provide leads to publishers, producers and other Music industry professionals." Visit website or send SASE for more information.

TIPS Also see the listing for Great American Song Contest in the Contests and Awards section of this book.

SOUTHWEST VIRGINIA SONGWRITERS ASSOCIATION

P.O. Box 698, Salem VA 24153. **E-mail:** svsasongwriters@gmail.com. **Website:** www.svsasongs.com. Accepts members of all ages and skill levels in all genres of Music. SVSA helps members improve their songwriting knowledge and skills through song critiques, workshops and discussions of related topics in an encouraging and supportive environment. SVSA offers performance opportunities, instruction, monthly meetings and a monthly newsletter. Applications accepted year-round. Membership fee: $20/year.

TEXAS ACCOUNTANTS & LAWYERS FOR THE ARTS

6001 Airport Blvd. Suite 2280-A, Austin TX 78752. (512)459-8252. **E-mail:** info@talarts.org. **Website:** www.talarts.org. TALA's members include accountants, attorneys, museums, theatre groups, dance groups, actors, artists, Musicians and filmmakers. Our members are of all age groups and represent all facets of their respective fields. TALA is a nonprofit organization that provides pro bono legal and accounting services to income-eligible artists from all disciplines and to nonprofit arts organizations. TALA also provides mediation services for resolving disputes as a low cost-nonadversarial alternative to litigation. Offers newsletter, lectures, library and workshops. Applications accepted year-round. Annual membership fees: students, $30; artists, $50; bands, $100; nonprofit organizations, $200.

TIPS TALA's speakers program presents low-cost seminars on topics such as The Music Business, Copyright and Trademark, and The Business of Writing. These seminars are held annually at a location in Houston. TALA's speaker's program also provides speakers for seminars by other organizations.

TEXAS MUSIC OFFICE

P.O. Box 13246, Austin TX 78711. (512)463-6666. **Fax:** (512)463-4114. **E-mail:** Music@governor.state. tx.us. **Website:** http://governor.state.tx.us/Music. **Contact:** Casey J. Monahan, director. "The Texas Music Office (TMO) is a state-funded business promotion office and information clearinghouse for the Texas Music industry. The TMO assists more than 14,000 individual clients each year, ranging from a new band trying to make statewide business contacts to BBC journalists seeking information on Down South Hip hop. The TMO is the sister office to the Texas Film Commission, both of which are within the Office of the Governor. The TMO serves the Texas Music industry by using its Business Referral Network: Texas Music Industry (7,880 Texas Music businesses in 96 Music business categories); Texas Music Events (625 Texas Music events); Texas Talent Register (8,036 Texas recording artists); Texas Radio Stations (942 Texas stations); U.S. Music Contacts; Classical Texas (detailed information for all classical Music organizations in Texas); and International (1,425 foreign businesses interested in Texas Music). Provides referrals to Texas Music businesses, talent and events in order to attract new business to Texas and/or to encourage Texas businesses and individuals to keep Music business in-state. Serves as a liaison between Music businesses and other government offices and agencies. Publicizes significant developments within the Texas Music industry."

TORONTO MUSICIANS' ASSOCIATION

15 Gervais Dr., Suite 500, Toronto ON M3C 1Y8 Canada. (416)421-1020. **Fax:** (416)421-7011. **E-mail:** info@tma149.ca. **Website:** www.torontoMusicians. org. "Local 149 of the American Federation of Musicians of the United States and Canada is the Professional Association for Musicians in the greater Toronto Area. A member driven association of 3,500 members, the TMA represents professional Musicians in all facets of Music in the greater Toronto area. Dedicated to the development of Musical talent and skills the Toronto Musicians' Association has for the past 100 years fostered the opportunity through the collective efforts of our members for professional Musicians to live and work in dignity while receiving fair compensation." Joining fee: $225; thereafter, members pay $63.75 per quarter.

VOLUNTEER LAWYERS FOR THE ARTS

1 E. 53rd St., 6th Floor, New York NY 10022. (212)319-2787, ext. 1. **Fax:** (212)752-6575. **E-mail:** vlany@vlany.org. **Website:** www.vlany.org. Purpose of organization: Volunteer Lawyers for the Arts is dedicated to providing free arts-related legal assistance to low-income artists and not-for-profit arts organizations in all creative fields. Over 1,000 attorneys in the New York area donate their time through VLA to artists and arts organizations unable to afford legal counsel. Everyone is welcome to use VLA's Art Law Line, a legal hotline for any artist or arts organization needing quick answers to arts-related questions. VLA also provides clinics, seminars and publications designed to educate artists on legal issues which affect their careers. Members receive discounts on publications and seminars as well as other benefits. Some of the many publications we carry are *All You Need to Know About the Music Business; Business and Legal Forms for Fine Artists, Photographers & Authors & Self-Publishers; Contracts for the Film & TV Industry*, plus many more.

WASHINGTON AREA MUSIC ASSOCIATION

6263 Occoquan Forest Dr., Manassas VA 20112. (703)368-3300. **Fax:** (703)393-1028. **E-mail:** doMusic@wamadc.com. **Website:** www.wamadc.com. Serves songwriters, Musicians and performers, managers, club owners and entertainment lawyers; "all those with an interest in the Washington Music scene." The organization is designed to promote the Washington, D.C., Music scene and increase its visibility. Its primary value to members is its seminars and networking opportunities. Offers lectures, newsletter, performance opportunities and workshops. WAMA sponsors the annual Washington Music Awards (The Wammies) and The Crosstown Jam or annual showcase of artists in the DC area. Applications accepted year-round. Membership fee: $35/year.

WEST COAST SONGWRITERS

1724 Laurel St., Suite 120, San Carlos CA 94070. (650)654-3966. **E-mail:** info@westcoastsongwriters. org; ian@westcoastsongwriters.org. **Website:** www. westcoastsongwriters.org. "Our 1,200 members are lyricists and composers from ages 16-80, from beginners to professional songwriters. No eligibility requirements. Our purpose is to provide the education and opportunities that will support our writers in creating and marketing outstanding songs. WCS provides support and direction through local networking and input from Los Angeles and Nashville Music industry leaders, as well as valuable marketing opportunities. Most songwriters need some form of collaboration, and by being a member they are exposed to other writers, ideas, critiquing, etc." Offers annual West Coast Songwriters Conference, "the largest event of its kind in northern California. This 2-day event held the second weekend in September features 16 seminars, 50 screening sessions (over 1,200 songs listened to by industry professionals) and a sunset concert with hit songwriters performing their songs." Also offers monthly visits from major publishers, songwriting classes, competitions, seminars conducted by hit songwriters (ONLINE) song-screening service for members who cannot attend due to time or location, a monthly e-newsletter, monthly performance opportunities and workshops Applications accepted year-round. Membership fees: $40/year for students; $90/year, regular individual; $119, bands; $150+, contributing members.

TIPS "WCS's functions draw local talent and nationally recognized names together. This is of a tremendous value to writers outside a major Music center. We are developing a strong songwriting community in Portland, and Northern and Southern California. We serve the San Jose, Monterey Bay, East Bay, San Francisco, Los Angeles, Sacramento and Portland, WA areas and we have the support of some outstanding writers and publishers from both Los Angeles and Nashville. They provide us with invaluable direction and inspiration."

RETREATS & COLONIES

//

This section provides information on retreats and artists' colonies. These are places for creatives, including songwriters, to find solitude and spend concentrated time focusing on their work. While a residency at a colony may offer participation in seminars, critiques or performances, the atmosphere of a colony or retreat is much more relaxed than that of a conference or workshop. Also, a songwriter's stay at a colony is typically anywhere from one to twelve weeks (sometimes longer), while time spent at a conference may only run from one to fourteen days.

Like conferences and workshops, however, artists' colonies and retreats span a wide range. Yaddo, perhaps the most well-known colony, limits its residencies to artists "working at a professional level in their field, as determined by a judging panel of professionals in the field." The Brevard Music Center offers residencies only to those involved in classical music. Despite different focuses, all artists' colonies and retreats have one thing in common: They are places where you may work undisturbed, usually in nature-oriented, secluded settings.

SELECTING A COLONY OR RETREAT

When selecting a colony or retreat, the primary consideration for many songwriters is cost, and you'll discover that arrangements vary greatly. Some colonies provide residencies as well as stipends for personal expenses. Some suggest donations of a certain amount. Still others offer residencies for substantial sums but have financial assistance available.

When investigating the various options, consider meal and housing arrangements and your family obligations. Some colonies provide meals for residents, while others require residents to pay for meals. Some colonies house artists in one main building; others provide separate cottages. A few have provisions for spouses and families. Others prohibit families altogether.

Overall, residencies at colonies and retreats are competitive. Since only a handful of spots are available at each place, you often must apply months in advance for the time period you desire. A number of locations are open year-round, and you may find planning to go during the "off-season" lessens your competition. Other colonies, however, are only available during certain months. In any case, be prepared to include a sample of your best work with your application. Also, know what project you'll work on while in residence and have alternative projects in mind in case the first one doesn't work out once you're there.

Each listing in this section details fee requirements, meal and housing arrangements, and space and time availability, as well as the retreat's surroundings, facilities and special activities. Of course, before making a final decision, send a SASE to the colonies or retreats that interest you to receive their most up-to-date details. Costs, application requirements and deadlines are particularly subject to change.

MUSICIAN'S RESOURCE

For other listings of songwriter-friendly colonies, see *Musician's Resource* (available from Watson-Guptill—www.watsonguptill.com), which not only provides information about conferences, workshops and academic programs but also residencies and retreats. Also check the Publications of Interest section in this book for newsletters and other periodicals providing this information.

BREVARD MUSIC CENTER

P.O. Box 312, Brevard NC 28712. (828)862-2100. **Fax:** (828)884-2036. **Website:** www.brevardmusic.org. **Contact:** Frank McConnell, director of operations. The Brevard Music Center is a community of student and professional musicians who aspire to ever-higher levels of artistry. Since all members of the community reside on campus, learning occurs constantly and is manifest through intensive practice and rehearsal and a challenging concert schedule. A consistently high level of public performance is a hallmark of the Brevard Music Center.

☻ THE TYRONE GUTHRIE CENTRE

Annaghmakerrig, Newbliss, County Monaghan Ireland. **E-mail:** info@tyroneguthrie.ie. **Website:** www.tyroneguthrie.ie. Offers year-round residencies. Artists may stay for anything from 1 week to 3 months in the Big House, or for up to 6 months at a time in one of the 5 self-catering houses in the old farmyard. Open to artists of all disciplines. Accommodates 13 in the big house and up to 7 in the farmyard cottages. Personal living quarters include bedroom with bathroom en suite. Offers a variety of workspaces. There is a music room for composers and musicians with a Yamaha C3M-PE conservative grand piano, a performance studio with a Yamaha upright, a photographic darkroom and a number of studios for visual artists, one of which is wheelchair accessible. At certain times of the year it is possible, by special arrangement, to accommodate groups of artists, symposiums, master classes, workshops and other collaborations.
COSTS Irish and European artists: €300/week for the big house; €150 for self-catering cottages; others pay €600 per week, all found, for a residency in the Big House and €300 per week (plus gas and electricity costs) for one of the self-catering farmyard houses. To qualify for a residency, it is necessary to show evidence of a significant level of achievement in the relevant field.

THE HAMBIDGE CENTER

105 Hambidge Court, Rabun Gap GA 30568. (706)746-5718. **Fax:** (706)746-9933. **E-mail:** center@hambidge.org; director@hambidge.org. **Website:** www.hambidge.org. **Contact:** Debra Sanders, office manager; Jamie Badoud, executive director. Hambidge provides a residency program that empowers talented artists to explore, develop, and express their creative voices. Situated on 600 acres in the mountains of north Georgia, Hambidge is a sanctuary of time and space that inspires artists working in a broad range of disciplines to create works of the highest caliber. Hambidge's Residency Program opens the first week of February and closes mid-to late-December through the month of January. Application deadlines are: January 15 for May-August; April 15 for September-December; September 15 for March-April of the following year.
COSTS Resident fellows pay $200/week. Several scholarships are available.

ISLE ROYALE NATIONAL PARK ARTIST-IN-RESIDENCE PROGRAM

800 E. Lakeshore Dr., Houghton MI 49931. (906)482-0984. **Fax:** (906)482-8753. **E-mail:** Greg_Blust@nps.gov. **Website:** www.nps.gov/getinvolved/artist-in-residence.htm. Offers 2-3 week residencies from mid-June to mid-September. Open to all art forms. Accommodates 1 artist with 1 companion at 1 time. Personal living quarters include cabin with shared outhouse. A canoe is provided for transportation. Offers a guest house at the site that can be used as a studio. The artist is asked to contribute a piece of work representative of their stay at Isle Royale, to be used by the park in an appropriate manner. During their residency, artists will be asked to share their experience (1 presentation per week of residency, about 1 hour/week) with the public by demonstration, talk, or other means.
REQUIREMENTS Deadline: applications should be postmarked or delievered by February 16. Send for application forms and guidelines. Accepts inquiries via fax or e-mail. A panel of professionals from various disciplines, and park representatives will choose the finalists. The selection is based on artistic integrity, ability to reside in a wilderness environment, a willingness to donate a finished piece of work inspired on the island, and the artist's ability to relate and interpret the park through their work.

KALANI OCEANSIDE RETREAT

RR2, Box 4500, Pahoa HI 96778. (808)965-7828. **Fax:** (808)965-0527. **Website:** www.kalani.com. **Contact:** Richard Koob, founder and director.
○ "Kalani Honua means harmony of heaven and earth, and this is what we aspire to. We welcome all in the spirit of aloha and are guided by the Hawai'ian tradition of `ohana (extended family), respecting our diversity yet sharing in unity. We invite you to open your heart to the

Big Island of Hawaii at Kalani Oceanside Retreat."

COSTS $76-235/night, lodging only. Full meal plan (3 chef-prepared meals/day) available for $42/day. Prices subject to change. Airport transportation by Kalani service $65/trip, or taxi $90/trip.

SITKA CENTER FOR ART & ECOLOGY

56605 Sitka Dr., Otis OR 97368. (541)994-5485. **Fax:** (541)994-8024. **E-mail:** info@sitkacenter.org. **Website:** www.sitkacenter.org.

COSTS Residency and housing provided. The resident is asked to provide some form of community service on behalf of Sitka.

VIRGINIA CENTER FOR THE CREATIVE ARTS

154 San Angelo Dr., Amherst VA 24521. (434)946-7236. **Fax:** (434)946-7239. **E-mail:** vcca@vcca.com. **Website:** www.vcca.com. Offers residencies year-round, typical residency lasts 2 weeks to 2 months. Open to originating artists: composers, writers, and visual artists. Accommodates 25 at one time. Personal living quarters include 22 single rooms, 2 double rooms, bathrooms shared with one other person. All meals are served. Kitchens for fellows' use available at studios and residence. The VCCA van goes into town twice a week. Fellows share their work regularly. Four studios have pianos. No transportation costs are covered. "Artists are accepted into the VCCA without regard for their ability to contribute financially to their residency. Daily cost is $180 per fellow. We ask fellows to contribute according to their ability."

COSTS Application fee: $30. Deadline: May 15 for October-January residency; September 15 for February-May residency; January 15 for June-September residency. Send SASE for application form or download from website. Applications are reviewed by panelists.

WORKSHOPS & CONFERENCES

//

For a songwriter just starting out, conferences and workshops can provide valuable learning opportunities. At conferences, songwriters can have their songs evaluated, hear suggestions for further improvement and receive feedback from music business experts. They are also excellent places to make valuable industry contacts. Workshops can help a songwriter improve his craft and learn more about the business of songwriting. They may involve classes on songwriting and the business, as well as lectures and seminars by industry professionals.

Each year, hundreds of workshops and conferences take place all over the country. Songwriters can choose from small regional workshops held in someone's living room to large national conferences such as South by Southwest in Austin, Texas, which hosts more than 6,000 industry people, songwriters and performers. Many songwriting organizations—national and local—host workshops that offer instruction on just about every songwriting topic imaginable, from lyric writing and marketing strategy to contract negotiation. Conferences provide songwriters the chance to meet one on one with publishing and record company professionals and give performers the chance to showcase their work for a live audience (usually consisting of industry people) during the conference. There are conferences and workshops that address almost every type of music, offering programs for songwriters, performers, musical playwrights and much more.

This section includes national and local workshops and conferences with a brief description of what they offer, when they are held and how much they cost to attend. Write or call any that interest you for further information. To find out what workshops or conferences take place in specific parts of the country, see the Geographic Index at the end of this book.

APPEL FARM ARTS AND MUSIC FESTIVAL

457 Shirley Road, P.O. Box 888, Elmer NJ 08318. (856)358-2472. **Fax:** (856)358-6513. **E-mail:** jdunaway@appelfarm.org; stimmons@appelfarm.org. **Website:** www.appelfarm.org. **Contact:** Sean Timmons, artistic director. Appel Farm's mission is "to provide people of all ages, cultures and economic backgrounds with a supportive, cooperative environment in which to explore the fine and performing arts." We believe that the arts are an exciting and essential part of the learning process and that artistic talent is innate and waiting to be developed in every person.

ASCAP I CREATE MUSIC EXPO

1 Lincoln Plaza, New York NY 10023. **E-mail:** expo@ascap.com. **Website:** www.ascap.com. "The ASCAP I Create Music EXPO puts you face-to-face with some of the world's most successful songwriters, composers, producers and music business leaders, all who willingly share their knowledge and expertise and give you the know-how to take your music to the next level." For more info and to register, visit the website.

ASCAP LESTER SILL SONGWRITERS WORKSHOP

7920 Sunset Blvd., 3rd Floor, Los Angeles CA 90046. **Website:** www.ascap.com. Annual workshop for advanced songwriters sponsored by the ASCAP Foundation. Re-named in 1995 to honor ASCAP's late Board member and industry pioneer Lester Sill, the workshop takes place over a four-week period and features prominent guest speakers from various facets of the music business. Workshop dates and deadlines vary from year to year. Applicants must submit 2 songs on a CD (cassette tapes not accepted), lyric sheets, brief bio and short explanation as to why they would like to participate, e-mail address, and telephone number. Limited number of participants are selected each year.

ASCAP MUSICAL THEATRE WORKSHOP

1 Lincoln Plaza, New York NY 10023. **Website:** www.ascap.com. Workshop is for musical theatre composers and lyricists only. Its purpose is to nurture and develop new musicals for the theatre. Offers programs for songwriters. Offers programs annually, usually April through May. Event took place in New York City. Four musical works are selected. Others are invited to audit the workshop. Participants are amateur and professional songwriters, composers and musical playwrights. Participants are selected by demo CD submission. Deadline: see website. Also available: the annual ASCAP/Disney Musical Theatre Workshop in Los Angeles. It takes place in January and February. Deadline is late November. Details similar to New York workshop as above.

BILLBOARD & THE HOLLYWOOD REPORTER FILM & TV MUSIC CONFERENCE

Sofitel LA, 8555 Beverly Blvd., Los Angeles CA 90048. (212)493-4026. **E-mail:** conferences@billboaRoad-com. **Website:** www.billboardevents.com. Promotes all music for film and television. Offers programs for songwriters and composers. Held annually in November. More than 350 songwriters/musicians participate in each event. Participants are professional songwriters, composers, producers, directors, etc. Conference panelists are selected by invitation. For registration information, including fees, call Nicole Carbone at (212)493-4263.

THE BMI LEHMAN ENGEL MUSICAL THEATRE WORKSHOP

7 World Trade Center, 250 Greenwich St., New York NY 10007. (212)230-3000. **Fax:** (212)262-2824. **E-mail:** theatreworkshop@bmi.com. **Website:** www.bmi.com. **Contact:** Patricia Cook, director. "BMI is a music licensing company which collects royalties for affiliated writers and publishers. We offer programs to musical theatre composers, lyricists and librettists. The BMI-Lehman Engel Musical Theatre Workshops were formed if an effort to refresh and stimulate professional writers, as well as to encourage and develop new creative talent for the musical theatre. Each workshop meets 1 afternoon a week for 2 hours at BMI, New York. Participants are professional songwriters, composers and playwrights. The BMI Lehman Musical Theatre Workshop Showcase presents the best of the workshop to producers, agents, record and publishing company execs, press and directors for possible option and production. Visit www.bmi.com/genres/entry/musical_theatre_workshop_application for application. Tape and lyrics of 3 compositions required with applications."

TIPS BMI also sponsors a jazz composers workshop. For more information, contact Raette Johnson at rjohnson@bmi.com.

CMJ MUSIC MARATHON & FILM FESTIVAL

1201 Broadway, Suite 706, New York NY 10001. (212)277-7120. **Fax:** (212)719-9396. **E-mail:** marketing@cmj.com. **Website:** www.cmj.com/marathon.

"Premier annual alternative music gathering of more than 9,000 music business and film professionals. Fall, NYC; October 21-25. Features 5 days and nights of more than 75 panels and workshops focusing on every facet of the industry; exclusive film screenings; keynote speeches by the world's most intriguing and controversial voices; exhibition area featuring live performance stage; over 1,000 of music's brightest and most visionary talents (from the unsigned to the legendary) performing over 5 evenings at more than 80 of NYC's most important music venues." Participants are selected by submitting demonstration tape. Visit website for application (through Sonicbids.com).

CUTTING EDGE C.E.

(Formerly the Cutting Edge Music Business Conference), New Orleans LA 70116. (504)945-1800. **E-mail:** eric@cuttingedgenola.com. **Website:** www.cuttingedgenola.com. Cutting Edge C.E. (formerly the Cutting Edge Music Business Conference) will again discuss "Hot Topics" and "Current Trends" in today's entertainment business. Attend conference sessions on Entertainment Law, Music Business, Film financing and tax credits, Roots Music, and the NewWorks Showcases. Check out the NOLA Downtown Festival and Cruisin' New Orleans Pro Gear Show at the Historic Carver Theater. Held at the InterContinental Hotel & the Hisotroical Carver Theater in New Orleans from August 21-23.

FOLK ALLIANCE ANNUAL CONFERENCE

509 Delaware St. #101, Kansas City MO 64105. (816)221-3655. **Fax:** (816)221-3658. **E-mail:** fa@folk. org. **Website:** www.folk.org. **Contact:** Louis Meyes, executive director. Conference/workshop topics change each year. Conference takes place late-February and lasts 4 days at a different location each year. 2,000-plus attendees include artists, agents, arts administrators, print/broadcast media, folklorists, folk societies, merchandisers, presenters, festivals, recording companies, etc. Artists wishing to showcase should contact the office for a showcase application form. Closing date for official showcase application is in November.

INDEPENDENT MUSIC CONFERENCE

304 Main Ave., PMB 287, Norwalk CT 06851. (203)606-4649. **E-mail:** IMC@intermixx.com. **Website:** www.indiemusicon.com. "The purpose of the IMC is to bring together rock, hip hop and acoustic music for of panels and showcases. Offers programs

for songwriters, composers and performers. 250 showcases at 20 clubs around the city. Also offer a DJ cutting contest." Held annually in the fall. 3,000 amateur and professional songwriters, composers, individual vocalists, bands, individual instrumentalists, attorneys, managers, agents, publishers, A&R, promotions, club owners, etc., participate each year. Send for application.

Ⓞ Formerly the Philadelphia Music Conference.

KERRVILLE FOLK FESTIVAL

Kerrville Festivals, Inc., P.O. Box 291466, Kerrville TX 78029. **E-mail:** info@kerrville-music.com. **Website:** www.kerrvillefolkfestival.com. **Contact:** Dalis Allen, producer. Hosts 3-day songwriters' school, a 4-day music business school and New Folk concert competition. Festival produced in late spring and early summer. Spring festival lasts 18 days and is held outdoors at Quiet Valley Ranch. 110 or more songwriters participate. Performers are professional songwriters and bands. Participants selected by submitting demo, by invitation only. Send cassette, or CD, promotional material and list of upcoming appearances. "Songwriter and music schools include lunch, experienced professional instructors, camping on ranch and concerts. Rustic facilities. Food available at reasonable cost. Audition materials accepted at above address. These three-day and four-day seminars include noon meals, handouts and camping on the ranch. Usually held during Kerrville Folk Festival, first and second week in June. Write or check the website for contest rules, schools and seminars information, and festival schedules. Also establishing a Phoenix Fund to provide assistance to ill or injured singer/songwriters who find themselves in distress."

Ⓞ Also see the listing for New Folk Concerts For Emerging Songwriters in the Contests & Awards section of this book.

LAMB'S RETREAT FOR SONGWRITERS

presented by Springfed Arts, a nonprofit organization, P.O. Box 304, Royal Oak MI 48068-0304. (248)589-3913. **E-mail:** johndlamb@ameritech.net. **Website:** www.springfed.org. **Contact:** John D. Lamb, director. Offers programs for songwriters on annual basis; November 6-9, and November 13-16, at The Birchwood Inn, Harbor Springs, MI. Sixty songwriters/musicians participate in each event. Participants are amateur and professional songwriters. Anyone can participate. Send for registration or e-mail. Deadline:

2 weeks before event begins. Fee: $300-575; includes all meals. Facilities are single/double occupancy lodging with private baths; 2 conference rooms and hospitality lodge. Offers song assignments, songwriting workshops, song swaps, open mic, and one-on-one mentoring. Faculty are noted songwriters. Partial scholarships may be available by writing: Blissfest Music Organization, Jim Gillespie, P.O. Box 441, Harbor Springs, MI 49740. Deadline: 2 weeks before event.

MANCHESTER MUSIC FESTIVAL

P.O. Box 33, 42 Dillingham Ave., Manchester VT 05254. (802)362-1956. **Fax:** (802)362-0711. **E-mail:** info@mmfvt.org. **Website:** www.mmfvt.org. **Contact:** Joana Genova, education director. Offers classical music education and performances. Summer program for young professional musicians offered in tandem with a professional concert series in the mountains of Manchester, Vermont. Up to 23 young professionals, age 19 and up, are selected by audition for the Young Artists Program, which provides instruction, performance and teaching opportunities, with full scholarship for all participants. Commissioning opportunities for new music, and performance opportunities for professional chamber ensembles and soloists for both summer and fall/winter concert series.

THE NEW HARMONY PROJECT

P.O. Box 441062, Indianapolis IN 46244-1062. (317)464-1103. **E-mail:** mhunter@newharmonyproject.org; jgrynheim@newharmonyproject.org. **Website:** www.newharmonyproject.org. **Contact:** Mead Hunter, artistic director; Joel Grynheim, project director.

○ "The purpose of The New Harmony Project shall be to create, nurture, and promote new works for stage, television and film that sensitively and truthfully explore the positive aspects of life. Our goal is to bring the writers who seek to produce uplifting, high-quality entertainment alternatives to our conference, surround them with professional resources, provide them with the opportunity to develop these works in a supportive and life-affirming environment that further enables their writing creativity and help each writer to tell their story well." Held May 18-31.

NEWPORT FOLK FESTIVAL

New Festival Productions, LLC, PO Box 3865, Newport RI 02840. **E-mail:** info@newportfolkfest.org.

Website: www.newportfolkfest.org. Held annually in mid-summer at the International Tennis Hall of Fame and Fort Adams State Park.

NEWPORT JAZZ FESTIVAL

New Festival Productions, LLC, Newport RI **E-mail:** jazz@newportjazzfest.org. **Website:** www.newportjazzfest.org. "Hailed by *The New York Times* as the festival that put jazz festivals on the map, the Newport Jazz Festival was founded by Jazz pianist George Wein in 1954 as the first outdoor music festival of its kind devoted entirely to Jazz, and is now universally acknowledged as the grandfather of all Jazz festivals. During the last half-century, the name Newport has become synonymous with the best in Jazz music. In its long illustrious history, the Newport Jazz Festival has presented a virtual pantheon of Jazz immortals alongside an array of rising young artists: Duke Ellington's 1956 rebirth framing Paul Gonzalves' epic solo; subject of the classic 1958 documentary "Jazz on a Summer's Day; origin of famous recordings by Thelonious Monk, John Coltrane and Miles Davis; showcase for emerging young masters including Wynton Marsalis, Diana Krall, Joshua Redman and Esperanza Spalding. Referred to as a Mecca of Jazz, the event draws thousands of people from all over the world to it's uniquely picturesque outdoor stages at the International Tennis Hall of Fame and Fort Adams State Park."

NORFOLK CHAMBER MUSIC FESTIVAL

P.O. Box 208246, New Haven CT 06520. **E-mail:** norfolk@yale.edu. **Website:** www.yale.edu/norfolk. Festival season of chamber music. Offers programs for composers and performers. Offers programs summer only. Approximately 45 fellows participate. Participants are up-and-coming composers and instrumentalists. Participants are selected by following a screening round. Auditions are held in New Haven, CT. Send for application. Deadline: mid-January. Fee: $50. "Held at the Ellen Battell Stoeckel Estate, the Festival offers a magnificent Music Shed with seating for 1,000, practice facilities, music library, dining hall, laundry and art gallery. Nearby are hiking, bicycling and swimming."

○ NORTH BY NORTHEAST MUSIC FESTIVAL AND CONFERENCE

189 Church St., Lower Level, Toronto ON M5B 1Y7 Canada. (416)863-6963. **Fax:** (416)863-0828. **E-mail:** info@nxne.com; michaelh@nowtoronto.com. **Web-**

site: www.nxne.com. **Contact:** Michael Hollett, managing director. "Our festival takes place mid-June at over 30 venues across downtown Toronto, drawing over 2,000 conference delegates, 500 bands and 50,000 music fans. Musical genres include everything from folk to funk, roots to rock, polka to punk and all points in between, bringing exceptional new talent, media front-runners, music business heavies and music fans from all over the world to Toronto." Participants include emerging and established songwriters, vocalists, composers, bands and instrumentalists. Festival performers are selected by submitting a CD and accompanying press kit or applying through sonicbids.com. Application forms are available by website or by calling the office. Submission period each year is from November 1 to the third weekend in January.

NSAI SONG CAMPS

1710 Roy Acuff Place, Nashville TN 37023. (800)321-6008; (615)256-335. **Fax:** (615)256-0034. **E-mail:** events@nashvillesongwriters.com; shannon@nashvillesongwriters.com. **Website:** www.nashvillesongwriters.com. Offers programs strictly for songwriters. Events held in late-July in Nashville. "We provide most meals and lodging is available. We also present an amazing evening of music presented by the faculty." Camps are 3-4 days long, with 36-112 participants, depending on the camp. "There are different levels of camps, some having preferred prerequisites. Each camp varies. Please call, e-mail or refer to website. It really isn't about the genre of music, but the quality of the song itself. Song Camp strives to strengthen the writer's vision and skills, therefore producing the better song. Song Camp is known as 'boot camp' for songwriters. It is guaranteed to catapult you forward in your writing! Participants are all aspiring songwriters led by a pro faculty. We do accept lyricists only and composers only with the hopes of expanding their scope." Participants are selected through submission of 2 songs with lyric sheet. Song Camp is open to NSAI members, although anyone can apply and upon acceptance join the organization. There is no formal application form. See website for membership and event information. Also see the listing for Nashville Songwriters Association International (NSAI) in the Organizations section of this book.

◐ ORFORD FESTIVAL

Orford Arts Centre, 3165 chemin du Parc, Orford QC J1X 7A2 Canada. (819)843-9871; (800)567-6155. **Fax:**

(819)843-7274. **E-mail:** info@arts-orfoRoadorg. **Website:** www.arts-orfoRoadorg. The Orford Arts Centre plays host to a world-class Academy of Music, which offers advanced training to particularly gifted young musicians who are at the beginning of a professional career in classical music. Together with internationally renowned professors and artists who are devoted to training the next generation, we are committed to providing our students with pedagogical activities that are as unique as they are enriching. In pursuit of its mission, the Centre abides by the following values: excellence, discipline, dedication, open-mindedness, respect and the will to surpass individual expectations.

◔ REGGAE SUMFEST

Shops 9 & 10 Parkway Plaza, Rose Hall, Montego Bay Jamaica. (876)953-8360. **Website:** http://reggaesumfest.com. **Contact:** Tina Mae Davis, festival coordinator. "Reggae Sumfest is a musical event to which we welcome 30,000+ patrons each year. The festival showcases the best of Dancehall and Reggae music, as well as top R&B/hip hop performers. The festival also offers delicious Jamaican cuisine as well as arts and crafts from all over the island. The main events of the festival is held at Catherine Hall, Montego Bay, Jamaica over a three-day period which usually falls in the third week of July, from Sunday to Saturday." Reggae Sumfest is presented by Summerfest Productions and accepts press kit submissions for persons wishing to perform at the festival between November and January each year. Send to address above.

THE SONGWRITERS GUILD OF AMERICA FOUNDATION

5120 Virginia Way, Suite C22, Brentwood TN 37027. (800)524-6742; (615)742-9945. **E-mail:** ny@songwritersguild.com; nash@songwritersguild.com; la@songwritersguild.com. **Website:** www.songwritersguild.com. **Contact:** Mark Saxon, director of operations. The Foundation is in charge of many events, including workshops in the NY, Nashville, and L.A. areas.

SOUTH BY SOUTHWEST MUSIC CONFERENCE

SXSW Headquarters, P.O. Box 685289, Austin TX 78768. **E-mail:** sxsw@sxsw.com. **Website:** www.sxsw.com. South by Southwest (SXSW) is a private company based in Austin, Texas, with a year-round staff of professionals dedicated to building and delivering conference and festival events for entertainment and related media industry professionals. Since 1987, SXSW has produced the internationally-recognized music and media conference and festival (SXSW). As the entertainment business adjusted to issues of future growth and development, in 1994, SXSW added conferences and festivals for the film industry (SXSW Film) as well as for the blossoming interactive media (SXSW Interactive Festival). Now three industry events converge in Austin during a Texas-sized week, mirroring the ever increasing convergence of entertainment/media outlets. The next SXSW Music Conference and Festival will be held in March. Offers panel discussions, "Crash Course" educational seminars and nighttime showcases. SXSW Music seeks out speakers who have developed unique ways to create and sell music. The conference includes over fifty sessions including a panel of label heads discussing strategy, interviews with notable artists, topical discussions, demo listening sessions and the mentor program. And when the sun goes down, a multitude of performances by musicians and songwriters from across the country and around the world populate the SXSW Music Festival, held in venues in central Austin." Write, e-mail or visit website for dates and registration instructions.

TIPS "Visit the website in August to apply for showcase consideraton. SXSW is also involved in North by Northeast (NXNE), held in Toronto, Canada in late Spring."

THE SWANNANOA GATHERING—CONTEMPORARY FOLK WEEK

Warren Wilson College, P.O. Box 9000, Asheville NC 28815-9000. (828)298-3434. **Fax:** (828)298-3434. **E-mail:** gathering@warren-wilson.edu. **Website:** www.swangathering.com. **Contact:** Jim Magill, director. "For anyone who ever wanted to make music for an audience, we offer a comprehensive week in artist development, including classes in songwriting, performance, and vocal coaching." For a brochure or other info, contact The Swannanoa Gathering. Takes place last week in July. Tuition: See website. Housing (including all meals): $385. Annual program of The Swannanoa Gathering Folk Arts Workshops.

WEST COAST SONGWRITERS CONFERENCE

(formerly Northern California Songwriters Association), 1724 Laurel St., Suite 120, San Carlos CA 94070. (650)654-3966. **E-mail:** info@westcoastsongwriters.

org. **Website:** www.westcoastsongwriters.org. "Conference offers opportunity and education; 16 seminars, 50 song screening sessions (1,500 songs reviewed), performance showcases, one on one sessions and concerts." Offers programs for lyricists, songwriters, composers and performers. "During the year we have competitive live Songwriter competitions. Winners go into the playoffs. Winners of the playoffs perform at the sunset concert at the conference." Event takes place second weekend in September at Foothill College, Los Altos Hills, CA. Over 500 songwriters/musicians participate in this event. Participants are songwriters, composers, musical playwrights, vocalists, bands, instrumentalists and those interested in a career in the music business. Send for application. Deadline: September 1. Fee: $150-280. "See our listing in the Organizations section."

WESTERN WIND WORKSHOP IN ENSEMBLE SINGING

263 W. 86th St., New York NY 10024. (212)873-2848. **E-mail:** workshops@westernwind.org; info@westernwind.org. **Website:** www.westernwind.org. **Contact:** William Zukoff, executive producer. Participants learn the art of ensemble singing—no conductor, one on-a-part. Workshops focus on blend, diction, phrasing, and production. Offers programs for performers. Limited talent-based scholarship available. Offers programs annually. Takes place June and August in the music department at Smith College, Northampton, MA. 70-80 songwriters and/or musicians participate in each event. Participants are amateur and professional vocalists. Anyone can participate. Send for application or register at their website. Arrangers' works are frequently studied and performed. Also offers additional workshops President's Day weekend in Brattleboro, VT and Columbus Day weekend in Woodstock, VT.

WINTER MUSIC CONFERENCE INC.

3450 NE 12 Terrace, Ft. Lauderdale FL 33334. (954)563-4444. **Fax:** (954)563-1599. **E-mail:** info@wintermusicconference.com. **Website:** www.wintermusicconference.com. Features educational seminars and showcases for dance, hip hop, alternative, and rap. Offers programs for songwriters and performers. Offers programs annually. Event takes place March of each year in Miami, Florida. 3,000 songwriters/musicians participate in each event. Participants are amateur and professional songwriters, composers, musi-

cal playwrights, vocalists, bands and instrumentalists. Participants are selected by submitting demo
tape. Send SASE, visit website or call for application.
Deadline: February. Event held at either nightclubs or
hotel with complete staging, lights and sound.

VENUES

THE 4TH AVENUE TAVERN

210 E. Fourth Ave., Olympia WA 98501. (360)951-7887. **E-mail:** the4thave@gmail.com. **Website:** www.the4thave.com. Music: indie, alternative, funk, rock, punk. The 4th Ave is home to one of the largest stages in Olympia. Booking is very selective. Only contact if you have a large draw in the South Sound area.

40 WATT CLUB

285 W. Washington St., Athens GA 30601. (706)549-7871. **E-mail:** velenavego@gmail.com. **Website:** www.40watt.com. Music: indie, rock, alternative.

123 PLEASANT STREET

123 Pleasant St., Morgantown WV 26505. (304)292-0800. **E-mail:** 123pleasantstreet@gmail.com. **Website:** www.123pleasantstreet.com. "An eclectic crowd can be expected any given night and is as diverse as the bands that grace our stage whether it be rock, bluegrass, punk, jazz, reggae, salsa, country, DJs, indie, hardcore, old time, or some mixture of some or all or the above." To book, send media, press kits 8x10 glossies, etc.

ABG'S BAR

190 W. Center St., Provo UT 84106. (801)373-1200. **E-mail:** booking@abgsbar.com. **Website:** www.abgsbar.com. Music: rock, alt-country, alternative, folk, blues, jazz.

✪ ACL LIVE AT THE MOODY THEATER

310 W. Willie Nelson Blvd., Austin TX 78701. (512)225-7999. **E-mail:** info@acl-live.com. **Website:** www.acl-live.com. Austin City Limits Live at The Moody Theater (ACL Live) is a state-of-the-art, 2,750-person capacity live music venue that hosts approximately 100 concerts a year.

✪ ANTONE'S

2015 E. Riverside Dr., Austin TX 78741. (512)800-4628. **Website:** www.antonesnightclub.com. Antone's Nightclub, the first club on 6th street, opened its doors in the summer of 1975 with the great Clifton Chenier. The venue, now located at the corner of 5th and Lavaca Street, was founded by legendary promoter Clifford Antone and has hosted such blues "greats" as Muddy Waters, B.B. King, Buddy Guy, John Lee Hooker, Pinetop Perkins, James Cotton and countless others.

✪ ARLENE'S GROCERY

95 Stanton St., New York NY 10002. (212)358-1633. **Fax:** (212)995-1719. **E-mail:** arlenesbooking@gmail.com. **Website:** www.arlenesgrocery.net. For booking, write the name of your band and any requested dates/timeframe for the show in the subject line of an e-mail. The body of the e-mail should contain a brief description of your music and instrumentation; links to your band's website, streaming music, an EPK, and social media pages; show history in New York City and estimated draw; and requested dates or timeframe. Usually booked at least 6 weeks out. Music: rock, alternate, indie, old school, new school, etc.

ARMADILLO'S BAR & GRILL

132 Dock St., Annapolis MD 21401. (401)280-0028. **E-mail:** armadillosannapolis@gmail.com; info@armadillosannapolis.com. **Website:** www.armadillosannapolis.com. "Armadillo's is the top choice for nightlife in downtown Annapolis. We are the only venue in town to provide two levels of live entertainment. Upstairs, Armadillo's brings you the hottest local and national bands, in a casual, intimate setting, while DJ's keep the crowd moving downstairs." All band bookings must go through Shook Productions & Media (www.shookpm.com). See website for details. Music: rock, acoustic, reggae, soul, pop, indie, alternative.

ART BAR

1211 Park St., Columbia SC 29201. (803)929-0198. **E-mail:** booking@artbarsc.com. **Website:** www.artbarsc.com. Booking guidelines available on website. Music: rock, alternative, indie, punk, hard rock, hip-hop.

ASHLAND COFFEE & TEA

100 N. Railroad Ave., Ashland VA 23005. (804)798-1702. **Fax:** (804)798-2573. **Website:** www.ashlandcoffeeandtea.com. "Join us most Thursdays, Fridays and Saturdays in our intimate 'Listening Room' for an evening of Americana, bluegrass, folk, blues, jazz, pop—you never know what we'll have on tap with our wide range of performers. Don't miss 'Homegrown Wednesday' featuring local Virginia talent, or the 'Songwriter's Showdown', a songwriting and vocal performance competition every Tuesday."

BACKBOOTH

37 W. Pine St., Orlando FL 32801. (407)999-2570. **E-mail:** bookings@backbooth.com. **Website:** www.backbooth.com. "BackBooth's reputation as a music venue has grown to being named one of the best live music venues in the city, according to Orlando Weekly, and still boasts the most impressive draft selection in downtown. With a capacity of 350, a large stage, a powerful sound/lighting system, balcony, and back bar area; the club still maintains a very comfortable and inviting, almost pub-like atmosphere with an Old English decor including wood work and dark curtains throughout. As a venue, Back Booth continues to play host to many popular national and regional acts, while remaining a favorite among locals. The club is also known for its dance parties; which are among the most popular and recognized in town. Whether it be for an intimate live performance, a rousing rock show, or a night of dancing and drinks, Back Booth is established in the heart of the central Florida community as a favorite destination." Music: reggae, acoustic, alternative, indie, pop, hip-hop, jam, roots, soul, gospel, funk, dubstep, country, rock, metal.

BACK EAST BAR & GRILL

9475 Briar Village Point, Colorado Springs CO 80920. (719)264-6161. **Website:** www.backeastbarandgrill.com. "We have created the perfect place for you to watch your favorite game and enjoy the incredible food and flavors that we have brought from home. We know you will enjoy every minute that you share with us. So sit back and have a drink, eat some great food, and enjoy your favorite team on one of our many TVs." Music: rock, alternative, R&B, blues, country, pop.

THE BARLEY STREET TAVERN

2735 N. 62nd St., Omaha NE 68104. (402)408-0028. **E-mail:** bookings@barleystreet.com. **Website:** www.barleystreet.com. "We have live music performances on scheduled nights, featuring some great local and regional performers, as well as, national touring acts. This is the music venue to find the best in all music styles." Music: rock, alternative, folk, indie, country, pop, Americana.

✛ THE BELL HOUSE

149 7th St., Brooklyn NY 11215. (718)643-6510. **Fax:** (718)369-3390. **E-mail:** info@thebellhouseny.com. **E-mail:** booking@thebellhouseny.com. **Website:** www.thebellhouseny.com. A 1920's warehouse converted into a beautiful music and events venue in Brooklyn, New York.

BERKELEY CAFE

217 W. Martin St., Raleigh NC 27601. (919)821-0777. **E-mail:** lakeboonee@bellsouth.net. **Contact:** Jim Shires. Music: rock, bluegrass, alternative, blues, punk, folk.

BILLY'S LOUNGE

1437 Wealthy SE, Grand Rapids MI 49506. (616)459-5757. **E-mail:** billysbooking@gmail.com. **Website:** www.billyslounge.com. "Billy's Lounge is a local hot spot in the Eastown Community. With our live music, a fully stocked bar, and dirt cheap drink specials on a nightly basis ... you can see why! billy's has a strong history in keeping with the tradition of service and entertainment. We pride ourselves on our support of local music, our abilities to drink, and the atmospheres we produce." Music: Blues, Rock, R&B, Americana, Hip-Hop, Jazz.

BLUE

650A Congress St., Portland ME 04101. (207)774-4111. **E-mail:** booking@portcityblue.com. **Website:** www.portcityblue.com. "Located in the heart of Portland's Arts District, Blue is Portland's most intimate live music venue. We present an array of music such as Celtic, Middle Eastern, Blues, Old Time, Jazz, Folk, and more."

THE BLUE DOOR

2805 N. McKinley Ave., Oklahoma City OK 73106. (405)524-0738. **E-mail:** bluedoormusic@yahoo.com. **Website:** www.bluedoorokc.com. **Contact:** Greg Johnson. "We have grown to become Oklahoma's premiere venue for performing songwriters, hosting such legends as Jimmy Webb, Joe Ely, Ramblin' Jack Elliott, David Lindley and Tom Rush. We love working with new songwriters who are developing their audience and always welcome the best in bluegrass, folk, rock, country and blues."

⊕ BLUE WHALE BAR

123 Astronaut E. S. Onizuka St., Los Angeles CA 90012. (213)620-0908. **Website:** www.bluewhalemusic.com. Blue Whale is a live jazz bar located in the heart of Little Tokyo, Los Angeles.

⊕ BOGART'S

2621 Vine St., Cincinnati OH 45219. (513)872-8801. **Fax:** (513)872-8805. **Website:** www.bogarts.com. The venue holds approximately 1,500 people, has six bars, three levels for concert viewing, two entrances, and an elevated stage. Bogart's has been recognized on the international stage for bringing the newest, and best, music and entertainment to the public for over two decades. Today, it is operated by Live Nation Inc., and continues the tradition of quality live entertainment that has been its forté since the building was built in 1890.

⊕ BOOTLEG BAR & THEATER

2220 Beverly Blvd., Los Angeles CA 90057. (213)389-3856. **E-mail:** sterling@foldsilverlake.com. **E-mail:** buyer@foldsilverlake.com. **Website:** www.foldsilverlake.com. "For booking inquiries, please provide your name, the band's name, a phone number, and e-mail address in all correspondences. Please list your targeted show dates, or even some details on how you got referred. Please don't e-mail mp3s and such as attachments, just e-mail the appropriate url or sound-clip address."

THE BOTTLENECK

737 New Hampshire, Lawrence KS 66044. (785)841-5483. **E-mail:** booking@pipelineproductions.com. **Website:** www.thebottlenecklive.com. "The Bottleneck is considered by many to be a Rock & Roll historical landmark. The Bottleneck cemented its status as a scheduled stop on many major-city, national tours, giving nearby University of Kansas students access to some of the best names in modern music." Music: indie, rock, alternative, folk, country, jazz, blues, funk, dance, ska, psychedelic.

THE BOTTLETREE

3719 Third Ave. S, Birmingham AL 35222. (205)533-6288. **Fax:** (205)533-7565. **E-mail:** info@thebottletree.com. **E-mail:** merrilee@thebottletree.com; booking@thebottletree.com. **Website:** www.thebottletree.com. **Contact:** Merrilee Challiss. Music: punk, indie, folk, rock, country, soul, alternative.

BOTTOM OF THE HILL

1233 17th St., San Francisco CA 94107. (415)621-4455. **E-mail:** booking@bottomofthehill.com. **Website:** www.bottomofthehill.com. **Contact:** Ramona Downey; Ursula Rodriguez, bookers. Music: alternative, rock, rockabilly, punk, hard rock.

⊕ BOWERY BALLROOM

6 Delancey St., New York NY 10002. (212)533-2111. **E-mail:** info@bowerypresents.com. **Website:** www.boweryballroom.com. **Contact:** Eddie Brusier. The best way to get a show at a Bowery Presents club is to send your press pack to: The Bowery Presents, c/o Eddie Bruiser, 156 Ludlow St., New York, NY 10002. Please list a New York City show history and allow 4-6 weeks before following up with an e-mail.

THE BRASS RAIL

1121 Broadway, Ft. Wayne IN 46802. (260)267-5303. **E-mail:** corey@brassrailfw.com. **Website:** www.brassrailfw.com. **Contact:** Corey Rader. Music: rock, punk, metal, alternative.

THE BREWERY

3009 Hillsborough St., Raleigh NC 27607. (919)838-6788. **Fax:** (919)838-6789. **E-mail:** tom@brewerync.com. **Website:** www.brewerync.com. "The Brewery has been a staple of the NC music scene since 1983. Having hosted some of the biggest names in the music industry, The Brewery is the perfect spot to see the best local musicians as well as the stars of tomorrow." Music: rock, pop, alternative, hip-hop.

THE BRICKYARD

129 N. Rock Island, Wichita KS 67202. (316)263-4044. **E-mail:** booking@brickyardoldtown.com. **Website:** www.brickyardoldtown.com. Music: rock, indie, alternative, punk, classic rock, country.

BROOKLYN BOWL

61 Wythe Ave., Brooklyn NY 11211. (718)963-3369. **E-mail:** rock.androll@brooklynbowl.com. **E-mail:** booking@brooklynbowl.com. **Website:** www.brooklynbowl.com. "Brooklyn Bowl redefines the entertainment experience for the 21st century. Centered around a 16-lane bowling alley, 600-capacity performance venue with live music 7 nights a week, and food by Blue Ribbon, Brooklyn Bowl stakes out expansive new territory, literally and conceptually, in the 23,000-square foot former Hecla Iron Works (1882), one block from the burgeoning waterfront." Music: rock, indie, hip-hop, R&B, alternative, punk, funk, folk, reggae, soul.

THE BROTHERHOOD LOUNGE

119 Capital Way N, Olympia WA 98501. (360)352-4153. **Website:** www.thebrotherhoodlounge.com. Music: soul, funk, rock, pop, hip-hop, R&B.

THE CACTUS CLUB

2496 S. Wentworth Ave., Milwaukee WI 53207. (414)897-0663. **E-mail:** cactuscl@execpc.com. **Website:** www.cactusclub.dostuff.info/. Music: punk, rock, alternative, indie, funk, pyschedelic.

CAFE 939

939 Boylston St., Boston MA 02215. (617)747-6040 or (617)747-6143. **E-mail:** 939booking@beklee.edu. **Website:** www.cafe939.com. "Cafe 939 showcases Berklee's emerging student performers and local Boston artists, as well as national acts seeking a more intimate, personal space in which to connect with their fans. The venue is open to the general public and aims to attract musicians and music fans from all walks of life." Music: rock, jazz, folk, Americana, bluegrass, hip-hop, electronica, pop, indie.

CAFE NINE

250 State St., New Haven CT 06511. (203)789-8281. **E-mail:** bookcafenine@gmail.com. **Website:** www. cafenine.com. **Contact:** Paul Mayer, booker. "Cafe Nine features live music from national, regional and local acts seven nights a week. Catch some of your

favorites getting back to their roots in our intimate setting or see tomorrows stars on their way to the stadiums." Music: indie, rock, alternative, jazz, punk, garage, alt-country.

CALEDONIA LOUNGE

256 W. Clayton St., Athens GA 30601. (706)549-5577. **E-mail:** booking@caledonialounge.com. **Website:** www.caledonialounge.com. Music: indie, rock, alternative, folk.

THE CANOPY CLUB

708 S. Goodwin Ave., Champaign-Urbana IL 61801. (217)344-2263. **E-mail:** mikea@jaytv.com. **Website:** www.canopyclub.com. **Contact:** Mike Armintrout. "In striving to achieve the highest level of entertainment, the Canopy Club prides itself on being able to offer entertainment for all walks of life. Whether you like rock, country, hip hop, jazz, funk, indie or anything in between, the Canopy Club has something to offer you. If you're a fan of live music and entertainment, the Canopy Club is your home in central Illinois!"

CASSELMAN'S BAR & VENUE

2620 Walnut St., Denver CO 80205. (720)242-8923. **Fax:** (877)667-7572. **E-mail:** booking@casselmans. com. **Website:** www.casselmans.com. "Casselman's is a multi-use live music and special events venue located in NoDo (NorthDowntown) Denver. Casselman's opened in 2009 and started to brand "NoDo" as the new entertainment and arts district of Denver. The name Casselman is the maiden name of our great grandmother and was carried as the middle name down to three members of the family business. Casselman's is a proud recipient of the Westword's 2010 Best New Club award!" Bookings should be completed electronically through the website. Music: pop, rock, R&B, hip-hop, alternative.

THE CAVE

452 1/2 W. Franklin St., Chapel Hill NC 27516. (919)968-9308. **E-mail:** cavencbooking@gmail.com. **Website:** www.caverntavern.com. Music: pop, rock, country, twang, folk, acoustic, funk, indie, punk, blues, bluegrass.
TIPS Use online booking form.

CHELSEA'S CAFE

2857 Perkins Road, Baton Rouge LA 70808. (225)387-3679. **E-mail:** dave@chelseascafe.com. **E-mail:** jb@ chelseascafe.com. **Website:** www.chelseascafe.com.

"Chelsea's Cafe is Baton Rouge's favorite place to relax, offering good food, drinks and live music in an intimate, casual atmosphere." Music: rock, indie, alternative, soul.

CHILKOOT CHARLIES

1068 W. Fireweed Ln., Suite A, Anchorage AK 99503. (907)279-1692. **E-mail:** promo@koots.com. **Website:** www.koots.com. "Chilkoot Charlie's features a rustic Alaska atmosphere with sawdust-covered floors, 3 stages, 3 dance floors and 10 bars (11 in the summertime!) with padded tree stumps and beer kegs for seating. Literally filled to the rafters with such things as famous band photos & autographs, huge beer can collections, hilarious gags, and tons of Alaska memorabilia, a person could wander around Chilkoot Charlie's for days and still not see everything." Music: rock, punk, metal, ska.

CHROME HORSE SALOON

1202 Third St. SE, Cedar Rapids IA 52401. (319)365-1234. **Fax:** (319)365-9795. **E-mail:** chromehorsesaloon@mchsi.com. **Website:** www.chromehorsesaloon.net. "In addition to weekly shows inside on Friday and Saturday nights, a series of Friday night outdoor concerts are held in the parking lot during the summer months. The bar also has hosted a variety of national acts, including The Jeff Healey Band, L.A. Guns, Saliva, Hank Williams III, Black Oak Arkansas, The Buckinghams, The Grass Roots, American Idol finalist Amanda Overmyer and Blues Traveler." Music: rock, funk, punk, indie, alternative.

CHURCHILL'S

5501 NE Second Ave., Miami FL 33137. (305)757-1807. **E-mail:** bookings@churchillspub.com. **Website:** www.churchillspub.com. Music: rock, alternative, indie, pop, jazz, hip-hop, electronica, acoustic.

CITY TAVERN

1402 Main St., Dallas TX 75201. (214)745-1402. **E-mail:** info@citytaverndowntown.com. **E-mail:** booking@citytaverndowntown.com. **Website:** www.citytaverndowntown.com. Music: country, rock, jam, pop, alternative.

CLUB 209

209 N. Boulder Ave., Tulsa OK 74103. (918)584-9944. **E-mail:** thegang@club209tulsa.com. **Website:** www.club209tulsa.com. Music: indie, Americana, alt-country, folk.

CLUB CONGRESS

311 E. Congress St., Tucson AZ 85701. (520)622-8848. **Fax:** (520)792-6366. **E-mail:** bookingashow@hotelcongress.com. **Website:** www.hotelcongress.com. **Contact:** David Slutes, entertainment and booking director. Music: rock, alternative, indie, folk, Americana.

THE CLUBHOUSE

1320 E. Broadway Road, Tempe AZ 85282. (460)968-3238. **E-mail:** clubhousegigs@hotmail.com. **Website:** www.clubhousemusicvenue.com. "A club that features the best in local, touring, and regional acts. Voted Best Local Music Venue by The New Times Magazine, We have been in the valley of the sun for 6 years hosting shows for all age groups on a nightly basis." Music: rock, punk, metal, alternative.

D.B.A.

618 Frenchmen St., New Orleans LA 70116. (504)942-3731. **E-mail:** booking@dbaneworleans.com. **E-mail:** dbaneworleans@yahoo.com. **Website:** www.dbabars.com/dbano. "We are proud to present some of New Orleans and the region's greatest musicians, and are privileged to have had appearances on our stage by greats such as Clarence "Gatemouth" Brown, David "Honeyboy" Edwards, Jimmy Buffet and Stevie Wonder. When in New Orleans, get away from the tourist traps of Bourbon Street and head down to the "Marigny," just downriver from the French Quarter, voted w/ Williamsburg, Brooklyn and the Inner Mission in San Francisco as one of the hippest neighborhoods in the country." Music: blues, jazz, R&B, Cajun.

THE DOGFISH BAR & GRILLE

128 Free St., Portland ME 04101. (207)772-5483. **E-mail:** michele@thedogfishcompany.com. **Website:** www.thedogfishcompany.com. **Contact:** Michele Arcand. "Great food, drink and service in a casual and unpretentious atmosphere and a great place to hear live local artists. The Dogfish Bar and Grille is an intimate, informal restaurant with a great dinner menu and daily specials. We have two very comfortable decks for those who enjoy eating outside, a dining room upstairs, and a friendly tavern on the ground floor. The Dogfish Bar and Grille books local, regional, and national talent most evenings of the week. The music is mostly acoustic, blues, and jazz. There is never a cover charge" Music: jazz, be-bop, blues, soul, jam, acoustic.

VENUES

THE DOUBLE DOOR INN

1218 Charlottetowne Ave., Charlotte NC 28204. (704)376-1446. **Fax:** (704)372-3057. **E-mail:** info@doubledoorinn.com. **E-mail:** maxxmusic2@gmail.com. **Website:** www.doubledoorinn.com. **Contact:** Gregg McGraw, main talent buyer/promoter. "Established in 1973 and recognized as the "Oldest Live Music Venue East of the Mississippi," the Double Door Inn oozes musical tradition. Looking at our walls, packed with 35 years of autographed photos, has been described as being like "viewing a timeline for live music in the Queen City." Also holding the title "Oldest Blues Club In The U.S. Under Original Ownership," the Double Door Inn strives to bring the best in local, regional, and national touring and recording artists to the discriminating music lover. Legendary performers like Eric Clapton, Stevie Ray Vaughn, Dave Alvin, Leon Russell, Buddy Guy, Junior Brown, Bob Margolin, and others, have graced the stage of our historic and intimate venue." Music: blues, rock, soul, pop, funk, jazz, bluegrass, acoustic, folk, alt-country, R&B, Americana, reggae.

DOUG FIR LOUNGE

830 E. Burnside, Portland OR 97214. (503)231-9663. **E-mail:** inquiries@dougfirlounge.com. **E-mail:** booking@dougfirlounge.com. **Website:** www.dougfirlounge.com. Music: rock, alternative, indie, funk, garage, pop, dance, folk, bluegrass, soul, Americana.

✚ THE DRINKERY

1150 Main St., Cincinnati OH 45202. (513)827-9357. **E-mail:** drinkerybooking@icloud.com. **Website:** www.drinkeryotr.com. **Contact:** Matt Ogden, booking. The Drinkery OTR is a music venue in Cincinnati, Ohio featuring local draft beer, quality craft bottles, and soothing, warm bourbons.

DUFFY'S TAVERN

1412 O St., Lincoln NE 68508. (402)474-3543. **E-mail:** management@duffyslincoln.com. **E-mail:** booking@duffyslincoln.com. **Website:** www.duffyslincoln.com. **Contact:** Jon Dell, booking and promotions. "We're known for a lot of things, but if you ask any of us, we will tell you that we're a music venue. Many national acts have graced our stage, including Nirvana, 311, Bright Eyes, the Boss Martians, Slobberbone, Wesley Willis, and many others. A lot of us think some of the local acts are even better, and on any Sunday or Wednesday night, you can be assured Duffy's stage will be jumping with some of the best original music

around." Music: rock, folk, Americana, indie, psychedelic, pop, hard rock.

THE ECHO

1822 Sunset Blvd., Los Angeles CA 90026. (213)413-8200. **Website:** www.attheecho.com. Music: funk, punk, rock, indie, folk, hip-hop, electronica, Mexicana, pop.

EL BAIT SHOP

200 SW Second St., Des Moines IA 50309. (515)284-1970. **E-mail:** info@elbaitshop.com. **E-mail:** music@elbaitshop.com. **Website:** www.elbaitshop.com. Music: rock, alternative, pop, indie, folk, country, Americana, blues, jam, bluegrass, psychedelic.

ELBOW ROOM

1855 Stephens, Missoula MT 59801. **E-mail:** paffer17@yahoo.com. **Website:** www.elbowroombar.com. **Contact:** Josh Paffhausen, owner and general manager. "With entertainment at least five nights a week, ranging from karaoke and red hot DJs to favorite local bands, and major headliners." Music: rock, alternative, country.

✚ EL REY THEATRE

5515 Wilshire Blvd., Los Angeles CA 90036. (323)936-6400. **E-mail:** booking@theelrey.com. **Website:** www.theelrey.com. The El Rey Theatre is an original art deco theater in the heart of the Miracle Mile, one of Los Angeles' preserved art deco districts. After over 50 years as a first run movie house, the El Rey was converted into a live music venue in 1994.

THE EMPTY BOTTLE

1035 N. Western Ave., Chicago IL 60622. (773)276-3600. **E-mail:** christen@emptybottle.com; bookingasst@emptybottle.com. **Website:** www.emptybottle.com. **Contact:** Christen Thomas, talent buyer. Music: rock, indie, psychedelic, anti-pop, garage, metal, country, dance, electronica, soul, blues, folk.

THE EMPTY GLASS

410 Elizabeth St., Charleston WV 25311. (304)345-3914. **E-mail:** booking@emptyglass.com. **Website:** www.emptyglass.com. Music: blues, jazz, rock, folk, bluegrass, indie.

EXIT/IN

2208 Elliston Place, Nashville TN 37203. (615)321-3340. **Website:** www.exitin.com. "The Exit/In began it's role as a Nashville music venue back in 1971. Since then countless shows and great memories have happened within these walls." Music: rock, country, alt-country, folk, punk, pop, psychedelic.

FAT CATZ MUSIC CLUB

440 Bourbon St., New Orleans LA 70130. (504)525-0303. **E-mail:** info@fatcatzmusicclub.com. "When you are looking for a great place to hang out in New Orleans, look no further! Stop by for a great time any day of the week. We have awesome music all the time, and our staff is second to none. Kick back, relax, and enjoy quality music with us! We have live bands EVERY night of the week that feature a large variety music styles." Music: R&B, rock, alternative, jazz, hip-hop, pop, blues.

THE FINELINE MUSIC CAFE

318 First Ave., Minneapolis MN 55401. (612)338-8100. **Fax:** (612)337-8416. **E-mail:** info@finelinemusic.com. **E-mail:** localbookings@finelinemusic.com; nationalbookings@finelinemusic.com. **Website:** www.finelinemusic.com. Music: rock, acoustic, indie, folk, alternative.

FREAKIN' FROG

4700 S. Maryland Pkwy., Suite 8, Las Vegas NV 89119. **E-mail:** info@freakinfrog.com. **E-mail:** music@freakinfrog.com. **Website:** www.freakinfrog.com. Music: pop, rock, punk, blues, alternative.

FREIGHT HOUSE DISTRICT

250 Evans Ave., Reno NV 89501. (775)334-7071. **E-mail:** info@freighthouse.com. **E-mail:** charlie@reno-aces.com. **Website:** www.freighthouse.com. Includes: Duffy's Ale House, 205 Lounge, Bugsy's Sports Bar and Grill, Arroyo Mexican Grill. Music: funk, rock, Latin, pop, dance, alternative, soul, reggae, blues.

THE FREQUENCY

121 W. Main St., Madison WI 53703. (608)819-8777. **E-mail:** contact@madisonfrequency.com. **E-mail:** madisonfrequency@gmail.com. **Website:** www.madisonfrequency.com. "A live music venue and night club located in downtown Madison near the capitol square. We host a wide variety of live music seven nights a week, featuring local, regional, national, and international acts playing rock, punk, metal, bluegrass, jazz, and indie."

GEORGE'S MAJESTIC LOUNGE

519 W. Dickson St., Fayetteville AR 72701. (479)527-6618. **E-mail:** saxsafe@aol.com. **Website:** www.georgesmajesticlounge.com. **Contact:** Brian Crowne, owner/operator/booking; Harold Weities, general manager. "George's is perhaps best known for the incredible musicians that have graced our stages, bringing the best in local, regional, and national acts through our doors. Some artists of note that have performed at Georges through the years include Robert Cray, Leon Russell, Little River Band, Delbert McClinton, Eddie Money, Pat Green, Derek Trucks, Sam Bush, Tower of Power, Leftover Salmon, Bob Margolin, Chubby Carrier, Tommy Castro, Coco Montoya, Anthony Gomes, Bernard Allison, Michael Burks, Charlie Robison, Cross Canadian Ragweed, Jason Boland, Dark Star Orchestra, Steve Kimock, Martin Fierro, North Mississippi Allstars, Robert Randolph, David Lindley, Big Smith, Cate Brothers, Oteil Burbridge, and so many more. Music: rock, folk, alternative, country, bluegrass, punk.

THE GOLDEN FLEECE TAVERN

132 W. Loockerman St., Dover DE 19904. (302)674-1776. **E-mail:** goldenfleecetavern@gmail.com; info@goldenfleecetavern.com. **Website:** www.thegoldenfleecetavern.com. Music: rock, indie, classic rock, pop, alternative.

THE GRAMOPHONE

4243 Manchester Ave., St. Louis MO 63110. (314)531-5700. **E-mail:** info@thegramophonelive.com. **Website:** www.thegramophonelive.com. "The Gramophone features an eclectic schedule of live music and DJs in an intimate concert setting." Music: hip-hop, funk, soul, indie, rock, Americana.

GREAT AMERICAN MUSIC HALL

859 O'Farrell St., San Francisco CA 94109. (415)885-0750. **E-mail:** dana@slims-sf.com. **Website:** www.slimpresents.com. **Contact:** Dana Smith, booking. "The past three decades at the Great American Music Hall have been full of music, with artists ranging from Duke Ellington, Sarah Vaughan and Count Basie to Van Morrison, the Grateful Dead and Bobby McFerrin." Music: contemporary pop, indie, jazz, folk, rock, alternative, Americana.

THE GREAT NORTHERN BAR & GRILL

27 Central Ave., Whitefish MT 59937. (406)862-2816. **E-mail:** info@greatnorthernbar.com. **Website:** www.greatnorthernbar.com. "The Great Northern Bar & Grill is the premiere destination in the Flathead Valley for good food, good music, and good times." Music: rock, alternative.

GREAT SCOTT

1222 Commonwealth Ave., Allston MA 02134. (617)566-9014. E-mail: submissions@greatscott-boston.com. Website: www.greatscottboston.com. Music: rock, metal, alternative, indie.

✪ GREEK THEATRE

2700 N. Vermont Ave., Los Angeles CA 90027. (323)665-5857. Fax: (323)666-8202. E-mail: your-contact@greektheatrela.com. Website: www.greek-theatrela.com. Music: theatrical, pop, family, rock, ethnic, comedy, etc. In the last 2 years, has booked Bruce Springsteen, Dave Matthews Band, Crosby, Stills, Nash & Young, James Taylor, Journey, and more.

THE GREEN LANTERN

497 W. Third St., Lexington KY 40508. (859)252-9539. E-mail: greenlanternbooking@gmail.com. Website: https://greenlanternlexington.tumblr.com. "Making the best neighborhood bar in Lex a reality." Music: rock, alternative, indie, folk, punk, metal.

GUNPOWDER LODGE

10092 Bel Air Road, Kingsville MD 21087. (410)256-2626. Website: www.thegunpowderlodge.com. Music: rock, indie, acoustic, classic rock.

HAL & MAL'S

200 S. Commerce St., Jackson MS 39204. (601)948-0888. E-mail: jane@halandmals.com. Website: www.halandmals.com. Contact: Jane Halbert. "The most talked about, upscale honky tonk in all of Mississippi. Here, art is made, music is played and locals gather to share community and celebrate the very best of Mississippi's creative spirit." Music: honky-tonk, country, rock, blues, classic rock, alternative.

HANK'S CAFE

1038 Nuuanu Ave., Honolulu HI 96817. (808)526-1411. Website: www.hankscafehawaii.com. Music: rock, doo-wop, dance, country, pop.

THE HAVEN

6700 Aloma Ave., Winter Park FL 32792. (407)673-2712. E-mail: maniacal_mojo_records@yahoo.com. Website: www.thehavenrocks.com. Contact: John "Clint" Pinder. The Haven is a 350-plus capacity venue with a full-liquor bar located in the Aloma Square Shopping Center in Winter Park, FL. Music: Alternative, Classic Rock, Cover Band, Funk, Jam Band, Metal, Punk, Reggae, Rock, and Singer/Songwrit-er—all types of live music with local, regional and national bands, and most shows are age 18 and up. TIPS See House P.A., Stage and Lighting Specs, Mains, Monitors, Microphones, Stage Dimensions, and Lighting Specs at: www.thehavenrocks.com/specs/.

HEADLINERS MUSIC HALL

1386 Lexington Road, Louisville KY 40206. (502)584-8088. E-mail: booking@headlinerslouis-ville.com. Website: www.headlinerslouisville.com. "Locally owned and operated, Headliners Music Hall is the premiere live entertainment venue of Louisville, Kentucky. We bring the best local and national acts to our stage, with fantastic sound and a fun atmosphere. We've had the privilege of hosting some amazing rock, metal, acoustic, hip-hop, and alternative bands such as My Morning Jacket, Jimmy Eat World, Neko Case, Clutch, Sharon Jones & The Dap Kings, Umphrey's McGee, Old Crow Medicine Show, Kings of Leon, Talib Kweli, Girl Talk and more." Music: rock, indie, punk, folk, reggae, soul, R&B, psychedelic.

THE HIDEOUT

1354 W. Wabansia, Chicago IL 60642. (773)227-4433. Website: www.hideoutchicago.com. "The Hideout is music, art, performance, plays, poetry, rock and rebellion." Music: indie, folk, rock, alternative, country.

HIGHLANDS TAP ROOM

1279 Bardstown Road, Louisville KY 40204. (502)459-2337. E-mail: booking@highlandstaproom.com. Website: www.highlandstaproom.com. "Fun, friendly neighborhood bar in the heart of the Highlands, Louisville, KY. Live entertainment seven days a week." Music: rock, acoustic, hip-hop, folk, blues, bluegrass, alt-country.

HIGH-NOON SALOON

701A E. Washington Ave., Madison WI 53703. (608)268-1122. E-mail: info@high-noon.com. E-mail: booking@high-noon.com. Website: www.high-noon.com. Contact: Cathy Dethmers, owner/manager. "Founded in 2004 in downtown Madison, Wisconsin, High Noon Saloon is a live music venue that features many different styles of music, including rock, alternative, metal, indie, alt-country, pop, punk, bluegrass, folk, jam, world music, and more.

We host large national acts, smaller touring bands from around the world, and lots of local music."

HI-TONE CAFE

412-414 N Cleveland St., Memphis TN 38104. (901)725-9999. **E-mail:** thehitonecafe@gmail.com. **Website:** www.hitonememphis.com. **Contact:** Jonathan Kiersky, general manager/talent buyer. Music: rock, alternative, indie, pop, alt-country, Americana, psych, metal, hip-hop, rap.

HODI'S HALF NOTE

167 N. College Ave., Fort Collins CO 80524. (970)472-2034. **E-mail:** booking@hodishalfnote. com. **Website:** www.hodishalfnote.com. **Contact:** Eric Imbrosciano, talent buyer.

⊕ HOTEL CAFÈ

1623 1/2 N. Cahuenga Blvd., Los Angeles CA 90028. (323)461-2040. **E-mail:** booking@hotelcafe.com. **E-mail:** marko@hotelcafe.com. **Website:** www.hotelcafe.com. For booking, e-mail a link to your website or online press kit. Include where you are from, other places you've played in LA, and your current draw in the LA area. Allow up to several weeks for a response, and at least 1-2 months for a booking.

HOT TUNA

2817 Shore Dr., Virginia Beach VA 23451. (757)481-2888. **E-mail:** rstreet@hottunavb.com. **Website:** www.hottunavb.com. Music: rock, acoustic, alternative, dance, pop.

HOUSE OF ROCK

511 Starr St., Corpus Christi TX 78401. **E-mail:** casey@texashouseofrock.com.

TIPS House of Rock was established on July 28th, 2005 in the heart of downtown Corpus Christi. Since our early years we have supported a wide range of entertainment including live music, art shows and many other cultural events. In addition to entertainment, we host private events, corporate events and fundraisers.

HOWLER'S COYOTE CAFE

4509 Liberty Ave., Pittsburgh PA 15224. (412)682-0320. **E-mail:** booking@howlerscoyotecafe.com. **Website:** www.howlerscoyotecafe.com. "Howler's Coyote Cafe is an independent mid-level music venue and bar in Pittsburgh's east end hosting local and national acts of all genres 5 days a week." Music: rock, alternative, pop, dance, blues, alt-country, punk, jam, psychedelic, folk, indie.

HUMPY'S

610 W. Sixth Ave., Anchorage AK 99501. (907)276-2337. **Website:** www.humpys.com. Music: folk, rock, metal, blues, Americana.

JEREMIAH BULLFROGS LIVE

4115 SW Huntoon St., Topeka KS 66604. (785)273-0606. **E-mail:** bullfrogslive@gmail.com. **Website:** www.bullfrogslive.com. **Contact:** Rob Fateley. Music: blues, soul, rock, alternative, dance.

JUANITA'S PARTY ROOM

614 President Clinton Ave., Little Rock AR 72201. (501)372-1228; (501)681-7552. **E-mail:** jsnyder@juanitas.com. **Website:** www.juanitas.com. **Contact:** James Snyder, general manager. Music: rock, reggae, alternative, country, alt-country, indie.

KILBY COURT

741 S. Kilby Ct., Salt Lake City UT 84101. (801)364-3538. **E-mail:** will@sartainandsaunders.com. **Website:** www.kilbycourt.com. **Contact:** Will Sartain, owner/talent buyer. Music: rock, alternative, Americana, indie, pop, ska, punk.

KNICKERBOCKERS

901 O St., Lincoln NE 68508. (402)476-6865. **Fax:** (402)420-2787. **E-mail:** mail@knickerbockers.net. **Website:** www.knickerbockers.net. Music: alternative, rock, metal, punk, indie, folk, electronica, Americana.

LARIMER LOUNGE

2721 Larimer St., Denver CO 80205. (303)296-1003. **E-mail:** james@larimerlounge.com. **Website:** www.larimerlounge.com; www.booklarimer.com. **Contact:** James Irvine, booking manager. Music: rock, pop, electronica, indie, garage, alternative.

LAUNCHPAD

618 Central Ave. SW, Albuquerque NM 87102. (505)764-8887. **Website:** www.launchpadrocks.com. Music: rock, punk, reggae, alternative.

LEADBETTERS TAVERN

1639 Thames St., Baltimore MD 21231. (410)675-4794. **E-mail:** leadbetterstavern2@gmail.com. **Website:** www.leadbetterstavern.com. Music: blues, rock, soul, jazz, punk, alternative, funk, pop, indie.

LIQUID LOUNGE

405 S. 8th St. #110, Boise ID 83702. (208)287-5379. **E-mail:** liquidbooking@gmail.com. **Website:** www.

liquidboise.com. Music: rock, reggae, funk, ska, blue-grass, dance, soul, folk, punk.

THE LOFT

2506 W. Colorado Ave., #C, Colorado Springs CO 80904. (719)445-9278. **Website:** www.loftmusicvenue. com. "We are here to bring you the best musical experience in Colorado Springs with an intimate atmosphere, amazing sound and GREAT music. We hope you come often and tell your friends about our place." Music: rock, pop, country, acoustic, indie, blues, jazz, bluegrass, folk.

THE LOST LEAF BAR & GALLERY

914 N. Fifth St., Phoenix AZ 85004. (602)481-4004. **E-mail:** solnotes@hotmail.com. **Website:** www.the-lostleaf.org. **Contact:** Tato Caraveo. Music: Latin, blues, salsa, hip-hop, R&B, funk, outlaw country, Americana.

THE LOUNGE AT HOTEL DONALDSON

101 Broadway, Fargo ND 58102. (701)478-1000 or (888)478-8768. **E-mail:** info@hoteldonaldson.com. **Website:** www.hoteldonaldson.com. **Contact:** Karen Stoker, founder/owner. Music: Americana, folk, indie, country, bluegrass.

LOW SPIRITS

2823 2nd St. NW, Albuquerque NM 87107. (505)433-9555. **Website:** www.lowspiritslive.com. Music: rock, indie, blues, alternative, folk.

LUCKEY'S CLUB CIGAR STORE

933 Olive St., Eugene OR 97401. (541)687-4643. **Web-site:** www.luckeysclub.com. **Contact:** Sam Hahn. "Today, Luckey's combines art nouveau decor, saloon sensibilities, serious pool players, cutting edge music, and a chair for everyone in the community. It still has echoes of the sounds, smells, pool games, and conversations from the past 100 years. It's like a time capsule with a hip twist." Music: folk, acoustic, blues, indie, Americana, rock.

MAD ANTHONY BREWING COMPANY

2002 Broadway, Ft. Wayne IN 46802. (260)426-2537. **E-mail:** madbrew@msn.com. **Website:** www.mad-brew.com. "A cool, laid back atmosphere, full food menu and weekly live music." Music: rock, jam, jazz, blues, funk, soul, pop.

THE MAJESTIC/MAGIC STICK

4140 Woodward Ave., Detroit MI 48201. (313)833-9700. **E-mail:** dave@majesticdetroit.com; traci@ma-jesticdetroit.com. **E-mail:** booking@majesticdetroit. com. **Website:** www.majesticdetroit.com. **Contact:** Dave Zainea, owner/general manager; Traci Zainea, talent buyer. The Majestic Theatre is steeped in history, designed by C. Howard Crane, it opened in 1915 as the largest theatre in the world of their kind. Since the mid 80's, The Majestic Theatre has been the site of memorable concerts featuring live music and entertainment from touring indie rock, blues, jazz, folk, hip hop and worldbeat artists. The Majestic has produced shows for The Black Keys, George Clinton, Black Eyed Peas, Flaming Lips, Wilco, Sheryl Crow, Dr. John, Yo La Tengo, Patti Smith, Sublime, Matt & Kim, Drake, Fleet Foxes, Decemberists, Yeah Yeah Yeahs, Foster The People, Jimmy Cliff, 311, Sonic Youth, Fela Kuti, and many more.

MAJESTIC THEATRE

115 King St., Madison WI 53703. (608)255-0901. **E-mail:** info2013@majesticmadison.com. **Website:** www.majesticmadison.com. Estab. 1906. The Majestic Theatre is a world-class venue located in Madison, WI, that hosts major national touring acts. Seeks established local and regional acts to open for high-profile headlining acts. Music: Acoustic, Alternative, Americana, Classic Rock, Country, Electronic/Dance/DJ, Folk, Funk, Hip-Hop/Rap, Jam Band, Metal, Pop, Punk, Reggae, Rock, Singer/Songwriter, Spoken Word, and Urban/R&B.

TIPS Contact/submit online at website.

MANGY MOOSE RESTAURANT & SALOON, THE

PO Box 590, Teton Village WY 83025. (307)733-4913. **E-mail:** management@mangymoose.net. **E-mail:** booking@mangymoose.net. **Website:** www.mangy-moose.net. Music: funk, punk, electronica, indie, folk, rock, bluegrass.

MARTIN'S DOWNTOWN BAR & GRILL

413 First St. SW, Roanoke VA 24015. (540)985-6278. **E-mail:** booking@martinsdowntown.com. **E-mail:** jason@martinsdowntown.com. **Website:** www.mar-tinsdowntown.com. Estab. 2005. Music: rock, jam band, reggae, grass, funk, ska.

MAXWELL'S

1039 Washington St., Hoboken NJ 07030. (201)653-7777. **E-mail:** info@maxwellsnj.com. **Website:** www. maxwellsnj.com. Music: rock, alternative, blues, punk, indie.

MELODY INN

3826 N. Illinois St., Indianapolis IN 46208. (317)923-4707. **E-mail:** melodyinn2001@gmail.com. **Website:** www.melodyindy.com. Music: punk, rock, metal, indie, pop, rockabilly, bluegrass.

MEMPHIS ON MAIN

55 E. Main St., Champaign IL 61820. (217)398-1097. **E-mail:** info@memphisonmain.com. **Website:** www.memphisonmain.com. Music: rock, classic rock, R&B, blues, soul, funk, folk, country, metal, rockabilly, punk, reggae.

MERCURY LOUNGE

1747 S. Boston Ave., Tulsa OK 74119. (918)382-0012. **E-mail:** mercuryloungetulsa@gmail.com. **Website:** www.mercurylounge918.com. Music: country, alt-country, Americana, blues, jazz, rock, reggae, rockabilly, pop.

MERCY LOUNGE/CANNERY BALLROOM

One Cannery Row, Nashville TN 37203. (615)251-3020. **E-mail:** info@mercylounge.com. **E-mail:** booking@mercylounge.com. **Website:** www.mercylounge.com. **Contact:** Andrew Mischke and Todd Ohlhauser, managers. "Since the doors to the Mercy Lounge first opened back in January of 2003, the cozy little club on Cannery Row has been both locally-favored and nationally-renowned. Building a reputation for showcasing the best in burgeoning buzz-bands and renowned national talents, the club has maintained its relevance by consistently offering reliable atmosphere and entertainment." Music: pop, country, rock, folk, Americana, indie, funk, soul, psychedelic.

THE MET

1005 Main Sr., Pawtucket RI 02860. (401)729-1005. **E-mail:** info@themetri.com. **Website:** www.themetri.com. Music: rock, funk, folk, blues, soul, punk, alternative.

THE MIDDLE EAST NIGHTCLUB

472 Massachusetts Ave., Cambridge MA 02139. (617)864-3278. **E-mail:** downstairs@mideastclub.com. **Website:** www.mideastclub.com. Downstairs room capacity is 575. Upstairs is 195. Parking garage is attached to the Meridian Hotel. Music: funk, rock, alternative, dance, pop, hip-hop, punk, Americana.

MILLCREEK TAVERN

4200 Chester Ave., University City, Philadelphia PA 19104. (215)222-9194; (215)222-1255. **Website:** www.millcreektavernphilly.com.

MILLER THEATRE

Columbia University School of the Arts, 2960 Broadway, MC 1801, New York NY 10027. (212)854-6205. **Website:** www.millertheatre.com. **Contact:** Melissa Smey, Executive Director. "Miller Theatre's mission is to develop the next generation of cultural consumers, to reinvigorate public enthusiasm in the arts nationwide by pioneering new approaches to programming, to educate the public by presenting specialized, informative programs inviting to a broad audience, to discover new and diverse repertoire and commission new works, and to share Columbia University's intellectual riches with the public." Music: dance, contemporary and early music, jazz, opera, and performance.

MILLY'S TAVERN

500 Commercial St., Manchester NH 03101. (603)625-4444. **E-mail:** info@millystavern.com. **Website:** www.millystavern.com. "There is always something happening in our lounge. Whether it's from 4-7 pm, or all night, you are bound to have a good time. We offer live music every Tuesday, Thursday, Friday and Saturday." Music: blues, rock, retro, funk, dance.

✪ THE MINT

6010 W. Pico Blvd., Los Angeles CA 90035. (323)954-9400. **Fax:** (323)938-2994. **E-mail:** booking@themintla.com. **Website:** www.themintla.com.

MISSISSIPPI STUDIOS

3939 N. Mississippi, Portland OR 97227. (503)288-3895. **E-mail:** info@mississippistudios.com; matt@mississippistudios.com; katherine@mississippistudios.com. **E-mail:** booking@mississippistudios.com. **Website:** www.mississippistudios.com. **Contact:** Matt King, talent buyer; Katherine Paul, booking assistant. "Portland's premier concert venue, offering guests the best sound and an intimate concert experience." Music: indie, folk, rock, Americana, alternative, pop, blues.

✪ MOHAWK

912 Red River St., Austin TX 78701. (512)666-0877. **E-mail:** cody@mohawkaustin.com. **E-mail:** patrick@mohawkaustin.com. **Website:** www.mohawkaustin.com. **Contact:** Cody R Cowan, general manager; Patrick Waites, booking and events. Venue known for rock shows. Values creative expression,

originality, and work ethic. Contact Patrick Waites with mp3 links only to be considered for booking.

THE MOHAWK PLACE

47 E. Mohawk Place, Buffalo NY 14203. (716)465-2368. **E-mail:** buffalomohawk@gmail.com. **E-mail:** erikspicoli@gmail.com. **Website:** www.themohawkplace.com. **Contact:** Erik Roesser, in-house booking agent. Music: indie, rock, alternative, punk.

◐ "We book shows predominantly through e-mail. Contact Erik Roesser or Nicholas Heim to book a show. Please understand we get a high volume of e-mails daily. In most cases, local bands get priority. If we are interested we will get back to you."

MOJO 13

1706 Philadelphia Ave., Wilmington DE 19809. (302)798-5798. **E-mail:** mojo13booking@gmail.com. **Website:** www.mojothirteen.com. "We play host to local and touring music acts as well as a whole host of other forms of entertainment that cater to the rock and roll lifestyle. We're looking to become the home away from home for the alternative minded music community here in Delaware and beyond... so if you've got a band, are a musician, entertainer or just a fan...please join us." Music: punk, rock, alternative, indie.

THE MONKEY HOUSE

30 Main St., Winooski VT 05404. (802)655-4563. **E-mail:** monkeybarmusic@gmail.com. **Website:** www.monkeyhousemusic.com. Music: folk, indie, hard rock, punk, rock, alternative, Americana, funk, blues.

MOTR PUB

1345 Main St., Cincinnati OH 45202. (513)381-6687. **Website:** www.motrpub.com. Music: rock, alternative, folk, indie, Americana.

THE M ROOM

15 W. Girard Ave., Philadelphia PA 19123. (215)739-5577. **E-mail:** booking@mroomphilly.com. **Website:** www.mroomphilly.com. Music: blues, folk, soul, bluegrass, classic rock, rock, alt-country, pop, jazz, electronica, dance.

MUSE MUSIC CAFE

115 N. University Ave., Provo UT 84106. (801)377-6873. **Website:** www.musemusiccafe.com. **Contact:** Justin Hyatt; Colin Hatch, general managers. "The hub of Music, Art and Culture in Utah Valley." Music: rock, hard rock, hip-hop, electronica, indie, alternative, pop, Americana.

THE MUSIC HALL AT CAPITAL ALE HOUSE

623 E. Main St., Richmond VA 23219. (804)780-2537. **E-mail:** booking@capitalalehouse.com. **Website:** www.capitalalehouse.com. Music: indie, rock, jazz, blues, pop.

⊕ MUSIC HALL OF WILLIAMSBURG

The Bowery Presents, 66 N. 6th St., Brooklyn NY 11211. **E-mail:** info@bowerypresents.com. **Website:** www.musichallofwilliamsburg.com. **Contact:** Eddie Bruiser. The best way to get a show at a Bowery Presents club is to send your press pack to: The Bowery Presents, c/o Eddie Bruiser, 156 Ludlow St., New York, NY 10002. Please list a New York City show history and allow 4-6 weeks before following up with an e-mail.

NATASHA'S BISTRO & BAR

112 Esplanade Alley, Lexington KY 40507. (888)259-6873; (859)259-2754. **Website:** www.bistro.beetnik.com. "Natasha's has hosted a wide variety of acts, including jazz, rock, world, comedy, pop, country, Americana, folk, singer/songwriter, indie and blues. Over The Rhine, Punch Brothers, Vienna Teng, Sara Watkins, Michelle Shocked, Richard Shindell, Patty Larkin,and Nellie McKay have all played recently on our stage."

THE NATIONAL UNDERGROUND NYC

159 E. Houston Street, New York NY 10002. (212)475-0611. **E-mail:** newyorkbooking@thenationalunderground.com. **Website:** www.thenationalunderground.com. **Contact:** Neeka DeGraw. "Musican brothers Joey & Gavin DeGraw opened The National Underground to provide a home for New York City and the nation's best independent musicians to showcase their talents to an appreciative audience. Featuring live music seven days and nights a week on two floors, The National Underground has more live bands performing per week then any club in New York City. We are a throwback NYC Rock/Americana/Country venue. Celebrity appearances have included Joss Stone, Norah Jones, Moby, John Popper of Blues Traveler, Robert Randolph, Billy Joe Armstrong of Green Day, Ryan Reynolds, Scarlett Johannson and NASCAR driver Jimmie Johnson. "

NECTAR'S

188 Main St., Burlington VT 05401. (802)658-4771. **E-mail:** booking@liveatnectars.com. **Website:** www.liveatnectars.com. "A long-standing landmark on Main Street in Burlington, Nectar's restaurant and bar has been the headquarters for thousands of local (and not-so local) music acts. From Phish to Led Loco, from reggae to rock, Nectar's Bar and Lounge is THE place to see live music in downtown Burlington." Music: blues, Americana, folk, rock, alternative, punk, indie, jazz, pop, dance, funk, psychedelic.

NEUMOS

925 E. Pike St., Seattle WA 98122. (206)709-9442. **Fax:** (206)219-5644. **E-mail:** steven@neumos.com; jason@neumos.com; eli@neumos.com. **Website:** www.neumos.com. "The Concert Hall side of the business has always been our priority, and the lifeline to all other things that surround it. We pride ourselves on our always relevant and carefully curated music calendar, light production and state of the art sound system. The Concert Hall has 3 full service bars, and a second floor with a nicely seated mezzanine and balcony over looking the showroom. The showroom is fitted with an ample size stage, merch area, and superior unobstructed sight lines. We play host to several musical genres, by national and local artists alike including but not excluded to indie rock, hip-hop, punk rock, DJ's, metal, singer/songwriters, country and much more."

NEUROLUX

111 N. 11th St., Boise ID 83702. (208)343-0886. **Website:** www.neurolux.com. Music: funk, indie, rock, reggae, folk, country, bluegrass.

THE NICK ROCKS

2514 10th Ave. S, Birmingham AL 35205. (205)252-3831. **E-mail:** nolenreevesmusic@mindspring.com. **Website:** www.thenickrocks.com. **Contact:** Dan Nolen, talent buyer. "The music heard almost every night of the week include local, regional and national acts. The diverse range of acts add to the appeal of an evening at the Nick. One can hear blues, rock, punk, emo, pop, country, metal, bluegrass, rock-a-billy, roots rock or whatever your genre of choice. The Nick has had it all. It is an upclose and personal room voted three times in a row as Birmingham's best live music venue by Birmingham Weekly."

NIETZSCHE'S

248 Allen St., Buffalo NY 14201. (716)886-8539. **Website:** www.nietzsches.com. Call for information regarding booking. Music: blues, jazz, rock, alternative, funk, soul.

⊕ NORTHSIDE TAVERN

4163 Hamilton Ave., Cincinnati OH 45223. (513)542-3603. **E-mail:** northsidetavern@gmail.com. **E-mail:** eddienst@me.com. **Website:** www.northside-tavern.com. Neighborhood tavern and free, original, live music venue in Cincinnati.

NORTH STAR BAR & RESTAURANT

2639 Poplar St., Philadelphia PA 19130. (215)787-0488. **E-mail:** booking@sunnydaymusic.com. **Website:** www.northstarbar.com. Music: rock, indie, psychedelic, pop, funk, jam, ska, punk, alternative.

THE OLD ROCK HOUSE

1200 S. Seventh St., St. Louis MO 63104. (314)588-0505. **E-mail:** info@oldrockhouse.com. **Website:** www.oldrockhouse.com. **Contact:** Tim Weber, co-owner. Music: rock, indie, alternative, punk, folk, pop.

ONE TRICK PONY GRILL & TAPROOM

136 E. Fulton, Grand Rapids MI 49503. (616)235-7669. **E-mail:** thepony@onetrick.biz. **Website:** www.onetrick.biz. **Contact:** Dan Verhil, owner. Music: acoustic, rock, country, blues.

ON STAGE DRINKS & GRINDS

802 Kapahulu Ave., Honolulu HI 96816. (808)738-0004. **Website:** www.onstagedrinksandgrinds.com. "Onstage is our ultimate living room. A cool, "off the beaten path," fun & comfortable spot to hang & chill. Equipped with a stage area complete with sound system, guitars, congas, and drums. We feature live music, and at times, surprise jams by well-known local artists that pop in. A kind of neat, underground music scene." Music: blues, rock, Hawaiian, acoustic.

PARADISE ROCK CLUB

967 Commonwealth Ave., Boston MA 02115. (617)547-0620. **E-mail:** informationdise@crossroadspresents.com. **E-mail:** paradiserockclub@gmail.com. **Website:** www.crossroadspresents.com. **Contact:** Lee Zazofsky, general manager. Music: pop, reggae, alternative, rock, indie, punk, hip-hop, Americana.
TIPS "Booking is handled by Crossroads Presents."

PARAMOUNT CENTER FOR THE ARTS

518 STATE ST, Bristol TN 37620. (423)274-8920. E-mail: info@theparamountcenter.com. **Website:** www.theparamountcenter.com. Built in 1931 and restored to its original splendor in 1991, the Paramount continues to grow as the Mountain Empire's premier performing arts center. Listed on the National Register of Historic Places, the Paramount is an excellent example of the art deco motion picture palaces built in the late 1920's and early 30's. The restoration retained the Paramount's opulent, richly embellished interior. The original Venetian-styled murals and the art deco ambience were faithfully recreated. The auditorium holds 756.

PARISH

214 E. 6th Street, Austin TX 78701. **E-mail:** Austen@theparishaustin.com. **Website:** www.theparishaustin.com. **Contact:** Austen Bailey, director of entertainment/booking. Located in the heart of downtown Austin in the historic district of 6th Street, The Parish is arguably the best indoor live music venue in Austin that offers the highest quality production for artists and events alike. With a 450 capacity, The Parish has hosted musical legends such as Pete Townshend, Slash, and Perry Farrell as well as independent artists such as Grizzly Bear and Yeasayer. It is an all-genres venue that provides an intimate, live music experience for all music fans.

✚ PARISH UNDERGROUND

214-B E. 6th St., Austin TX 78701. (512)494-6078. E-mail: booking@parishunderground.com. **Website:** www.parishunderground.com. Parish Underground is a beautiful room located directly below the world-renowned venue, Parish (see separate listing). At night, patrons can enjoy a live performance on stage featuring the best local and national acts.

PETE'S CANDY STORE

709 Lorimer Street, Brooklyn NY 11211. **E-mail:** booking@petescandystore.com. **Website:** www.petescandystore.com.
TIPS "We listen to all submissions and contact those acts which we are planning on booking. This follow up may take from anywhere from a week to a month. We do not confirm submissions, nor follow up with acts which we are not planning on booking. Please do not contact us to see if we received your submission, as the volume is quite high. We prefer to receive links to websites with songs/videos. Please do not include

links to Myspace sites. PLEASE DO NOT SEND AUDIO FILES."

PJ'S LAGER HOUSE

1254 Michigan Ave., Detroit MI 48226. (313)961-4668. **E-mail:** info@pjslagerhouse.com. **E-mail:** lagerhousebooking@yahoo.com. **Website:** www.pjslagerhouse.com. "PJ's features the best of Detroit's original rock'n'roll. Up and coming and established acts along with a variety of touring bands occupy PJ's stage most nights." Music: rock, alternative, hard rock, pop, folk, indie, punk.

PLOUGH AND STARS

912 Massachusetts Ave., Cambridge MA 02139. (617)576-0032. **Website:** www.ploughandstars.com. "The Plough and Stars Irish pub and restaurant in Cambridge has become a favorite of locals and visitors alike. With it's warm cozy atmosphere and great music scene, The Plough has become a staple of the Cambridge community. There is live music nearly every night." Music: alternative, pop, rock, indie, psychedelic, acoustic, folk.

PLUSH

340 E. Sixth St., Tucson AZ 85705. (502)798-1298. E-mail: booking@plushtucson.com. **Website:** www.plushtucson.com. **Contact:** Kris Kerry. "Dynamic and comfy! Plush, yet affordable! Come hither and partake. PLUSH is dedicated to Tucson's live music scene. YES, we book 'em live! Talented local, regional, and national touring acts 5-7 nights a week. AND our rooms and sound system were designed to sound good and look good so you feeeeel good!" Music: rock, indie, garage, electronica, alt-country, rockabilly.

POSITIVE PIE

22 State St., Montpelier VT 05602. (802)229-0453. E-mail: info@positivepie.com. **E-mail:** music@positivepie.com. **Website:** www.positivepie.com. Music: hip-hop, pop, R&B.

THE POUR HOUSE

1977 Maybank Hwy., Charleston SC 29412. (843)571-4343. **E-mail:** alex@charlestonpourhouse.com. **Website:** www.charlestonpourhouse.com. **Contact:** Alex Harris, owner/booking. Music: bluegrass, classic rock, indie, rock, funk, folk, country.

THE QUARTER

2504 13th St., Gulfport MS 39501. (228)863-2650. E-mail: info@thequarterbar.com. **E-mail:** manager@thequarterbar.com. "Our goal is to provide the coast with live music up to 5 nights a week or more in a relaxing French Quarter-like atmosphere." Music: metal, pop, rock, country, blues, classic rock.

RECORD BAR

1020 Westport Road, Kansas City MO 64111. (816)753-5207. **E-mail:** booking@therecordbar.com. **Website:** www.therecordbar.com. "We strive to provide our guests with diverse live entertainment, special events and gourmet food in a comfortable atmosphere. You'll see the best of the Kansas City music scene, as well as nationally known touring artists." Music: rock, punk, indie, jazz, swing, folk, pop, alternative.

RED SQUARE

136 Church St., Burlington VT 05401. (802)859-8909. **E-mail:** info@redsquarevt.com; booking@redsquarevt.com. **Website:** www.redsquarevt.com. Music: jazz, blues, rock, reggae.

RHYTHM & BREWS

2308 4th St., Tuscaloosa AL 35401. (205)750-2992. **Website:** www.rhythmnbrews.com. "Rhythm & Brews first opened in Tuscaloosa, AL. The club has the reputation of being the premiere location for the best live bands in the region. From dance music to performances by Nashville recording artists, the music you find at Rhythm & Brews will please all. We are committed to bringing you a fun and friendly atmosphere by offering a wide variety of drinks, great service, and great entertainment." Music: pop, rock, country, blues.

RICK'S BAR

2721 Main Ave., Fargo ND 58103. (701)232-8356. **Fax:** (701)232-1095. **E-mail:** meghanc@ricks-bar.com. **Website:** www.ricks-bar.com. **Contact:** Meghan Carik. Music: rock, metal, alternative.

ROCK ISLAND LIVE

101 N. Rock Island, Wichita KS 67202. (316)303-9800. **E-mail:** rockislandlivemusic@gmail.com. **Website:** www.rockislandlive.tumblr.com. Music: rock, alternative, pop, indie, dance.

✚ ROCKWOOD MUSIC HALL

196 Allen St., New York NY 10002. (212)477-4155. **E-mail:** info@rockwoodmusichall.com. **Website:** www.rockwoodmusichall.com. Those interested in booking should send an e-mail with links to your web pages, official and social, audio and video. Do not include attachments, only links. Each submission is reviewed and responses are sent/if when there is an opening.

SAINT VITUS BAR

1120 MANHATTAN AVENUE, Brooklyn NY 11222. **E-mail:** saintvitusbar@gmail.com; bookingsaintvitusbar@gmail.com. **Website:** www.saintvitusbar.com. Saint Vitus, a gothic-themed bar in Greenpoint, Brooklyn, named after a Black Sabbath song, is actually a welcoming spot for downing cheap beers and listening to Pantera.

SAM BONDS GARAGE

407 Blair, Eugene OR 97405. (541)431-6603. **E-mail:** info@sambonds.com. **E-mail:** bondsbooking@hotmail.com. **Website:** www.sambonds.com. "Opened in 1995, we've strived to represent the uniqueness of the neighborhood with a warm, laid back atmosphere, always changing local and regional microbrew selection, a full bar, quality vittles and of course, one of the west coast's best places to see diverse local, regional and worldly entertainment on a nightly basis." Music: bluegrass, rock, Irish jam, funk, alternative, folk, Americana.

SANTA FE SOL

37 Fire Place, Santa Fe NM 87508. (505)474-7322. **Website:** www.solsantafelive.com. Music: rock, Mexicana, Latin, alternative.

SCHUBAS TAVERN

3159 N. Southport, Chicago IL 60657. (773)525-2508. **E-mail:** rucins@schubas.com. **Website:** www.schubas.com. Paul Massarro, production manager. **Contact:** Matt Rucins, talent buyer. Schubas presents a diverse line-up of live music seven nights a week. From Honky-Tonk to Indie Rock, from Americana to Jazz, from Pop to Country.

◗ Building is a brick and masonry neo-Gothic neighborhood landmark built in 1903.

TIPS "Have a confirmed show? Use the Media and Retail link on the website to help better promote your show. Advance your show with our Production Manager, Paul Massarro. Send any promotional materials (posters, cds, bios, photos) to Rob Jensen."

SHANK HALL

1434 N. Farewell Ave., Milwaukee WI 53202. (414)276-7288. **E-mail:** shank@wi.rr.com. **Website:** www.shankhall.com. Music: indie, rock, alternative, Americana, pop, folk, bluegrass.

THE SHED

15094 Mills Road, Gulfport MS 39503. (228)875-8577. **E-mail:** contact@theshedbbq.com. **E-mail:** booking@

theshedbbq.com. **Website:** www.theshedbbq.com. **Contact:** Brett Orrison, entertainment director. Music: blues, folk, country, bluegrass, rock, alternative.

SILVER DOLLAR

3439 Thorpe Constantine Ave., Charleston SC 29455. (843)580-6092. **Website:** www.charlestoncocktail.com/silverdollar.html. Music: rock, pop, dance, hiphop, R&B, funk.

THE SLOWDOWN

729 N. 14th St., Omaha NE 68102. (402)345-7569. **E-mail:** info@theslowdown.com. **Website:** www.theslowdown.com. Music: rock, indie, alternative, psychedelic, punk, folk, pop.

THE SMILING MOOSE

1306 E. Carson St., Pittsburgh PA 15203. (412)431-4668. **Website:** www.smiling-moose.com. Music: rock, alt-country, indie, country, acoustic, pop, garbage, funk, hip-hop, metal.

SMITH'S OLDE BAR

1578 Piedmont Ave., Atlanta GA 30307. (404)875-1522. **E-mail:** nolenreevesbooking@gmail.com. **Website:** www.smithsoldebar.com. **Contact:** Dan Nolen, talent buyer. "Smith's Olde Bar is an Atlanta institution, offering some of the best music to be found anywhere in the city. Our atmosphere is very relaxed, and you can find something good to eat and something fun to do almost every night." Music: rock, indie, punk, hip-hop, alternative, garage, bluegrass, reggae, jazz, funk.

THE SPACE

295 Treadwell St., New Haven CT 06514. (203)288-6400. **E-mail:** spacebooking@gmail.com. **Website:** www.thespacect.com. **Contact:** Steve Rodgers; Natalie Tuttle. "The Space (since 2003) exists to build a safe, positive community for people of all ages through music and the arts. Physically, we are a listening room venue located in an unlikely industrial park in a sleepy suburb of New Haven." Music: alternative, rock, blues, Latin, folk, pop, indie, dance, hip-hop, Americana.

THE SPANISH MOON

1109 Highland Road, Baton Rouge LA 70802. (225)383-6666. **E-mail:** moonbooking@hotmail.com. **Website:** www.thespanishmoon.com. **Contact:** Aaron Scruggs, talent buyer/booking manager. Music: rock, pop, dubstep, indie, alternative, Americana.

THE SPOT UNDERGROUND

101 Richmond St., Second Floor, Providence RI 02903. (401)383-7133. **E-mail:** 725@TheSpotProvidence.com. **E-mail:** thespotunderground@gmail.com. **Website:** www.thespotprovidence.com. Music: rock, indie, world, hip-hop, R&B, funk, dance, jam, pop.

STRANGE BREW TAVERN

88 Market St., Manchester NH 03101. (603)666-4292. **E-mail:** info@strangebrewtavern.net. **Website:** www.strangebrewtavern.net. Music: blues, acoustic, rock, alternative.

SULLY'S PUB

2701 Park St., Hartford CT 06106. (860)231-8881. **E-mail:** sully@sullyspub.com; rob@sullyspub.com. **Website:** www.sullyspub.com. **Contact:** Darrell "Sully" Sullivan, owner; Rob Salter, manager. "This mantra though is an important one in any community. Original Music must be supported on every level of society. Sully's is proud to stand on the front lines of musical evolution. Blazing a trail with the very musicians composing and performing." Music: pop, rock, alternative, indie.

THE BELL HOUSE

149 7th Street, Brooklyn NY 11215. (718)643-6510. **E-mail:** booking@thebellhouseny.com; info@thebellhouseny.com. **Website:** www.thebellhouseny.com. In the Fall of 2008, a 1920's warehouse was converted into The Bell House. Called "a welcome oasis" by TimeOut, The Bell House is a magnificent two-room music and events venue located in the Gowanus section of Brooklyn. The Main Room boasts 25-foot wooden arched ceilings, a 450-square foot stage, and unobstructed views from any part of the room.

THE CHANCE

6 Crannell Street, Poughkeepsie NY (845)471-1966. **E-mail:** info@thechancetheater.com. **Website:** www.thechancetheater.com. Built in 1912, The Chance Theater has had a long history as a performing arts venue and has welcomed legendary acts such as The Police, The Ramones, Muddy Waters, Pete Seeger and Charles Mingus.

THE WHITE RABBIT

(210)737-2221. **E-mail:** thewhiterabbit@yahoo.com. **Website:** www.sawhiterabbit.com. Located in San Antonio, Texas, The White Rabbit plays host to a mix of local, up-and-coming and nationally recognized acts and over the years, has become one of the city's premiere venues for live entertainment.

⊕ TIN ROOF

160 E. Freedom Way, Ste. 150, Cincinnati OH 45202. (513)381-2176. **Website:** www.tinroof.com. Tin Roof is a live music restaurant and bar with a laid-back atmosphere.

TOAD

1912 Massachusetts Ave., Cambridge MA 02140. (617)499-6992. **E-mail:** info@toadcambridge.com. **E-mail:** bookagig@toadcambridge.com. **Website:** www. toadcambridge.com. **Contact:** Billy BeaRoad "Toad is a small neighborhood bar and music club featuring live music seven nights a week." Music: folk, alternative, rock, acoustic, Americana, indie.

TRACTOR TAVERN

5213 Ballard Ave. NW, Seattle WA 98107. (206)789-3599. **E-mail:** schedule@tractortavern.com. **E-mail:** booking@tractortavern.com. **Website:** www.tractortavern.com. "The Tractor hosts live shows 5-7 nights a week featuring a wide range of local and national acts. Check out all of your favorite rock, alternative country, rockabilly, groove & psychedelia, celtic, cajun & zydeco, folk, blues, jazz, and bluegrass acts to name a few."

THE TREE BAR

887 Chambers Road, Columbus OH 43212. (614)725-0955. **Website:** www.treebarcolumbus.com. Music: rock, classic rock, alternative, indie, Americana, folk, pop.

TRIPLE CROWN

206 N. Edward Gary St., San Marcos TX 78666. (512)396-2236. **E-mail:** booking@triplecrownlive. com. **Website:** www.triplecrownlive.com. **Contact:** Eric Shaw. Music: rock, country, Americana, jazz, blues, bluegrass, punk, hip-hop, folk.

TRIPLE ROCK SOCIAL CLUB

629 Cedar Ave., Minneapolis MN 55454. (612)333-7399. **Fax:** (612)333-7703. **E-mail:** info@triplerocksocialclub.com. **E-mail:** booking@triplerocksocialclub. com. **Website:** www.triplerocksocialclub.com. Estab. 2003. The Triple Rock has become one of the big destination punk, indie rock and underground hip hop clubs in the Twin Cities—a good-sized music venue with a capacity of 400. The Triple Rock is owned and operated by the members of punk rock band Dillinger Four. Music: Acoustic, Alternative, Blues, Classic Rock, Country, Cover Band, Electronic/Dance/DJ, Folk, Funk, Goth, Hip-Hop/Rap, Jam Band, Metal, Pop, Punk, Reggae, Rock, Singer/Songwriter, Soul, and Urban/R&B.

TIPS To advance shows that have been confirmed, please e-mail: zartan@triplerocksocialclub.com.

TROCADERO

1003 Arch St., Philadelphia PA 19107. (215)922-6888. **E-mail:** trocadero@thetroc.com. **Website:** www.thetroc.com. Music: pop, indie, Americana, alternative, rock, hip-hop, rap, folk, bluegrass.

TROUBADOUR

9081 Santa Monica Blvd., West Hollywood CA 90069. (310)276-1158. **Website:** www.troubadour.com. Estab. 1958. "The Troubadour is rich with musical history. Elton John, Billy Joel, James Taylor and Joni Mitchell have all made debuts at the Troubadour. The legendary musical line-ups at the Troubadour continue til today. The Troubadour schedule features a wide arrangement of musical performances. Nada Surf, Bob Schneider, The Morning Benders and Manchester Orchestra were some of the performances featured on the Troubadour schedule for 2010." Music: pop, indie, alternative, rock, hip-hop, Americana, jazz, blues. ⊙ To contact use form online at www.www.troubadour.com/contact-booking/. See also lighting plot, stage layout, technical rider links at same site.

TURF CLUB

1601 University Ave. W, St. Paul MN 55104. (651)647-0486. **E-mail:** booking@turfclub.net. **Website:** www.turfclub.net. "Turf Club is a perfect setting for rock. The long, prominent bar scales one side of the narrow interior; the stage is at the back and the entire space is enveloped in dark woods. The music is loud, the crowd is devoted." Music: rock, indie, alternative, punk, classic rock.

THE UNDERGROUND

555 E. Fourth St., Reno NV 89512. (775)410-5993. **E-mail:** contact@renounderground.com. **Website:** www.renounderground.com. Use online booking forms. "The Underground is one of Reno's largest music venues and cannot be classified easily. Shows here range from all-ages top 40 parties, national, regional and local artist concerts. The music style varies wildly depending on the night, with shows ranging from hardcore to world beat, just about any other

VENUES

genre you can think of." Music: rock, alternative, pop, funk, hip-hop, Latin, World, acoustic, jazz, electronica, reggae, dubstep.

UNDERGROUND 119

119 S. President St., Jackson MS 39201. (601)352-2322. **E-mail:** underground119music@gmail.com. **E-mail:** booking@underground119.com. **Website:** www.underground119.com. **Contact:** Bill Ellison, entertainment director. Music: blues, jazz, bluegrass, country, funk, rock, alternative.

UNION POOL

484 Union Ave., Brooklyn NY 11211. (718)609-0484. **E-mail:** booking@union-pool.com. **Website:** www.union-pool.com. Music: rock, indie, alternative, Americana.

UPSTATE CONCERT HALL

1208 Rte 146, Clifton Park NY 12065. (518)371-0012. **Website:** www.upstateconcerthall.com.

TIPS To book your own show please e-mail: Dave@upstateconcerthall.com; To get booked on an existing bill please e-mail: Tetoll@nycap.rr.com.

URBAN LOUNGE

241 S. 500 E, Salt Lake City UT 84102. (801)824-1000. **E-mail:** will@sartainandsaunders.com. **Website:** www.theurbanloungeslc.com. **Contact:** Will Sartain. "The Urban Lounge has been a staple in the Salt Lake City, Utah music community for more than a decade. What started off as a local live music bar has flourished into a regular stop for headlining national acts-hosting a variety of music from independent artists of all genres including rock, hip hop, folk, electronic, reggae, experimental. Nearly every night of the week you can find a fresh take on a familiar scene."

VAUDEVILLE MEWS

212 Fourth St., Des Moines IA 50309. (515)243-3270. **E-mail:** info@vaudevillemews.com. **E-mail:** booking@vaudevillemews.com. **Website:** www.vaudevillemews.com. Music: folk, pop, blues, rock, alternative, Americana, hip-hop, soul, rap, country, hard rock, electronica.

THE VISULITE THEATRE

1615 Elizabeth Ave., Charlotte NC 28204. (704)358-9200. **Fax:** (704)258-9299. **E-mail:** info@visulite.com. **E-mail:** booking@visulite.com. **Website:** www.visulite.com. Music: rock, pop, funk, Americana, indie, blues, folk.

✚ THE WAY STATION

683 Washington Ave., Brooklyn NY 11238. (347)627-4949. **E-mail:** bookingtws@gmail.com. **Website:** www.waystationbk.blogspot.com. **Contact:** Andy Heidel, proprietor. For booking, send an e-mail with a short introduction and a link to hear your music or watch videos. Looking for one set of 40-45 minutes. Books 3 months in advance. If your band has already played at The Way Station, contact gailaheidel@yahoo.com with 2-3 dates to re-book.

THE WEBSTER UNDERGROUND

21 Webster St., Hartford CT 06114. (860)246-8001. **E-mail:** booking@webstertheater.com. **Website:** www.webstertheater.com. "The Main Theater is a great room for sizeable events or concerts. Book now and share the same stage that launched careers such as Staind, Marilyn Manson, Sevendust, Incubus, 311, Jay Z, Method Man, Godsmack, Fall Out Boy, and many more. The Underground is our intimate room equipped for shows and more- perfect for national, regional, locals that are looking to create their own show in a historic room." Music: rock, reggae, punk, alternative, pop, soul, indie, funk, hard rock.

WHISKY A GO-GO

8901 W. Sunset Blvd., West Hollywood CA 90069. (310)360-1110. **E-mail:** mproductionsrocks@gmail.com; booking@whiskyagogo.com. **Website:** www.whiskyagogo.com. **Contact:** Luke Iblings; Jake Perry; Cynthia Lempitsky. "As long as there has been a Los Angeles rock scene, there has been the Whisky A Go-Go. An anchor on the Sunset Strip since it's opening in 1964, the Whisky A Go-Go has played host to rock 'n' roll's most important bands, from the Doors, Janis Joplin, and Led Zeppelin to today's up and coming new artists." Music: hip-hop, rock, punk, metal, alternative, reggae, pop, classic rock, indie, Americana.

WHITE WATER TAVERN

2500 W. Seventh St., Little Rock AR 72205. (501)375-8400. **E-mail:** whitewaterbooking@gmail.com. **Website:** www.whitewatertavern.com. Music: rock, country, alternative, Americana, punk.

✚ THE WILTERN

3790 Wilshire Blvd., Los Angeles CA 90010. (800)653-8000; (213)388-1400. **Website:** www.thewiltern.net. Music: rock/pop.

THE WINCHESTER

12112 Madison Ave., Cleveland OH 44107. (216)226-5681. **E-mail:** jams@thewinchester.net. **Website:** www.thewinchester.net. Estab. 2002. Music: blues, jazz, prog, fusion, rock, classic rock, alternative, rockabilly, alt-country, bluegrass and swing/big band. The Winchester Music Hall is well known for featuring the best musicians both nationally and locally.

WOODLANDS TAVERN

1200 W. Third Ave., Columbus OH 43212. (614)299-4987 or (614)406-4799. **E-mail:** booking@woodlandstavern.com; promotions@woodlandstavern.com. **Website:** www.woodlandstavern.com. **Contact:** Paul Painter, booking. Music: bluegrass, acoustic, psychedelic, reggae, jam, funk, rock, classic rock, jazz, blues.

WORMY DOG SALOON

311 E. Sheridan Ave., Oklahoma City OK 73104. (405)601-6276. **E-mail:** booking@wormydog.com. **Website:** www.wormydog.com. Music: country, bluegrass, rock, Americana, rockabilly, folk.

YOUNG AVENUE DELI

2119 Young Ave., Memphis TN 38104. (901)278-0034 or (901)274-7080. **E-mail:** phillip@youngavenuedeli.com. **Website:** www.youngavenuedeli.com. **Contact:** Phillip Stroud. Music: rock, country, pop, folk.

STATE & PROVINCIAL GRANTS

///

Arts councils in the United States and Canada provide assistance to artists (including song-writers) in the form of fellowships or grants. These grants can be substantial and confer prestige upon recipients; however, **only state or province residents are eligible**. Because deadlines and available support vary annually, query first or check websites for updated guidelines.

UNITED STATES ARTS AGENCIES

ALABAMA STATE COUNCIL ON THE ARTS, 201 Monroe St., Montgomery, AL 36130-1800. (334)242-4076. Website: www.arts.state.al.us.

ALASKA STATE COUNCIL ON THE ARTS, 161 Klevin Street, Suite 102, Anchorage, AK 99508-1506. (907)269-6610 or (888)278-7424. E-mail: aksca.info@alaska.gov. Website: www.eed.state.ak.us/aksca.

ARIZONA COMMISSION ON THE ARTS, 417 W. Roosevelt St., Phoenix, AZ 85003-1326. (602)771-6501. E-mail: info@azarts.gov. Website: www.azarts.gov.

ARKANSAS ARTS COUNCIL, 323 Center Street, Suite 1500, Little Rock, AR 72201-2606. (501)324-9766. E-mail: info@arkansasarts.com. Website: www.arkansasarts.com.

CALIFORNIA ARTS COUNCIL, 1300 I St., Suite 930, Sacramento, CA 95814. (916)322-6555 or (800)201-6201. E-mail: info@arts.ca.gov. Website: www.cac.ca.gov.

COLORADO COUNCIL ON THE ARTS, 1625 Broadway, Suite 2700, Denver, CO 80202. (303)892-3802. E-mail: online form. Website: www.coloradocreativeindustries.org.

CONNECTICUT COMMISSION ON CULTURE & TOURISM, Arts Division, One Constitution Plaza, 755 Main St., Hartford, CT 06103. (860)256-2800. Website: www.cultureandtourism.org.

DELAWARE DIVISION OF THE ARTS, Carvel State Office Bldg., 4th Floor, 820 N. French St., Wilmington, DE 19801. (302)577-8278 (New Castle Co.) or (302)739-5304 (Kent or Sussex Counties). E-mail: delarts@state.de.us. Website: www.artsdel.org.

DISTRICT OF COLUMBIA COMMISSION ON THE ARTS & HUMANITIES, 200 I Street, SE, Washington, DC 20003. (202)724-5613. E-mail: cah@dc.gov. Website: www.dcarts.dc.gov.

FLORIDA COUNCIL ON ARTS AND CULTURE, Florida Division of Cultural Affairs, 329 North Meridian Street, Tallahassee, FL 32308. (850)245-6470. E-mail: info@florida-arts.org. Website: www.florida-arts.org.

GEORGIA COUNCIL FOR THE ARTS, 75 Fifth Street, NW, Suite 1200, Atlanta, GA 30308. (404)685-2787. E-mail: gaarts@gaarts.org. Website: www.gaarts.org.

GUAM COUNCIL ON THE ARTS & HUMANITIES AGENCY, P.O. Box 2950, Hagatna GU 96932. (671)646-2781. Website: www.guamcaha.net.

HAWAII STATE FOUNDATION ON CULTURE & THE ARTS, 2500 S. Hotel St., 2nd Floor, Honolulu, HI 96813. (808)586-0300. Website: http.hawaii.gov/sfca.

IDAHO COMMISSION ON THE ARTS, 2410 N. Old Penitentiary Road, Boise, ID 83712. (208)334-2119 or (800)278-3863. E-mail: info@arts.idaho.gov. Website: www.arts.idaho.gov.

ILLINOIS ARTS COUNCIL, James R. Thompson Center, 100 W. Randolph, Suite 10-500, Chicago, IL 60601. (312)814-6750. E-mail: iac.info@illinois.gov. Website: www.arts.illinois.gov.

INDIANA ARTS COMMISSION, 100 North Senate Avenue, Room N505, Indianapolis, IN 46204. (317)232-1268. E-mail: IndianaArtsCommission@iac.in.gov. Website: www.in.gov/arts.

IOWA ARTS COUNCIL, 600 E. Locust, Des Moines, IA 50319-0290. (515)242-6194. Website: www.iowaartscouncil.org.

KANSAS CITY - ARTSKC - REGIONAL ARTS COUNCIL, 906 Grand, Suite 10B, Kansas City, MO 64106. (816)221-1777. Website: www.artsks.org.

KENTUCKY ARTS COUNCIL, 21st Floor, Capital Plaza Tower, 500 Mero St., Frankfort, KY 40601-1987. (888)833-2787. E-mail: kyarts@ky.gov. Website: www.artscouncil.ky.gov.

LOUISIANA DIVISION OF THE ARTS, Capitol Annex Bldg., 1051 N. 3rd St., 4th Floor, Room #420, Baton Rouge, LA 70804. (225)342-8180. Website: www.crt.louisiana.gov/cultural-development/arts/index.

MAINE ARTS COMMISSION, 193 State St., 25 State House Station, Augusta, ME 04333-0025. (207)287-2724. E-mail: MaineArts.info@maine.gov. Website: www.mainearts.maine.gov.

MARYLAND STATE ARTS COUNCIL, 175 W. Ostend St., Suite E, Baltimore, MD 21230. (410)767-6555. E-mail: msac@msac.org. Website: www.msac.org.

MASSACHUSETTS CULTURAL COUNCIL, 10 St. James Ave., 3rd Floor, Boston, MA 02116-3803. (617)727-3668. E-mail: mcc@art.state.ma.us. Website: www.massculturalcouncil.org.

MICHIGAN COUNCIL FOR ARTS AND CULTURAL AFFAIRS, 300 N. Washington Square, Lansing, MI, 48913. (888)522-0103. E-mail: Online form. Website: www.michiganbusiness.org/community/council-arts-cultural-affairs.

MINNESOTA STATE ARTS BOARD, Park Square Court, 400 Sibley St., Suite 200, St. Paul, MN 55101-1928. (651)215-1600 or (800)866-2787. E-mail: msab@arts.state.mn.us. Website: www.arts.state.mn.us.

MISSISSIPPI ARTS COMMISSION, 501 N. West St., Suite 701B, Woolfolk Bldg., Jackson, MS 39201. (601)359-6030. Website: www.arts.state.ms.us.

MISSOURI ARTS COUNCIL, 815 Olive St., Suite 16, St. Louis, MO 63101-1503. (314)340-6845 or (866)407-4752. E-mail: moarts@ded.mo.gov. Website: www.missouriartscouncil.org.

MONTANA ARTS COUNCIL, PO Box 202201, Helena MT 59620-2201. (406)444-6430. E-mail: mac@mt.gov. Website: www.art.mt.gov.

NATIONAL ASSEMBLY OF STATE ARTS AGENCIES, 1029 Vermont Ave. NW, 2nd Floor, Washington, DC 20005. (202)347-6352. E-mail: nasaa@nasaa-arts.org. Website: www.nasaa-arts.org.

NEBRASKA ARTS COUNCIL, 1004 Farnam St., Plaza Level, Omaha, NE 68102. (402)595-2122 or (800)341-4067. Website: www.nebraskaartscouncil.org.

NEVADA ARTS COUNCIL, 716 N. Carson St., Suite A, Carson City, NV 89701. (775)687-6680. E-mail: infonvartscouncil@nevadaculture.org. Website: www.nac.nevadaculture.org.

NEW HAMPSHIRE STATE COUNCIL ON THE ARTS, 19 Pillsbury Street, 1st Floor, Concord, NH 03301. (603)271-2789. Website: www.nh.gov/nharts.

NEW JERSEY STATE COUNCIL ON THE ARTS, 225 W. State St., P.O. Box 306, Trenton, NJ 08625-0306. (609)292-6130. Website: www.artscouncil.nj.gov.

NEW MEXICO ARTS, Bataan Memorial Building, 407 Galisteo St. Suite 270, Santa Fe, NM 87501. (505)827-6490 or (800)879-4278. Website: www.nmarts.org.

NEW YORK STATE COUNCIL ON THE ARTS, 300 Park Ave. South, 10th Floor, New York, NY 10010. (212)459-8800. Website: www.nysca.org.

NORTH CAROLINA ARTS COUNCIL, 109 East Jones St., Cultural Resources Building, Raleigh, NC 27601. (919)807-6500. E-mail: ncarts@ncdcr.gov. Website: www.ncarts.org.

NORTH DAKOTA COUNCIL ON THE ARTS, 1600 E. Century Ave., Suite 6, Bismarck, ND 58503. (701)328-7590. Website: www.nd.gov/arts.

COMMONWEALTH COUNCIL FOR ARTS AND CULTURE (NORTHERN MARIANA ISLANDS), P.O. Box 5553, CHRB, Saipan, MP 96950. (670)322-9982 or (670)322-9983. E-mail: galaidi@vzpacifica.net. Website: www.geocities.com/ccacarts/ccacwebsite.html.

OHIO ARTS COUNCIL, 30 East broad Street, 33rd Floor, Columbus, OH 43215-3414. (614)466-2613. Website: www.oac.state.oh.us.

OKLAHOMA ARTS COUNCIL, Jim Thorpe Building, 2101 N. Lincoln Blvd., Suite 640, Oklahoma City, OK 73105. (405)521-2931. E-mail: okarts@arts.ok.gov. Website: www.arts.ok.gov.

OREGON ARTS COMMISSION, 775 Summer St. NE, Suite 200, Salem, OR 97301-1280. (503)986-0082. E-mail: oregon.artscomm@state.or.us. Website: www.oregonartscommission.org.

PENNSYLVANIA COUNCIL ON THE ARTS, 216 Finance Bldg., Harrisburg, PA 17120. (717)787-6883. Website: www.pacouncilonthearts.org.

INSTITUTE OF PUERTO RICAN CULTURE, E-mail: info@IPRAC.org. Website: www.iprac.org.

RHODE ISLAND STATE COUNCIL ON THE ARTS, One Capitol Hill, Third Floor, Providence, RI 02908. (401)222-3880. E-mail: info@arts.ri.gov. Website: www.arts.ri.gov.

SOUTH CAROLINA ARTS COMMISSION, 1800 Gervais St., Columbia, SC 29201. (803)734-8696. E-mail: info@arts.sc.gov. Website: www.southcarolinaarts.com.

SOUTH DAKOTA ARTS COUNCIL, 711 E. Wells Ave., Pierre, SD 57501-3369. (605)773-3301. E-mail: sdac@state.sd.us. Website: www.artscouncil.sd.gov.

TENNESSEE ARTS COMMISSION, 401 Charlotte Ave., Nashville, TN 37243-0780. (615)741-1701. Website: www.tn.gov/arts.

TEXAS COMMISSION ON THE ARTS, E.O. Thompson Office Building, 920 Colorado, Suite 501, Austin TX 78701. (512)463-5535. E-mail: front.desk@arts.state.tx.us. Website: www.arts.texas.gov.

UTAH DIVISION OF ARTS AND MUSEUMS, 617 E. South Temple, Salt Lake City, UT 84102-1177. (801)236-7555. Website: www.heritage.utah.gov/utah-division-of-arts-museums.

VERMONT ARTS COUNCIL, 136 State St., Drawer 33, Montpelier, VT 05633-6001. (802)828-3291. E-mail: online form. Website: www.vermontartscouncil.org.

VIRGIN ISLANDS COUNCIL ON THE ARTS, 5070 Norre Gade, St. Thomas, VI 00802-6872. (340)774-5984. Website: www.vicouncilonarts.org.

VIRGINIA COMMISSION FOR THE ARTS, 1001 East Broad Street, Suite 330, Richmond, VA 23219. (804)225-3132. E-mail: arts@arts.virginia.gov. Website: www.arts.virginia.gov.

WASHINGTON STATE ARTS COMMISSION, P.O. Box 42675, Olympia, WA 98504-2675. (360)753-3860. E-mail: online form Website: www.arts.wa.gov.

WEST VIRGINIA COMMISSION ON THE ARTS, The Cultural Center, Capitol Complex, 1900 Kanawha Blvd. E., Charleston, WV 25305-0300. (304)558-0220. Website: www.wvculture.org/arts.

WISCONSIN ARTS BOARD, PO Box 8690, Madison, WI 53708-8690. (608)266-0190. E-mail: artsboard@wisconsin.gov. Website: www.artsboaRoadwisconsin.gov.

WYOMING ARTS COUNCIL, 2320 Capitol Ave., Cheyenne, WY 82002. (307)777-7742. E-mail: online form. Website: www.wyoarts.state.wy.us.

CANADIAN PROVINCIAL ARTS AGENCIES

ALBERTA FOUNDATION FOR THE ARTS, 10708-105 Ave., Edmonton, AB T5H 0A1. (780)427-9968. E-mail: online form. Website: www.affta.ab.ca.

BRITISH COLUMBIA ARTS COUNCIL, P.O. Box 9819, Stn. Prov. Govt., Victoria, BC V8W 9W3. (250)356-1718. E-mail: BCArtsCouncil@gov.bc.ca. Website: www.bcartscouncil.ca.

THE CANADA COUNCIL FOR THE ARTS, 150 Elgin St., P.O. Box 1047, Ottawa, ON K1P 5V8. (613)566-4414 or (800)263-5588 (within Canada). E-mail: info@canadacouncil.ca. Website: www.canadacouncil.ca.

MANITOBA ARTS COUNCIL, 525-93 Lombard Ave., Winnipeg, MB R3B 3B1. (204)945-2237 or (866)994-2787 (in Manitoba). E-mail: info@artscouncil.mb.ca. Website: www.artscouncil.mb.ca.

NEW BRUNSWICK ARTS BOARD (NBAB), 634 Queen St., Suite 300, Fredericton, NB E3B 1C2. (506)444-4444 or (866)460-2787. Website: www.artsnb.ca.

NEWFOUNDLAND & LABRADOR ARTS COUNCIL, P.O. Box 98, St. John's, NL A1C 5H5. (709)726-2212 or (866)726-2212. E-mail: nlacmail@nlac.ca. Website: www.nlac.ca.

NOVA SCOTIA DEPARTMENT OF TOURISM, CULTURE, AND HERITAGE, 1741 Brunswick St., 3rd Floor, P. O. Box 456, STN Central, Halifax, NS B3J 2R5. (902)424-5000. Website: www.cch. novascotia.ca.

ONTARIO ARTS COUNCIL, 151 Bloor St. W., 5th Floor, Toronto, ON M5S 1T6. (416)961-1660 or (800)387-0058 (in Ontario). E-mail: info@arts.on.ca. Website: www.arts.on.ca.

PRINCE EDWARD ISLAND COUNCIL OF THE ARTS, 115 Richmond St., Charlottetown, PE C1A 1H7. (902)368-4410 or (888)734-2784. E-mail: info@peiartscouncil.com. Website: www. peiartscouncil.com.

QUÉBEC COUNCIL FOR ARTS & LITERATURE, 79 boul. René-Lévesque Est, 3e étage, Québec, QC G1R 5N5. (418)643-1707 or (800)897-1707. E-mail: info@calq.gouv.qc.ca. Website: www. calq. gouv.qc.ca.

THE SASKATCHEWAN ARTS BOARD, 1355 Broad St., Regina, SK S4R 7V1. (306)787-4056 or (800)667-7526 (Saskatchewan only). E-mail: sab@artsboaRoadsk.ca. Website: www.arts-boaRoadsk.ca.

YUKON ARTS FUNDING PROGRAM, Cultural Services Branch, Dept. of Tourism & Culture, Government of Yukon, Box 2703 (L-3), Whitehorse, YT Y1A 2C6. (867)667-8589 or (800)661-0408 (in Yukon). E-mail: arts@gov.yk.ca. Website: www.tc.gov.yk.ca/216.html.

PUBLICATIONS OF INTEREST

Knowledge about the music industry is essential for both creative and business success, and staying informed requires keeping up with constantly changing information. Updates on the evolving trends in the music business are available to you in the form of music magazines, music trade papers, and books. There is a publication aimed at almost every type of musician, songwriter, and music fan, from the most technical knowledge of amplification systems to gossip about your favorite singer. These publications can enlighten and inspire you, and provide information vital in helping you become a more well-rounded, educated, and, ultimately, successful musical artist.

What follows is a cross-section of all types of magazines and books you may find interesting. From songwriters' newsletters and glossy music magazines to tip sheets and how-to books, there should be something listed here that you'll enjoy and benefit from.

PERIODICALS

ALTERNATIVE PRESS, 1305 West 80th Street, Suite 214, Cleveland, OH 44102-3045. (216)631-1510. E-mail: subscriptions@altpress.com. Website: http://altpress.com. *Reviews, news, and features for alternative and indie music fans.*

AMERICAN SONGWRITER MAGAZINE, 113 19th Avenue South Nashville, TN 37203. (615)321-6096. E-mail: info@americansongwriter.com. Website: www.americansongwriter.com. *Bimonthly publication for and about songwriters.*

ARTROCKER MAGAZINE, 43 Chute House, Stockwell Park Road, Brixton, SW9 0DW. (216)631-1510. E-mail: info@artrockermagazine.com. Website: http://artrockermagazine.com. *Monthly magazine involved in music promotion and publishing.*

BACK STAGE (NYC), 770 Broadway, 15th Floor, New York, NY 10003. (212)493-4420.

BACK STAGE (LA), 5055 Wilshire Blvd., Los Angeles, CA 90036. (323)525-2358 or (800)745-8922. Website: www.backstage.com. *Weekly East and West Coast performing-artist trade papers.*

BASS PLAYER, 28 E. 28 St., 12th Floor, New York, NY 10016. (800)234-1831. E-mail: bassplayer@ neodata.com. Website: www.bassplayer.com. *Monthly magazine for bass players with lessons, interviews, articles, and transcriptions.*

BILLBOARD, 770 Broadway, 7th Floor, New York, NY 10003. (800)684-1873. E-mail: subscriptions@billboaRoadbiz. Website: www.billboaRoadcom. *Weekly industry trade magazine.*

CANADIAN MUSICIAN, 23 Hannover Dr., Suite 7, St. Catharines, ON L2W 1A3 Canada. (877)746-4692. Website: www.canadianmusician.com. *Bimonthly publication for amateur and professional Canadian musicians.*

CCM MAGAZINE, 402 BNA Drive, Suite 400, Nashville, TN 37217. (800)527-5226. E-mail: online form. Website: www.ccmagazine.com. *Online magazine focusing on Christian singers and performers.*

CHART ATTACK, 200-41 Britain St., Toronto, ON M5A 1R7 Canada. (416)363-3101. E-mail: hello@chartattack.com. Website: www.chartattack.com. *Monthly magazine covering the Canadian and international music scenes.*

CMJ NEW MUSIC REPORT/CMJ NEW MUSIC MONTHLY, 151 W. 25th St., 12 Floor, New York, NY 10001. (917)606-1908. Website: www.cmj.com. *Weekly college radio and alternative music tip sheet.*

COUNTRY LINE MAGAZINE, 16150 S. IH-35, Buda, TX 78610. (512)295-8400. E-mail: editor@ countrylinemagazine.com. Website: www.countrylinemagazine.com. *Monthly Texas-only country music cowboy and lifestyle magazine.*

ENTERTAINMENT LAW & FINANCE, Website: www.lawjournalnewsletters.com/ljn_entertainment. *Monthly newsletter covering music industry contracts, lawsuit filings, court rulings, and legislation.*

EXCLAIM!, 7849A Bloor St. W., Toronto, ON M6G 1M3 Canada. (416)535-9735. E-mail: exclaim@exclaim.ca. Website: www.exclaim.ca. *Canadian music monthly covering all genres of non-mainstream music.*

FAST FORWARD, Disc Makers, 7905 N. Rt. 130, Pennsauken, NJ 08110-1402. (800)468-9353. Website: www.discmakers.com/music/ffwd. *Quarterly newsletter featuring companies and products for performing and recording artists in the independent music industry. Provides custom CD and DVD packaging and promotional materials.*

GAMUT: ONLINE JOURNAL OF MUSIC THOERY, Website: http://trace.tennessee.edu/gamut. *Peer-reviewed online journal of the Music Theory Society of the Mid-Atlantic. A journal of criticism, commentary, research, and scholarship.*

GUITAR PLAYER, P.O Box 469073 Escondido, CA 92046. (800)289-9839. Website: www.guitar-player.com. *Monthly guitar magazine with transcriptions, columns, and interviews, including occasional articles on songwriting.*

JAZZTIMES, 8737 10801 Margate Road, Silver Spring, MD 20910-3921. (617)315-9155. Website: www.jazztimes.com. *10 issues/year magazine covering the American jazz scene.*

MOJO, 189 Shaftesbury Avenue, London, WC2H 8JG. Website: www.mojo4music.com. E-mail: MOJO@bauermedia.co.uk. *Monthly UK maagzine focusing on classic rock acts as well as emerging rock and indie bands.*

MUSIC CONNECTION MAGAZINE, Website: www.musicconnection.com. *Monthy music industry trade publication.*

MUSIC ROW MAGAZINE, 1231 17th Ave. S, Nashville, TN 37212. (615)349-2171. E-mail: info@musicrow.com. Website: www.musicrow.com. *Biweekly Nashville industry publication.*

MUSIC WEEK, Suncourt House, 18-26 Essex Road, Islington, London, UK N1 8LN. Website: www.musicweek.com. *UK industry publication with music news, data, analysis, and opinions.*

NEW MUSICAL EXPRESS (NME), NME, 9th Floor, Blue Fin Building, London, UK SE1 0SU. Website: www.nme.com. *UK weekly publication of music journalism.*

OFFBEAT MAGAZINE, 421 Frenchman St., Suite 200, New Orleans, LA 70116. (504)944-4300. E-mail: offbeat@offbeat.com. Website: www.offbeat.com. *Monthly magazine covering Louisiana music and artists.*

PERFORMER MAGAZINE, PO Box 348, Somerville, MA 02143. E-mail: editorial@performermag.com. (617) 627-9200. Website: www.performermag.com. *Focuses on independent musicians, those unsigned and on small labels, and their success in a DIY environment.*

THE PERFORMING SONGWRITER, Performing Songwriter Enterprises, LLC P.O. Box 158989, Nashville, TN 37215. (800)883-7664. E-mail: order@performingsongwriter.com. Website: www.performingsongwriter.com. *Bimonthly songwriters' magazine.*

SING OUT!, P.O. Box 5460, Bethlehem, PA 18015. (888)SING-OUT. Fax: (215)895-3052. E-mail: info@singout.org. Website: www.singout.org. *Quarterly folk music magazine.*

SONG CAST, Song Cast Distribution, 2926 State Road, Suite 111, Cuyahoga Falls, OH 44223. E-mail: info@songcastmusic.com. Offers assistance selling music through online retail sites like iTunes or Amazon.

SONGLINK INTERNATIONAL, 23 Belsize Crescent, London NW3 5QY England. +44 (0) 207-794-2540. Fax: +44(0)207-794-7393. Website: www.songlink.com. *10 issues/year newsletter including details of recording artists looking for songs; contact details for industry sources; also news and features on the music business.*

SOUND ON SOUND, Media House, Trafalgar Way, Bar Hill, Cambridge, CB23 8SQ, UK. +44 (0)1954 789888. Website: www.soundonsound.com. *Monthly music technology magazine with online forum.*

VARIETY, 5700 Wilshire Blvd., Suite 120, Los Angeles CA 90036. (323)857-6600. Fax: (323)857-0494. Website: www.variety.com. *Weekly entertainment trade newspaper.*

WORDS AND MUSIC, 41 Valleybrook Dr., Toronto ON M3B 2S6 Canada. (416)445-8700. Website: www.socan.ca. *Monthly songwriters' magazine.*

BOOKS & DIRECTORIES

1000 SONGWRITING IDEAS: MUSIC PRO GUIDES, by Lisa Aschmann, Hal Leonard Corporation, P.O. Box 13819, Milwaukee, WI 53213. (415)947-6615. E-mail: books@musicplayer.com. Website: www.halleonardbooks.com.

101 SONGWRITING WRONGS & HOW TO RIGHT THEM, by Pat & Pete Luboff, Writer's Digest Books, 10151 Carver Road, Suite. 200, Blue Ash, OH 45242. (800)448-0915. Website: www.writersdigest.com.

THE A&R REGISTRY, by Ritch Esra, SRS Publishing, 7510 Sunset Blvd. #1041, Los Angeles, CA 90046-3418. (800)377-7411 or (800)552-7411. E-mail: musicregistry@compuserve.com.

THE BILLBOARD GUIDE TO MUSIC PUBLICITY, rev. ed., by Jim Pettigrew, Jr., Billboard Books, 1745 Broadway, New York, NY 10019. (212)782-9000.

BREAKIN' INTO NASHVILLE, by Jennifer Ember Pierce, Madison Books, University Press of America, 4501 Forbes Road, Suite 200, Lanham, MD 20706. (800)462-6420.

CMJ DIRECTORY, 1201 Broadway, Suite 706, New York, NY 10001. (917)591-4661. Website: www.cmj.com.

THE CRAFT AND BUSINESS OF SONGWRITING, by John Braheny, Writer's Digest Books, 10151 Carver Road, Suite. 200, Blue Ash, OH 45242. (800)448-0915. Website: www.writersdigest.com.

THE CRAFT OF LYRIC WRITING, by Sheila Davis, Writer's Digest Books, 10151 Carver Road, Suite. 200, Blue Ash, OH 45242 (800)448-0915. Website: www.writersdigest.com.

DISC MAKERS, by Jason Ojalvo, Disc Makers, 7905 N. Rt. 130, Pennsauken, NJ 08110. (800)468-9353. E-mail: discman@discmakers.com. Website: www.discmakers.com.

HOLLYWOOD CREATIVE DIRECTORY, 3000 W. Olympic Blvd. #2525, Santa Monica, CA 90404. (800)815-0503. Website: www.hcdonline.com. *Lists producers in film and TV.*

THE HOLLYWOOD REPORTER, The Writers Store, 3510 West Magnolia Blvd., Burbank, CA, 91505. (800)272-8927. Website: www.hollywoodreporter.com.

HOW TO GET SOMEWHERE IN THE MUSIC BUSINESS FROM NOWHERE WITH NOTHING, by Mary Dawson, CQK Books, CQK Music Group, 2221 Justin Road, Suite 119-142, Flower Mound, TX 75028. (972)317-2720. Fax: (972)317-4737. Website: www.FromNowhereWithNothing.com.

HOW TO PROMOTE YOUR MUSIC SUCCESSFULLY ON THE INTERNET, by David Nevue, Midnight Rain Productions, 228 Stags Leap Ct., Eugene, OR 97402. (541741-3262. Website: www.rain-music.com.

HOW TO MAKE IT IN THE NEW MUSIC BUSINESS: LESSONS, TIPS, AND INSPIRATIONS FROM MUSIC'S BIGGEST AND BEST, by Robert Wolff, Billboard Books, 1745 Broadway, New York, NY 10019. (212)782-9000.. Website: www.billboaRoadcom.

HOW YOU CAN BREAK INTO THE MUSIC BUSINESS: WITHOUT BREAKING YOUR HEART, YOUR DREAM, OR YOUR BANK ACCOUNT, by Marty Garrett, Lonesome Wind Corporation, (800)210-4416.

LOUISIANA MUSIC DIRECTORY, OffBeat, Inc., 421 Frenchmen St., Suite 200, New Orleans, LA 70116. (504)944-4300. Website: www.offbeat.com.

LYDIAN CHROMATIC CONCEPT OF TONAL ORGANIZATION, VOLUME ONE: THE ART AND SCIENCE OF TONAL GRAVITY, by George Russell, Concept Publishing Company, 258 Harvard St., #296, Brookline, MA 02446-2904. E-mail: lydconcept@aol.com. Website: www.lydianchromaticconcept.com.

MELODY IN SONGWRITING, by Jack Perricone, Berklee Press, 1140 Boylston St., Boston, MA 02215. (617)747-2146. E-mail: info@berkleepress.com. Website: www.berkleepress.com.

MUSIC ATTORNEY LEGAL & BUSINESS AFFAIRS REGISTRY, by Ritch Esra and Steve Trumbull, SRS Publishing, 7510 Sunset Blvd. #1041, Los Angeles, CA 90046-3418. (800)552-7411. E-mail: musicregistry@compuserve.com or srspubl@aol.com.

THE MUSIC BUSINESS REGISTRY, by Ritch Esra, SRS Publishing, 7510 Sunset Blvd. #1041, Los Angeles, CA 90046-3418. (800)552-7411. E-mail: musicregistry@compuserve.com or srspubl@aol.com. Website: www.musicregistry.com.

MUSIC DIRECTORY CANADA, 7th ed., Norris-Whitney Communications Inc., 23 Hannover Dr., Suite 7, St. Catherines, ON L2W 1A3 Canada. (877)RING-NWC. E-mail: mail@nor.com. Website: http://nor.com. www.musicdirectorycanada.com

MUSIC LAW: HOW TO RUN YOUR BAND'S BUSINESS, by Richard Stin, Nolo Press, 950 Parker St., Berkeley, CA 94710-9867. (510)549-1976. Website: www.nolo.com.

MUSIC, MONEY AND SUCCESS: THE INSIDER'S GUIDE TO THE MUSIC INDUSTRY, by Jeffrey Brabec and Todd Brabec, Schirmer Books, 180 Madison Avenue, 24th Floor New York, NY 10016. (212) 254-2100.

THE MUSIC PUBLISHER REGISTRY, by Ritch Esra, SRS Publishing, 7510 Sunset Blvd. #1041, Los Angeles, CA 90046-3418. (800)552-7411. E-mail: musicregistry@compuserve.com or srspubl@aol.com.

MUSIC PUBLISHING: A SONGWRITER'S GUIDE, rev. ed., by Randy Poe, Writer's Digest Books, 10151 Carver Road, Suite. 200, Blue Ash, OH 45242. (800)448-0915. Website: www.writersdigest.com.

THE MUSICIAN'S GUIDE TO MAKING & SELLING YOUR OWN CDS & CASSETTES, by Jana Stanfield, Writer's Digest Books, 10151 Carver Road, Suite, 200, Blue Ash, OH 45242. (800)448-0915. Website: www.writersdigest.com.

MUSICIANS' PHONE BOOK, THE LOS ANGELES MUSIC INDUSTRY DIRECTORY, Get Yourself Some Publishing, 28336 Simsalido Ave., Canyon Country, CA 91351. (805)299-2405. E-mail: mpb@earthlink.net. Website: www.musiciansphonebook.com.

NASHVILLE MUSIC BUSINESS DIRECTORY, by Mark Dreyer, NMBD Publishing, 9 Music Square S., Suite 210, Nashville, TN 37203. (615)826-4141. E-mail: nmbd@nashvilleconnection.com. Website: www.nashvilleconnection.com.

NASHVILLE'S UNWRITTEN RULES: INSIDE THE BUSINESS OF THE COUNTRY MUSIC MACHINE, by Dan Daley, Overlook Press, 141 Wooster Street New York, NY 10012. (212) 673-2210. E-mail: sales@overlookny.com.

THE REAL DEAL—HOW TO GET SIGNED TO A RECORD LABEL FROM A TO Z, by Daylle Deanna Schwartz, Billboard Books, 1745 Broadway, New York, NY 10019. (212)782-9000.

RECORDING INDUSTRY SOURCEBOOK, Music Books Plus, 4600 Witmer Industrial Estates, Suite 6, Niagra Falls, NY 14305. (800)265-8481. Website: www.musicbooksplus.com.

REHARMONIZATION TECHNIQUES, by Randy Felts, Berklee Press, 1140 Boylston St., Boston, MA 02215. (617)747-2146. E-mail: info@berkleepress.com. Website: www.berkleepress.com.

THE SONGWRITERS IDEA BOOK, by Sheila Davis, Writer's Digest Books, 10151 Carver Road, Suite. 200, Blue Ash, OH 45242. (800)448-0915. Website: www.writersdigest.com.

SONGWRITER'S MARKET GUIDE TO SONG & DEMO SUBMISSION FORMATS, Writer's Digest Books, 10151 Carver Road, Suite 200, Blue Ash, OH 45242. (800)448-0915. Website: www.writersdigest.com.

SONGWRITER'S PLAYGROUND—INNOVATIVE EXERCISES IN CREATIVE SONGWRITING, by Barbara L. Jordan, Creative Music Marketing, 1085 Commonwealth Ave., Suite 323, Boston, MA 02215. (617)926-8766. Website: www.songwritersplayground.com

THE SONGWRITER'S WORKSHOP: HARMONY, by Jimmy Kachulis, Berklee Press, 1140 Boylston St., Boston, MA 02215. (617)747-2146. E-mail: info@berkleepress.com. Website: www.berkleepress.com.

THE SONGWRITER'S WORKSHOP: MELODY, by Jimmy Kachulis, Berklee Press, 1140 Boylston St., Boston, MA 02215. (617)747-2146. E-mail: info@berkleepress.com. Website: www.berkleepress.com.

SONGWRITING AND THE CREATIVE PROCESS, by Steve Gillette, Sing Out! Publications, P.O. Box 5640, Bethlehem, PA 18015-0253. (888)SING-OUT. E-mail: singout@libertynet.org. Website: www.singout.org/sopubs.html.

SONGWRITING: ESSENTIAL GUIDE TO LYRIC FORM AND STRUCTURE, by Pat Pattison, Berklee Press, 1140 Boylston St., Boston, MA 02215. (617)747-2146. E-mail: info@berkleepress.com. Website: www.berkleepress.com.

SONGWRITING: ESSENTIAL GUIDE TO RHYMING, by Pat Pattison, Berklee Press, 1140 Boylston St., Boston, MA 02215. (617)747-2146. E-mail: info@berkleepress.com. Website: www.berkleepress.com.

THE SONGWRITING SOURCEBOOK: HOW TO TURN CHORDS INTO GREAT SONGS, by Rikky Rooksby, Hal Leonard Corporation, P.O. Box 13819, Milwaukee, WI 53213. (415)947-6615. E-mail: books@musicplayer.com. Website: www.halleonardbooks.com.

SONGWRITING STRATEGIES: A 360-DEGREE APPROACH, by Mark Simos, Hal Leonard Corporation, P.O. Box 13819, Milwaukee, WI 53213. (415)947-6615. E-mail: books@musicplayer.com. Website: www.halleonardbooks.com.

SONGWRITING WITHOUT BOUNDARIES, by Pat Pattison, 10151 Carver Road, Suite. 200, Blue Ash, OH 45242. (800)448-0915. Website: www.writersdigest.com.

THE SOUL OF THE WRITER, by Susan Tucker with Linda Lee Strother, Journey Publishing, P.O. Box 92411, Nashville, TN 37209. (615)952-4894. Website: www.journeypublishing.com.

SUCCESSFUL LYRIC WRITING, by Sheila Davis, Writer's Digest Books, 10151 Carver Road, Suite 200, Blue Ash, OH 45242. (800)448-0915. Website: www.writersdigest.com.

THIS BUSINESS OF MUSIC MARKETING AND PROMOTION, by Tad Lathrop and Jim Pettigrew, Jr., Billboard Books, Watson-Guptill Publications, 1745 Broadway. New York, NY 10019. (212)782-9000. E-mail: info@watsonguptill.com.

TIM SWEENEY'S GUIDE TO RELEASING INDEPENDENT RECORDS, by Tim Sweeney, TSA Books, 31805 Highway 79 S., Temecula, CA 92592. (909)303-9506. E-mail: info@tsamusic.com. Website: www.tsamusic.com.

TIM SWEENEY'S GUIDE TO SUCCEEDING AT MUSIC CONVENTIONS, by Tim Sweeney, TSA Books, 31805 Highway 79 S., Temecula, CA 92592. (909)303-9506. Website: www.tsamusic.com.

TEXAS MUSIC INDUSTRY DIRECTORY, Texas Music Office, Office of the Governor, P.O. Box 13246, Austin, TX 78711. (512)463-6666. E-mail: music@governor.state.tx.us. Website: www.enjoytexasmusic.com.

TUNESMITH: INSIDE THE ART OF SONGWRITING, by Jimmy Webb, Hyperion, 1500 Broadway, 3rd Floor, New York, NY 10036. (800)759-0190.

VOLUNTEER LAWYERS FOR THE ARTS GUIDE TO COPYRIGHT FOR MUSICIANS AND COMPOSERS, One E. 53rd St., 6th Floor, New York, NY 10022. (212)319-2787.

WRITING BETTER LYRICS, by Pat Pattison, Writer's Digest Books, 10151 Carver Road, Suite 200, Blue Ash, OH 45242. (800)448-0915. Website: www.writersdigest.com.

WRITING MUSIC FOR HIT SONGS, by Jai Josefs, Schirmer Trade Books, Music Sales Corporation, 257 Park Ave. S., New York, NY 10010. (212)254-2100.

THE YELLOW PAGES OF ROCK, The Album Network, 120 N. Victory Blvd., Burbank, CA 91502. (800)222-4382. Fax: (818)955-9048. E-mail: ypinfo@yprock.com.

WEBSITES OF INTEREST

The Internet provides a wealth of information for songwriters and performers, and the number of sites devoted to music grows each day. Below is a list of websites that can offer you information, links to other music sites, contact with other songwriters, and places to showcase your songs. Due to the dynamic nature of the online world, this is certainly not a comprehensive list, but it gives you a place to start on your Internet journey as you search for opportunities to get your music heard.

ABOUT.COM MUSICIANS' EXCHANGE www.musicians.about.com/
Site features headlines and articles of interest to independent musicians and songwriters, as well as links and label profiles.

ABSOLUTE PUNK www.absolutepunk.net
Searchable online community focusing on punk and rock music, including news, reviews, articles, interviews, and forums to discuss music and pop culture.

AMERICAN MUSIC CENTER www.amc.net
Classical and jazz archives. Includes a list of organizations and contacts for composers.

AMERICAN SOCIETY OF COMPOSERS, AUTHORS AND PUBLISHERS (ASCAP) www.ascap.com
Database of works in ASCAP's repertoire. Includes performer, songwriter, and publisher information as well as membership information and industry news.

***AMERICAN SONGWRITER MAGAZINE* HOMEPAGE** www.americansongwriter.com
This is the official homepage for *American Songwriter* magazine. Features an online article archive, e-mail newsletter, and links.

BANDCAMP www.bandcamp.com

An online music store and platform for artist promotion that caters mainly to independent artists.

BEAIRD MUSIC GROUP DEMOS www.beairdmusicgroup.com

Nashville demo service which offers a variety of demo packages.

BILLBOARD.COM www.billboard.com

Industry news and searchable online database of music companies by subscription.

THE BLUES FOUNDATION www.blues.org

Nonprofit organization located in Memphis, TN, website contains information on the foundation, membership, and events.

BROADCAST MUSIC, INC. (BMI) www.bmi.com

Offers lists of song titles, writers, and publishers of the BMI repertoire. Includes membership information and general information on songwriting and licensing.

THE BUZZ FACTOR www.thebuzzfactor.com

Website offers free tips on music marketing and self-promotion.

BUZZNET www.buzznet.com

Searchable networking and news site featuring music, pop culture, photos, videos, concert reviews, and more.

CDBABY www.cdbaby.com

An online CD store dedicated to the sales of independent music.

CADENZA www.cadenza.org

Online resource for contemporary and classical music and musicians, including methods of contacting other musicians.

CHORUS AMERICA www.chorusamerica.org

The website for Chorus America, a national organization for professional and volunteer choruses. Includes job listings and professional development information.

FINETUNE www.finetune.com

Internet radio/streaming audio. User can create personalized channels and playlists online.

FILM MUSIC NETWORK www.filmmusicworld.com or www.filmmusic.net

Network of links, news, and job listings within the film music world.

GET SIGNED www.getsigned.com

Interviews with musicians, songwriters, and industry veterans, how-to business information, and more.

GOVERNMENT LIAISON SERVICES www.trademarkinfo.com

An intellectual property research firm. Offers a variety of trademark searches.

GUITAR NINE RECORDS www.guitar9.com

Offers articles on songwriting, music theory, guitar techniques, etc.

GOOGLE www.google.com

Online search engine can be used to look up music, information, lyrics.

HARMONY CENTRAL www.harmony-central.com

Online community for musicians with in-depth reviews and discussions.

HARRY FOX AGENCY www.harryfox.com

Offers a comprehensive FAQ about licensing songs for use in recording, performance, and film.

THE HOBNOB www.hobnob.net

Offers a directory allowing artists, engineers, and producers to connect and collaborate.

ILIKE www.ilike.com

Music networking site. Signed and unsigned artists can sign up for free artists' page and upload songs and events. Works with other social networks such as www.facebook.com.

INDEPENDENT DISTRIBUTION NETWORK www.idnmusic.com

Website of independent bands distributing their music with advice on everything from starting a band to finding labels.

INDEPENDENT SONGWRITER WEB MAGAZINE www.independentsongwriter.com

Independent music reviews, classifieds, message board, and chat sessions.

INDIE-MUSIC.COM www.indie-music.com

Website of how-to articles, record label directory, links to musicians and venue listings.

JAZZ CORNER www.jazzcorner.com

Portal for the websites of jazz musicians and organizations. Includes the jazz video share, jukebox, and the "Speakeasy" bulletin board.

JUST PLAIN FOLKS www.jpfolks.com or www.justplainfolks.org

Website for songwriting organization featuring message boards, lyric feedback forums, member profiles, music, contact listings, chapter homepages, and more.

LAST.FM www.last.fm

Music tracking and social networking site.

LI'L HANK'S GUIDE FOR SONGWRITERS IN L.A. www.halsguide.com

Website for songwriters with information on clubs, publishers, books, etc. Links to other songwriting sites.

LIVE365 www.live365.com/index.live

Internet radio/audio stream search engine.

LIVEJOURNAL www.livejournal.com

Social networking community using open source technology, music communities provide news, interviews, and reviews.

LOS ANGELES GOES UNDERGROUND www.lagu.somaweb.org

Website dedicated to underground rock bands from Los Angeles and Hollywood.

LYRIC IDEAS www.lyricideas.com

Offers songwriting prompts, themes, and creative techniques for songwriting.

LYRICIST www.lyricist.com

Site offers advice, tips, and events in the music industry.

MI2N (THE MUSIC INDUSTRY NEWS NETWORK) www.mi2n.com

Offers news on happenings in the music industry and career postings.

THE MUSE'S MUSE www.musesmuse.com

Classifieds, catalog of music samples, songwriting articles, newsletter, and chat room.

MOG www.mog.com

Internet radio/streaming audio. Contains music news and concert reviews, personalized recommendations.

MUSIC BOOKS PLUS www.musicbooksplus.com

Online bookstore dedicated to music books on every music-related topic, plus a free newsletter.

MUSIC PUBLISHERS ASSOCIATION www.mpa.org

Ofers directories for music publishers and imprints, copyright resource center, and information on the organization.

MUSIC YELLOW PAGES www.musicyellowpages.com

Listings of music-related businesses.

MYSPACE www.myspace.com

Social networking site featuring music Web pages for musicians and songwriters.

NASHVILLE SONGWRITERS ASSOCIATION INTERNATIONAL (NSAI) www.nashvillesongwriters.com
Official NSAI homepage. Offers news, links, online registration, and message board for members.

NATIONAL ASSOCIATION OF COMPOSERS USA (NACUSA) www.music-usa.org/nacusa
A nonprofit organization devoted to the promotion and performance of American concert hall music.

NATIONAL MUSIC PUBLISHERS ASSOCIATION www.nmpa.org
Organization's online site filled with information about copyright, legislation, and other concerns of the music publishing world.

ONLINE ROCK www.onlinerock.com
Range of membership options including a free option, offers webpage services, articles, chat rooms, links, and more.

OPERA AMERICA www.operaamerica.org
Website of Opera America features information on advocacy and awareness programs, publications, conference schedules, and more.

PANDORA www.pandora.com
A site created by the founders of the Music Genome Project; a searchable music radio/streaming audio site.

PERFORMER MAG www.performermag.com
Offers articles, music, industry news, classifieds, and reviews.

PERFORMING SONGWRITER MAGAZINE HOMEPAGE www.performingsongwriter.com
Official homepage for the magazine features articles and links.

PITCHFORK www.pitchforkmedia.com
Offers indie news, reviews, media, and features.

PUBLIC DOMAIN MUSIC www.pdinfo.com
Articles on public domain works and copyright, including public domain song lists, research sources, tips, and FAQs.

PUMP AUDIO www.pumpaudio.com
License music for film and television on a non-exclusive basis. No submission fees, rights retained by songwriter.

PUREVOLUME www.purevolume.com

Music hosting site with searchable database of songs by signed and unsigned artists. Musicians and songwriters can upload songs and events.

THE RECORDING PROJECT www.recordingproject.com

Online community for musicians and recording artists, every level welcome.

RECORD PRODUCER.COM www.record-producer.com

Extensive site dedicated to audio engineering and record production. Offers a free newsletter, online instruction, and e-books on various aspects of record production and audio engineering.

ROCK AND ROLL HALL OF FAME + MUSEUM www.rockhall.com

Website for the Rock and Roll Hall of Fame and Museum, including events listings, visitor info, and more.

SESAC INC. www.sesac.com

Website for performing rights organization with songwriter profiles, industry news updates, licensing information, and links to other sites.

SINGERSONGWRITER www.singersongwriter.ws

Resources for singer-songwriters, including an extensive list, featured resources, and lists of radio stations organized geographically.

SLACKER www.slacker.com

Internet radio/streaming audio. User can create personalized channels and playlists online.

SOMA FM www.somafm.com

Internet underground/alternative radio with commercial-free broadcasting from San Francisco.

SONG CATALOG www.songcatalog.com

Online song catalog database for licensing.

SONGLINK www.songlink.com

Offers opportunities to pitch songs to music publishers for specific recording projects and industry news.

SONGRAMP www.songramp.com

Online songwriting organization with message boards, blogs, news, and streaming music channels. Offers variety of membership packages.

SONGSALIVE! www.songsalive.org

Online songwriters organization and community.

SONGWRITER 101 www.songwriter101.com
> Offers articles, industry news, and message boards.

SONGWRITER'S GUILD OF AMERICA (SGA) www.songwritersguild.com
> Industry news, member services information, newsletters, contract reviews, and more.

SONGWRITER'S RESOURCE NETWORK www.songwritersresourcenetwork.com
> News and education resource for songwriters, lyricists, and composers.

SONGWRITERUNIVERSE www.songwriteruniverse.com
> In-depth articles, business information, education, and recommended reading.

THE SONGWRITING EDUCATION RESOURCE www.craftofsongwriting.com
> An educational website for songwriters. Offers discussion boards, articles, and links.

SONIC BIDS www.sonicbids.com
> Features an online press kit with photos, bio, music samples, date calendar. Free trial period first month for artists/bands to sign up, newsletter.

SOUNDCLOUD www.soundcloud.com
> An online audio distribution platform which allows collaboration, promotion, and distribution of audio recordings.

SOUNDPEDIA www.soundpedia.com
> Internet Radio/streaming audio. User can create personalized channels and playlists online.

STARPOLISH www.starpolish.com
> Features articles and interviews about the music industry.

SUMMERSONGS SONGWRITING CAMPS www.summersongs.com
> Information about songwriting camps, staff, and online registration.

TAXI www.taxi.com
> Independent A&R vehicle that shops demos to A&R professionals.

TUNECORE www.tunecore.com
> Service that allows musicians to sell their music digitally via online retailers such as iTunes, Amazon, Spotify, and more.

UNITED STATES COPYRIGHT OFFICE www.copyright.gov
> Homepage for the US Copyright office. Offers information on registering songs.

THE VELVET ROPE www.velvetrope.com
> Famous/infamous online music industry message board.

WEIRDO MUSIC www.weirdomusic.com

Online music magazine with articles, reviews, downloads, and links to Internet radio shows.

YAHOO! www.new.music.yahoo.com

Search engine with radio station guide, music industry news, and listings.

YOUTUBE www.youtube.com

Social networking site which hosts audiovisual content. Searchable database provides links to music videos, interviews, and more.

GLOSSARY

A CAPPELLA. Choral singing without accompaniment.

AAA FORM. A song form in which every verse has the same melody, often used for songs that tell a story.

AABA, ABAB. A commonly used song pattern consisting of two verses, a bridge, and a verse, or a repeated pattern of verse and bridge, where the verses are musically the same.

A&R DIRECTOR. Record company executive in charge of the Artists and Repertoire Department who is responsible for finding and developing new artists and matching songs with artists.

A/C. Adult contemporary music.

ADVANCE. Money paid to the songwriter or recording artist, which is then recouped before regular royalty payment begins. Sometimes called "up front" money, advances are deducted from royalties.

AFIM. Association for Independent Music (formerly NAIRD). Organization for independent record companies, distributors, retailers, manufacturers, etc.

AFM. American Federation of Musicians. A union for musicians and arrangers.

AFTRA. American Federation of Television and Radio Artists. A union for performers.

AIMP. Association of Independent Music Publishers.

AIRPLAY. The radio broadcast of a recording.

AOR. Album-Oriented Rock. A radio format that primarily plays selections from rock albums as opposed to hit singles.

ARRANGEMENT. An adaptation of a composition for a recording or performance, with consideration for the melody, harmony, instrumentation, tempo, style, etc.

ASCAP. American Society of Composers, Authors, and Publishers. A performing rights society. (See the "Organizations" section.)

ASSIGNMENT. Transfer of song rights from writer to publisher.

AUDIO VISUAL INDEX (AVI). A database containing title and production information for cue sheets which are available from a performing rights organization. Currently, BMI, ASCAP, SOCAN, PRS, APRA, and SACEM contribute their cue-sheet listings to the AVI.

AUDIOVISUAL. Refers to presentations that use audio backup for visual material.

BACKGROUND MUSIC. Music used that creates mood and supports the spoken dialogue of a radio program or visual action of an audiovisual work. Not feature or theme music.

B&W. Black and white.

BED. Prerecorded music used as background material in commercials. In rap music, often refers to the sampled and looped drums and music over which the rapper performs.

BLACK BOX. Theater without fixed stage or seating arrangements, capable of a variety of formations. Usually a small space, often attached to a major theater complex, used for workshops or experimental works calling for small casts and limited sets.

BMI. Broadcast Music, Inc. A performing rights society. (See the "Organizations" section.)

BOOKING AGENT. Person who schedules performances for entertainers.

BOOTLEGGING. Unauthorized recording and selling of a song.

BUSINESS MANAGER. Person who handles the financial aspects of artistic careers.

BUZZ. Attention an act generates through the media and word of mouth.

B/W. Backed with. Usually refers to the B-side of a single.

C&W. Country and western.

CATALOG. The collected songs of one writer or all songs handled by one publisher.

CD. Compact Disc.

CD-R. A recordable CD.

CD-ROM. Compact Disc-Read Only Memory. A computer information storage medium capable of holding enormous amounts of data. Information on a CD-ROM cannot be deleted. A computer user must have a CD-ROM drive to access a CD-ROM.

CHAMBER MUSIC. Any music suitable for performance in a small audience area or chamber.

CHAMBER ORCHESTRA. A miniature orchestra usually containing one instrument per part.

CHART. The written arrangement of a song.

CHARTS. The trade magazines' lists of the best-selling records.

CHR. Contemporary Hit Radio. Top-40 pop music.

COLLABORATION. Two or more artists, writers, etc., working together on a single project; for instance, a playwright and a songwriter creating a musical together.

COMPACT DISC. A small disc (about 4.7 inches in diameter) holding digitally encoded music that is read by a laser beam in a CD player.

COMPOSERS. The men and women who create musical compositions for motion pictures and other audiovisual works or the creators of classical music compositions.

COPUBLISH. Two or more parties own publishing rights to the same song.

COPYRIGHT. The exclusive legal right giving the creator of a work the power to control the publishing, reproduction, and sales of the work. Although a song is technically copyrighted at the time it is written, the best legal protection of that copyright comes through registering the copyright with the Library of Congress.

COPYRIGHT INFRINGEMENT. Unauthorized use of a copyrighted song or portions thereof.

COVER RECORDING. A new version of a previously recorded song.

CROSSOVER. A song that becomes popular in two or more musical categories (e.g., country and pop).

CUT. Any finished recording; a selection from an LP. Also, to record.

DAT. Digital Audio Tape. A professional and consumer audiocassette format for recording and playing back digitally encoded material. DAT cassettes are approximately one-third smaller than conventional audiocassettes.

DCC. Digital Compact Cassette. A consumer audio cassette format for recording and playing back digitally encoded tape. DCC tapes are the same size as analog cassettes.

DEMO. A recording of a song submitted as a demonstration of a writer's or artist's skills.

DERIVATIVE WORK. A work derived from another work, such as a translation, musical arrangement, sound recording, or motion-picture version.

DISTRIBUTOR. Wholesale marketing agent responsible for getting records from manufacturers to retailers.

DONUT. A jingle with singing at the beginning and end and an instrumental background in the middle. Ad copy is recorded over the middle section.

E-MAIL. Electronic mail. Computer address where a company or individual can be reached via modem.

ENGINEER. A specially trained individual who operates recording studio equipment.

ENHANCED CD. General term for an audio CD that also contains multimedia computer information. It is playable in both standard CD players and CD-ROM drives.

EP. Extended-Play record, CD, or cassette containing more selections than a standard single, but fewer than a standard album.

EPK. Electronic press kit. Usually contains photos, sound files, bio information, reviews, tour dates, etc., posted online. Sonicbids.com is a popular EPK hosting website.

FINAL MIX. The art of combining all the various sounds that take place during the recording session into a two-track stereo or mono tape. Reflects the total product and all of the energies and talents the artist, producer, and engineer have put into the project.

FLY SPACE. The area above a stage from which set pieces are lowered and raised during a performance.

FOLIO. A softcover collection of printed music prepared for sale.

FOLLOWING. A fanbase committed to going to gigs and buying albums.

FOREIGN RIGHTS SOCIETIES. Performing rights societies other than domestic which have reciprocal agreements with ASCAP and BMI for the collection of royalties accrued by foreign radio, television airplay, and other public performance of the above groups' writer members.

HARRY FOX AGENCY. Organization that collects mechanical royalties.

GRAMMY. Music industry awards presented by the National Academy of Recording Arts and Sciences.

HIP-HOP. A dance-oriented musical style derived from a combination of disco, rap, and R&B.

HIT. A song or record that achieves Top-40 status.

HOOK. A memorable "catch" phrase or melody line that is repeated in a song.

HOUSE. Dance music created by remixing samples from other songs.

HYPERTEXT. Words or groups of words in an electronic document that are linked to other text, such as a definition or a related document. Hypertext can also be linked to illustrations.

INDIE. An independent record label, music publisher, or producer.

INFRINGEMENT. A violation of the exclusive rights granted by the copyright law to a copyright owner.

INTERNET. A worldwide network of computers that offers access to a wide variety of electronic resources.

IPS. Inches per second, a speed designation for tape recording.

IRC. International reply coupon, necessary for the return of materials sent out of the country. Available at most post offices.

JINGLE. Usually a short verse set to music, designed as a commercial message.

LEAD SHEET. Written version (melody, chord symbols, and lyric) of a song.

LEADER. Plastic (non-recordable) tape at the beginning and between songs for ease in selection.

LIBRETTO. The text of an opera or any long choral work. The booklet containing such text.

LISTING. Block of information in this book about a specific company.

LP. Designation for long-playing record played at 33⅓rpm.

LYRIC SHEET. A typed or written copy of a song's lyrics.

MARKET. A potential song or music buyer. Also a demographic division of the record-buying public.

MASTER. Edited and mixed tape used in the production of records; the best or original copy of a recording from which copies are made.

MD. MiniDisc. A 2.5-inch disk for recording and playing back digitally encoded music.

MECHANICAL RIGHT. The right to profit from the physical reproduction of a song.

MECHANICAL ROYALTY. Money earned from record, tape, and CD sales.

MIDI. Musical instrument digital interface. Universal standard interface that allows musical instruments to communicate with each other and computers.

MINI DISC. (see MD above.)

MIX. To blend a multi-track recording into the desired balance of sound, usually to a two-track stereo master.

MODEM. MOdulator/DEModulator. A computer device used to send data from one computer to another via telephone line.

MOR. Middle of the road. Easy-listening popular music.

MP3. File format of a relatively small size that stores audio files on a computer. Music saved in MP3 format can be played only with an MP3 player (which can be downloaded onto a computer).

MS. Manuscript.

MULTIMEDIA. Computers and software capable of integrating text, sound, photographic-quality images, animation, and video.

MUSIC BED. (see Bed above.)

MUSIC JOBBER. A wholesale distributor of printed music.

MUSIC LIBRARY. A business that purchases canned music, which can then be bought by producers of radio and TV commercials, films, videos, and audiovisual productions to use however they wish.

MUSIC PUBLISHER. A company that evaluates songs for commercial potential, finds artists to record them, finds other uses (such as TV or film) for the songs, collects income generated by the songs, and protects copyrights from infringement.

MUSIC ROW. An area of Nashville, TN, encompassing Sixteenth, Seventeenth and Eighteenth Avenues where most of the major publishing houses, recording studios, mastering labs, songwriters, singers, promoters, etc., practice their trade.

NARAS. National Academy of Recording Arts and Sciences.

THE NATIONAL ACADEMY OF SONGWRITERS (NAS). The largest U.S. songwriters' association. (See the "Organizations" section.)

NEEDLE-DROP. Refers to a type of music library. A needle-drop music library is a licensed library that allows producers to borrow music on a rate schedule. The price depends on how the music will be used.

NETWORK. A group of computers electronically linked to share information and resources.

NMPA. National Music Publishers Association.

ONE-OFF. A deal between songwriter and publisher that includes only one song or project at a time. No future involvement is implicated. Many times a single-song contract accompanies a one-off deal.

ONE-STOP. A wholesale distributor who sells small quantities of records to "mom-and-pop" record stores, retailers, and jukebox operators.

OPERETTA. Light, humorous, satiric plot, or poem set to cheerful, light music with occasional spoken dialogue.

OVERDUB. To record an additional part (vocal or instrumental) onto a basic multi-track recording.

PARODY. A satirical imitation of a literary or musical work. Permission from the owner of the copyright is sometimes required before commercial exploitation of a parody.

PAYOLA. Dishonest payment to broadcasters in exchange for airplay.

PERFORMING RIGHTS. A specific right granted by U.S. copyright law protecting a composition from being publicly performed without the owner's permission.

PERFORMING RIGHTS ORGANIZATION. An organization that collects income from the public performance of songs written by its members and then proportionally distributes this income to the individual copyright holder based on the number of performances of each song.

PERSONAL MANAGER. A person who represents artists to develop and enhance their careers. Personal managers may negotiate contracts, hire and dismiss other agencies and personnel relating to the artist's career, review material, help with artist promotions, and perform many other services.

PIRACY. The unauthorized reproduction and selling of printed or recorded music.

PITCH. To attempt to solicit interest for a song by audition.

PLAYLIST. List of songs a radio station will play.

POINTS. A negotiable percentage paid to producers and artists for records sold.

PRODUCER. Person who supervises every aspect of a recording project.

PRODUCTION COMPANY. Company specializing in producing jingle packages for advertising agencies. May also refer to companies specializing in audiovisual programs.

PROFESSIONAL MANAGER. Member of a music publisher's staff who screens submitted material and tries to get the company's catalog of songs recorded.

PROSCENIUM. Permanent architectural arch in a theater that separates the stage from the audience.

PUBLIC DOMAIN. Any composition with an expired, lapsed, or invalid copyright, therefore belonging to everyone.

PURCHASE LICENSE. Fee paid for music used from a stock music library.

QUERY. A letter of inquiry to an industry professional soliciting his interest.

R&B. Rhythm and blues.

RACK JOBBER. Distributors who lease floor space from department stores and put in racks of albums.

RATE. The percentage of royalty as specified by contract.

RELEASE. Any record issued by a record company.

RESIDUALS. In advertising or television, payments to singers and musicians for use of a performance.

RIAA. Recording Industry Association of America.

ROYALTY. Percentage of money earned from the sale of records or use of a song.

RPM. Revolutions per minute. Refers to phonograph turntable speed.

SAE. Self-addressed envelope (with no postage attached).

SASE. Self-addressed stamped envelope.

SATB. The abbreviation for parts in choral music, meaning Soprano, Alto, Tenor, and Bass.

SCORE. A complete arrangement of all the notes and parts of a composition (vocal or instrumental) written out on staves. A full score, or orchestral score, depicts every orchestral part on a separate staff and is used by a conductor.

SELF-CONTAINED. A band or recording act that writes all their own material.

SESAC. A performing rights organization, originally the Society of European Stage Authors and Composers. (see the "Organizations" section.)

SFX. Sound effects.

SHOP. To pitch songs to a number of companies or publishers.

SINGLE. 45rpm record with only one song per side. A 12£ single refers to a long version of one song on a 12£ disc, usually used for dance music.

SKA. Up-tempo dance music influenced primarily by reggae and punk, usually featuring horns, saxophone, and bass.

SOCAN. Society of Composers, Authors and Music Publishers of Canada. A Canadian performing rights organization. (see the "Organizations" section.)

SOLICITED. Songs or materials that have been requested.

SONG PLUGGER. A songwriter representative whose main responsibility is promoting uncut songs to music publishers, record companies, artists, and producers.

SONG SHARK. Person who deals with songwriters deceptively for his own profit.

SOUNDSCAN. A company that collates the register tapes of reporting stores to track the actual number of albums sold at the retail level.

SOUNDTRACK. The audio, including music and narration, of a film, videotape, or audiovisual program.

SPACE STAGE. Open stage that features lighting and, perhaps, projected scenery.

SPLIT PUBLISHING. To divide publishing rights between two or more publishers.

STAFF SONGWRITER. A songwriter who has an exclusive agreement with a publisher.

STATUTORY ROYALTY RATE. The maximum payment for mechanical rights guaranteed by law that a record company may pay the songwriter and his publisher for each record, CD, or tape sold.

SUBPUBLISHING. Certain rights granted by a U.S. publisher to a foreign publisher in exchange for promoting the U.S. catalog in his territory.

SYNCHRONIZATION. Technique of timing a musical soundtrack to action on film or video.

TAKE. Either an attempt to record a vocal or instrument part or an acceptable recording of a performance.

TEJANO. A musical form begun in the late 1970s by regional bands in south Texas, its style reflects a blended Mexican-American culture. Incorporates elements of rock, country, R&B, and jazz, and often features accordion and twelve-string guitar.

THRUST STAGE. Stage with audience on three sides and a stagehouse or wall on the fourth side.

TOP 40. The first forty songs on the pop music charts at any given time. Also refers to a style of music which emulates that heard on the current Top 40.

TRACK. Divisions of a recording tape (e.g., 24-track tape) that can be individually recorded in the studio, and then mixed into a finished master.

TRADES. Publications covering the music industry.

12-SINGLE. A 12-inch record containing one or more remixes of a song, originally intended for dance club play.

UNSOLICITED. Songs or materials that were not requested and are not expected.

VOCAL SCORE. An arrangement of vocal music detailing all vocal parts and condensing all accompanying instrumental music into one piano part.

WEBSITE. An address on the World Wide Web that can be accessed by computer modem. It may contain text, graphics, and sound.

WING SPACE. The offstage area surrounding the playing stage in a theater, unseen by the audience, where sets and props are hidden, actors wait for cues, and stagehands prepare to change sets.

WORLD MUSIC. A general music category that includes most musical forms originating outside the U.S. and Europe, including reggae and calypso. World music finds its roots primarily in the Caribbean, Latin America, Africa, and the South Pacific.

WORLD WIDE WEB (WWW). An Internet resource that utilizes hypertext to access information. It also supports formatted text, illustrations, and sounds, depending on the user's computer capabilities.

GENERAL INDEX

CATEGORY INDEX

RECORD COMPANIES

RECORD PRODUCERS

MANAGERS & BOOKING AGENTS